THE
NEIL GAIMAN
LIBRARY

A STUDY IN EMERALD

ADAPTATION SCRIPT
RAFAEL ALBUQUERQUE AND
RAFAEL SCAVONE

ART
RAFAEL ALBUQUERQUE

COLORS
DAVE STEWART

LETTERS
TODD KLEIN

COVER
RAFAEL ALBUQUERQUE

MURDER MYSTERIES

ADAPTATION SCRIPT AND ART
P. CRAIG RUSSELL

COLORS
LOVERN KINDZIERSKI

LETTERS
GALEN SHOWMAN

MYSTERIES DEMYSTIFIED
ORIGINALLY PUBLISHED IN *THE ART OF P. CRAIG RUSSELL*
DURWIN S. TALON

COVER
P. CRAIG RUSSELL

HOW TO TALK TO GIRLS AT PARTIES

ADAPTATION SCRIPT, ART, AND LETTERS
FÁBIO MOON AND
GABRIEL BÁ

COVER
FÁBIO MOON AND
GABRIEL BÁ

FORBIDDEN BRIDES
OF THE FACELESS SLAVES IN THE SECRET
HOUSE OF THE NIGHT OF DREAD DESIRE

ADAPTATION SCRIPT AND ART
SHANE OAKLEY

COLORS
(PAGES 5, 12–14, 18–25, 32–36, 40–42)
NICK FILARDI

LETTERS
TODD KLEIN

COVER
SHANE OAKLEY

COVER BY
FÁBIO MOON

THE NEIL GAIMAN LIBRARY

· VOLUME I ·

STORIES AND WORDS BY
NEIL GAIMAN

PUBLISHER
MIKE RICHARDSON

COLLECTION EDITOR
DANIEL CHABON

COLLECTION ASSISTANT EDITOR
CHUCK HOWITT

DESIGNER
CINDY CACEREZ-SPRAGUE

DIGITAL ART TECHNICIAN
ADAM PRUETT

A STUDY IN EMERALD
EDITORIAL
EDITOR DANIEL CHABON
ASSISTANT EDITOR BRETT ISRAEL

HOW TO TALK TO GIRLS AT PARTIES
EDITORIAL
EDITOR DIANA SCHUTZ
ASSISTANT EDITOR AARON WALKER

MURDER MYSTERIES
EDITORIAL
FIRST EDITION EDITOR SCOTT ALLIE
SECOND EDITION EDITOR DANIEL CHABON

FORBIDDEN BRIDES
EDITORIAL
EDITOR DANIEL CHABON
ASSISTANT EDITOR CARDNER CLARK

SPECIAL THANKS TO CAT MIHOS, MERRILEE HEIFETZ, AND SARAH-KATE FENELON

EXECUTIVE VICE PRESIDENT NEIL HANKERSON • CHIEF FINANCIAL OFFICER TOM WEDDLE • VICE PRESIDENT OF PUBLISHING RANDY STRADLEY • CHIEF BUSINESS DEVELOPMENT OFFICER NICK McWHORTER • CHIEF INFORMATION OFFICER DALE LaFOUNTAIN • VICE PRESIDENT OF MARKETING MATT PARKINSON • VICE PRESIDENT OF PRODUCTION AND SCHEDULING VANESSA TODD-HOLMES • VICE PRESIDENT OF BOOK TRADE AND DIGITAL SALES MARK BERNARDI • GENERAL COUNSEL KEN LIZZI • EDITOR IN CHIEF DAVE MARSHALL • EDITORIAL DIRECTOR DAVEY ESTRADA • SENIOR BOOKS EDITOR CHRIS WARNER • DIRECTOR OF SPECIALTY PROJECTS CARY GRAZZINI • ART DIRECTOR LIA RIBACCHI • DIRECTOR OF DIGITAL ART AND PREPRESS MATT DRYER SENIOR DIRECTOR OF LICENSED PUBLICATIONS MICHAEL GOMBOS • DIRECTOR OF CUSTOM PROGRAMS KARI YADRO • DIRECTOR OF INTERNATIONAL LICENSING KARI TORSON • DIRECTOR OF TRADE SALES SEAN BRICE

This volume collects *A Study in Emerald*, *Murder Mysteries*, *How to Talk to Girls at Parties*, and *Forbidden Brides of the Faceless Slaves in the Secret House of the Night of Dread Desire*.

THE NEIL GAIMAN LIBRARY™
© 2020 Neil Gaiman. A Study in Emerald™ © 2003, 2018, 2020 Neil Gaiman. All rights reserved. Neil Gaiman's Murder Mysteries™ text © 1992, 2002, 2014, 2020 Neil Gaiman. Neil Gaiman's Murder Mysteries™ adaptation and illustrations © 2002, 2014, 2020 P. Craig Russell. How to Talk to Girls at Parties™ © 2006, 2016, 2020 Neil Gaiman. All rights reserved. How to Talk to Girls at Parties™ adaptation and artwork © 2016, 2020 Fábio Moon and Gabriel Bá. Neil Gaiman's Forbidden Brides of the Faceless Slaves in the Secret House of the Night of Dread Desire™ © 2004, 2017, 2020 Neil Gaiman. All rights reserved. Neil Gaiman's Forbidden Brides of the Faceless Slaves in the Secret House of the Night of Dread Desire™ artwork © 2017, 2020 Shane Oakley.

All other material, unless otherwise specified, © 2020 Dark Horse Comics LLC. Dark Horse Books® and the Dark Horse logo are trademarks of Dark Horse Comics LLC, registered in various categories and countries. All rights reserved. No portion of this publication may be reproduced or transmitted, in any form or by any means, without the express written permission of Dark Horse Comics LLC. Names, characters, places, and incidents featured in this publication either are the product of the author's imagination or are used fictitiously. Any resemblance to actual persons (living or dead), events, institutions, or locales, without satiric intent, is coincidental.

Published by Dark Horse Books
A division of Dark Horse Comics LLC
10956 SE Main Street, Milwaukie, OR 97222

DarkHorse.com
Facebook.com/DarkHorseComics   Twitter.com/DarkHorseComics
To find a comics shop in your area, visit comicshoplocator.com.

First hardcover edition: May 2020
ISBN 978-1-50671-593-3

10 9 8 7 6 5 4 3 2
Printed in China

Library of Congress Cataloging-in-Publication Data

Names: Gaiman, Neil, author. | Albuquerque, Rafael, 1981- author, artist. | Stewart, Dave, colourist. | Klein, Todd, letterer. | Russell, P. Craig, author, artist. | Kindzierski, Lovern, 1954- colourist. | Showman, Galen, letterer. | Moon, Fábio, author, artist. | Bá, Gabriel, author, artist. | Oakley, Shane, author, artist. | Filardi, Nick, colourist.
Title: The Neil Gaiman library / story and words by Neil Gaiman.
Other titles: Graphic novels. Selections
Description: First hardcover edition. | Milwaukie, OR : Dark Horse Books, 2020- | Summary: "Collects the full graphic novels A Study in Emerald, Murder Mysteries, How to Talk to Girls at Parties, and Forbidden Brides of the Faceless Slaves in the Secret House of the Night of Dread Desire"-- Provided by publisher.
Identifiers: LCCN 2019057534 | ISBN 9781506715933 (v. 1 ; hardcover) | ISBN 9781506715964 (v. 1 ; ebook)
Subjects: LCSH: Graphic novels.
Classification: LCC PN6737.G3 A6 2020 | DDC 741.5/942--dc23
LC record available at https://lccn.loc.gov/2019057534

TABLE OF CONTENTS

A STUDY IN EMERALD
PAGE 7

MURDER MYSTERIES
PAGE 81

HOW TO TALK TO GIRLS AT PARTIES
PAGE 151

FORBIDDEN BRIDES
OF THE FACELESS SLAVES IN THE SECRET HOUSE
OF THE NIGHT OF DREAD DESIRE
PAGE 215

BONUS CONTENT
PAGE 255

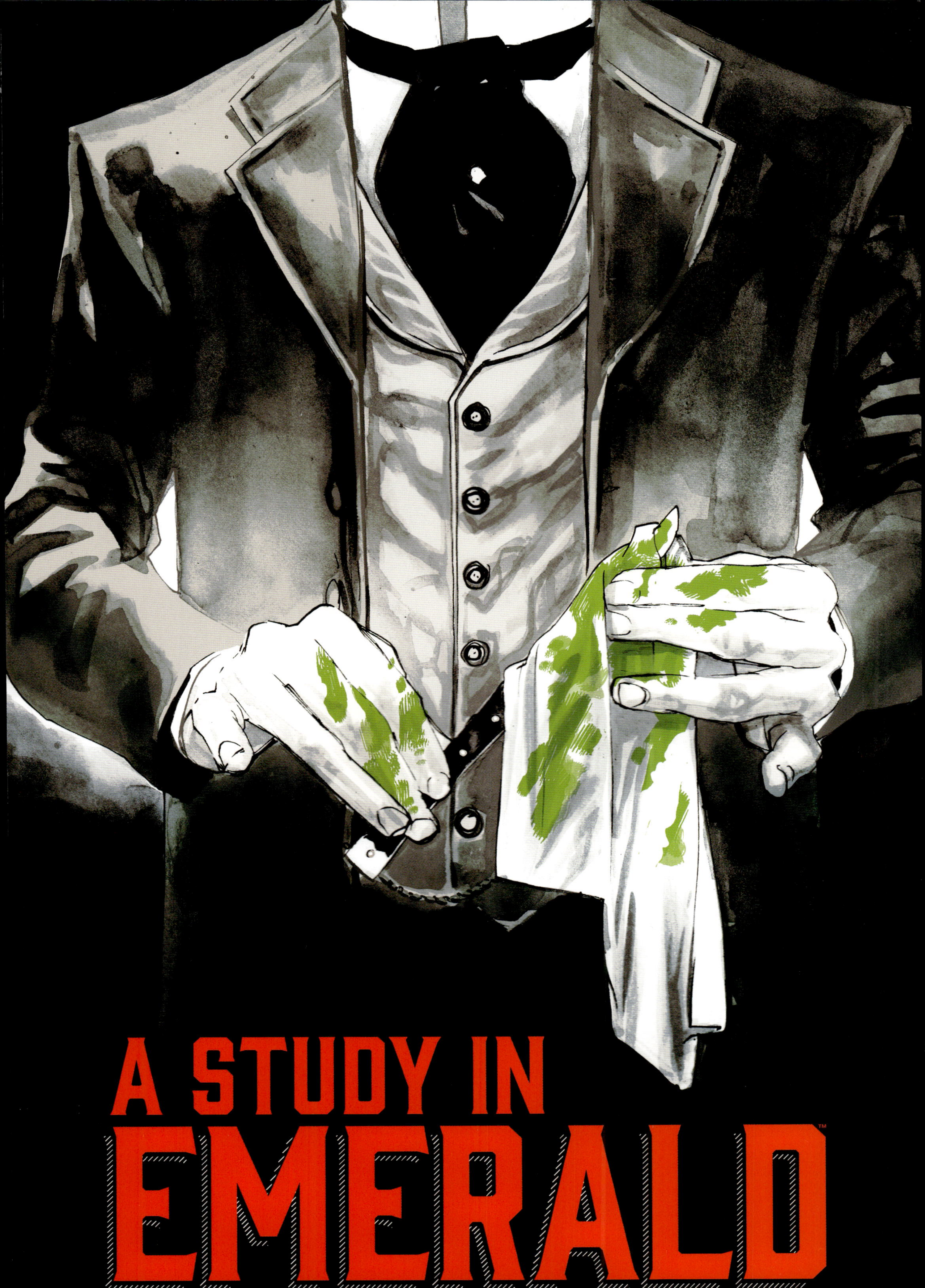
A STUDY IN
EMERALD™

THE NEW FRIEND

THE STRAND PLAYERS

PRESENTS

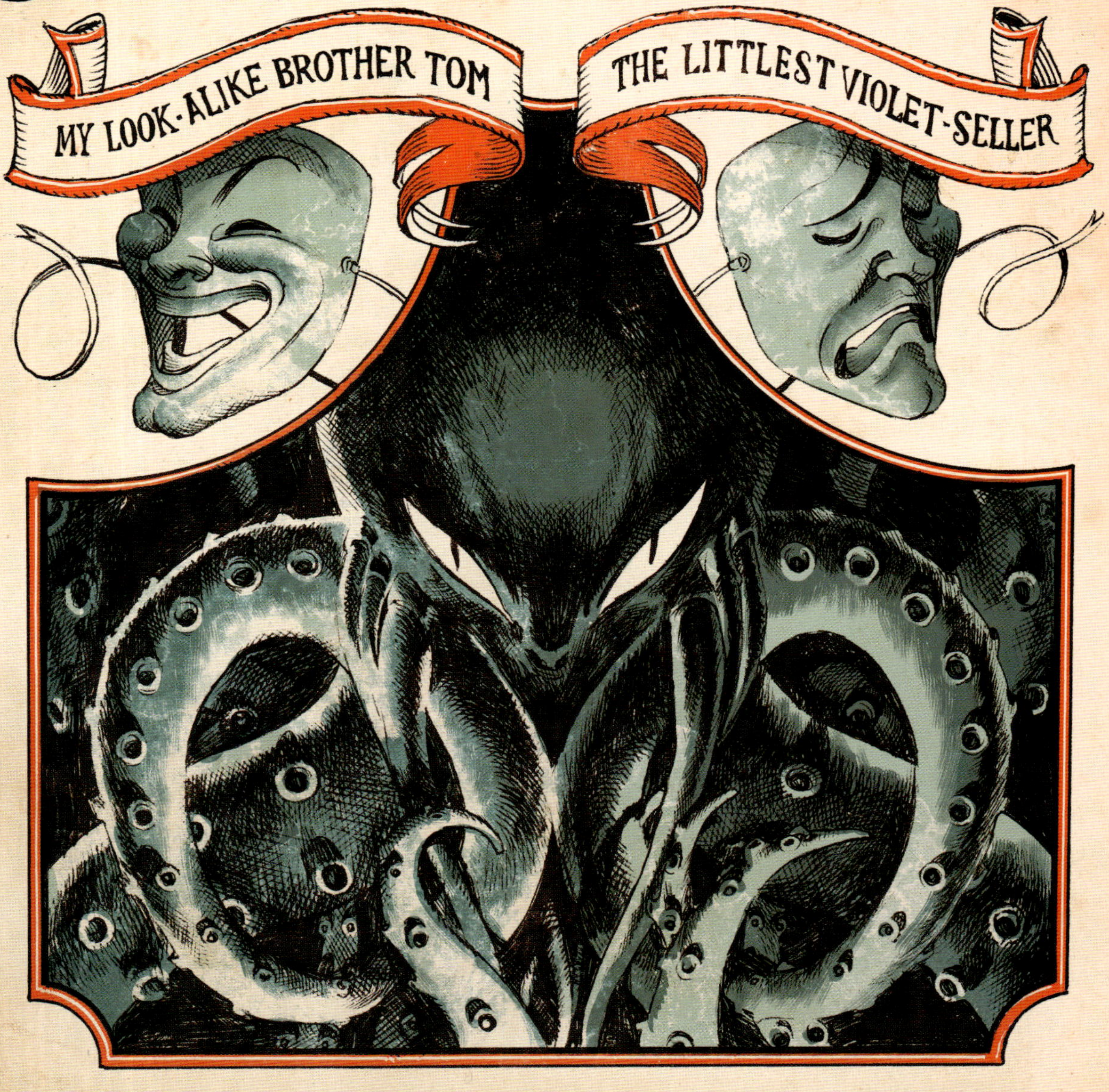
MY LOOK-ALIKE BROTHER TOM
THE LITTLEST VIOLET-SELLER

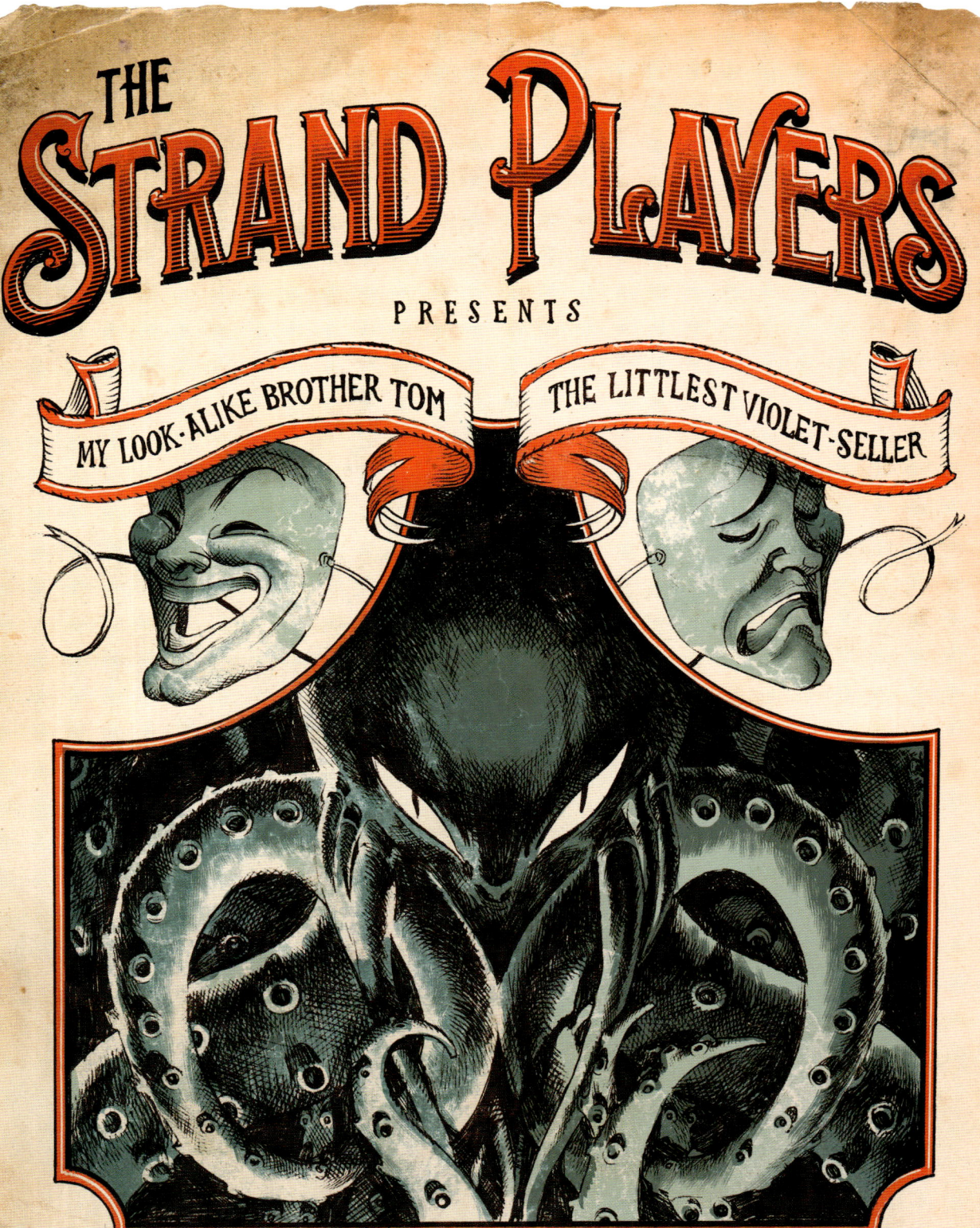

THE GREAT OLD ONES COME

Fresh from Their Stupendous European Tour, where they performed before several of the **CROWNED HEADS OF EUROPE**, garnering their **plaudits** and **praise** with **magnificent dramatic performances**, combining both **COMEDY** and **TRAGEDY**, the **Strand Players** wish to make it known that they shall be appearing at the **Royal Court Theatre, Drury Lane**, for a **LIMITED ENGAGEMENT** in April, at which they will present *"My Look-Alike Brother Tom!" "The Littlest Violet-Seller"* and *"The Great Old Ones Come,"* (this last an Historical Epic of Pageantry and Delight); each an entire play in one act!
Tickets are available now from the Box Office.

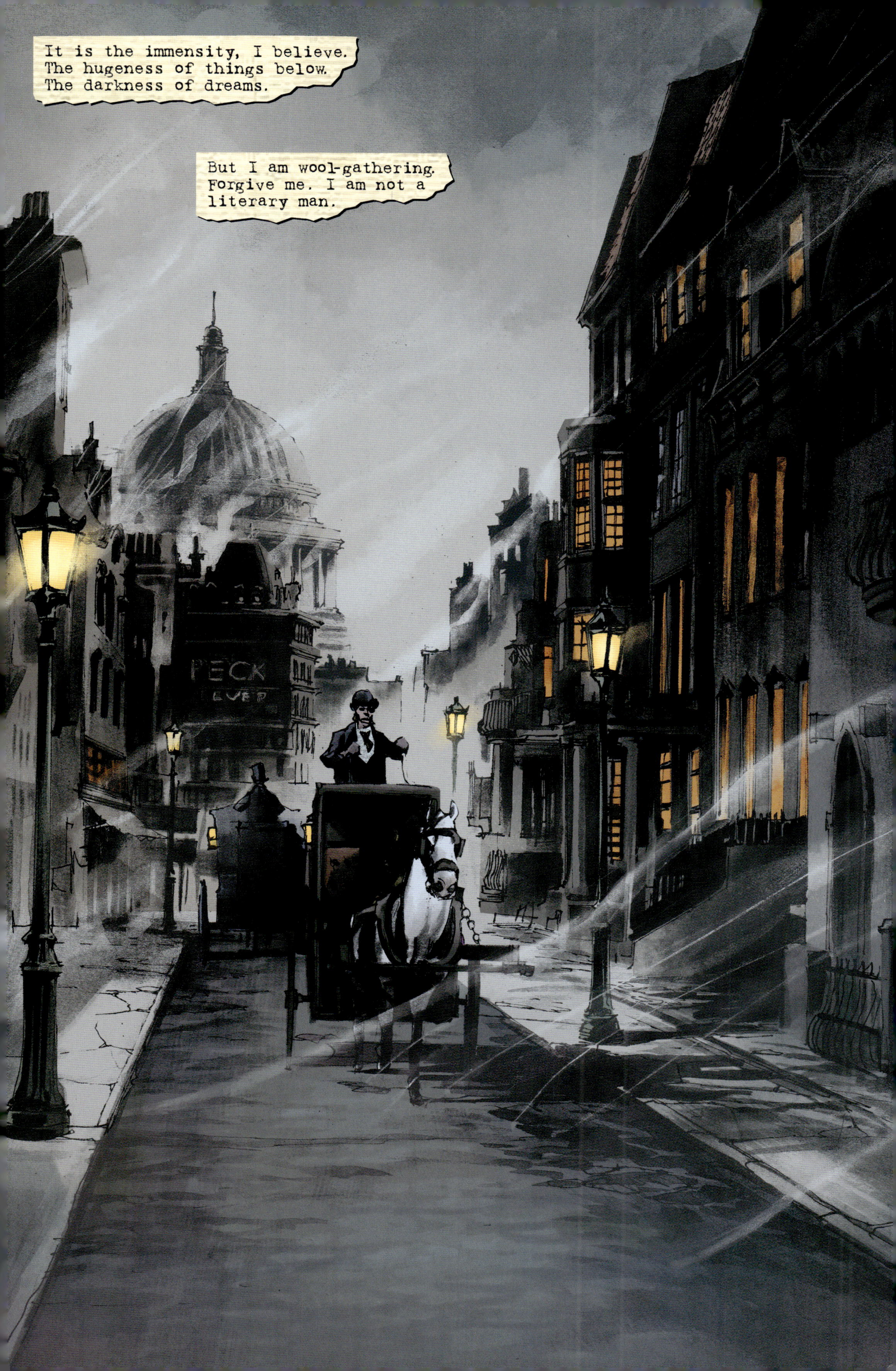
It is the immensity, I believe. The hugeness of things below. The darkness of dreams.
But I am wool-gathering. Forgive me. I am not a literary man.

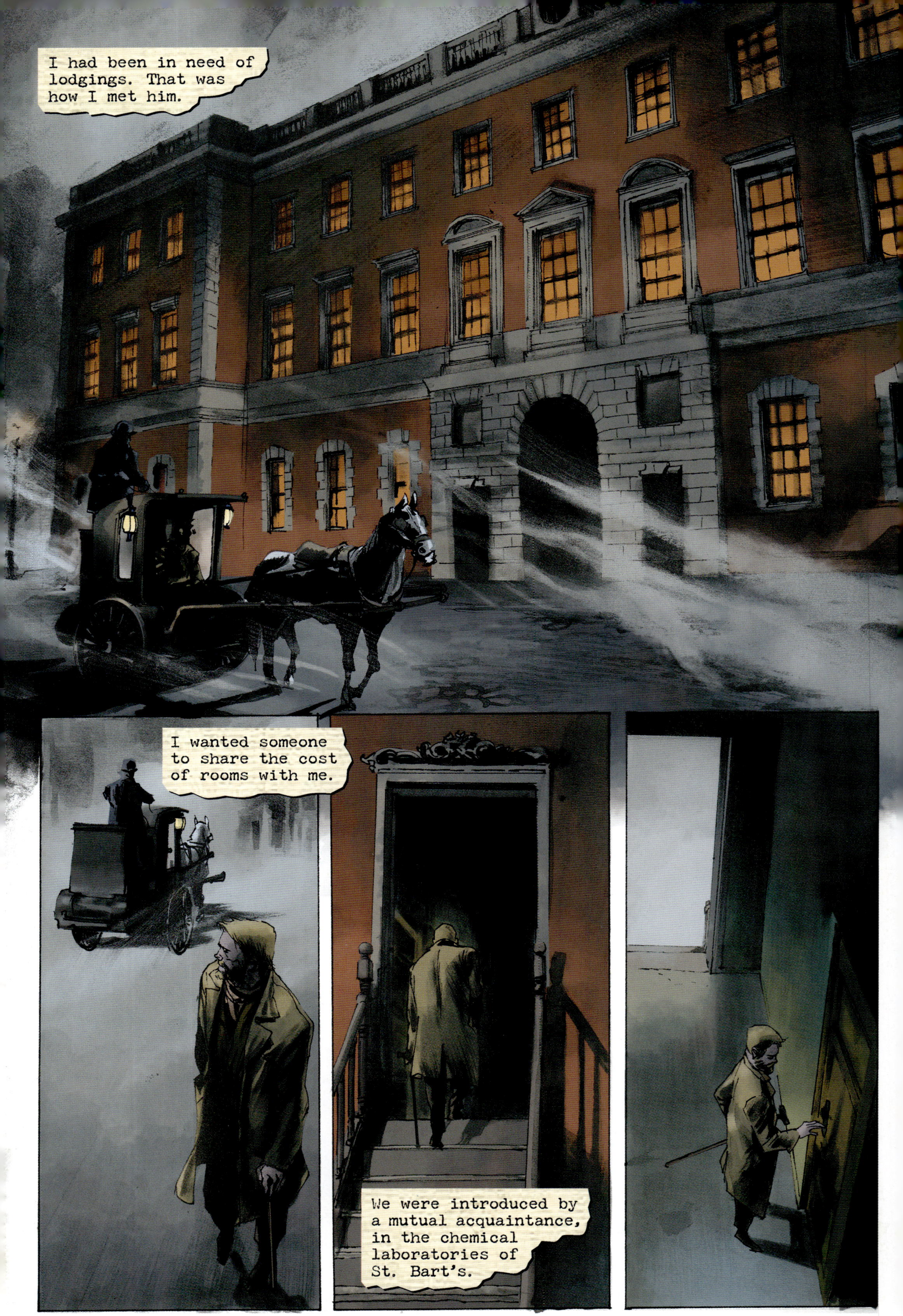
I had been in need of lodgings. That was how I met him.
I wanted someone to share the cost of rooms with me.
We were introduced by a mutual acquaintance, in the chemical laboratories of St. Bart's.

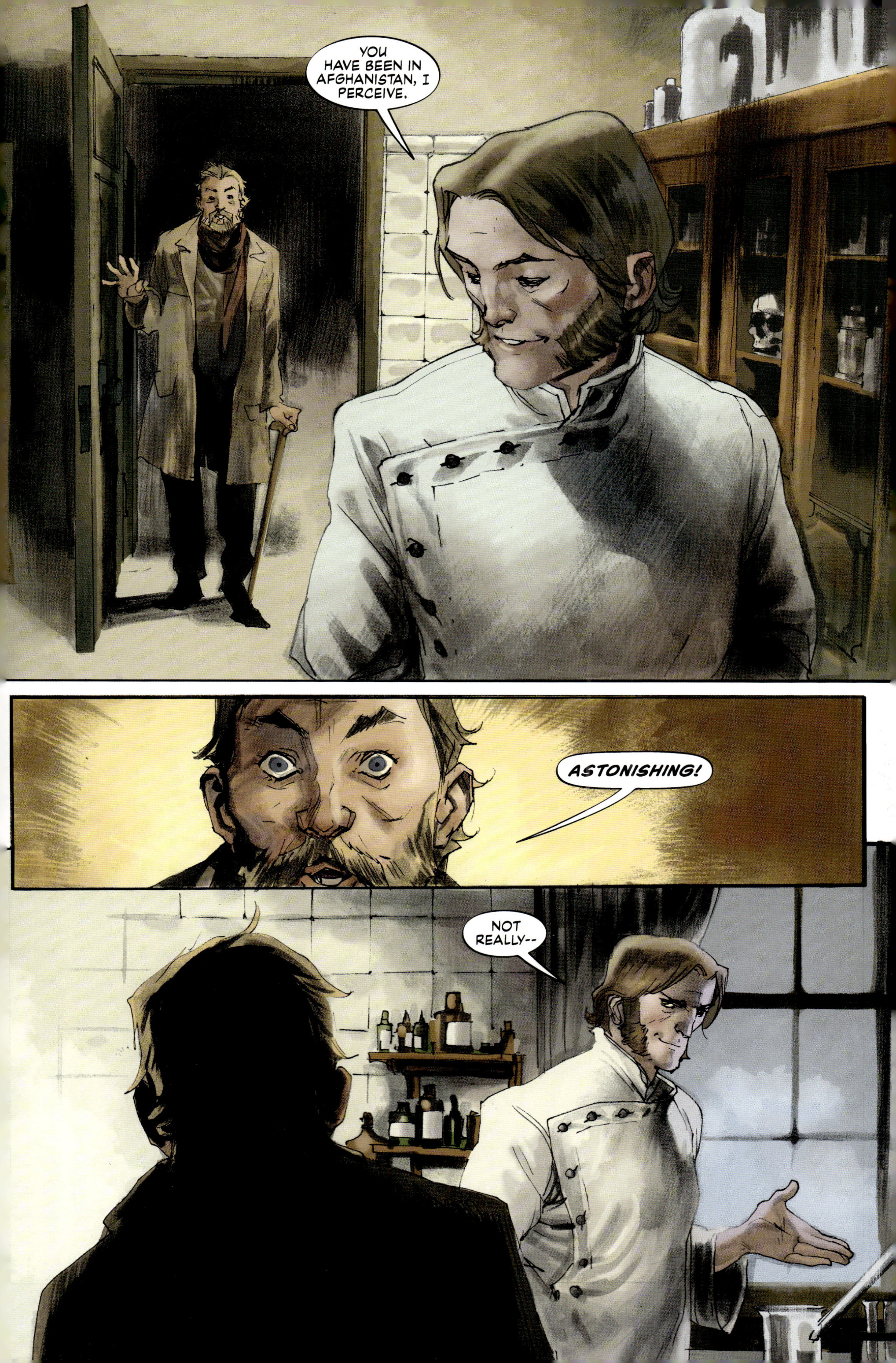
YOU HAVE BEEN IN AFGHANISTAN, I PERCEIVE.
ASTONISHING!
NOT REALLY--

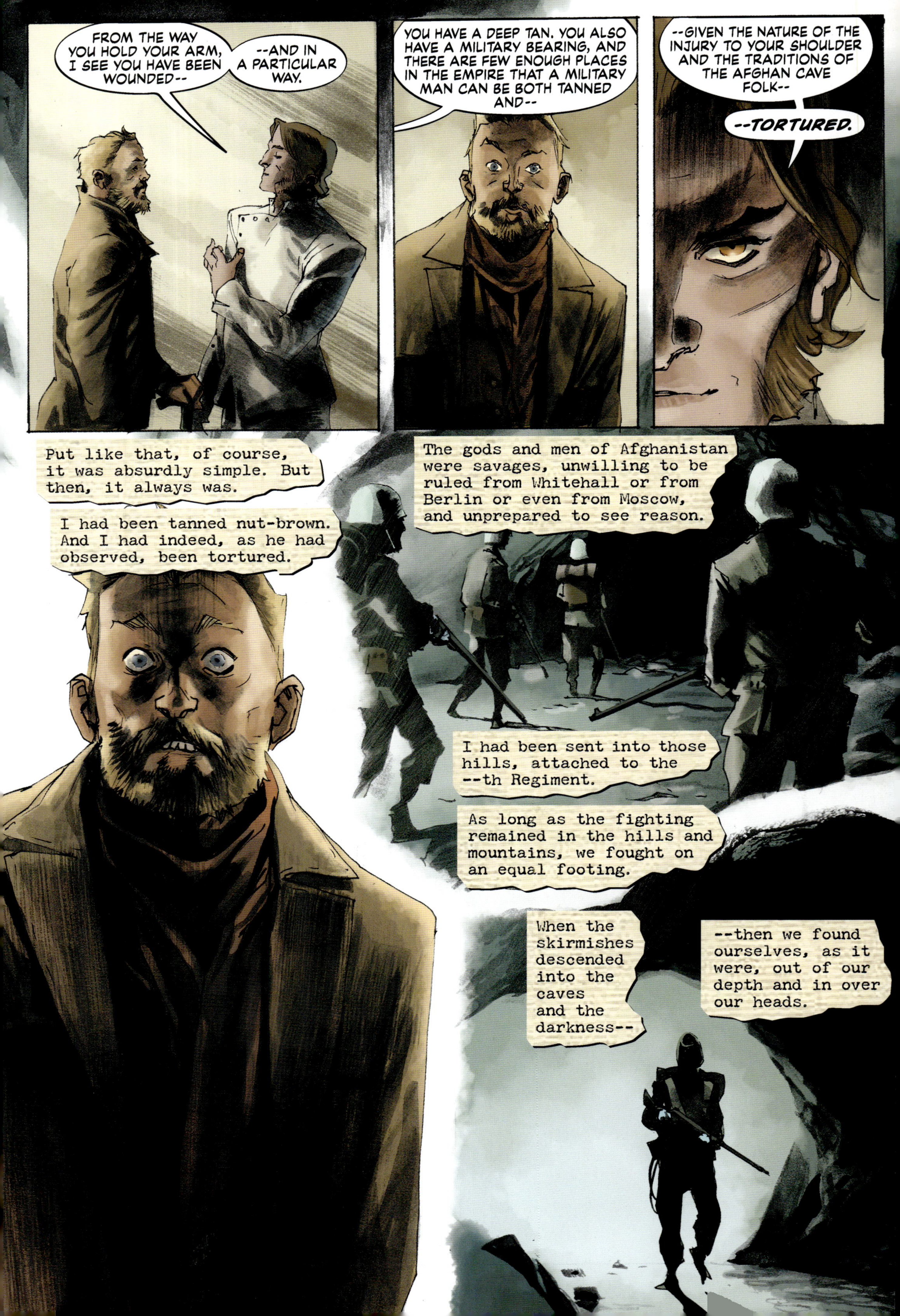
FROM THE WAY YOU HOLD YOUR ARM, I SEE YOU HAVE BEEN WOUNDED--
--AND IN A PARTICULAR WAY.
YOU HAVE A DEEP TAN. YOU ALSO HAVE A MILITARY BEARING, AND THERE ARE FEW ENOUGH PLACES IN THE EMPIRE THAT A MILITARY MAN CAN BE BOTH TANNED AND--
--GIVEN THE NATURE OF THE INJURY TO YOUR SHOULDER AND THE TRADITIONS OF THE AFGHAN CAVE FOLK--
--TORTURED.
Put like that, of course, it was absurdly simple. But then, it always was.
I had been tanned nut-brown. And I had indeed, as he had observed, been tortured.
The gods and men of Afghanistan were savages, unwilling to be ruled from Whitehall or from Berlin or even from Moscow, and unprepared to see reason.
I had been sent into those hills, attached to the --th Regiment.
As long as the fighting remained in the hills and mountains, we fought on an equal footing.
When the skirmishes descended into the caves and the darkness--
--then we found ourselves, as it were, out of our depth and in over our heads.

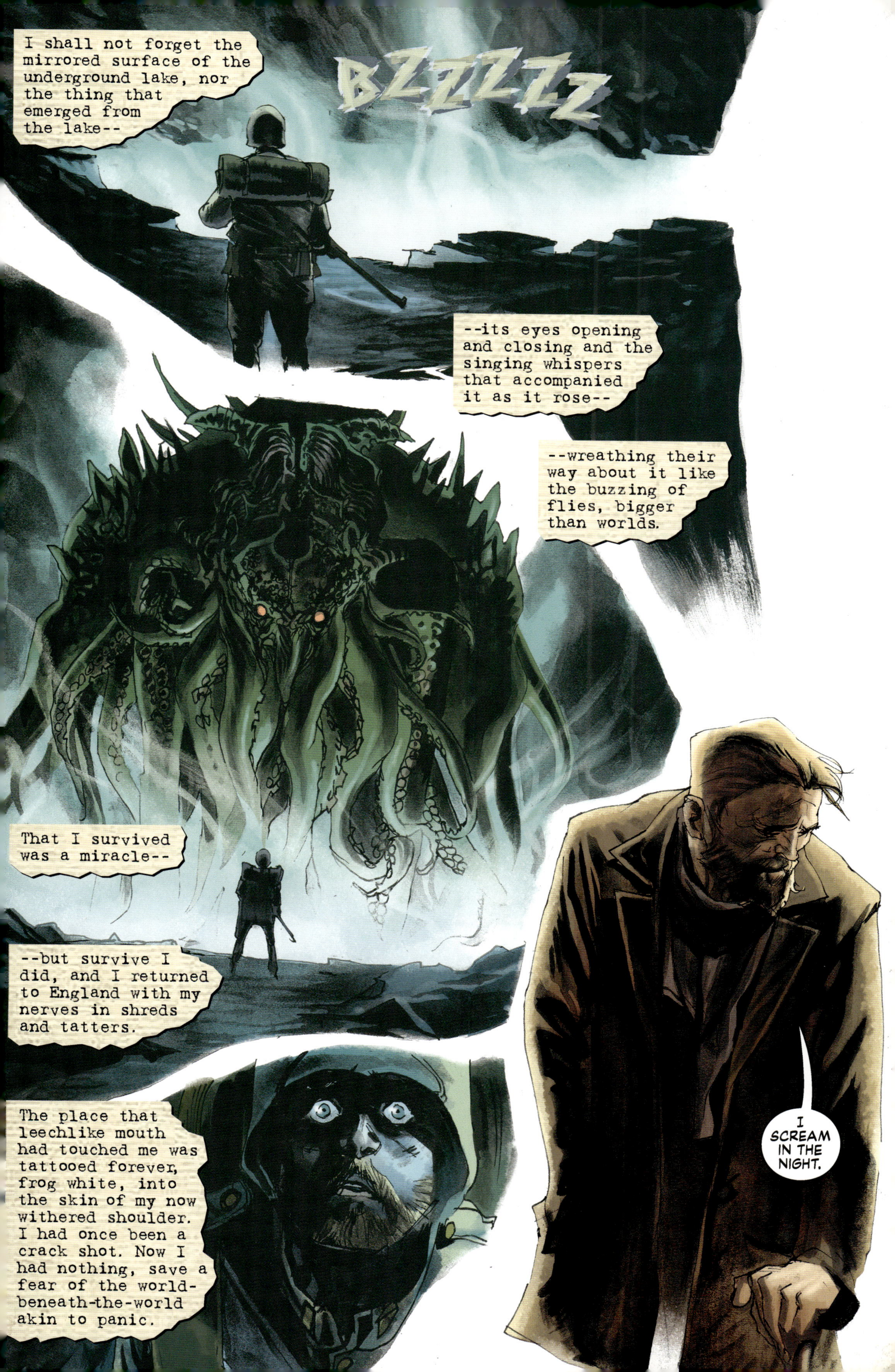
I shall not forget the mirrored surface of the underground lake, nor the thing that emerged from the lake--
BZZZZZ
--its eyes opening and closing and the singing whispers that accompanied it as it rose--
--wreathing their way about it like the buzzing of flies, bigger than worlds.
That I survived was a miracle--
--but survive I did, and I returned to England with my nerves in shreds and tatters.
The place that leechlike mouth had touched me was tattooed forever, frog white, into the skin of my now withered shoulder. I had once been a crack shot. Now I had nothing, save a fear of the world-beneath-the-world akin to panic.
I SCREAM IN THE NIGHT.

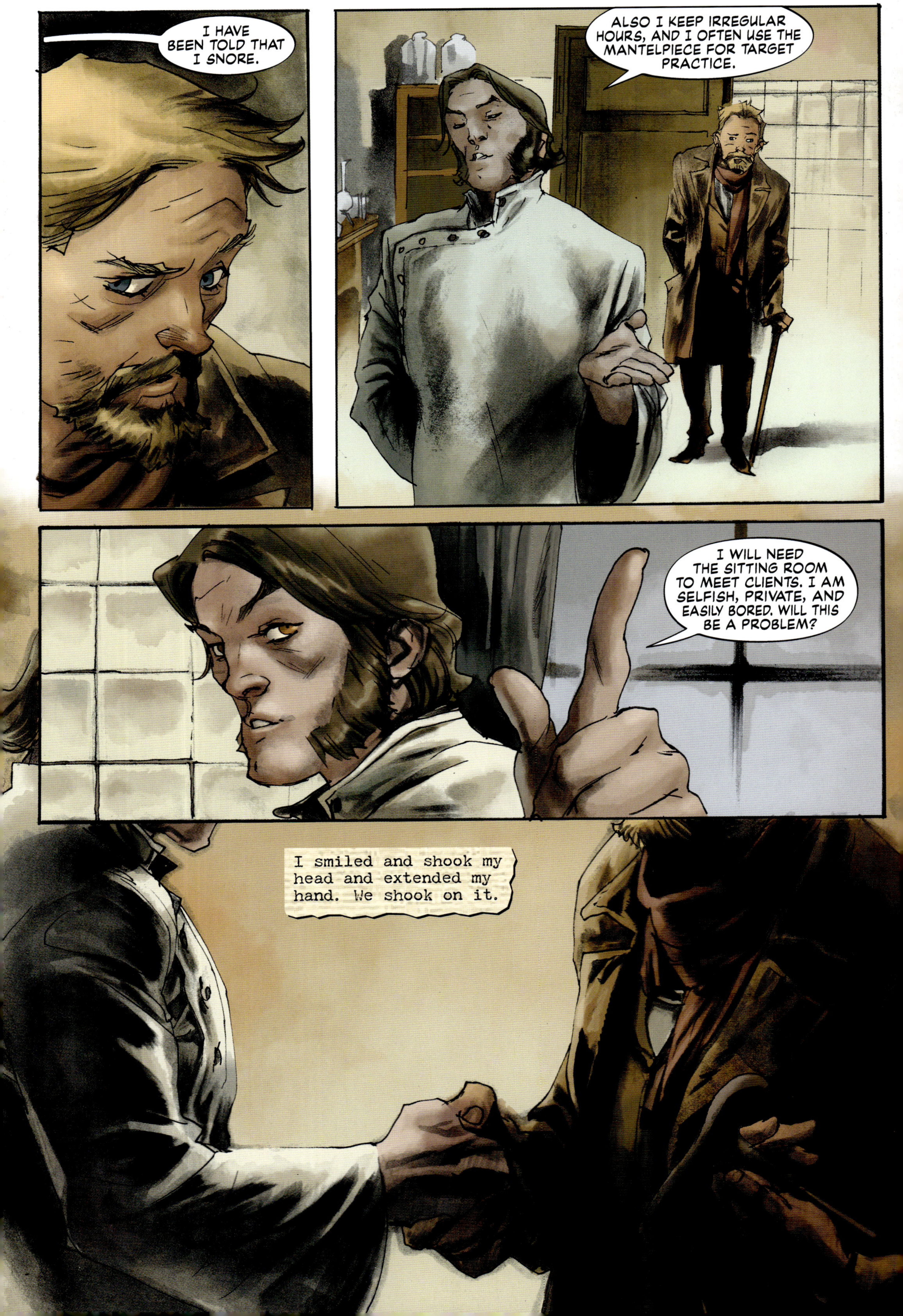
I HAVE BEEN TOLD THAT I SNORE.
ALSO I KEEP IRREGULAR HOURS, AND I OFTEN USE THE MANTELPIECE FOR TARGET PRACTICE.
I WILL NEED THE SITTING ROOM TO MEET CLIENTS. I AM SELFISH, PRIVATE, AND EASILY BORED. WILL THIS BE A PROBLEM?
I smiled and shook my head and extended my hand. We shook on it.

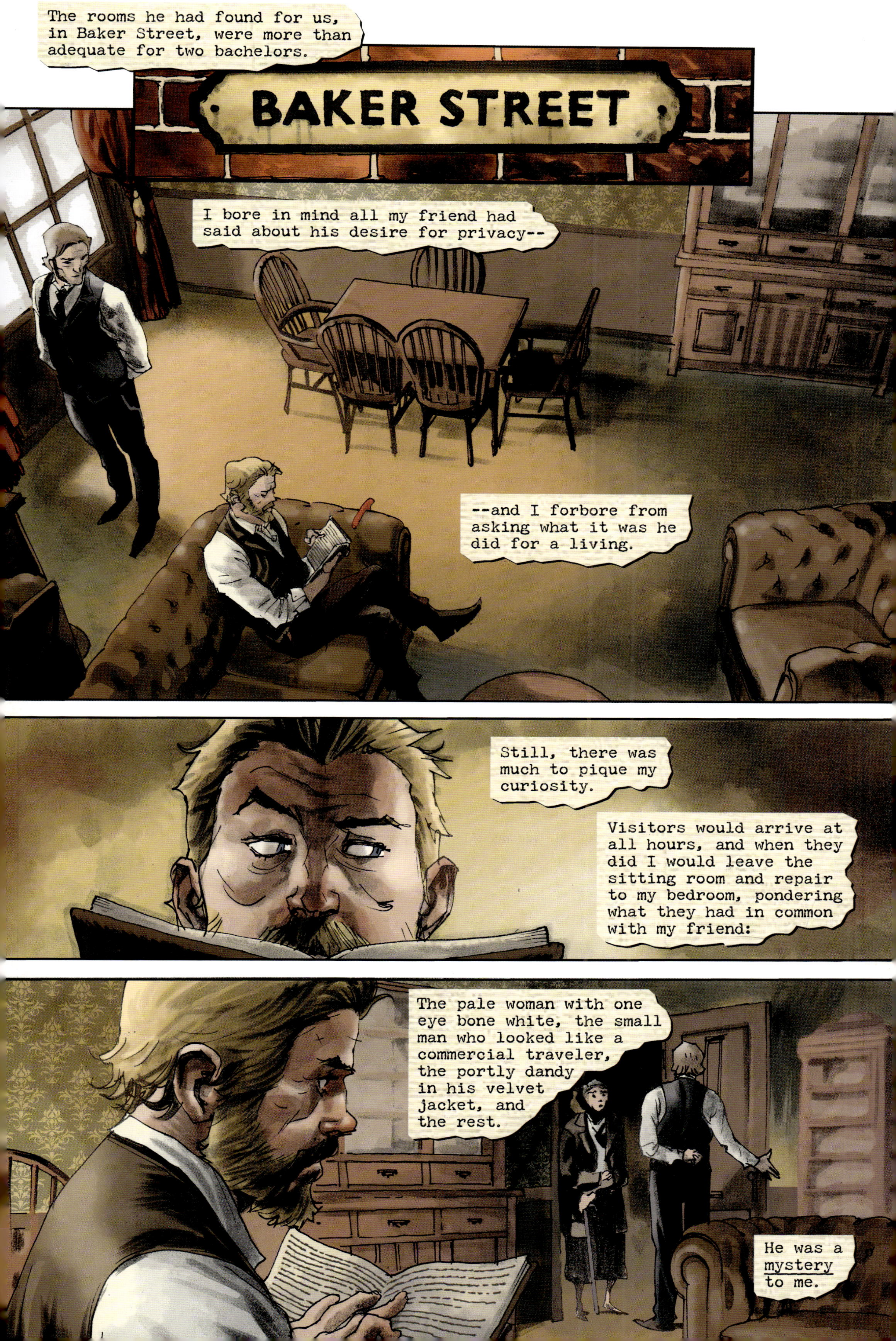
The rooms he had found for us, in Baker Street, were more than adequate for two bachelors.
BAKER STREET
I bore in mind all my friend had said about his desire for privacy--
--and I forbore from asking what it was he did for a living.
Still, there was much to pique my curiosity.
Visitors would arrive at all hours, and when they did I would leave the sitting room and repair to my bedroom, pondering what they had in common with my friend:
The pale woman with one eye bone white, the small man who looked like a commercial traveler, the portly dandy in his velvet jacket, and the rest.
He was a mystery to me.

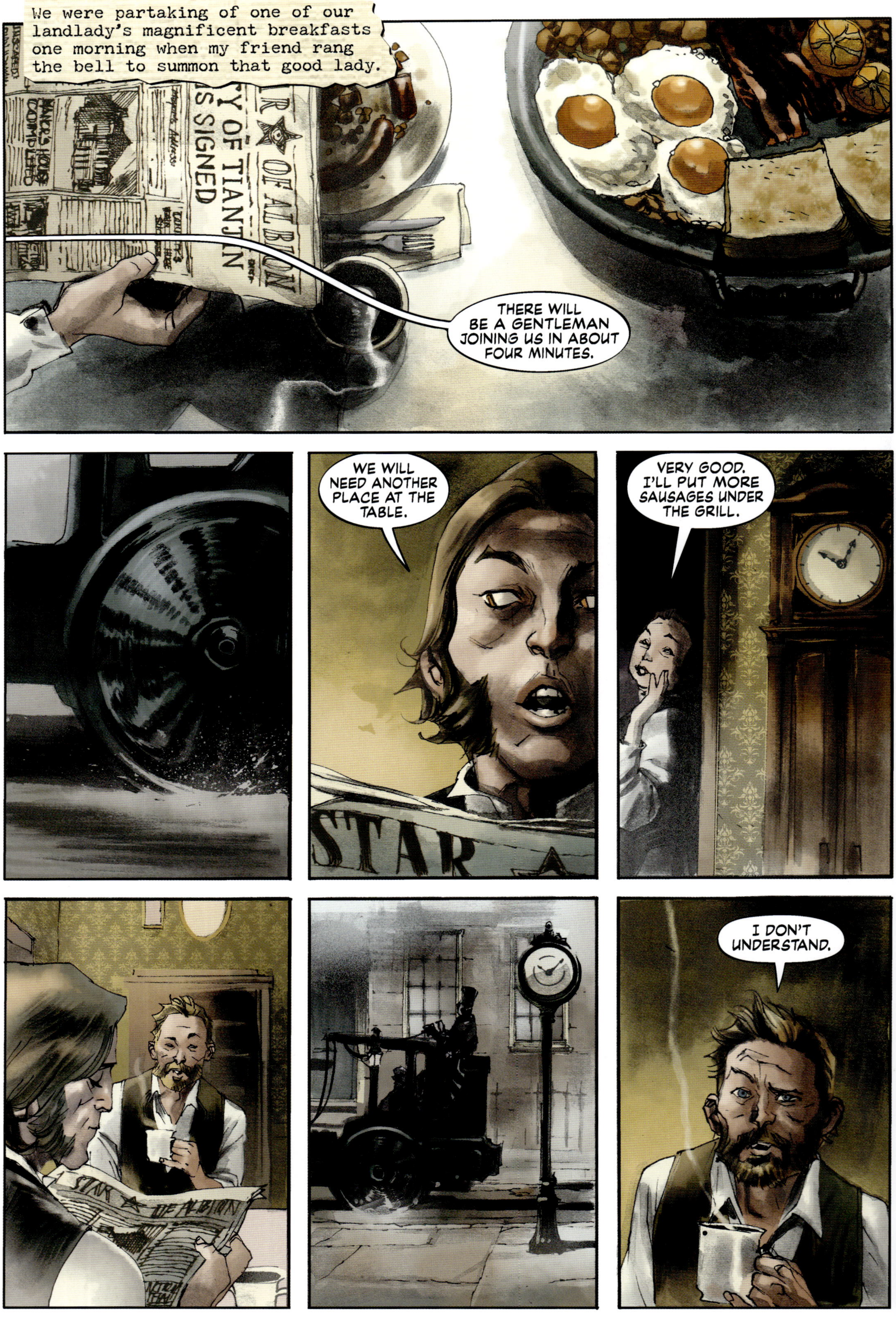
We were partaking of one of our landlady's magnificent breakfasts one morning when my friend rang the bell to summon that good lady.
STAR OF ALBION
TREATY OF TIANJIN IS SIGNED
THERE WILL BE A GENTLEMAN JOINING US IN ABOUT FOUR MINUTES.
WE WILL NEED ANOTHER PLACE AT THE TABLE.
VERY GOOD. I'LL PUT MORE SAUSAGES UNDER THE GRILL.
I DON'T UNDERSTAND.

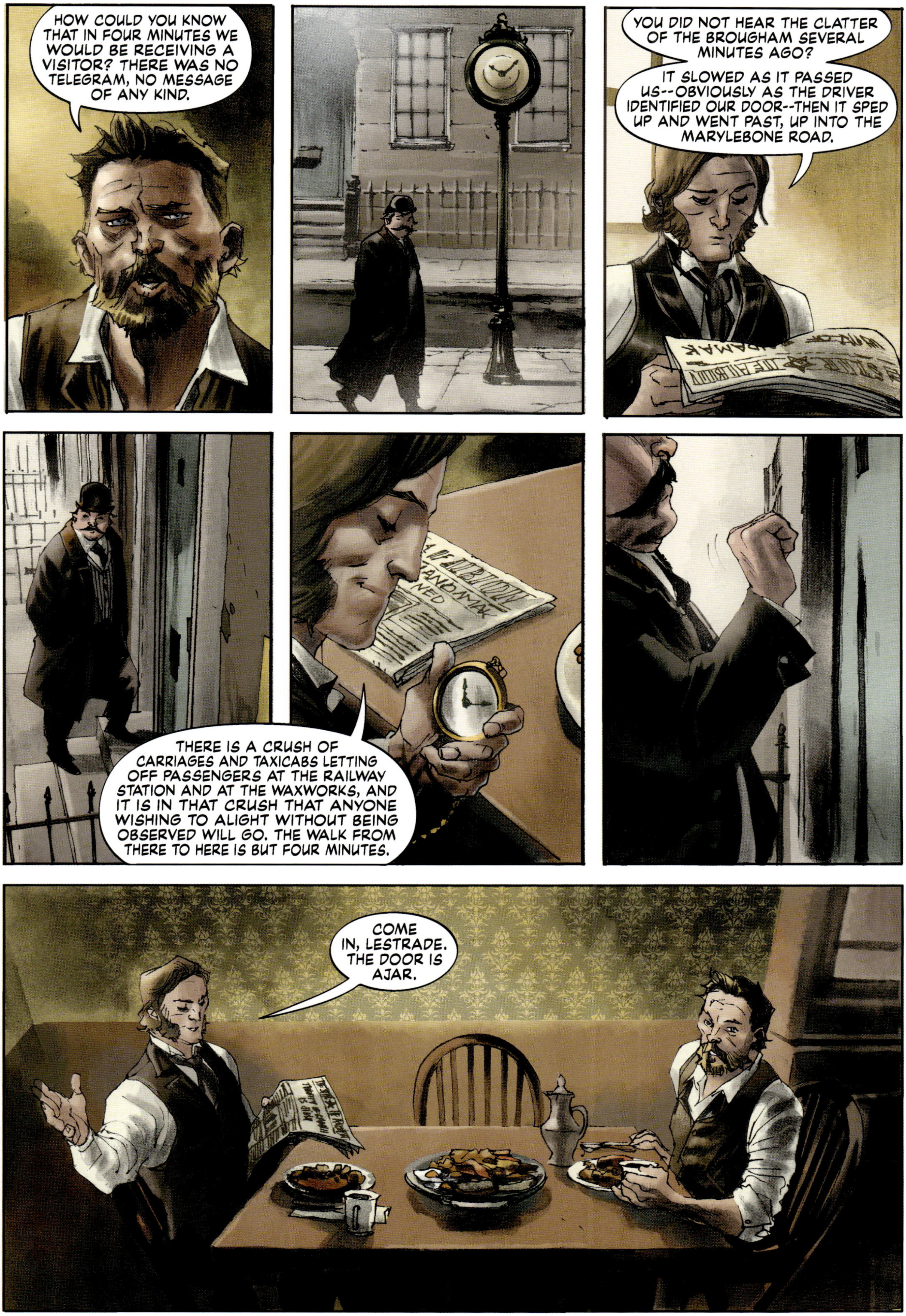
HOW COULD YOU KNOW THAT IN FOUR MINUTES WE WOULD BE RECEIVING A VISITOR? THERE WAS NO TELEGRAM, NO MESSAGE OF ANY KIND.
YOU DID NOT HEAR THE CLATTER OF THE BROUGHAM SEVERAL MINUTES AGO?
IT SLOWED AS IT PASSED US--OBVIOUSLY AS THE DRIVER IDENTIFIED OUR DOOR--THEN IT SPED UP AND WENT PAST, UP INTO THE MARYLEBONE ROAD.
THERE IS A CRUSH OF CARRIAGES AND TAXICABS LETTING OFF PASSENGERS AT THE RAILWAY STATION AND AT THE WAXWORKS, AND IT IS IN THAT CRUSH THAT ANYONE WISHING TO ALIGHT WITHOUT BEING OBSERVED WILL GO. THE WALK FROM THERE TO HERE IS BUT FOUR MINUTES.
COME IN, LESTRADE. THE DOOR IS AJAR.

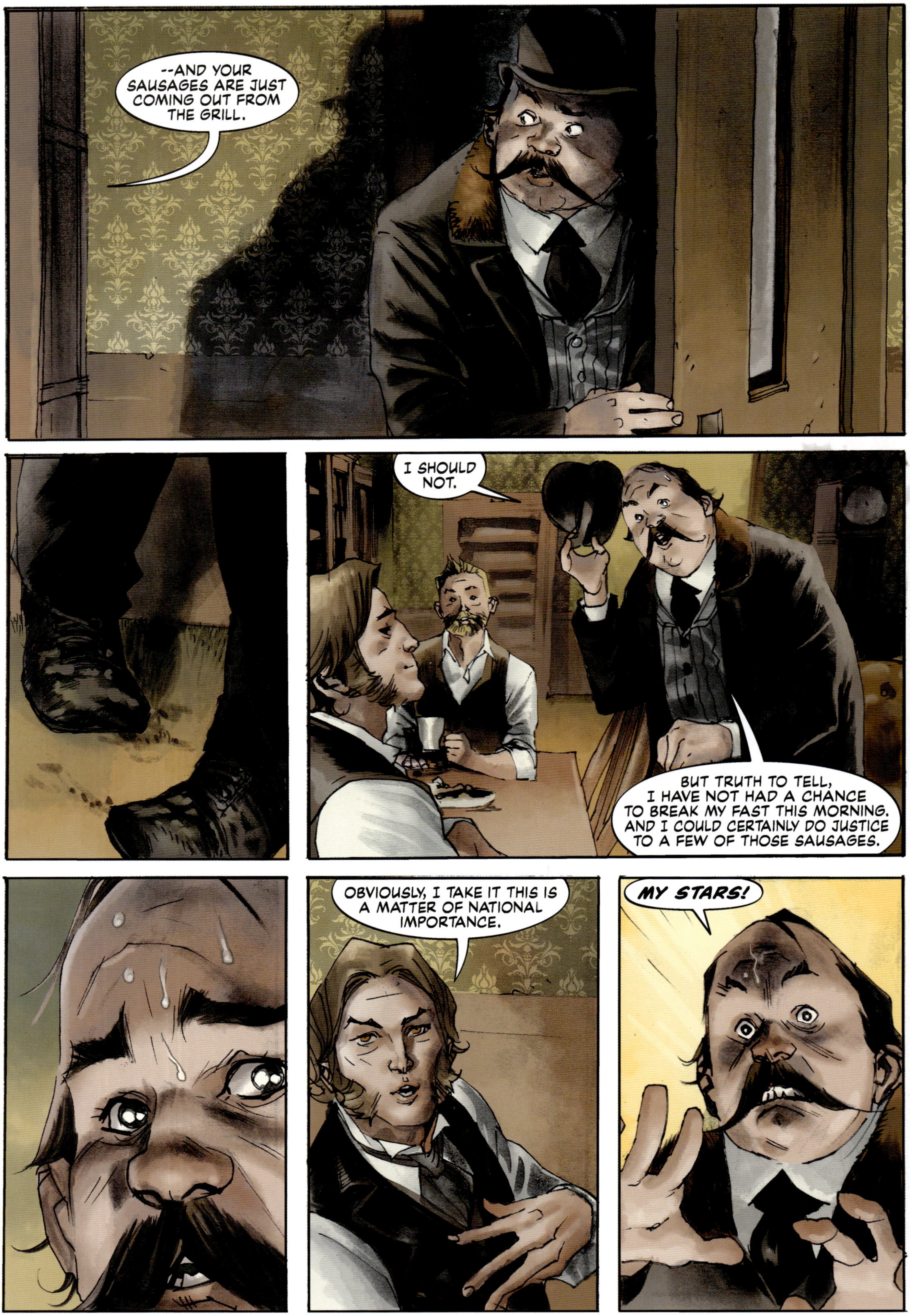
--AND YOUR SAUSAGES ARE JUST COMING OUT FROM THE GRILL.
I SHOULD NOT.
BUT TRUTH TO TELL, I HAVE NOT HAD A CHANCE TO BREAK MY FAST THIS MORNING. AND I COULD CERTAINLY DO JUSTICE TO A FEW OF THOSE SAUSAGES.
OBVIOUSLY, I TAKE IT THIS IS A MATTER OF NATIONAL IMPORTANCE.
MY STARS!

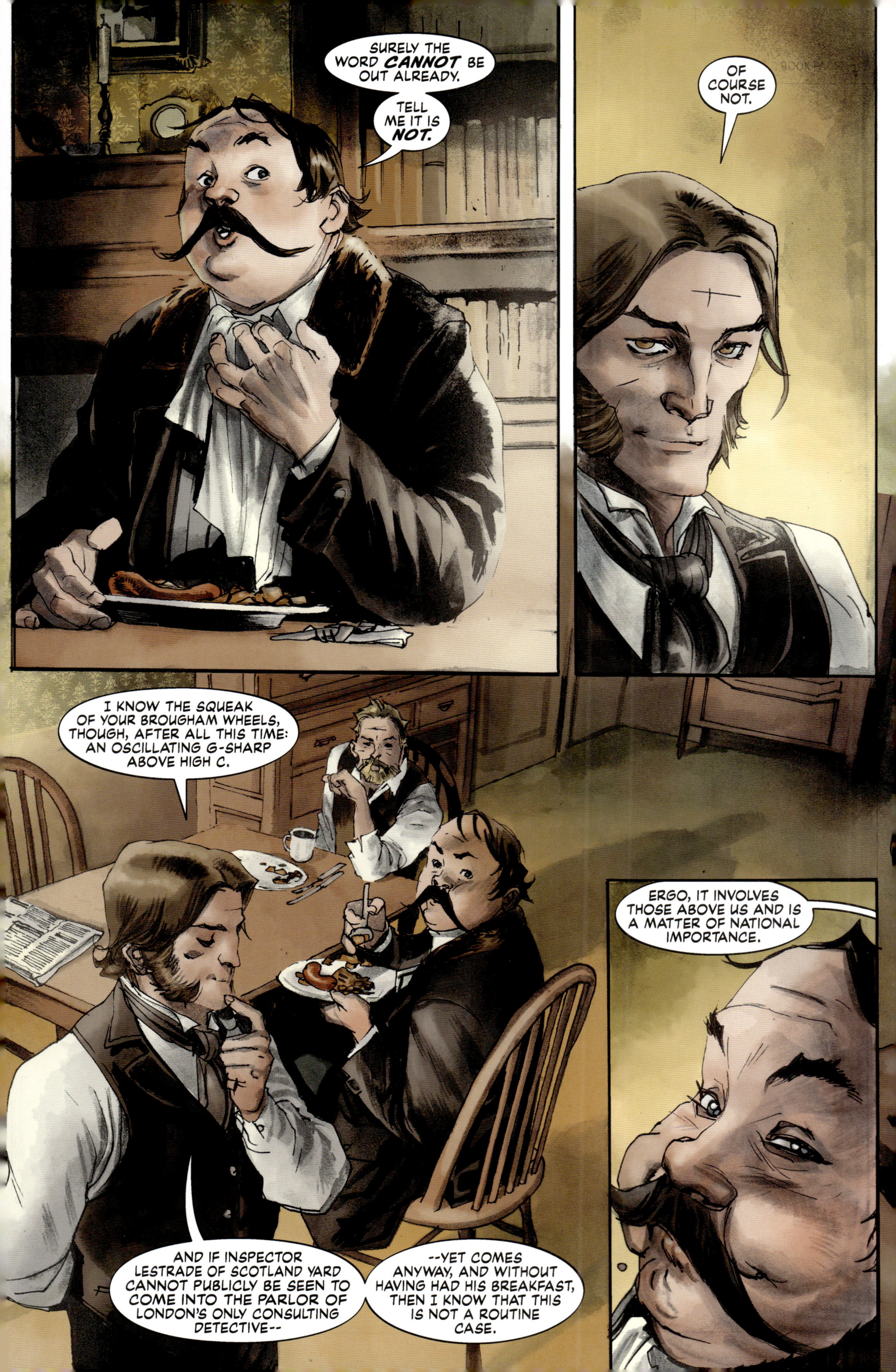
SURELY THE WORD **CANNOT** BE OUT ALREADY.
TELL ME IT IS **NOT.**
OF COURSE NOT.
I KNOW THE SQUEAK OF YOUR BROUGHAM WHEELS, THOUGH, AFTER ALL THIS TIME: AN OSCILLATING G-SHARP ABOVE HIGH C.
AND IF INSPECTOR LESTRADE OF SCOTLAND YARD CANNOT PUBLICLY BE SEEN TO COME INTO THE PARLOR OF LONDON'S ONLY CONSULTING DETECTIVE--
--YET COMES ANYWAY, AND WITHOUT HAVING HAD HIS BREAKFAST, THEN I KNOW THAT THIS IS NOT A ROUTINE CASE.
ERGO, IT INVOLVES THOSE ABOVE US AND IS A MATTER OF NATIONAL IMPORTANCE.

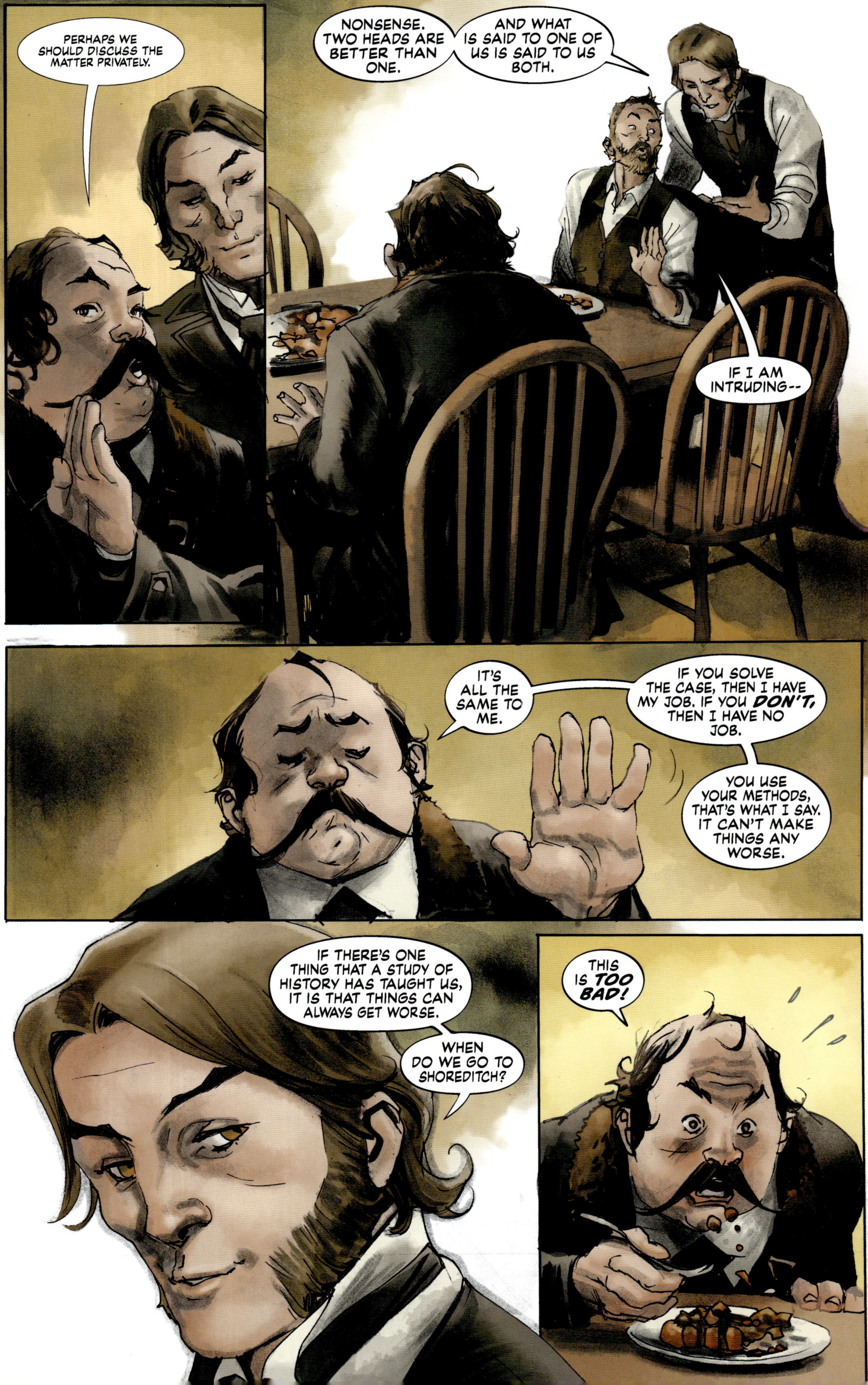
PERHAPS WE SHOULD DISCUSS THE MATTER PRIVATELY.
NONSENSE. TWO HEADS ARE BETTER THAN ONE.
AND WHAT IS SAID TO ONE OF US IS SAID TO US BOTH.
IF I AM INTRUDING--
IT'S ALL THE SAME TO ME.
IF YOU SOLVE THE CASE, THEN I HAVE MY JOB. IF YOU ***DON'T,*** THEN I HAVE NO JOB.
YOU USE YOUR METHODS, THAT'S WHAT I SAY. IT CAN'T MAKE THINGS ANY WORSE.
IF THERE'S ONE THING THAT A STUDY OF HISTORY HAS TAUGHT US, IT IS THAT THINGS CAN ALWAYS GET WORSE.
WHEN DO WE GO TO SHOREDITCH?
THIS IS ***TOO BAD!***

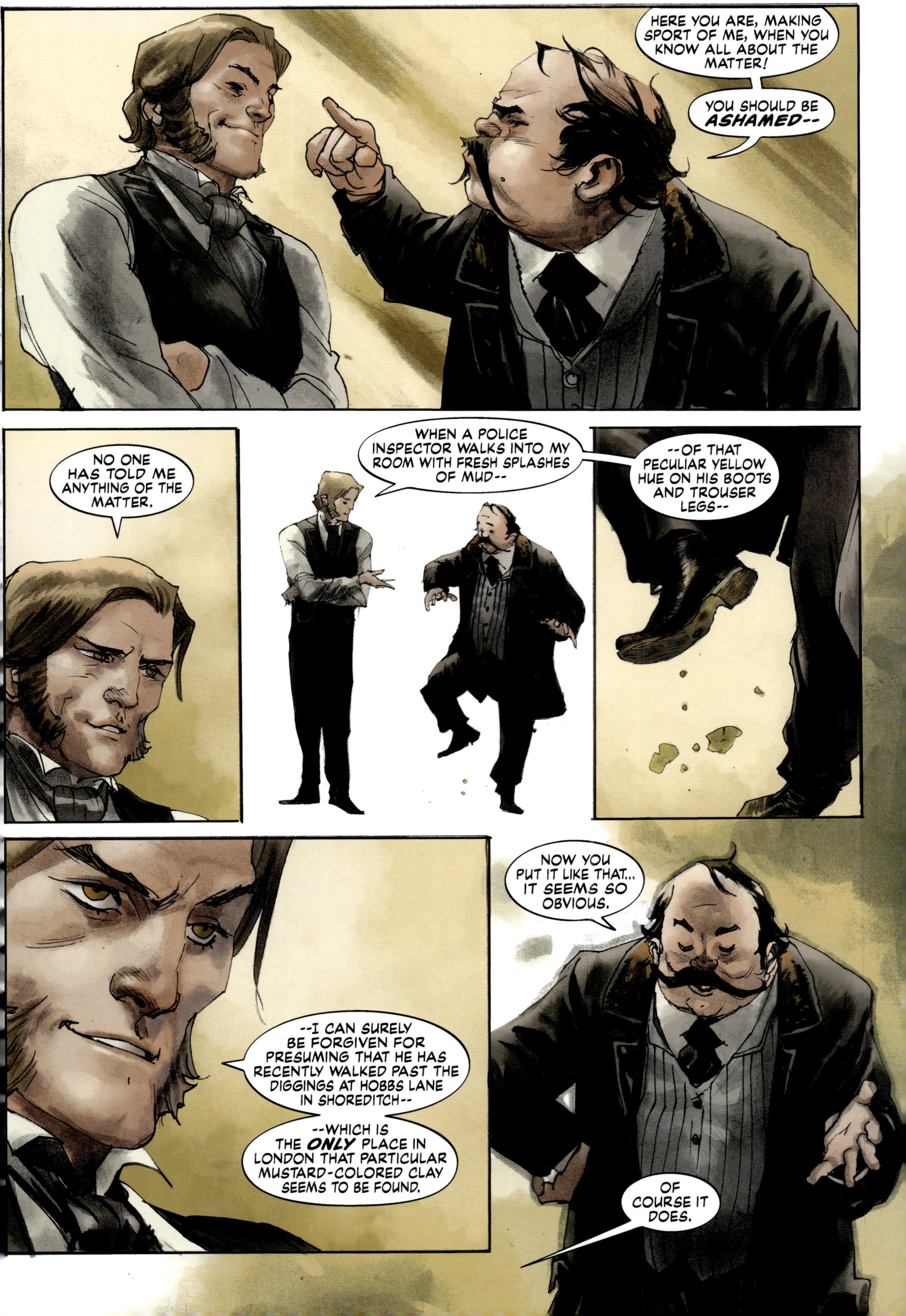
HERE YOU ARE, MAKING SPORT OF ME, WHEN YOU KNOW ALL ABOUT THE MATTER!
YOU SHOULD BE ASHAMED--
NO ONE HAS TOLD ME ANYTHING OF THE MATTER.
WHEN A POLICE INSPECTOR WALKS INTO MY ROOM WITH FRESH SPLASHES OF MUD--
--OF THAT PECULIAR YELLOW HUE ON HIS BOOTS AND TROUSER LEGS--
--I CAN SURELY BE FORGIVEN FOR PRESUMING THAT HE HAS RECENTLY WALKED PAST THE DIGGINGS AT HOBBS LANE IN SHOREDITCH--
--WHICH IS THE ONLY PLACE IN LONDON THAT PARTICULAR MUSTARD-COLORED CLAY SEEMS TO BE FOUND.
NOW YOU PUT IT LIKE THAT... IT SEEMS SO OBVIOUS.
OF COURSE IT DOES.

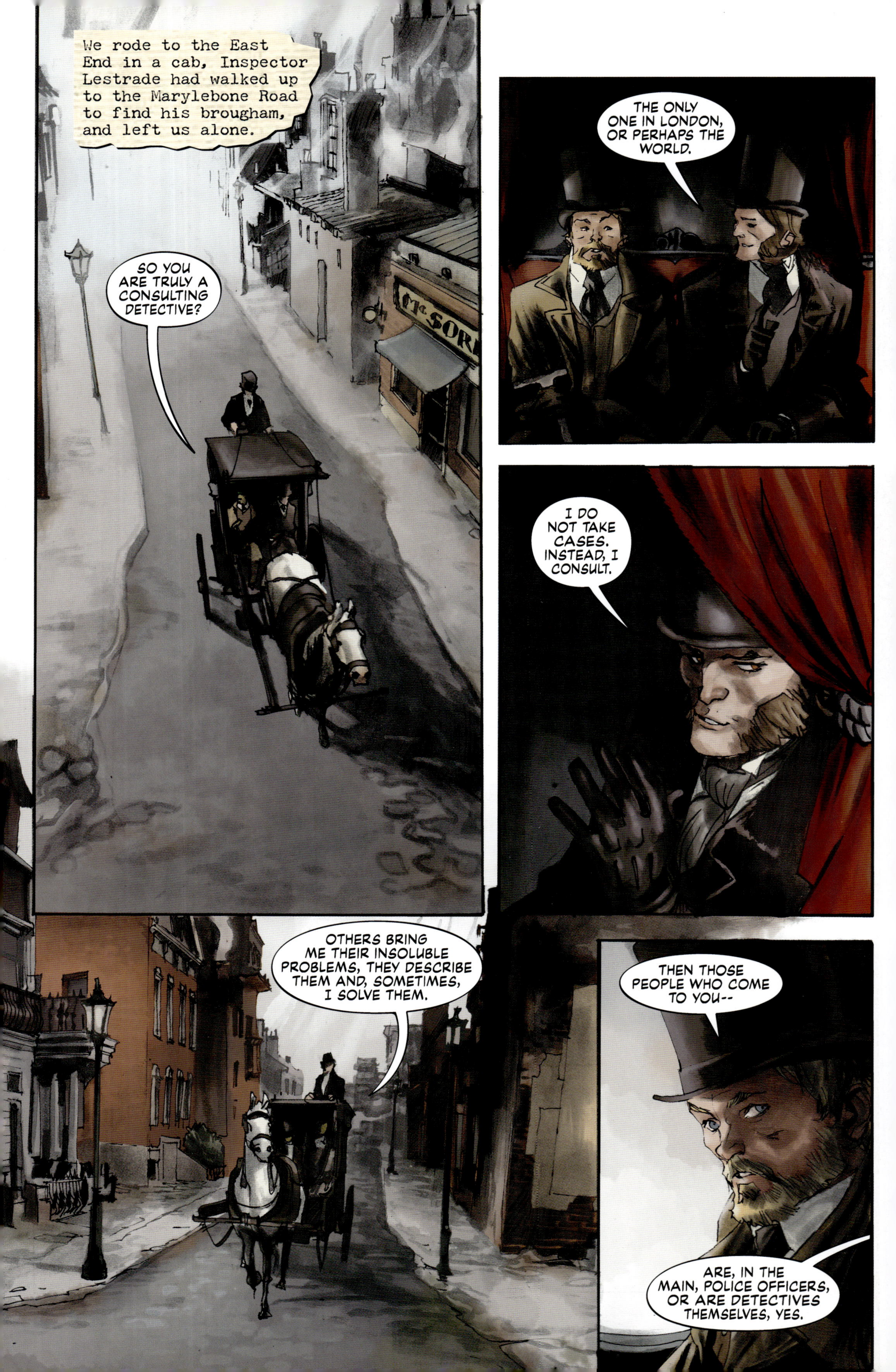
We rode to the East End in a cab, Inspector Lestrade had walked up to the Marylebone Road to find his brougham, and left us alone.
SO YOU ARE TRULY A CONSULTING DETECTIVE?
THE ONLY ONE IN LONDON, OR PERHAPS THE WORLD.
I DO NOT TAKE CASES. INSTEAD, I CONSULT.
OTHERS BRING ME THEIR INSOLUBLE PROBLEMS, THEY DESCRIBE THEM AND, SOMETIMES, I SOLVE THEM.
THEN THOSE PEOPLE WHO COME TO YOU--
ARE, IN THE MAIN, POLICE OFFICERS, OR ARE DETECTIVES THEMSELVES, YES.

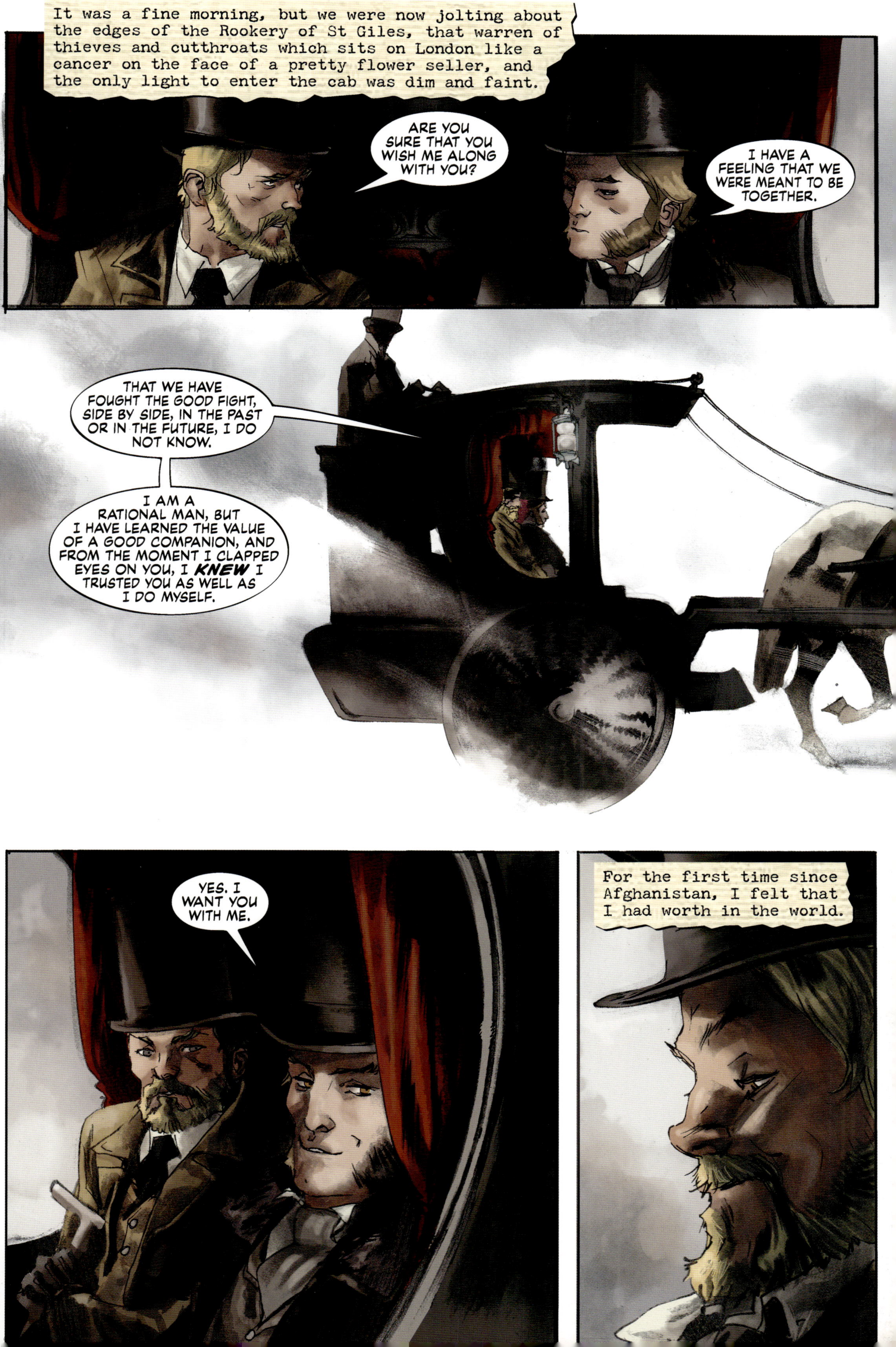
It was a fine morning, but we were now jolting about the edges of the Rookery of St Giles, that warren of thieves and cutthroats which sits on London like a cancer on the face of a pretty flower seller, and the only light to enter the cab was dim and faint.
ARE YOU SURE THAT YOU WISH ME ALONG WITH YOU?
I HAVE A FEELING THAT WE WERE MEANT TO BE TOGETHER.
THAT WE HAVE FOUGHT THE GOOD FIGHT, SIDE BY SIDE, IN THE PAST OR IN THE FUTURE, I DO NOT KNOW.
I AM A RATIONAL MAN, BUT I HAVE LEARNED THE VALUE OF A GOOD COMPANION, AND FROM THE MOMENT I CLAPPED EYES ON YOU, I ***KNEW*** I TRUSTED YOU AS WELL AS I DO MYSELF.
YES. I WANT YOU WITH ME.
For the first time since Afghanistan, I felt that I had worth in the world.

THE ROOM

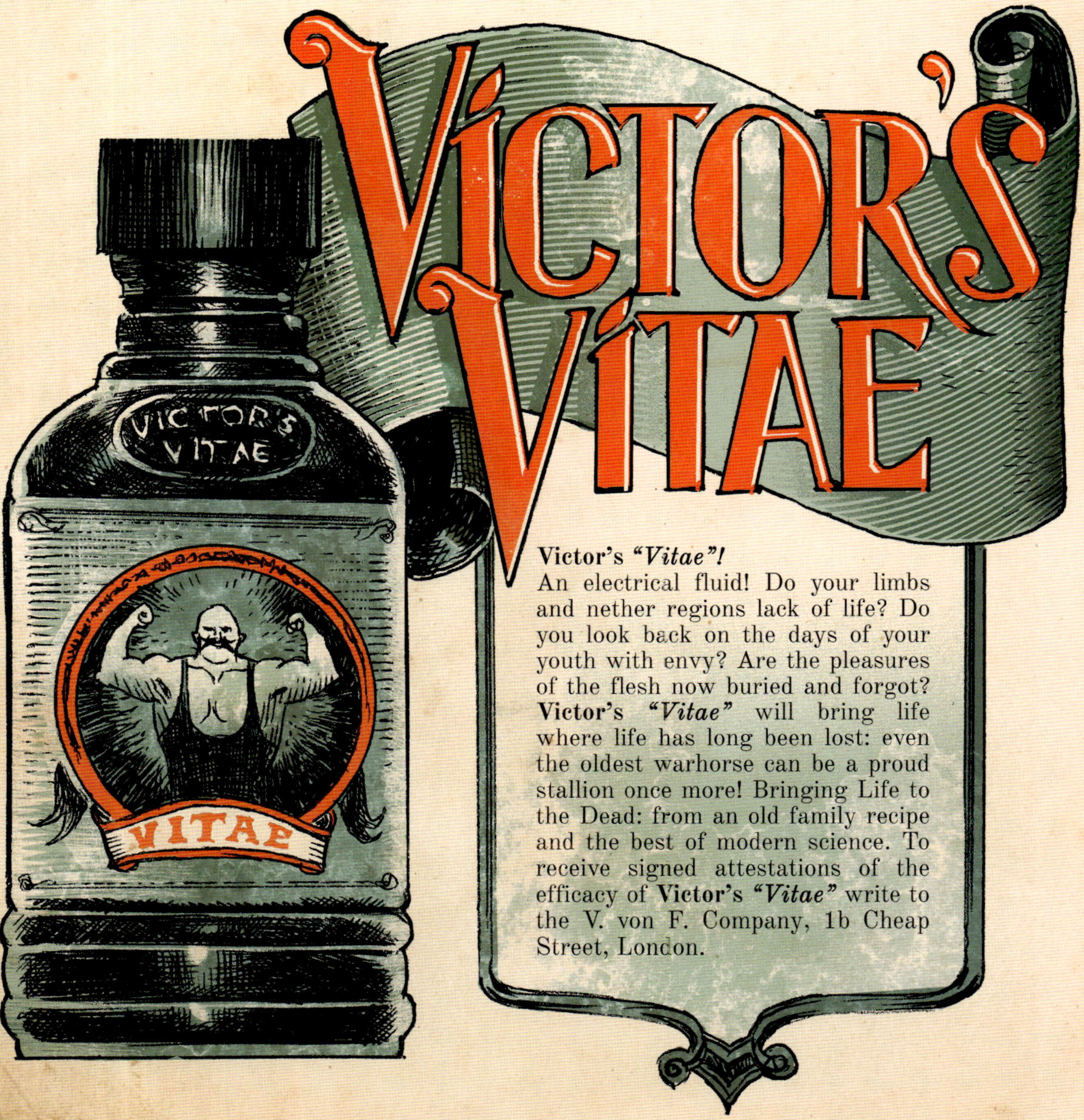
VICTOR'S VITAE
VICTOR'S VITAE
VITAE
Victor's ***"Vitae"!***
An electrical fluid! Do your limbs and nether regions lack of life? Do you look back on the days of your youth with envy? Are the pleasures of the flesh now buried and forgot? **Victor's** ***"Vitae"*** will bring life where life has long been lost: even the oldest warhorse can be a proud stallion once more! Bringing Life to the Dead: from an old family recipe and the best of modern science. To receive signed attestations of the efficacy of **Victor's** ***"Vitae"*** write to the V. von F. Company, 1b Cheap Street, London.

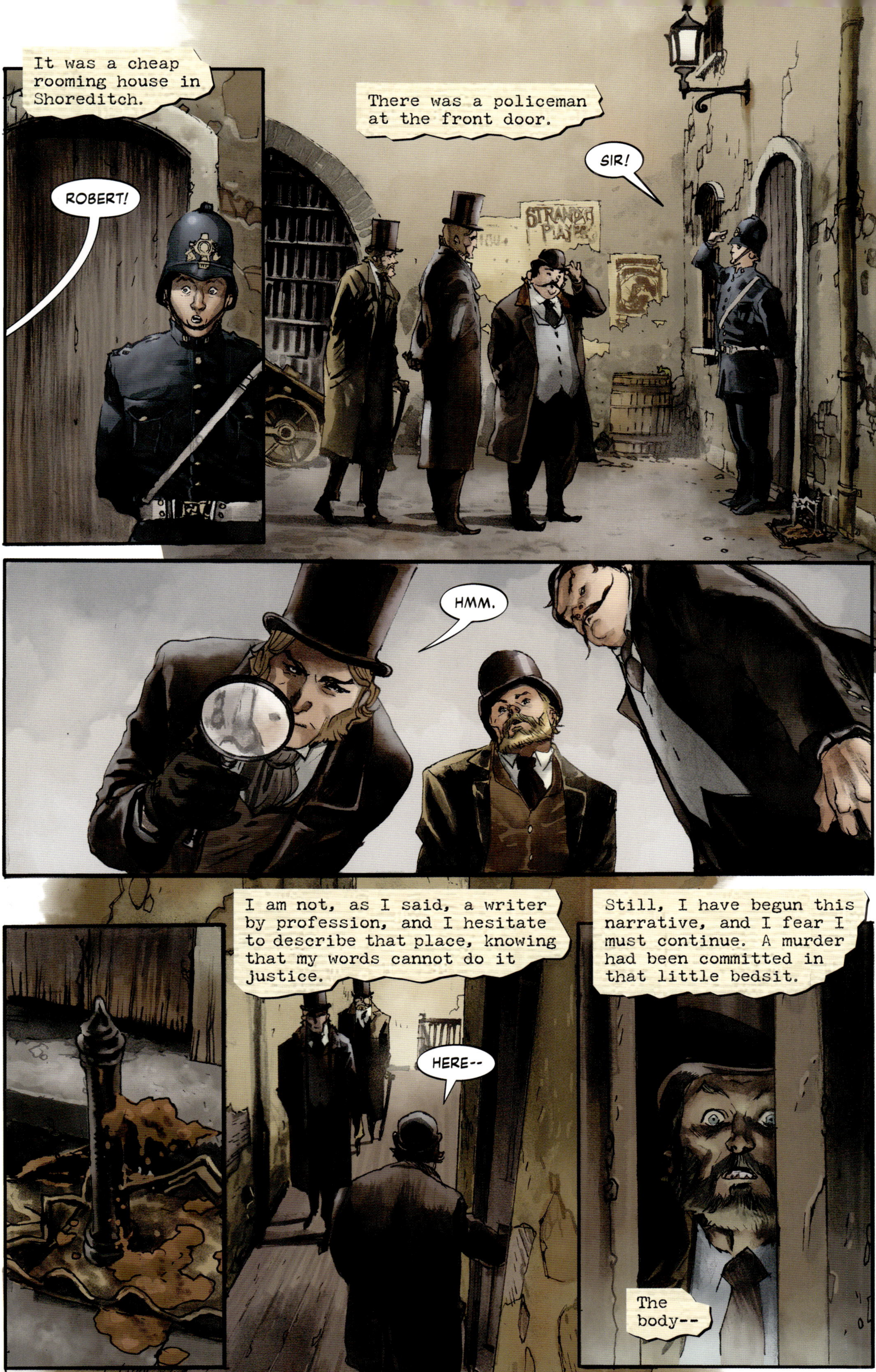
It was a cheap rooming house in Shoreditch.
ROBERT!
There was a policeman at the front door.
SIR!
HMM.
I am not, as I said, a writer by profession, and I hesitate to describe that place, knowing that my words cannot do it justice.
HERE--
Still, I have begun this narrative, and I fear I must continue. A murder had been committed in that little bedsit.
The body--

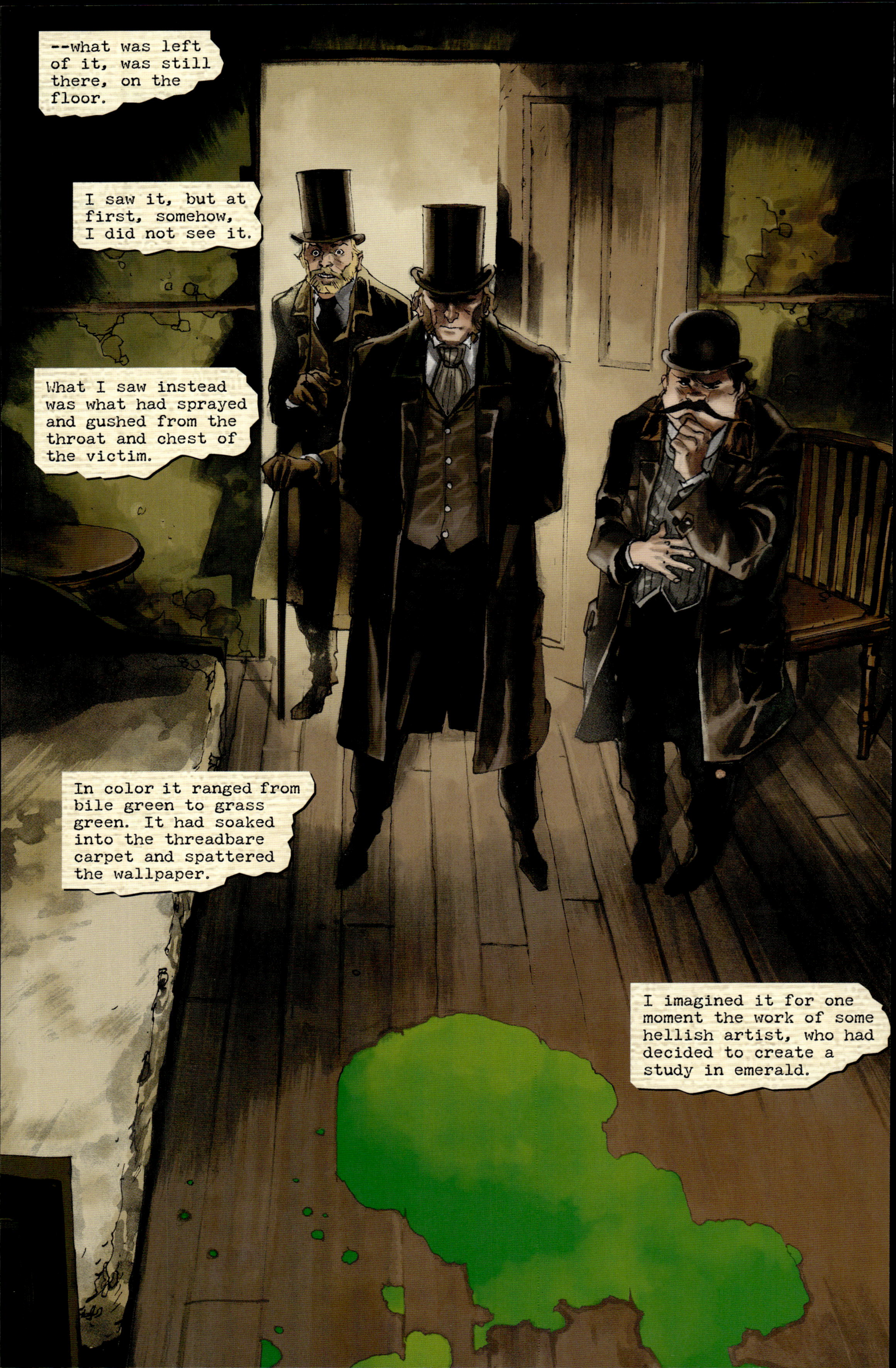
--what was left of it, was still there, on the floor.
I saw it, but at first, somehow, I did not see it.
What I saw instead was what had sprayed and gushed from the throat and chest of the victim.
In color it ranged from bile green to grass green. It had soaked into the threadbare carpet and spattered the wallpaper.
I imagined it for one moment the work of some hellish artist, who had decided to create a study in emerald.

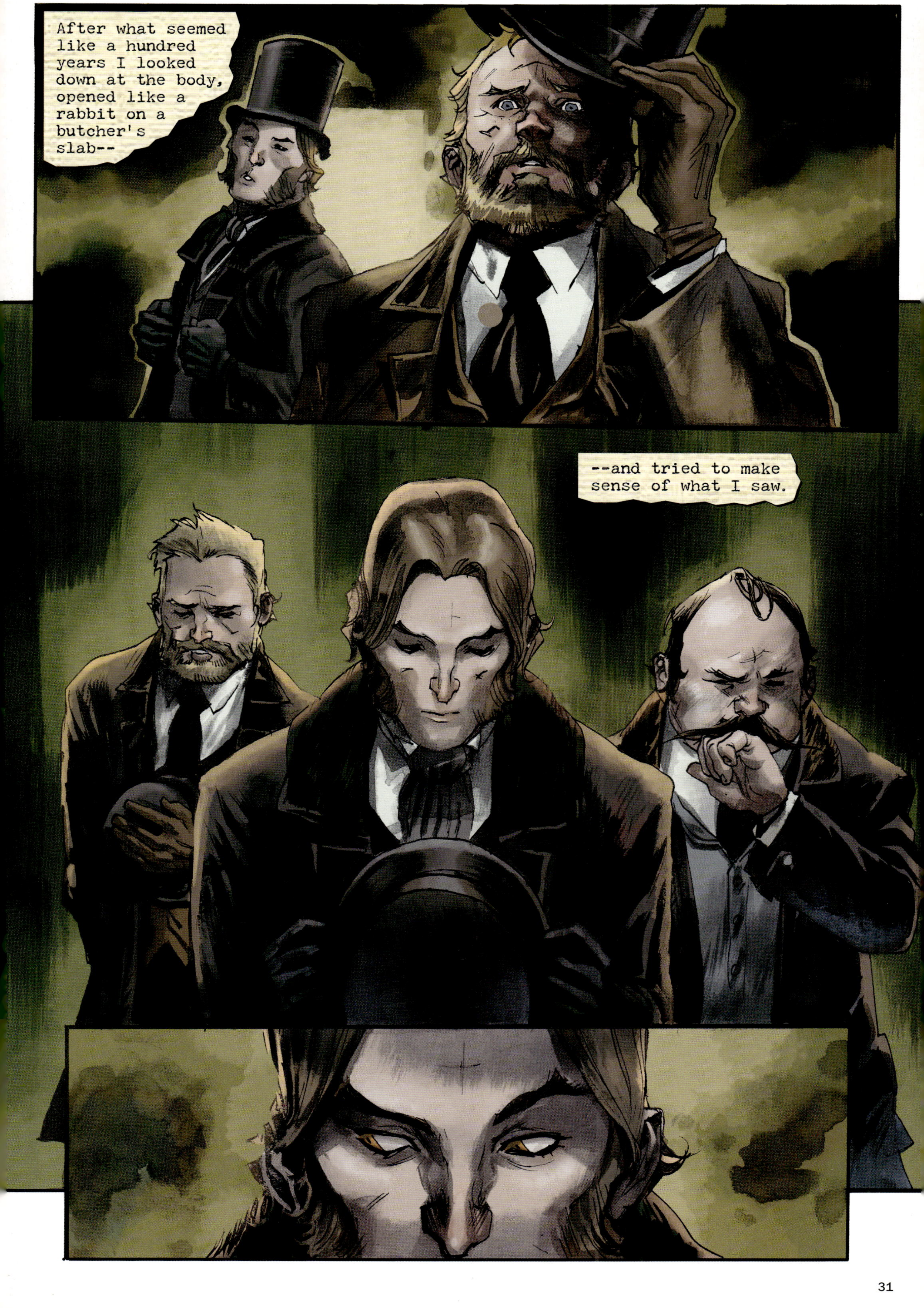
After what seemed like a hundred years I looked down at the body, opened like a rabbit on a butcher's slab--
--and tried to make sense of what I saw.

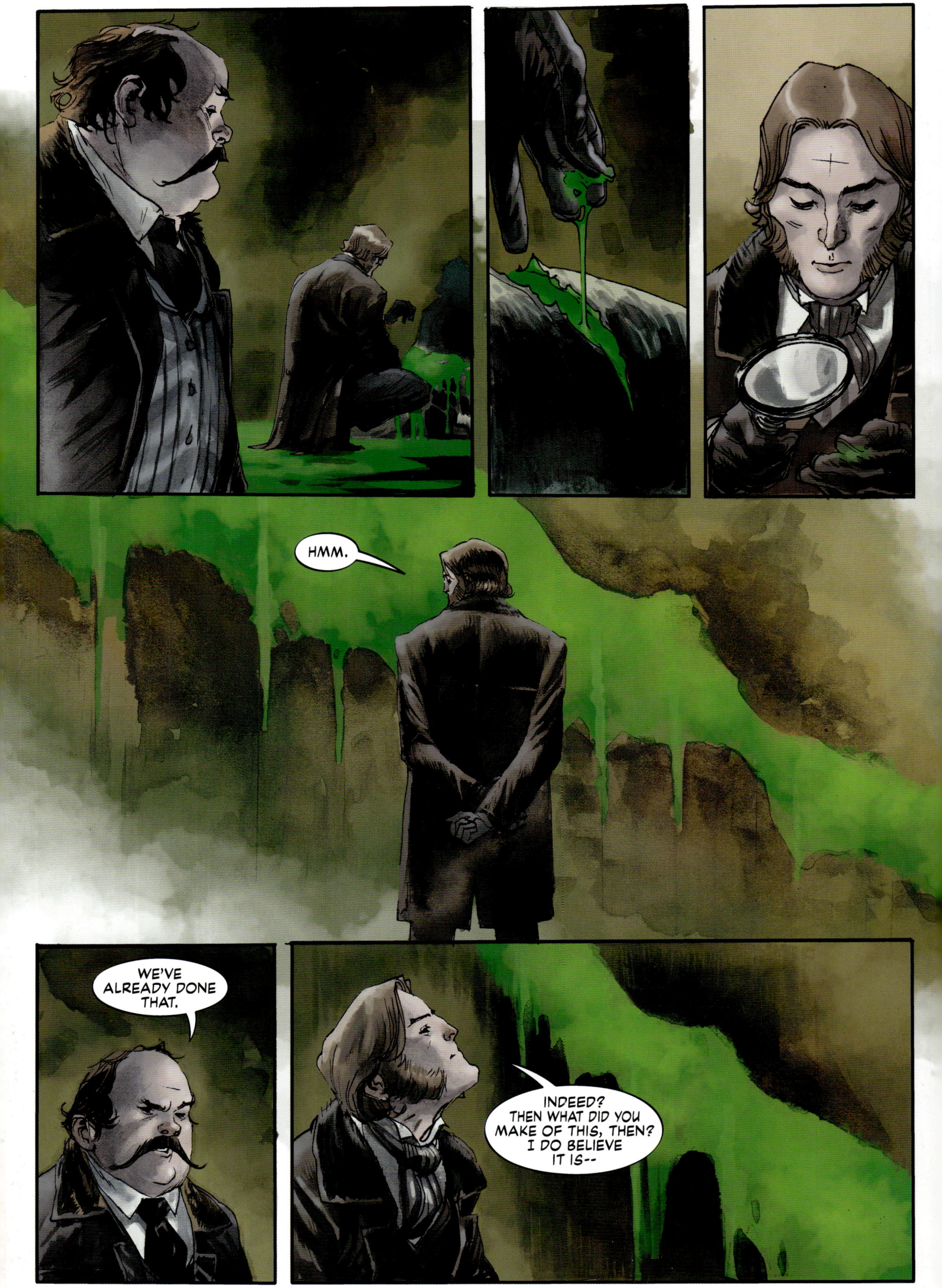
HMM.
WE'VE ALREADY DONE THAT.
INDEED? THEN WHAT DID YOU MAKE OF THIS, THEN? I DO BELIEVE IT IS--

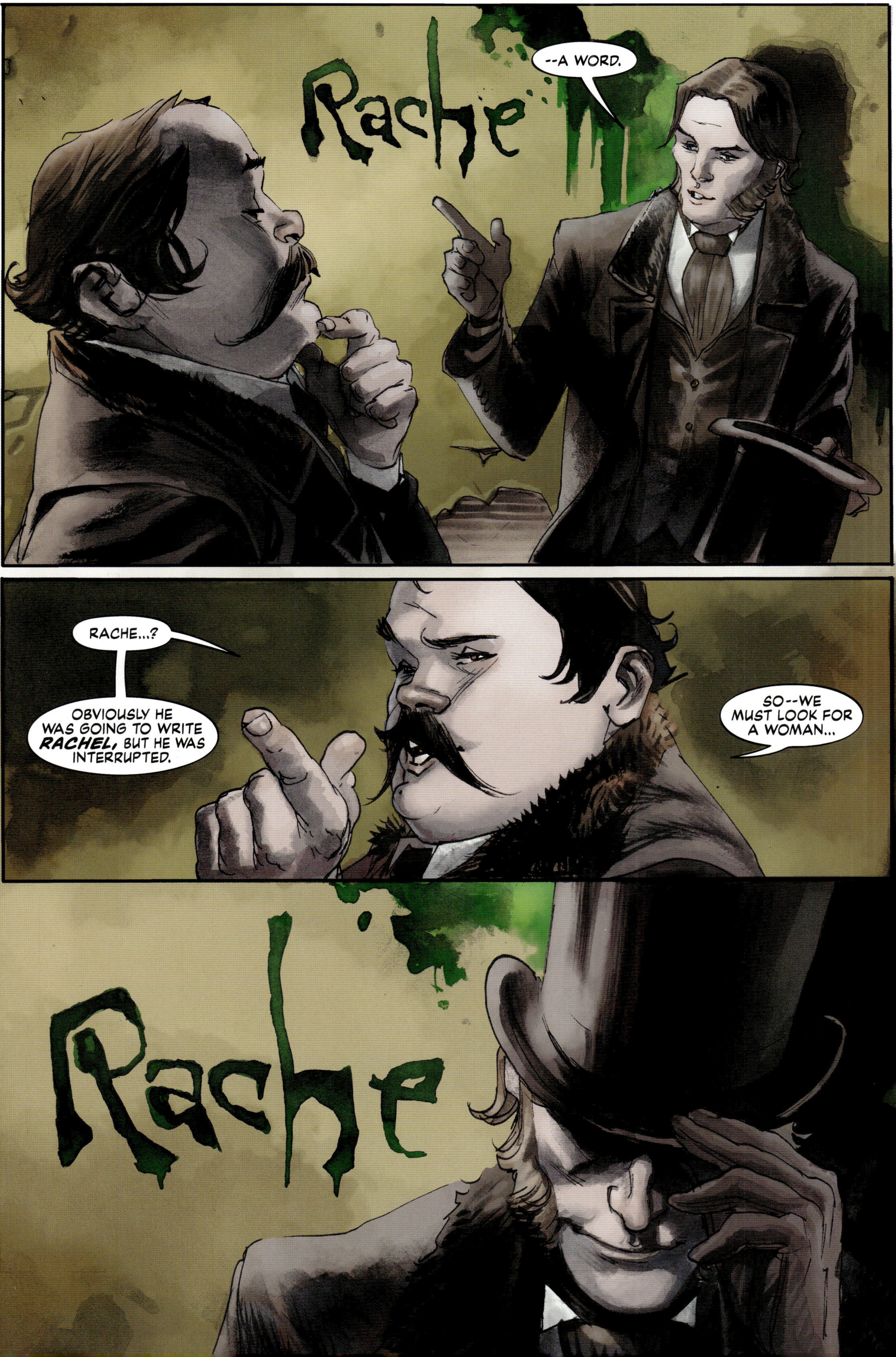
Rache
--A WORD.
RACHE...?
OBVIOUSLY HE WAS GOING TO WRITE RACHEL, BUT HE WAS INTERRUPTED.
SO--WE MUST LOOK FOR A WOMAN...
Rache

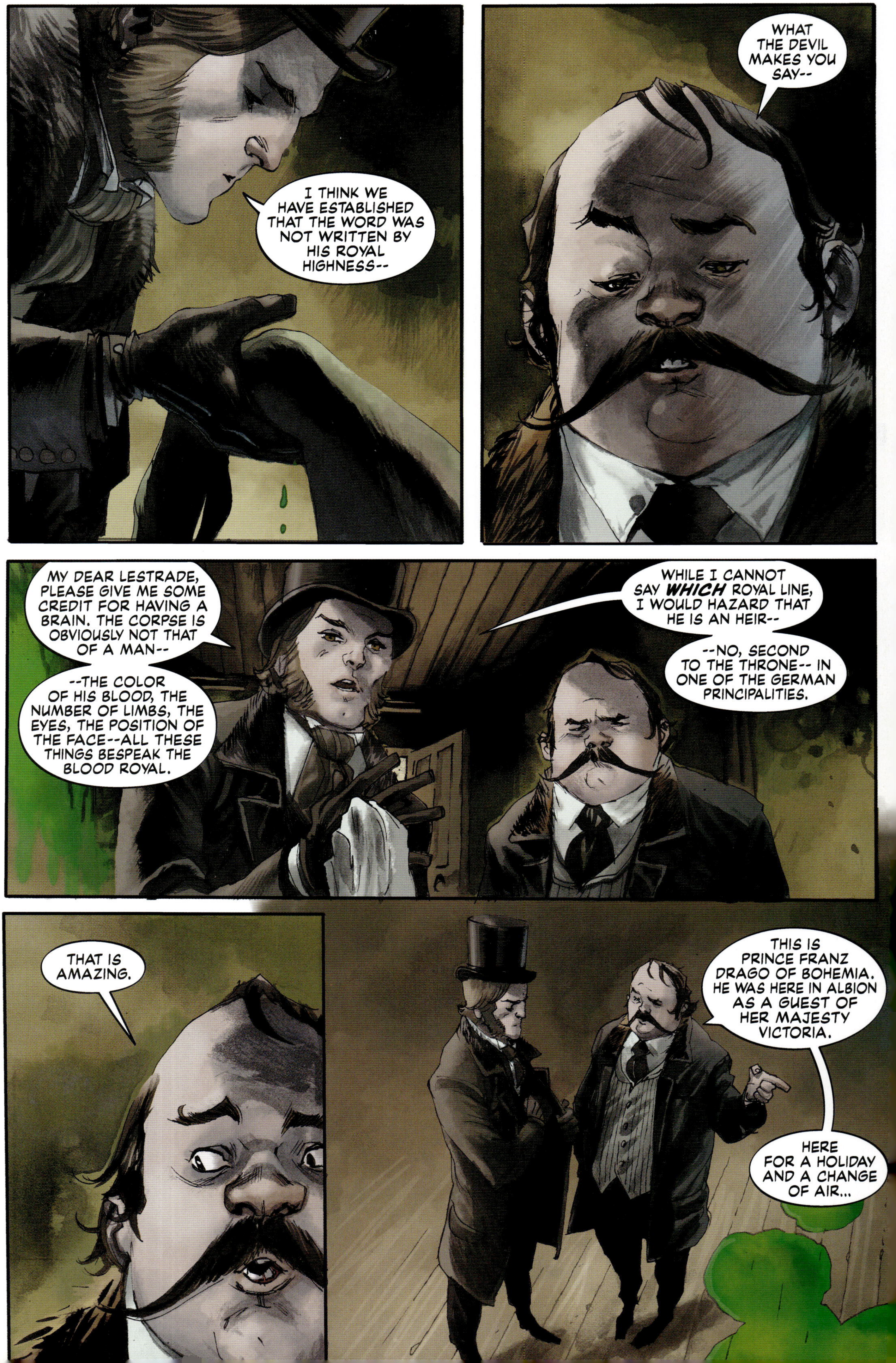
I THINK WE HAVE ESTABLISHED THAT THE WORD WAS NOT WRITTEN BY HIS ROYAL HIGHNESS--
WHAT THE DEVIL MAKES YOU SAY--
MY DEAR LESTRADE, PLEASE GIVE ME SOME CREDIT FOR HAVING A BRAIN. THE CORPSE IS OBVIOUSLY NOT THAT OF A MAN--
--THE COLOR OF HIS BLOOD, THE NUMBER OF LIMBS, THE EYES, THE POSITION OF THE FACE--ALL THESE THINGS BESPEAK THE BLOOD ROYAL.
WHILE I CANNOT SAY *WHICH* ROYAL LINE, I WOULD HAZARD THAT HE IS AN HEIR--
--NO, SECOND TO THE THRONE-- IN ONE OF THE GERMAN PRINCIPALITIES.
THAT IS AMAZING.
THIS IS PRINCE FRANZ DRAGO OF BOHEMIA. HE WAS HERE IN ALBION AS A GUEST OF HER MAJESTY VICTORIA.
HERE FOR A HOLIDAY AND A CHANGE OF AIR...

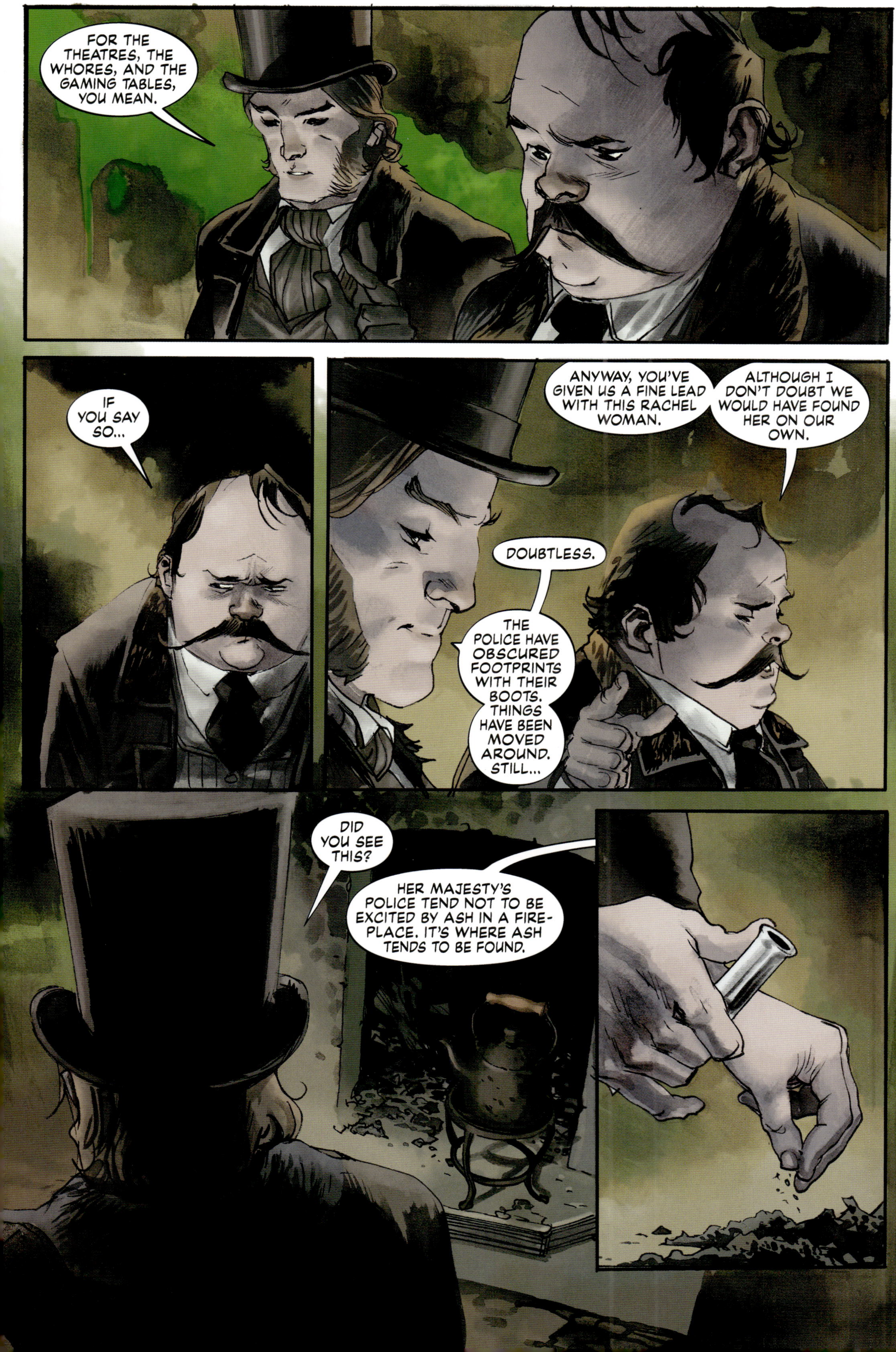
FOR THE THEATRES, THE WHORES, AND THE GAMING TABLES, YOU MEAN.
IF YOU SAY SO...
ANYWAY, YOU'VE GIVEN US A FINE LEAD WITH THIS RACHEL WOMAN.
ALTHOUGH I DON'T DOUBT WE WOULD HAVE FOUND HER ON OUR OWN.
DOUBTLESS.
THE POLICE HAVE OBSCURED FOOTPRINTS WITH THEIR BOOTS. THINGS HAVE BEEN MOVED AROUND. STILL...
DID YOU SEE THIS?
HER MAJESTY'S POLICE TEND NOT TO BE EXCITED BY ASH IN A FIRE-PLACE. IT'S WHERE ASH TENDS TO BE FOUND.

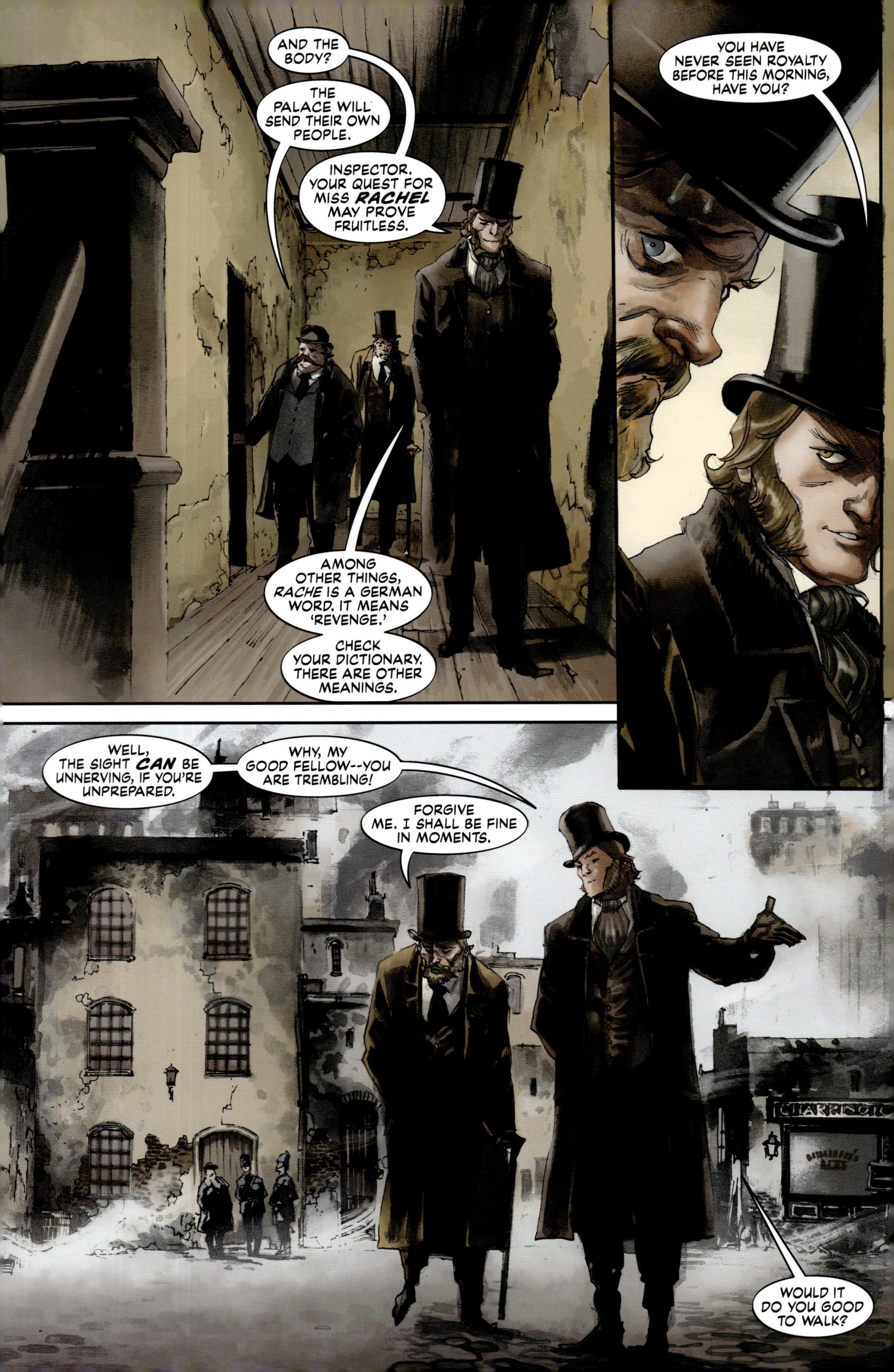
AND THE BODY?
THE PALACE WILL SEND THEIR OWN PEOPLE.
INSPECTOR. YOUR QUEST FOR MISS RACHEL MAY PROVE FRUITLESS.
AMONG OTHER THINGS, RACHE IS A GERMAN WORD. IT MEANS 'REVENGE.'
CHECK YOUR DICTIONARY. THERE ARE OTHER MEANINGS.
YOU HAVE NEVER SEEN ROYALTY BEFORE THIS MORNING, HAVE YOU?
WELL, THE SIGHT CAN BE UNNERVING, IF YOU'RE UNPREPARED.
WHY, MY GOOD FELLOW--YOU ARE TREMBLING!
FORGIVE ME. I SHALL BE FINE IN MOMENTS.
WOULD IT DO YOU GOOD TO WALK?

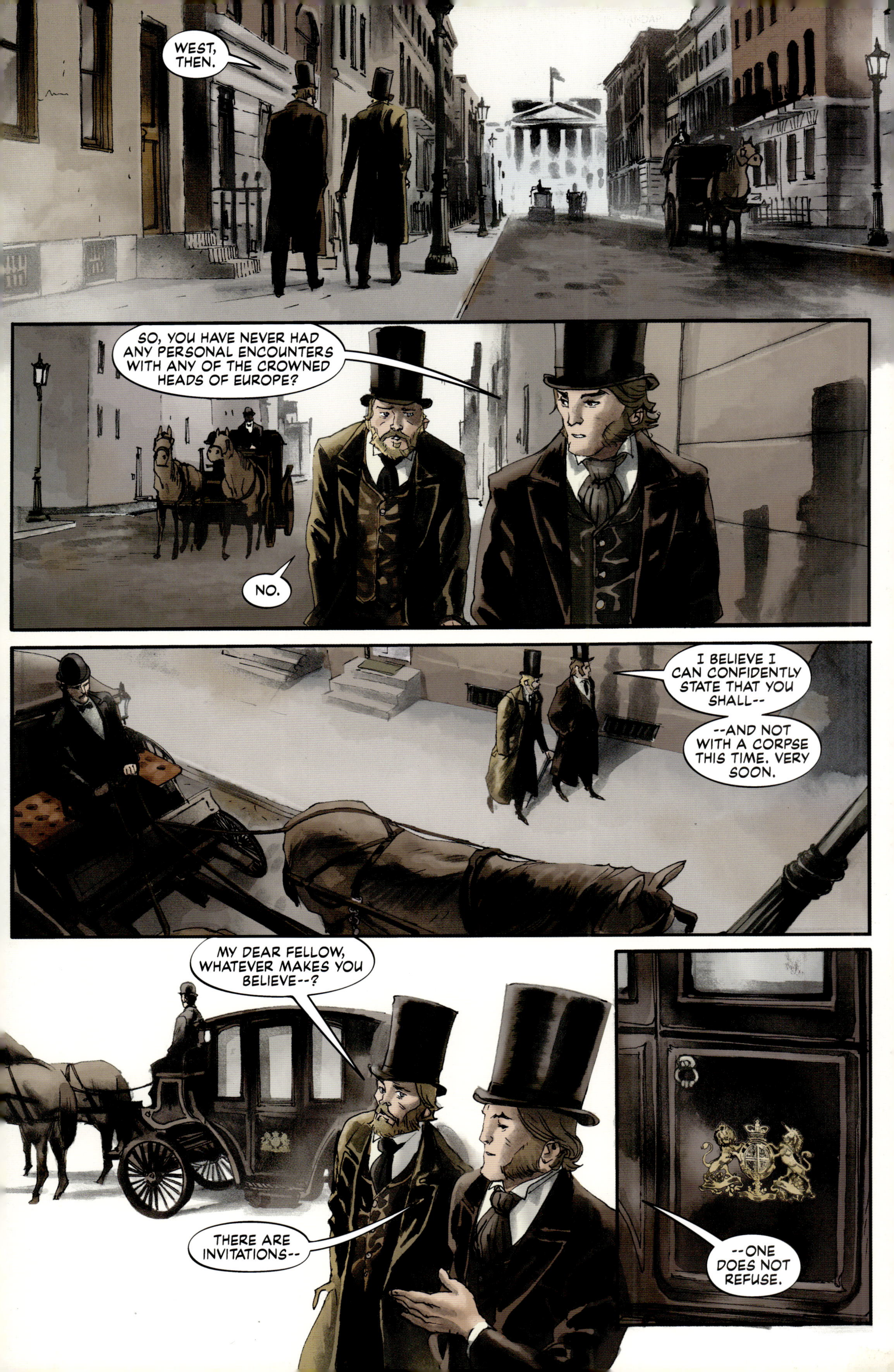
WEST, THEN.
SO, YOU HAVE NEVER HAD ANY PERSONAL ENCOUNTERS WITH ANY OF THE CROWNED HEADS OF EUROPE?
NO.
I BELIEVE I CAN CONFIDENTLY STATE THAT YOU SHALL--
--AND NOT WITH A CORPSE THIS TIME. VERY SOON.
MY DEAR FELLOW, WHATEVER MAKES YOU BELIEVE--?
THERE ARE INVITATIONS--
--ONE DOES NOT REFUSE.

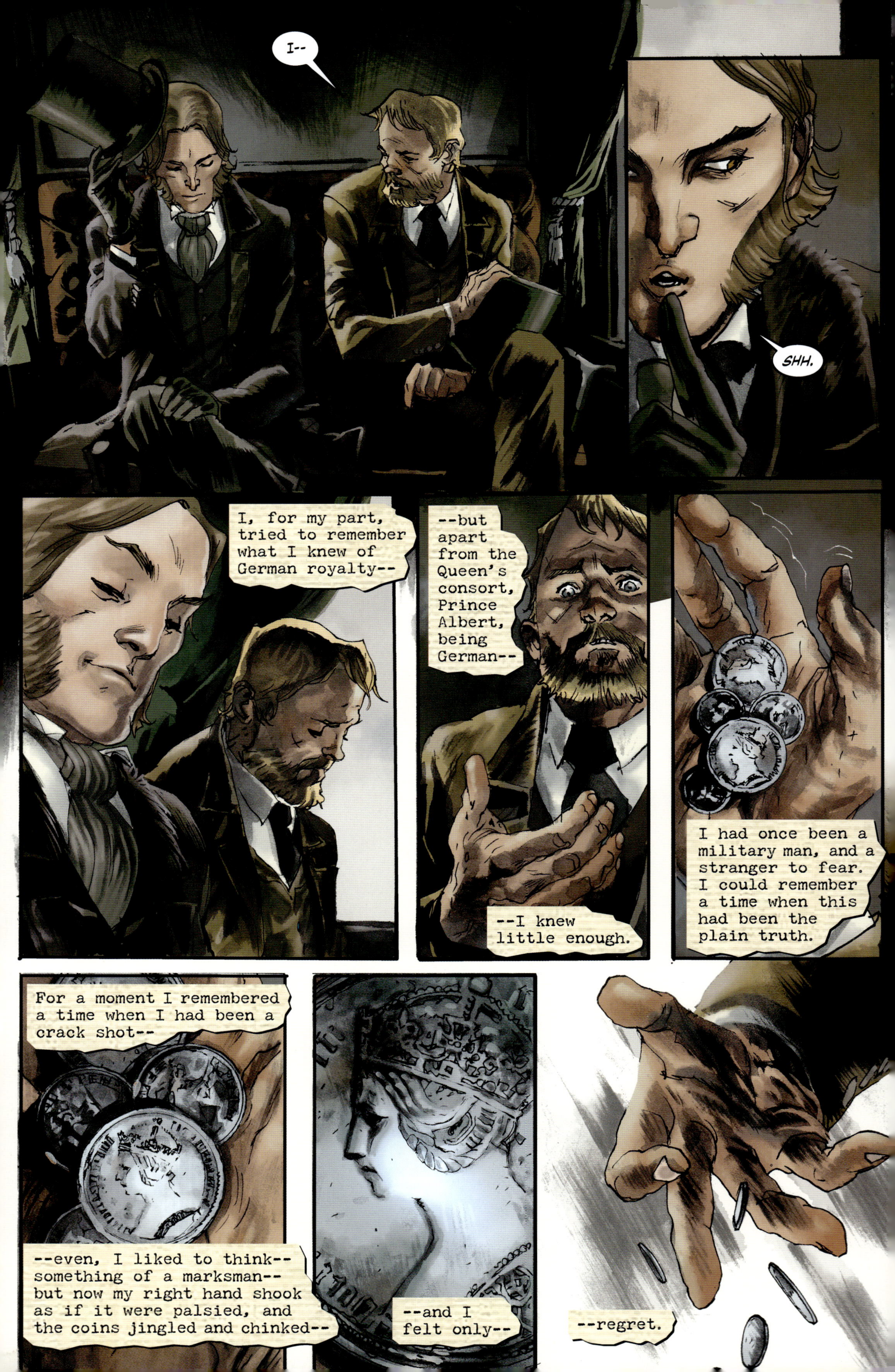
I--
SHH.
I, for my part, tried to remember what I knew of German royalty--
--but apart from the Queen's consort, Prince Albert, being German--
--I knew little enough.
I had once been a military man, and a stranger to fear. I could remember a time when this had been the plain truth.
For a moment I remembered a time when I had been a crack shot--
--even, I liked to think--something of a marksman--but now my right hand shook as if it were palsied, and the coins jingled and chinked--
--and I felt only--
--regret.

THE PALACE

before

At Long Last Doctor Henry Jekyll is proud to announce the general release of the world-renowned **"Jekyll's Powders"** for popular consumption. No longer the province of the privileged few. **Release the Inner You!** For Inner and Outer Cleanliness! **TOO MANY PEOPLE**, both men and women, suffer from **CONSTIPATION OF THE SOUL!**

Relief is immediate and cheap – with Jekyll's powders! *(Available in Vanilla and Original Mentholatum Formulations.)*

JEKYLL'S POWDERS

after

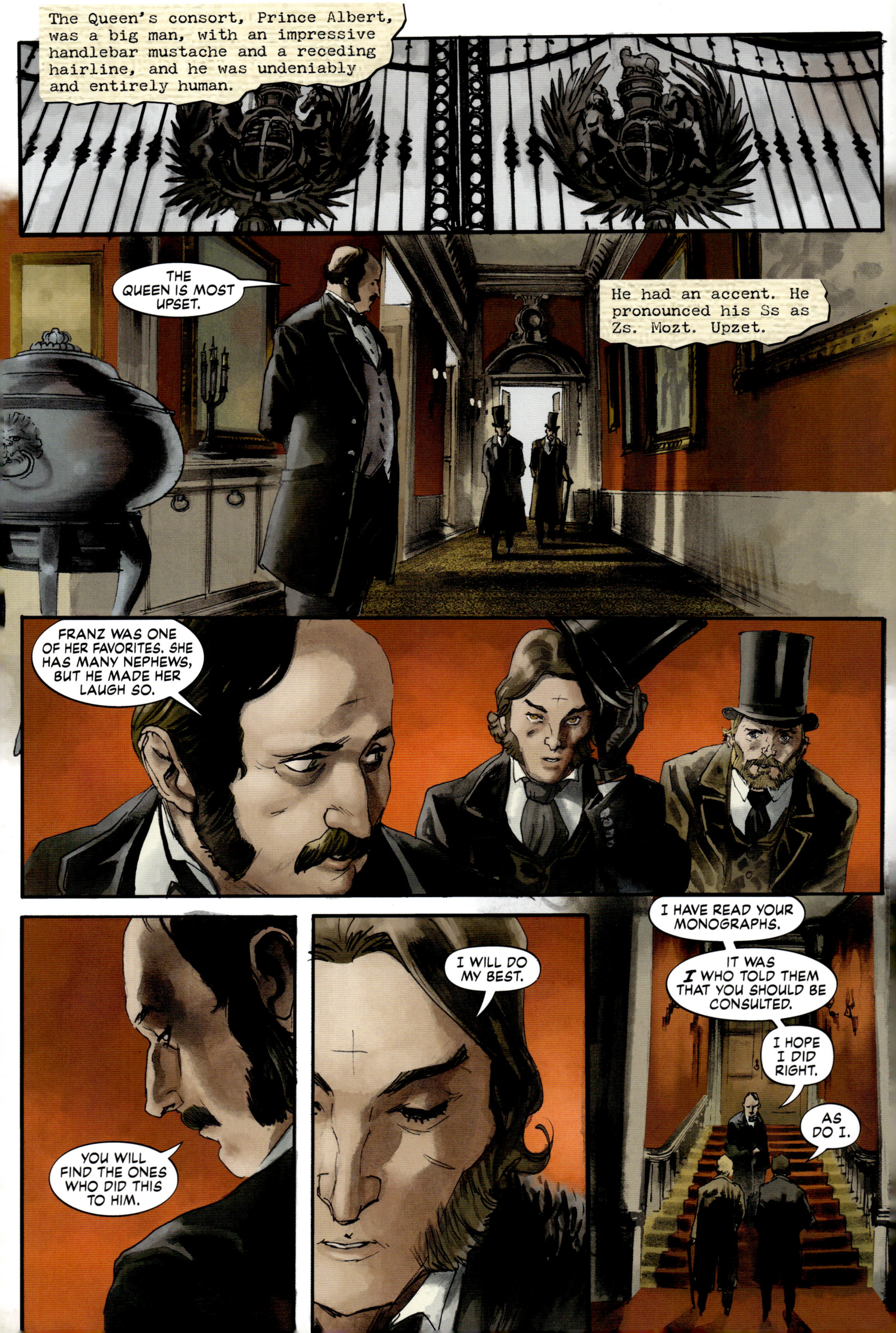
The Queen's consort, Prince Albert, was a big man, with an impressive handlebar mustache and a receding hairline, and he was undeniably and entirely human.
THE QUEEN IS MOST UPSET.
He had an accent. He pronounced his Ss as Zs. Mozt. Upzet.
FRANZ WAS ONE OF HER FAVORITES. SHE HAS MANY NEPHEWS, BUT HE MADE HER LAUGH SO.
YOU WILL FIND THE ONES WHO DID THIS TO HIM.
I WILL DO MY BEST.
I HAVE READ YOUR MONOGRAPHS.
IT WAS I WHO TOLD THEM THAT YOU SHOULD BE CONSULTED.
I HOPE I DID RIGHT.
AS DO I.

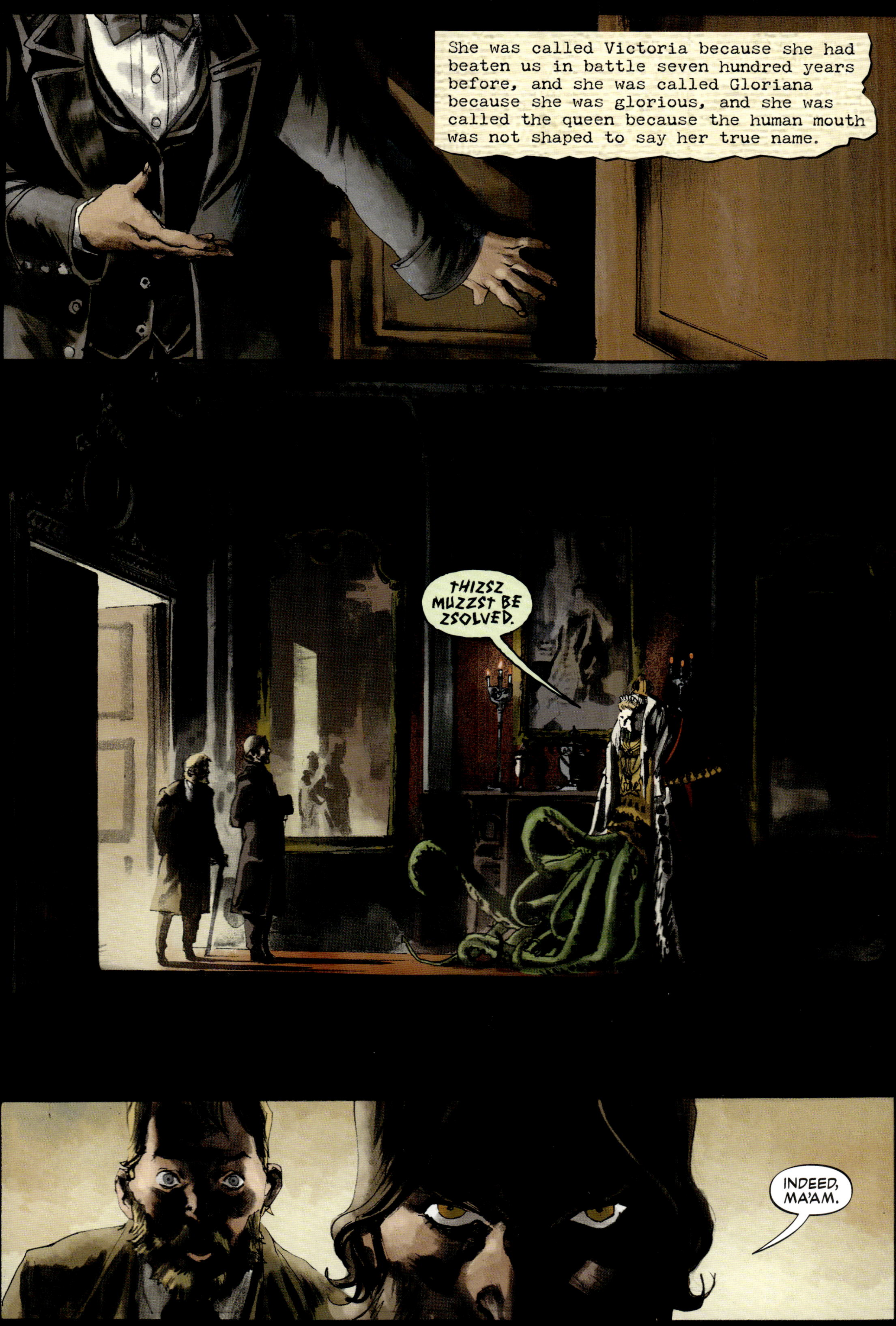
She was called Victoria because she had beaten us in battle seven hundred years before, and she was called Gloriana because she was glorious, and she was called the queen because the human mouth was not shaped to say her true name.
THIZSZ MUZZST BE ZSOLVED.
INDEED, MA'AM.

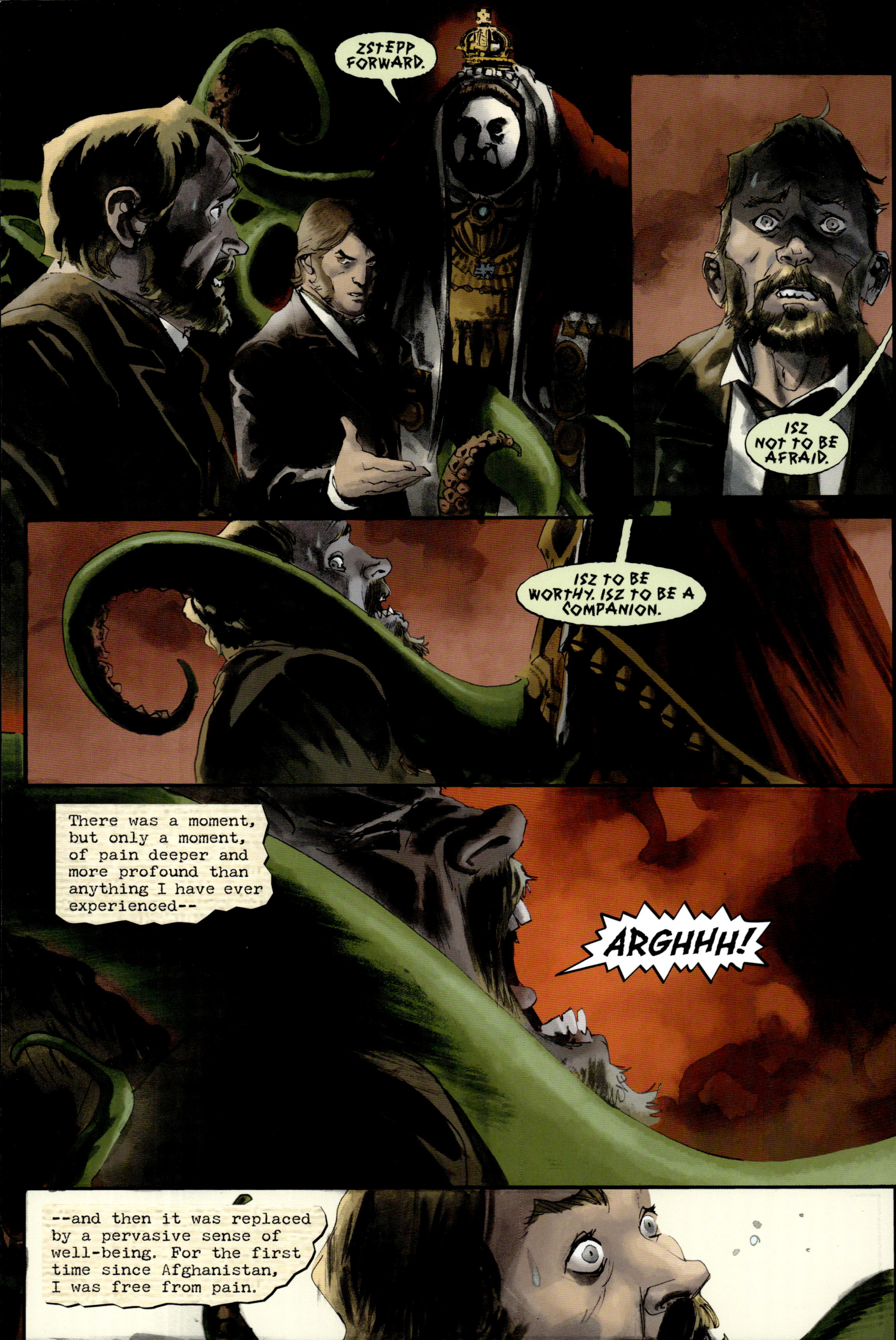
ZSTEPP FORWARD.
ISZ NOT TO BE AFRAID.
ISZ TO BE WORTHY. ISZ TO BE A COMPANION.
There was a moment, but only a moment, of pain deeper and more profound than anything I have ever experienced--
ARGHHH!
--and then it was replaced by a pervasive sense of well-being. For the first time since Afghanistan, I was free from pain.

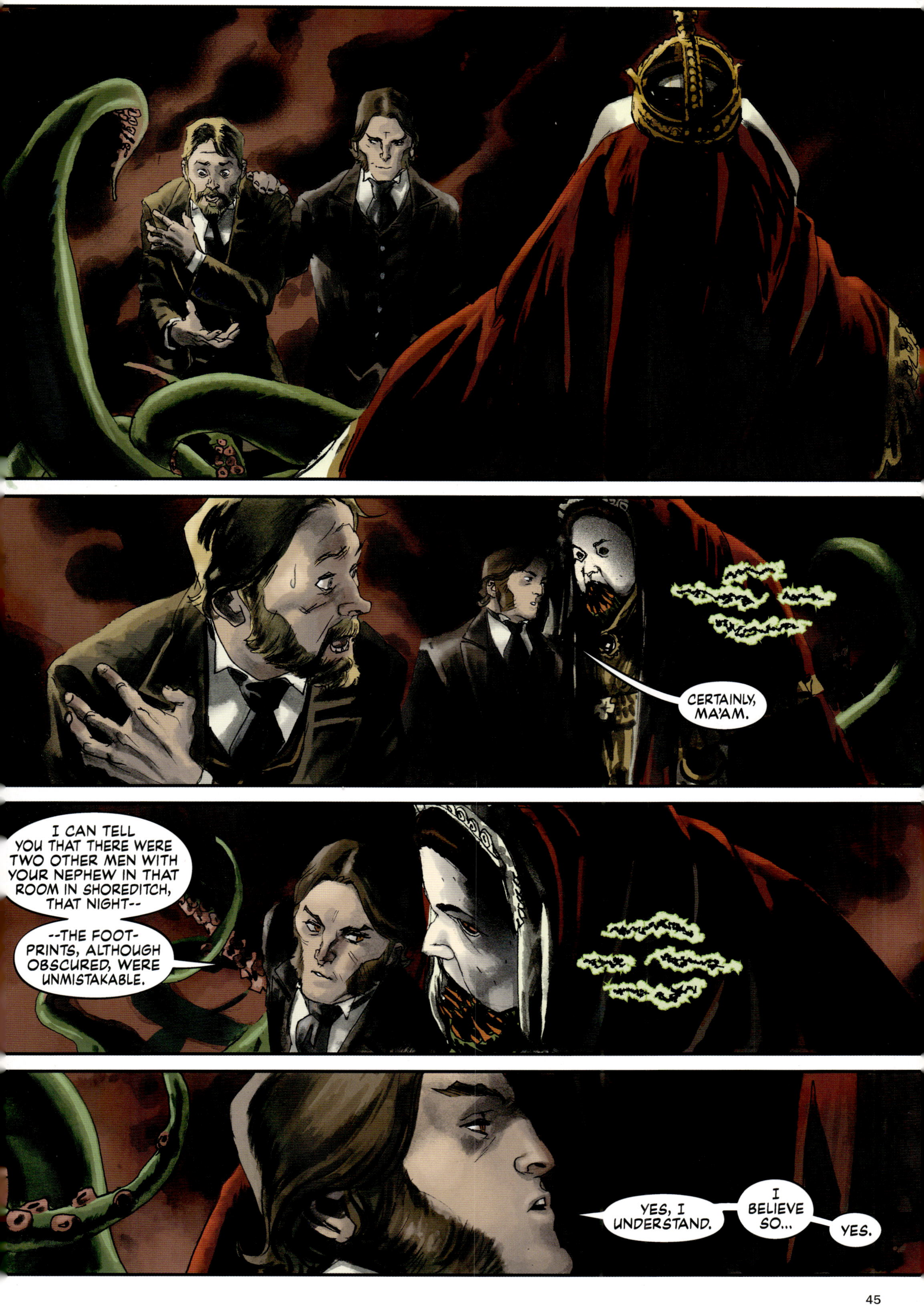
CERTAINLY, MA'AM.
I CAN TELL YOU THAT THERE WERE TWO OTHER MEN WITH YOUR NEPHEW IN THAT ROOM IN SHOREDITCH, THAT NIGHT--
--THE FOOT-PRINTS, ALTHOUGH OBSCURED, WERE UNMISTAKABLE.
YES, I UNDERSTAND.
I BELIEVE SO...
YES.

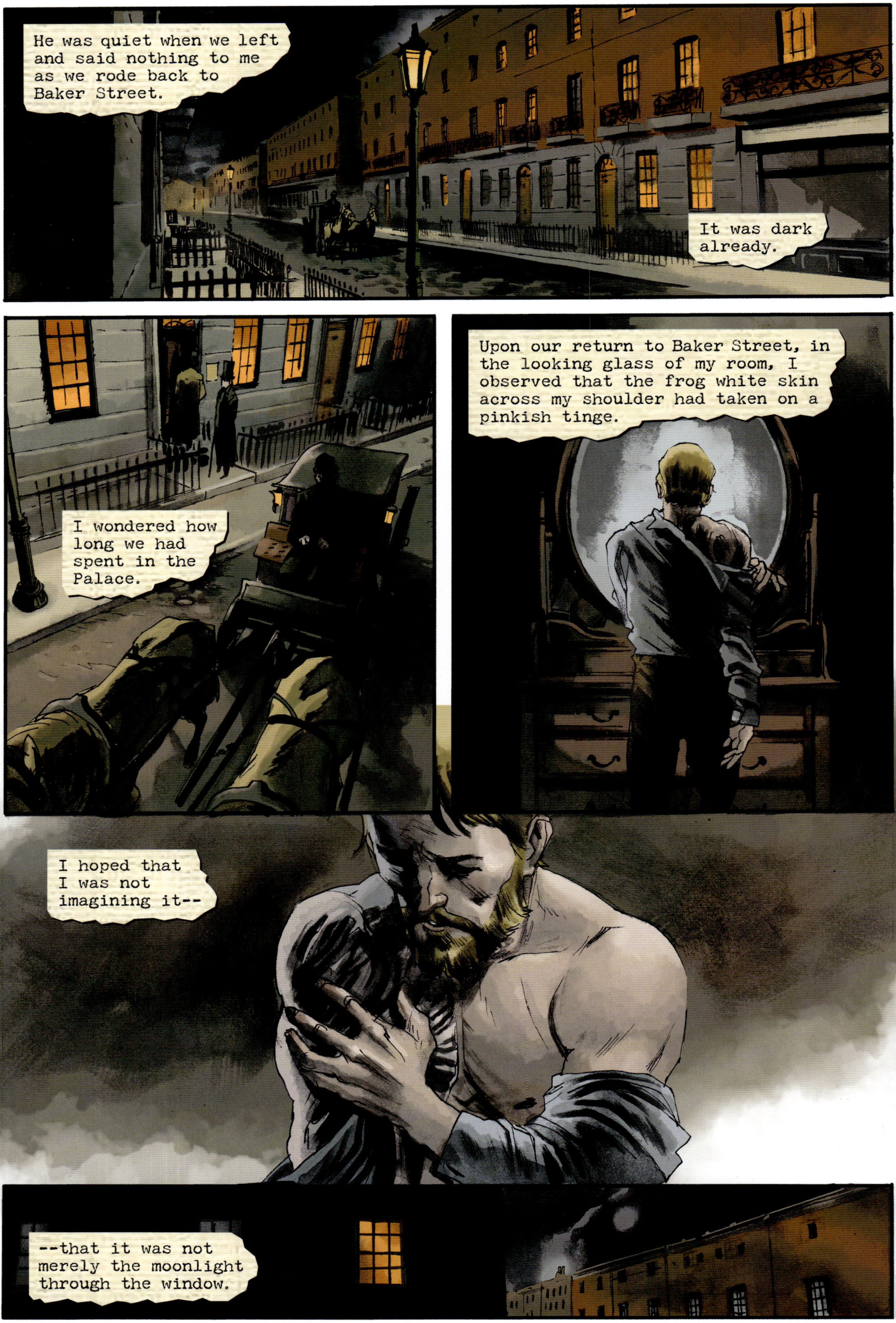
He was quiet when we left and said nothing to me as we rode back to Baker Street.
It was dark already.
I wondered how long we had spent in the Palace.
Upon our return to Baker Street, in the looking glass of my room, I observed that the frog white skin across my shoulder had taken on a pinkish tinge.
I hoped that I was not imagining it--
--that it was not merely the moonlight through the window.

THE PERFORMANCE

EXSANGUINATOR V. TEPES

LIVER COMPLAINTS?!
BILIOUS ATTACKS?!
NEURASTHENIC DISTURBANCES?!
QUINSY?!
ARTHRITIS?!

These are just a handful of the *complaints* for which a professional **EXSANGUINATION** can be the *remedy*. In our offices we have sheaves of **TESTIMONIALS** which can be inspected by the public at *any time*. Do not put your health in the hands of *amateurs*!! We have been doing this for a very long time: **V. TEPES - PROFESSIONAL EXSANGUINATOR.** (Remember! It is pronounced *Tzsep-pesh*!) Romania, Paris, London, Whitby. **You've tried the rest - NOW TRY THE BEST!!**

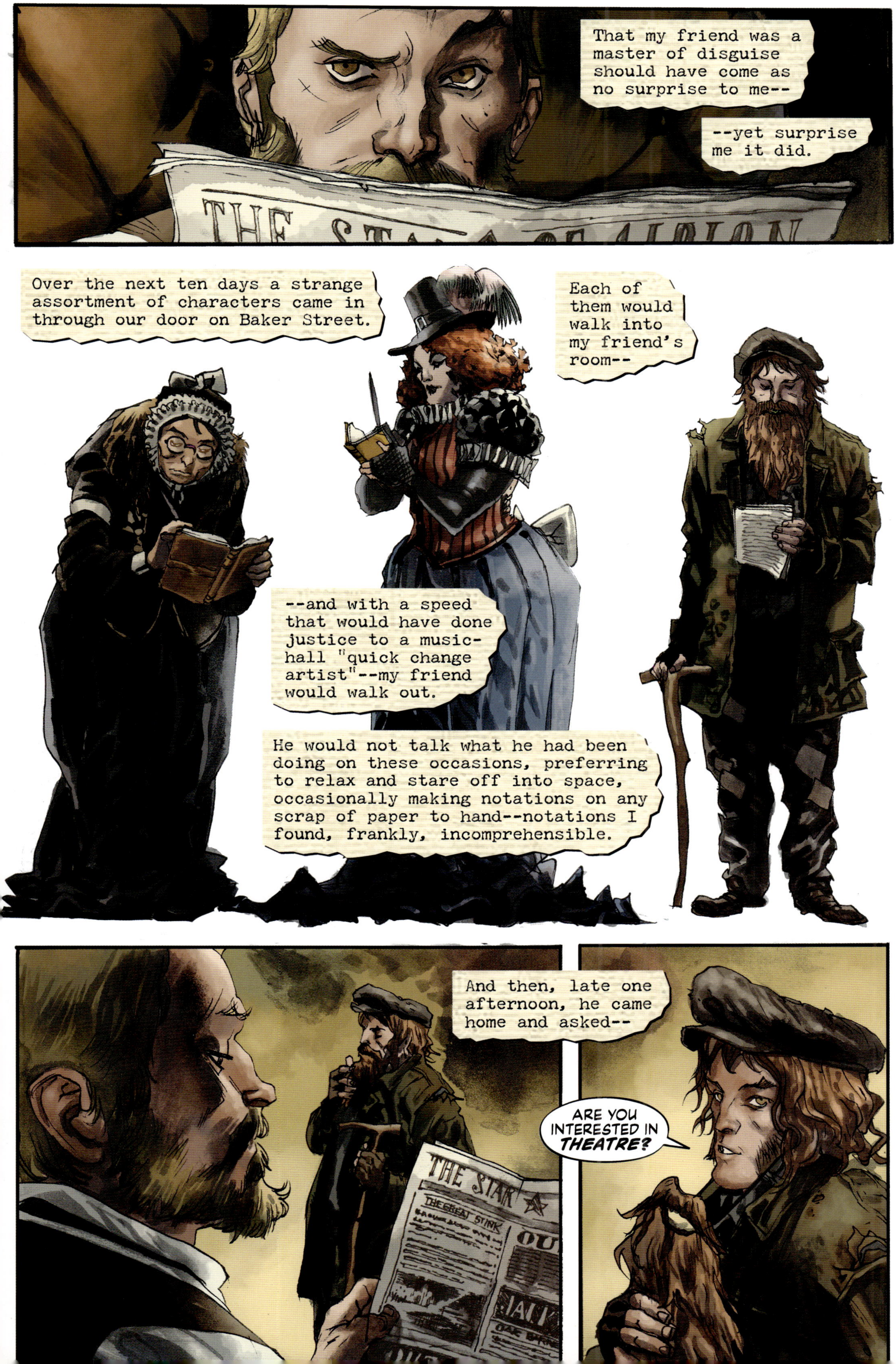
That my friend was a master of disguise should have come as no surprise to me--
--yet surprise me it did.
Over the next ten days a strange assortment of characters came in through our door on Baker Street.
Each of them would walk into my friend's room--
--and with a speed that would have done justice to a music-hall "quick change artist"--my friend would walk out.
He would not talk what he had been doing on these occasions, preferring to relax and stare off into space, occasionally making notations on any scrap of paper to hand--notations I found, frankly, incomprehensible.
And then, late one afternoon, he came home and asked--
THE STAR
THE GREAT STINK
ARE YOU INTERESTED IN *THEATRE?*

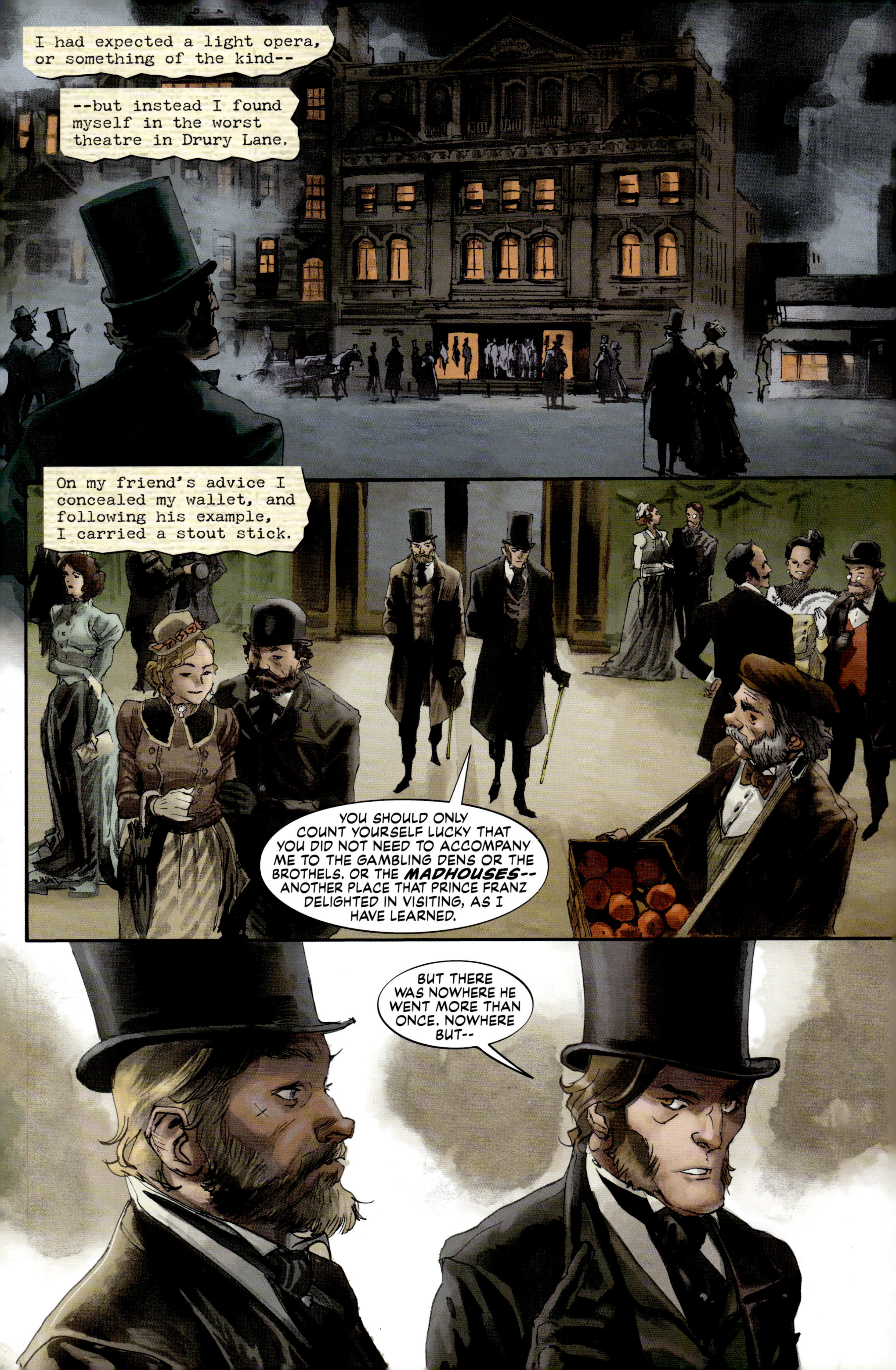
I had expected a light opera, or something of the kind--
--but instead I found myself in the worst theatre in Drury Lane.
On my friend's advice I concealed my wallet, and following his example, I carried a stout stick.
YOU SHOULD ONLY COUNT YOURSELF LUCKY THAT YOU DID NOT NEED TO ACCOMPANY ME TO THE GAMBLING DENS OR THE BROTHELS. OR THE MADHOUSES-- ANOTHER PLACE THAT PRINCE FRANZ DELIGHTED IN VISITING, AS I HAVE LEARNED.
BUT THERE WAS NOWHERE HE WENT MORE THAN ONCE. NOWHERE BUT--

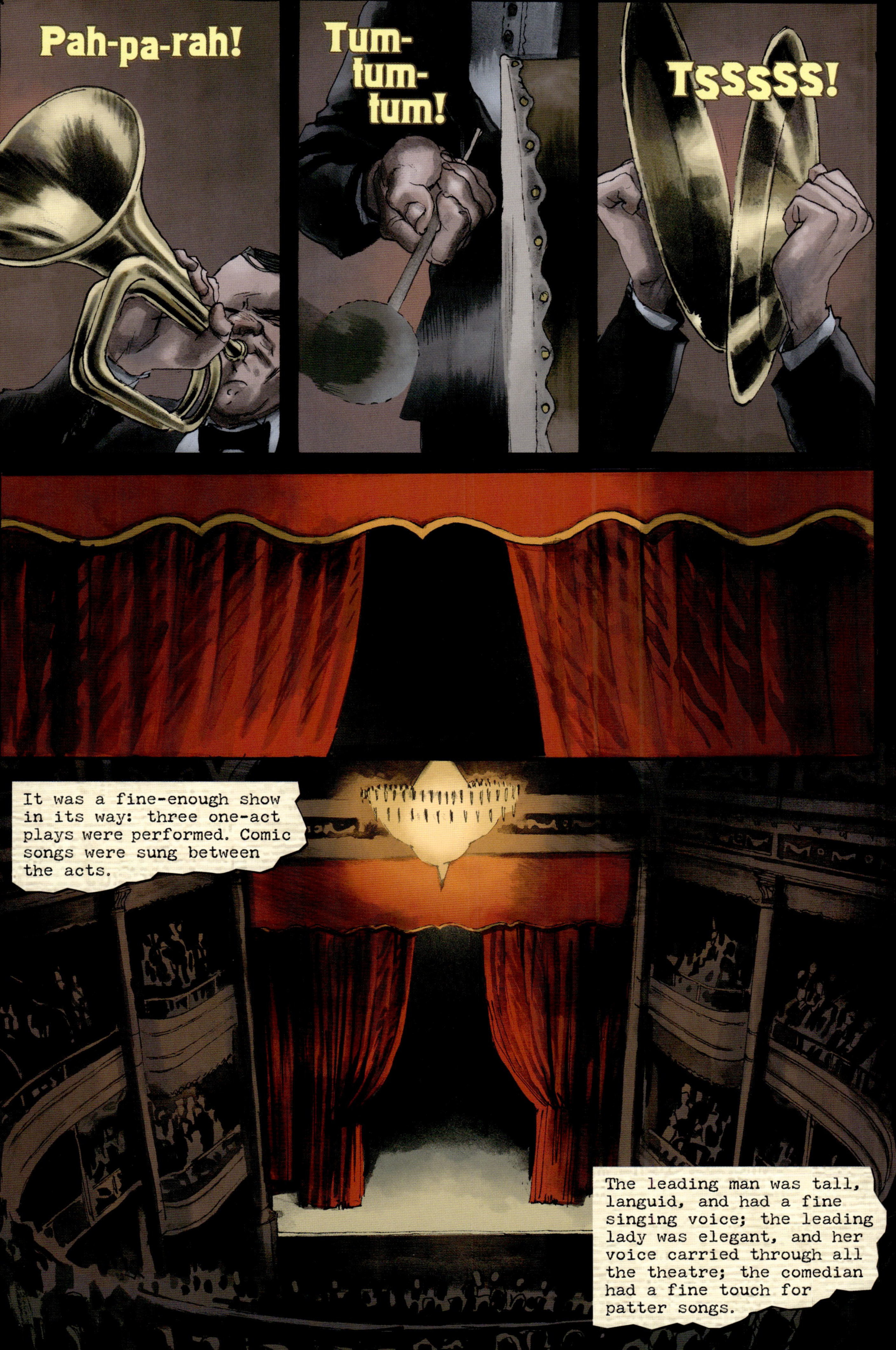
Pah-pa-rah!
Tum-tum-tum!
TSSSSS!
It was a fine-enough show in its way: three one-act plays were performed. Comic songs were sung between the acts.
The leading man was tall, languid, and had a fine singing voice; the leading lady was elegant, and her voice carried through all the theatre; the comedian had a fine touch for patter songs.

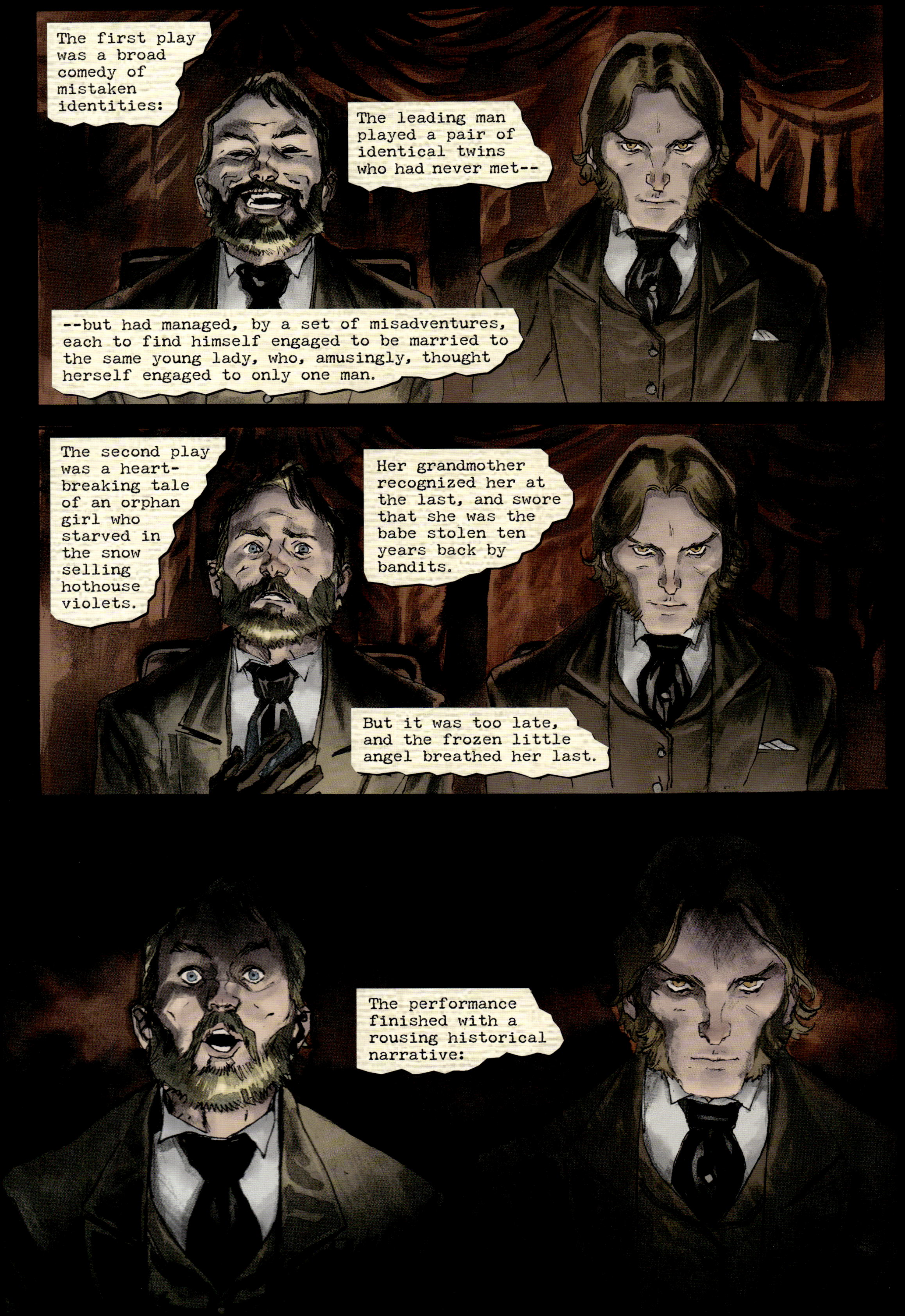
The first play was a broad comedy of mistaken identities:
The leading man played a pair of identical twins who had never met--
--but had managed, by a set of misadventures, each to find himself engaged to be married to the same young lady, who, amusingly, thought herself engaged to only one man.
The second play was a heart-breaking tale of an orphan girl who starved in the snow selling hothouse violets.
Her grandmother recognized her at the last, and swore that she was the babe stolen ten years back by bandits.
But it was too late, and the frozen little angel breathed her last.
The performance finished with a rousing historical narrative:

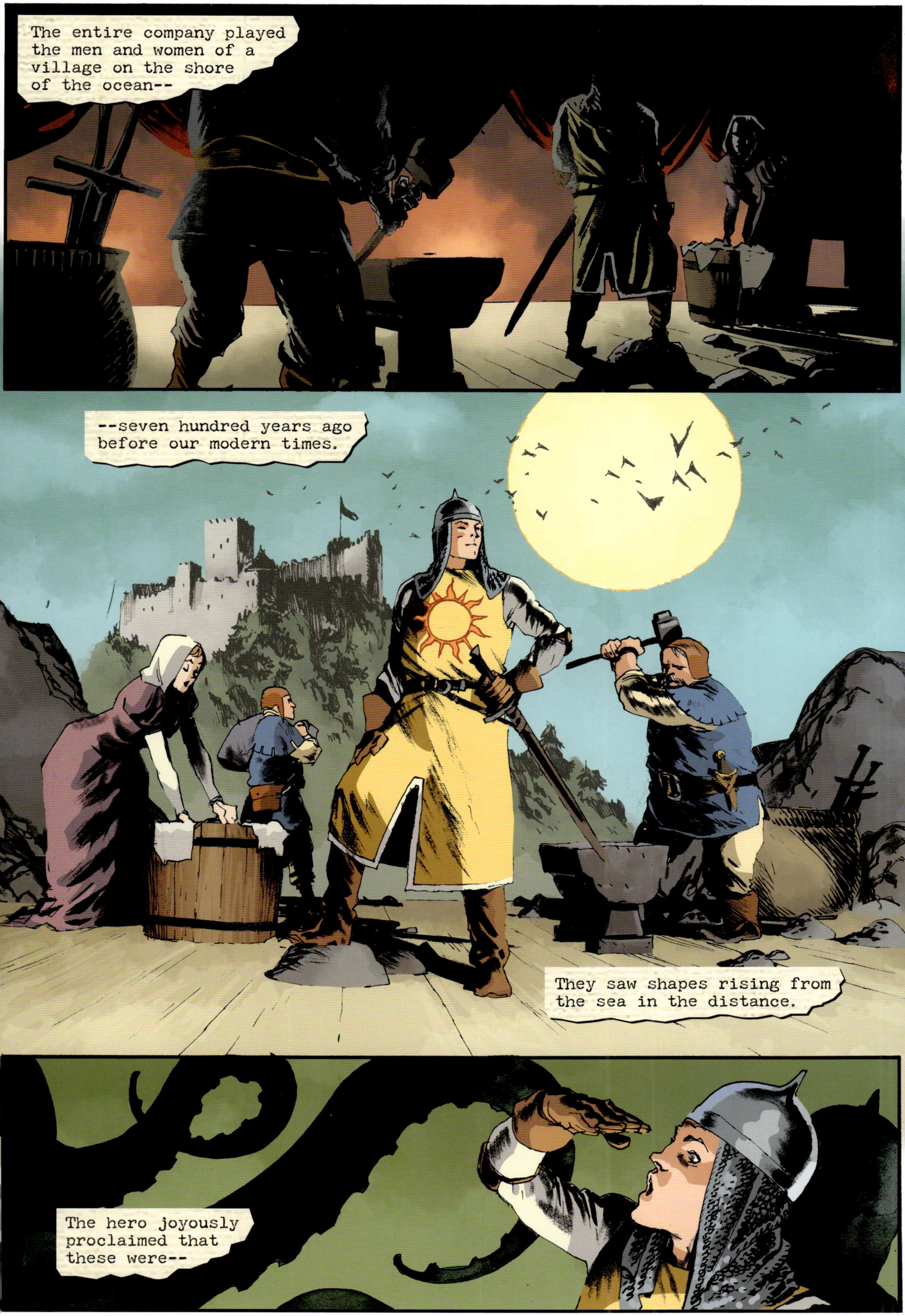
The entire company played the men and women of a village on the shore of the ocean--
--seven hundred years ago before our modern times.
They saw shapes rising from the sea in the distance.
The hero joyously proclaimed that these were--

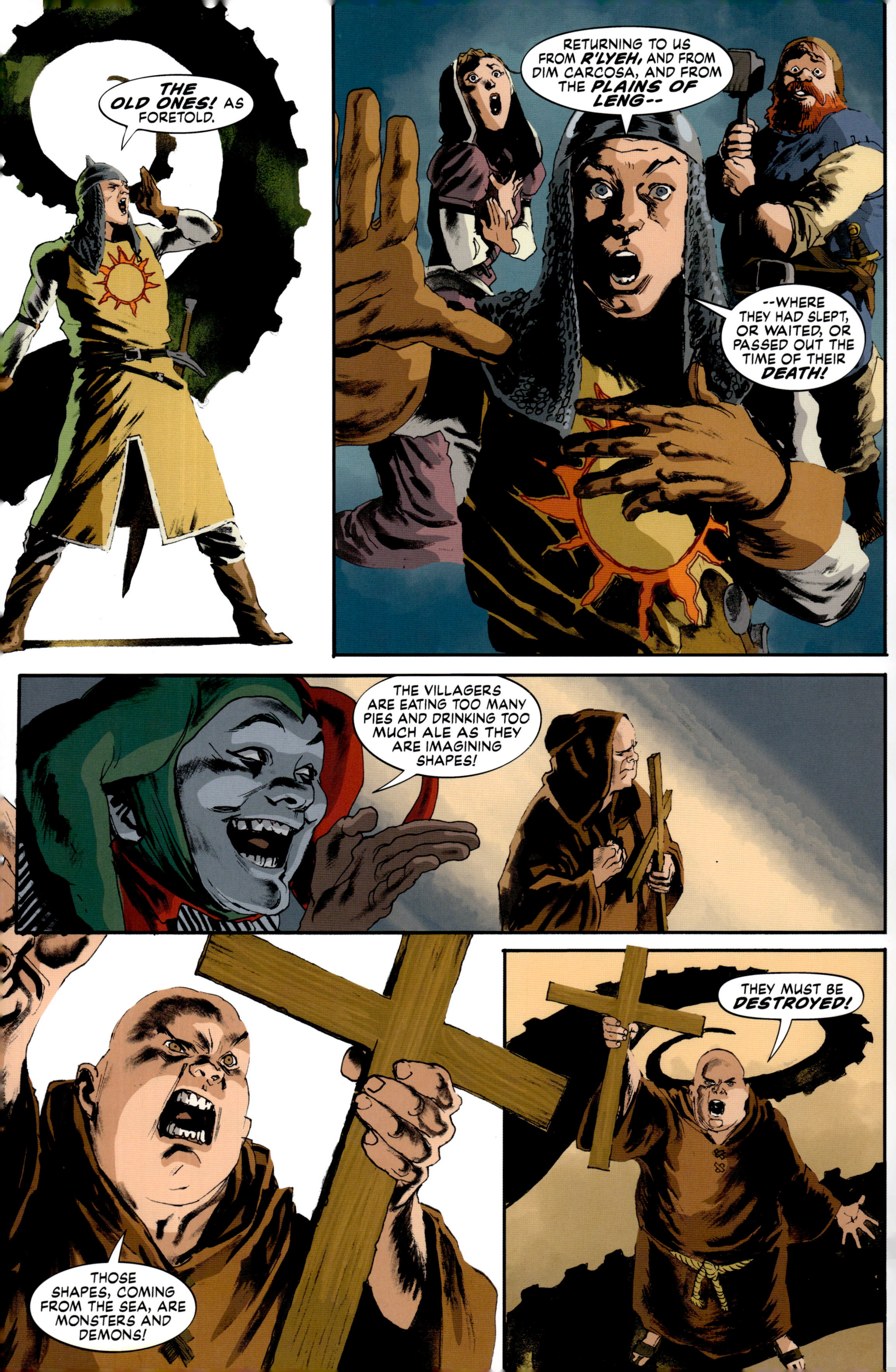
THE OLD ONES! AS FORETOLD.
RETURNING TO US FROM R'LYEH, AND FROM DIM CARCOSA, AND FROM THE PLAINS OF LENG--
--WHERE THEY HAD SLEPT, OR WAITED, OR PASSED OUT THE TIME OF THEIR DEATH!
THE VILLAGERS ARE EATING TOO MANY PIES AND DRINKING TOO MUCH ALE AS THEY ARE IMAGINING SHAPES!
THOSE SHAPES, COMING FROM THE SEA, ARE MONSTERS AND DEMONS!
THEY MUST BE DESTROYED!

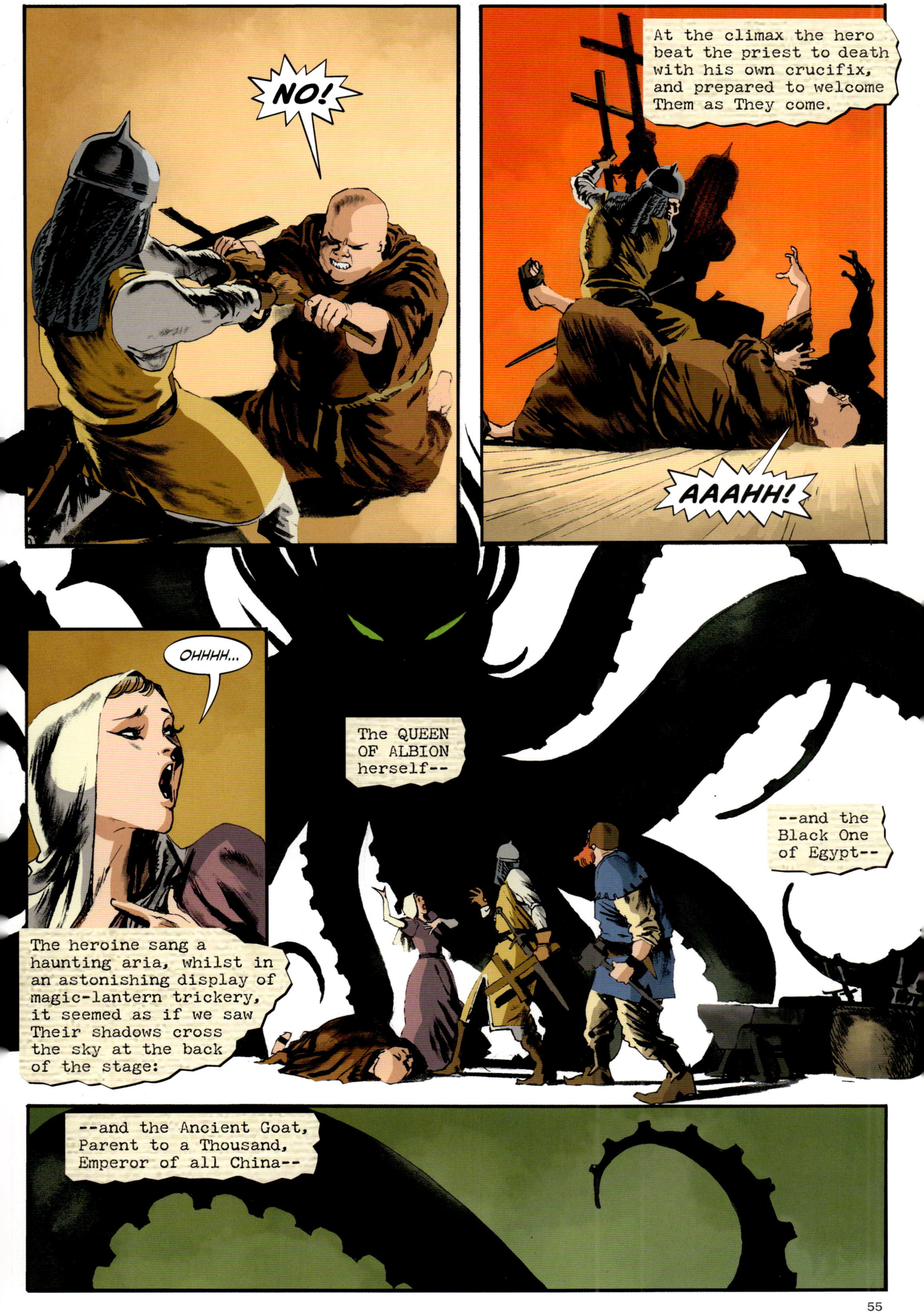
NO!
At the climax the hero beat the priest to death with his own crucifix, and prepared to welcome Them as They come.
AAAHH!
OHHHH...
The heroine sang a haunting aria, whilst in an astonishing display of magic-lantern trickery, it seemed as if we saw Their shadows cross the sky at the back of the stage:
The QUEEN OF ALBION herself--
--and the Black One of Egypt--
--and the Ancient Goat, Parent to a Thousand, Emperor of all China--

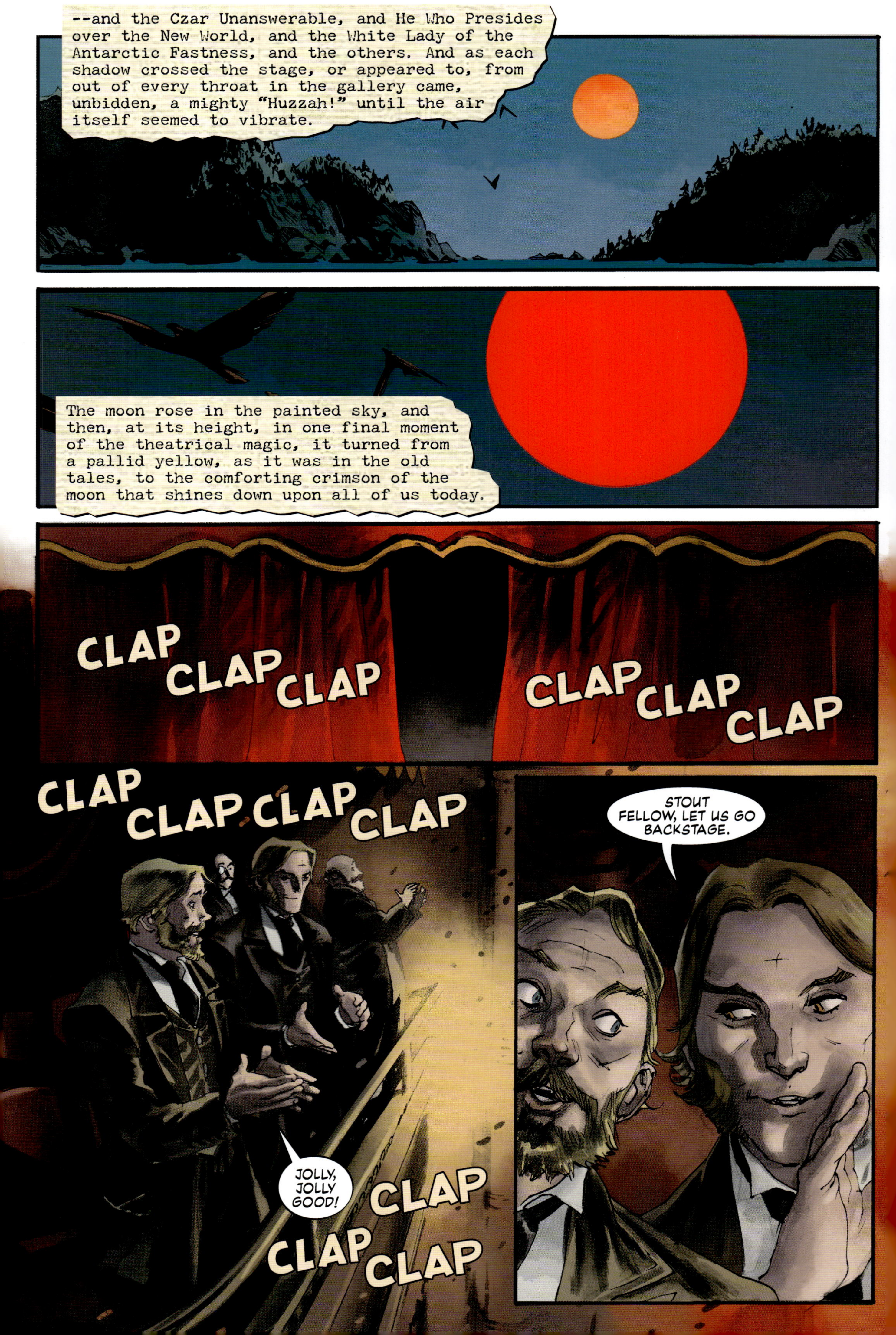
--and the Czar Unanswerable, and He Who Presides over the New World, and the White Lady of the Antarctic Fastness, and the others. And as each shadow crossed the stage, or appeared to, from out of every throat in the gallery came, unbidden, a mighty "Huzzah!" until the air itself seemed to vibrate.
The moon rose in the painted sky, and then, at its height, in one final moment of the theatrical magic, it turned from a pallid yellow, as it was in the old tales, to the comforting crimson of the moon that shines down upon all of us today.
CLAP CLAP CLAP
CLAP CLAP CLAP
CLAP CLAP CLAP CLAP
JOLLY, JOLLY GOOD!
CLAP CLAP CLAP
STOUT FELLOW, LET US GO BACKSTAGE.

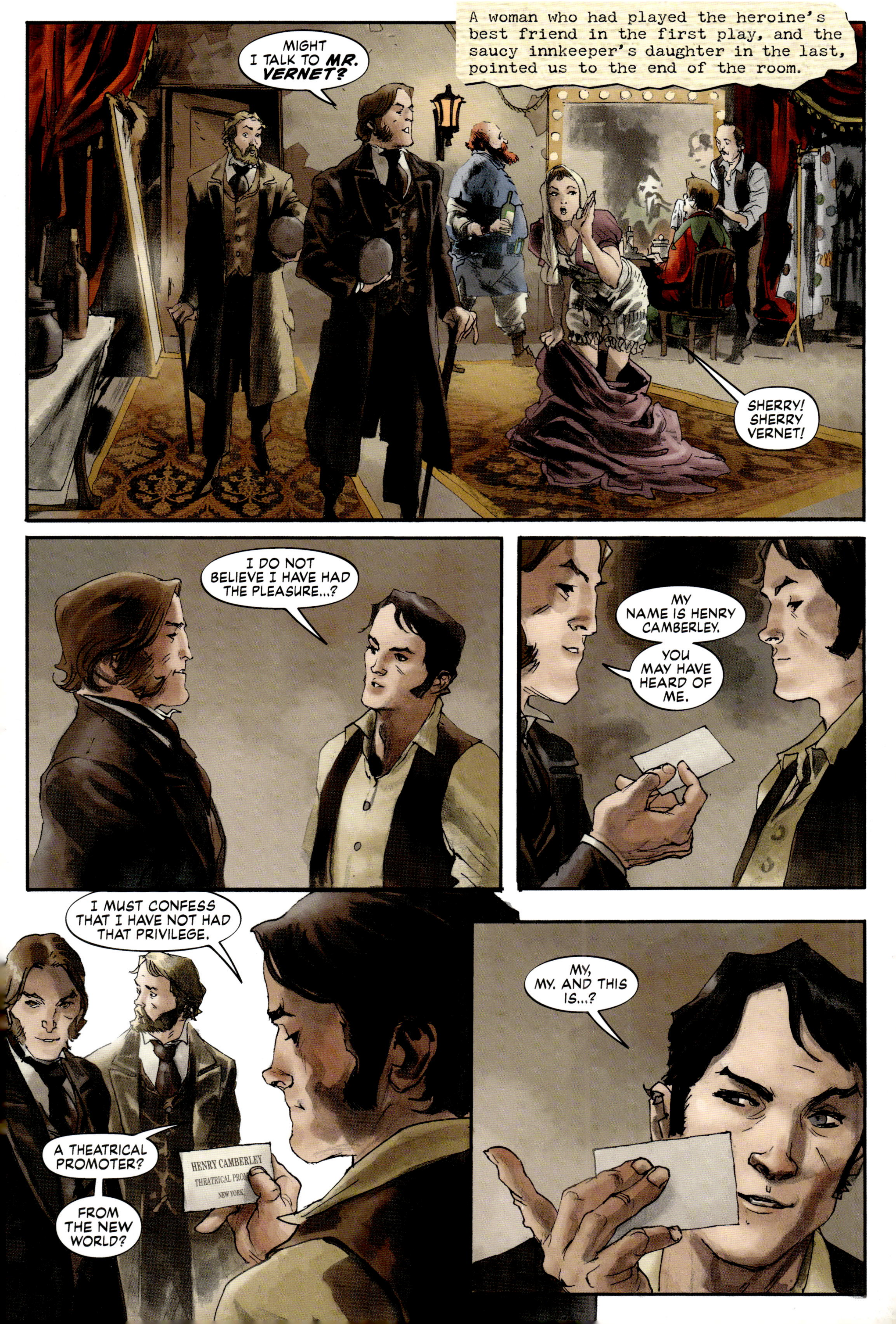
A woman who had played the heroine's best friend in the first play, and the saucy innkeeper's daughter in the last, pointed us to the end of the room.
MIGHT I TALK TO *MR. VERNET?*
SHERRY! SHERRY VERNET!
I DO NOT BELIEVE I HAVE HAD THE PLEASURE...?
MY NAME IS HENRY CAMBERLEY.
YOU MAY HAVE HEARD OF ME.
I MUST CONFESS THAT I HAVE NOT HAD THAT PRIVILEGE.
A THEATRICAL PROMOTER?
FROM THE NEW WORLD?
MY, MY. AND THIS IS...?

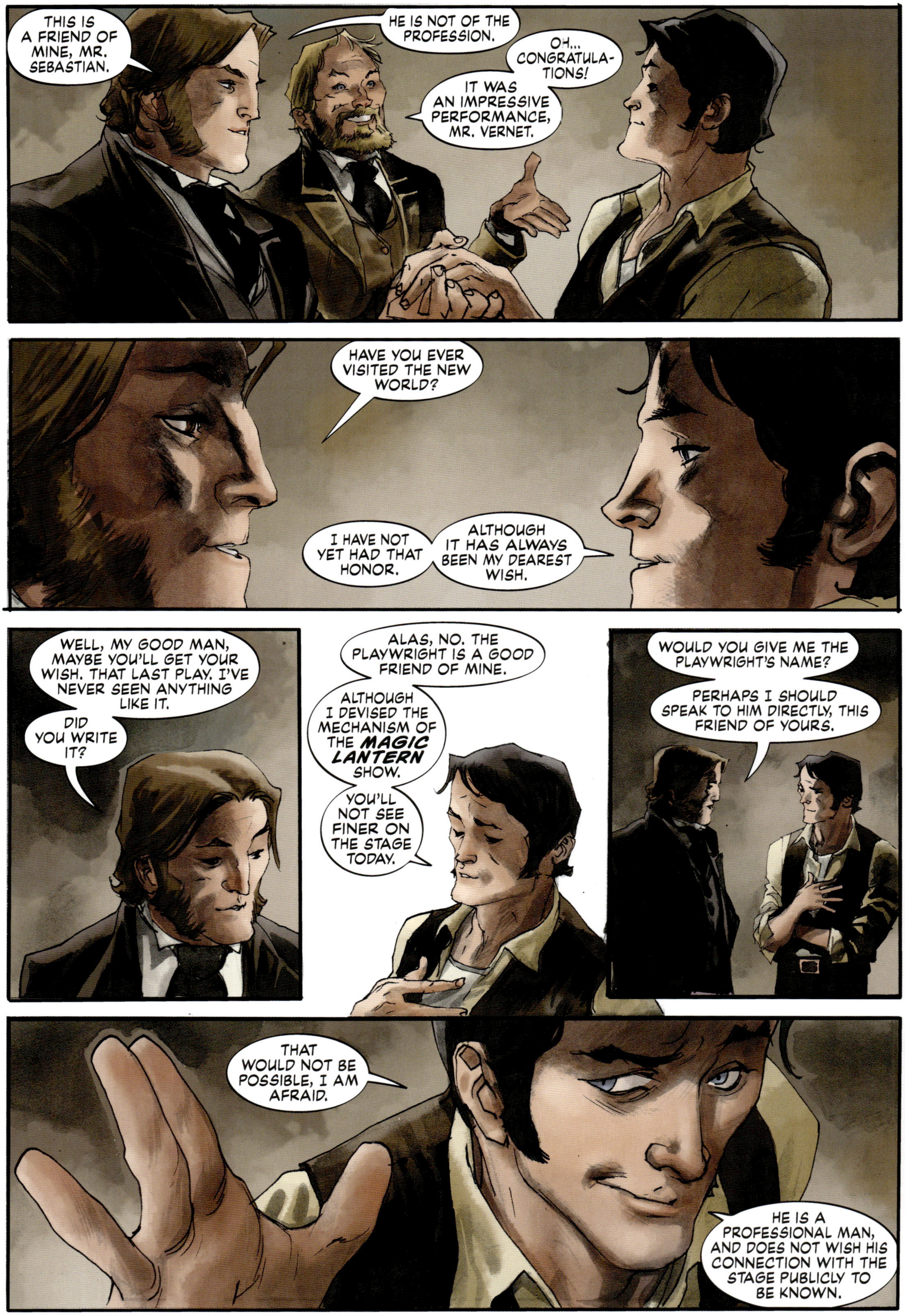

THIS IS A FRIEND OF MINE, MR. SEBASTIAN.
HE IS NOT OF THE PROFESSION.
OH... CONGRATULATIONS!
IT WAS AN IMPRESSIVE PERFORMANCE, MR. VERNET.
HAVE YOU EVER VISITED THE NEW WORLD?
I HAVE NOT YET HAD THAT HONOR.
ALTHOUGH IT HAS ALWAYS BEEN MY DEAREST WISH.
WELL, MY GOOD MAN, MAYBE YOU'LL GET YOUR WISH. THAT LAST PLAY. I'VE NEVER SEEN ANYTHING LIKE IT.
DID YOU WRITE IT?
ALAS, NO. THE PLAYWRIGHT IS A GOOD FRIEND OF MINE.
ALTHOUGH I DEVISED THE MECHANISM OF THE MAGIC LANTERN SHOW.
YOU'LL NOT SEE FINER ON THE STAGE TODAY.
WOULD YOU GIVE ME THE PLAYWRIGHT'S NAME?
PERHAPS I SHOULD SPEAK TO HIM DIRECTLY, THIS FRIEND OF YOURS.
THAT WOULD NOT BE POSSIBLE, I AM AFRAID.
HE IS A PROFESSIONAL MAN, AND DOES NOT WISH HIS CONNECTION WITH THE STAGE PUBLICLY TO BE KNOWN.

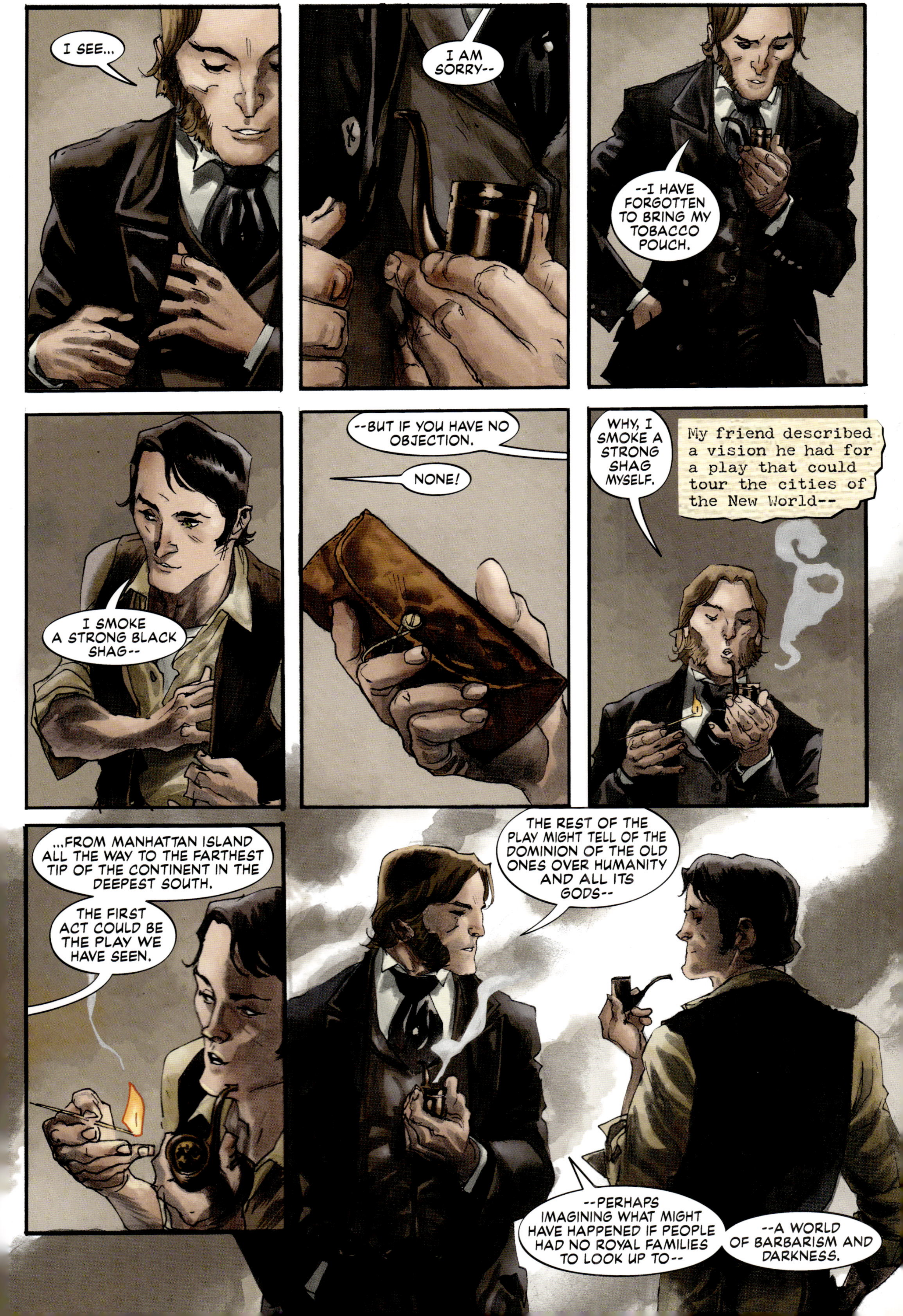
I SEE...
I AM SORRY--
--I HAVE FORGOTTEN TO BRING MY TOBACCO POUCH.
I SMOKE A STRONG BLACK SHAG--
--BUT IF YOU HAVE NO OBJECTION.
NONE!
WHY, I SMOKE A STRONG SHAG MYSELF.
My friend described a vision he had for a play that could tour the cities of the New World--
...FROM MANHATTAN ISLAND ALL THE WAY TO THE FARTHEST TIP OF THE CONTINENT IN THE DEEPEST SOUTH.
THE FIRST ACT COULD BE THE PLAY WE HAVE SEEN.
THE REST OF THE PLAY MIGHT TELL OF THE DOMINION OF THE OLD ONES OVER HUMANITY AND ALL ITS GODS--
--PERHAPS IMAGINING WHAT MIGHT HAVE HAPPENED IF PEOPLE HAD NO ROYAL FAMILIES TO LOOK UP TO--
--A WORLD OF BARBARISM AND DARKNESS.

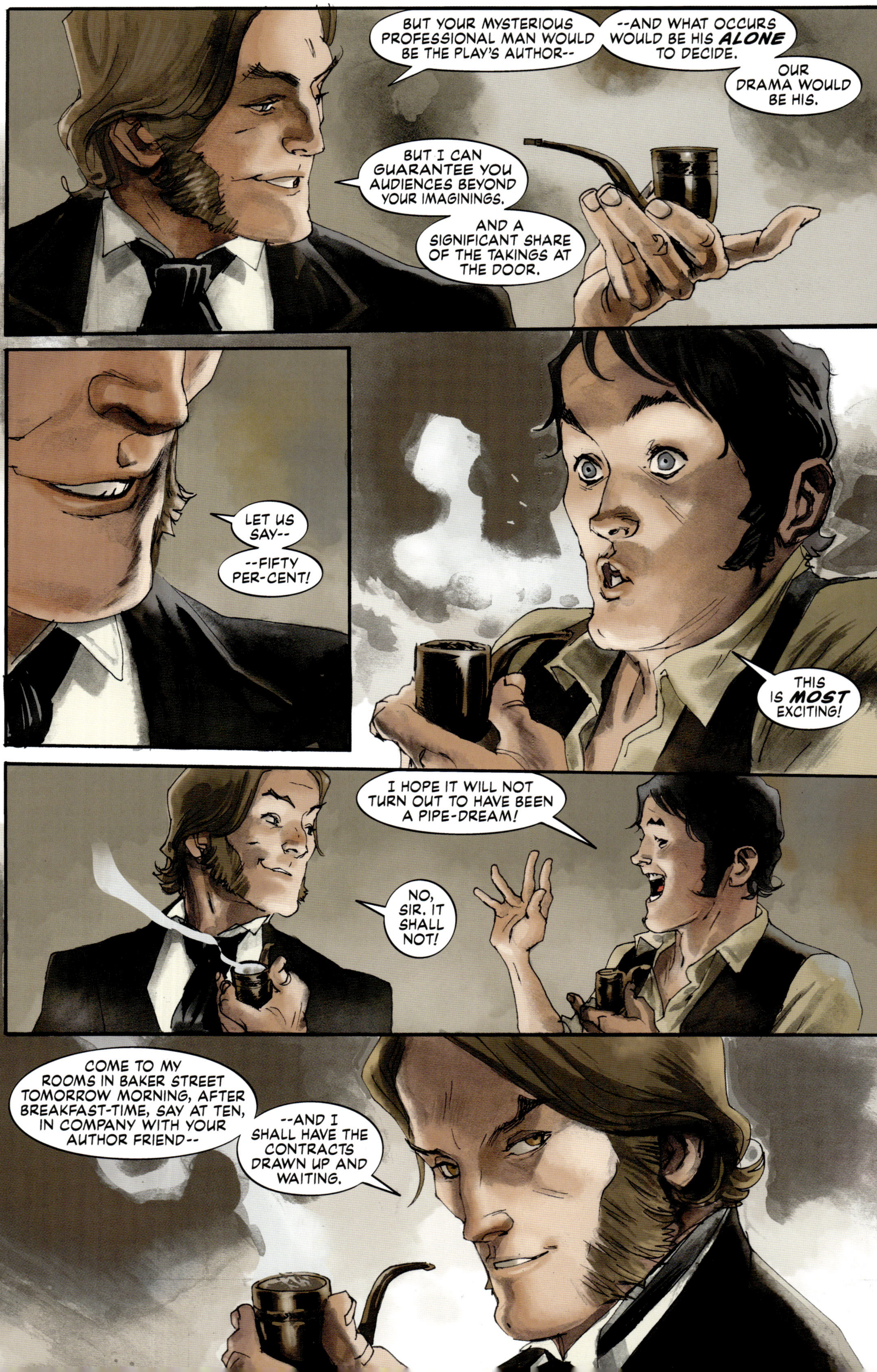
BUT YOUR MYSTERIOUS PROFESSIONAL MAN WOULD BE THE PLAY'S AUTHOR--
--AND WHAT OCCURS WOULD BE HIS **ALONE** TO DECIDE.
OUR DRAMA WOULD BE HIS.
BUT I CAN GUARANTEE YOU AUDIENCES BEYOND YOUR IMAGININGS.
AND A SIGNIFICANT SHARE OF THE TAKINGS AT THE DOOR.
LET US SAY--
--FIFTY PER-CENT!
THIS IS **MOST** EXCITING!
I HOPE IT WILL NOT TURN OUT TO HAVE BEEN A PIPE-DREAM!
NO, SIR. IT SHALL NOT!
COME TO MY ROOMS IN BAKER STREET TOMORROW MORNING, AFTER BREAKFAST-TIME, SAY AT TEN, IN COMPANY WITH YOUR AUTHOR FRIEND--
--AND I SHALL HAVE THE CONTRACTS DRAWN UP AND WAITING.

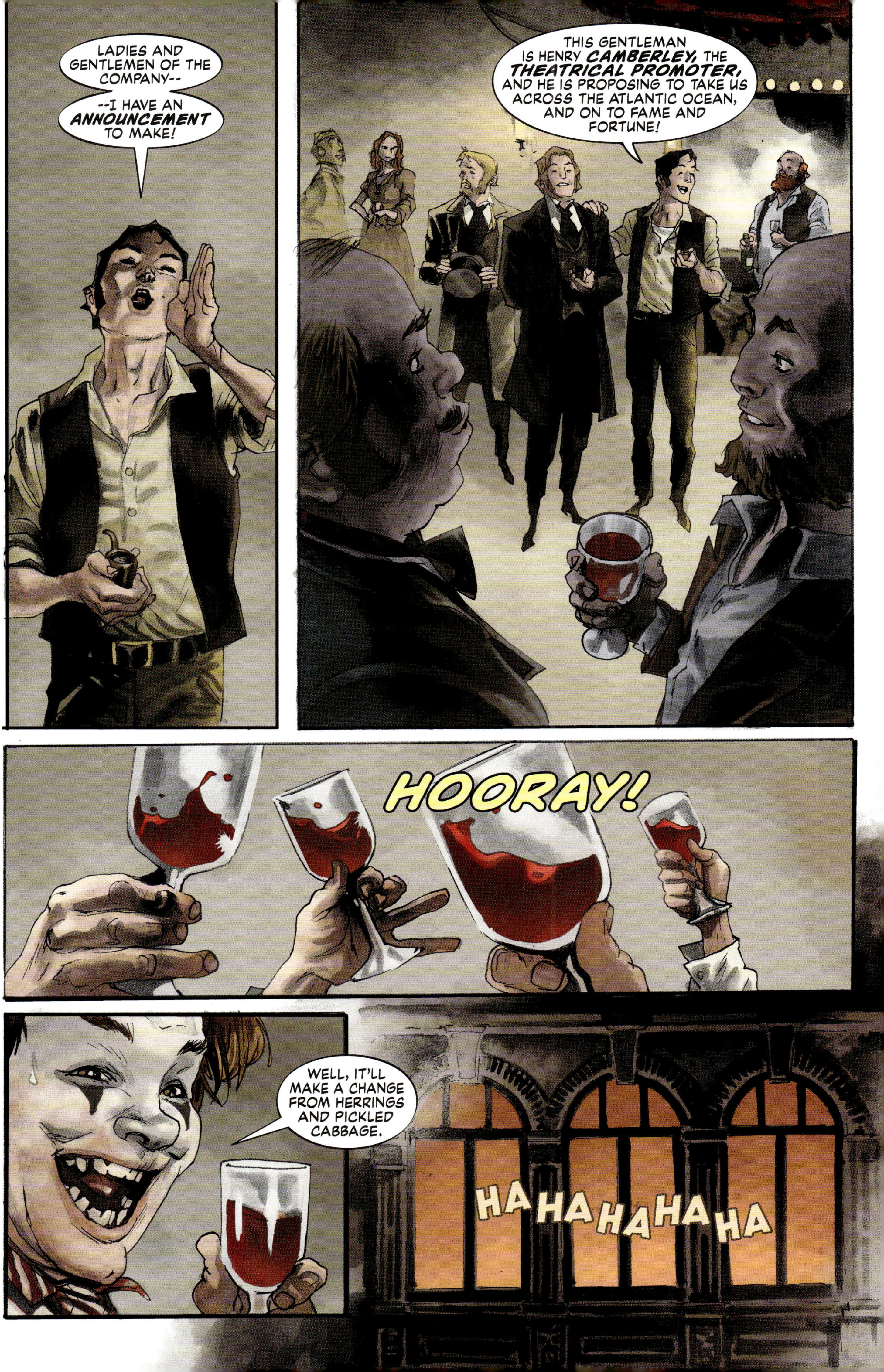
LADIES AND GENTLEMEN OF THE COMPANY--
--I HAVE AN ANNOUNCEMENT TO MAKE!
THIS GENTLEMAN IS HENRY CAMBERLEY, THE THEATRICAL PROMOTER, AND HE IS PROPOSING TO TAKE US ACROSS THE ATLANTIC OCEAN, AND ON TO FAME AND FORTUNE!
HOORAY!
WELL, IT'LL MAKE A CHANGE FROM HERRINGS AND PICKLED CABBAGE.
HAHAHAHAHAHA

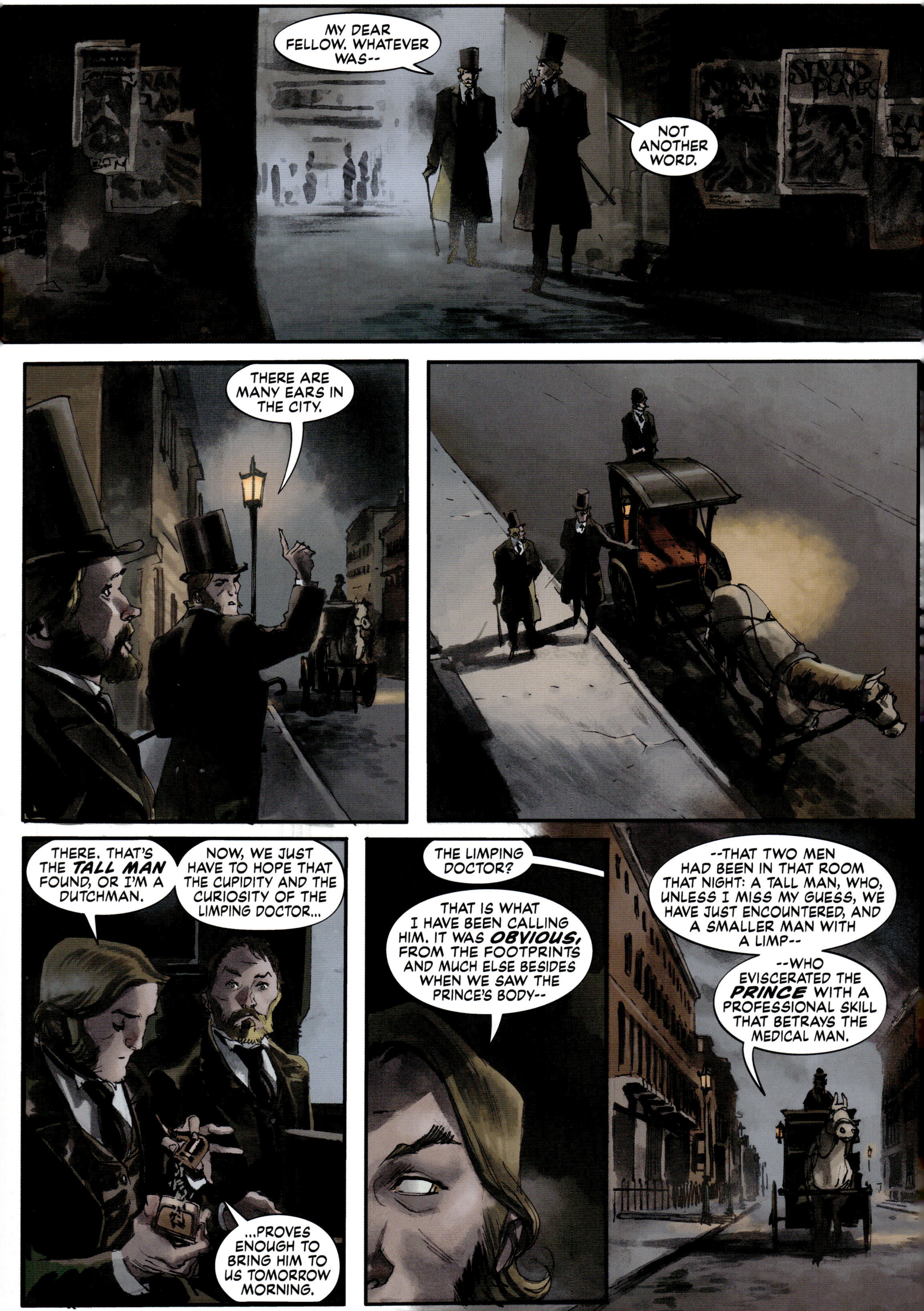
MY DEAR FELLOW. WHATEVER WAS--
NOT ANOTHER WORD.
STRAND PLAYERS
THERE ARE MANY EARS IN THE CITY.
THERE. THAT'S THE TALL MAN FOUND, OR I'M A DUTCHMAN.
NOW, WE JUST HAVE TO HOPE THAT THE CUPIDITY AND THE CURIOSITY OF THE LIMPING DOCTOR...
...PROVES ENOUGH TO BRING HIM TO US TOMORROW MORNING.
THE LIMPING DOCTOR?
THAT IS WHAT I HAVE BEEN CALLING HIM. IT WAS OBVIOUS, FROM THE FOOTPRINTS AND MUCH ELSE BESIDES WHEN WE SAW THE PRINCE'S BODY--
--THAT TWO MEN HAD BEEN IN THAT ROOM THAT NIGHT: A TALL MAN, WHO, UNLESS I MISS MY GUESS, WE HAVE JUST ENCOUNTERED, AND A SMALLER MAN WITH A LIMP--
--WHO EVISCERATED THE PRINCE WITH A PROFESSIONAL SKILL THAT BETRAYS THE MEDICAL MAN.

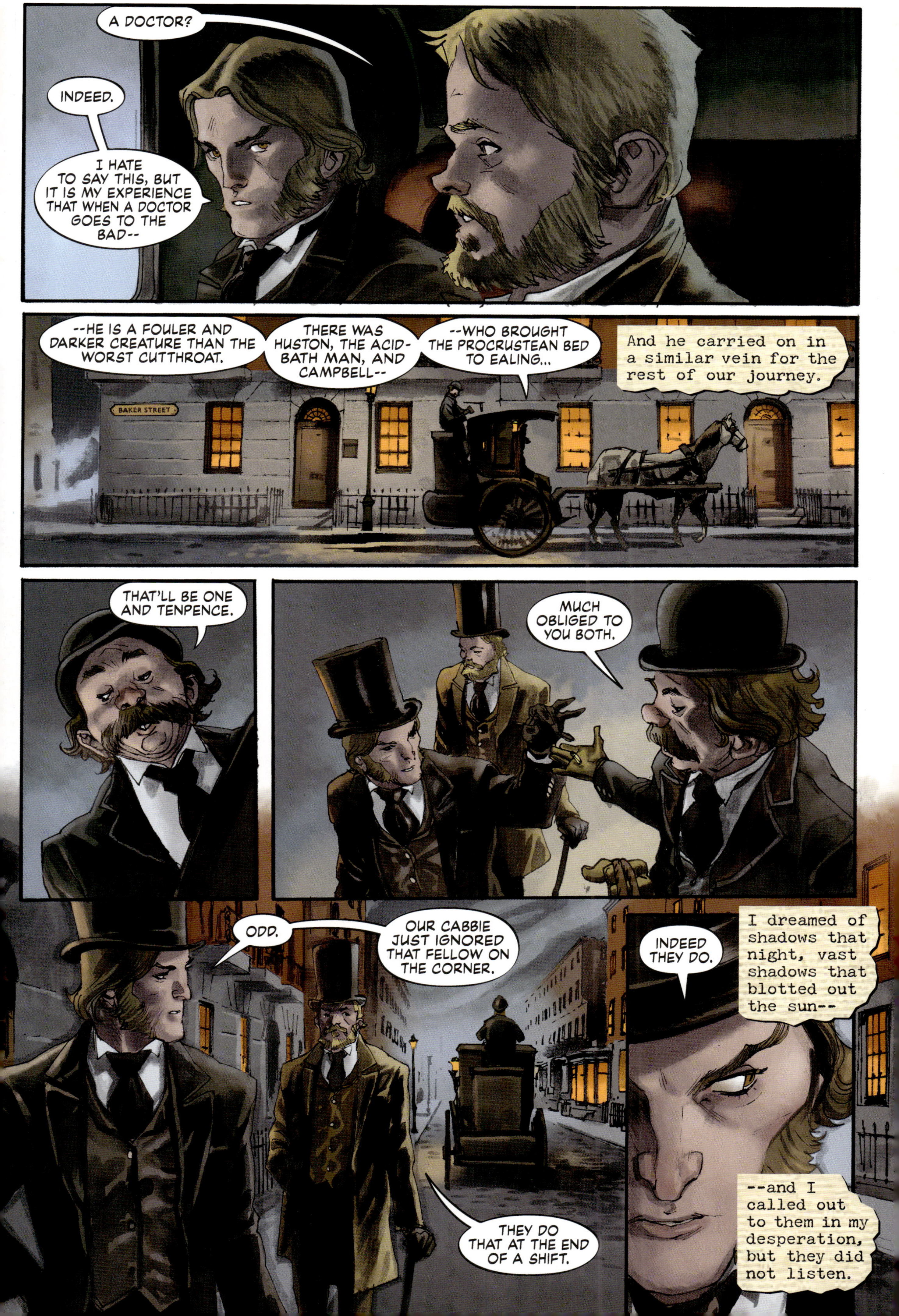
A DOCTOR?
INDEED.
I HATE TO SAY THIS, BUT IT IS MY EXPERIENCE THAT WHEN A DOCTOR GOES TO THE BAD--
--HE IS A FOULER AND DARKER CREATURE THAN THE WORST CUTTHROAT.
THERE WAS HUSTON, THE ACID-BATH MAN, AND CAMPBELL--
--WHO BROUGHT THE PROCRUSTEAN BED TO EALING...
And he carried on in a similar vein for the rest of our journey.
BAKER STREET
THAT'LL BE ONE AND TENPENCE.
MUCH OBLIGED TO YOU BOTH.
ODD.
OUR CABBIE JUST IGNORED THAT FELLOW ON THE CORNER.
THEY DO THAT AT THE END OF A SHIFT.
INDEED THEY DO.
I dreamed of shadows that night, vast shadows that blotted out the sun--
--and I called out to them in my desperation, but they did not listen.

THE SKIN AND THE PIT

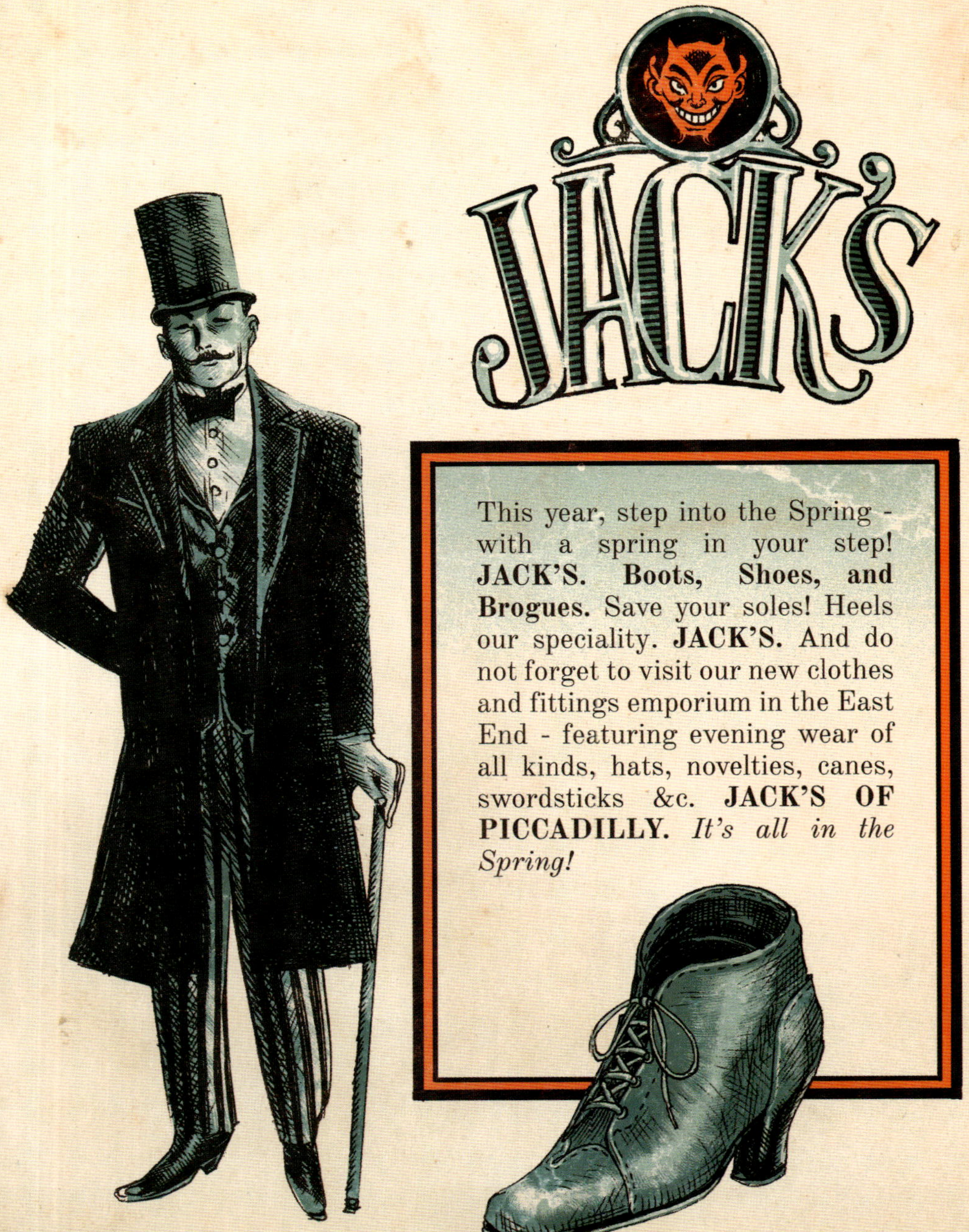
JACK'S
This year, step into the Spring - with a spring in your step! **JACK'S. Boots, Shoes, and Brogues.** Save your soles! Heels our speciality. **JACK'S.** And do not forget to visit our new clothes and fittings emporium in the East End - featuring evening wear of all kinds, hats, novelties, canes, swordsticks &c. **JACK'S OF PICCADILLY.** *It's all in the Spring!*

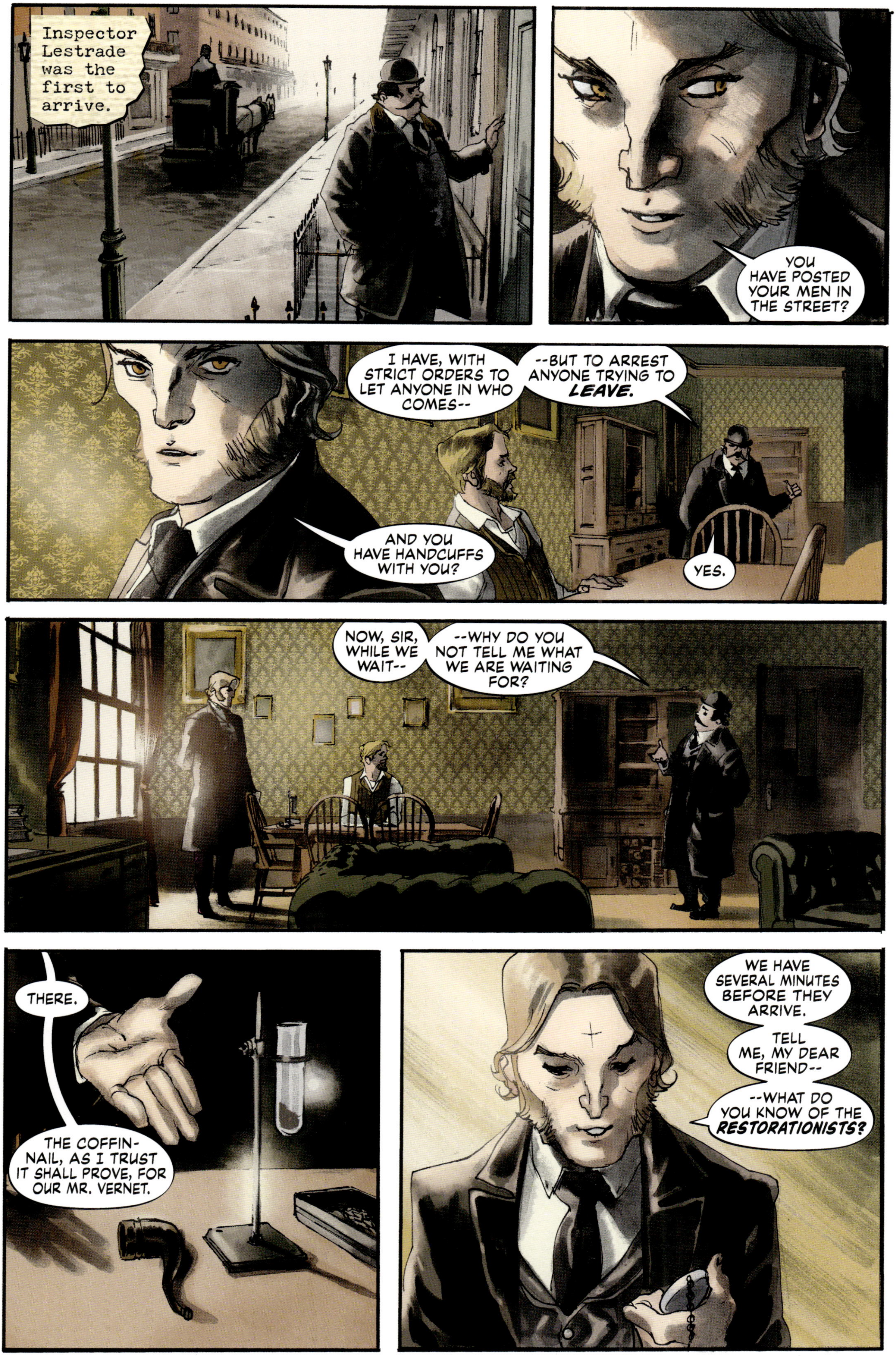

Inspector Lestrade was the first to arrive.
YOU HAVE POSTED YOUR MEN IN THE STREET?
I HAVE, WITH STRICT ORDERS TO LET ANYONE IN WHO COMES--
--BUT TO ARREST ANYONE TRYING TO LEAVE.
AND YOU HAVE HANDCUFFS WITH YOU?
YES.
NOW, SIR, WHILE WE WAIT--
--WHY DO YOU NOT TELL ME WHAT WE ARE WAITING FOR?
THERE.
THE COFFIN-NAIL, AS I TRUST IT SHALL PROVE, FOR OUR MR. VERNET.
WE HAVE SEVERAL MINUTES BEFORE THEY ARRIVE.
TELL ME, MY DEAR FRIEND--
--WHAT DO YOU KNOW OF THE RESTORATIONISTS?

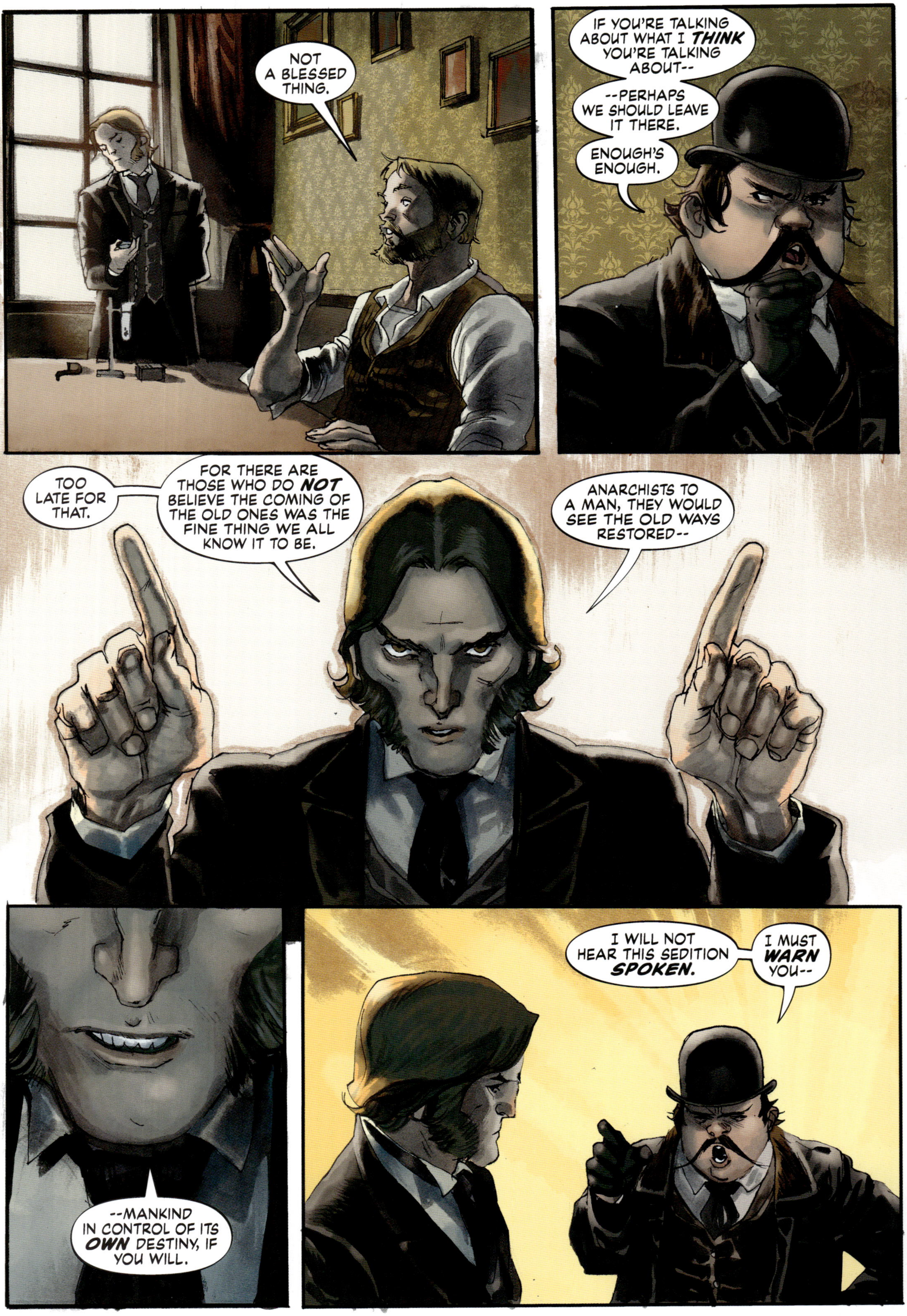
NOT A BLESSED THING.
IF YOU'RE TALKING ABOUT WHAT I THINK YOU'RE TALKING ABOUT--
--PERHAPS WE SHOULD LEAVE IT THERE.
ENOUGH'S ENOUGH.
TOO LATE FOR THAT.
FOR THERE ARE THOSE WHO DO NOT BELIEVE THE COMING OF THE OLD ONES WAS THE FINE THING WE ALL KNOW IT TO BE.
ANARCHISTS TO A MAN, THEY WOULD SEE THE OLD WAYS RESTORED--
--MANKIND IN CONTROL OF ITS OWN DESTINY, IF YOU WILL.
I WILL NOT HEAR THIS SEDITION SPOKEN.
I MUST WARN YOU--

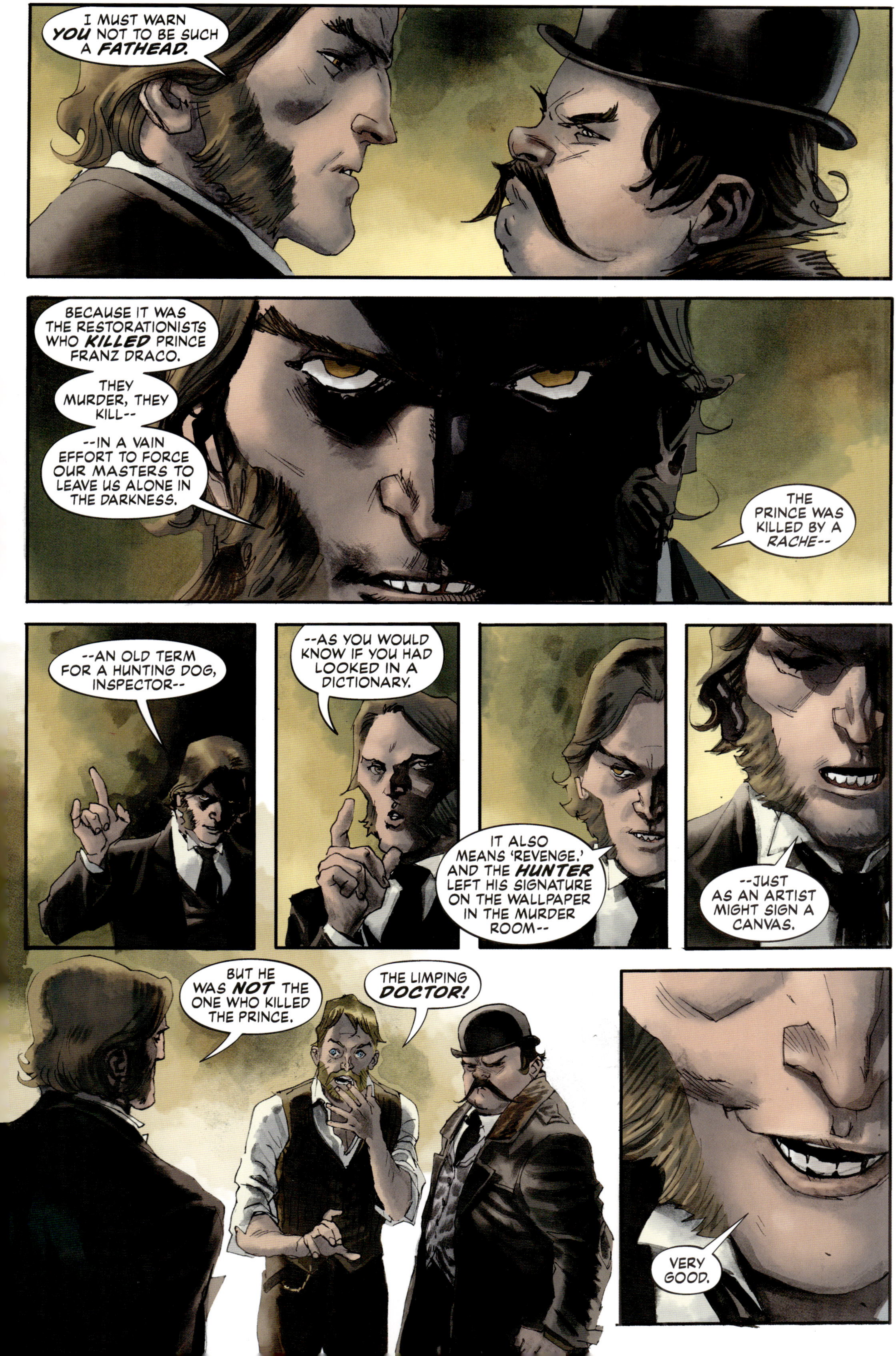
I MUST WARN YOU NOT TO BE SUCH A FATHEAD.
BECAUSE IT WAS THE RESTORATIONISTS WHO KILLED PRINCE FRANZ DRACO.
THEY MURDER, THEY KILL--
--IN A VAIN EFFORT TO FORCE OUR MASTERS TO LEAVE US ALONE IN THE DARKNESS.
THE PRINCE WAS KILLED BY A RACHE--
--AN OLD TERM FOR A HUNTING DOG, INSPECTOR--
--AS YOU WOULD KNOW IF YOU HAD LOOKED IN A DICTIONARY.
IT ALSO MEANS 'REVENGE.' AND THE HUNTER LEFT HIS SIGNATURE ON THE WALLPAPER IN THE MURDER ROOM--
--JUST AS AN ARTIST MIGHT SIGN A CANVAS.
BUT HE WAS NOT THE ONE WHO KILLED THE PRINCE.
THE LIMPING DOCTOR!
VERY GOOD.

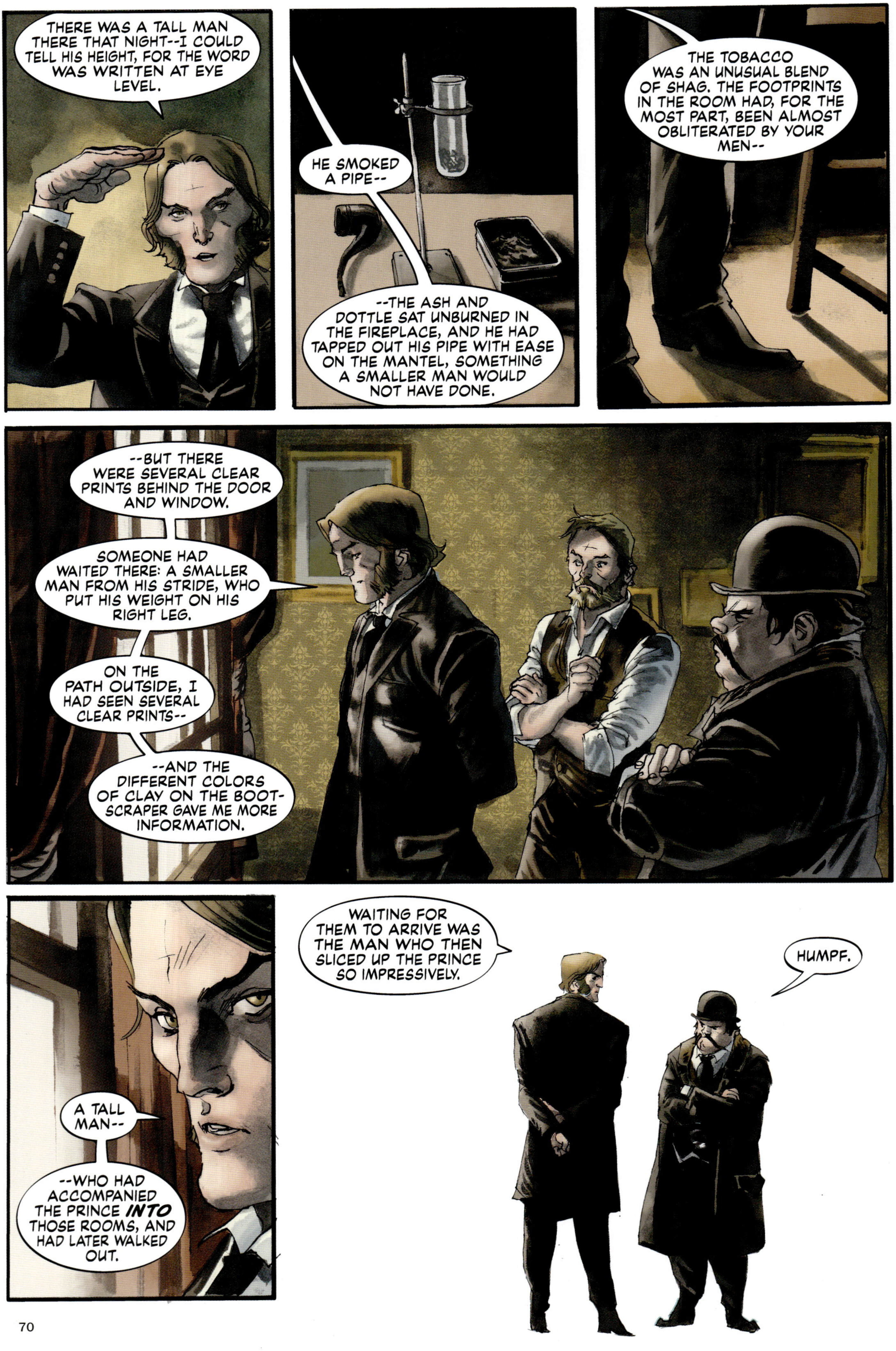
THERE WAS A TALL MAN THERE THAT NIGHT--I COULD TELL HIS HEIGHT, FOR THE WORD WAS WRITTEN AT EYE LEVEL.
HE SMOKED A PIPE--
--THE ASH AND DOTTLE SAT UNBURNED IN THE FIREPLACE, AND HE HAD TAPPED OUT HIS PIPE WITH EASE ON THE MANTEL, SOMETHING A SMALLER MAN WOULD NOT HAVE DONE.
THE TOBACCO WAS AN UNUSUAL BLEND OF SHAG. THE FOOTPRINTS IN THE ROOM HAD, FOR THE MOST PART, BEEN ALMOST OBLITERATED BY YOUR MEN--
--BUT THERE WERE SEVERAL CLEAR PRINTS BEHIND THE DOOR AND WINDOW.
SOMEONE HAD WAITED THERE: A SMALLER MAN FROM HIS STRIDE, WHO PUT HIS WEIGHT ON HIS RIGHT LEG.
ON THE PATH OUTSIDE, I HAD SEEN SEVERAL CLEAR PRINTS--
--AND THE DIFFERENT COLORS OF CLAY ON THE BOOT-SCRAPER GAVE ME MORE INFORMATION.
A TALL MAN--
--WHO HAD ACCOMPANIED THE PRINCE ***INTO*** THOSE ROOMS, AND HAD LATER WALKED OUT.
WAITING FOR THEM TO ARRIVE WAS THE MAN WHO THEN SLICED UP THE PRINCE SO IMPRESSIVELY.
HUMPF.

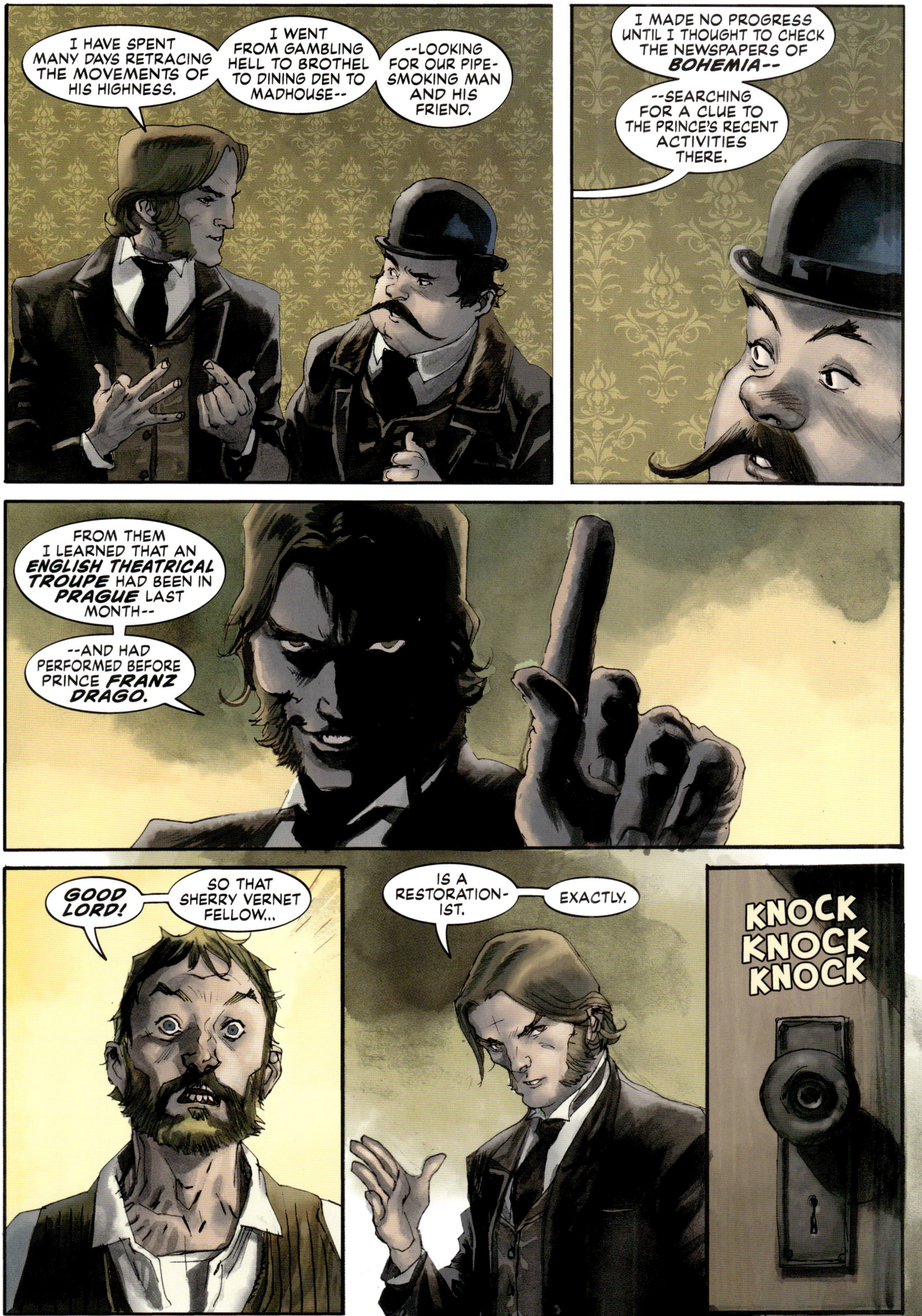
I HAVE SPENT MANY DAYS RETRACING THE MOVEMENTS OF HIS HIGHNESS.
I WENT FROM GAMBLING HELL TO BROTHEL TO DINING DEN TO MADHOUSE--
--LOOKING FOR OUR PIPE-SMOKING MAN AND HIS FRIEND.
I MADE NO PROGRESS UNTIL I THOUGHT TO CHECK THE NEWSPAPERS OF ***BOHEMIA***--
--SEARCHING FOR A CLUE TO THE PRINCE'S RECENT ACTIVITIES THERE.
FROM THEM I LEARNED THAT AN ***ENGLISH THEATRICAL TROUPE*** HAD BEEN IN ***PRAGUE*** LAST MONTH--
--AND HAD PERFORMED BEFORE PRINCE ***FRANZ DRAGO.***
GOOD LORD!
SO THAT SHERRY VERNET FELLOW...
IS A RESTORATION-IST.
EXACTLY.
KNOCK KNOCK KNOCK

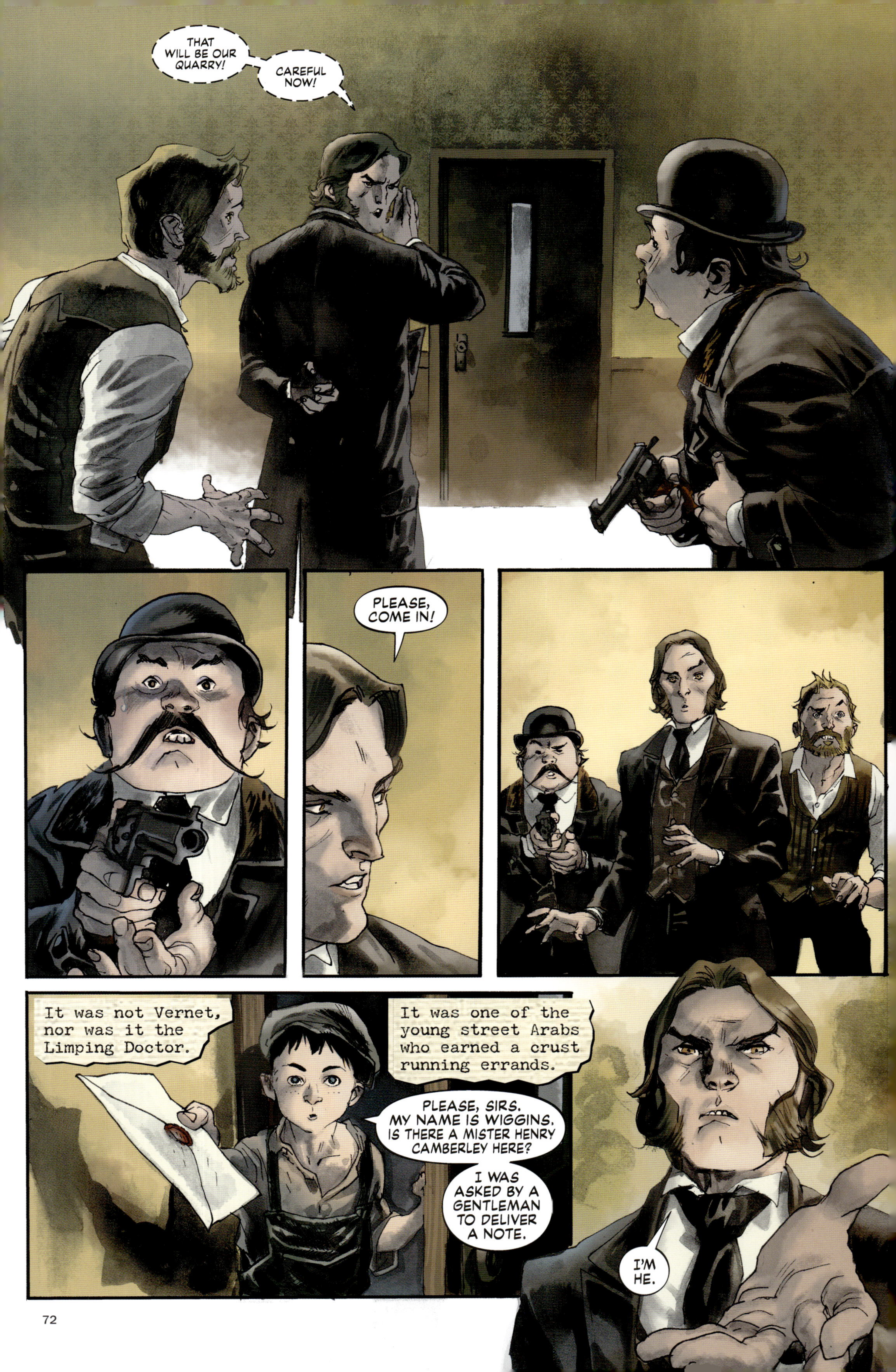
THAT WILL BE OUR QUARRY!
CAREFUL NOW!
PLEASE, COME IN!
It was not Vernet, nor was it the Limping Doctor.
It was one of the young street Arabs who earned a crust running errands.
PLEASE, SIRS. MY NAME IS WIGGINS. IS THERE A MISTER HENRY CAMBERLEY HERE?
I WAS ASKED BY A GENTLEMAN TO DELIVER A NOTE.
I'M HE.

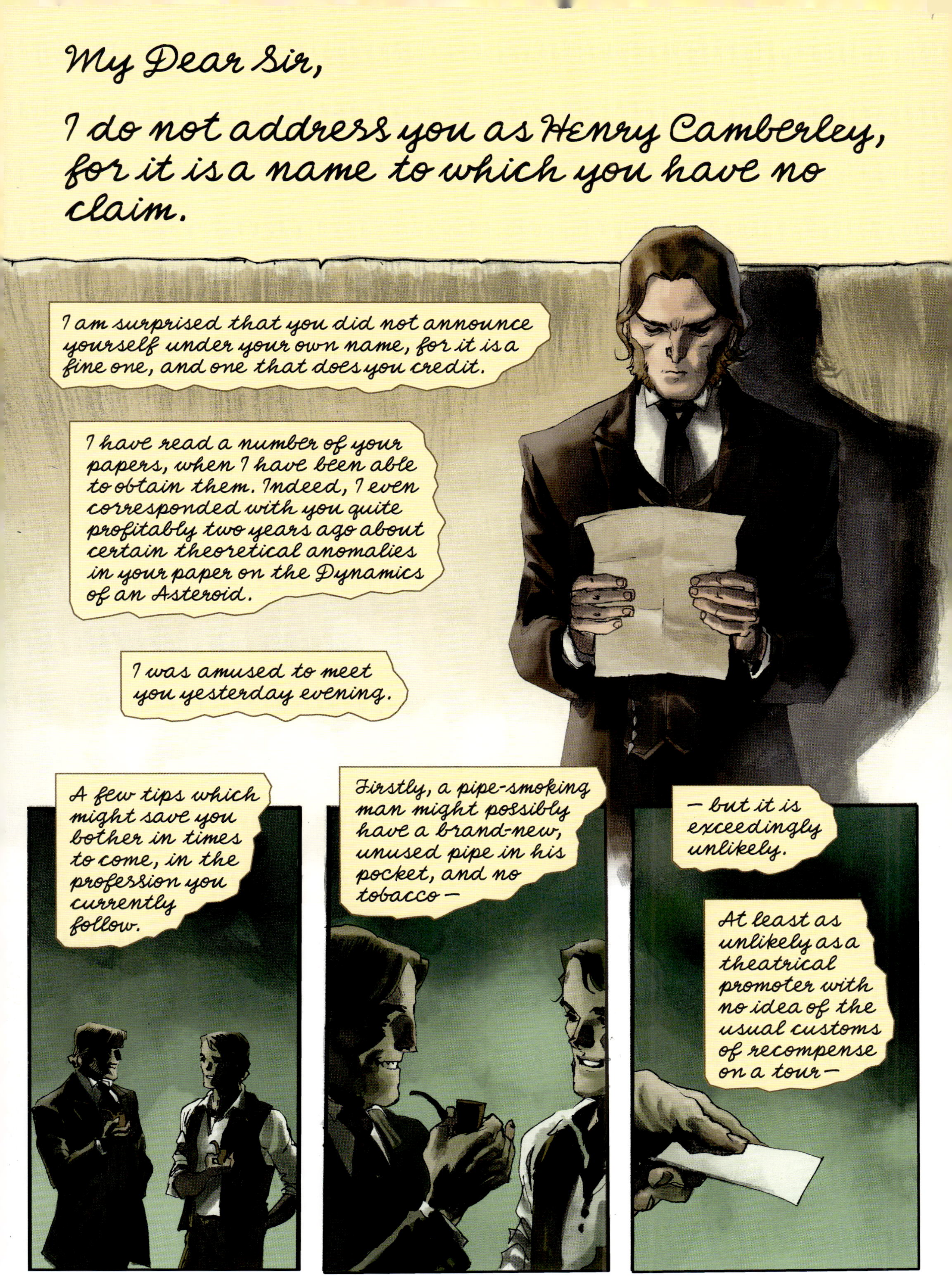
My Dear Sir,
I do not address you as Henry Camberley, for it is a name to which you have no claim.
I am surprised that you did not announce yourself under your own name, for it is a fine one, and one that does you credit.
I have read a number of your papers, when I have been able to obtain them. Indeed, I even corresponded with you quite profitably two years ago about certain theoretical anomalies in your paper on the Dynamics of an Asteroid.
I was amused to meet you yesterday evening.
A few tips which might save you bother in times to come, in the profession you currently follow.
Firstly, a pipe-smoking man might possibly have a brand-new, unused pipe in his pocket, and no tobacco—
—but it is exceedingly unlikely.
At least as unlikely as a theatrical promoter with no idea of the usual customs of recompense on a tour—

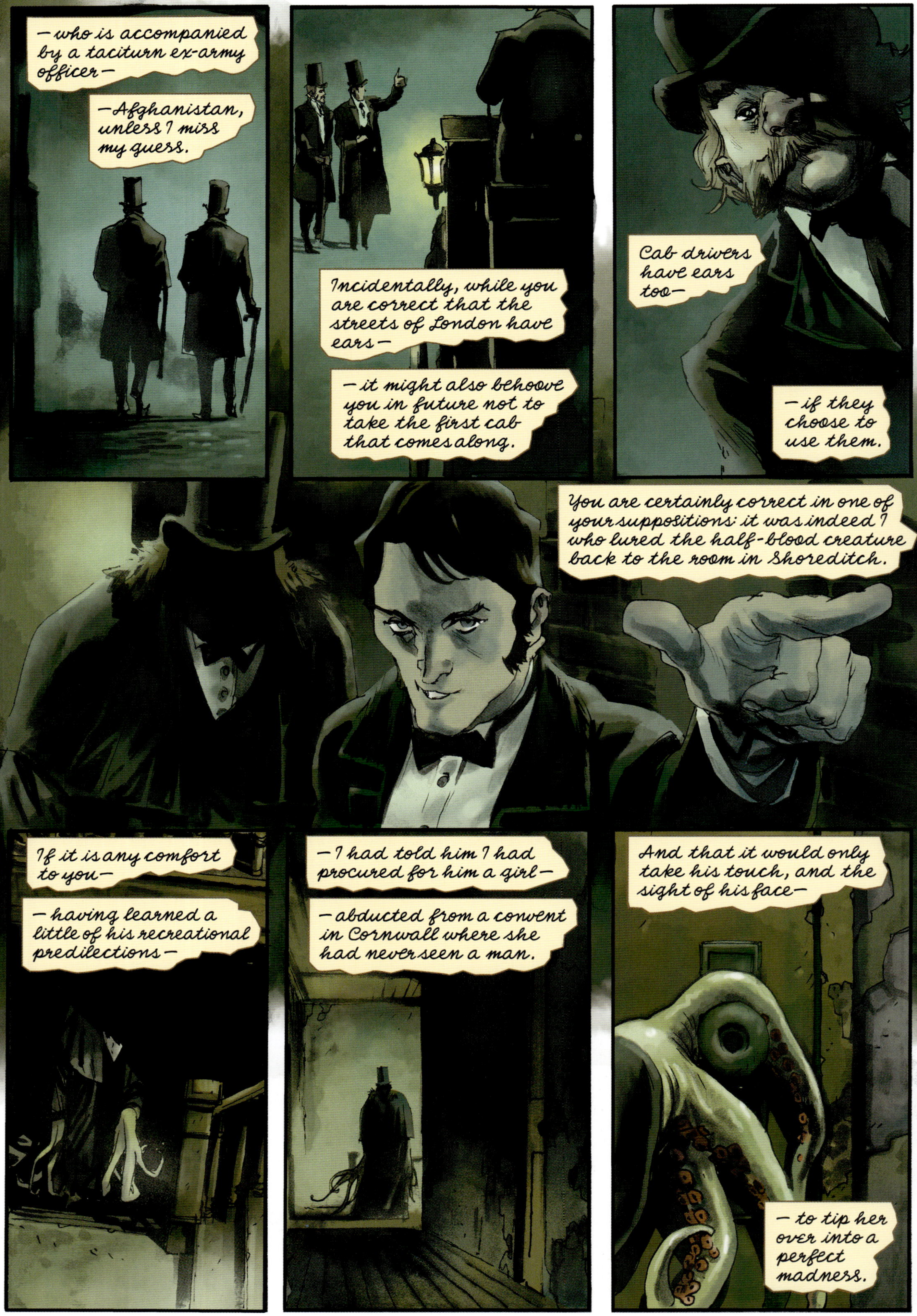

—who is accompanied by a taciturn ex-army officer—
—Afghanistan, unless I miss my guess.
Incidentally, while you are correct that the streets of London have ears—
—it might also behoove you in future not to take the first cab that comes along.
Cab drivers have ears too—
—if they choose to use them.
You are certainly correct in one of your suppositions: it was indeed I who lured the half-blood creature back to the room in Shoreditch.
If it is any comfort to you—
—having learned a little of his recreational predilections—
—I had told him I had procured for him a girl—
—abducted from a convent in Cornwall where she had never seen a man.
And that it would only take his touch, and the sight of his face—
—to tip her over into a perfect madness.

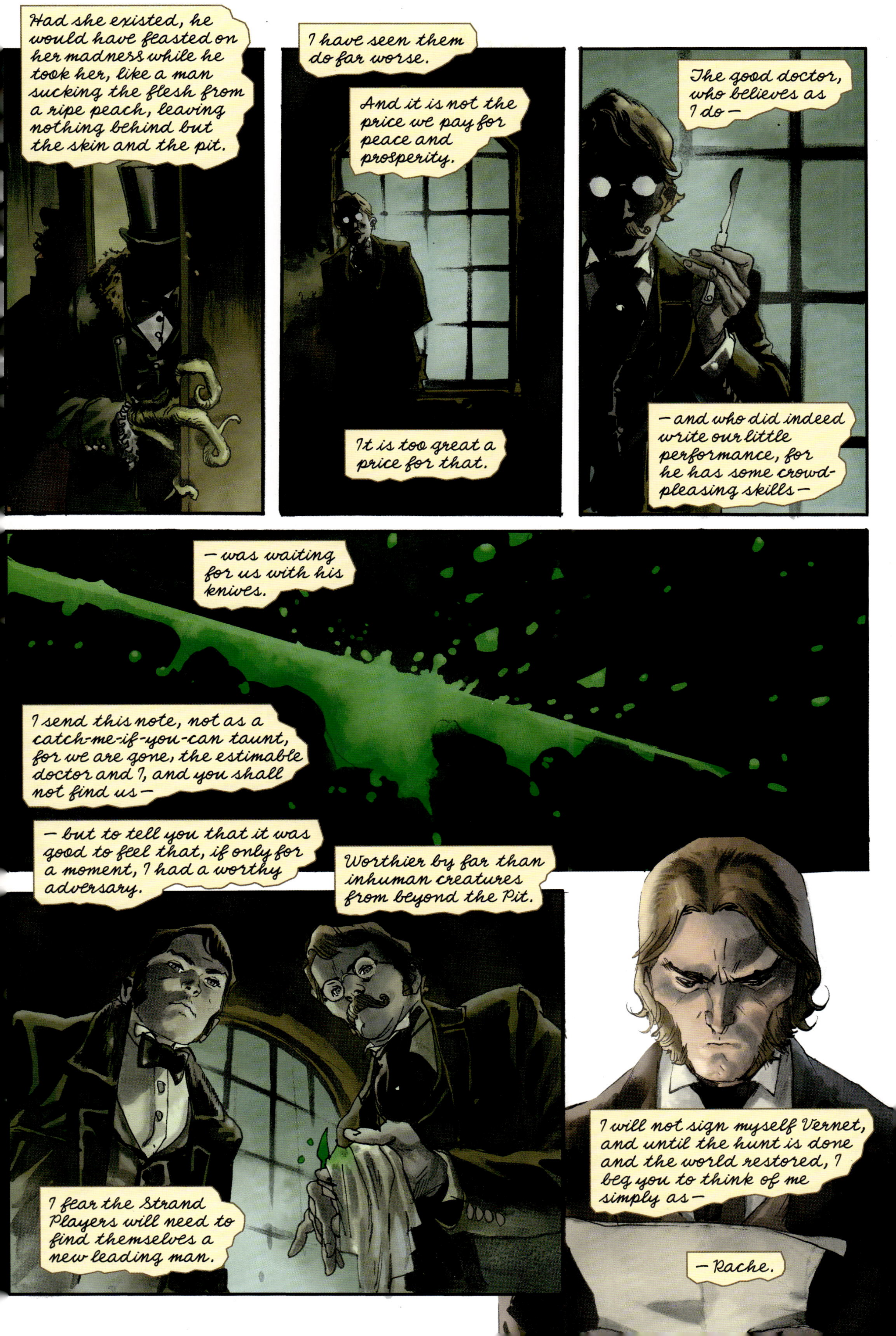
Had she existed, he would have feasted on her madness while he took her, like a man sucking the flesh from a ripe peach, leaving nothing behind but the skin and the pit.
I have seen them do far worse.
And it is not the price we pay for peace and prosperity.
It is too great a price for that.
The good doctor, who believes as I do—
—and who did indeed write our little performance, for he has some crowd-pleasing skills—
—was waiting for us with his knives.
I send this note, not as a catch-me-if-you-can taunt, for we are gone, the estimable doctor and I, and you shall not find us—
—but to tell you that it was good to feel that, if only for a moment, I had a worthy adversary.
Worthier by far than inhuman creatures from beyond the Pit.
I fear the Strand Players will need to find themselves a new leading man.
I will not sign myself Vernet, and until the hunt is done and the world restored, I beg you to think of me simply as—
—Rache.

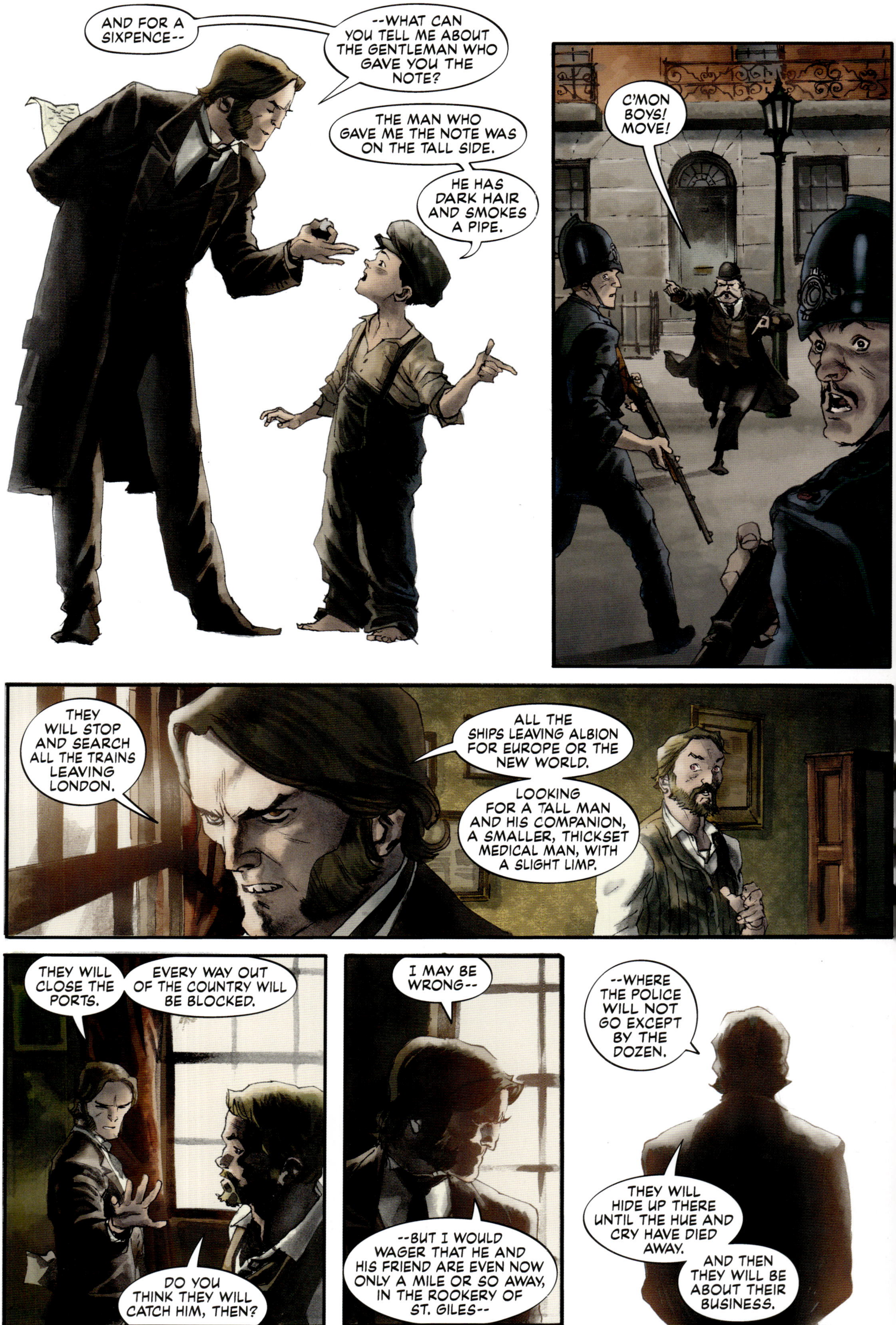
AND FOR A SIXPENCE--
--WHAT CAN YOU TELL ME ABOUT THE GENTLEMAN WHO GAVE YOU THE NOTE?
THE MAN WHO GAVE ME THE NOTE WAS ON THE TALL SIDE.
HE HAS DARK HAIR AND SMOKES A PIPE.
C'MON BOYS! MOVE!
THEY WILL STOP AND SEARCH ALL THE TRAINS LEAVING LONDON.
ALL THE SHIPS LEAVING ALBION FOR EUROPE OR THE NEW WORLD.
LOOKING FOR A TALL MAN AND HIS COMPANION, A SMALLER, THICKSET MEDICAL MAN, WITH A SLIGHT LIMP.
THEY WILL CLOSE THE PORTS.
EVERY WAY OUT OF THE COUNTRY WILL BE BLOCKED.
DO YOU THINK THEY WILL CATCH HIM, THEN?
I MAY BE WRONG--
--BUT I WOULD WAGER THAT HE AND HIS FRIEND ARE EVEN NOW ONLY A MILE OR SO AWAY, IN THE ROOKERY OF ST. GILES--
--WHERE THE POLICE WILL NOT GO EXCEPT BY THE DOZEN.
THEY WILL HIDE UP THERE UNTIL THE HUE AND CRY HAVE DIED AWAY.
AND THEN THEY WILL BE ABOUT THEIR BUSINESS.

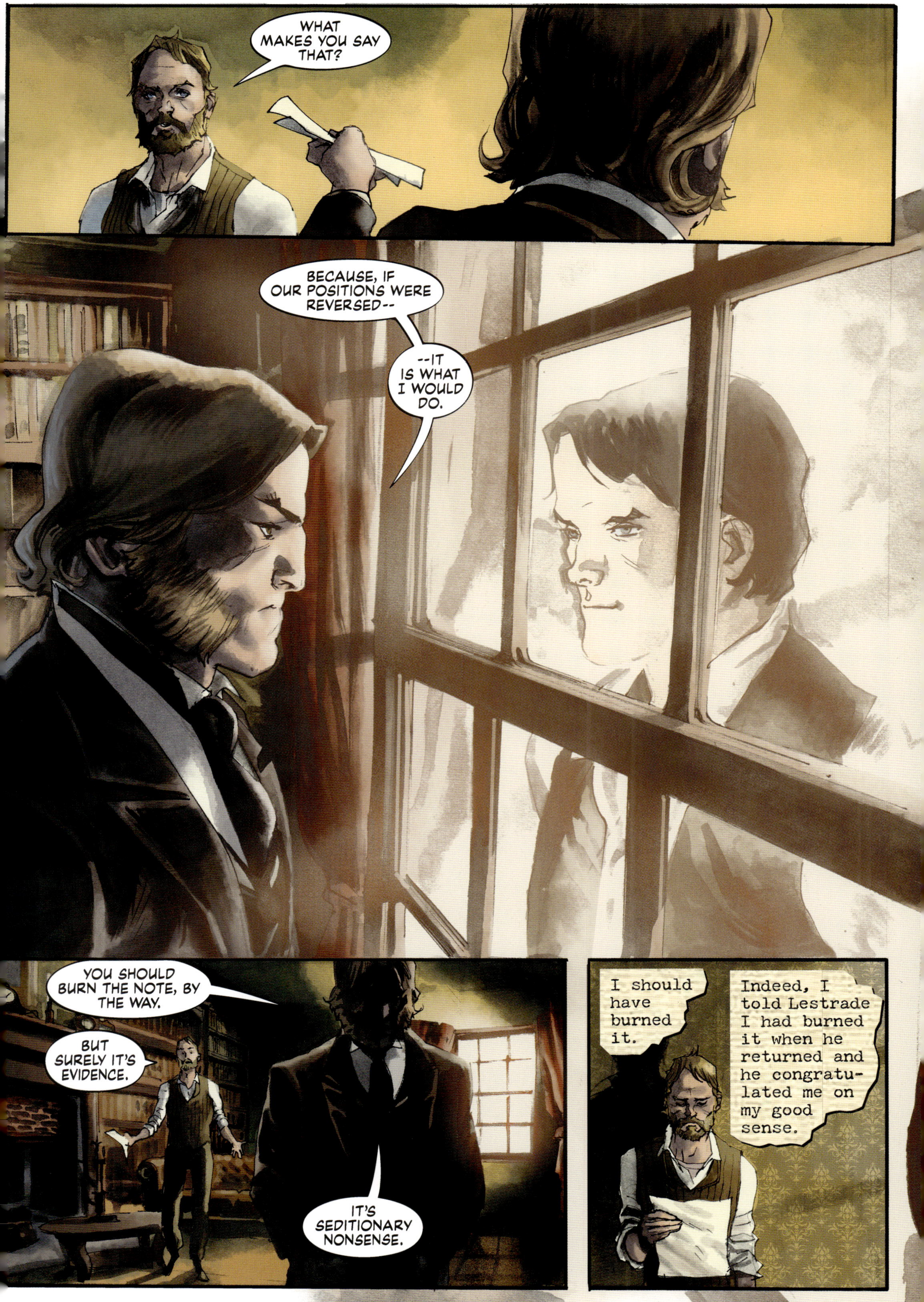
WHAT MAKES YOU SAY THAT?
BECAUSE, IF OUR POSITIONS WERE REVERSED--
--IT IS WHAT I WOULD DO.
YOU SHOULD BURN THE NOTE, BY THE WAY.
BUT SURELY IT'S EVIDENCE.
IT'S SEDITIONARY NONSENSE.
I should have burned it.
Indeed, I told Lestrade I had burned it when he returned and he congratulated me on my good sense.

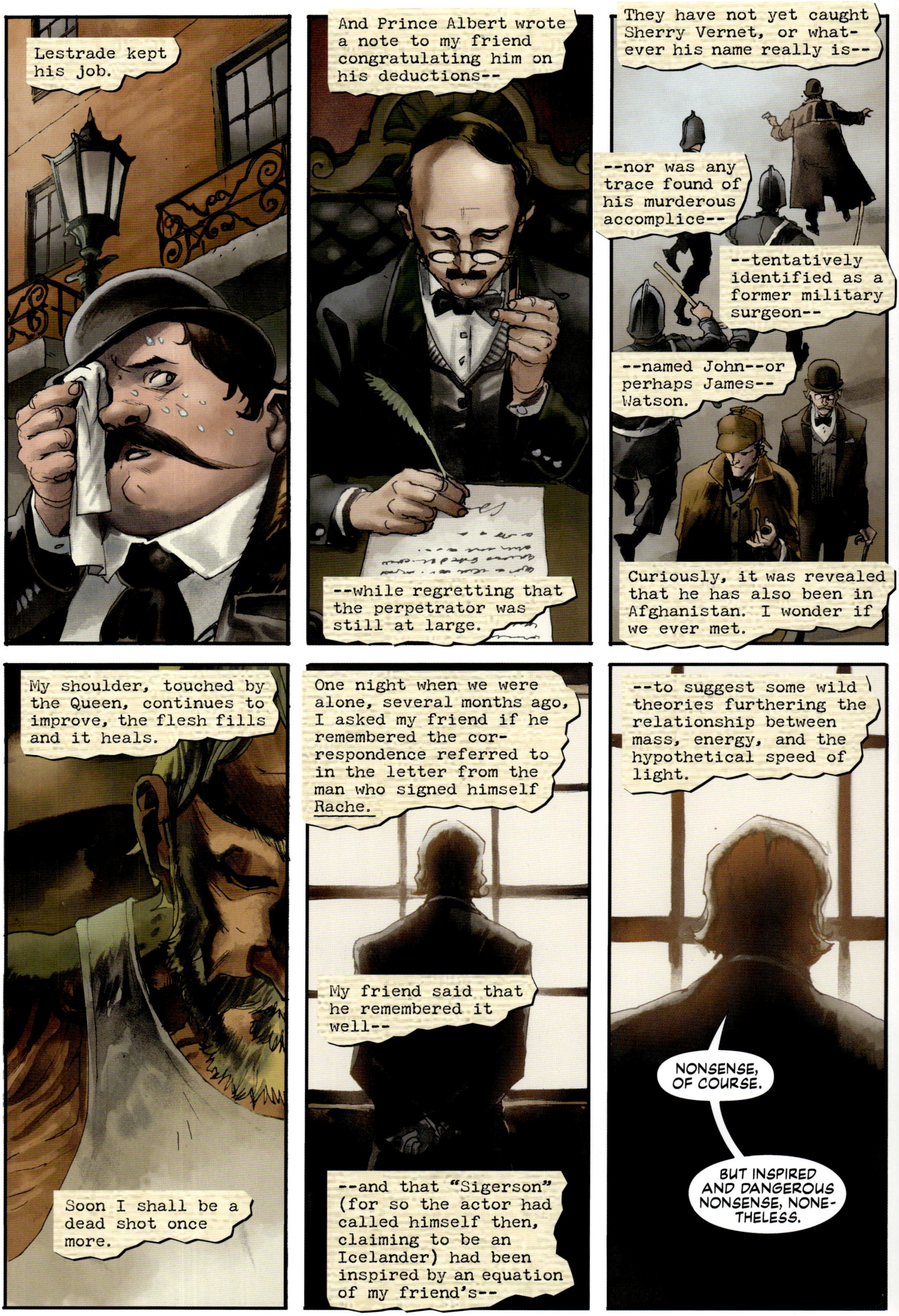
Lestrade kept his job.
And Prince Albert wrote a note to my friend congratulating him on his deductions--
--while regretting that the perpetrator was still at large.
They have not yet caught Sherry Vernet, or whatever his name really is--
--nor was any trace found of his murderous accomplice--
--tentatively identified as a former military surgeon--
--named John--or perhaps James--Watson.
Curiously, it was revealed that he has also been in Afghanistan. I wonder if we ever met.
My shoulder, touched by the Queen, continues to improve, the flesh fills and it heals.
Soon I shall be a dead shot once more.
One night when we were alone, several months ago, I asked my friend if he remembered the correspondence referred to in the letter from the man who signed himself Rache.
My friend said that he remembered it well--
--and that "Sigerson" (for so the actor had called himself then, claiming to be an Icelander) had been inspired by an equation of my friend's--
--to suggest some wild theories furthering the relationship between mass, energy, and the hypothetical speed of light.
NONSENSE, OF COURSE.
BUT INSPIRED AND DANGEROUS NONSENSE, NONETHELESS.

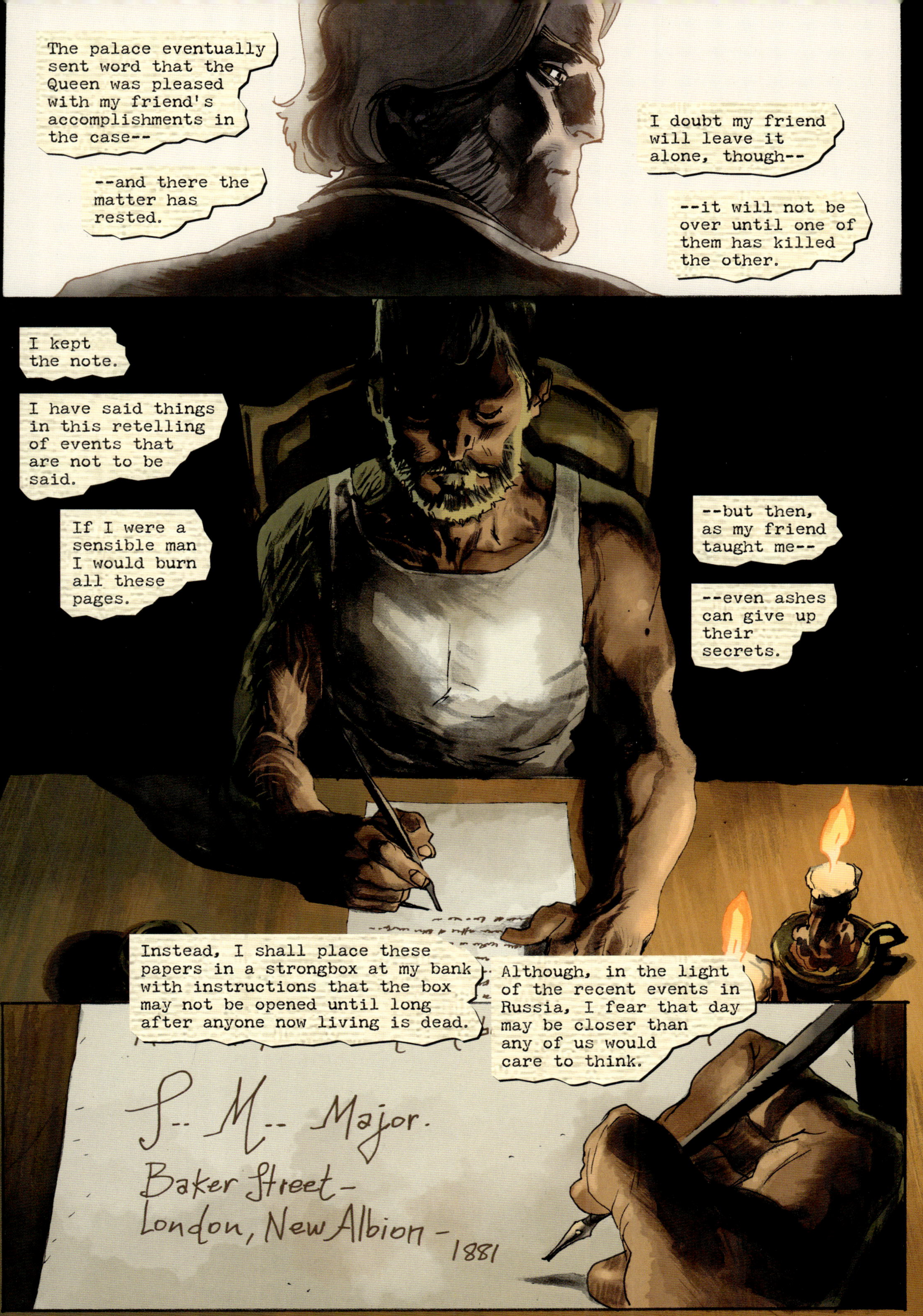
The palace eventually sent word that the Queen was pleased with my friend's accomplishments in the case--
--and there the matter has rested.
I doubt my friend will leave it alone, though--
--it will not be over until one of them has killed the other.
I kept the note.
I have said things in this retelling of events that are not to be said.
If I were a sensible man I would burn all these pages.
--but then, as my friend taught me--
--even ashes can give up their secrets.
Instead, I shall place these papers in a strongbox at my bank with instructions that the box may not be opened until long after anyone now living is dead.
Although, in the light of the recent events in Russia, I fear that day may be closer than any of us would care to think.
S-- M-- Major.
Baker Street-
London, New Albion - 1881

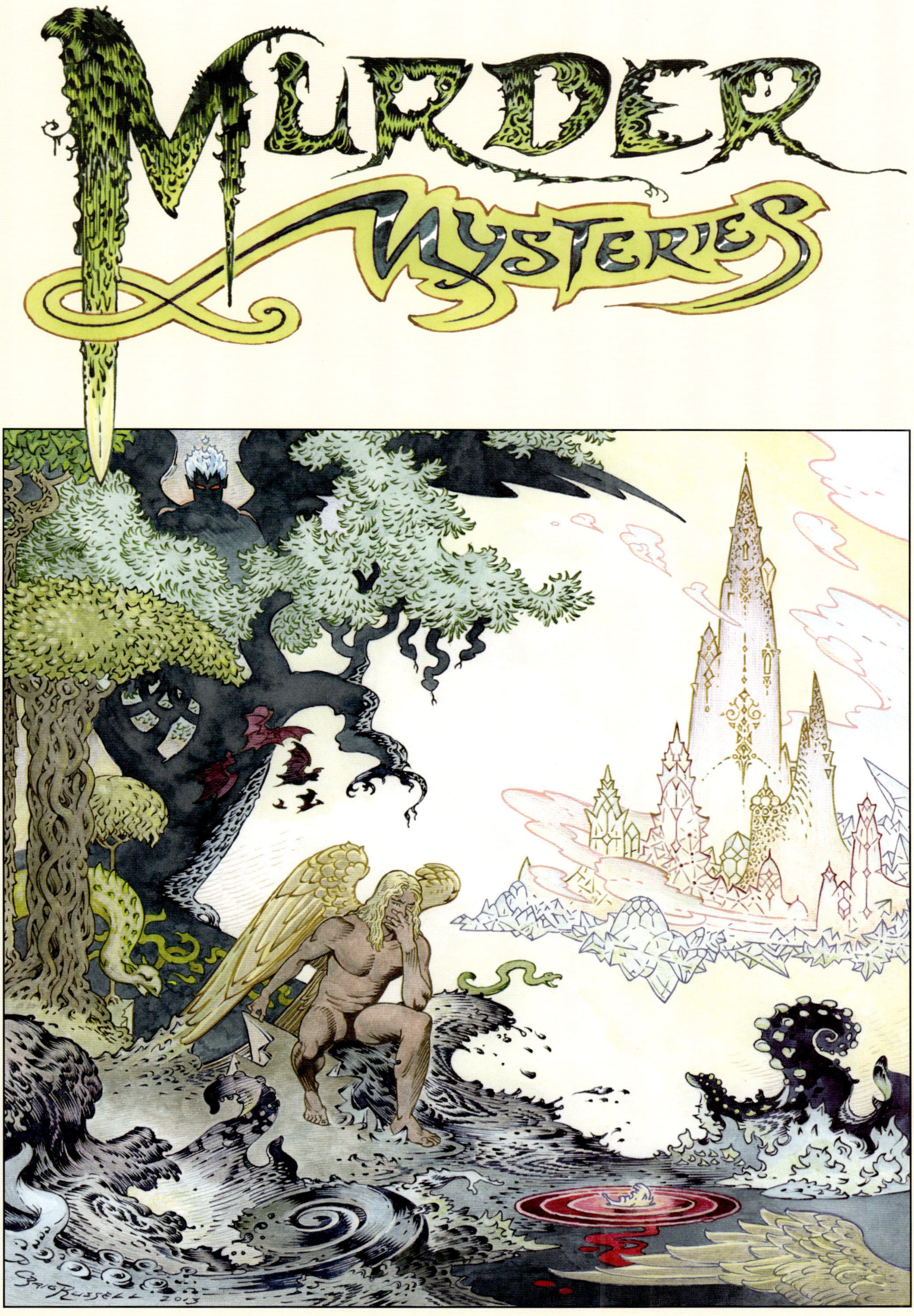
Murder
Mysteries

PROLOGUE

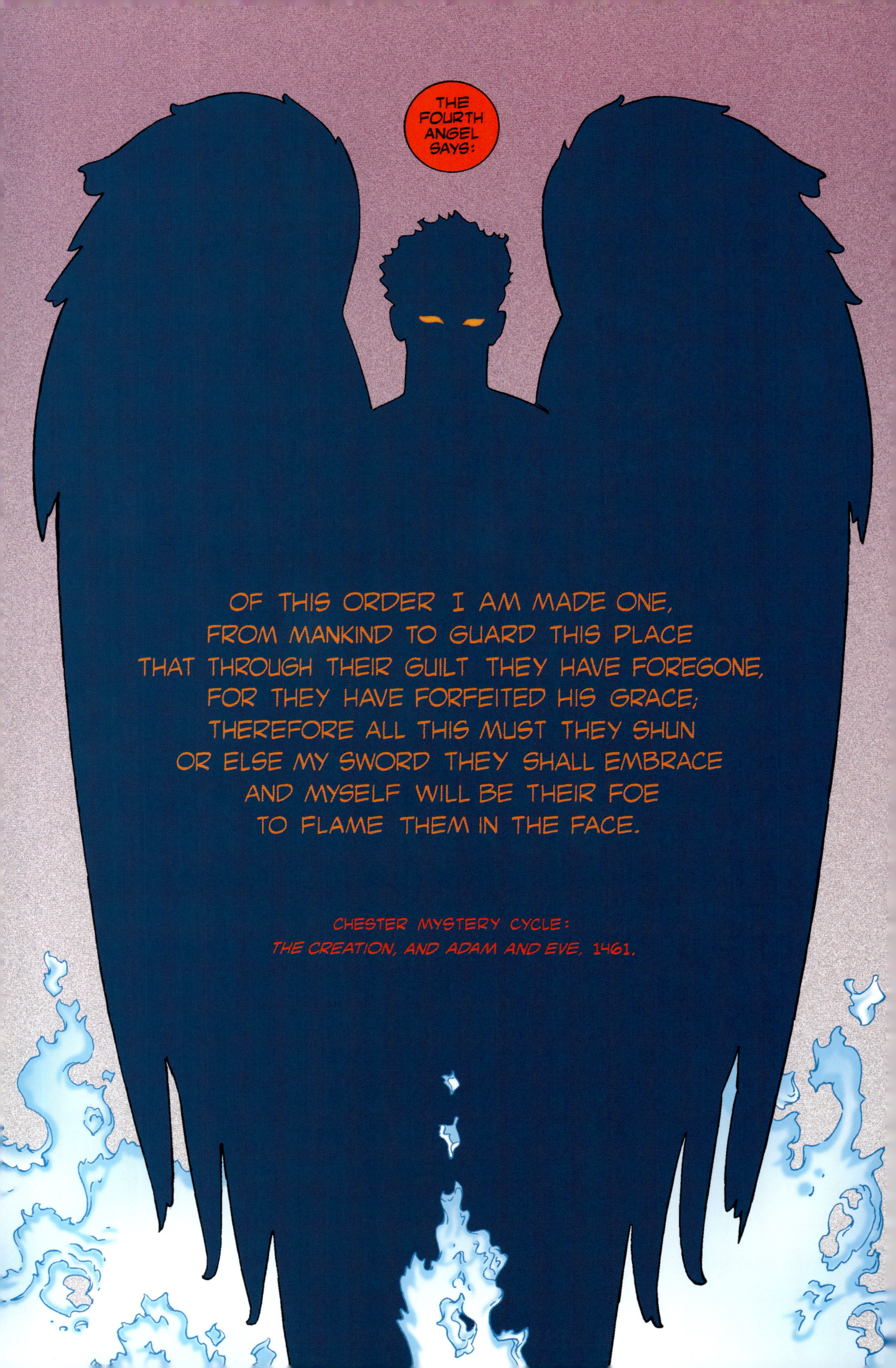
THE FOURTH ANGEL SAYS:
OF THIS ORDER I AM MADE ONE,
FROM MANKIND TO GUARD THIS PLACE
THAT THROUGH THEIR GUILT THEY HAVE FOREGONE,
FOR THEY HAVE FORFEITED HIS GRACE;
THEREFORE ALL THIS MUST THEY SHUN
OR ELSE MY SWORD THEY SHALL EMBRACE
AND MYSELF WILL BE THEIR FOE
TO FLAME THEM IN THE FACE.
CHESTER MYSTERY CYCLE:
THE CREATION, AND ADAM AND EVE, 1461.

NO!
THIS IS MAD-NESS...
YOU DON'T UNDERSTAND... PLEASE, JUST...
NO!
FOR THE LOVE OF GOD...
NO!

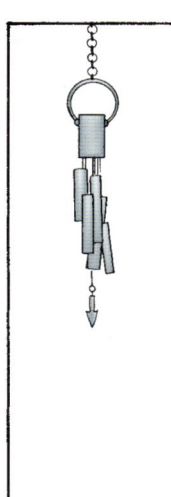

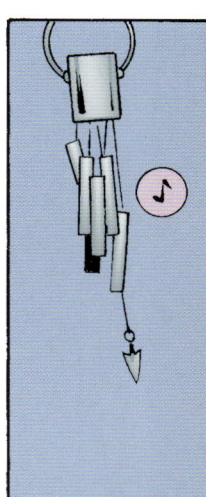

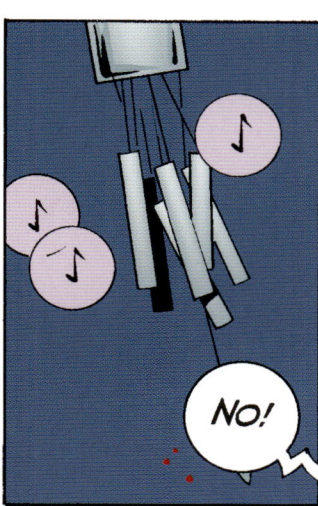

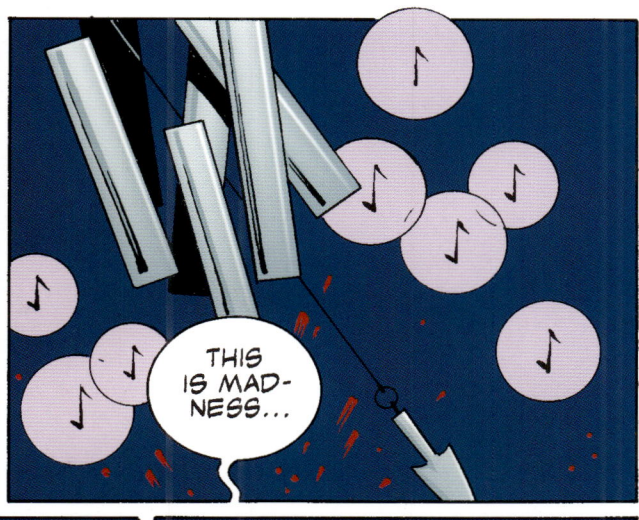

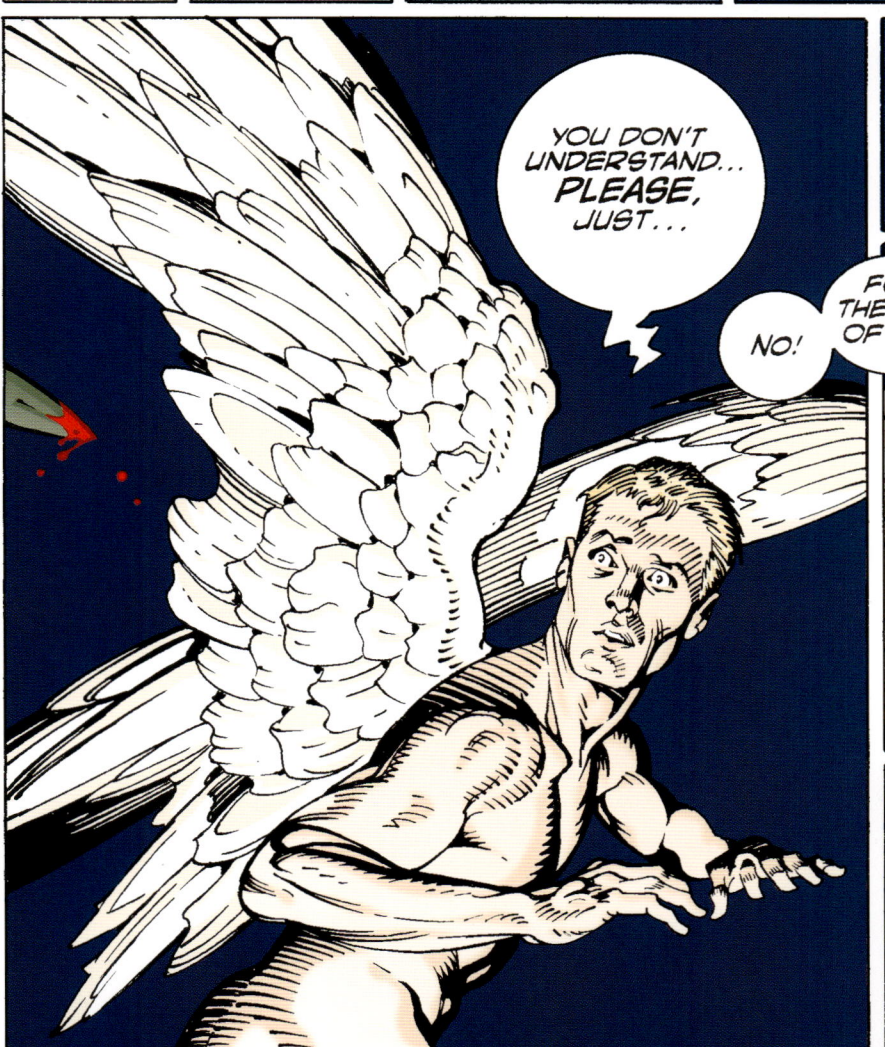

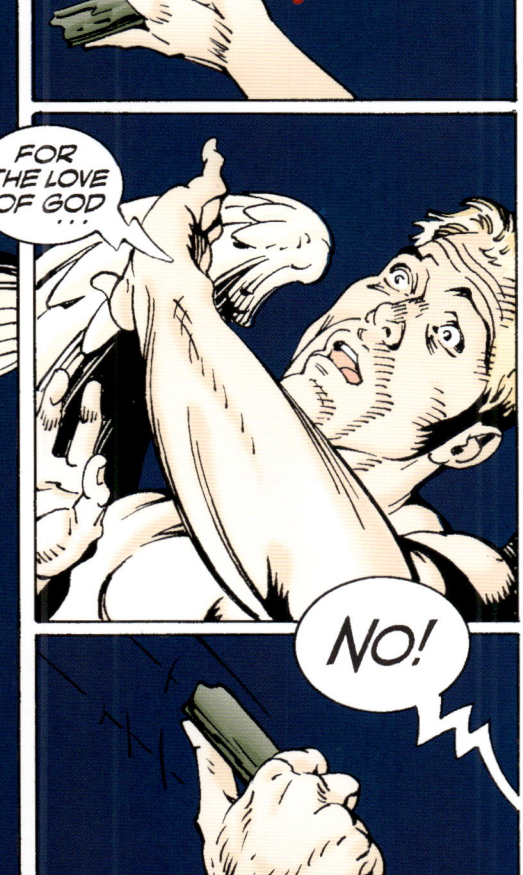

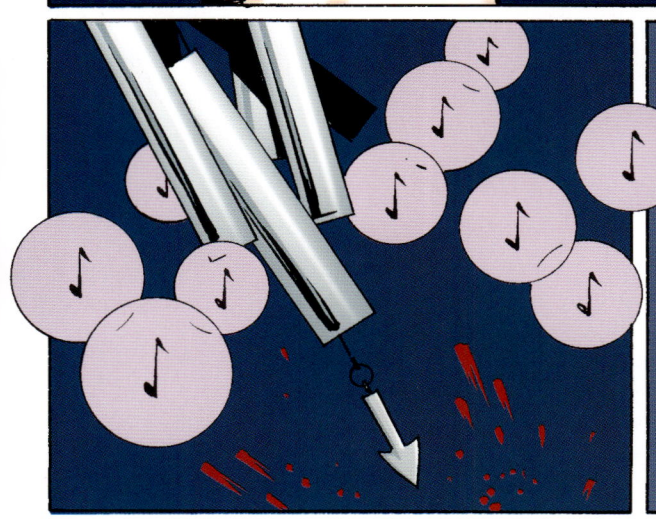

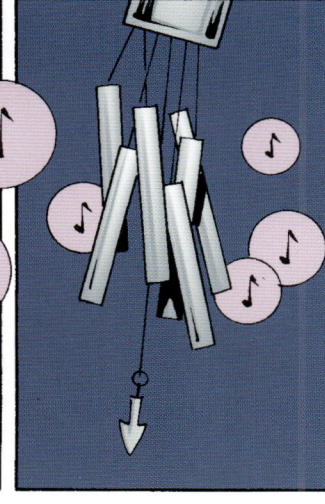

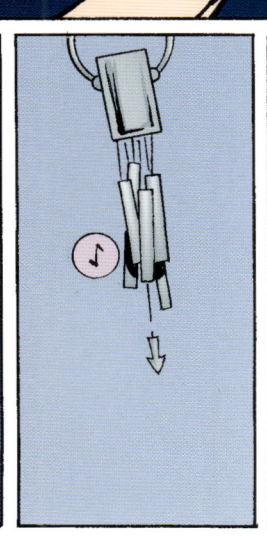

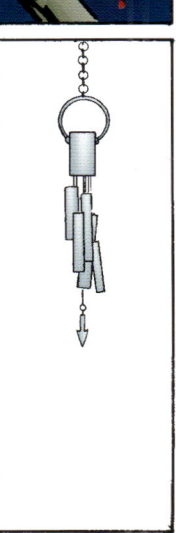

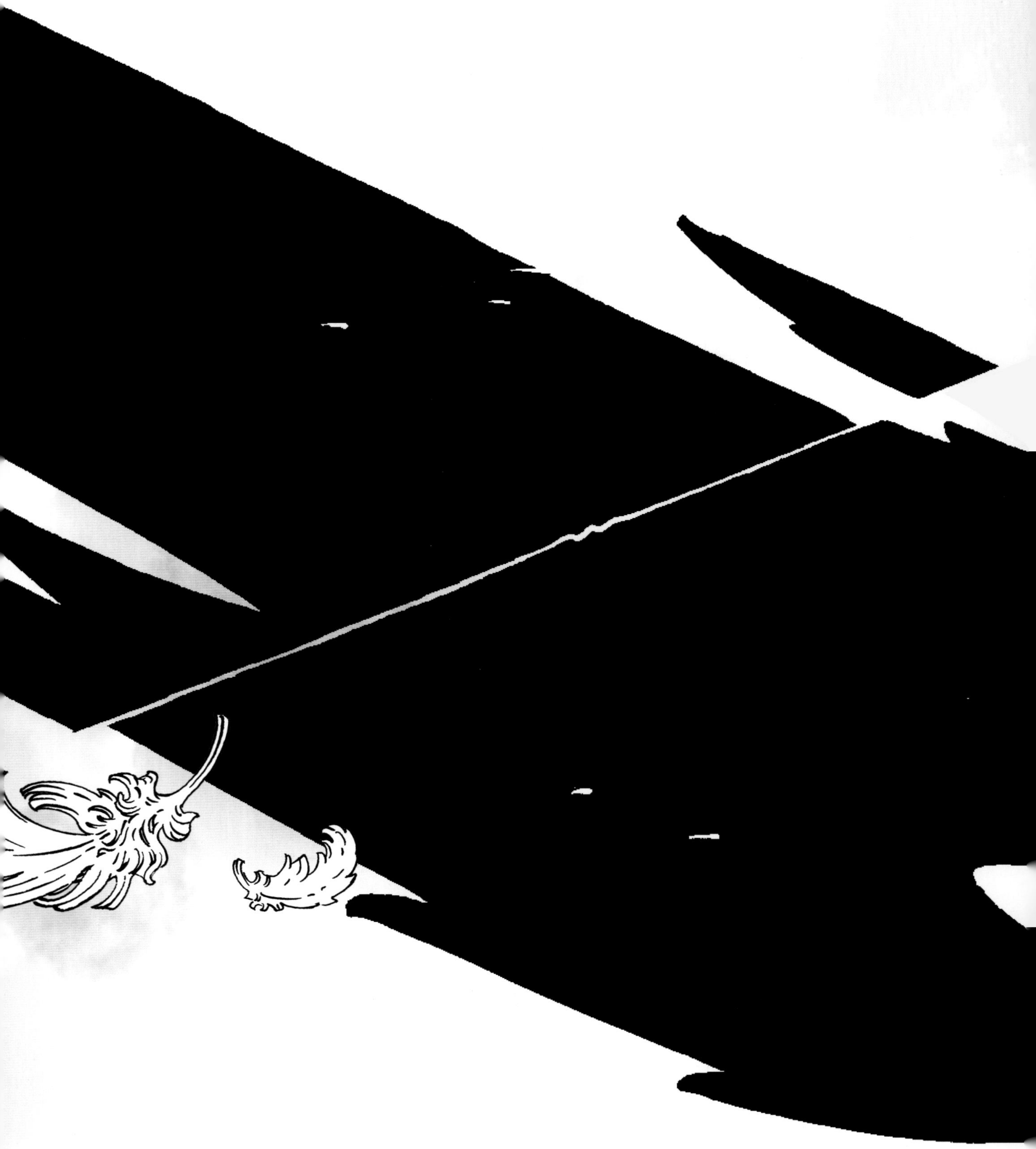

MURDER MYSTERIES

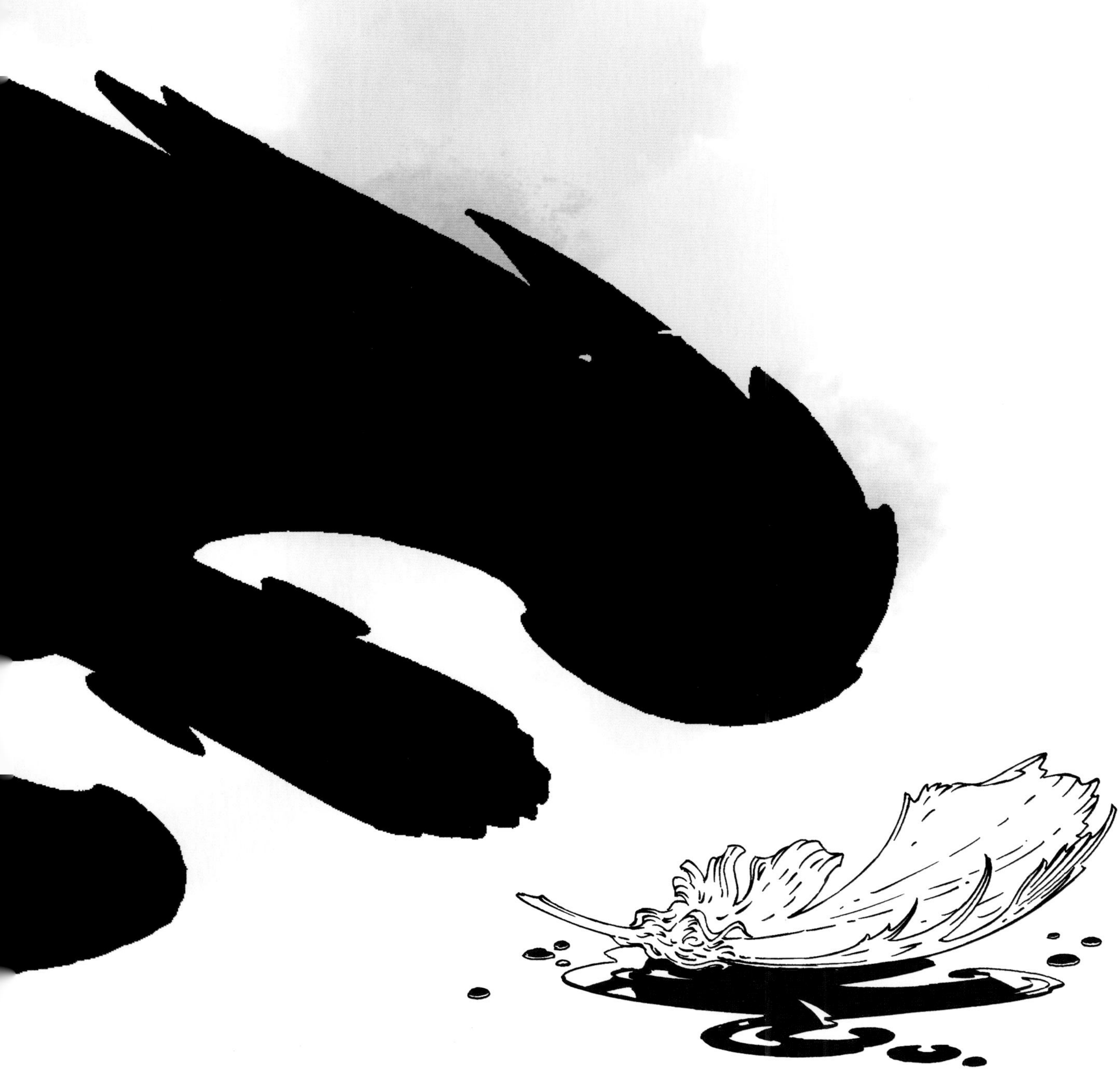

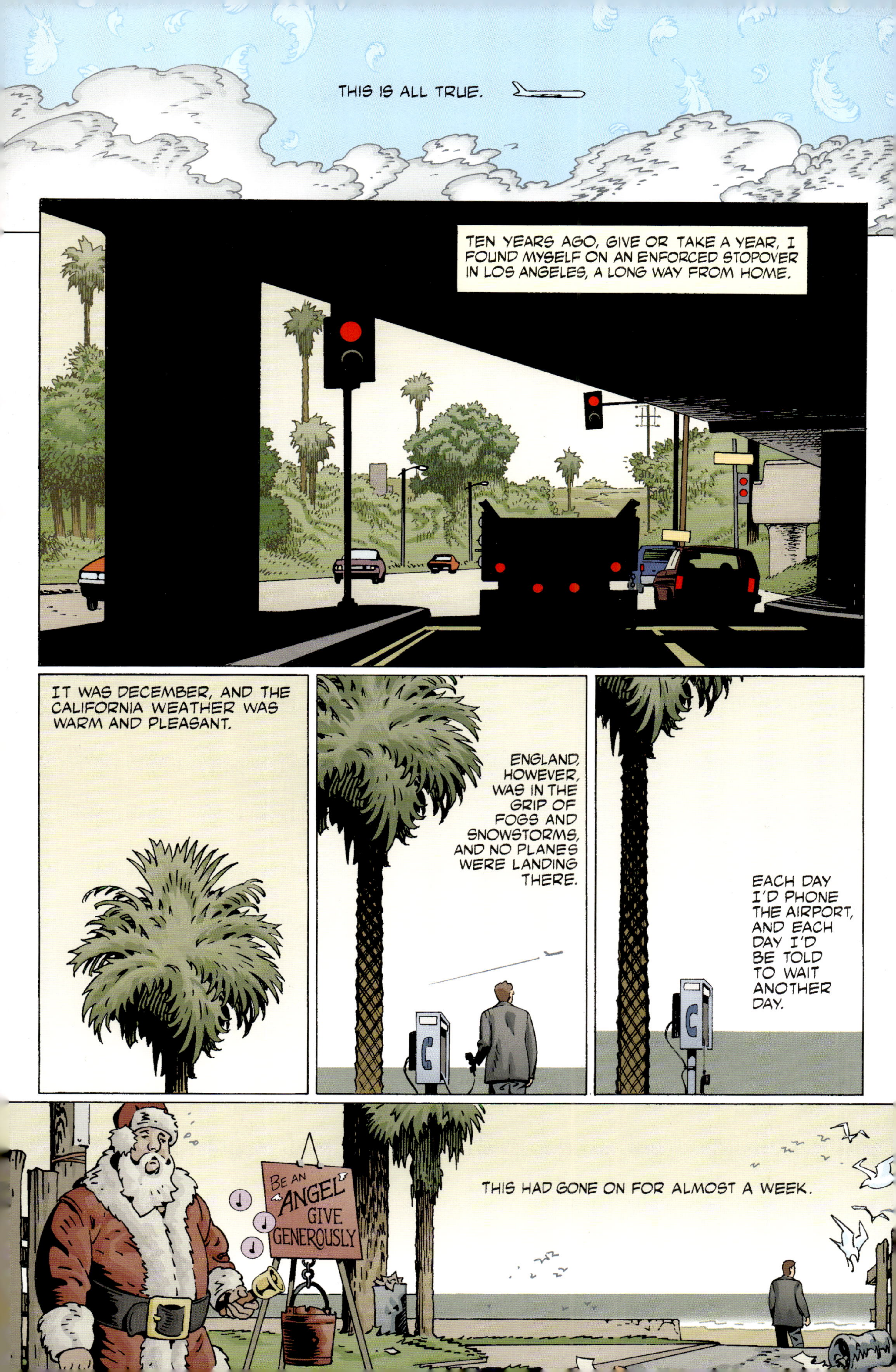
THIS IS ALL TRUE.
TEN YEARS AGO, GIVE OR TAKE A YEAR, I FOUND MYSELF ON AN ENFORCED STOPOVER IN LOS ANGELES, A LONG WAY FROM HOME.
IT WAS DECEMBER, AND THE CALIFORNIA WEATHER WAS WARM AND PLEASANT.
ENGLAND, HOWEVER, WAS IN THE GRIP OF FOGS AND SNOWSTORMS, AND NO PLANES WERE LANDING THERE.
EACH DAY I'D PHONE THE AIRPORT, AND EACH DAY I'D BE TOLD TO WAIT ANOTHER DAY.
BE AN ANGEL GIVE GENEROUSLY
THIS HAD GONE ON FOR ALMOST A WEEK.

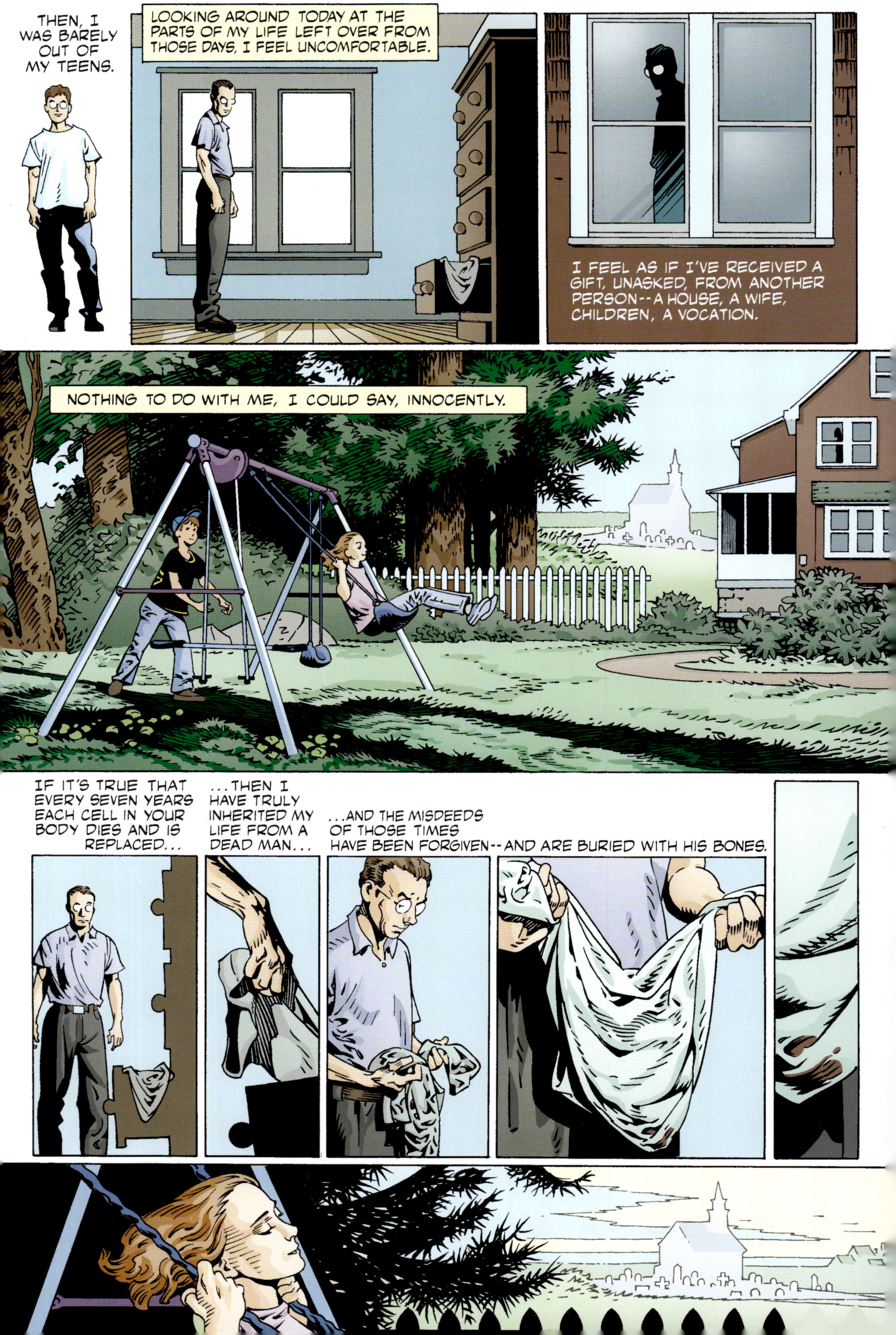
THEN, I WAS BARELY OUT OF MY TEENS.
LOOKING AROUND TODAY AT THE PARTS OF MY LIFE LEFT OVER FROM THOSE DAYS, I FEEL UNCOMFORTABLE.
I FEEL AS IF I'VE RECEIVED A GIFT, UNASKED, FROM ANOTHER PERSON--A HOUSE, A WIFE, CHILDREN, A VOCATION.
NOTHING TO DO WITH ME, I COULD SAY, INNOCENTLY.
IF IT'S TRUE THAT EVERY SEVEN YEARS EACH CELL IN YOUR BODY DIES AND IS REPLACED...
...THEN I HAVE TRULY INHERITED MY LIFE FROM A DEAD MAN...
...AND THE MISDEEDS OF THOSE TIMES HAVE BEEN FORGIVEN--AND ARE BURIED WITH HIS BONES.

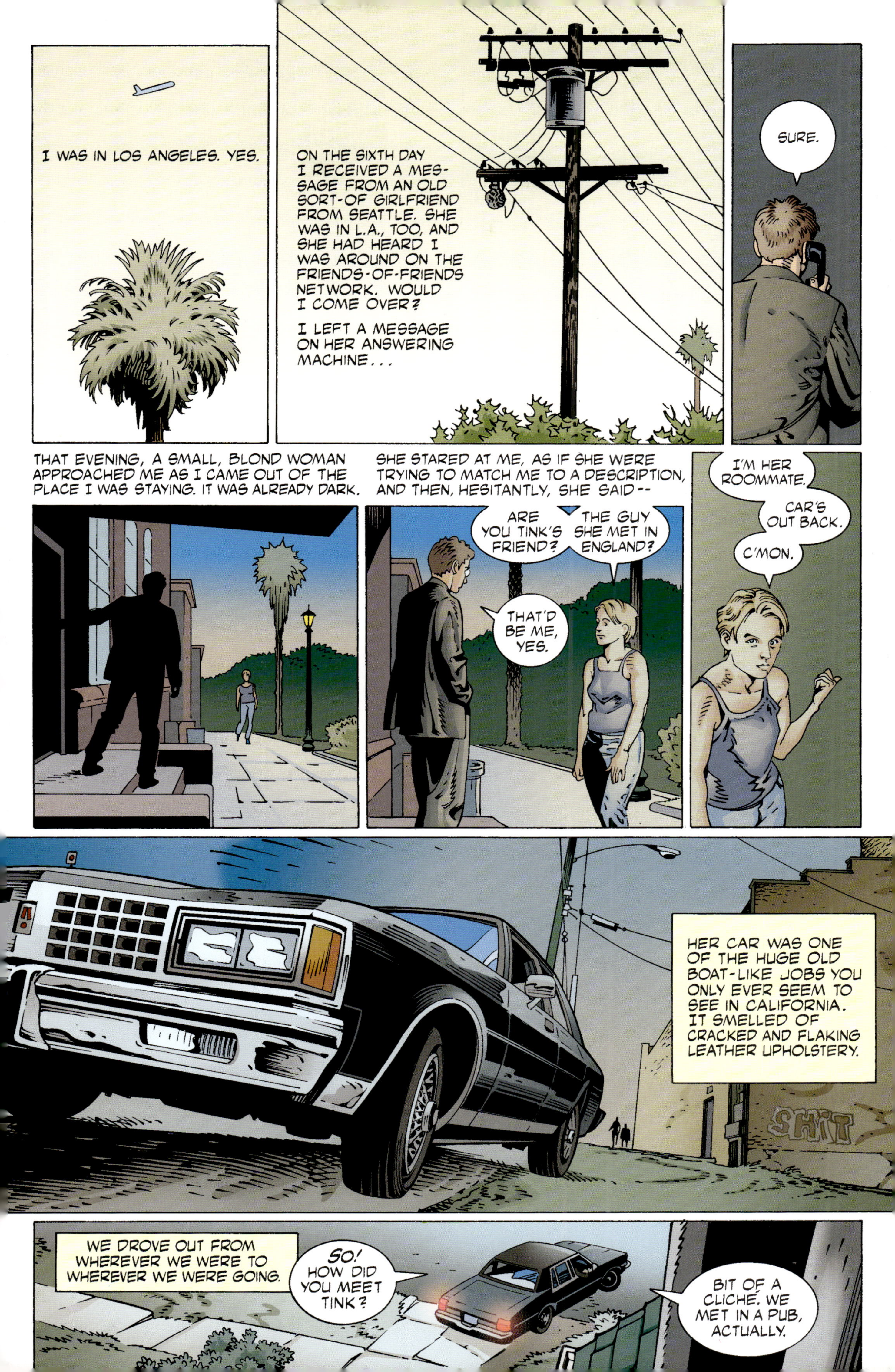

I WAS IN LOS ANGELES. YES.
ON THE SIXTH DAY I RECEIVED A MESSAGE FROM AN OLD SORT-OF GIRLFRIEND FROM SEATTLE. SHE WAS IN L.A., TOO, AND SHE HAD HEARD I WAS AROUND ON THE FRIENDS-OF-FRIENDS NETWORK. WOULD I COME OVER?
I LEFT A MESSAGE ON HER ANSWERING MACHINE...
SURE.
THAT EVENING, A SMALL, BLOND WOMAN APPROACHED ME AS I CAME OUT OF THE PLACE I WAS STAYING. IT WAS ALREADY DARK.
SHE STARED AT ME, AS IF SHE WERE TRYING TO MATCH ME TO A DESCRIPTION, AND THEN, HESITANTLY, SHE SAID--
ARE YOU TINK'S FRIEND?
THE GUY SHE MET IN ENGLAND?
THAT'D BE ME, YES.
I'M HER ROOMMATE.
CAR'S OUT BACK.
C'MON.
HER CAR WAS ONE OF THE HUGE OLD BOAT-LIKE JOBS YOU ONLY EVER SEEM TO SEE IN CALIFORNIA. IT SMELLED OF CRACKED AND FLAKING LEATHER UPHOLSTERY.
SHIT
WE DROVE OUT FROM WHEREVER WE WERE TO WHEREVER WE WERE GOING.
SO! HOW DID YOU MEET TINK?
BIT OF A CLICHÉ. WE MET IN A PUB, ACTUALLY.

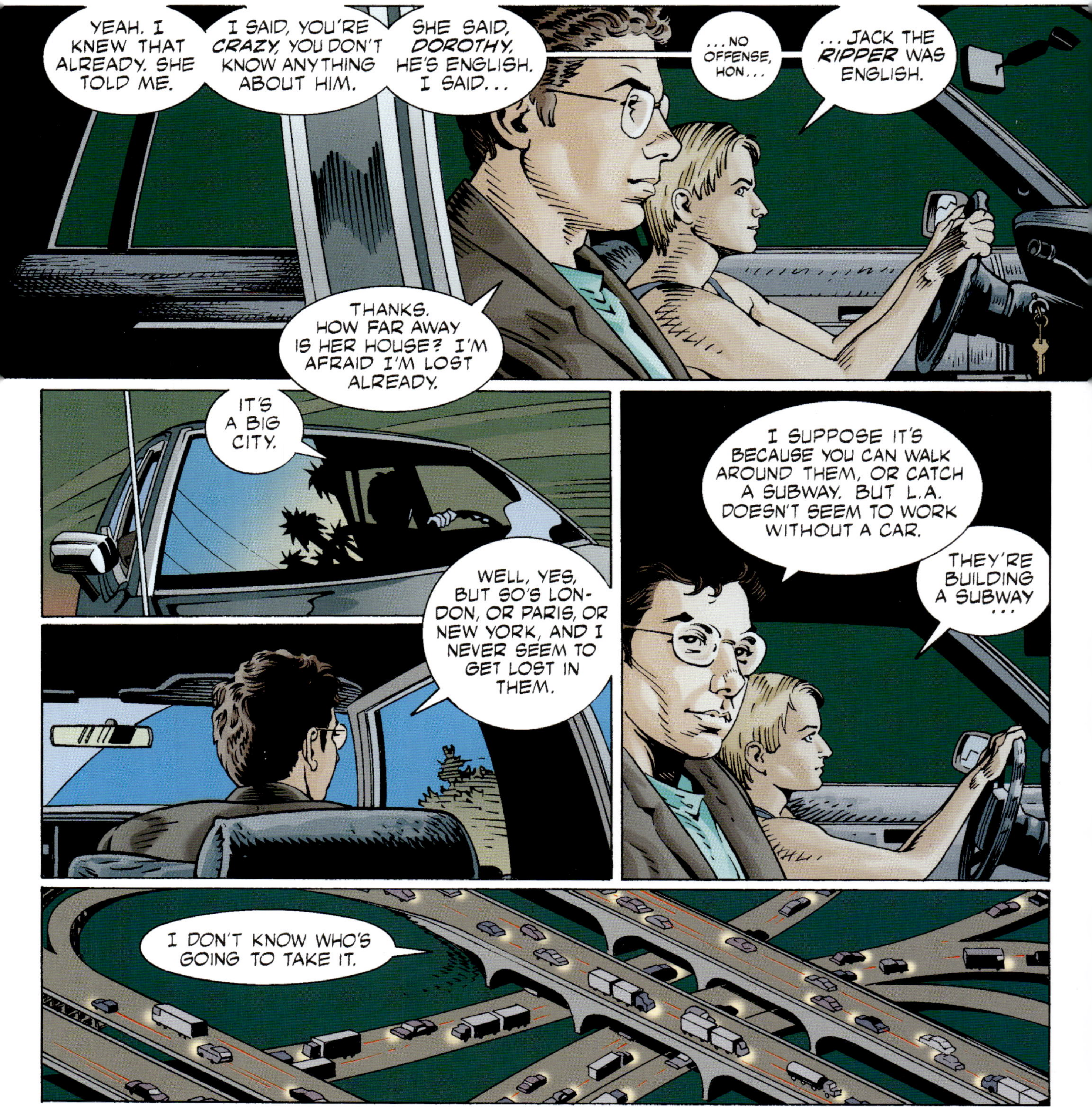
YEAH. I KNEW THAT ALREADY. SHE TOLD ME.
I SAID, YOU'RE *CRAZY,* YOU DON'T KNOW ANYTHING ABOUT HIM.
SHE SAID, *DOROTHY,* HE'S ENGLISH. I SAID...
...NO OFFENSE, HON...
...JACK THE *RIPPER* WAS ENGLISH.
THANKS. HOW FAR AWAY IS HER HOUSE? I'M AFRAID I'M LOST ALREADY.
IT'S A BIG CITY.
WELL, YES, BUT SO'S LONDON, OR PARIS, OR NEW YORK, AND I NEVER SEEM TO GET LOST IN THEM.
I SUPPOSE IT'S BECAUSE YOU CAN WALK AROUND THEM, OR CATCH A SUBWAY. BUT L.A. DOESN'T SEEM TO WORK WITHOUT A CAR.
THEY'RE BUILDING A SUBWAY...
I DON'T KNOW WHO'S GOING TO TAKE IT.

LOS ANGELES WAS AT THAT TIME A COMPLETE MYSTERY TO ME--AND I CANNOT SAY I UNDERSTAND IT MUCH BETTER NOW. MEMORIES OF L.A. FOR ME ARE LINKED BY RIDES IN OTHER PEOPLE'S CARS, WITH NO SENSE THERE OF THE SHAPE OF THE CITY, OF THE RELATIONSHIPS BETWEEN THE PEOPLE AND THE PLACE.

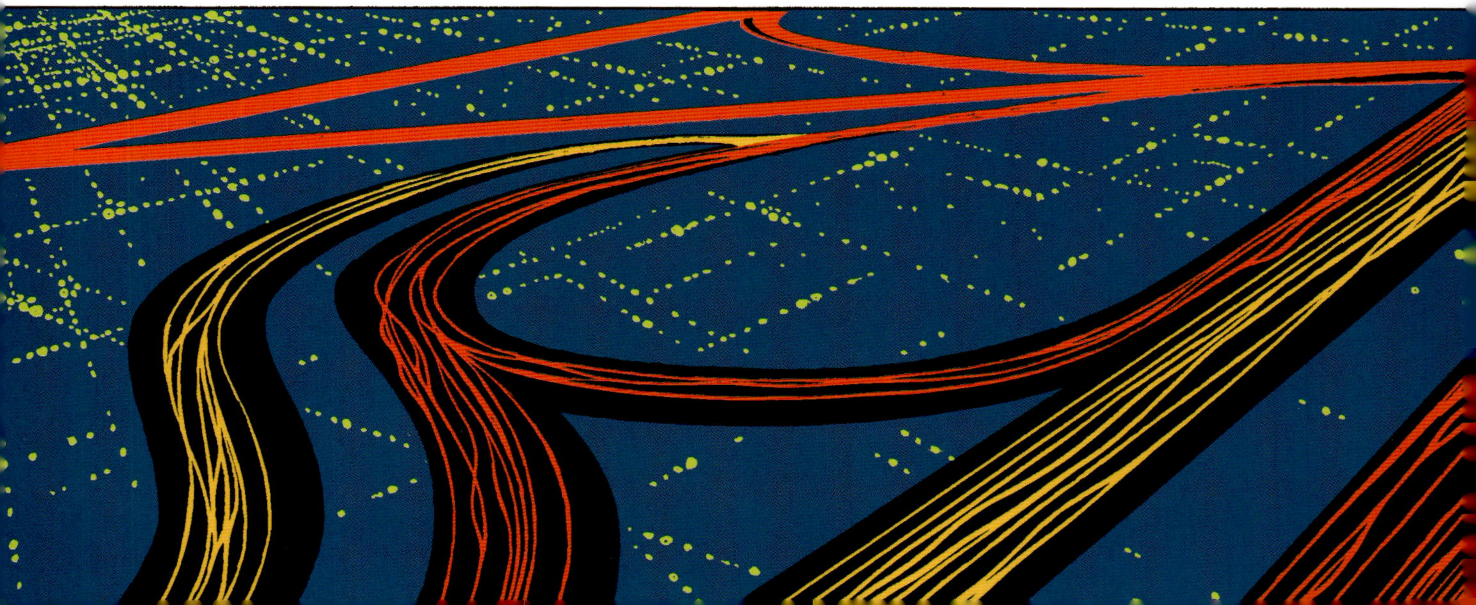

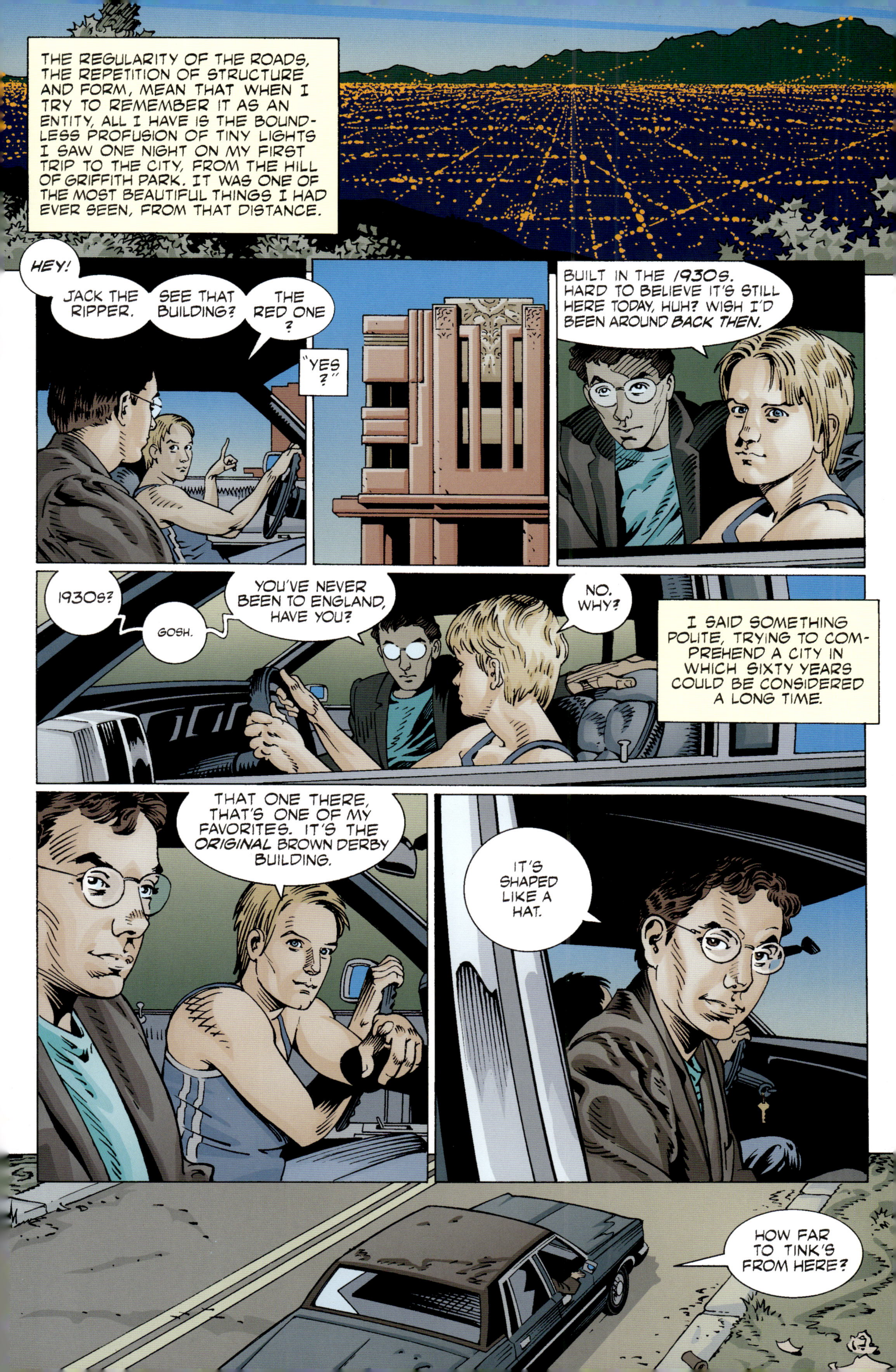
THE REGULARITY OF THE ROADS, THE REPETITION OF STRUCTURE AND FORM, MEAN THAT WHEN I TRY TO REMEMBER IT AS AN ENTITY, ALL I HAVE IS THE BOUNDLESS PROFUSION OF TINY LIGHTS I SAW ONE NIGHT ON MY FIRST TRIP TO THE CITY, FROM THE HILL OF GRIFFITH PARK. IT WAS ONE OF THE MOST BEAUTIFUL THINGS I HAD EVER SEEN, FROM THAT DISTANCE.
HEY!
JACK THE RIPPER.
SEE THAT BUILDING?
THE RED ONE?
"YES?"
BUILT IN THE 1930s. HARD TO BELIEVE IT'S STILL HERE TODAY, HUH? WISH I'D BEEN AROUND BACK THEN.
1930s?
GOSH.
YOU'VE NEVER BEEN TO ENGLAND, HAVE YOU?
NO. WHY?
I SAID SOMETHING POLITE, TRYING TO COMPREHEND A CITY IN WHICH SIXTY YEARS COULD BE CONSIDERED A LONG TIME.
THAT ONE THERE, THAT'S ONE OF MY FAVORITES. IT'S THE ORIGINAL BROWN DERBY BUILDING.
IT'S SHAPED LIKE A HAT.
HOW FAR TO TINK'S FROM HERE?

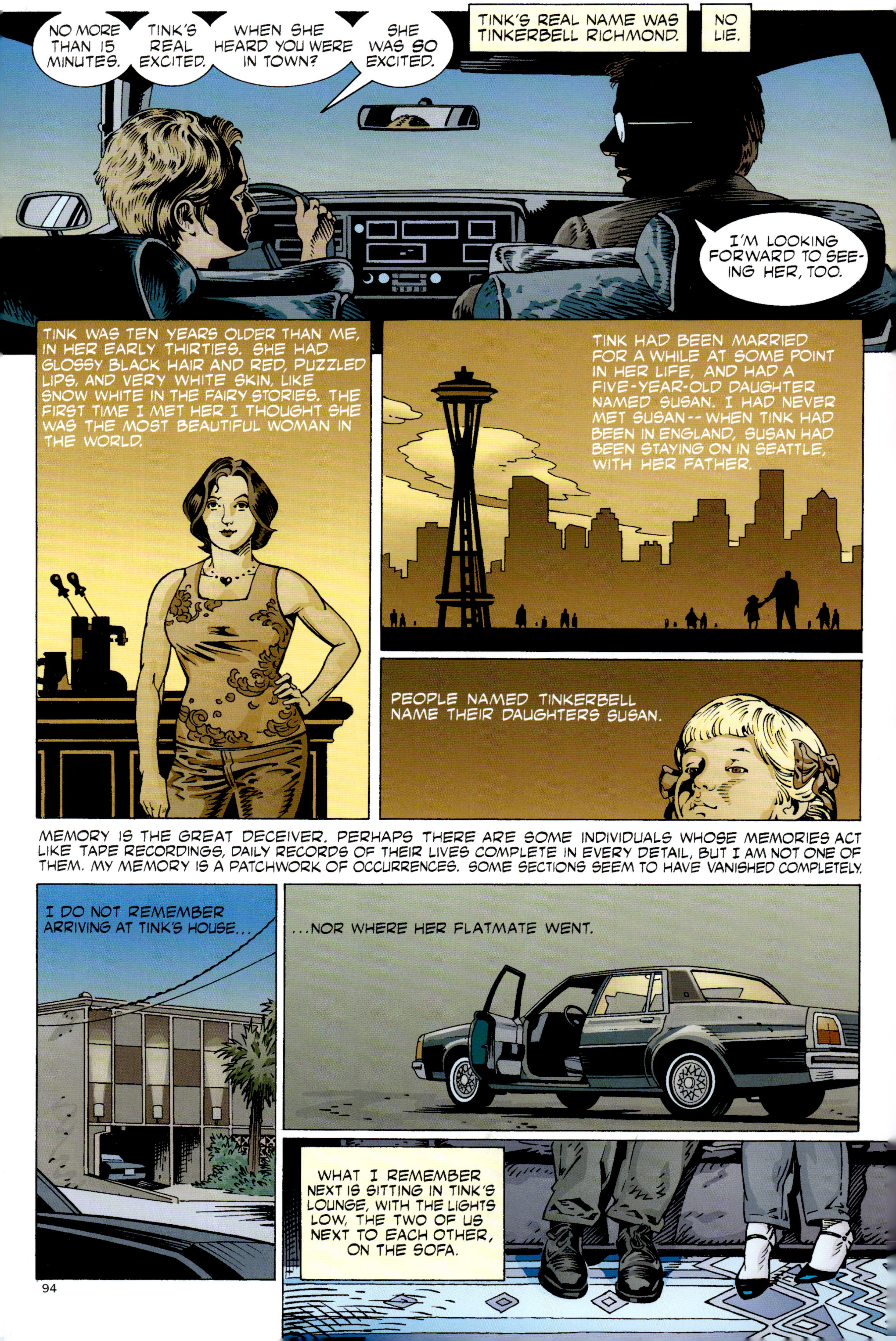
NO MORE THAN 15 MINUTES.
TINK'S REAL EXCITED.
WHEN SHE HEARD YOU WERE IN TOWN?
SHE WAS SO EXCITED.
TINK'S REAL NAME WAS TINKERBELL RICHMOND.
NO LIE.
I'M LOOKING FORWARD TO SEE-ING HER, TOO.
TINK WAS TEN YEARS OLDER THAN ME, IN HER EARLY THIRTIES. SHE HAD GLOSSY BLACK HAIR AND RED, PUZZLED LIPS, AND VERY WHITE SKIN, LIKE SNOW WHITE IN THE FAIRY STORIES. THE FIRST TIME I MET HER I THOUGHT SHE WAS THE MOST BEAUTIFUL WOMAN IN THE WORLD.
TINK HAD BEEN MARRIED FOR A WHILE AT SOME POINT IN HER LIFE, AND HAD A FIVE-YEAR-OLD DAUGHTER NAMED SUSAN. I HAD NEVER MET SUSAN-- WHEN TINK HAD BEEN IN ENGLAND, SUSAN HAD BEEN STAYING ON IN SEATTLE, WITH HER FATHER.
PEOPLE NAMED TINKERBELL NAME THEIR DAUGHTERS SUSAN.
MEMORY IS THE GREAT DECEIVER. PERHAPS THERE ARE SOME INDIVIDUALS WHOSE MEMORIES ACT LIKE TAPE RECORDINGS, DAILY RECORDS OF THEIR LIVES COMPLETE IN EVERY DETAIL, BUT I AM NOT ONE OF THEM. MY MEMORY IS A PATCHWORK OF OCCURRENCES. SOME SECTIONS SEEM TO HAVE VANISHED COMPLETELY.
I DO NOT REMEMBER ARRIVING AT TINK'S HOUSE...
...NOR WHERE HER FLATMATE WENT.
WHAT I REMEMBER NEXT IS SITTING IN TINK'S LOUNGE, WITH THE LIGHTS LOW, THE TWO OF US NEXT TO EACH OTHER, ON THE SOFA.

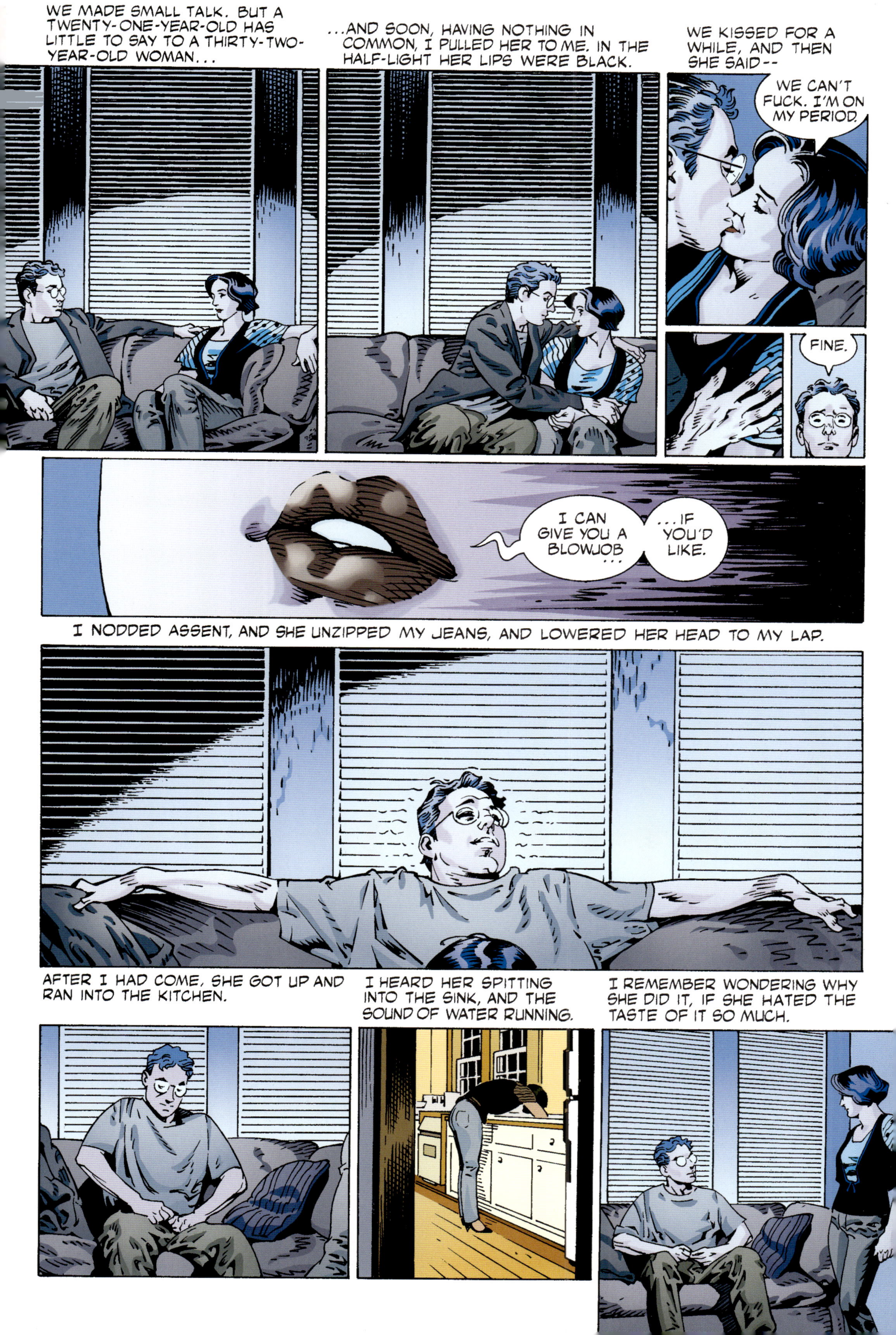
WE MADE SMALL TALK. BUT A TWENTY-ONE-YEAR-OLD HAS LITTLE TO SAY TO A THIRTY-TWO-YEAR-OLD WOMAN...
...AND SOON, HAVING NOTHING IN COMMON, I PULLED HER TO ME. IN THE HALF-LIGHT HER LIPS WERE BLACK.
WE KISSED FOR A WHILE, AND THEN SHE SAID--
WE CAN'T FUCK. I'M ON MY PERIOD.
FINE.
I CAN GIVE YOU A BLOWJOB...
...IF YOU'D LIKE.
I NODDED ASSENT, AND SHE UNZIPPED MY JEANS, AND LOWERED HER HEAD TO MY LAP.
AFTER I HAD COME, SHE GOT UP AND RAN INTO THE KITCHEN.
I HEARD HER SPITTING INTO THE SINK, AND THE SOUND OF WATER RUNNING.
I REMEMBER WONDERING WHY SHE DID IT, IF SHE HATED THE TASTE OF IT SO MUCH.

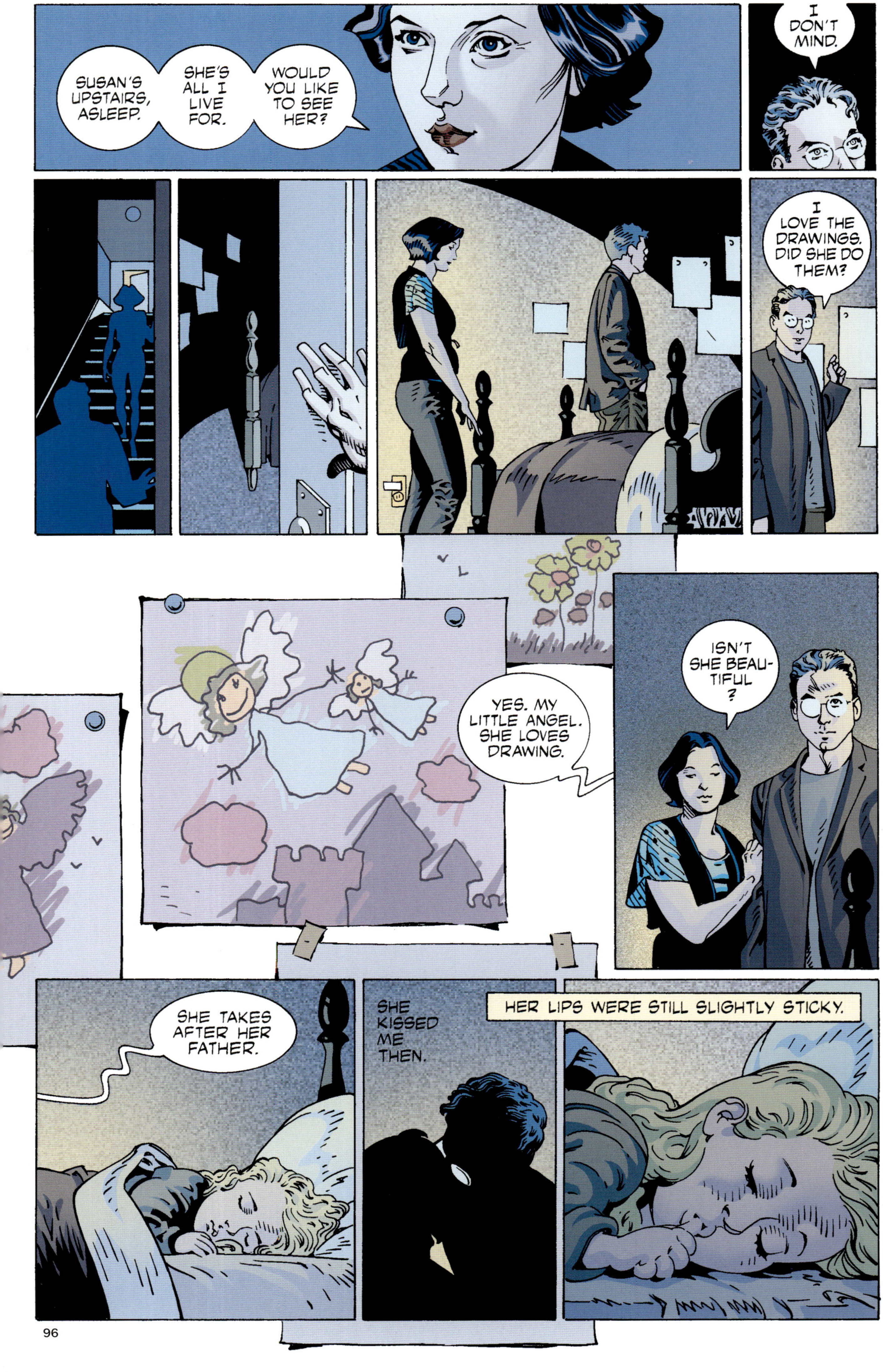
SUSAN'S UPSTAIRS, ASLEEP.
SHE'S ALL I LIVE FOR.
WOULD YOU LIKE TO SEE HER?
I DON'T MIND.
I LOVE THE DRAWINGS. DID SHE DO THEM?
YES. MY LITTLE ANGEL. SHE LOVES DRAWING.
ISN'T SHE BEAUTIFUL?
SHE TAKES AFTER HER FATHER.
SHE KISSED ME THEN.
HER LIPS WERE STILL SLIGHTLY STICKY.

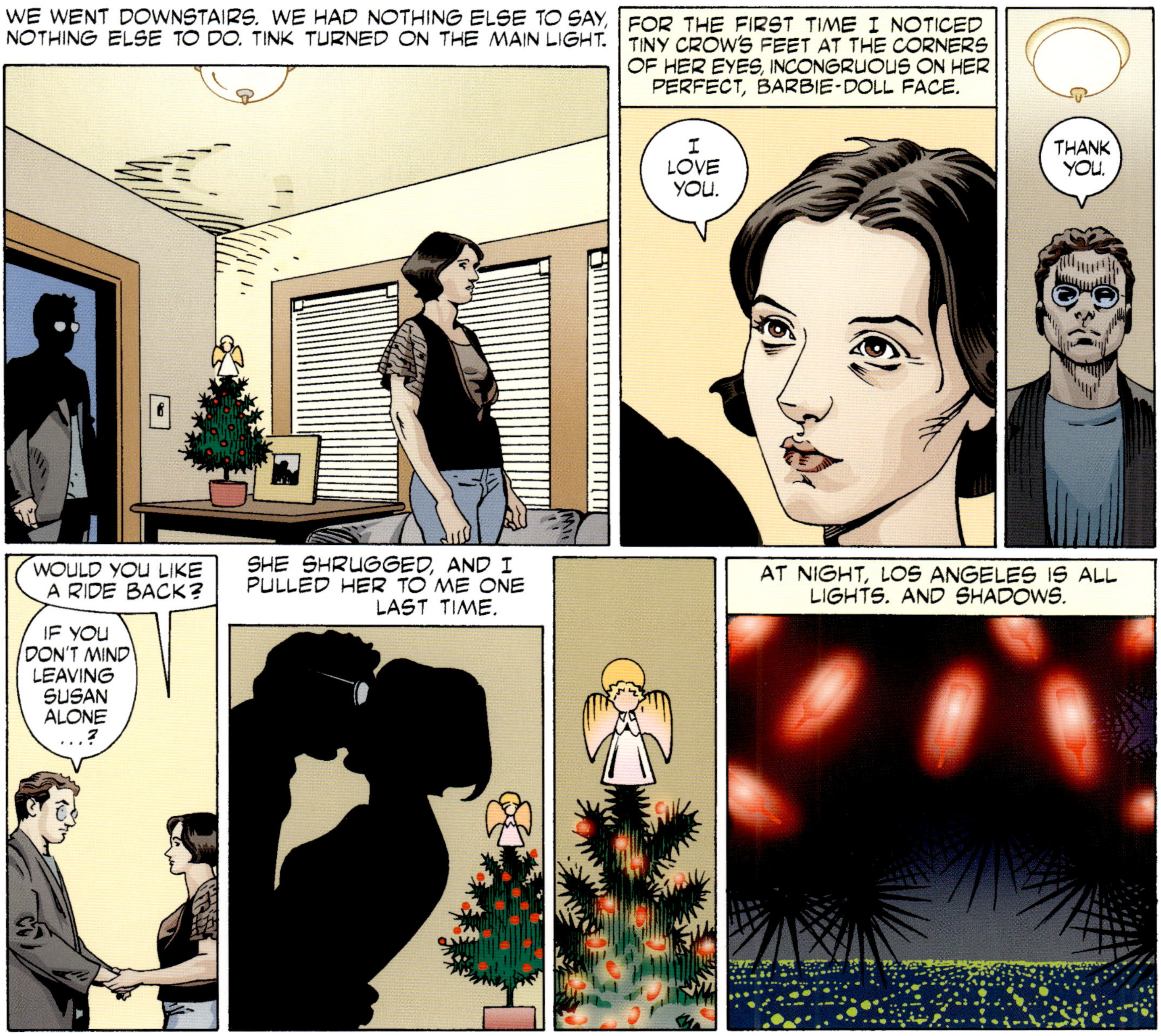
WE WENT DOWNSTAIRS. WE HAD NOTHING ELSE TO SAY, NOTHING ELSE TO DO. TINK TURNED ON THE MAIN LIGHT.
FOR THE FIRST TIME I NOTICED TINY CROW'S FEET AT THE CORNERS OF HER EYES, INCONGRUOUS ON HER PERFECT, BARBIE-DOLL FACE.
I LOVE YOU.
THANK YOU.
WOULD YOU LIKE A RIDE BACK?
IF YOU DON'T MIND LEAVING SUSAN ALONE . . .?
SHE SHRUGGED, AND I PULLED HER TO ME ONE LAST TIME.
AT NIGHT, LOS ANGELES IS ALL LIGHTS. AND SHADOWS.

A BLANK, HERE, IN MY MIND. I SIMPLY DON'T REMEMBER WHAT HAPPENED NEXT. SHE MUST HAVE DRIVEN ME BACK TO THE PLACE I WAS STAYING--HOW ELSE WOULD I HAVE GOTTEN THERE? I DO NOT EVEN REMEMBER KISSING HER GOODBYE. PERHAPS I SIMPLY WAITED ON THE SIDEWALK AND WATCHED HER DRIVE AWAY.

PERHAPS.

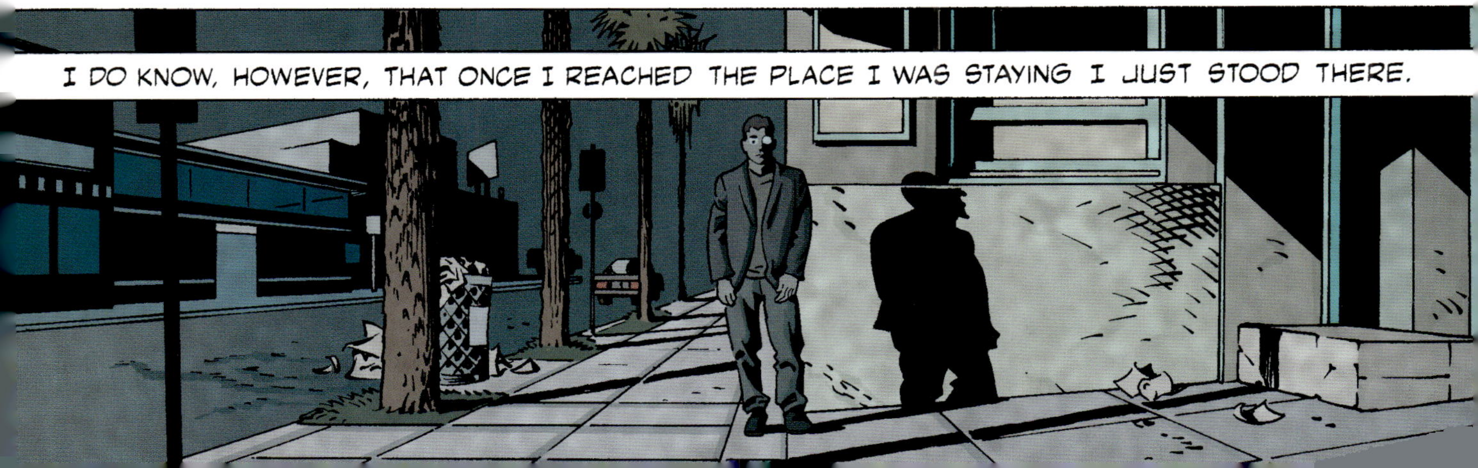
I DO KNOW, HOWEVER, THAT ONCE I REACHED THE PLACE I WAS STAYING I JUST STOOD THERE.

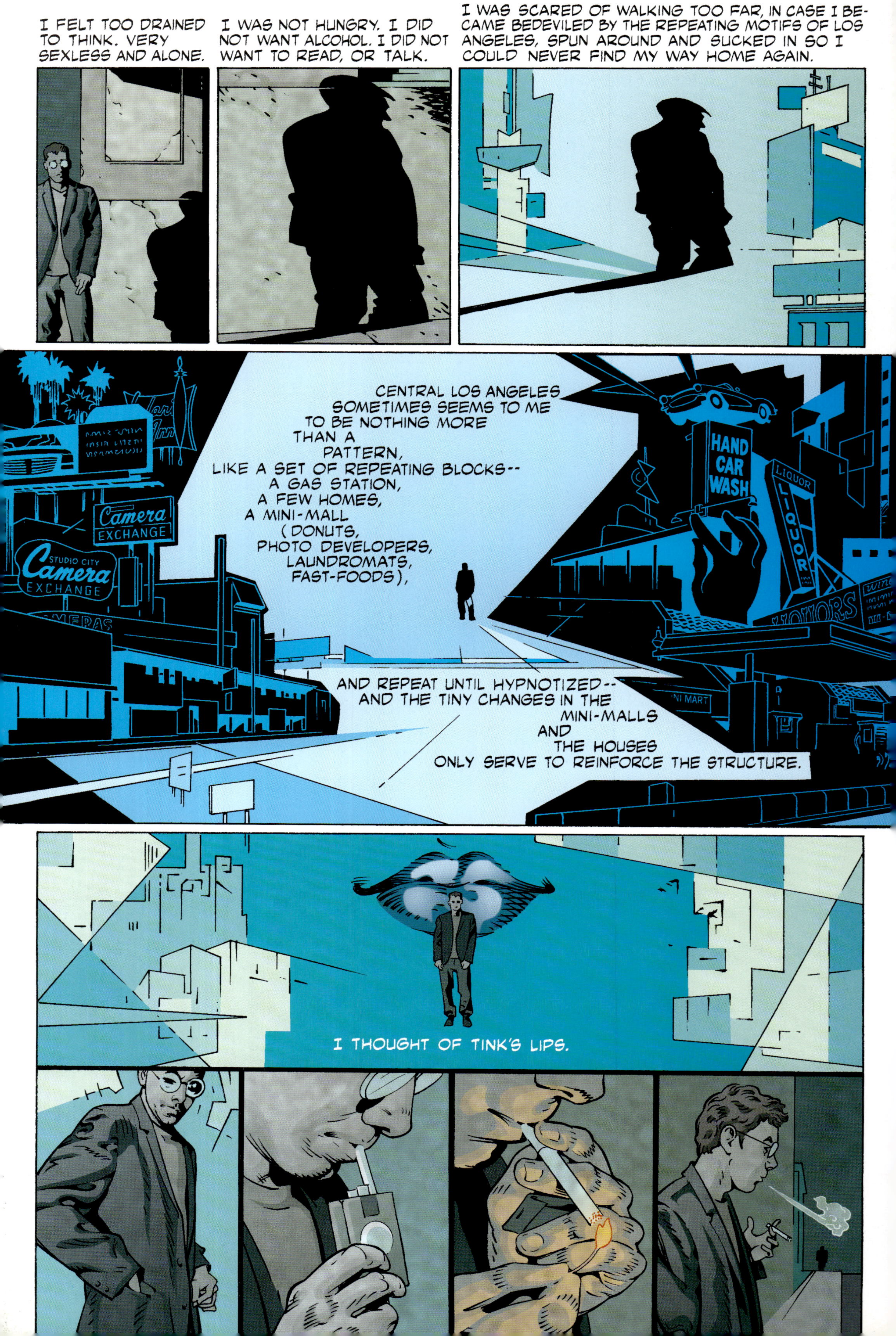
I FELT TOO DRAINED TO THINK. VERY SEXLESS AND ALONE.
I WAS NOT HUNGRY. I DID NOT WANT ALCOHOL. I DID NOT WANT TO READ, OR TALK.
I WAS SCARED OF WALKING TOO FAR, IN CASE I BECAME BEDEVILED BY THE REPEATING MOTIFS OF LOS ANGELES, SPUN AROUND AND SUCKED IN SO I COULD NEVER FIND MY WAY HOME AGAIN.
CENTRAL LOS ANGELES SOMETIMES SEEMS TO ME TO BE NOTHING MORE THAN A PATTERN, LIKE A SET OF REPEATING BLOCKS-- A GAS STATION, A FEW HOMES, A MINI-MALL (DONUTS, PHOTO DEVELOPERS, LAUNDROMATS, FAST-FOODS),
AND REPEAT UNTIL HYPNOTIZED-- AND THE TINY CHANGES IN THE MINI-MALLS AND THE HOUSES ONLY SERVE TO REINFORCE THE STRUCTURE.
Camera EXCHANGE
STUDIO CITY Camera EXCHANGE
HAND CAR WASH
LIQUOR
LIQUOR
I THOUGHT OF TINK'S LIPS.

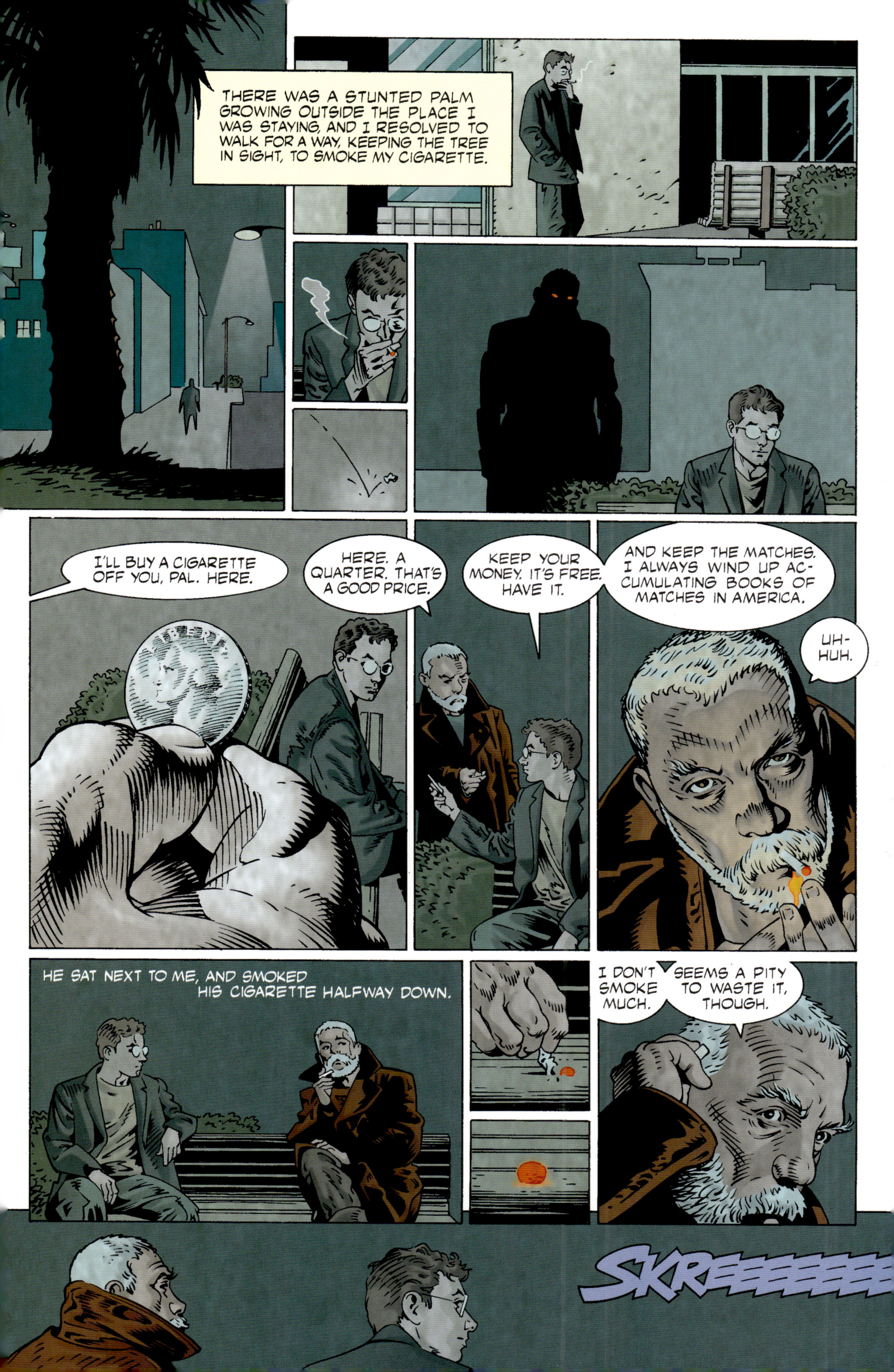
THERE WAS A STUNTED PALM GROWING OUTSIDE THE PLACE I WAS STAYING, AND I RESOLVED TO WALK FOR A WAY, KEEPING THE TREE IN SIGHT, TO SMOKE MY CIGARETTE.
I'LL BUY A CIGARETTE OFF YOU, PAL. HERE.
HERE. A QUARTER. THAT'S A GOOD PRICE.
KEEP YOUR MONEY. IT'S FREE. HAVE IT.
AND KEEP THE MATCHES. I ALWAYS WIND UP AC-CUMULATING BOOKS OF MATCHES IN AMERICA.
UH-HUH.
HE SAT NEXT TO ME, AND SMOKED HIS CIGARETTE HALFWAY DOWN.
I DON'T SMOKE MUCH.
SEEMS A PITY TO WASTE IT, THOUGH.
SKREEEEEEEE

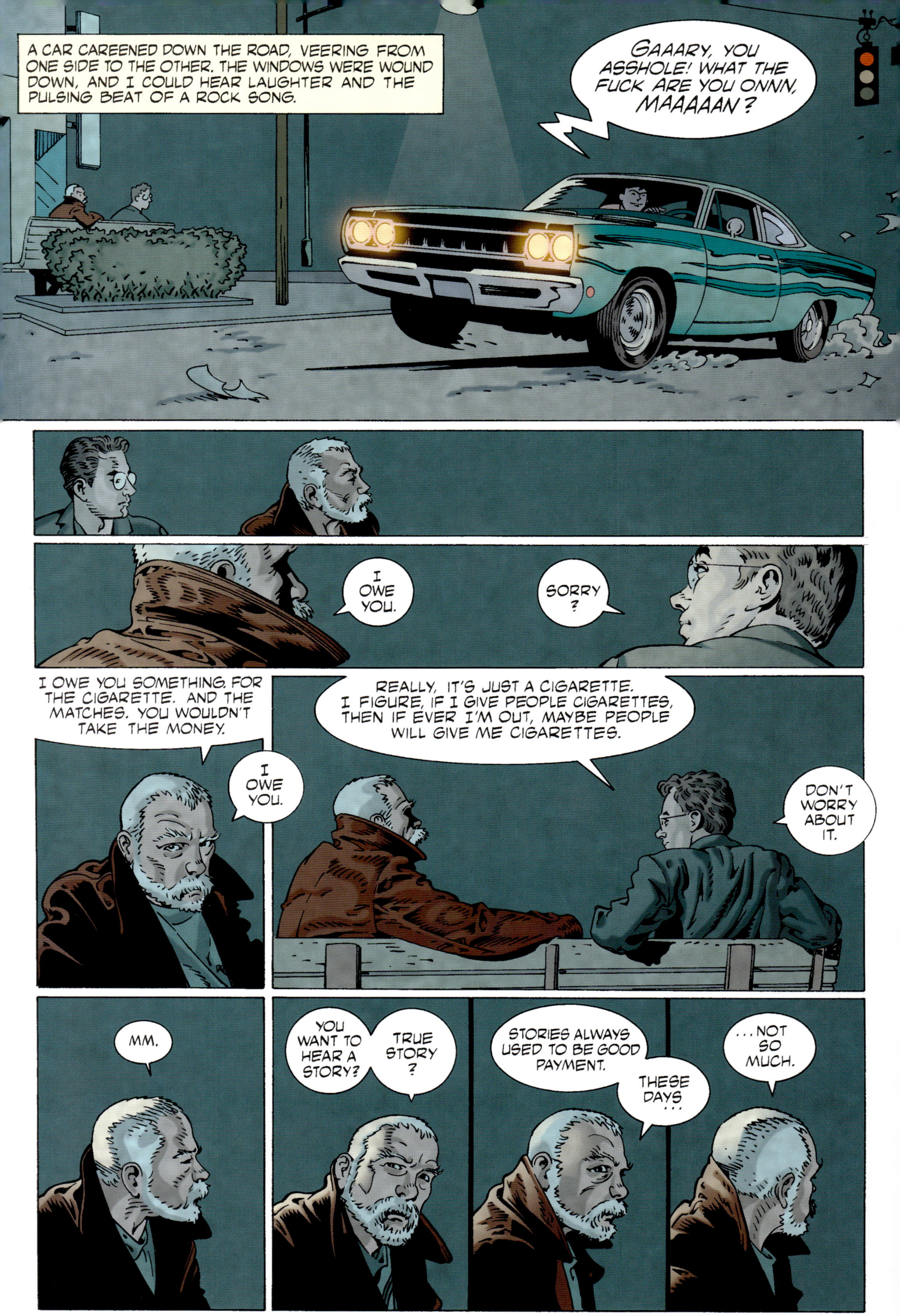
A CAR CAREENED DOWN THE ROAD, VEERING FROM ONE SIDE TO THE OTHER. THE WINDOWS WERE WOUND DOWN, AND I COULD HEAR LAUGHTER AND THE PULSING BEAT OF A ROCK SONG.
GAAARY, YOU ASSHOLE! WHAT THE FUCK ARE YOU ONNN, MAAAAAN?
I OWE YOU.
SORRY?
I OWE YOU SOMETHING. FOR THE CIGARETTE. AND THE MATCHES. YOU WOULDN'T TAKE THE MONEY.
I OWE YOU.
REALLY, IT'S JUST A CIGARETTE. I FIGURE, IF I GIVE PEOPLE CIGARETTES, THEN IF EVER I'M OUT, MAYBE PEOPLE WILL GIVE ME CIGARETTES.
DON'T WORRY ABOUT IT.
MM.
YOU WANT TO HEAR A STORY?
TRUE STORY?
STORIES ALWAYS USED TO BE GOOD PAYMENT.
THESE DAYS...
...NOT SO MUCH.

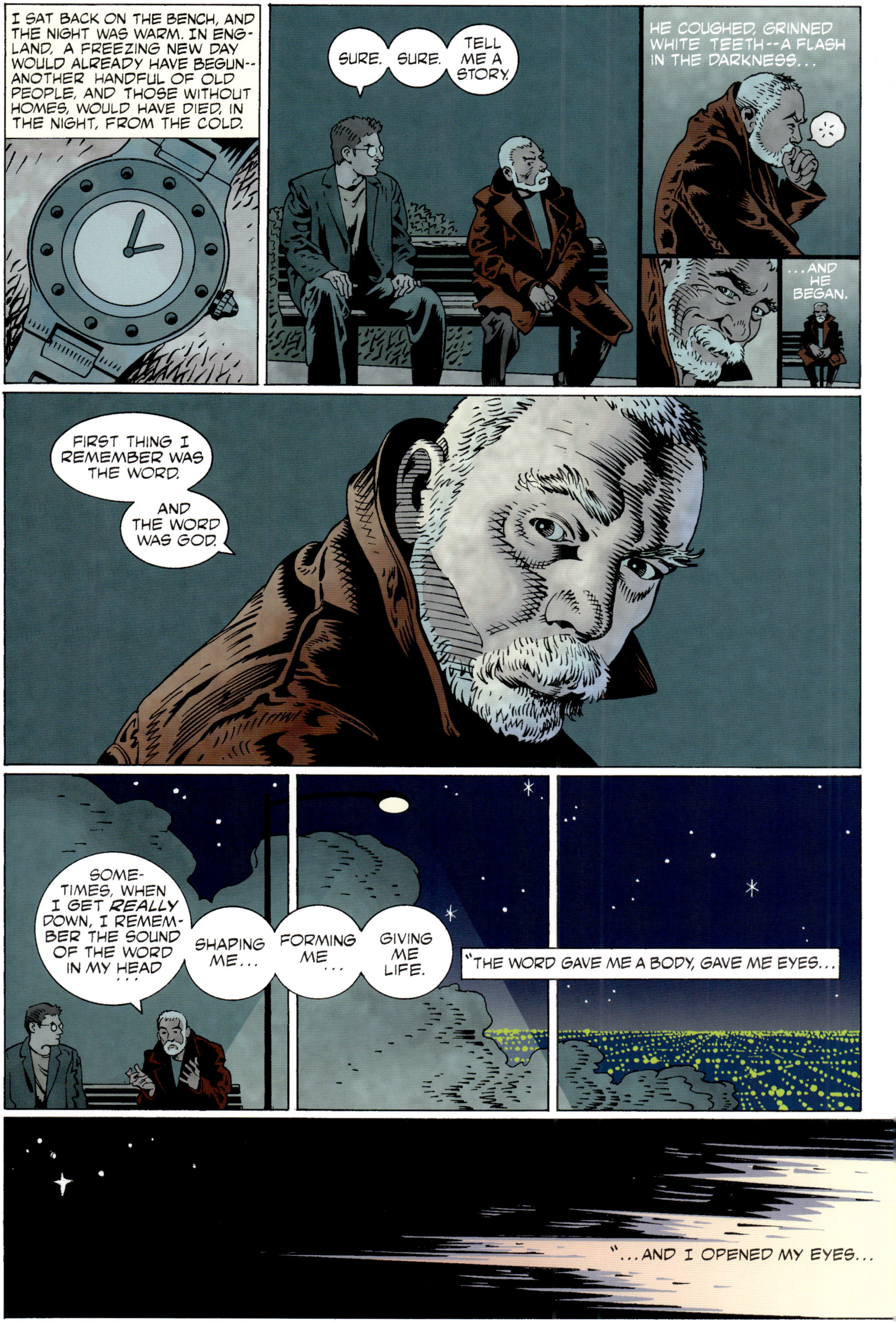
I SAT BACK ON THE BENCH, AND THE NIGHT WAS WARM. IN ENGLAND, A FREEZING NEW DAY WOULD ALREADY HAVE BEGUN--ANOTHER HANDFUL OF OLD PEOPLE, AND THOSE WITHOUT HOMES, WOULD HAVE DIED, IN THE NIGHT, FROM THE COLD.
SURE.
SURE.
TELL ME A STORY.
HE COUGHED, GRINNED WHITE TEETH--A FLASH IN THE DARKNESS...
...AND HE BEGAN.
FIRST THING I REMEMBER WAS THE WORD.
AND THE WORD WAS GOD.
SOMETIMES, WHEN I GET *REALLY* DOWN, I REMEMBER THE SOUND OF THE WORD IN MY HEAD...
SHAPING ME...
FORMING ME...
GIVING ME LIFE.
"THE WORD GAVE ME A BODY, GAVE ME EYES...
"...AND I OPENED MY EYES...

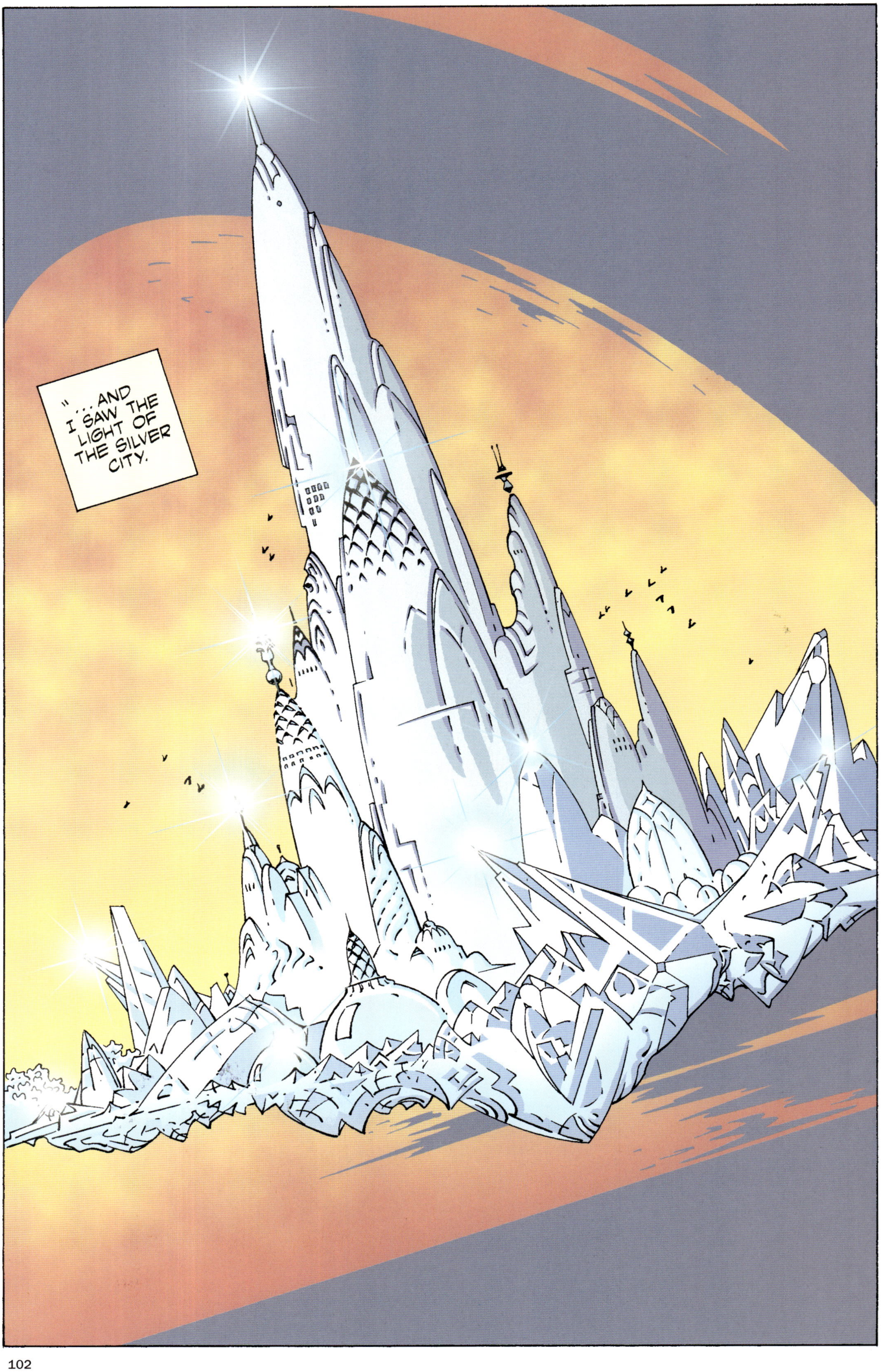
"...AND I SAW THE LIGHT OF THE SILVER CITY.

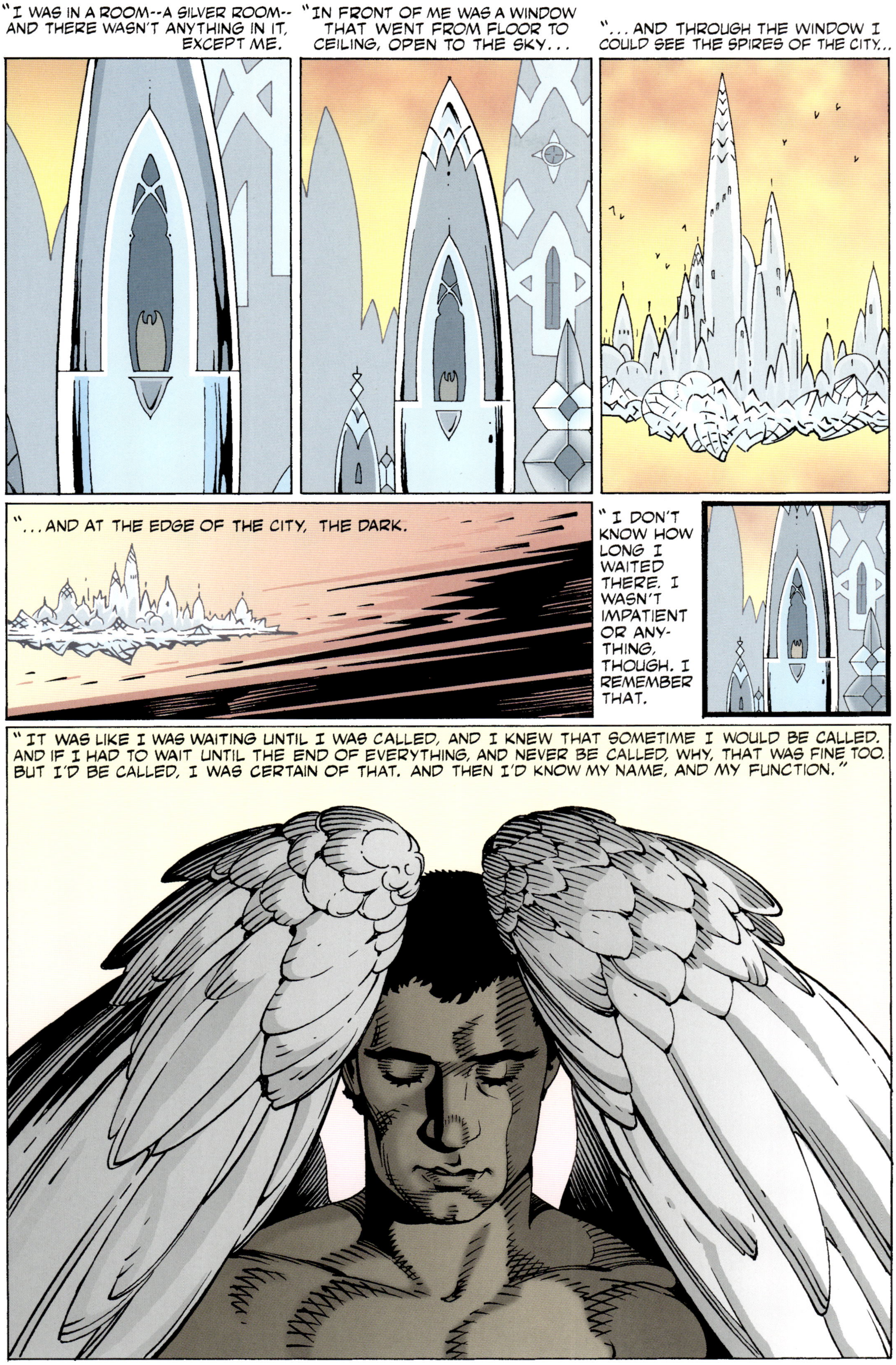
"I WAS IN A ROOM--A SILVER ROOM-- AND THERE WASN'T ANYTHING IN IT, EXCEPT ME.
"IN FRONT OF ME WAS A WINDOW THAT WENT FROM FLOOR TO CEILING, OPEN TO THE SKY...
"...AND THROUGH THE WINDOW I COULD SEE THE SPIRES OF THE CITY...
"...AND AT THE EDGE OF THE CITY, THE DARK.
"I DON'T KNOW HOW LONG I WAITED THERE. I WASN'T IMPATIENT OR ANY-THING, THOUGH. I REMEMBER THAT.
"IT WAS LIKE I WAS WAITING UNTIL I WAS CALLED, AND I KNEW THAT SOMETIME I WOULD BE CALLED. AND IF I HAD TO WAIT UNTIL THE END OF EVERYTHING, AND NEVER BE CALLED, WHY, THAT WAS FINE TOO. BUT I'D BE CALLED, I WAS CERTAIN OF THAT. AND THEN I'D KNOW MY NAME, AND MY FUNCTION."

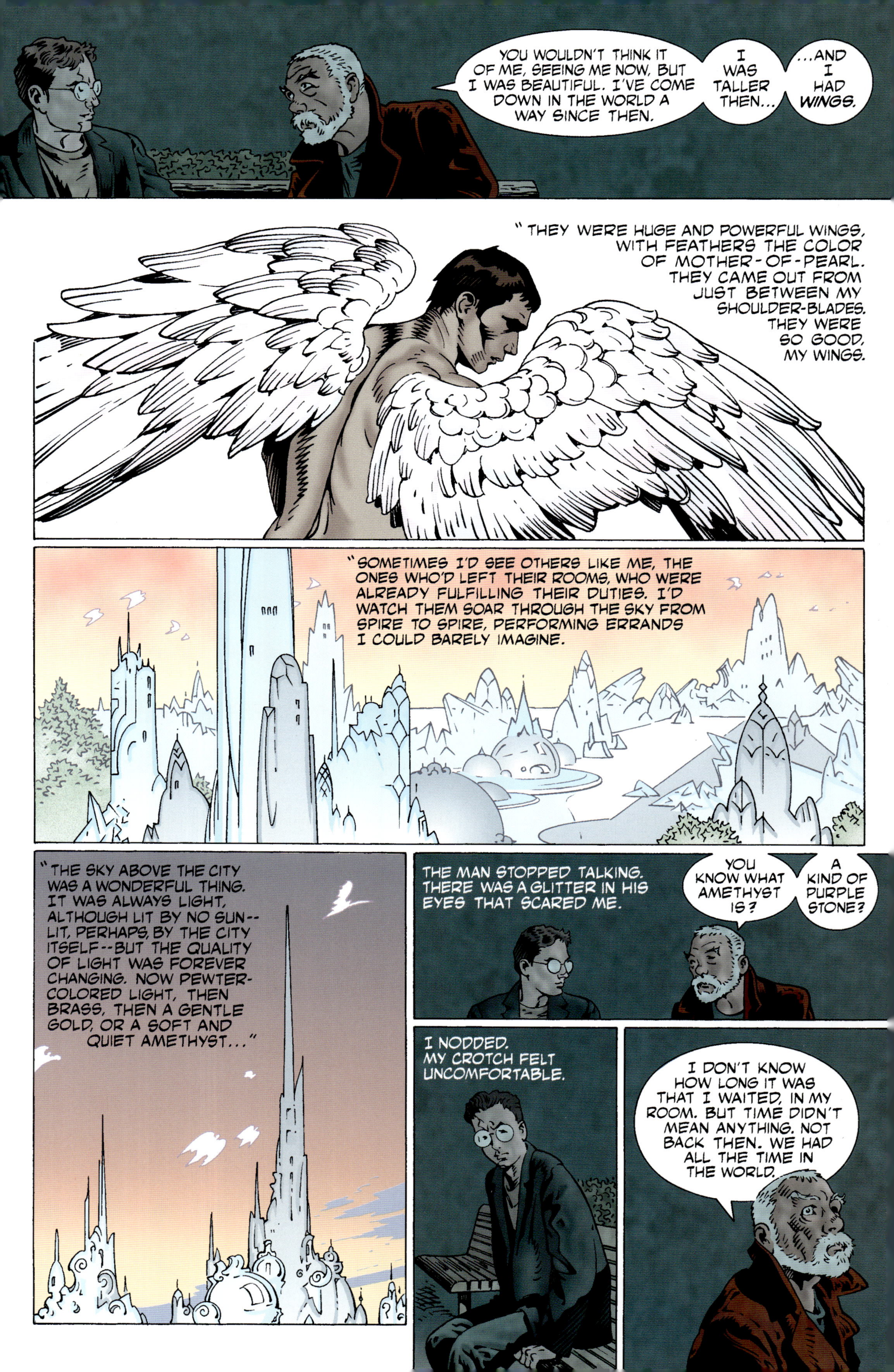
YOU WOULDN'T THINK IT OF ME, SEEING ME NOW, BUT I WAS BEAUTIFUL. I'VE COME DOWN IN THE WORLD A WAY SINCE THEN.
I WAS TALLER THEN...
...AND I HAD *WINGS.*
"THEY WERE HUGE AND POWERFUL WINGS, WITH FEATHERS THE COLOR OF MOTHER-OF-PEARL. THEY CAME OUT FROM JUST BETWEEN MY SHOULDER-BLADES. THEY WERE SO GOOD, MY WINGS.
"SOMETIMES I'D SEE OTHERS LIKE ME, THE ONES WHO'D LEFT THEIR ROOMS, WHO WERE ALREADY FULFILLING THEIR DUTIES. I'D WATCH THEM SOAR THROUGH THE SKY FROM SPIRE TO SPIRE, PERFORMING ERRANDS I COULD BARELY IMAGINE.
"THE SKY ABOVE THE CITY WAS A WONDERFUL THING. IT WAS ALWAYS LIGHT, ALTHOUGH LIT BY NO SUN--LIT, PERHAPS, BY THE CITY ITSELF--BUT THE QUALITY OF LIGHT WAS FOREVER CHANGING. NOW PEWTER-COLORED LIGHT, THEN BRASS, THEN A GENTLE GOLD, OR A SOFT AND QUIET AMETHYST..."
THE MAN STOPPED TALKING. THERE WAS A GLITTER IN HIS EYES THAT SCARED ME.
YOU KNOW WHAT AMETHYST IS?
A KIND OF PURPLE STONE?
I NODDED. MY CROTCH FELT UNCOMFORTABLE.
I DON'T KNOW HOW LONG IT WAS THAT I WAITED, IN MY ROOM. BUT TIME DIDN'T MEAN ANYTHING. NOT BACK THEN. WE HAD ALL THE TIME IN THE WORLD.

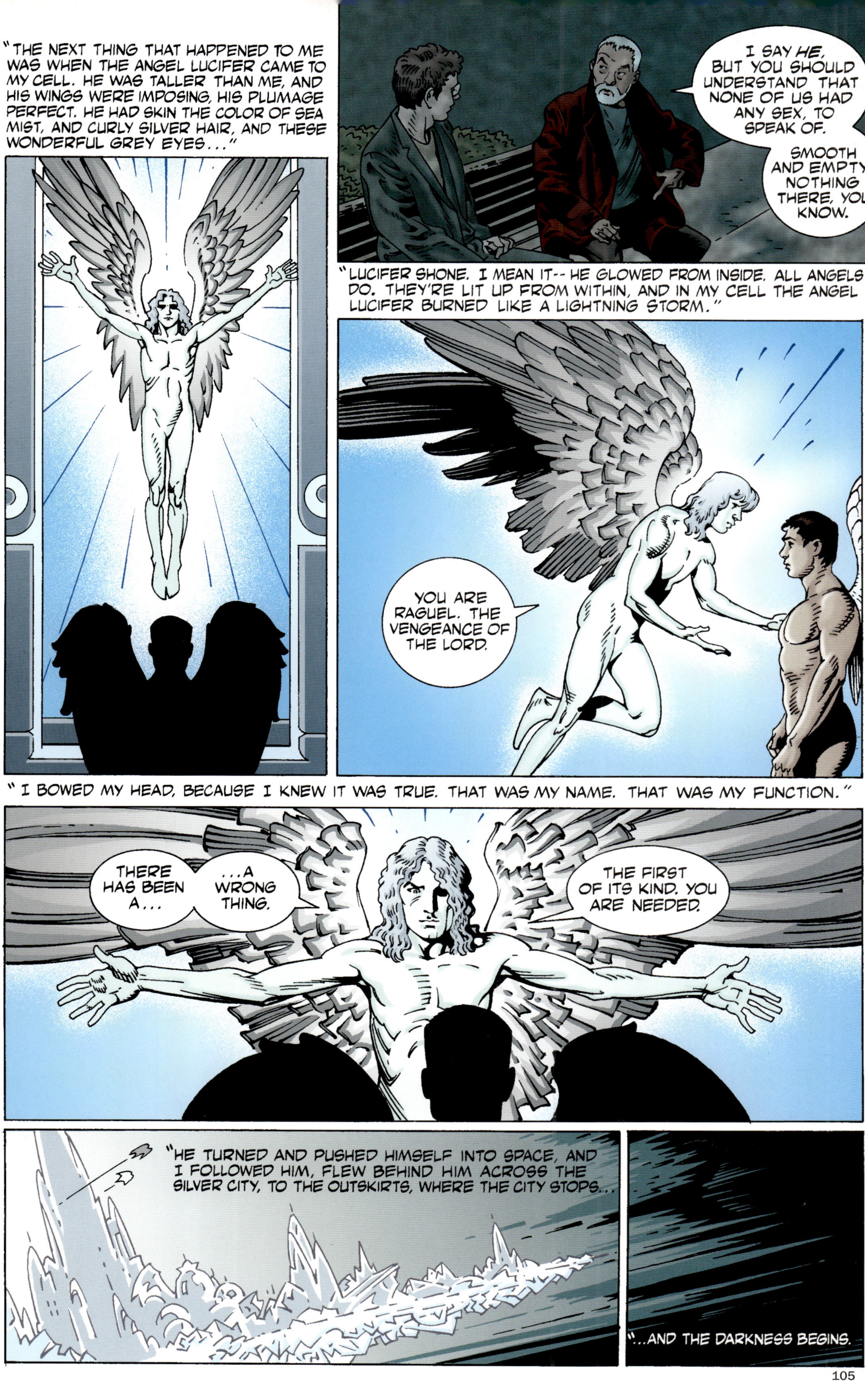
"THE NEXT THING THAT HAPPENED TO ME WAS WHEN THE ANGEL LUCIFER CAME TO MY CELL. HE WAS TALLER THAN ME, AND HIS WINGS WERE IMPOSING, HIS PLUMAGE PERFECT. HE HAD SKIN THE COLOR OF SEA MIST, AND CURLY SILVER HAIR, AND THESE WONDERFUL GREY EYES..."
I SAY *HE*, BUT YOU SHOULD UNDERSTAND THAT NONE OF US HAD ANY SEX, TO SPEAK OF.
SMOOTH AND EMPTY. NOTHING THERE, YOU KNOW.
"LUCIFER SHONE. I MEAN IT-- HE GLOWED FROM INSIDE. ALL ANGELS DO. THEY'RE LIT UP FROM WITHIN, AND IN MY CELL THE ANGEL LUCIFER BURNED LIKE A LIGHTNING STORM."
YOU ARE RAGUEL. THE VENGEANCE OF THE LORD.
" I BOWED MY HEAD, BECAUSE I KNEW IT WAS TRUE. THAT WAS MY NAME. THAT WAS MY FUNCTION."
THERE HAS BEEN A...
...A WRONG THING.
THE FIRST OF ITS KIND. YOU ARE NEEDED.
"HE TURNED AND PUSHED HIMSELF INTO SPACE, AND I FOLLOWED HIM, FLEW BEHIND HIM ACROSS THE SILVER CITY, TO THE OUTSKIRTS, WHERE THE CITY STOPS...
"...AND THE DARKNESS BEGINS.

"AND IT WAS THERE, UNDER A VAST SILVER SPIRE, THAT WE DESCENDED TO THE STREET..."

"...AND I SAW THE DEAD ANGEL.

"THE BODY LAY, CRUMBLED AND BROKEN, ON THE SILVER SIDEWALK.

"ITS WINGS WERE CRUSHED UNDERNEATH IT AND A FEW LOOSE FEATHERS HAD ALREADY BLOWN INTO THE SILVER GUTTER.

"THE BODY WAS ALMOST DARK. NOW AND AGAIN, A LIGHT WOULD FLASH INSIDE IT, AN OCCASIONAL FLICKER OF COLD FIRE IN THE CHEST, OR IN THE EYES, OR IN THE SEXLESS GROIN, AS THE LAST OF THE GLOW OF LIFE LEFT IT FOREVER.

"IT WAS VERY BEAUTIFUL, EVEN IN DEATH.

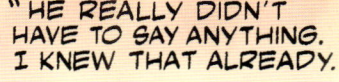

"IT WOULD HAVE BROKEN YOUR HEART."

YOU MUST FIND WHO WAS RESPONSIBLE FOR THIS, AND HOW-- AND TAKE THE VENGEANCE OF THE NAME ON WHOEVER CAUSED THIS THING TO HAPPEN.

"HE REALLY DIDN'T HAVE TO SAY ANYTHING. I KNEW THAT ALREADY.

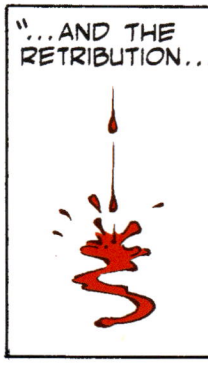

"THE HUNT...

"...AND THE RETRIBUTION...

"...IT WAS WHAT I WAS CREATED FOR, IN THE BEGINNING...

"...IT WAS WHAT I *WAS*."

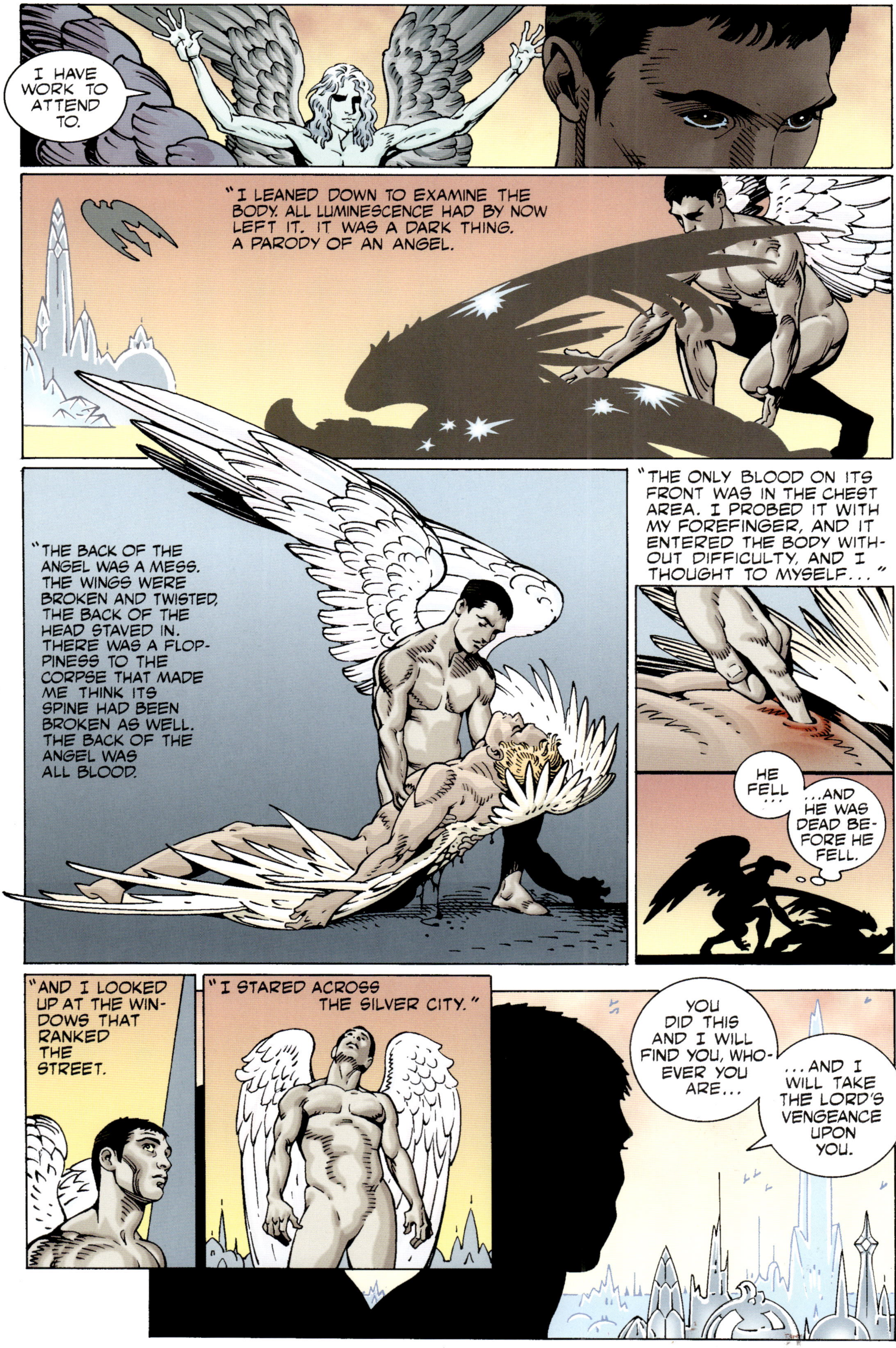
I HAVE WORK TO ATTEND TO.
"I LEANED DOWN TO EXAMINE THE BODY. ALL LUMINESCENCE HAD BY NOW LEFT IT. IT WAS A DARK THING. A PARODY OF AN ANGEL.
"THE BACK OF THE ANGEL WAS A MESS. THE WINGS WERE BROKEN AND TWISTED, THE BACK OF THE HEAD STAVED IN. THERE WAS A FLOPPINESS TO THE CORPSE THAT MADE ME THINK ITS SPINE HAD BEEN BROKEN AS WELL. THE BACK OF THE ANGEL WAS ALL BLOOD.
"THE ONLY BLOOD ON ITS FRONT WAS IN THE CHEST AREA. I PROBED IT WITH MY FOREFINGER, AND IT ENTERED THE BODY WITHOUT DIFFICULTY, AND I THOUGHT TO MYSELF..."
HE FELL...
...AND HE WAS DEAD BEFORE HE FELL.
"AND I LOOKED UP AT THE WINDOWS THAT RANKED THE STREET.
"I STARED ACROSS THE SILVER CITY."
YOU DID THIS AND I WILL FIND YOU, WHOEVER YOU ARE...
...AND I WILL TAKE THE LORD'S VENGEANCE UPON YOU.

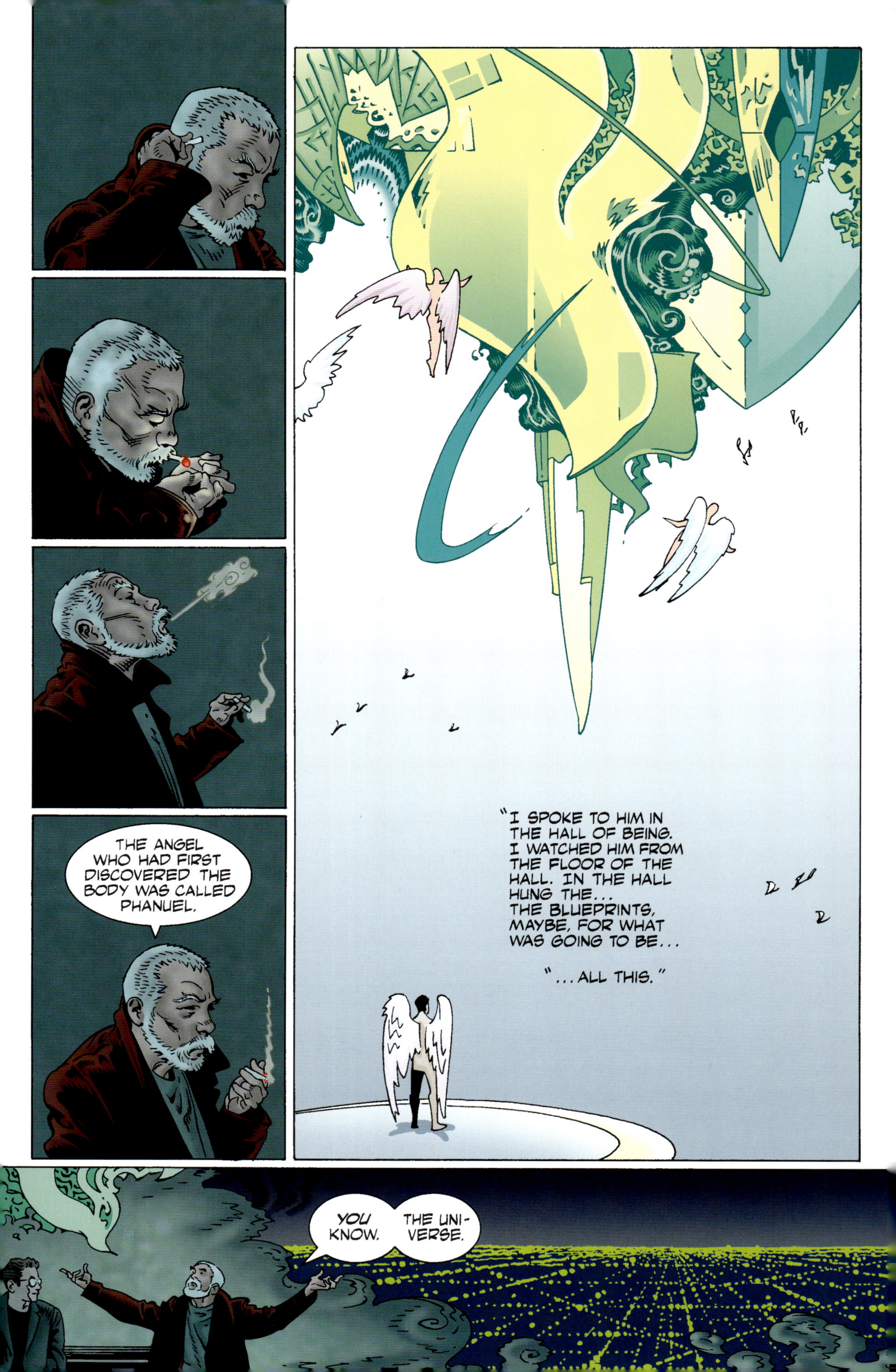
THE ANGEL WHO HAD FIRST DISCOVERED THE BODY WAS CALLED PHANUEL.
"I SPOKE TO HIM IN THE HALL OF BEING. I WATCHED HIM FROM THE FLOOR OF THE HALL. IN THE HALL HUNG THE... THE BLUEPRINTS, MAYBE, FOR WHAT WAS GOING TO BE...
"...ALL THIS."
YOU KNOW.
THE UNI-VERSE.

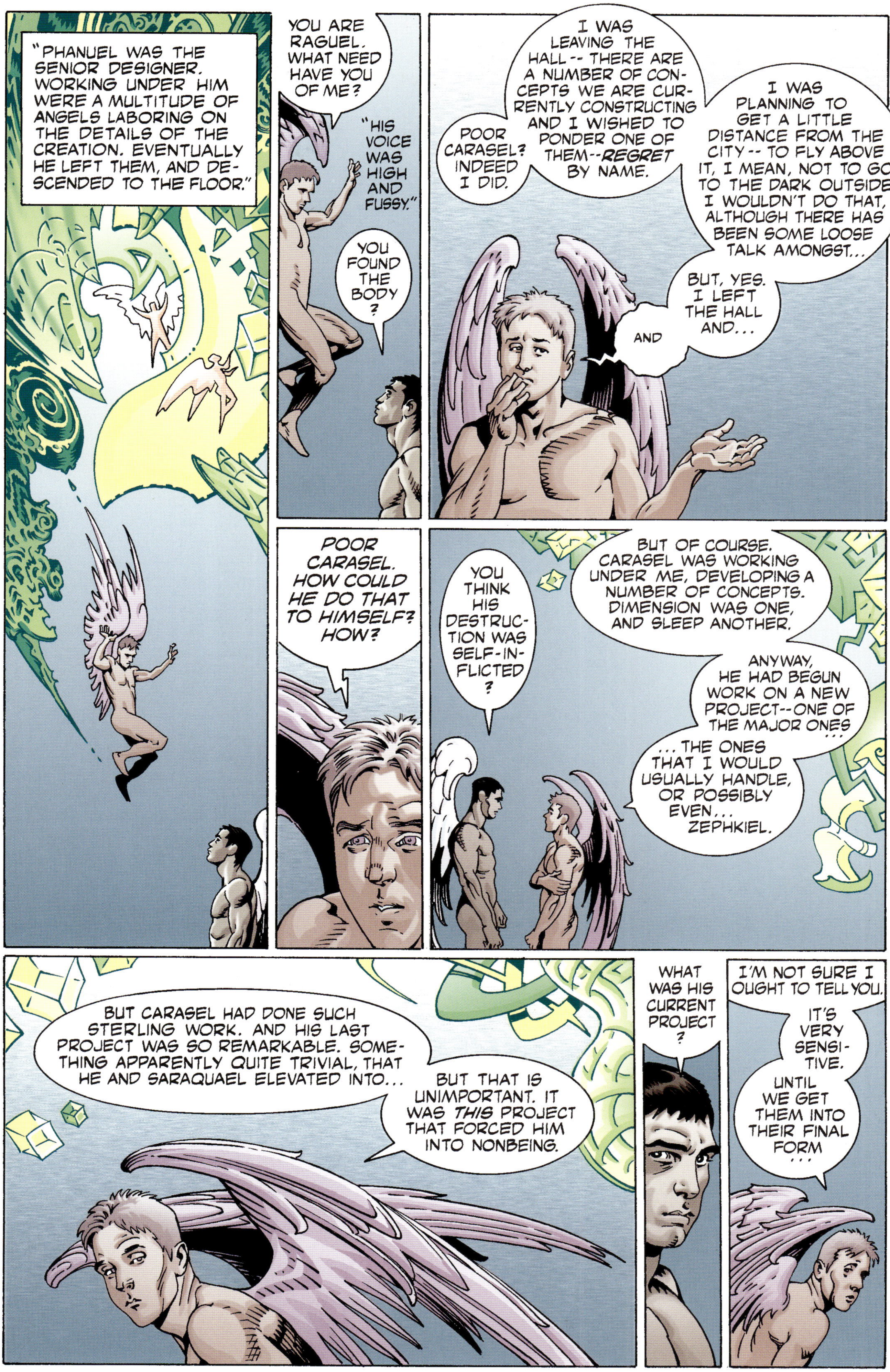
"PHANUEL WAS THE SENIOR DESIGNER. WORKING UNDER HIM WERE A MULTITUDE OF ANGELS LABORING ON THE DETAILS OF THE CREATION. EVENTUALLY HE LEFT THEM, AND DESCENDED TO THE FLOOR."
YOU ARE RAGUEL. WHAT NEED HAVE YOU OF ME?
"HIS VOICE WAS HIGH AND FUSSY."
YOU FOUND THE BODY?
POOR CARASEL? INDEED I DID.
I WAS LEAVING THE HALL -- THERE ARE A NUMBER OF CONCEPTS WE ARE CURRENTLY CONSTRUCTING AND I WISHED TO PONDER ONE OF THEM--*REGRET* BY NAME.
I WAS PLANNING TO GET A LITTLE DISTANCE FROM THE CITY -- TO FLY ABOVE IT, I MEAN, NOT TO GO TO THE DARK OUTSIDE. I WOULDN'T DO THAT, ALTHOUGH THERE HAS BEEN SOME LOOSE TALK AMONGST...
BUT, YES. I LEFT THE HALL AND...
AND
POOR CARASEL. HOW COULD HE DO THAT TO HIMSELF? HOW?
YOU THINK HIS DESTRUCTION WAS SELF-INFLICTED?
BUT OF COURSE. CARASEL WAS WORKING UNDER ME, DEVELOPING A NUMBER OF CONCEPTS. DIMENSION WAS ONE, AND SLEEP ANOTHER.
ANYWAY, HE HAD BEGUN WORK ON A NEW PROJECT--ONE OF THE MAJOR ONES...
...THE ONES THAT I WOULD USUALLY HANDLE, OR POSSIBLY EVEN... ZEPHKIEL.
BUT CARASEL HAD DONE SUCH STERLING WORK. AND HIS LAST PROJECT WAS SO REMARKABLE. SOMETHING APPARENTLY QUITE TRIVIAL, THAT HE AND SARAQUAEL ELEVATED INTO...
BUT THAT IS UNIMPORTANT. IT WAS *THIS* PROJECT THAT FORCED HIM INTO NONBEING.
WHAT WAS HIS CURRENT PROJECT?
I'M NOT SURE I OUGHT TO TELL YOU.
IT'S VERY SENSITIVE.
UNTIL WE GET THEM INTO THEIR FINAL FORM...

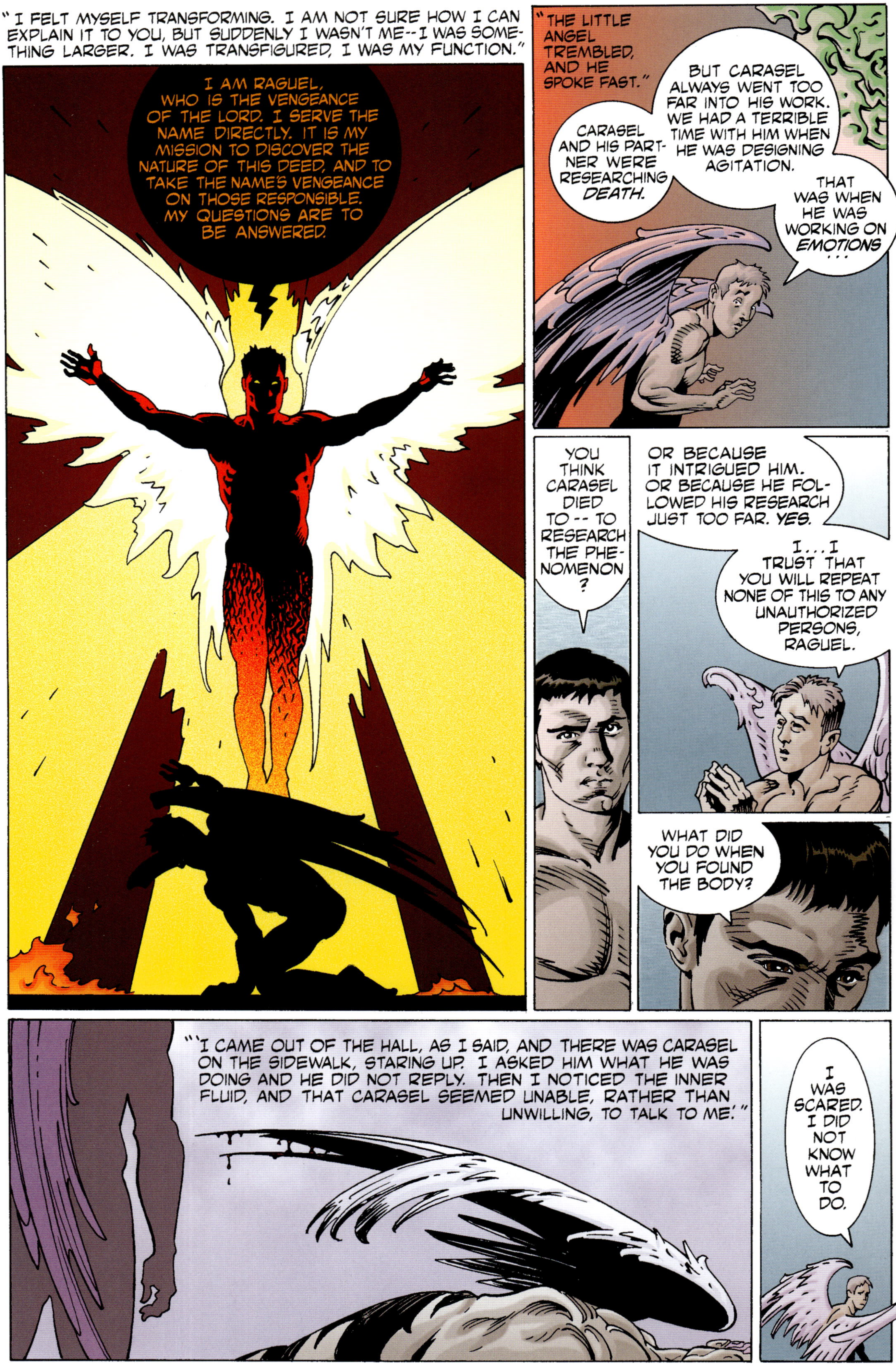
"I FELT MYSELF TRANSFORMING. I AM NOT SURE HOW I CAN EXPLAIN IT TO YOU, BUT SUDDENLY I WASN'T ME--I WAS SOMETHING LARGER. I WAS TRANSFIGURED, I WAS MY FUNCTION."
I AM RAGUEL, WHO IS THE VENGEANCE OF THE LORD. I SERVE THE NAME DIRECTLY. IT IS MY MISSION TO DISCOVER THE NATURE OF THIS DEED, AND TO TAKE THE NAME'S VENGEANCE ON THOSE RESPONSIBLE. MY QUESTIONS ARE TO BE ANSWERED.
"THE LITTLE ANGEL TREMBLED, AND HE SPOKE FAST."
CARASEL AND HIS PARTNER WERE RESEARCHING *DEATH*.
BUT CARASEL ALWAYS WENT TOO FAR INTO HIS WORK. WE HAD A TERRIBLE TIME WITH HIM WHEN HE WAS DESIGNING AGITATION.
THAT WAS WHEN HE WAS WORKING ON *EMOTIONS* . . .
YOU THINK CARASEL DIED TO -- TO RESEARCH THE PHENOMENON?
OR BECAUSE IT INTRIGUED HIM. OR BECAUSE HE FOLLOWED HIS RESEARCH JUST TOO FAR. *YES*.
I... I TRUST THAT YOU WILL REPEAT NONE OF THIS TO ANY UNAUTHORIZED PERSONS, RAGUEL.
WHAT DID YOU DO WHEN YOU FOUND THE BODY?
"'I CAME OUT OF THE HALL, AS I SAID, AND THERE WAS CARASEL ON THE SIDEWALK, STARING UP. I ASKED HIM WHAT HE WAS DOING AND HE DID NOT REPLY. THEN I NOTICED THE INNER FLUID, AND THAT CARASEL SEEMED UNABLE, RATHER THAN UNWILLING, TO TALK TO ME.'"
I WAS SCARED. I DID NOT KNOW WHAT TO DO.

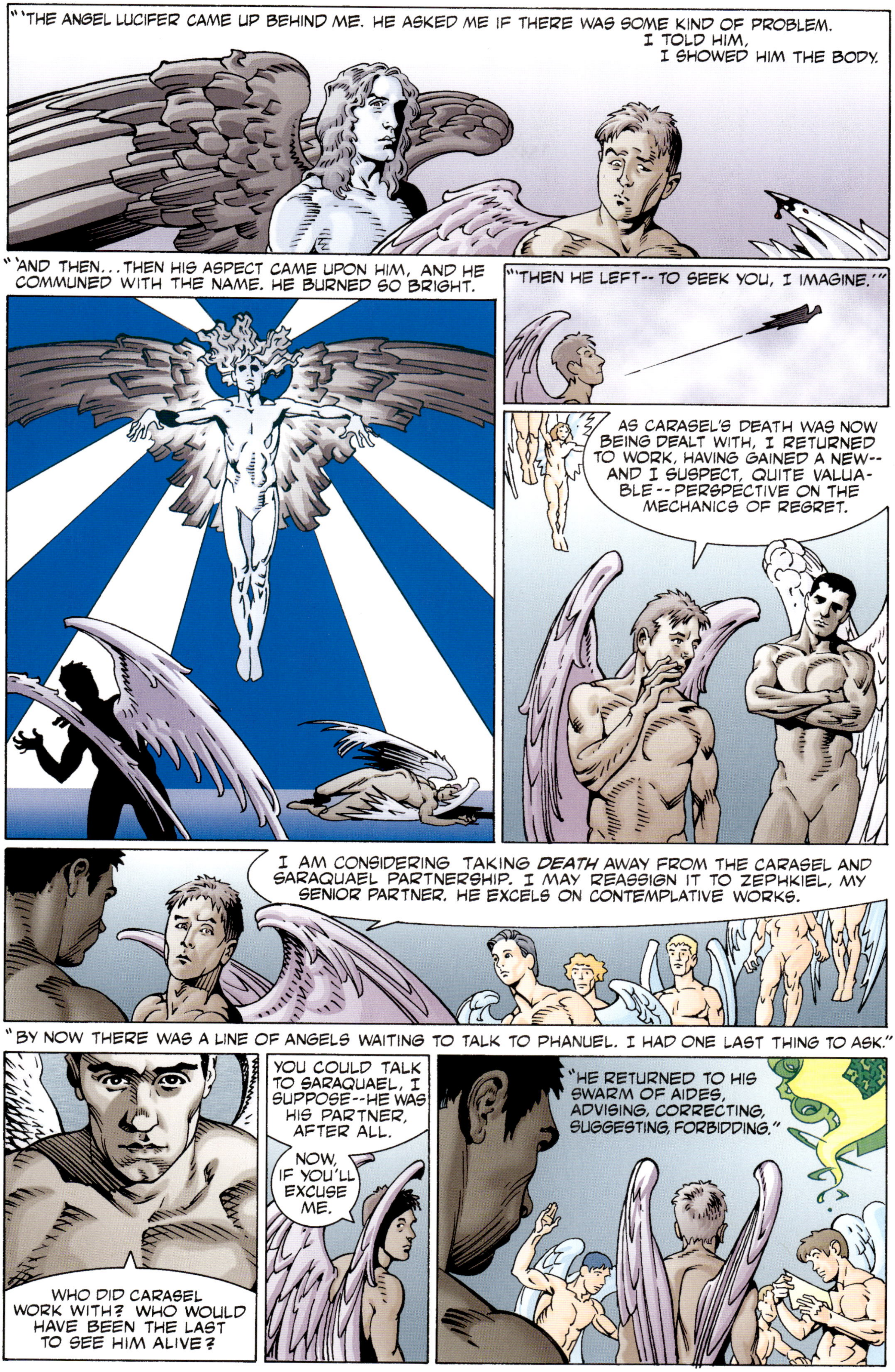
"'THE ANGEL LUCIFER CAME UP BEHIND ME. HE ASKED ME IF THERE WAS SOME KIND OF PROBLEM. I TOLD HIM, I SHOWED HIM THE BODY.
"'AND THEN... THEN HIS ASPECT CAME UPON HIM, AND HE COMMUNED WITH THE NAME. HE BURNED SO BRIGHT.
"'THEN HE LEFT-- TO SEEK YOU, I IMAGINE.'"
AS CARASEL'S DEATH WAS NOW BEING DEALT WITH, I RETURNED TO WORK, HAVING GAINED A NEW-- AND I SUSPECT, QUITE VALUABLE-- PERSPECTIVE ON THE MECHANICS OF REGRET.
I AM CONSIDERING TAKING *DEATH* AWAY FROM THE CARASEL AND SARAQUAEL PARTNERSHIP. I MAY REASSIGN IT TO ZEPHKIEL, MY SENIOR PARTNER. HE EXCELS ON CONTEMPLATIVE WORKS.
"BY NOW THERE WAS A LINE OF ANGELS WAITING TO TALK TO PHANUEL. I HAD ONE LAST THING TO ASK."
WHO DID CARASEL WORK WITH? WHO WOULD HAVE BEEN THE LAST TO SEE HIM ALIVE?
YOU COULD TALK TO SARAQUAEL, I SUPPOSE--HE WAS HIS PARTNER, AFTER ALL.
NOW, IF YOU'LL EXCUSE ME.
"HE RETURNED TO HIS SWARM OF AIDES, ADVISING, CORRECTING, SUGGESTING, FORBIDDING."

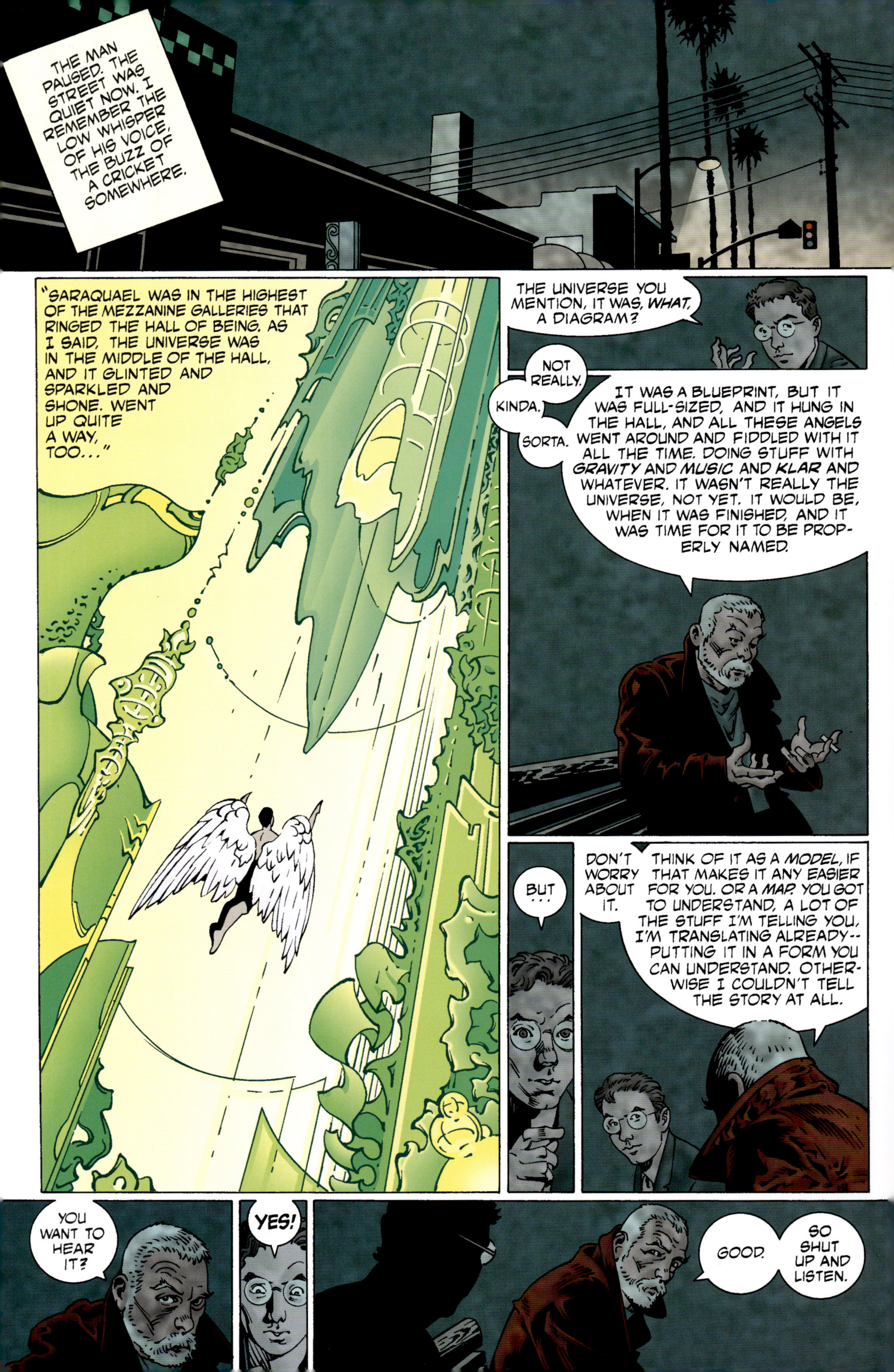
THE MAN PAUSED. THE STREET WAS QUIET NOW. I REMEMBER THE LOW WHISPER OF HIS VOICE, THE BUZZ OF A CRICKET SOMEWHERE.
"SARAQUAEL WAS IN THE HIGHEST OF THE MEZZANINE GALLERIES THAT RINGED THE HALL OF BEING. AS I SAID, THE UNIVERSE WAS IN THE MIDDLE OF THE HALL, AND IT GLINTED AND SPARKLED AND SHONE. WENT UP QUITE A WAY, TOO..."
THE UNIVERSE YOU MENTION, IT WAS, WHAT, A DIAGRAM?
NOT REALLY.
KINDA.
SORTA.
IT WAS A BLUEPRINT, BUT IT WAS FULL-SIZED, AND IT HUNG IN THE HALL, AND ALL THESE ANGELS WENT AROUND AND FIDDLED WITH IT ALL THE TIME. DOING STUFF WITH GRAVITY AND MUSIC AND KLAR AND WHATEVER. IT WASN'T REALLY THE UNIVERSE, NOT YET. IT WOULD BE, WHEN IT WAS FINISHED, AND IT WAS TIME FOR IT TO BE PROPERLY NAMED.
BUT...
DON'T WORRY ABOUT IT.
THINK OF IT AS A MODEL, IF THAT MAKES IT ANY EASIER FOR YOU. OR A MAP. YOU GOT TO UNDERSTAND, A LOT OF THE STUFF I'M TELLING YOU, I'M TRANSLATING ALREADY-- PUTTING IT IN A FORM YOU CAN UNDERSTAND. OTHERWISE I COULDN'T TELL THE STORY AT ALL.
YOU WANT TO HEAR IT?
YES!
GOOD.
SO SHUT UP AND LISTEN.

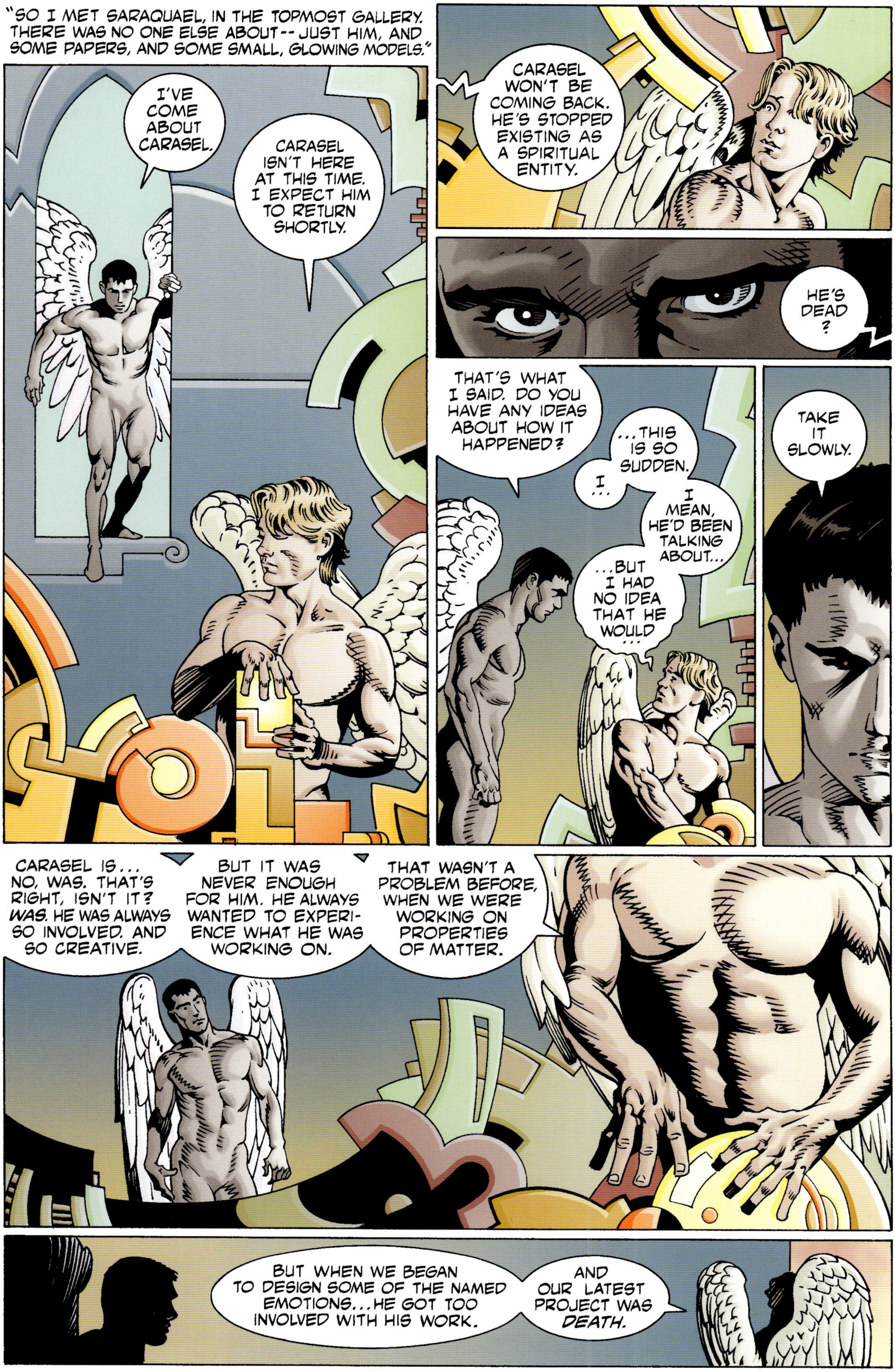
"SO I MET SARAQUAEL, IN THE TOPMOST GALLERY. THERE WAS NO ONE ELSE ABOUT -- JUST HIM, AND SOME PAPERS, AND SOME SMALL, GLOWING MODELS."
I'VE COME ABOUT CARASEL.
CARASEL ISN'T HERE AT THIS TIME. I EXPECT HIM TO RETURN SHORTLY.
CARASEL WON'T BE COMING BACK. HE'S STOPPED EXISTING AS A SPIRITUAL ENTITY.
HE'S DEAD?
THAT'S WHAT I SAID. DO YOU HAVE ANY IDEAS ABOUT HOW IT HAPPENED?
I...
...THIS IS SO SUDDEN.
I MEAN, HE'D BEEN TALKING ABOUT...
...BUT I HAD NO IDEA THAT HE WOULD...
TAKE IT SLOWLY.
CARASEL IS... NO, WAS. THAT'S RIGHT, ISN'T IT? *WAS.* HE WAS ALWAYS SO INVOLVED. AND SO CREATIVE.
BUT IT WAS NEVER ENOUGH FOR HIM. HE ALWAYS WANTED TO EXPERIENCE WHAT HE WAS WORKING ON.
THAT WASN'T A PROBLEM BEFORE, WHEN WE WERE WORKING ON PROPERTIES OF MATTER.
BUT WHEN WE BEGAN TO DESIGN SOME OF THE NAMED EMOTIONS...HE GOT TOO INVOLVED WITH HIS WORK.
AND OUR LATEST PROJECT WAS *DEATH.*

"HE STOOD UP AND WALKED TO THE WINDOW. THERE WAS NO VIEW OF THE SILVER CITY FROM HIS WINDOW--JUST A REFLECTED GLOW FROM THE CITY AND THE SKY BEHIND US, HANGING IN THE AIR, AND BEYOND THAT, THE DARK."

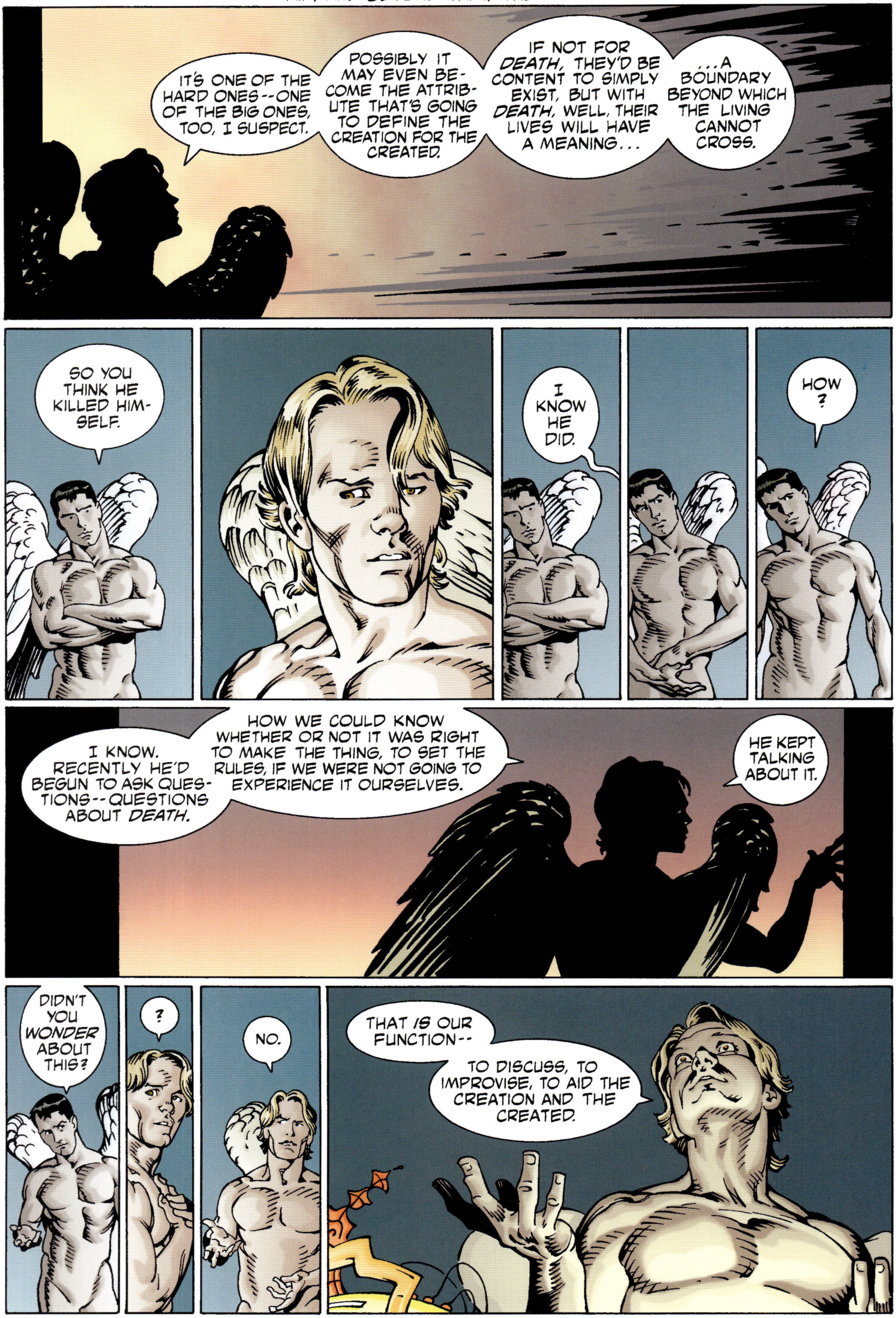
IT'S ONE OF THE HARD ONES--ONE OF THE BIG ONES, TOO, I SUSPECT.
POSSIBLY IT MAY EVEN BECOME THE ATTRIBUTE THAT'S GOING TO DEFINE THE CREATION FOR THE CREATED.
IF NOT FOR *DEATH*, THEY'D BE CONTENT TO SIMPLY EXIST, BUT WITH *DEATH*, WELL, THEIR LIVES WILL HAVE A MEANING...
...A BOUNDARY BEYOND WHICH THE LIVING CANNOT CROSS.
SO YOU THINK HE KILLED HIMSELF.
I KNOW HE DID.
HOW?
I KNOW. RECENTLY HE'D BEGUN TO ASK QUESTIONS--QUESTIONS ABOUT *DEATH*.
HOW WE COULD KNOW WHETHER OR NOT IT WAS RIGHT TO MAKE THE THING, TO SET THE RULES, IF WE WERE NOT GOING TO EXPERIENCE IT OURSELVES.
HE KEPT TALKING ABOUT IT.
DIDN'T YOU *WONDER* ABOUT THIS?
?
NO.
THAT *IS* OUR FUNCTION--
TO DISCUSS, TO IMPROVISE, TO AID THE CREATION AND THE CREATED.

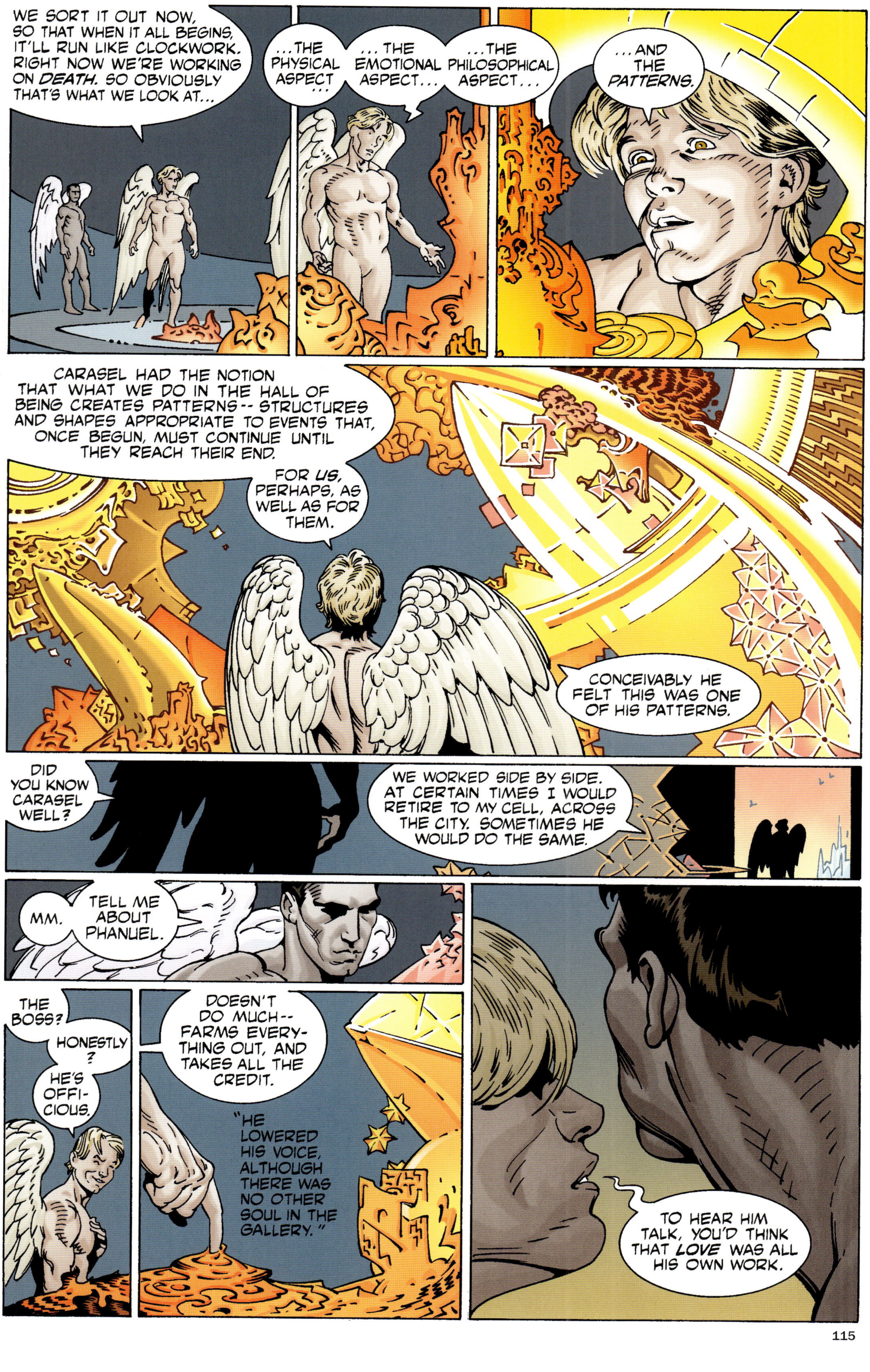

WE SORT IT OUT NOW, SO THAT WHEN IT ALL BEGINS, IT'LL RUN LIKE CLOCKWORK. RIGHT NOW WE'RE WORKING ON *DEATH*. SO OBVIOUSLY THAT'S WHAT WE LOOK AT...
...THE PHYSICAL ASPECT...
...THE EMOTIONAL ASPECT...
...THE PHILOSOPHICAL ASPECT...
...AND THE *PATTERNS*.
CARASEL HAD THE NOTION THAT WHAT WE DO IN THE HALL OF BEING CREATES PATTERNS-- STRUCTURES AND SHAPES APPROPRIATE TO EVENTS THAT, ONCE BEGUN, MUST CONTINUE UNTIL THEY REACH THEIR END.
FOR *US*, PERHAPS, AS WELL AS FOR THEM.
CONCEIVABLY HE FELT THIS WAS ONE OF HIS PATTERNS.
DID YOU KNOW CARASEL WELL?
WE WORKED SIDE BY SIDE. AT CERTAIN TIMES I WOULD RETIRE TO MY CELL, ACROSS THE CITY. SOMETIMES HE WOULD DO THE SAME.
MM.
TELL ME ABOUT PHANUEL.
THE BOSS?
HONESTLY?
HE'S OFFICIOUS.
DOESN'T DO MUCH-- FARMS EVERYTHING OUT, AND TAKES ALL THE CREDIT.
"HE LOWERED HIS VOICE, ALTHOUGH THERE WAS NO OTHER SOUL IN THE GALLERY."
TO HEAR HIM TALK, YOU'D THINK THAT *LOVE* WAS ALL HIS OWN WORK.

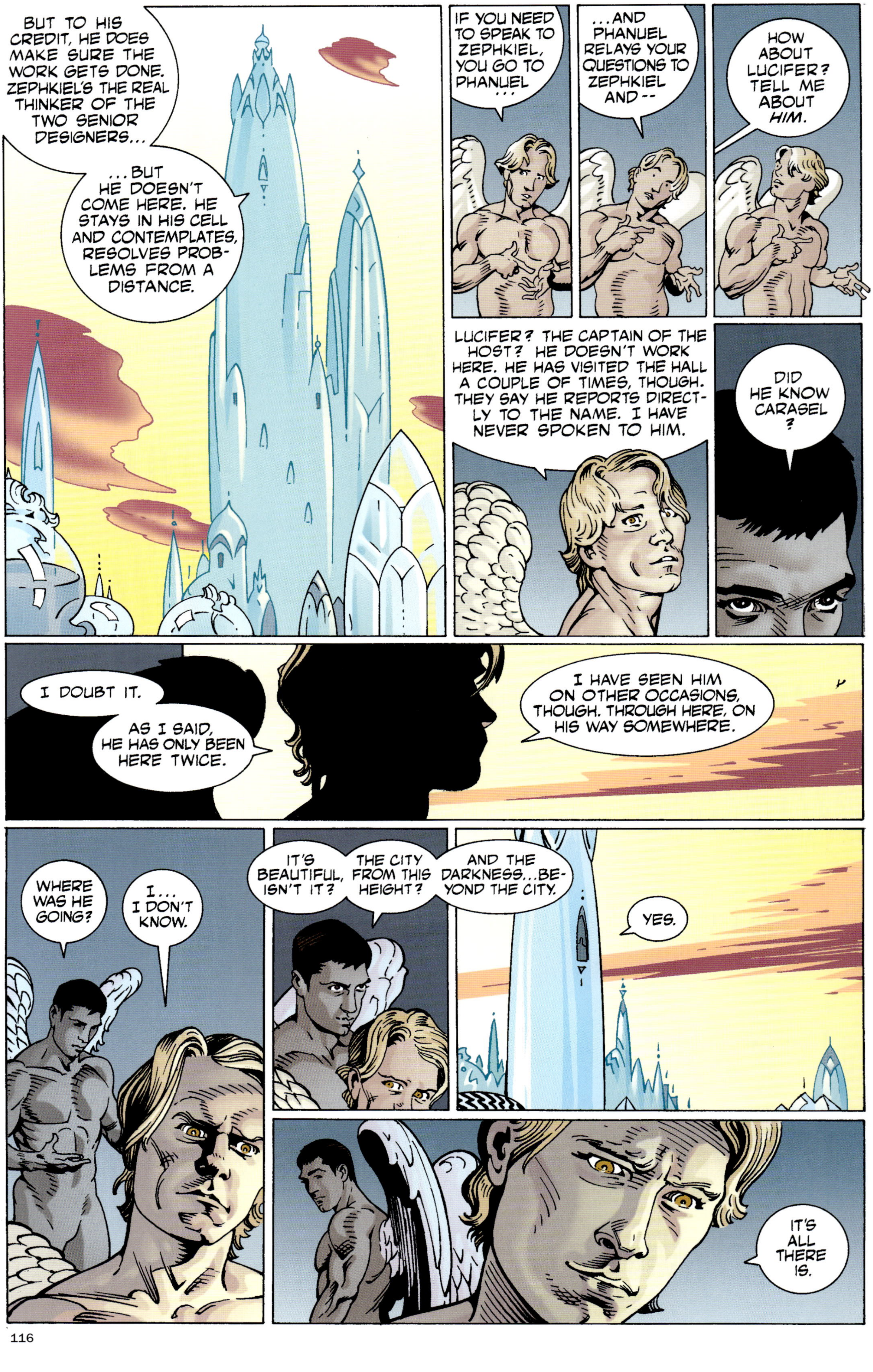
BUT TO HIS CREDIT, HE DOES MAKE SURE THE WORK GETS DONE. ZEPHKIEL'S THE REAL THINKER OF THE TWO SENIOR DESIGNERS...
...BUT HE DOESN'T COME HERE. HE STAYS IN HIS CELL AND CONTEMPLATES, RESOLVES PROBLEMS FROM A DISTANCE.
IF YOU NEED TO SPEAK TO ZEPHKIEL, YOU GO TO PHANUEL...
...AND PHANUEL RELAYS YOUR QUESTIONS TO ZEPHKIEL AND--
HOW ABOUT LUCIFER? TELL ME ABOUT *HIM*.
LUCIFER? THE CAPTAIN OF THE HOST? HE DOESN'T WORK HERE. HE HAS VISITED THE HALL A COUPLE OF TIMES, THOUGH. THEY SAY HE REPORTS DIRECTLY TO THE NAME. I HAVE NEVER SPOKEN TO HIM.
DID HE KNOW CARASEL?
I DOUBT IT.
AS I SAID, HE HAS ONLY BEEN HERE TWICE.
I HAVE SEEN HIM ON OTHER OCCASIONS, THOUGH. THROUGH HERE, ON HIS WAY SOMEWHERE.
WHERE WAS HE GOING?
I... I DON'T KNOW.
IT'S BEAUTIFUL, ISN'T IT?
THE CITY FROM THIS HEIGHT?
AND THE DARKNESS...BEYOND THE CITY.
YES.
IT'S ALL THERE IS.

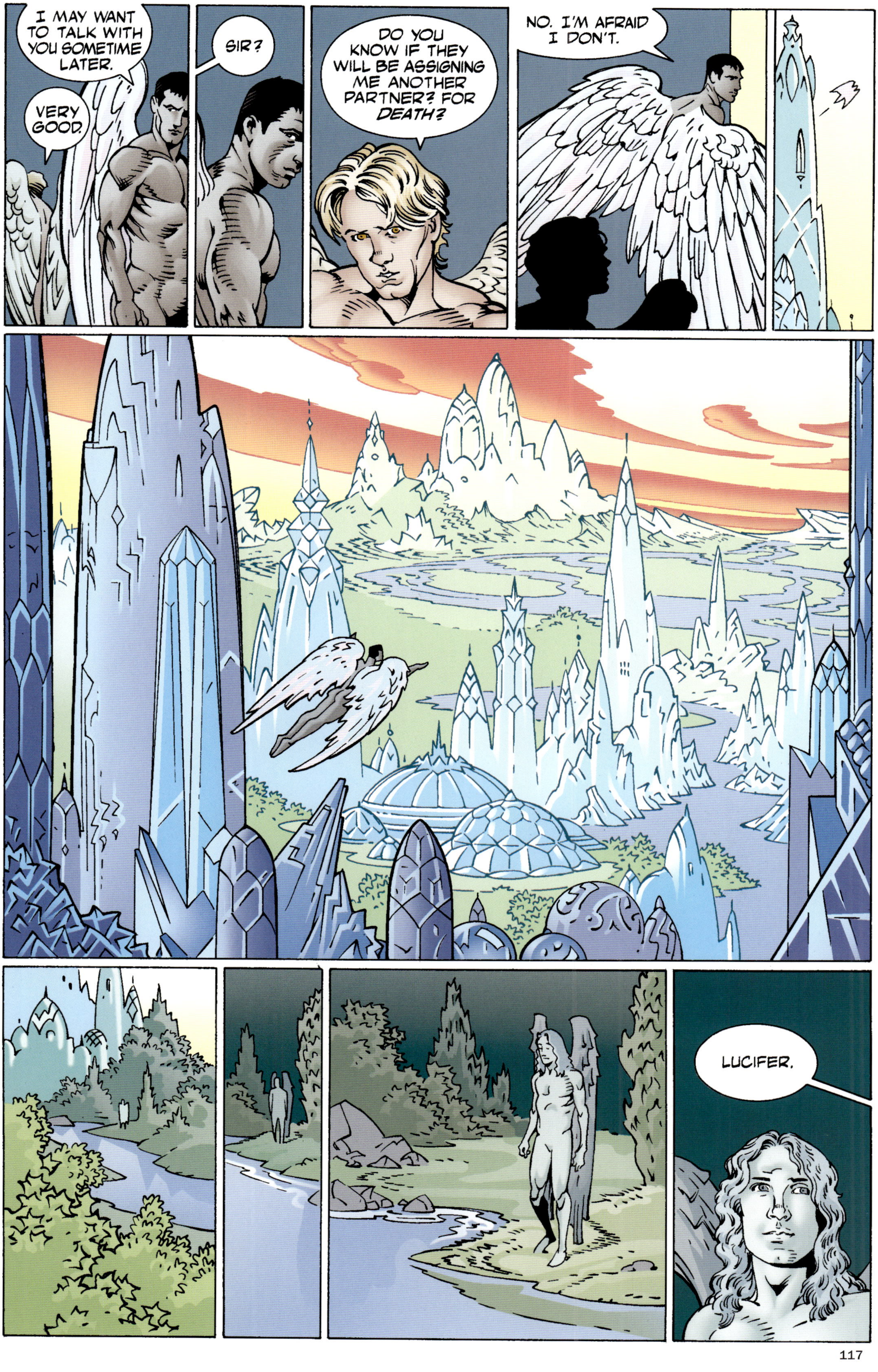
I MAY WANT TO TALK WITH YOU SOMETIME LATER.
VERY GOOD.
SIR?
DO YOU KNOW IF THEY WILL BE ASSIGNING ME ANOTHER PARTNER? FOR DEATH?
NO. I'M AFRAID I DON'T.
LUCIFER.

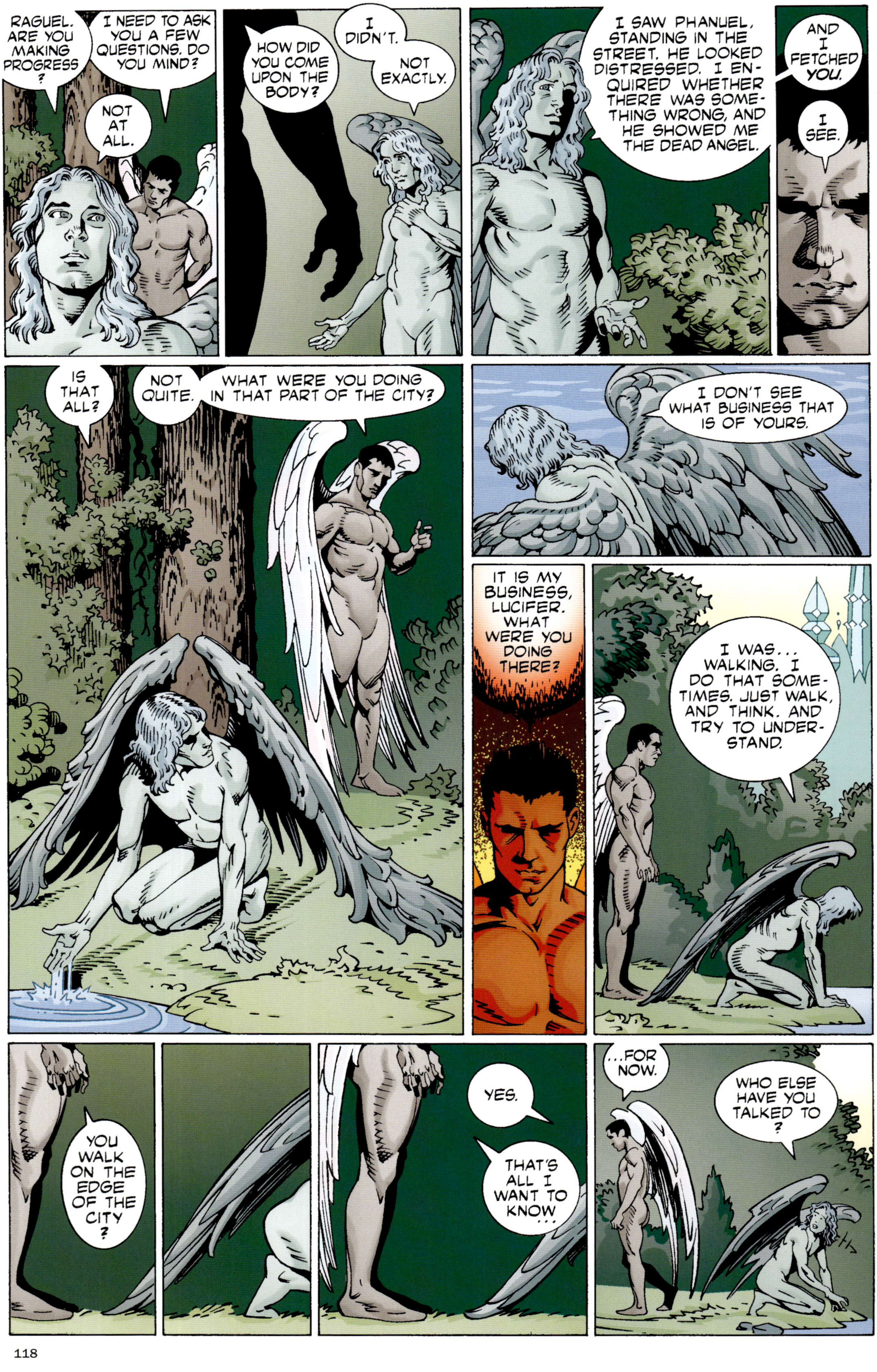
RAGUEL. ARE YOU MAKING PROGRESS?
I NEED TO ASK YOU A FEW QUESTIONS. DO YOU MIND?
NOT AT ALL.
HOW DID YOU COME UPON THE BODY?
I DIDN'T.
NOT EXACTLY.
I SAW PHANUEL, STANDING IN THE STREET. HE LOOKED DISTRESSED. I ENQUIRED WHETHER THERE WAS SOMETHING WRONG, AND HE SHOWED ME THE DEAD ANGEL.
AND I FETCHED YOU.
I SEE.
IS THAT ALL?
NOT QUITE.
WHAT WERE YOU DOING IN THAT PART OF THE CITY?
I DON'T SEE WHAT BUSINESS THAT IS OF YOURS.
IT IS MY BUSINESS, LUCIFER. WHAT WERE YOU DOING THERE?
I WAS... WALKING. I DO THAT SOMETIMES. JUST WALK, AND THINK. AND TRY TO UNDERSTAND.
YOU WALK ON THE EDGE OF THE CITY?
YES.
THAT'S ALL I WANT TO KNOW...
...FOR NOW.
WHO ELSE HAVE YOU TALKED TO?

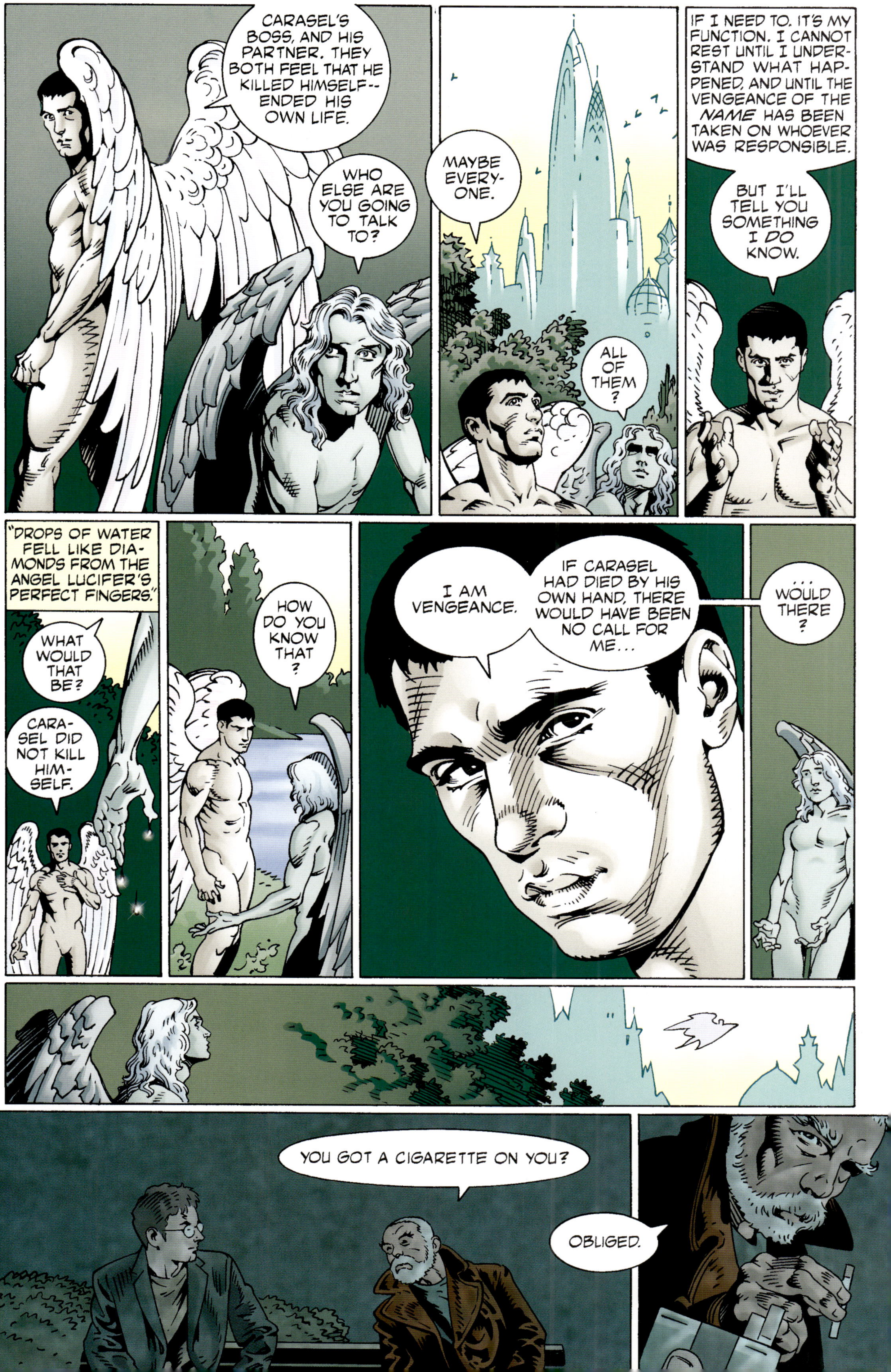
CARASEL'S BOSS, AND HIS PARTNER. THEY BOTH FEEL THAT HE KILLED HIMSELF-- ENDED HIS OWN LIFE.
WHO ELSE ARE YOU GOING TO TALK TO?
MAYBE EVERY-ONE.
ALL OF THEM?
IF I NEED TO. IT'S MY FUNCTION. I CANNOT REST UNTIL I UNDER-STAND WHAT HAP-PENED, AND UNTIL THE VENGEANCE OF THE NAME HAS BEEN TAKEN ON WHOEVER WAS RESPONSIBLE.
BUT I'LL TELL YOU SOMETHING I DO KNOW.
"DROPS OF WATER FELL LIKE DIA-MONDS FROM THE ANGEL LUCIFER'S PERFECT FINGERS."
WHAT WOULD THAT BE?
CARA-SEL DID NOT KILL HIM-SELF.
HOW DO YOU KNOW THAT?
I AM VENGEANCE.
IF CARASEL HAD DIED BY HIS OWN HAND, THERE WOULD HAVE BEEN NO CALL FOR ME...
...WOULD THERE?
YOU GOT A CIGARETTE ON YOU?
OBLIGED.

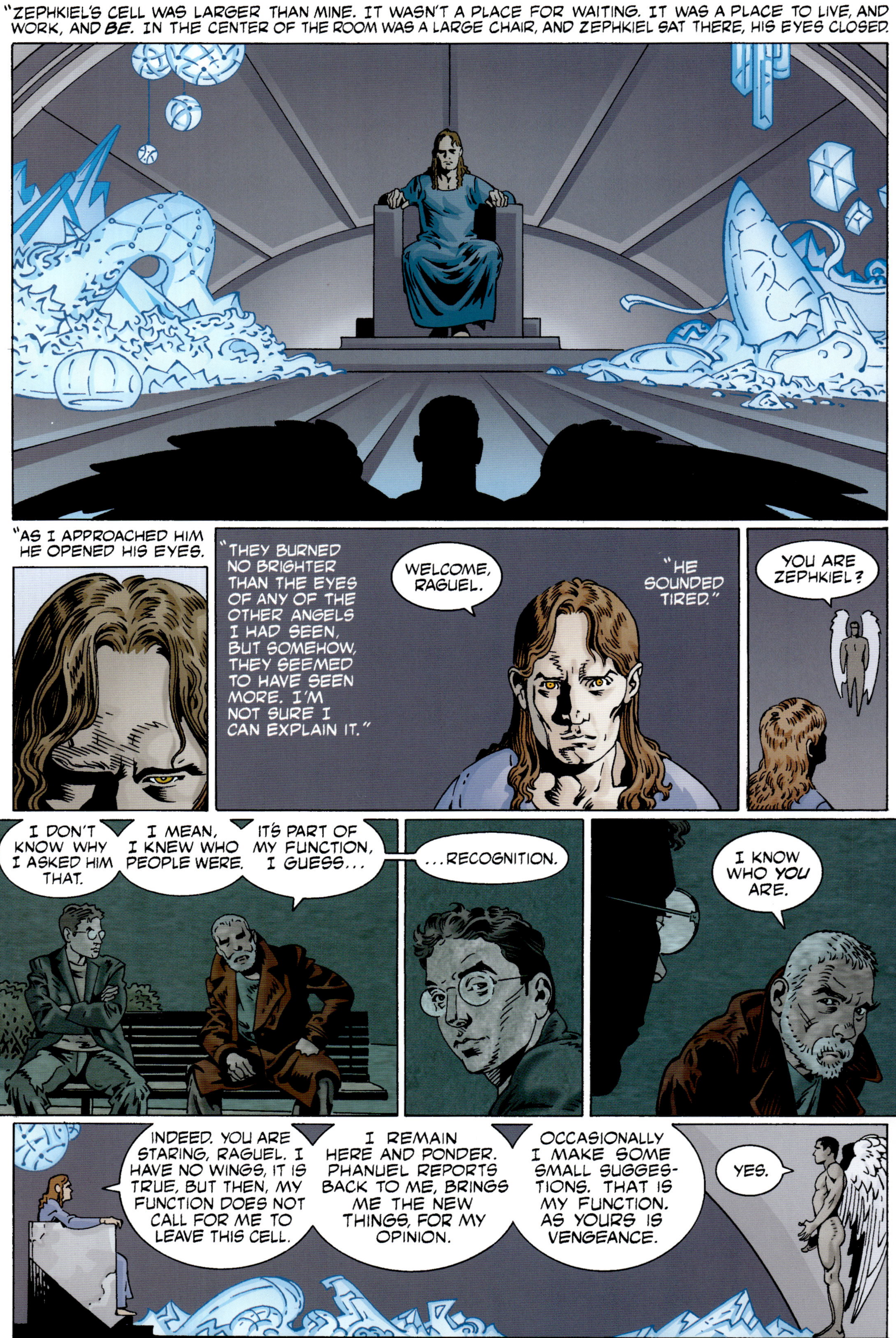
"ZEPHKIEL'S CELL WAS LARGER THAN MINE. IT WASN'T A PLACE FOR WAITING. IT WAS A PLACE TO LIVE, AND WORK, AND *BE.* IN THE CENTER OF THE ROOM WAS A LARGE CHAIR, AND ZEPHKIEL SAT THERE, HIS EYES CLOSED.
"AS I APPROACHED HIM HE OPENED HIS EYES.
"THEY BURNED NO BRIGHTER THAN THE EYES OF ANY OF THE OTHER ANGELS I HAD SEEN, BUT SOMEHOW, THEY SEEMED TO HAVE SEEN MORE. I'M NOT SURE I CAN EXPLAIN IT."
WELCOME, RAGUEL.
"HE SOUNDED TIRED."
YOU ARE ZEPHKIEL?
I DON'T KNOW WHY I ASKED HIM THAT.
I MEAN, I KNEW WHO PEOPLE WERE.
IT'S PART OF MY FUNCTION, I GUESS...
...RECOGNITION.
I KNOW WHO *YOU* ARE.
INDEED. YOU ARE STARING, RAGUEL. I HAVE NO WINGS, IT IS TRUE, BUT THEN, MY FUNCTION DOES NOT CALL FOR ME TO LEAVE THIS CELL.
I REMAIN HERE AND PONDER. PHANUEL REPORTS BACK TO ME, BRINGS ME THE NEW THINGS, FOR MY OPINION.
OCCASIONALLY I MAKE SOME SMALL SUGGES-TIONS. THAT IS MY FUNCTION. AS YOURS IS VENGEANCE.
YES.

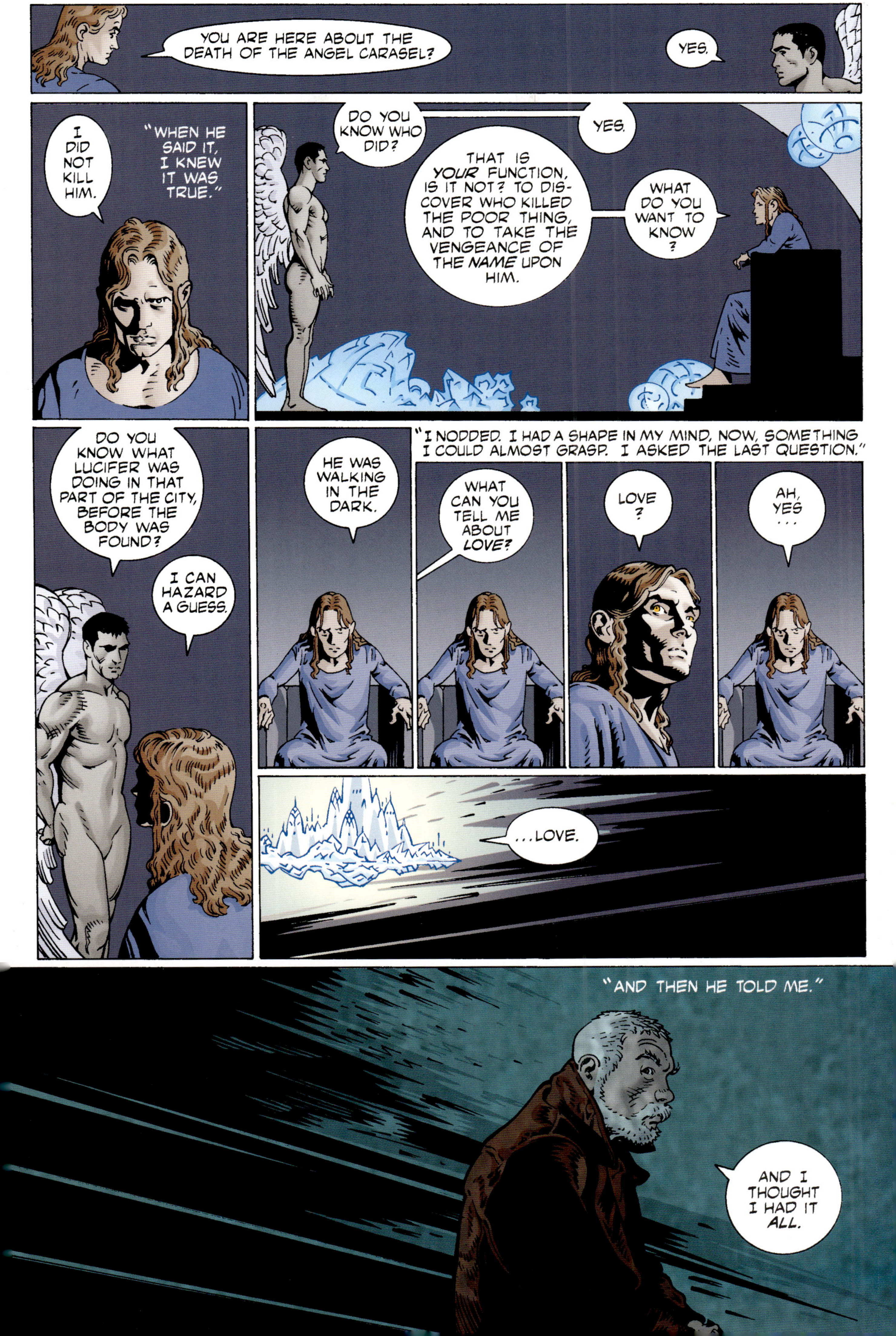

YOU ARE HERE ABOUT THE DEATH OF THE ANGEL CARASEL?
YES.
I DID NOT KILL HIM.
"WHEN HE SAID IT, I KNEW IT WAS TRUE."
DO YOU KNOW WHO DID?
YES.
THAT IS YOUR FUNCTION, IS IT NOT? TO DISCOVER WHO KILLED THE POOR THING, AND TO TAKE THE VENGEANCE OF THE NAME UPON HIM.
WHAT DO YOU WANT TO KNOW?
DO YOU KNOW WHAT LUCIFER WAS DOING IN THAT PART OF THE CITY, BEFORE THE BODY WAS FOUND?
I CAN HAZARD A GUESS.
HE WAS WALKING IN THE DARK.
"I NODDED. I HAD A SHAPE IN MY MIND, NOW, SOMETHING I COULD ALMOST GRASP. I ASKED THE LAST QUESTION."
WHAT CAN YOU TELL ME ABOUT LOVE?
LOVE?
AH, YES . . .
. . . LOVE.
"AND THEN HE TOLD ME."
AND I THOUGHT I HAD IT ALL.

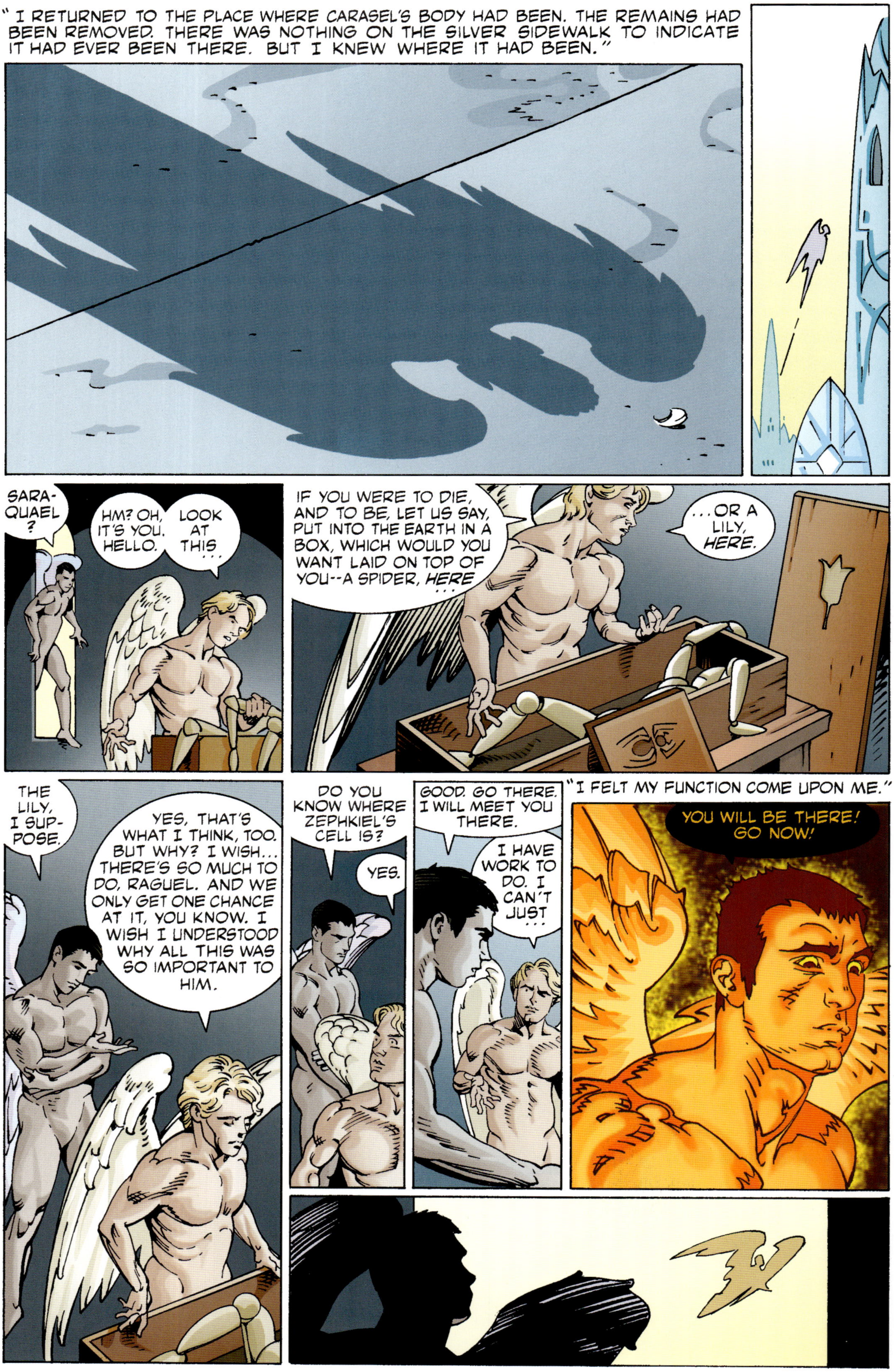
"I RETURNED TO THE PLACE WHERE CARASEL'S BODY HAD BEEN. THE REMAINS HAD BEEN REMOVED. THERE WAS NOTHING ON THE SILVER SIDEWALK TO INDICATE IT HAD EVER BEEN THERE. BUT I KNEW WHERE IT HAD BEEN."
SARAQUAEL?
HM? OH, IT'S YOU. HELLO.
LOOK AT THIS...
IF YOU WERE TO DIE, AND TO BE, LET US SAY, PUT INTO THE EARTH IN A BOX, WHICH WOULD YOU WANT LAID ON TOP OF YOU--A SPIDER, HERE...
...OR A LILY, HERE.
THE LILY, I SUPPOSE.
YES, THAT'S WHAT I THINK, TOO. BUT WHY? I WISH... THERE'S SO MUCH TO DO, RAGUEL. AND WE ONLY GET ONE CHANCE AT IT, YOU KNOW. I WISH I UNDERSTOOD WHY ALL THIS WAS SO IMPORTANT TO HIM.
DO YOU KNOW WHERE ZEPHKIEL'S CELL IS?
YES.
GOOD. GO THERE. I WILL MEET YOU THERE.
I HAVE WORK TO DO. I CAN'T JUST...
"I FELT MY FUNCTION COME UPON ME."
YOU WILL BE THERE! GO NOW!

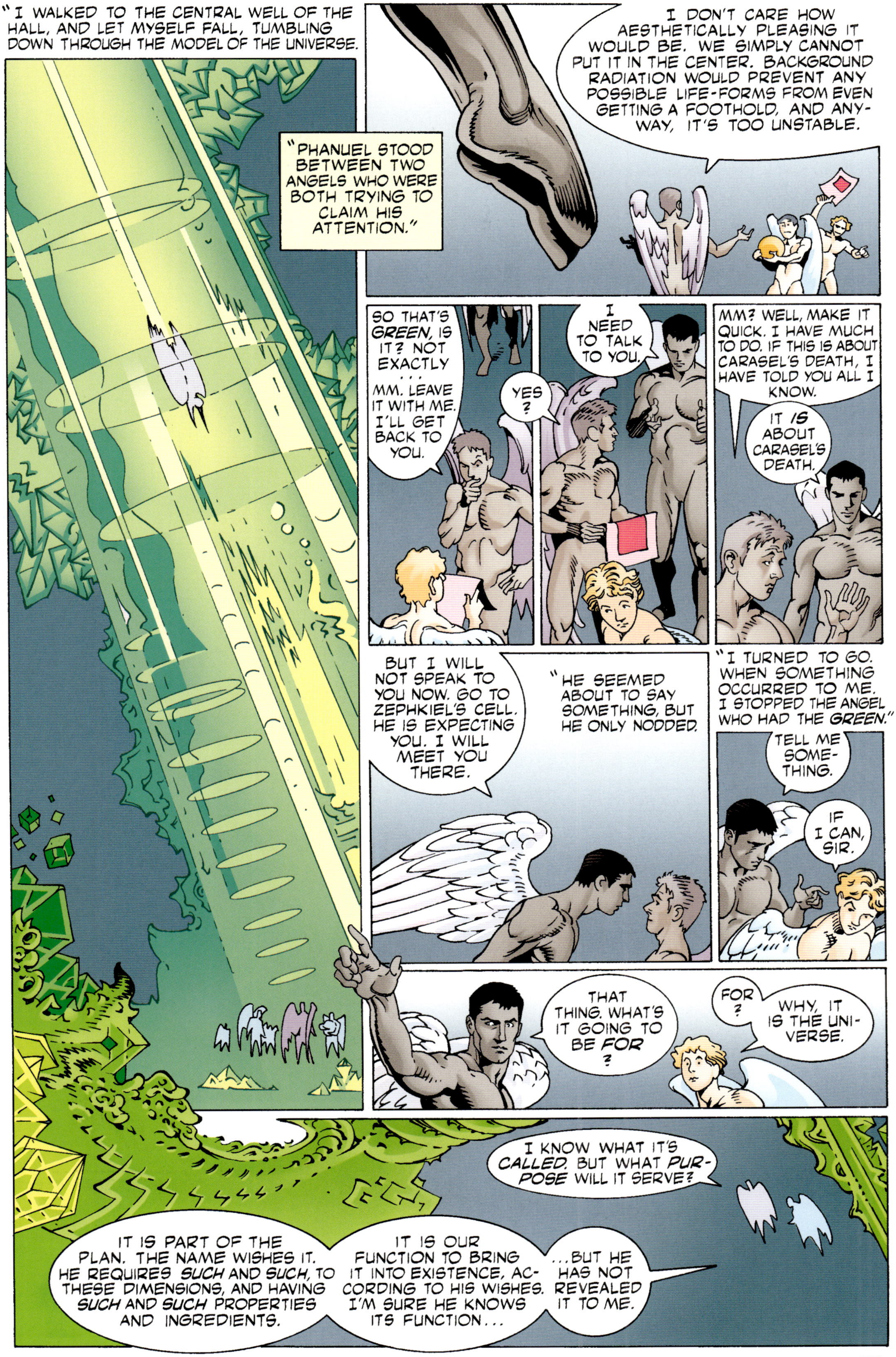
"I WALKED TO THE CENTRAL WELL OF THE HALL, AND LET MYSELF FALL, TUMBLING DOWN THROUGH THE MODEL OF THE UNIVERSE.
"PHANUEL STOOD BETWEEN TWO ANGELS WHO WERE BOTH TRYING TO CLAIM HIS ATTENTION."
I DON'T CARE HOW AESTHETICALLY PLEASING IT WOULD BE. WE SIMPLY CANNOT PUT IT IN THE CENTER. BACKGROUND RADIATION WOULD PREVENT ANY POSSIBLE LIFE-FORMS FROM EVEN GETTING A FOOTHOLD, AND ANYWAY, IT'S TOO UNSTABLE.
SO THAT'S GREEN, IS IT? NOT EXACTLY . . . MM. LEAVE IT WITH ME. I'LL GET BACK TO YOU.
YES?
I NEED TO TALK TO YOU.
MM? WELL, MAKE IT QUICK. I HAVE MUCH TO DO. IF THIS IS ABOUT CARASEL'S DEATH, I HAVE TOLD YOU ALL I KNOW.
IT IS ABOUT CARASEL'S DEATH.
BUT I WILL NOT SPEAK TO YOU NOW. GO TO ZEPHKIEL'S CELL. HE IS EXPECTING YOU. I WILL MEET YOU THERE.
"HE SEEMED ABOUT TO SAY SOMETHING, BUT HE ONLY NODDED.
"I TURNED TO GO. WHEN SOMETHING OCCURRED TO ME. I STOPPED THE ANGEL WHO HAD THE GREEN."
TELL ME SOMETHING.
IF I CAN, SIR.
THAT THING. WHAT'S IT GOING TO BE FOR?
FOR?
WHY, IT IS THE UNIVERSE.
I KNOW WHAT IT'S CALLED. BUT WHAT PURPOSE WILL IT SERVE?
IT IS PART OF THE PLAN. THE NAME WISHES IT. HE REQUIRES SUCH AND SUCH, TO THESE DIMENSIONS, AND HAVING SUCH AND SUCH PROPERTIES AND INGREDIENTS.
IT IS OUR FUNCTION TO BRING IT INTO EXISTENCE, ACCORDING TO HIS WISHES. I'M SURE HE KNOWS ITS FUNCTION . . .
. . . BUT HE HAS NOT REVEALED IT TO ME.

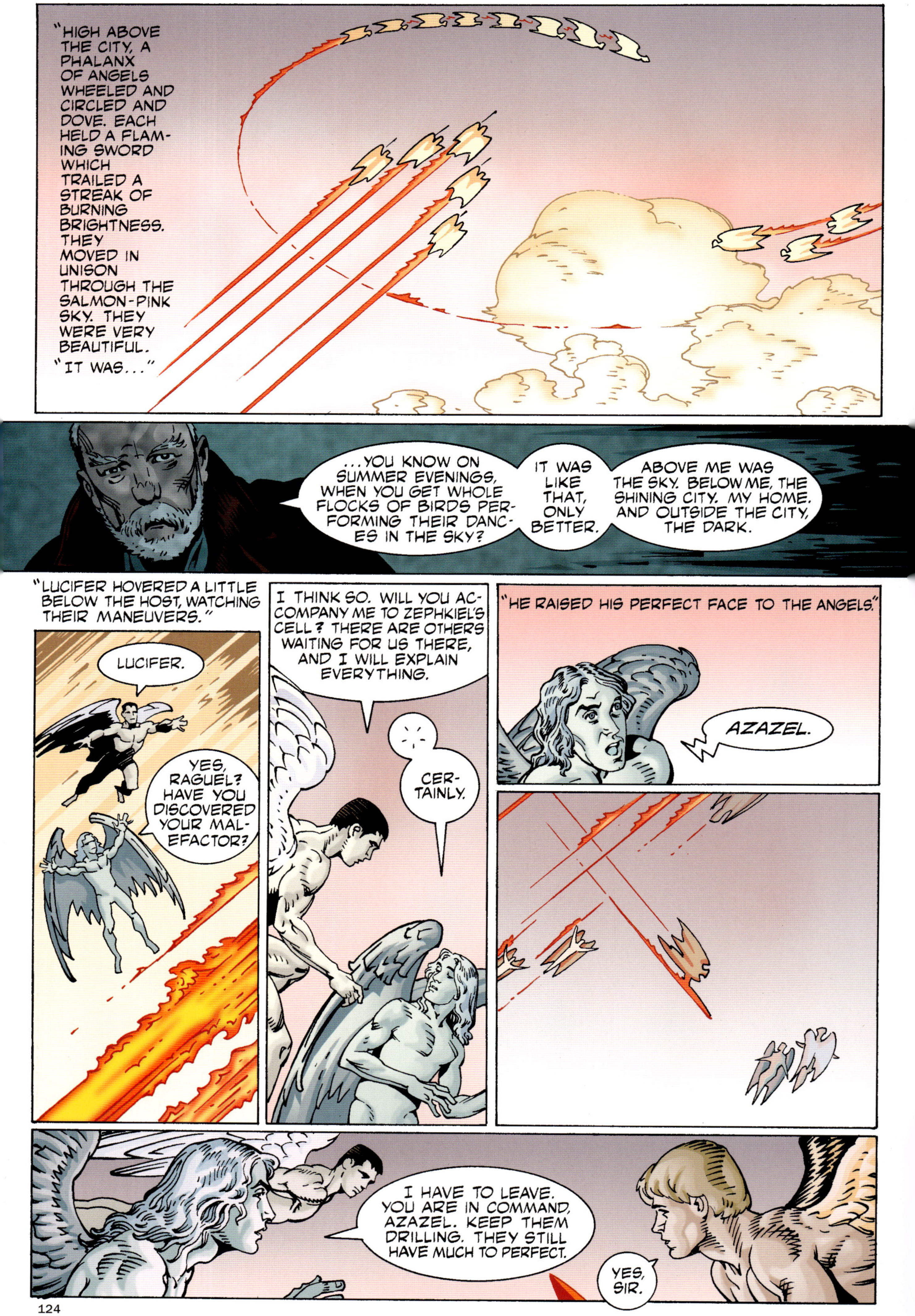
"HIGH ABOVE THE CITY, A PHALANX OF ANGELS WHEELED AND CIRCLED AND DOVE. EACH HELD A FLAMING SWORD WHICH TRAILED A STREAK OF BURNING BRIGHTNESS. THEY MOVED IN UNISON THROUGH THE SALMON-PINK SKY. THEY WERE VERY BEAUTIFUL.
"IT WAS..."
...YOU KNOW ON SUMMER EVENINGS, WHEN YOU GET WHOLE FLOCKS OF BIRDS PERFORMING THEIR DANCES IN THE SKY?
IT WAS LIKE THAT, ONLY BETTER.
ABOVE ME WAS THE SKY. BELOW ME, THE SHINING CITY. MY HOME. AND OUTSIDE THE CITY, THE DARK.
"LUCIFER HOVERED A LITTLE BELOW THE HOST, WATCHING THEIR MANEUVERS."
LUCIFER.
YES, RAGUEL? HAVE YOU DISCOVERED YOUR MALEFACTOR?
I THINK SO. WILL YOU ACCOMPANY ME TO ZEPHKIEL'S CELL? THERE ARE OTHERS WAITING FOR US THERE, AND I WILL EXPLAIN EVERYTHING.
CERTAINLY.
"HE RAISED HIS PERFECT FACE TO THE ANGELS."
AZAZEL.
I HAVE TO LEAVE. YOU ARE IN COMMAND, AZAZEL. KEEP THEM DRILLING. THEY STILL HAVE MUCH TO PERFECT.
YES, SIR.

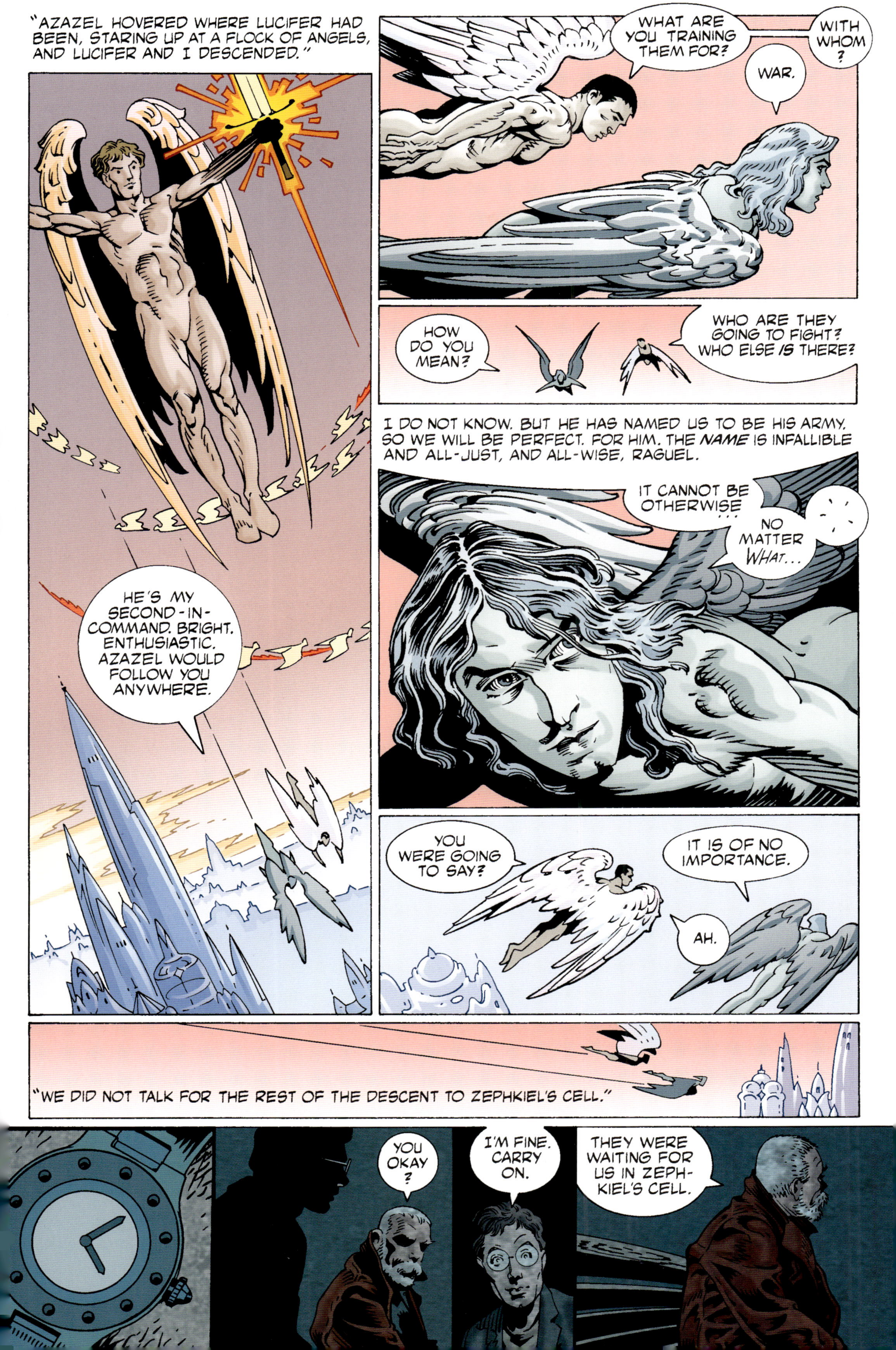
"AZAZEL HOVERED WHERE LUCIFER HAD BEEN, STARING UP AT A FLOCK OF ANGELS, AND LUCIFER AND I DESCENDED."
HE'S MY SECOND-IN-COMMAND. BRIGHT. ENTHUSIASTIC. AZAZEL WOULD FOLLOW YOU ANYWHERE.
WHAT ARE YOU TRAINING THEM FOR?
WITH WHOM ?
WAR.
HOW DO YOU MEAN?
WHO ARE THEY GOING TO FIGHT? WHO ELSE *IS* THERE?
I DO NOT KNOW. BUT HE HAS NAMED US TO BE HIS ARMY. SO WE WILL BE PERFECT. FOR HIM. THE *NAME* IS INFALLIBLE AND ALL-JUST, AND ALL-WISE, RAGUEL.
IT CANNOT BE OTHERWISE . . .
NO MATTER *WHAT*...
YOU WERE GOING TO SAY?
IT IS OF NO IMPORTANCE.
AH.
"WE DID NOT TALK FOR THE REST OF THE DESCENT TO ZEPHKIEL'S CELL."
YOU OKAY ?
I'M FINE. CARRY ON.
THEY WERE WAITING FOR US IN ZEPH-KIEL'S CELL.

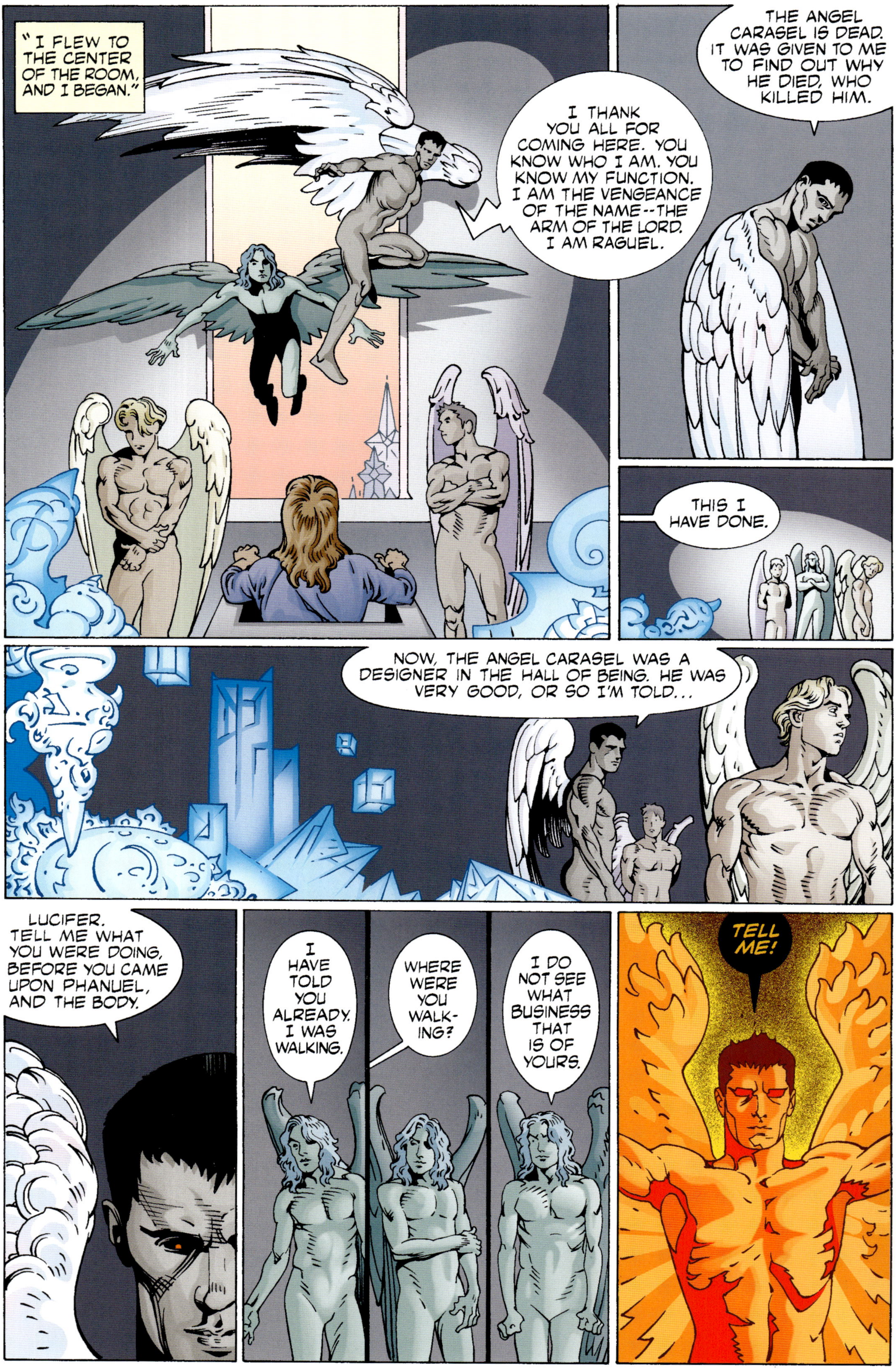
"I FLEW TO THE CENTER OF THE ROOM, AND I BEGAN."
I THANK YOU ALL FOR COMING HERE. YOU KNOW WHO I AM. YOU KNOW MY FUNCTION. I AM THE VENGEANCE OF THE NAME--THE ARM OF THE LORD. I AM RAGUEL.
THE ANGEL CARASEL IS DEAD. IT WAS GIVEN TO ME TO FIND OUT WHY HE DIED, WHO KILLED HIM.
THIS I HAVE DONE.
NOW, THE ANGEL CARASEL WAS A DESIGNER IN THE HALL OF BEING. HE WAS VERY GOOD, OR SO I'M TOLD...
LUCIFER. TELL ME WHAT YOU WERE DOING, BEFORE YOU CAME UPON PHANUEL, AND THE BODY.
I HAVE TOLD YOU ALREADY. I WAS WALKING.
WHERE WERE YOU WALKING?
I DO NOT SEE WHAT BUSINESS THAT IS OF YOURS.
TELL ME!

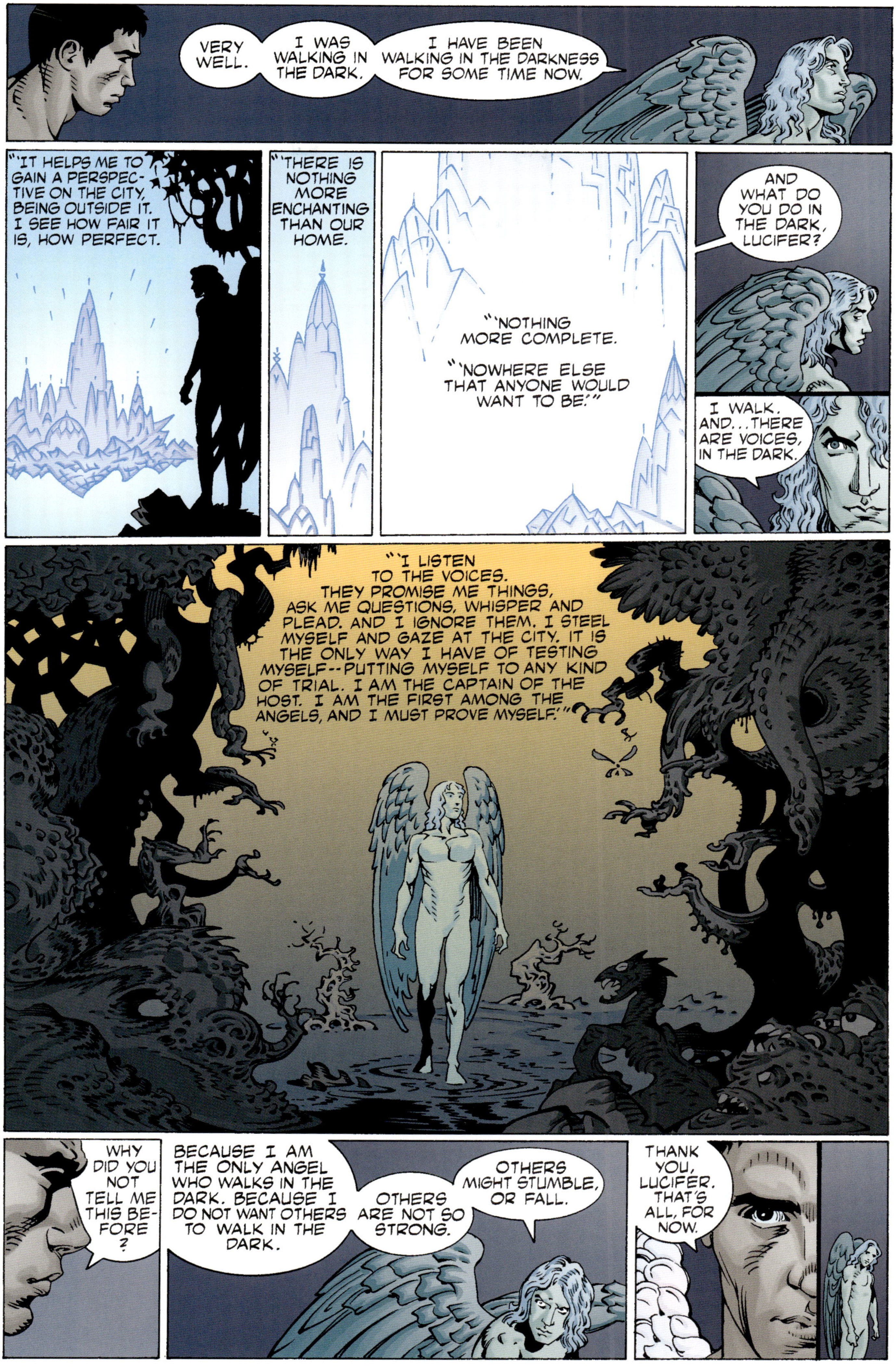
VERY WELL.
I WAS WALKING IN THE DARK.
I HAVE BEEN WALKING IN THE DARKNESS FOR SOME TIME NOW.
"IT HELPS ME TO GAIN A PERSPECTIVE ON THE CITY, BEING OUTSIDE IT. I SEE HOW FAIR IT IS, HOW PERFECT.
"'THERE IS NOTHING MORE ENCHANTING THAN OUR HOME.
"'NOTHING MORE COMPLETE.
"'NOWHERE ELSE THAT ANYONE WOULD WANT TO BE.'"
AND WHAT DO YOU DO IN THE DARK, LUCIFER?
I WALK. AND...THERE ARE VOICES, IN THE DARK.
"'I LISTEN TO THE VOICES. THEY PROMISE ME THINGS, ASK ME QUESTIONS, WHISPER AND PLEAD. AND I IGNORE THEM. I STEEL MYSELF AND GAZE AT THE CITY. IT IS THE ONLY WAY I HAVE OF TESTING MYSELF--PUTTING MYSELF TO ANY KIND OF TRIAL. I AM THE CAPTAIN OF THE HOST. I AM THE FIRST AMONG THE ANGELS, AND I MUST PROVE MYSELF.'"
WHY DID YOU NOT TELL ME THIS BEFORE?
BECAUSE I AM THE ONLY ANGEL WHO WALKS IN THE DARK. BECAUSE I DO NOT WANT OTHERS TO WALK IN THE DARK.
OTHERS ARE NOT SO STRONG.
OTHERS MIGHT STUMBLE, OR FALL.
THANK YOU, LUCIFER. THAT'S ALL, FOR NOW.

PHANUEL. HOW LONG HAVE YOU BEEN TAKING CREDIT FOR CARASEL'S WORK?

WH...

WELL?

I... I WOULD NOT TAKE CREDIT FOR ANOTHER'S WORK.

BUT YOU DID TAKE CREDIT FOR LOVE.

...YES, I DID.

WOULD YOU CARE TO EXPLAIN TO US ALL WHAT LOVE IS?

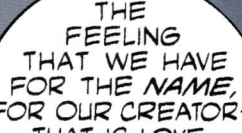

"HE GLANCED AROUND UNCOMFORTABLY."

IT'S A FEELING OF DEEP AFFECTION FOR ANOTHER BEING, OFTEN COMBINED WITH PASSION OR DESIRE -- A NEED TO BE WITH ANOTHER.

THE FEELING THAT WE HAVE FOR THE NAME, FOR OUR CREATOR -- THAT IS LOVE... AMONGST OTHER THINGS.

LOVE WILL BE AN IMPULSE WHICH WILL INSPIRE AND RUIN IN EQUAL MEASURE.

WE ARE VERY... AHH...

PROUD OF IT.

WHO DID THE MAJORITY OF THE WORK ON LOVE? NO, DON'T ANSWER. LET ME ASK THE OTHERS FIRST.

ZEPHKIEL? WHEN PHANUEL PASSED THE DETAILS OF LOVE TO YOU FOR APPROVAL, WHO DID HE TELL YOU WAS RESPONSIBLE FOR IT?

HE TOLD ME IT WAS HIS PROJECT.

THANK YOU, SIR.

NOW, SARAQUAEL, WHOSE WAS LOVE?

MINE. MINE AND CARASEL'S. PERHAPS MORE HIS THAN MINE, BUT WE WORKED ON IT TOGETHER.

YOU KNEW THAT PHANUEL WAS CLAIMING THE CREDIT FOR IT?

YES, AND YOU PERMITTED THIS?

HE -- HE PROMISED US THAT HE WOULD GIVE US A GOOD PROJECT OF OUR OWN TO FOLLOW. HE PROMISED THAT IF WE SAID NOTHING WE WOULD BE GIVEN MORE BIG PROJECTS...

...AND HE WAS TRUE TO HIS WORD.

HE GAVE US DEATH.

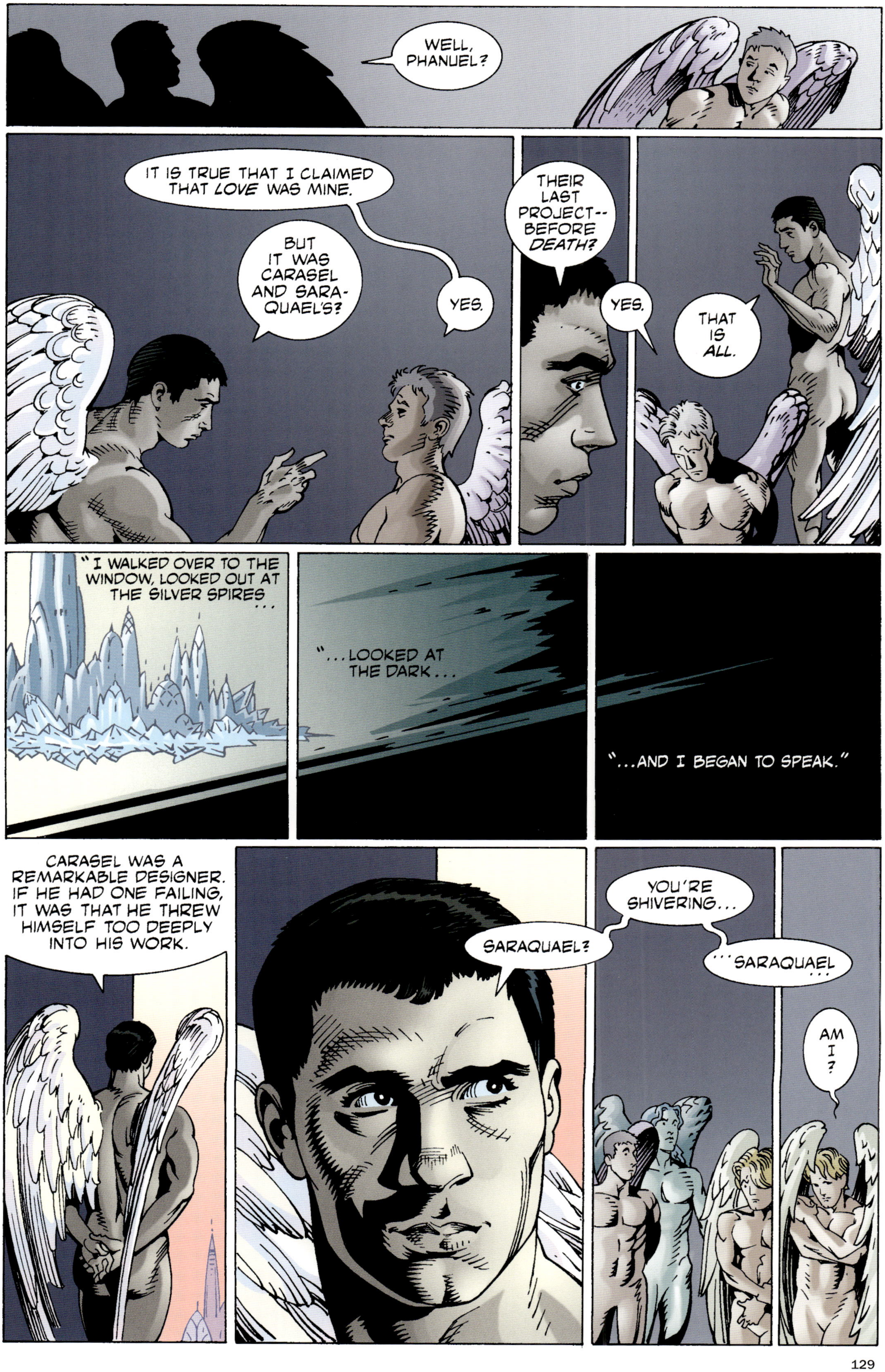
WELL, PHANUEL?
IT IS TRUE THAT I CLAIMED THAT LOVE WAS MINE.
BUT IT WAS CARASEL AND SARAQUAEL'S?
YES.
THEIR LAST PROJECT--BEFORE DEATH?
YES.
THAT IS ALL.
"I WALKED OVER TO THE WINDOW, LOOKED OUT AT THE SILVER SPIRES . . .
". . . LOOKED AT THE DARK . . .
". . . AND I BEGAN TO SPEAK."
CARASEL WAS A REMARKABLE DESIGNER. IF HE HAD ONE FAILING, IT WAS THAT HE THREW HIMSELF TOO DEEPLY INTO HIS WORK.
SARAQUAEL?
YOU'RE SHIVERING . . .
. . . SARAQUAEL . . .
AM I?

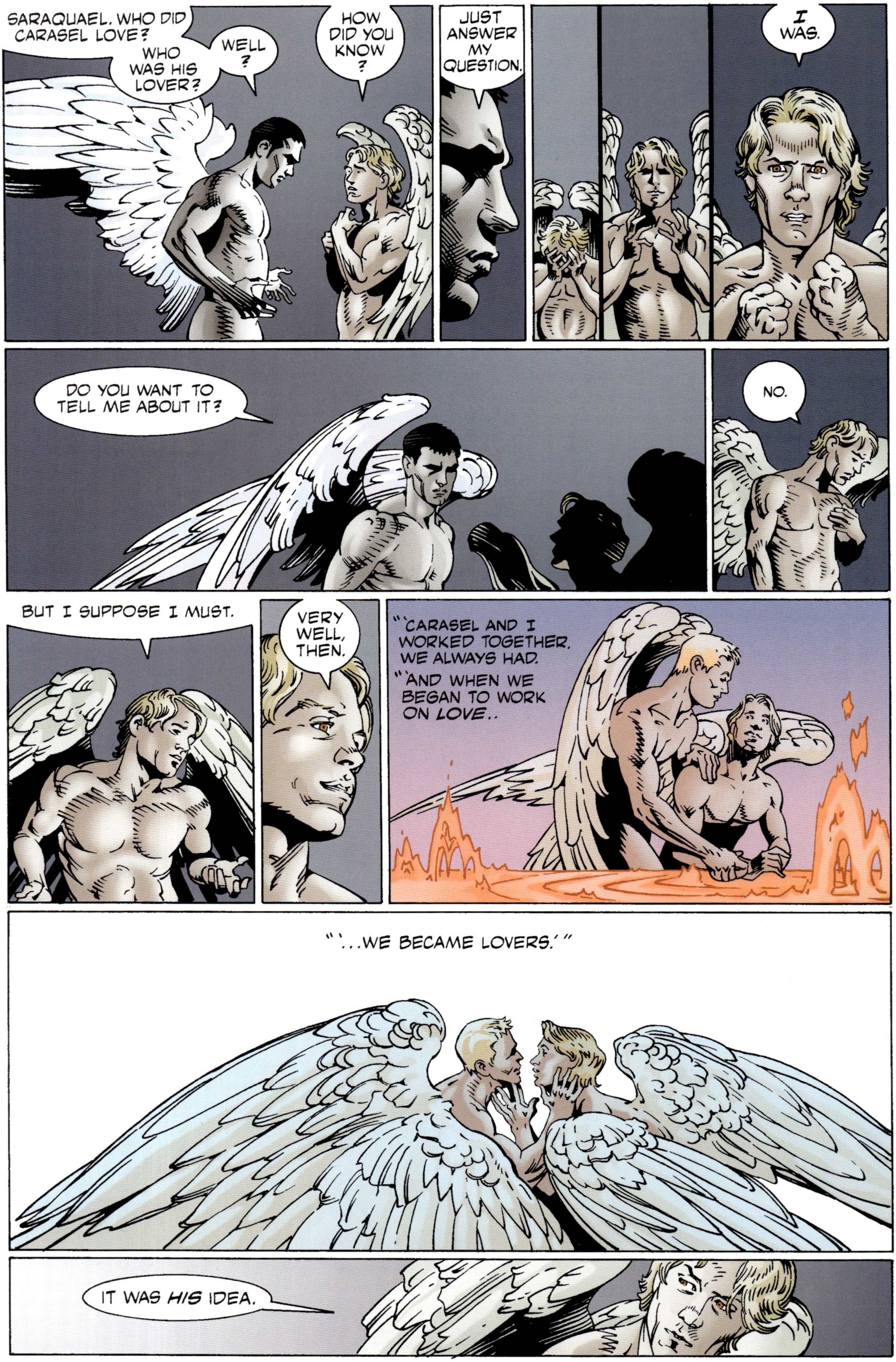
SARAQUAEL, WHO DID CARASEL LOVE?
WHO WAS HIS LOVER?
WELL?
HOW DID YOU KNOW?
JUST ANSWER MY QUESTION.
I WAS.
DO YOU WANT TO TELL ME ABOUT IT?
NO.
BUT I SUPPOSE I MUST.
VERY WELL, THEN.
"CARASEL AND I WORKED TOGETHER. WE ALWAYS HAD.
"AND WHEN WE BEGAN TO WORK ON LOVE..
"'...WE BECAME LOVERS.'"
IT WAS HIS IDEA.

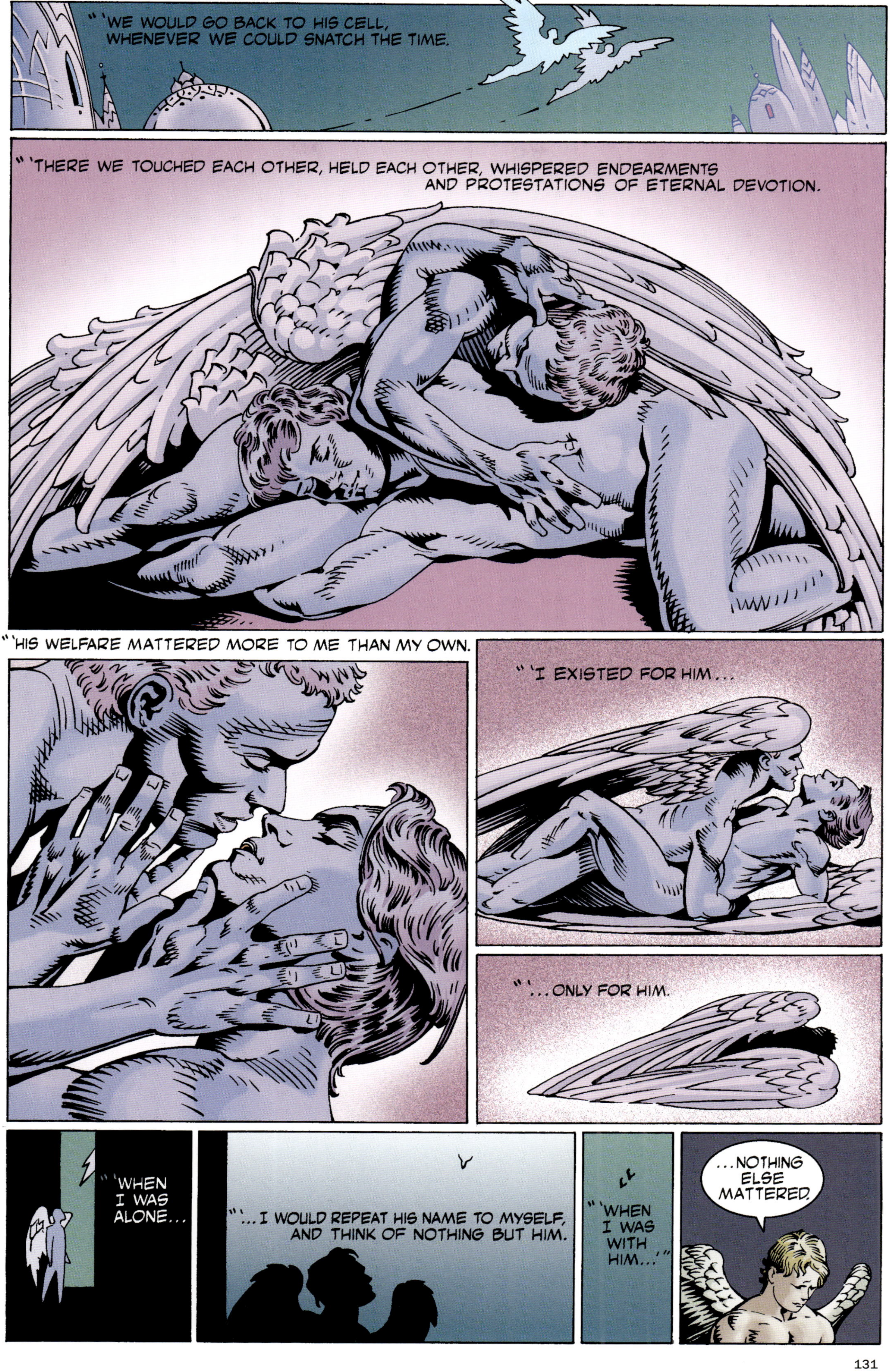
"'WE WOULD GO BACK TO HIS CELL, WHENEVER WE COULD SNATCH THE TIME.
"'THERE WE TOUCHED EACH OTHER, HELD EACH OTHER, WHISPERED ENDEARMENTS AND PROTESTATIONS OF ETERNAL DEVOTION.
"'HIS WELFARE MATTERED MORE TO ME THAN MY OWN.
"'I EXISTED FOR HIM...
"'...ONLY FOR HIM.
"'WHEN I WAS ALONE...
"'...I WOULD REPEAT HIS NAME TO MYSELF, AND THINK OF NOTHING BUT HIM.
"'WHEN I WAS WITH HIM...'"
...NOTHING ELSE MATTERED.

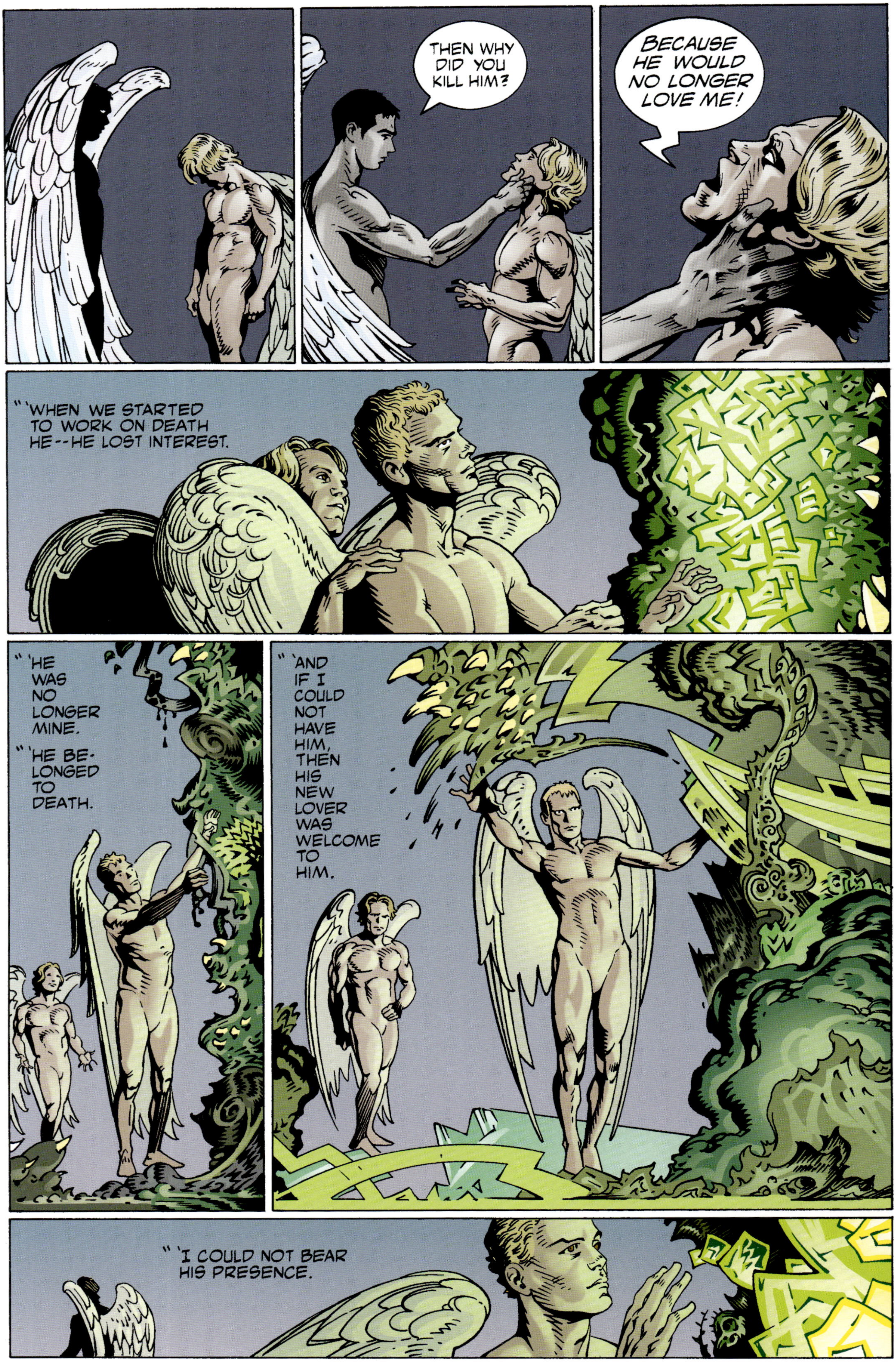
THEN WHY DID YOU KILL HIM?
BECAUSE HE WOULD NO LONGER LOVE ME!
"'WHEN WE STARTED TO WORK ON DEATH HE--HE LOST INTEREST.
"'HE WAS NO LONGER MINE.
"'HE BE-LONGED TO DEATH.
"'AND IF I COULD NOT HAVE HIM, THEN HIS NEW LOVER WAS WELCOME TO HIM.
"'I COULD NOT BEAR HIS PRESENCE.

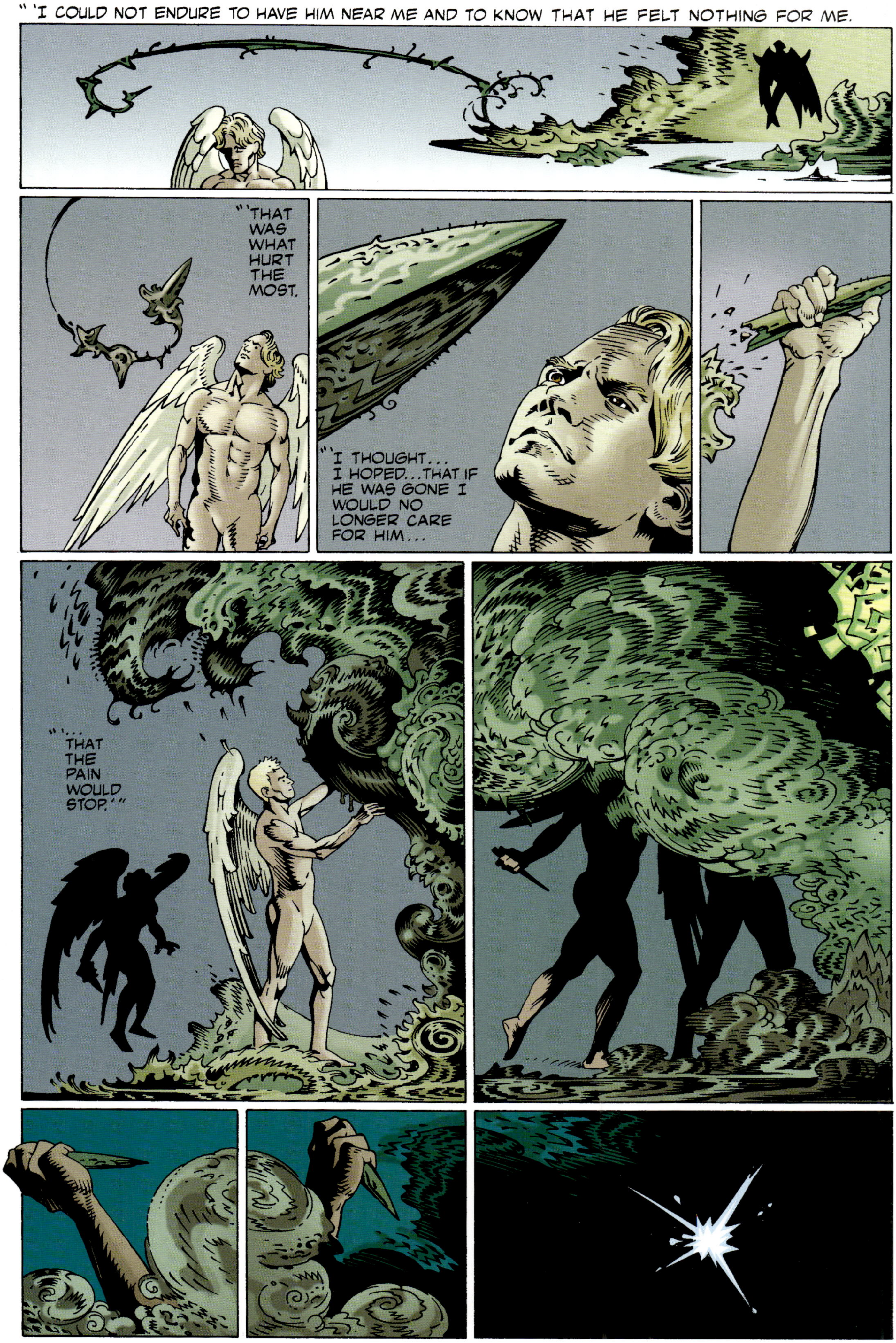
" 'I COULD NOT ENDURE TO HAVE HIM NEAR ME AND TO KNOW THAT HE FELT NOTHING FOR ME.
" 'THAT WAS WHAT HURT THE MOST.
" 'I THOUGHT... I HOPED...THAT IF HE WAS GONE I WOULD NO LONGER CARE FOR HIM...
" '...THAT THE PAIN WOULD STOP.' "

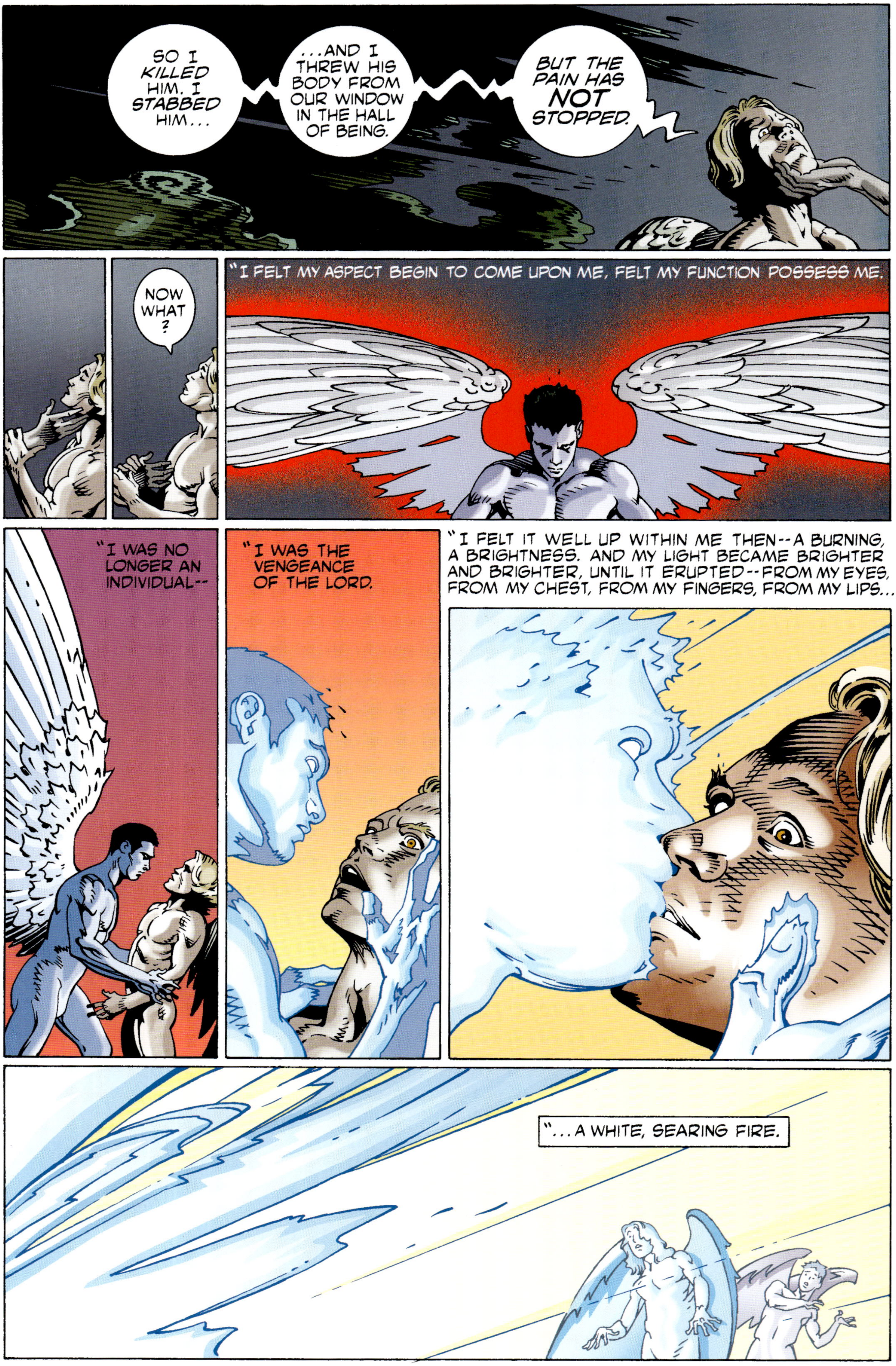
SO I KILLED HIM. I STABBED HIM...
...AND I THREW HIS BODY FROM OUR WINDOW IN THE HALL OF BEING.
BUT THE PAIN HAS NOT STOPPED.
NOW WHAT?
"I FELT MY ASPECT BEGIN TO COME UPON ME, FELT MY FUNCTION POSSESS ME.
"I WAS NO LONGER AN INDIVIDUAL--
"I WAS THE VENGEANCE OF THE LORD.
"I FELT IT WELL UP WITHIN ME THEN--A BURNING, A BRIGHTNESS. AND MY LIGHT BECAME BRIGHTER AND BRIGHTER, UNTIL IT ERUPTED--FROM MY EYES, FROM MY CHEST, FROM MY FINGERS, FROM MY LIPS...
"...A WHITE, SEARING FIRE.

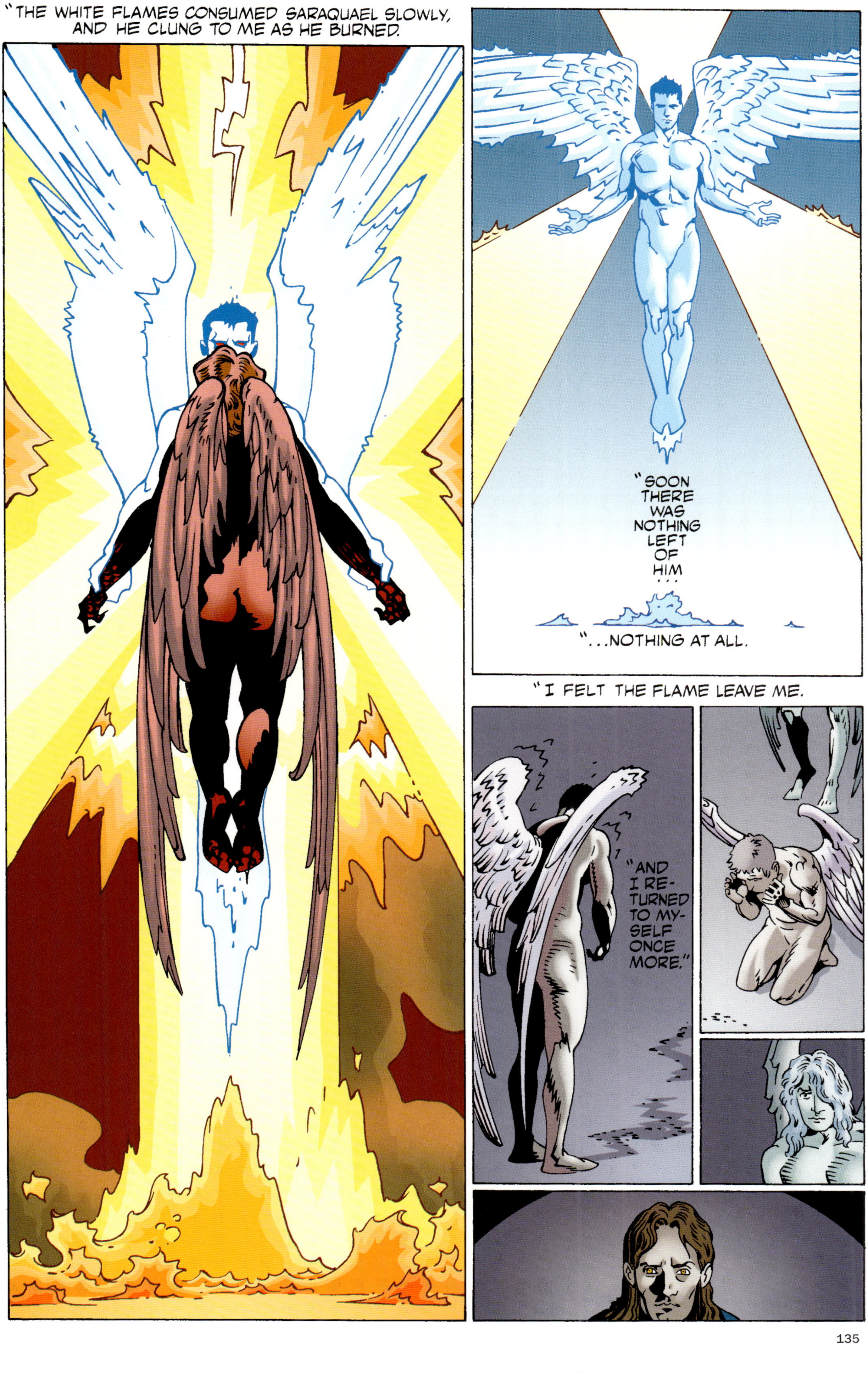
"THE WHITE FLAMES CONSUMED SARAQUAEL SLOWLY, AND HE CLUNG TO ME AS HE BURNED.
"SOON THERE WAS NOTHING LEFT OF HIM . . .
"...NOTHING AT ALL.
"I FELT THE FLAME LEAVE ME.
"AND I RETURNED TO MYSELF ONCE MORE."

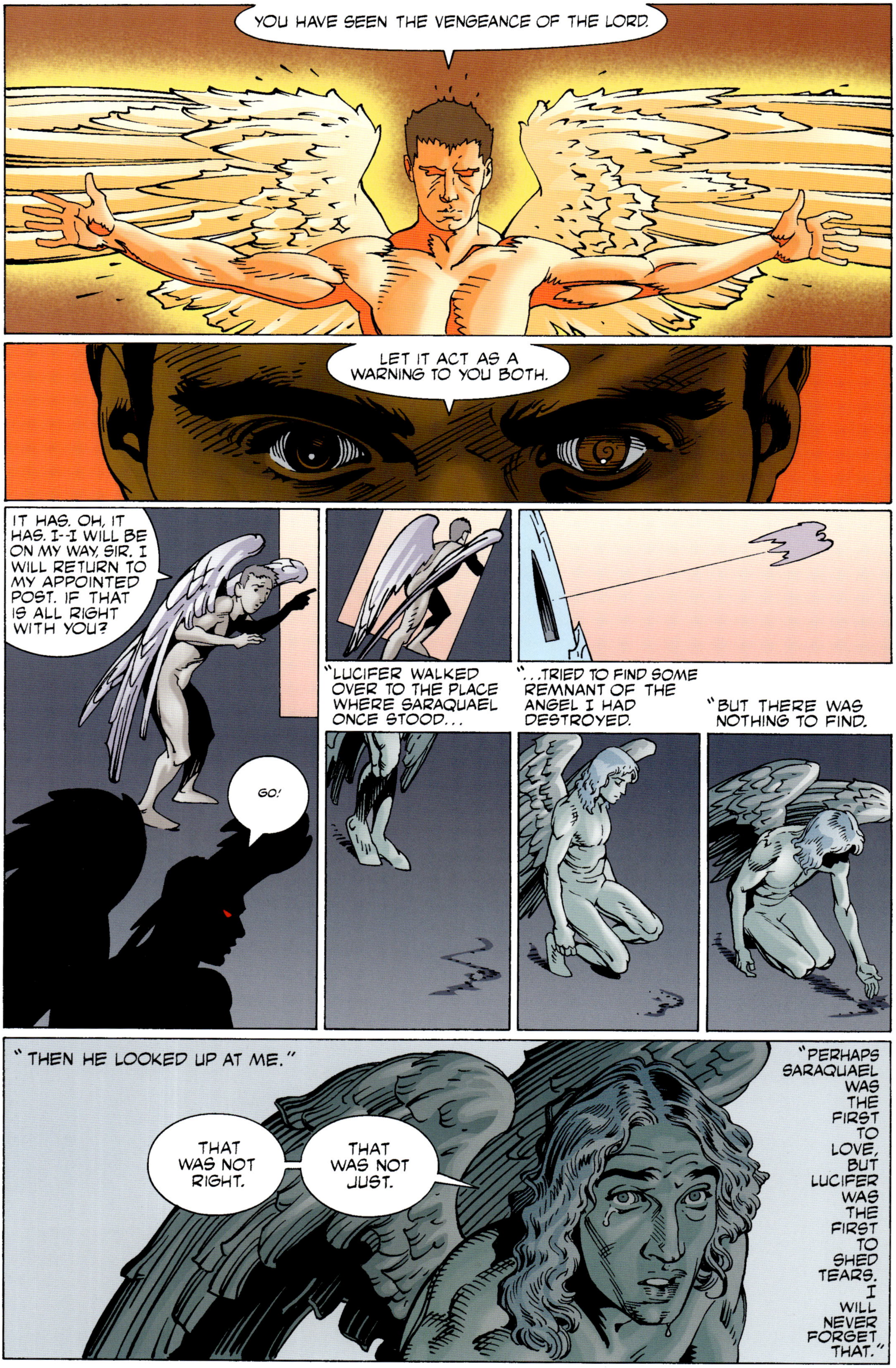
YOU HAVE SEEN THE VENGEANCE OF THE LORD.
LET IT ACT AS A WARNING TO YOU BOTH.
IT HAS. OH, IT HAS. I--I WILL BE ON MY WAY, SIR. I WILL RETURN TO MY APPOINTED POST. IF THAT IS ALL RIGHT WITH YOU?
GO!
"LUCIFER WALKED OVER TO THE PLACE WHERE SARAQUAEL ONCE STOOD...
"...TRIED TO FIND SOME REMNANT OF THE ANGEL I HAD DESTROYED.
"BUT THERE WAS NOTHING TO FIND.
"THEN HE LOOKED UP AT ME."
THAT WAS NOT RIGHT.
THAT WAS NOT JUST.
"PERHAPS SARAQUAEL WAS THE FIRST TO LOVE, BUT LUCIFER WAS THE FIRST TO SHED TEARS. I WILL NEVER FORGET THAT."

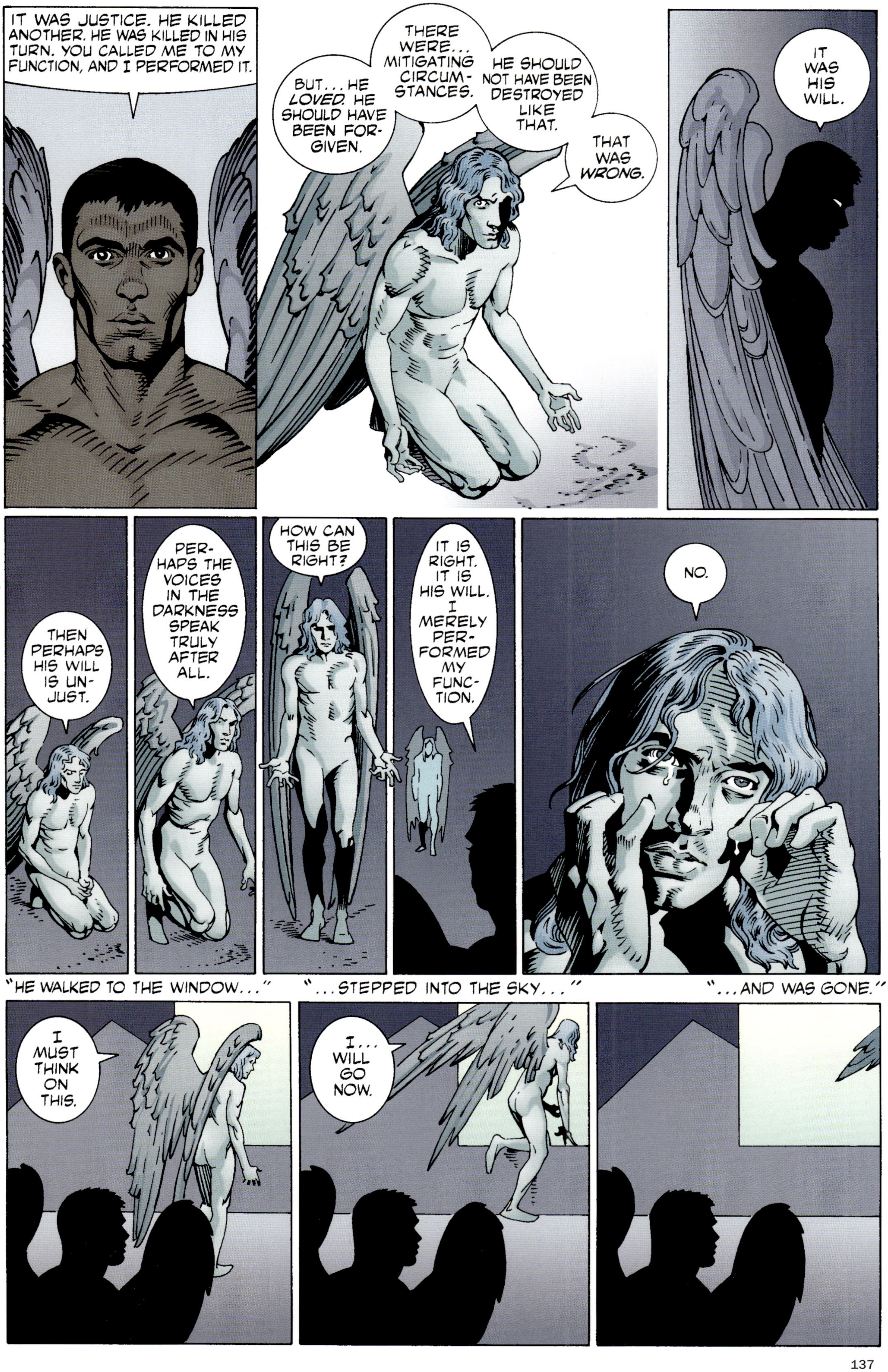
IT WAS JUSTICE. HE KILLED ANOTHER. HE WAS KILLED IN HIS TURN. YOU CALLED ME TO MY FUNCTION, AND I PERFORMED IT.
BUT... HE *LOVED*. HE SHOULD HAVE BEEN FORGIVEN.
THERE WERE... MITIGATING CIRCUMSTANCES.
HE SHOULD NOT HAVE BEEN DESTROYED LIKE THAT.
THAT WAS *WRONG*.
IT WAS HIS WILL.
THEN PERHAPS HIS WILL IS UNJUST.
PERHAPS THE VOICES IN THE DARKNESS SPEAK TRULY AFTER ALL.
HOW CAN THIS BE RIGHT?
IT IS RIGHT. IT IS HIS WILL. I MERELY PERFORMED MY FUNCTION.
NO.
"HE WALKED TO THE WINDOW..."
I MUST THINK ON THIS.
"...STEPPED INTO THE SKY..."
I... WILL GO NOW.
"...AND WAS GONE."

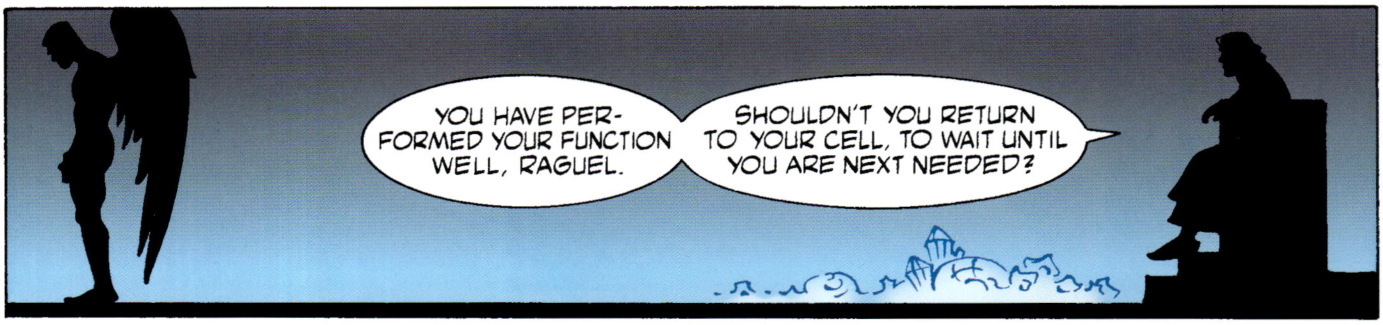
YOU HAVE PERFORMED YOUR FUNCTION WELL, RAGUEL.
SHOULDN'T YOU RETURN TO YOUR CELL, TO WAIT UNTIL YOU ARE NEXT NEEDED?

THE MAN ON THE BENCH TURNED TOWARDS ME. HIS EYES SOUGHT MINE. UNTIL NOW IT HAD SEEMED--FOR MOST OF HIS NARRATIVE--THAT HE WAS SCARCELY AWARE OF ME. NOW IT FELT AS IF HE HAD DISCOVERED ME, AND THAT HE SPOKE TO ME ALONE, RATHER THAN TO THE AIR, OR THE CITY OF LOS ANGELES, AND HE SAID--

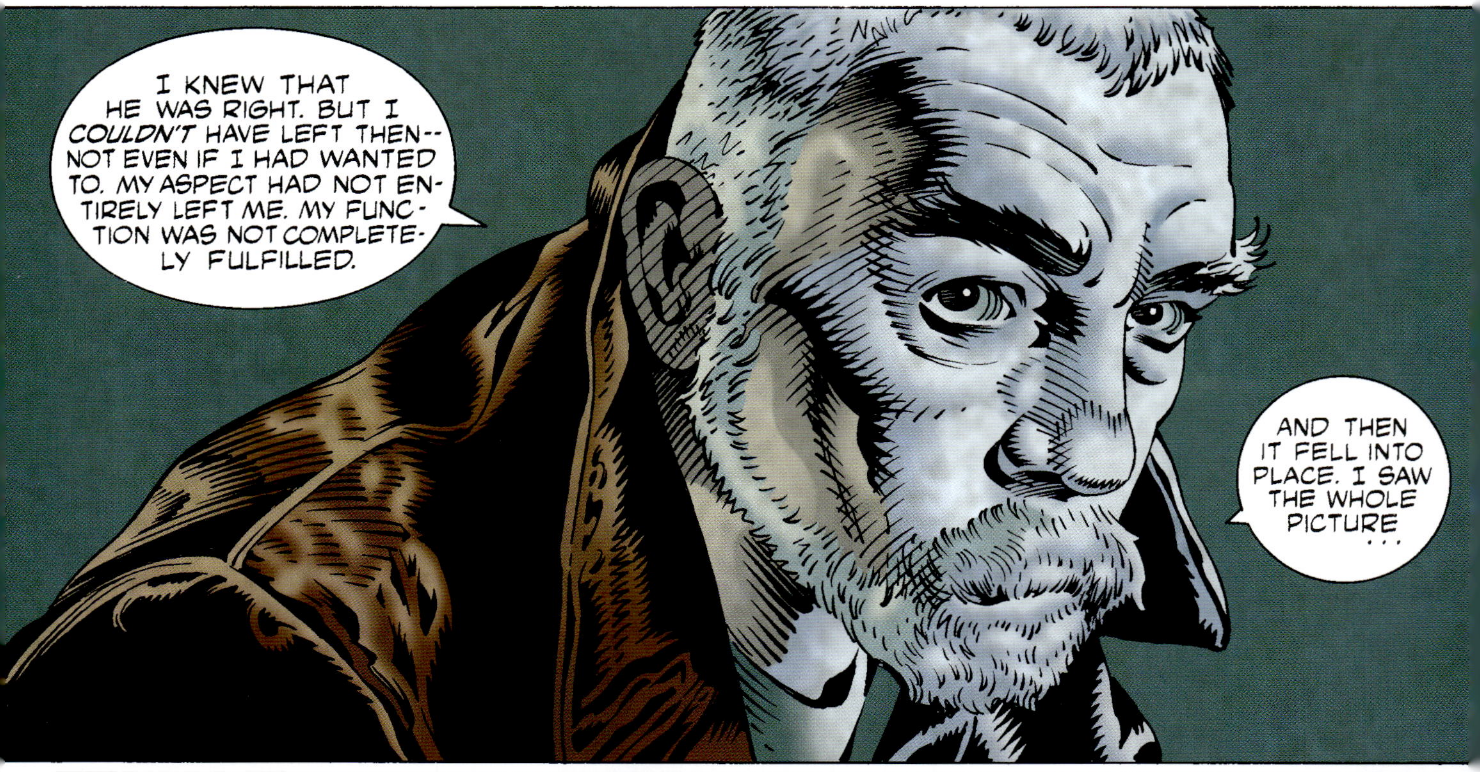
I KNEW THAT HE WAS RIGHT. BUT I *COULDN'T* HAVE LEFT THEN--NOT EVEN IF I HAD WANTED TO. MY ASPECT HAD NOT ENTIRELY LEFT ME. MY FUNCTION WAS NOT COMPLETELY FULFILLED.
AND THEN IT FELL INTO PLACE. I SAW THE WHOLE PICTURE . . .

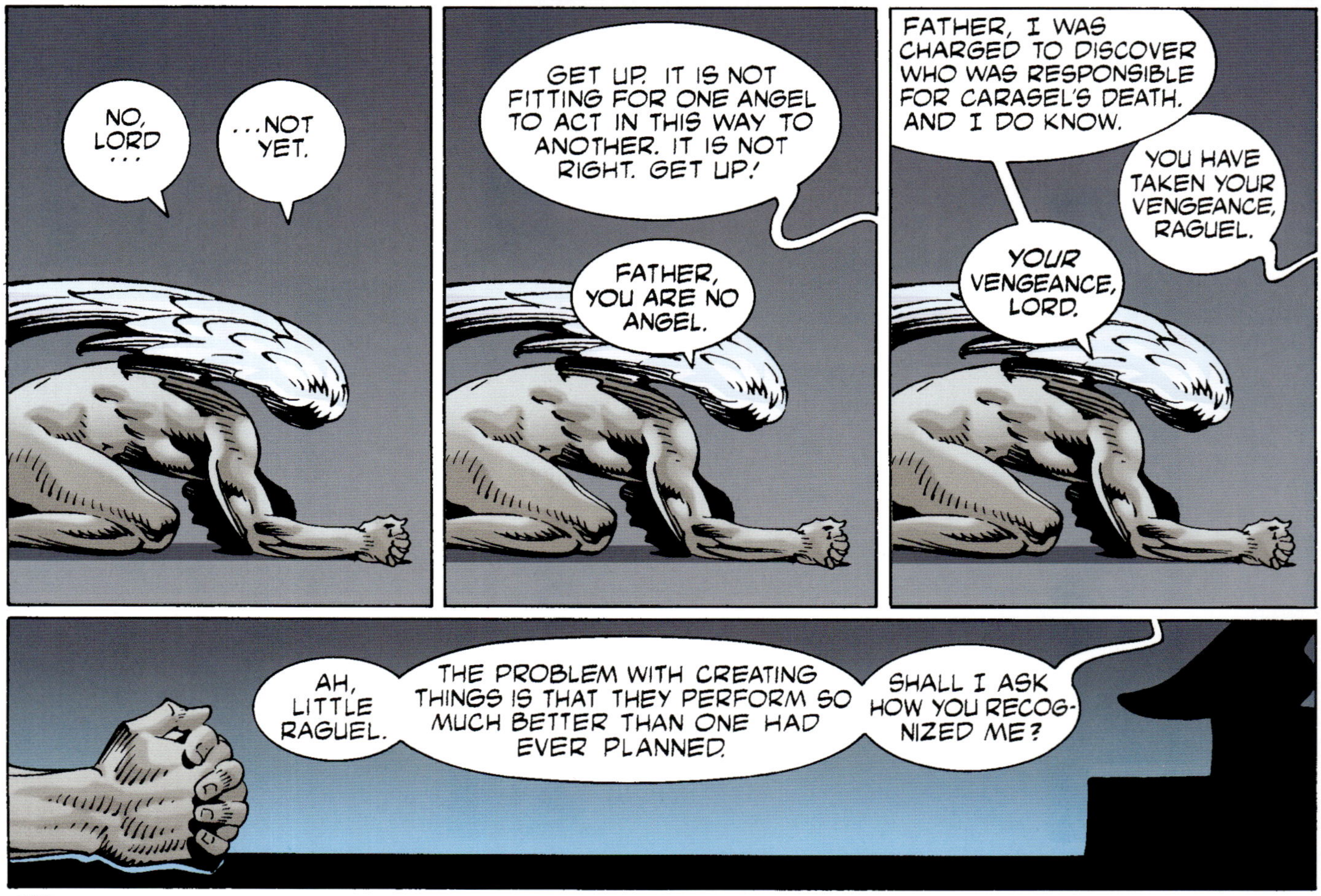
NO, LORD . . .
. . .NOT YET.
GET UP. IT IS NOT FITTING FOR ONE ANGEL TO ACT IN THIS WAY TO ANOTHER. IT IS NOT RIGHT. GET UP!
FATHER, YOU ARE NO ANGEL.
FATHER, I WAS CHARGED TO DISCOVER WHO WAS RESPONSIBLE FOR CARASEL'S DEATH. AND I DO KNOW.
YOU HAVE TAKEN YOUR VENGEANCE, RAGUEL.
YOUR VENGEANCE, LORD.
AH, LITTLE RAGUEL.
THE PROBLEM WITH CREATING THINGS IS THAT THEY PERFORM SO MUCH BETTER THAN ONE HAD EVER PLANNED.
SHALL I ASK HOW YOU RECOGNIZED ME?

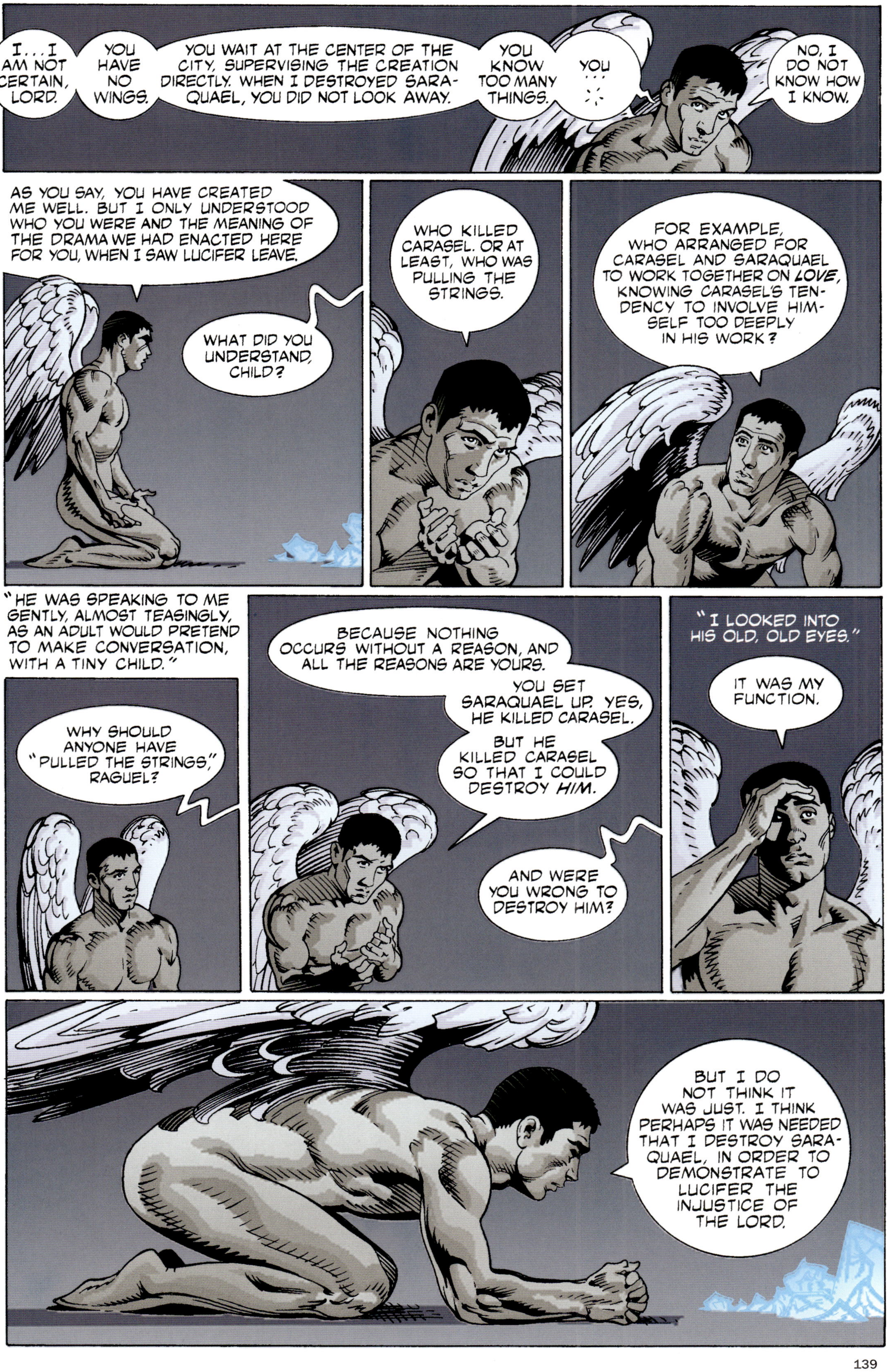

I... I AM NOT CERTAIN, LORD.
YOU HAVE NO WINGS.
YOU WAIT AT THE CENTER OF THE CITY, SUPERVISING THE CREATION DIRECTLY. WHEN I DESTROYED SARAQUAEL, YOU DID NOT LOOK AWAY.
YOU KNOW TOO MANY THINGS.
YOU ...
NO, I DO NOT KNOW HOW I KNOW.
AS YOU SAY, YOU HAVE CREATED ME WELL. BUT I ONLY UNDERSTOOD WHO YOU WERE AND THE MEANING OF THE DRAMA WE HAD ENACTED HERE FOR YOU, WHEN I SAW LUCIFER LEAVE.
WHAT DID YOU UNDERSTAND, CHILD?
WHO KILLED CARASEL. OR AT LEAST, WHO WAS PULLING THE STRINGS.
FOR EXAMPLE, WHO ARRANGED FOR CARASEL AND SARAQUAEL TO WORK TOGETHER ON LOVE, KNOWING CARASEL'S TENDENCY TO INVOLVE HIMSELF TOO DEEPLY IN HIS WORK?
"HE WAS SPEAKING TO ME GENTLY, ALMOST TEASINGLY, AS AN ADULT WOULD PRETEND TO MAKE CONVERSATION, WITH A TINY CHILD."
WHY SHOULD ANYONE HAVE "PULLED THE STRINGS," RAGUEL?
BECAUSE NOTHING OCCURS WITHOUT A REASON, AND ALL THE REASONS ARE YOURS.
YOU SET SARAQUAEL UP. YES, HE KILLED CARASEL.
BUT HE KILLED CARASEL SO THAT I COULD DESTROY HIM.
AND WERE YOU WRONG TO DESTROY HIM?
"I LOOKED INTO HIS OLD, OLD EYES."
IT WAS MY FUNCTION.
BUT I DO NOT THINK IT WAS JUST. I THINK PERHAPS IT WAS NEEDED THAT I DESTROY SARAQUAEL, IN ORDER TO DEMONSTRATE TO LUCIFER THE INJUSTICE OF THE LORD.

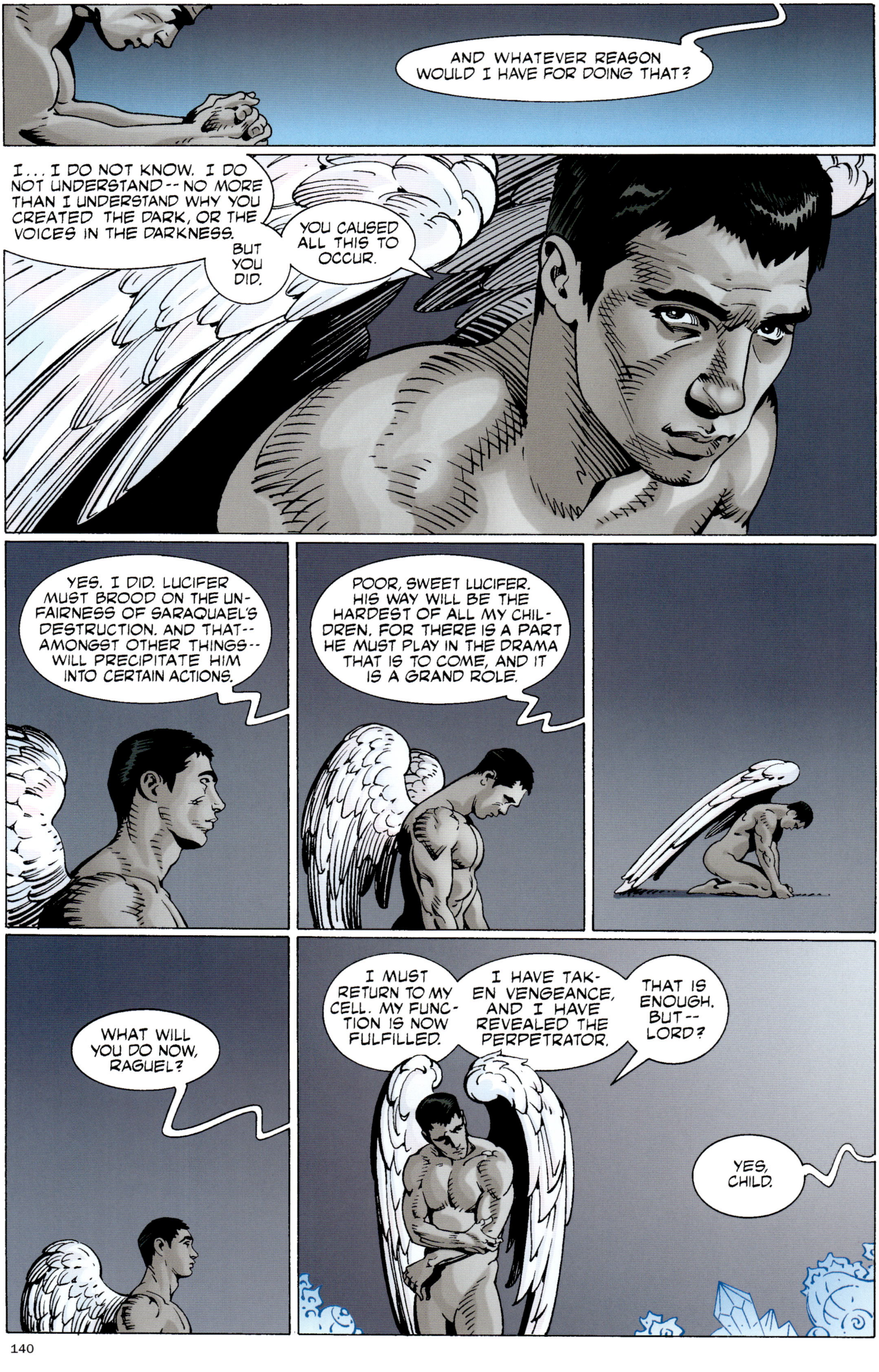
AND WHATEVER REASON WOULD I HAVE FOR DOING THAT?
I... I DO NOT KNOW. I DO NOT UNDERSTAND-- NO MORE THAN I UNDERSTAND WHY YOU CREATED THE DARK, OR THE VOICES IN THE DARKNESS.
BUT YOU DID.
YOU CAUSED ALL THIS TO OCCUR.
YES. I DID. LUCIFER MUST BROOD ON THE UNFAIRNESS OF SARAQUAEL'S DESTRUCTION. AND THAT-- AMONGST OTHER THINGS-- WILL PRECIPITATE HIM INTO CERTAIN ACTIONS.
POOR, SWEET LUCIFER. HIS WAY WILL BE THE HARDEST OF ALL MY CHILDREN. FOR THERE IS A PART HE MUST PLAY IN THE DRAMA THAT IS TO COME, AND IT IS A GRAND ROLE.
WHAT WILL YOU DO NOW, RAGUEL?
I MUST RETURN TO MY CELL. MY FUNCTION IS NOW FULFILLED.
I HAVE TAKEN VENGEANCE, AND I HAVE REVEALED THE PERPETRATOR.
THAT IS ENOUGH. BUT-- LORD?
YES, CHILD.

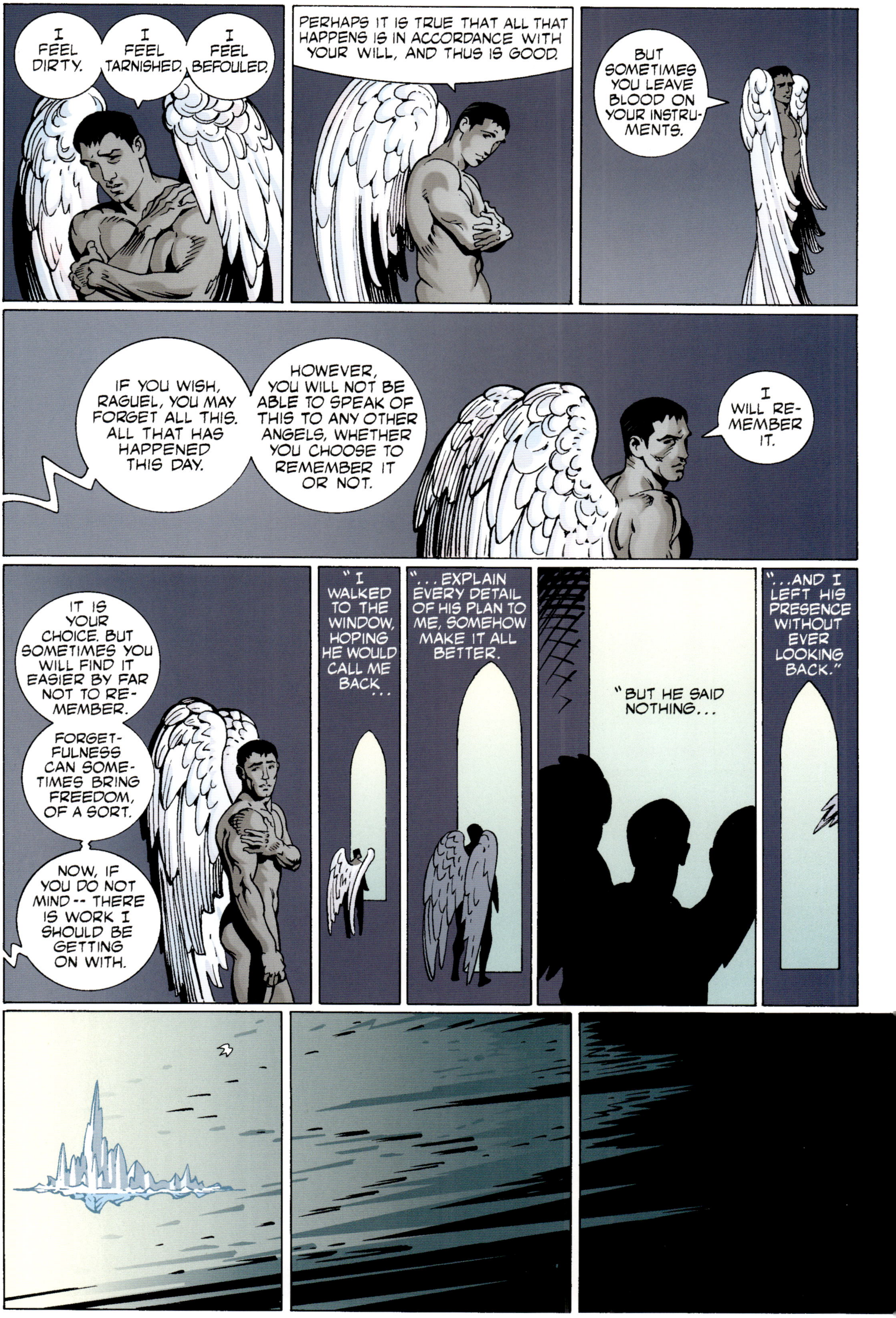
I FEEL DIRTY.
I FEEL TARNISHED.
I FEEL BEFOULED.
PERHAPS IT IS TRUE THAT ALL THAT HAPPENS IS IN ACCORDANCE WITH YOUR WILL, AND THUS IS GOOD.
BUT SOMETIMES YOU LEAVE BLOOD ON YOUR INSTRU-MENTS.
IF YOU WISH, RAGUEL, YOU MAY FORGET ALL THIS. ALL THAT HAS HAPPENED THIS DAY.
HOWEVER, YOU WILL NOT BE ABLE TO SPEAK OF THIS TO ANY OTHER ANGELS, WHETHER YOU CHOOSE TO REMEMBER IT OR NOT.
I WILL RE-MEMBER IT.
IT IS YOUR CHOICE. BUT SOMETIMES YOU WILL FIND IT EASIER BY FAR NOT TO RE-MEMBER.
FORGET-FULNESS CAN SOME-TIMES BRING FREEDOM, OF A SORT.
NOW, IF YOU DO NOT MIND -- THERE IS WORK I SHOULD BE GETTING ON WITH.
"I WALKED TO THE WINDOW, HOPING HE WOULD CALL ME BACK...
"...EXPLAIN EVERY DETAIL OF HIS PLAN TO ME, SOMEHOW MAKE IT ALL BETTER.
"BUT HE SAID NOTHING...
"...AND I LEFT HIS PRESENCE WITHOUT EVER LOOKING BACK."

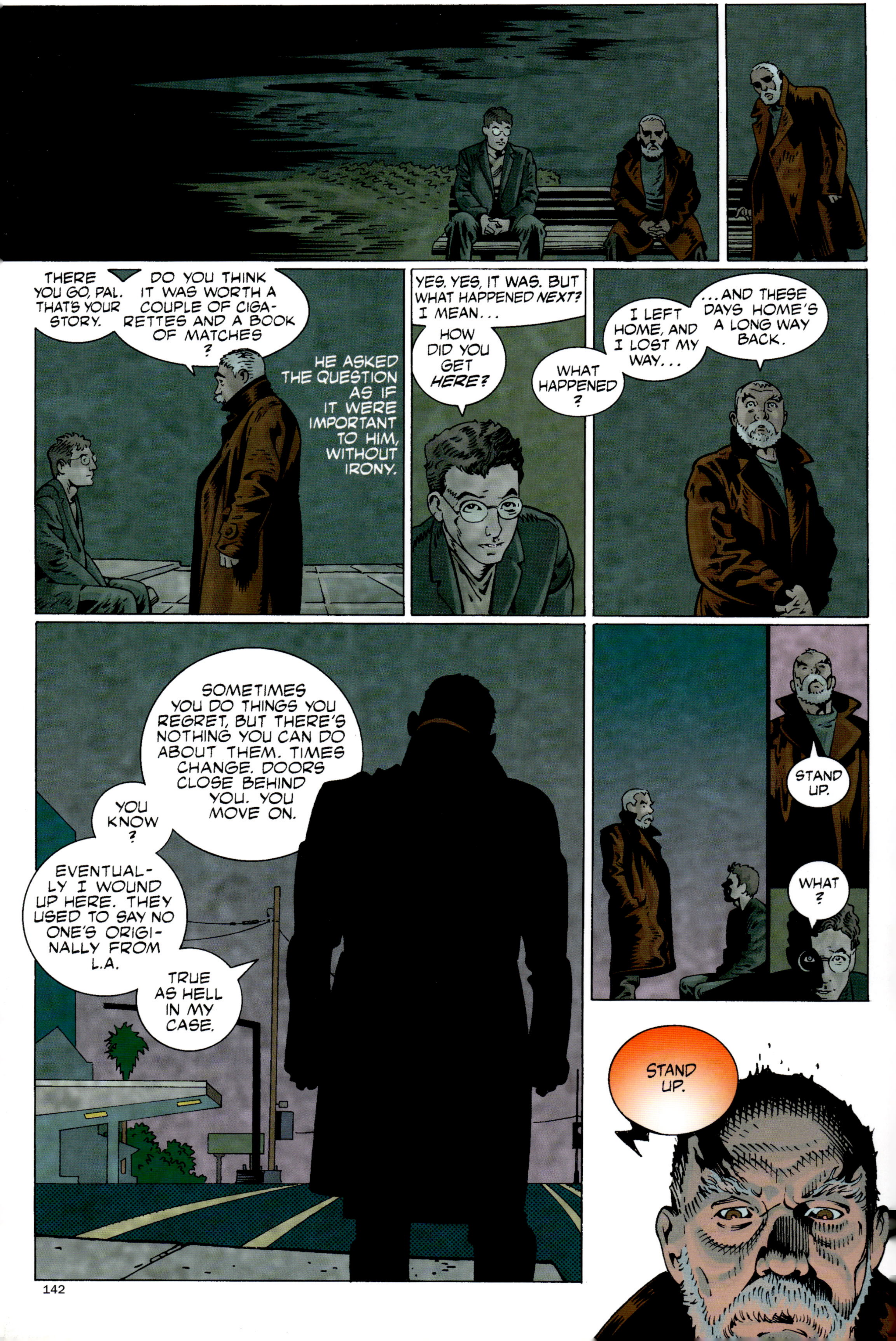
THERE YOU GO, PAL. THAT'S YOUR STORY.
DO YOU THINK IT WAS WORTH A COUPLE OF CIGARETTES AND A BOOK OF MATCHES?
HE ASKED THE QUESTION AS IF IT WERE IMPORTANT TO HIM, WITHOUT IRONY.
YES. YES, IT WAS. BUT WHAT HAPPENED NEXT? I MEAN...
HOW DID YOU GET HERE?
WHAT HAPPENED?
I LEFT HOME, AND I LOST MY WAY...
...AND THESE DAYS HOME'S A LONG WAY BACK.
YOU KNOW?
SOMETIMES YOU DO THINGS YOU REGRET, BUT THERE'S NOTHING YOU CAN DO ABOUT THEM. TIMES CHANGE. DOORS CLOSE BEHIND YOU. YOU MOVE ON.
EVENTUALLY I WOUND UP HERE. THEY USED TO SAY NO ONE'S ORIGINALLY FROM L.A.
TRUE AS HELL IN MY CASE.
STAND UP.
WHAT?
STAND UP.

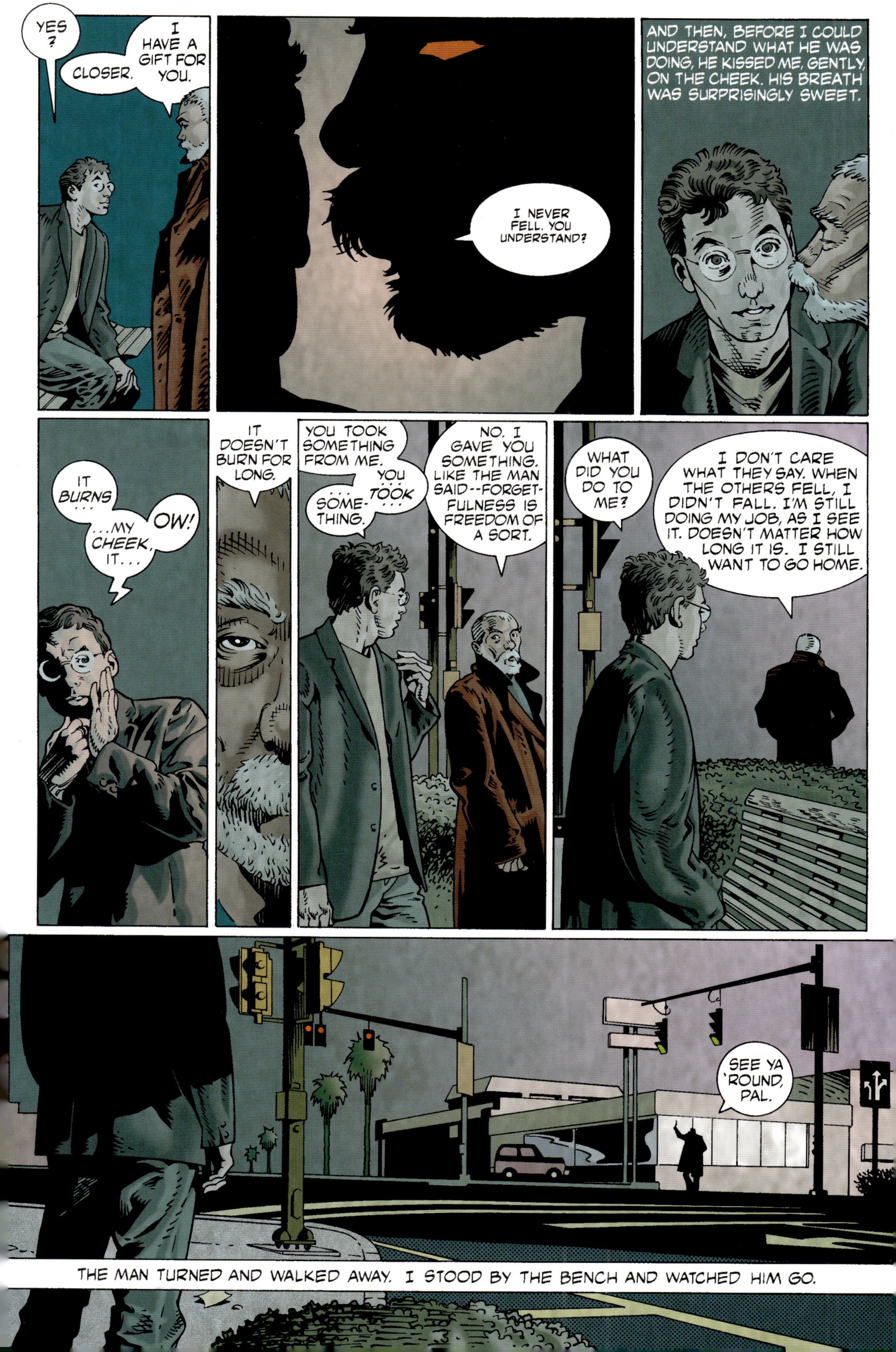
YES?
I HAVE A GIFT FOR YOU.
CLOSER.
I NEVER FELL. YOU UNDERSTAND?
AND THEN, BEFORE I COULD UNDERSTAND WHAT HE WAS DOING, HE KISSED ME, GENTLY, ON THE CHEEK. HIS BREATH WAS SURPRISINGLY SWEET.
IT BURNS...
...MY CHEEK, IT...
OW!
IT DOESN'T BURN FOR LONG.
YOU TOOK SOMETHING FROM ME.
YOU ... TOOK ...
... SOMETHING.
NO. I GAVE YOU SOMETHING. LIKE THE MAN SAID--FORGETFULNESS IS FREEDOM OF A SORT.
WHAT DID YOU DO TO ME?
I DON'T CARE WHAT THEY SAY. WHEN THE OTHERS FELL, I DIDN'T FALL. I'M STILL DOING MY JOB, AS I SEE IT. DOESN'T MATTER HOW LONG IT IS. I STILL WANT TO GO HOME.
SEE YA 'ROUND, PAL.
THE MAN TURNED AND WALKED AWAY. I STOOD BY THE BENCH AND WATCHED HIM GO.

I FELT LIKE HE HAD TAKEN SOMETHING FROM ME, ALTHOUGH I COULD NO LONGER REMEMBER WHAT. AND I FELT LIKE SOMETHING HAD BEEN LEFT IN ITS PLACE.

ABSOLUTION, PERHAPS, OR INNOCENCE...

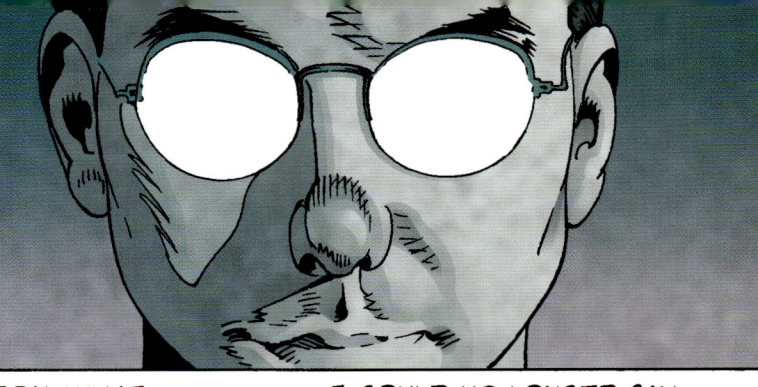

...ALTHOUGH OF WHAT...

...OR FROM WHAT...

...I COULD NO LONGER SAY.

AN IMAGE FROM SOMEWHERE -- A SCRIBBLED DRAWING, OF TWO ANGELS IN FLIGHT ABOVE A PERFECT CITY, AND OVER THE IMAGE, A CHILD'S PERFECT HANDPRINT, WHICH STAINS THE WHITE PAPER BLOOD RED.

IT CAME INTO MY MIND UNBIDDEN, AND I NO LONGER KNOW WHAT IT MEANT.

I STOOD UP.

IT WAS TOO DARK TO SEE THE FACE OF MY WATCH, BUT I KNEW I WOULD GET NO SLEEP THAT DAY.

I WALKED BACK TO THE PLACE I WAS STAYING, TO THE HOUSE BY THE STUNTED PALM TREE.

I THOUGHT ABOUT ANGELS, AND ABOUT TINK...

...AND I WONDERED WHETHER LOVE AND DEATH WENT HAND IN HAND.

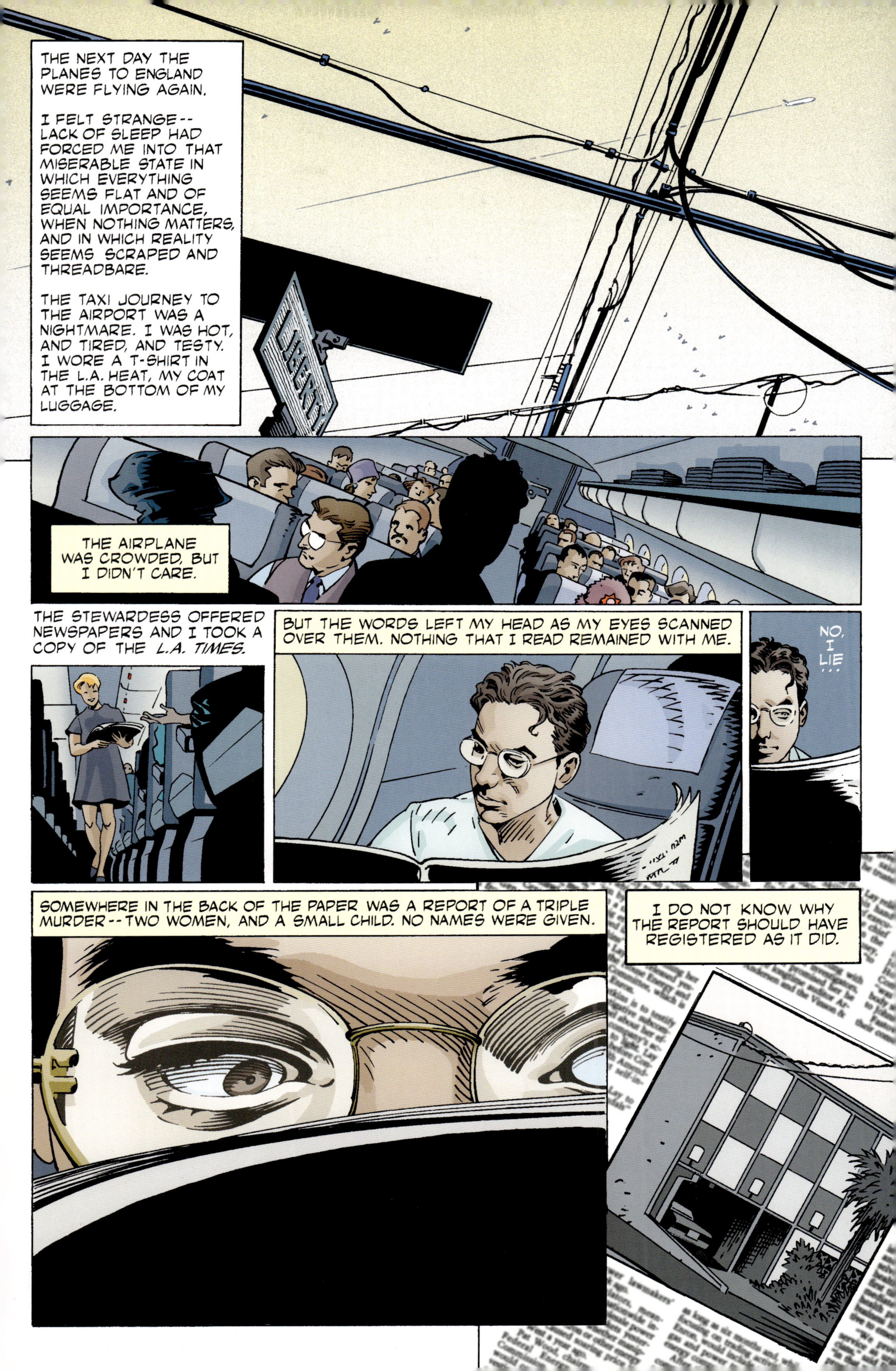
THE NEXT DAY THE PLANES TO ENGLAND WERE FLYING AGAIN.
I FELT STRANGE--LACK OF SLEEP HAD FORCED ME INTO THAT MISERABLE STATE IN WHICH EVERYTHING SEEMS FLAT AND OF EQUAL IMPORTANCE, WHEN NOTHING MATTERS, AND IN WHICH REALITY SEEMS SCRAPED AND THREADBARE.
THE TAXI JOURNEY TO THE AIRPORT WAS A NIGHTMARE. I WAS HOT, AND TIRED, AND TESTY. I WORE A T-SHIRT IN THE L.A. HEAT, MY COAT AT THE BOTTOM OF MY LUGGAGE.
LIBERTY
THE AIRPLANE WAS CROWDED, BUT I DIDN'T CARE.
THE STEWARDESS OFFERED NEWSPAPERS AND I TOOK A COPY OF THE *L.A. TIMES.*
BUT THE WORDS LEFT MY HEAD AS MY EYES SCANNED OVER THEM. NOTHING THAT I READ REMAINED WITH ME.
NO, I LIE...
SOMEWHERE IN THE BACK OF THE PAPER WAS A REPORT OF A TRIPLE MURDER--TWO WOMEN, AND A SMALL CHILD. NO NAMES WERE GIVEN.
I DO NOT KNOW WHY THE REPORT SHOULD HAVE REGISTERED AS IT DID.

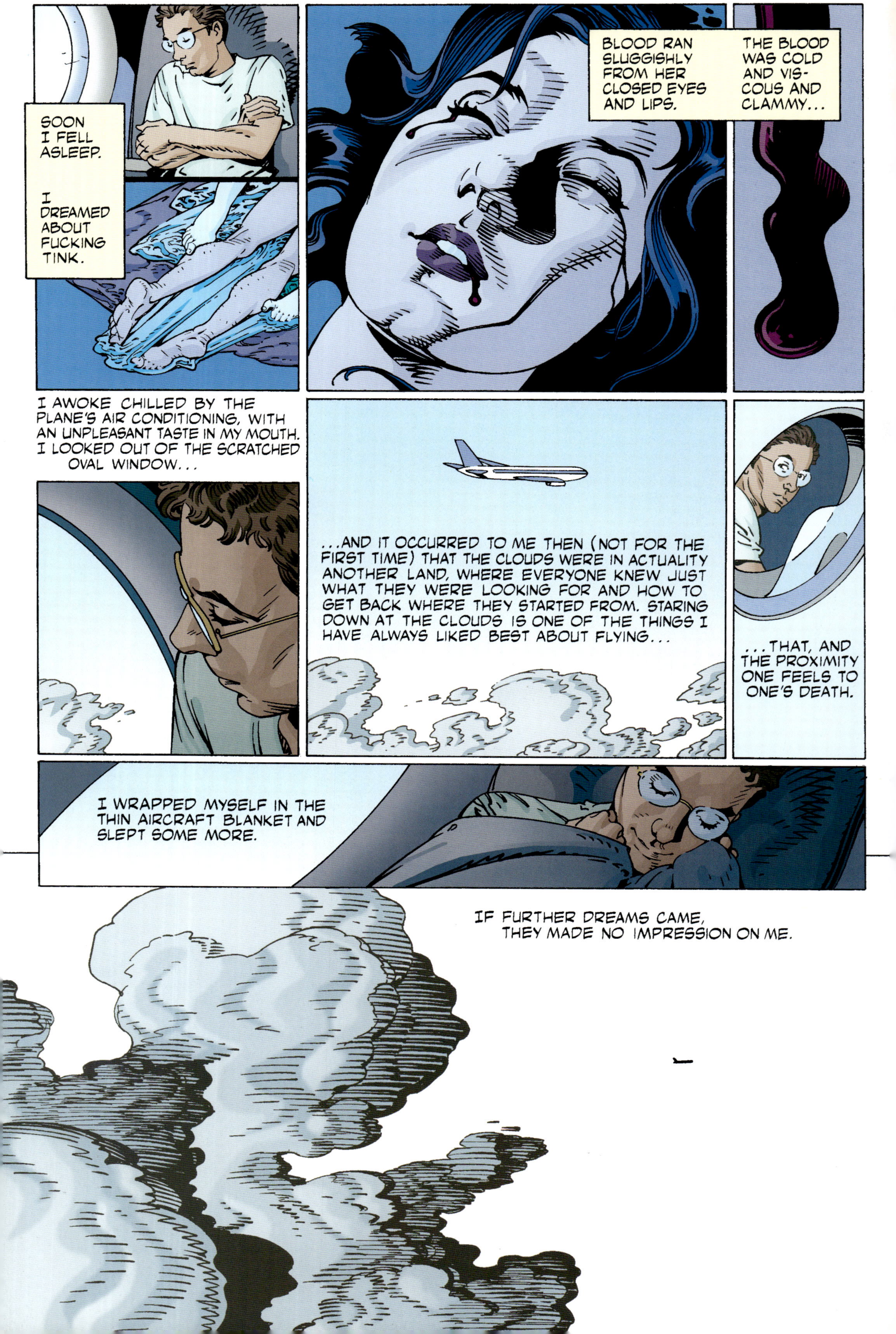
SOON I FELL ASLEEP.
I DREAMED ABOUT FUCKING TINK.
BLOOD RAN SLUGGISHLY FROM HER CLOSED EYES AND LIPS.
THE BLOOD WAS COLD AND VIS-COUS AND CLAMMY...
I AWOKE CHILLED BY THE PLANE'S AIR CONDITIONING, WITH AN UNPLEASANT TASTE IN MY MOUTH. I LOOKED OUT OF THE SCRATCHED OVAL WINDOW...
...AND IT OCCURRED TO ME THEN (NOT FOR THE FIRST TIME) THAT THE CLOUDS WERE IN ACTUALITY ANOTHER LAND, WHERE EVERYONE KNEW JUST WHAT THEY WERE LOOKING FOR AND HOW TO GET BACK WHERE THEY STARTED FROM. STARING DOWN AT THE CLOUDS IS ONE OF THE THINGS I HAVE ALWAYS LIKED BEST ABOUT FLYING...
...THAT, AND THE PROXIMITY ONE FEELS TO ONE'S DEATH.
I WRAPPED MYSELF IN THE THIN AIRCRAFT BLANKET AND SLEPT SOME MORE.
IF FURTHER DREAMS CAME, THEY MADE NO IMPRESSION ON ME.

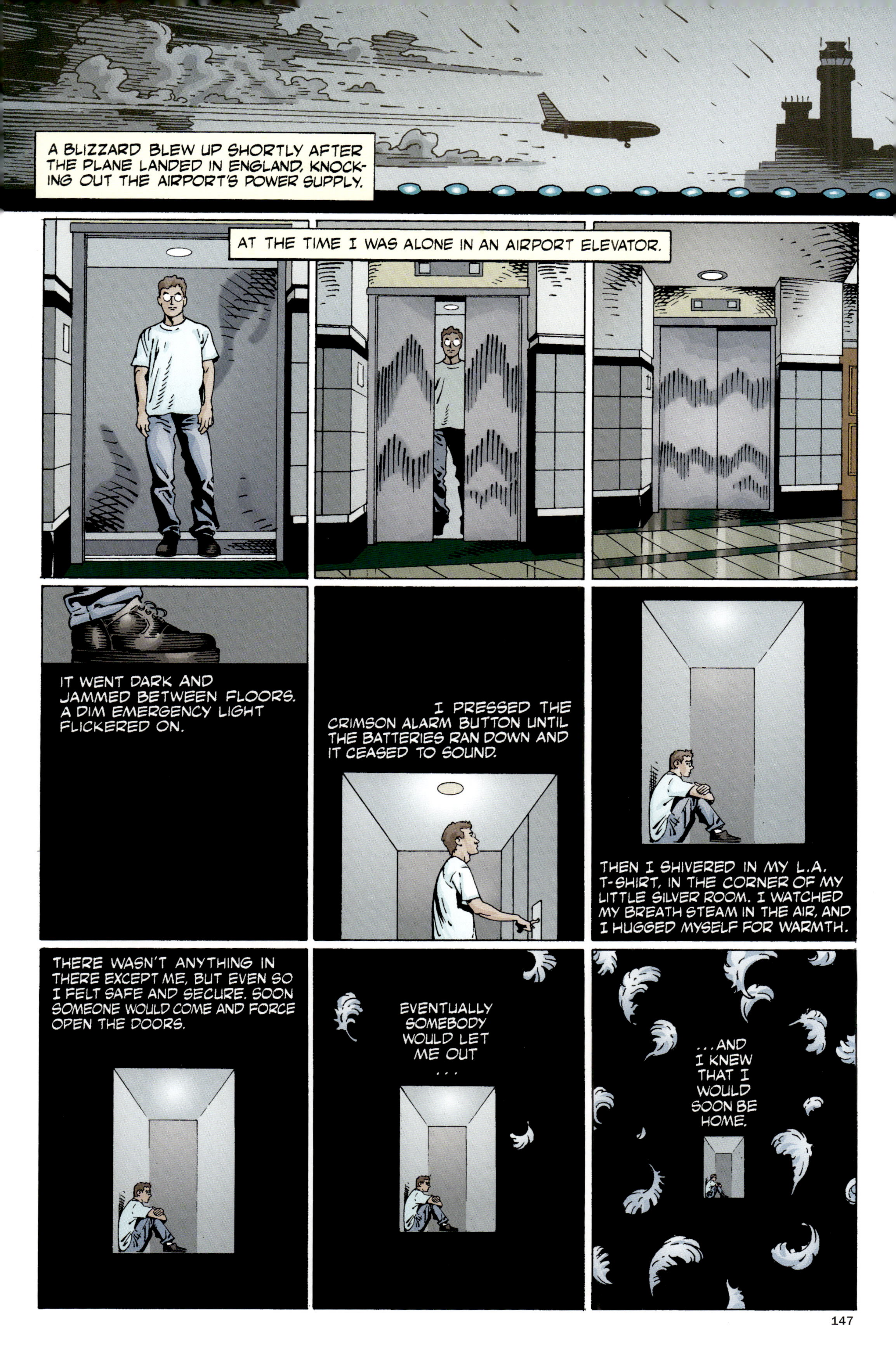
A BLIZZARD BLEW UP SHORTLY AFTER THE PLANE LANDED IN ENGLAND, KNOCKING OUT THE AIRPORT'S POWER SUPPLY.
AT THE TIME I WAS ALONE IN AN AIRPORT ELEVATOR.
IT WENT DARK AND JAMMED BETWEEN FLOORS. A DIM EMERGENCY LIGHT FLICKERED ON.
I PRESSED THE CRIMSON ALARM BUTTON UNTIL THE BATTERIES RAN DOWN AND IT CEASED TO SOUND.
THEN I SHIVERED IN MY L.A. T-SHIRT, IN THE CORNER OF MY LITTLE SILVER ROOM. I WATCHED MY BREATH STEAM IN THE AIR, AND I HUGGED MYSELF FOR WARMTH.
THERE WASN'T ANYTHING IN THERE EXCEPT ME, BUT EVEN SO I FELT SAFE AND SECURE. SOON SOMEONE WOULD COME AND FORCE OPEN THE DOORS.
EVENTUALLY SOMEBODY WOULD LET ME OUT ...
...AND I KNEW THAT I WOULD SOON BE HOME.

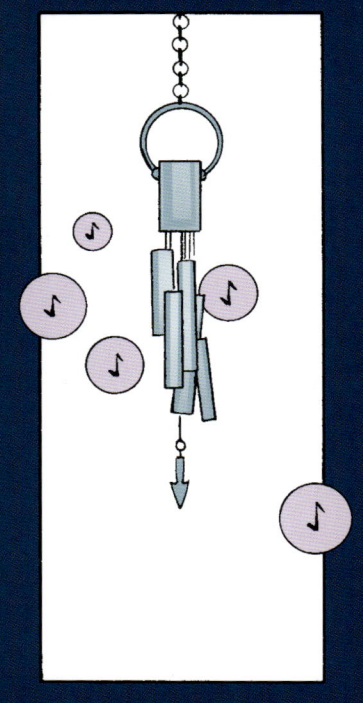

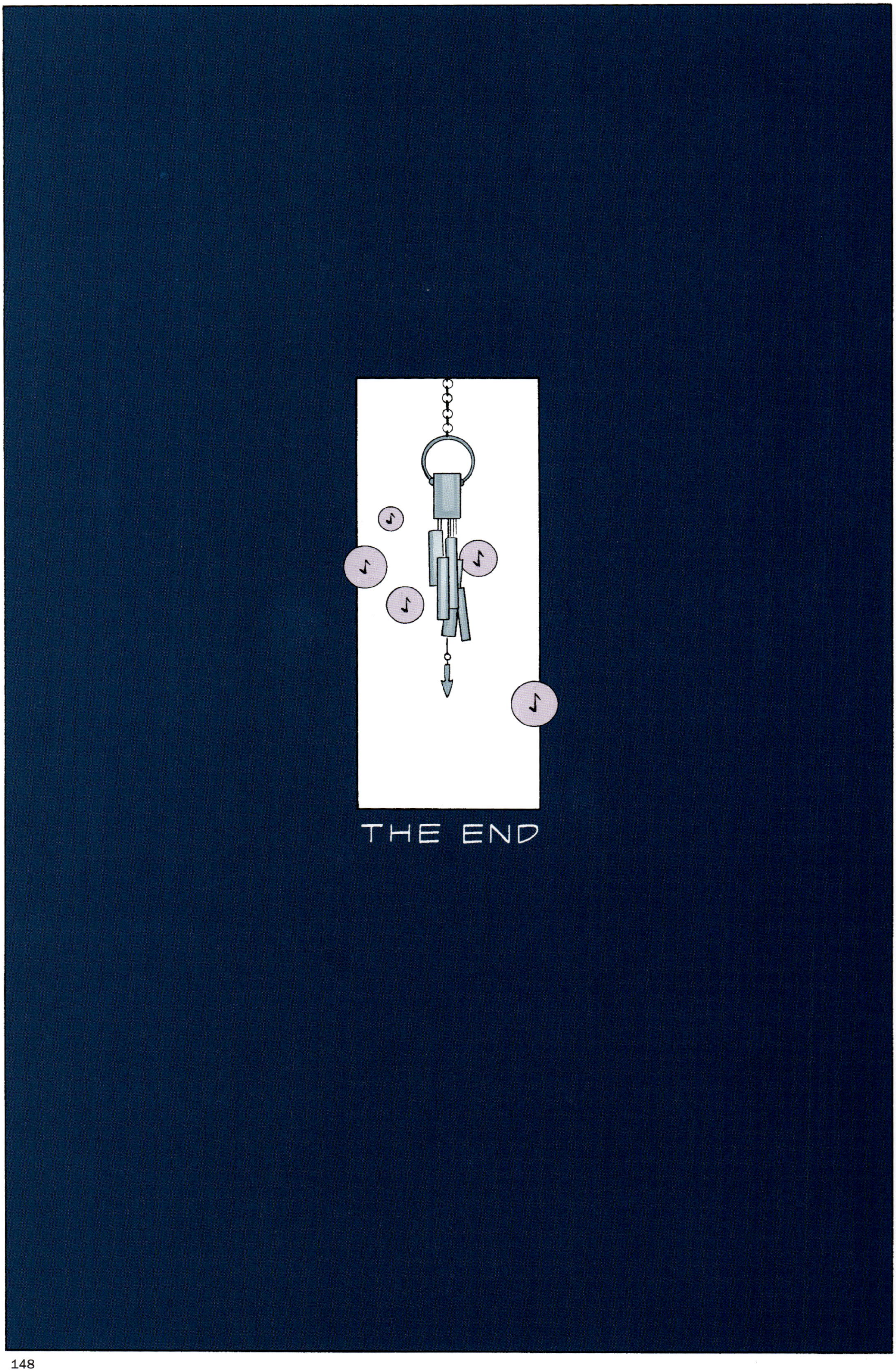

THE END

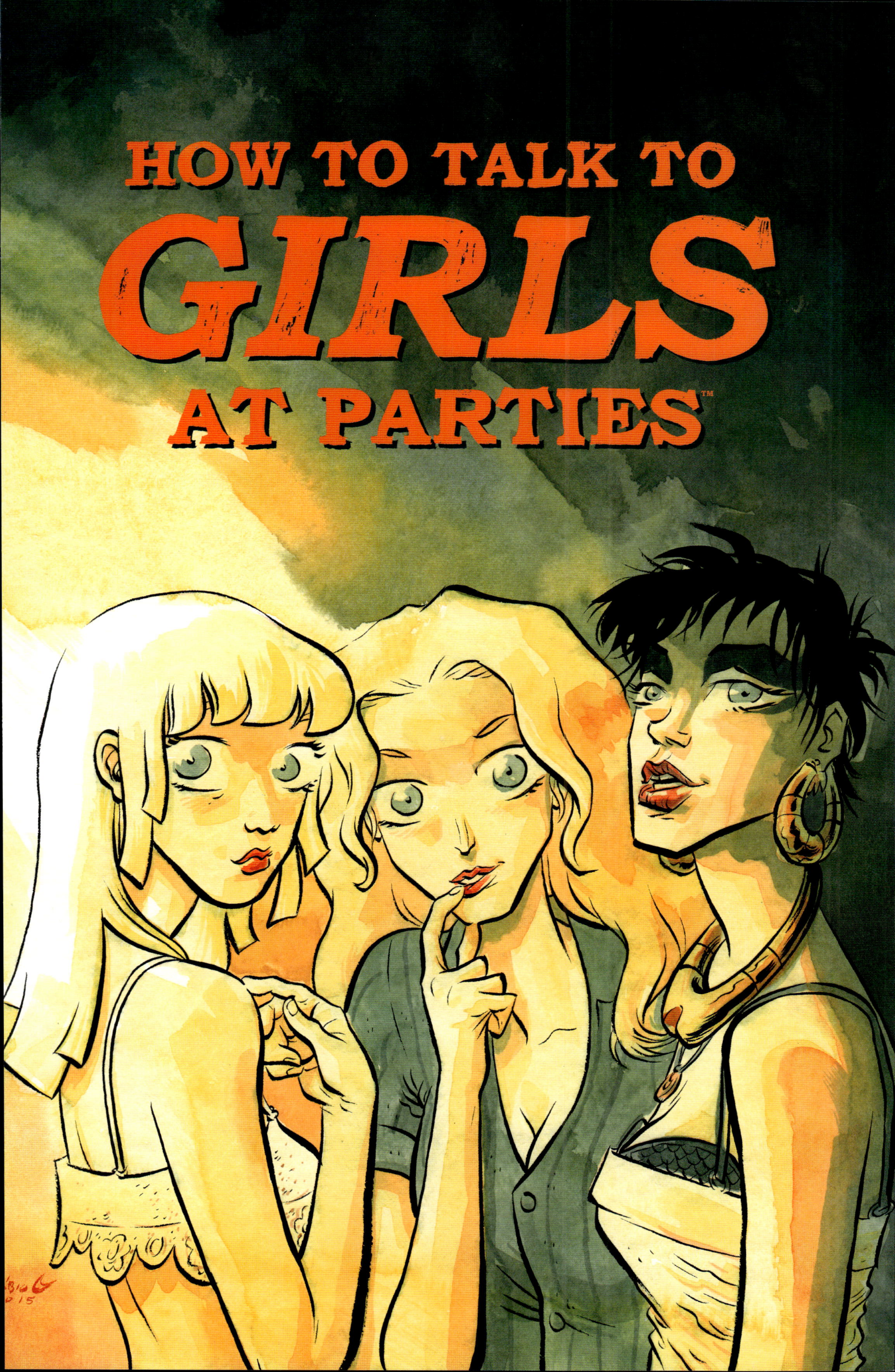
HOW TO TALK TO
GIRLS
AT PARTIES™

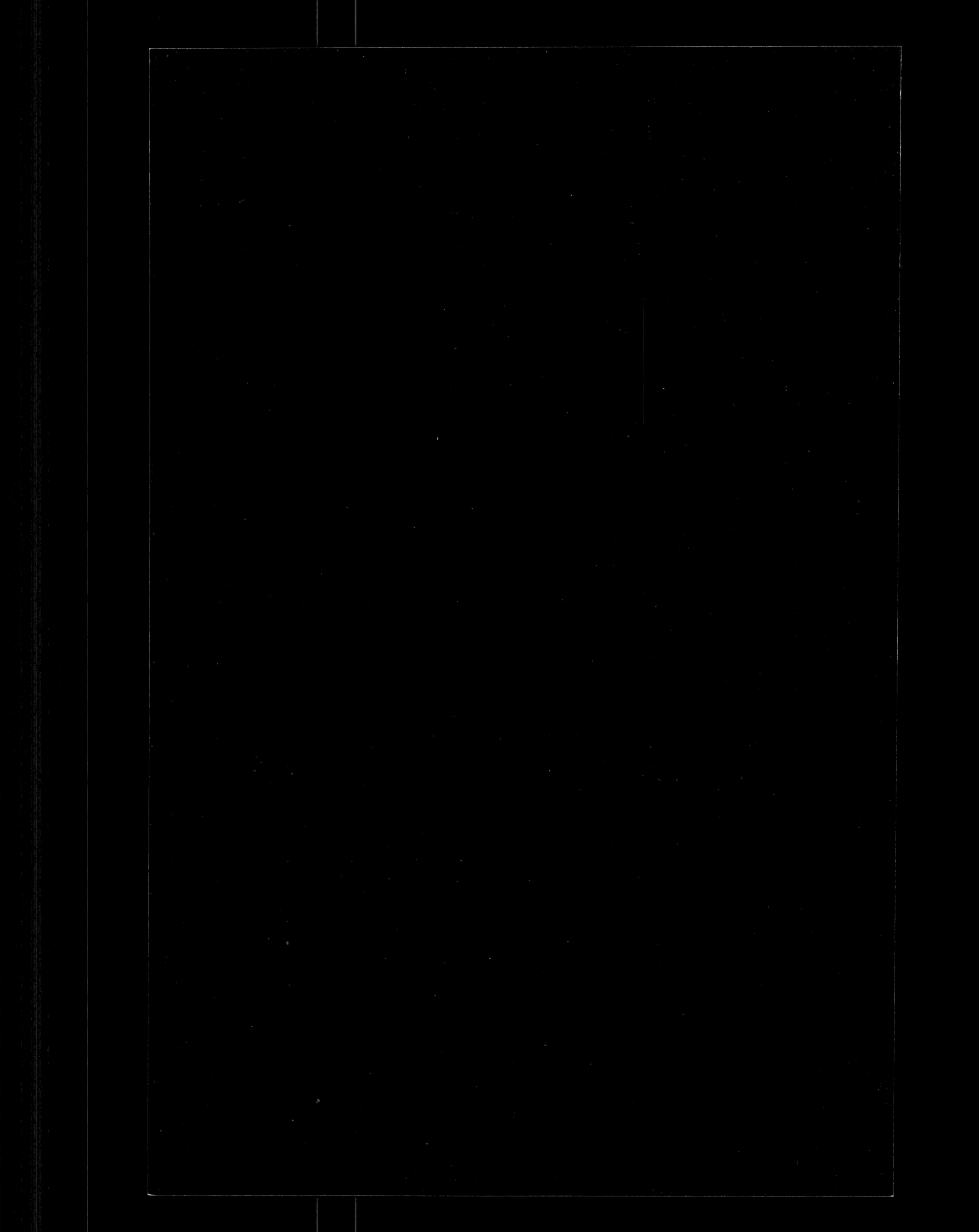

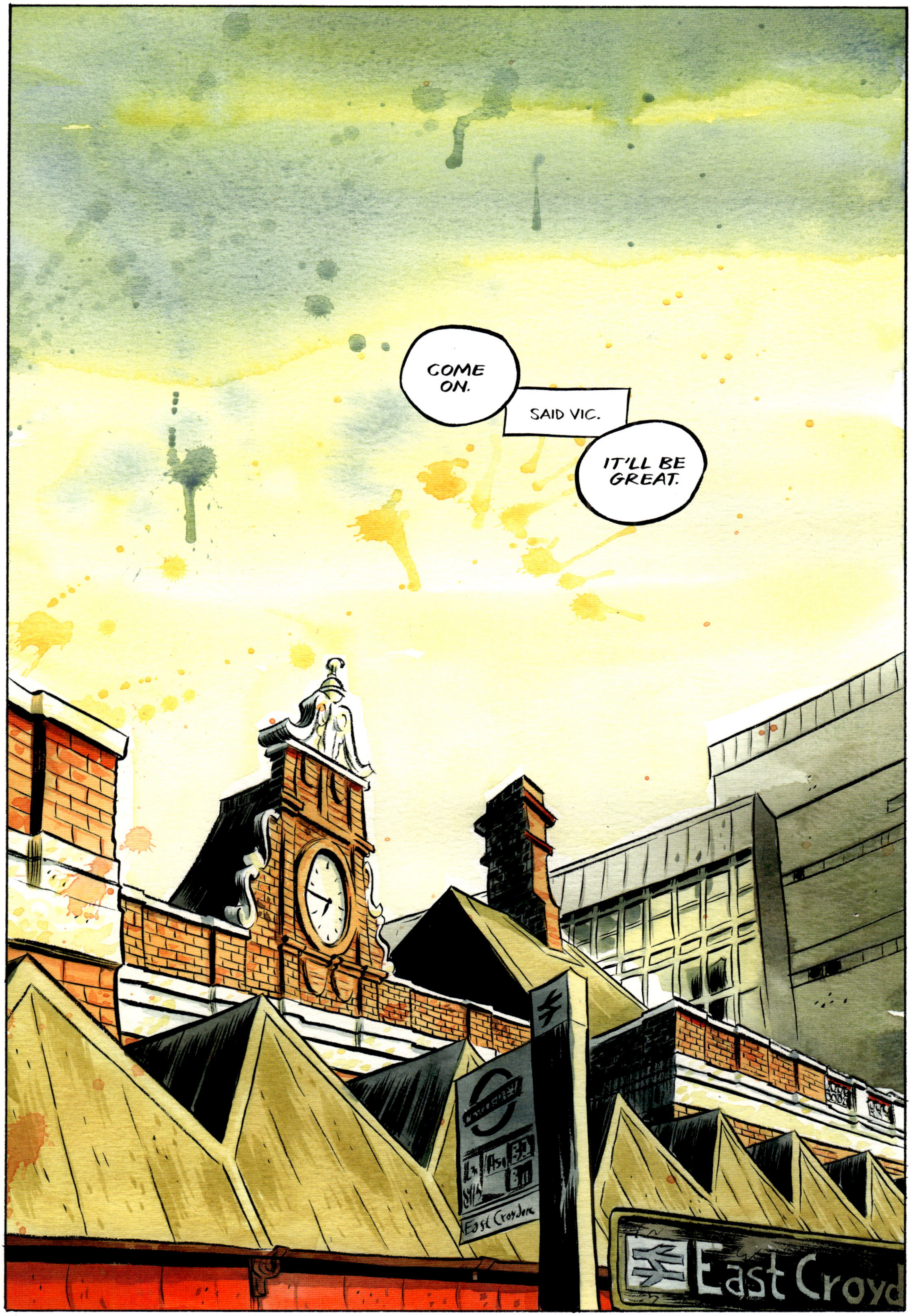
COME ON.
SAID VIC.
IT'LL BE GREAT.
East Croydon
East Croyd

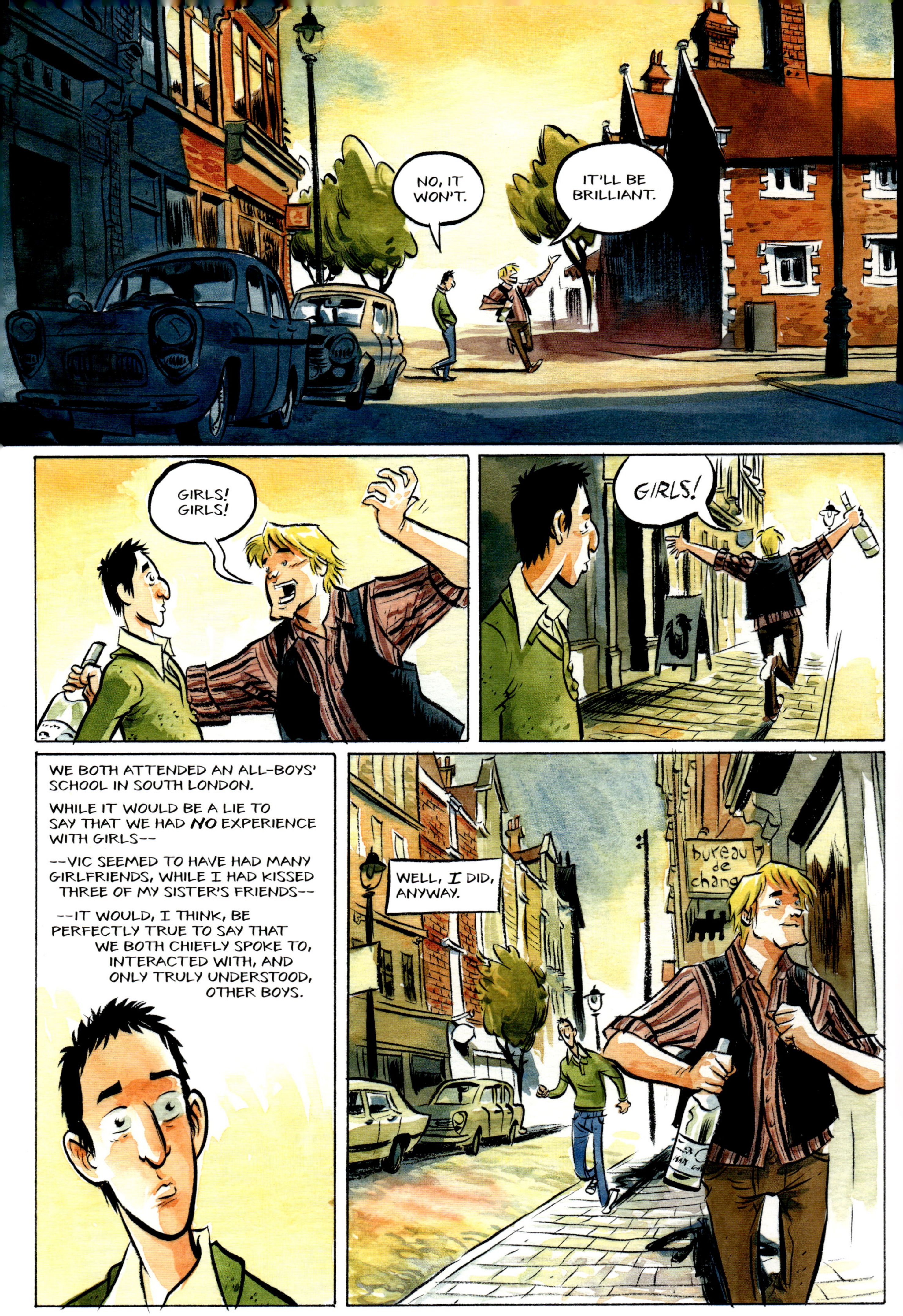
NO, IT WON'T.
IT'LL BE BRILLIANT.
GIRLS! GIRLS!
GIRLS!
WE BOTH ATTENDED AN ALL-BOYS' SCHOOL IN SOUTH LONDON.
WHILE IT WOULD BE A LIE TO SAY THAT WE HAD *NO* EXPERIENCE WITH GIRLS--
--VIC SEEMED TO HAVE HAD MANY GIRLFRIENDS, WHILE I HAD KISSED THREE OF MY SISTER'S FRIENDS--
--IT WOULD, I THINK, BE PERFECTLY TRUE TO SAY THAT WE BOTH CHIEFLY SPOKE TO, INTERACTED WITH, AND ONLY TRULY UNDERSTOOD, OTHER BOYS.
WELL, *I* DID, ANYWAY.
bureau de chang

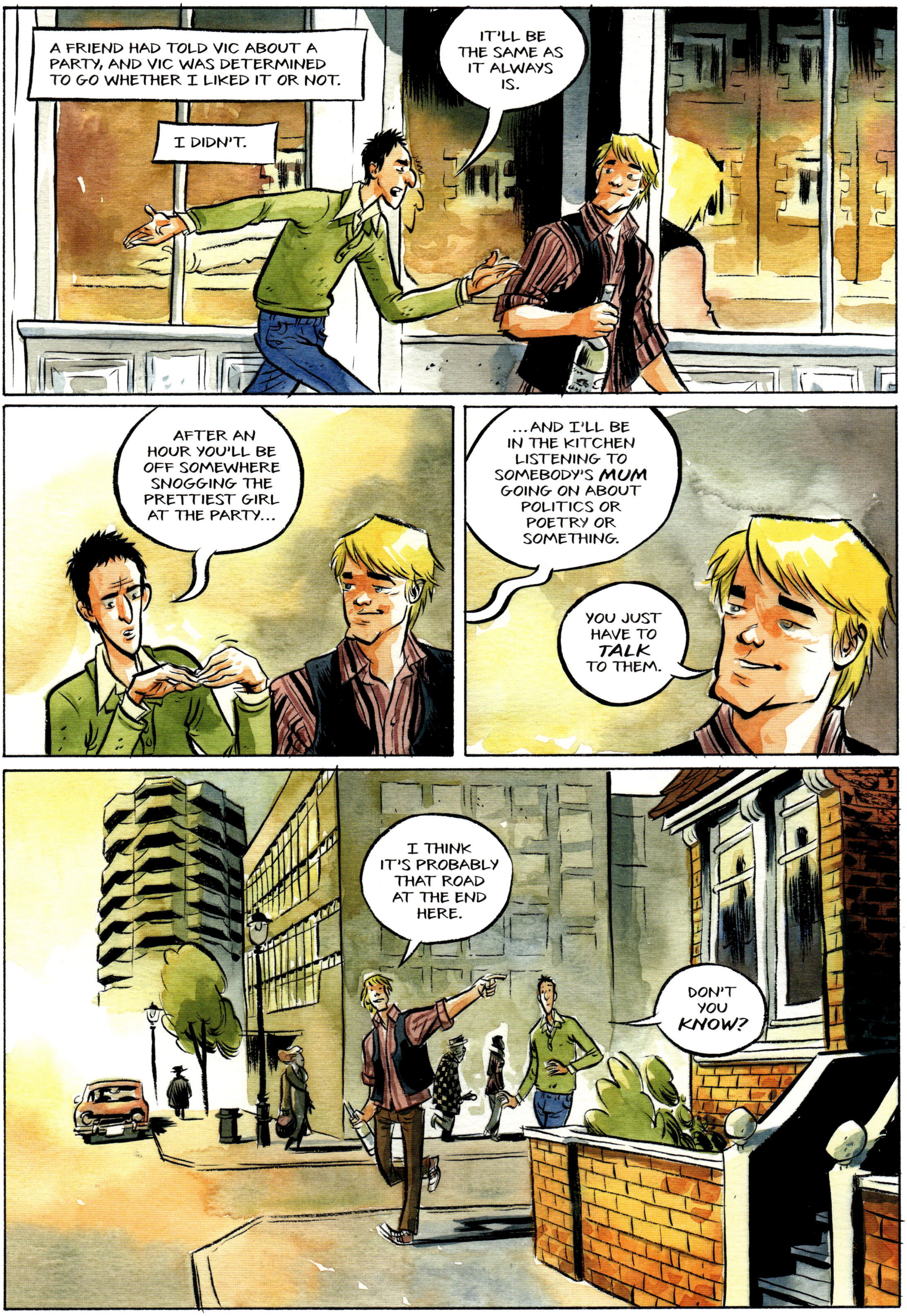
A FRIEND HAD TOLD VIC ABOUT A PARTY, AND VIC WAS DETERMINED TO GO WHETHER I LIKED IT OR NOT.
I DIDN'T.
IT'LL BE THE SAME AS IT ALWAYS IS.
AFTER AN HOUR YOU'LL BE OFF SOMEWHERE SNOGGING THE PRETTIEST GIRL AT THE PARTY...
...AND I'LL BE IN THE KITCHEN LISTENING TO SOMEBODY'S MUM GOING ON ABOUT POLITICS OR POETRY OR SOMETHING.
YOU JUST HAVE TO TALK TO THEM.
I THINK IT'S PROBABLY THAT ROAD AT THE END HERE.
DON'T YOU KNOW?

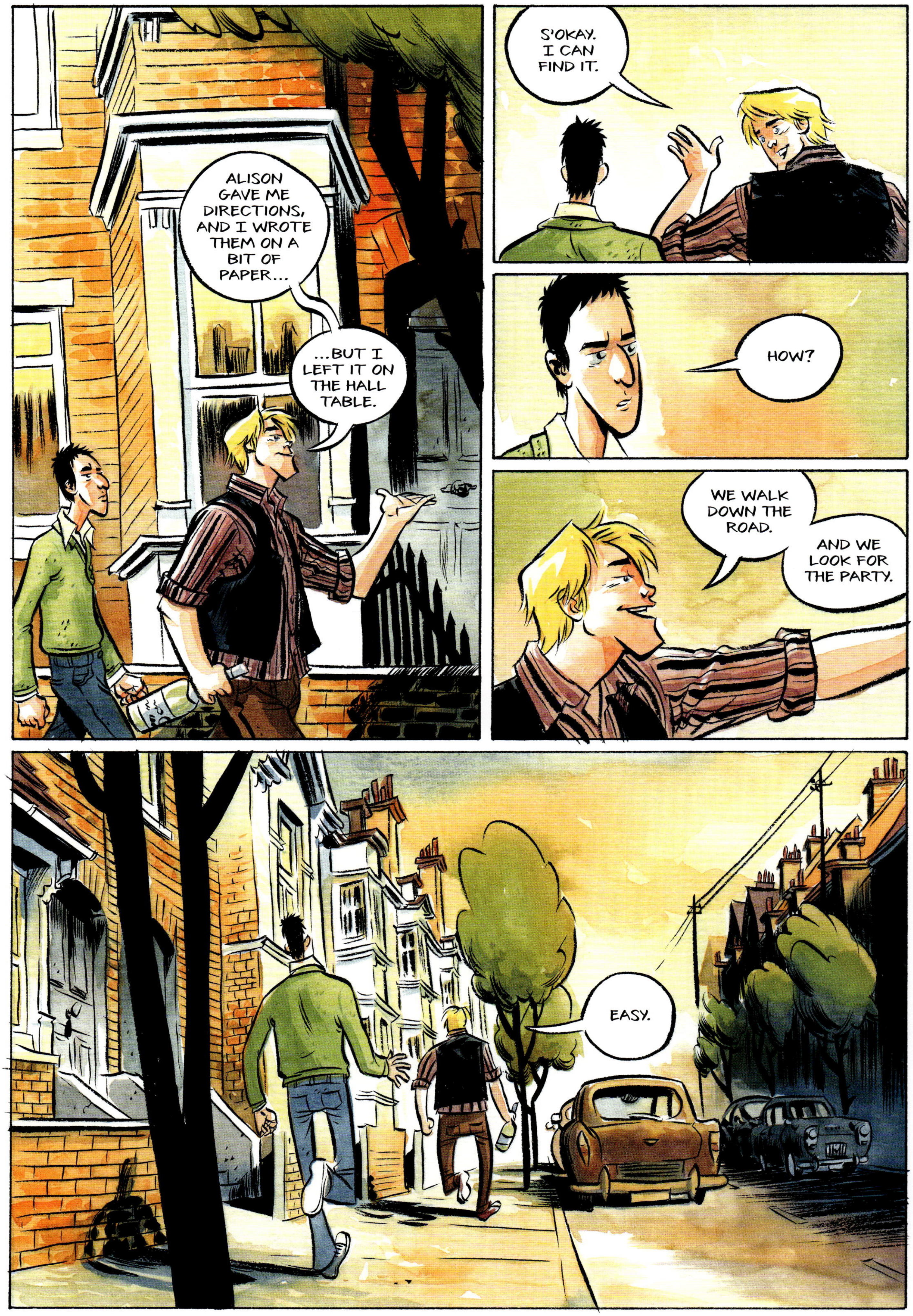
ALISON GAVE ME DIRECTIONS, AND I WROTE THEM ON A BIT OF PAPER...
...BUT I LEFT IT ON THE HALL TABLE.
S'OKAY. I CAN FIND IT.
HOW?
WE WALK DOWN THE ROAD.
AND WE LOOK FOR THE PARTY.
EASY.

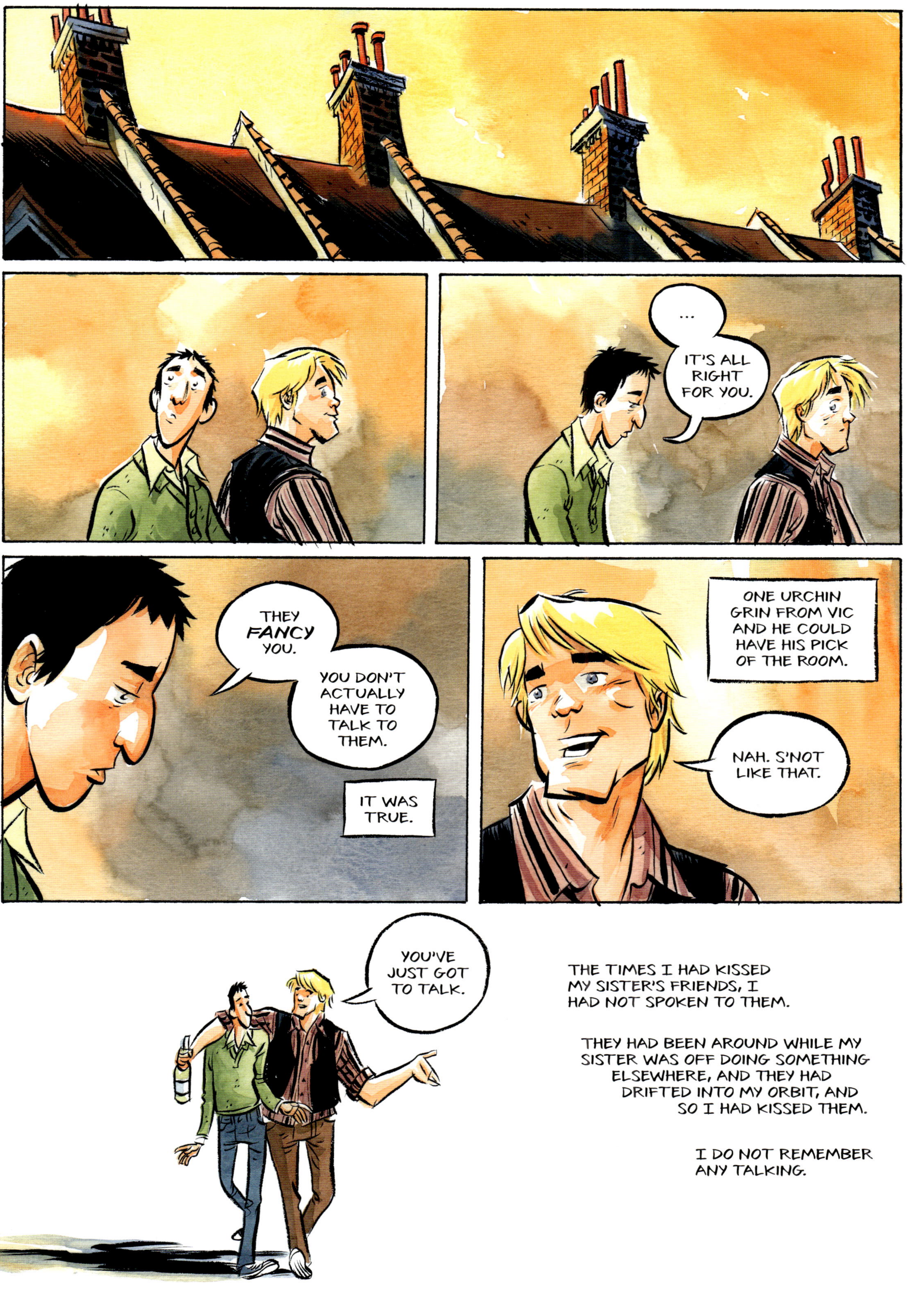
...
IT'S ALL RIGHT FOR YOU.
THEY FANCY YOU.
YOU DON'T ACTUALLY HAVE TO TALK TO THEM.
IT WAS TRUE.
ONE URCHIN GRIN FROM VIC AND HE COULD HAVE HIS PICK OF THE ROOM.
NAH. S'NOT LIKE THAT.
YOU'VE JUST GOT TO TALK.
THE TIMES I HAD KISSED MY SISTER'S FRIENDS, I HAD NOT SPOKEN TO THEM.
THEY HAD BEEN AROUND WHILE MY SISTER WAS OFF DOING SOMETHING ELSEWHERE, AND THEY HAD DRIFTED INTO MY ORBIT, AND SO I HAD KISSED THEM.
I DO NOT REMEMBER ANY TALKING.

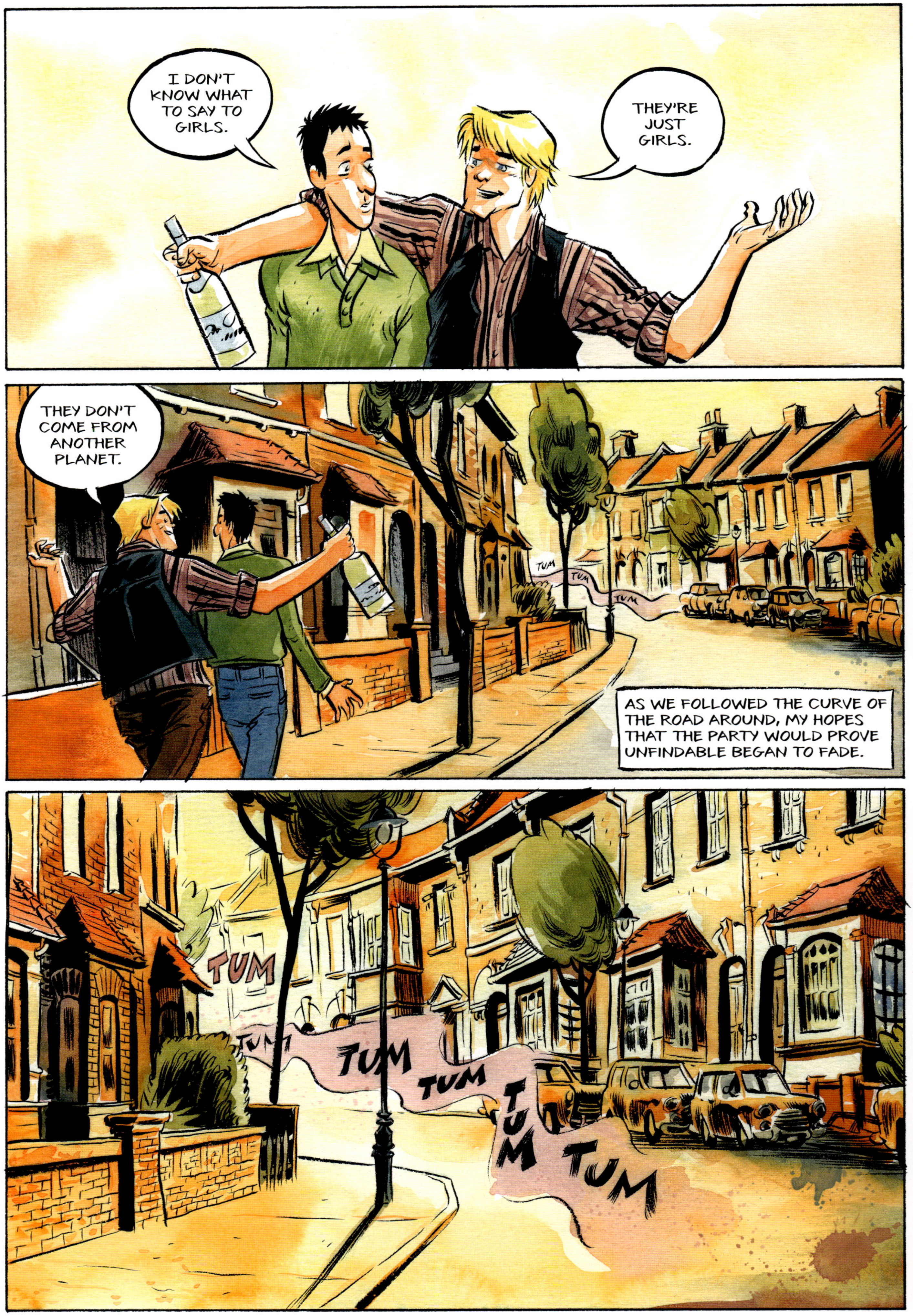
I DON'T KNOW WHAT TO SAY TO GIRLS.
THEY'RE JUST GIRLS.
THEY DON'T COME FROM ANOTHER PLANET.
TUM
TUM
TUM
AS WE FOLLOWED THE CURVE OF THE ROAD AROUND, MY HOPES THAT THE PARTY WOULD PROVE UNFINDABLE BEGAN TO FADE.
TUM
TUM
TUM
TUM
TUM
TUM

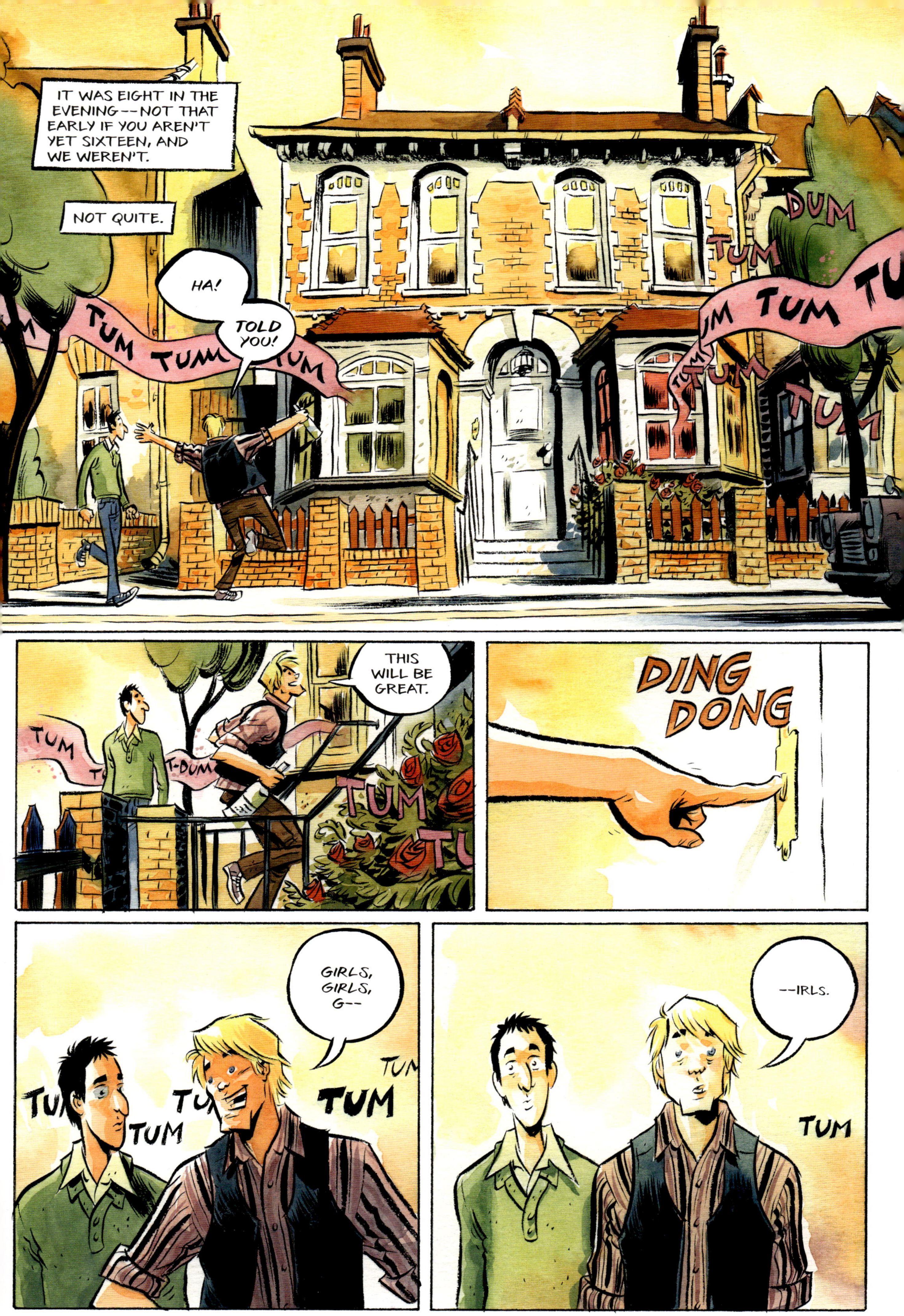
IT WAS EIGHT IN THE EVENING--NOT THAT EARLY IF YOU AREN'T YET SIXTEEN, AND WE WEREN'T.
NOT QUITE.
HA!
TOLD YOU!
TUM TUM TUM
DUM TUM
TUM TUM
THIS WILL BE GREAT.
TUM
T-DUM
TUM
DING DONG
GIRLS, GIRLS, G--
TUM
TUM
TUM
--IRLS.
TUM

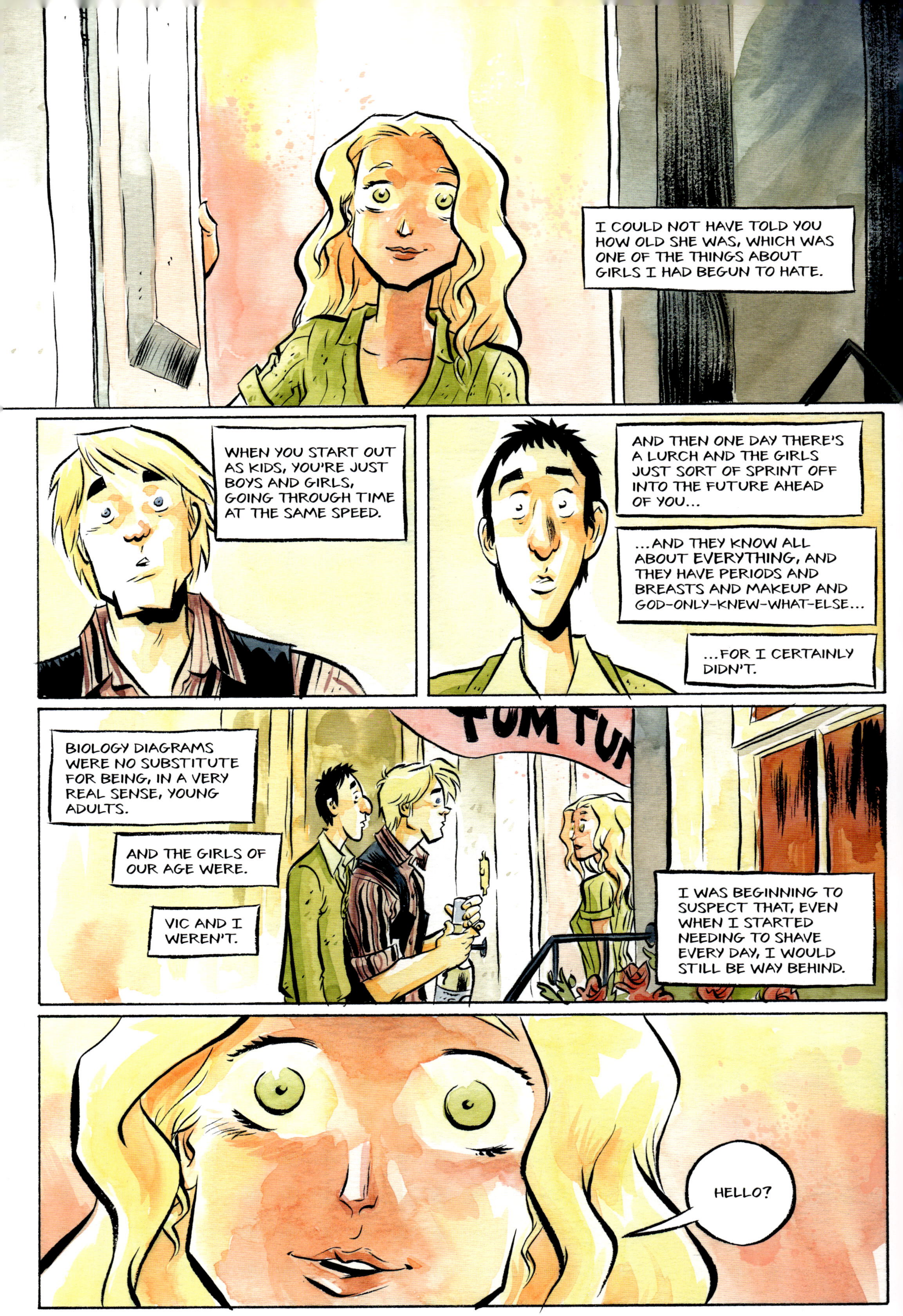
I COULD NOT HAVE TOLD YOU HOW OLD SHE WAS, WHICH WAS ONE OF THE THINGS ABOUT GIRLS I HAD BEGUN TO HATE.
WHEN YOU START OUT AS KIDS, YOU'RE JUST BOYS AND GIRLS, GOING THROUGH TIME AT THE SAME SPEED.
AND THEN ONE DAY THERE'S A LURCH AND THE GIRLS JUST SORT OF SPRINT OFF INTO THE FUTURE AHEAD OF YOU...
...AND THEY KNOW ALL ABOUT EVERYTHING, AND THEY HAVE PERIODS AND BREASTS AND MAKEUP AND GOD-ONLY-KNEW-WHAT-ELSE...
...FOR I CERTAINLY DIDN'T.
BIOLOGY DIAGRAMS WERE NO SUBSTITUTE FOR BEING, IN A VERY REAL SENSE, YOUNG ADULTS.
AND THE GIRLS OF OUR AGE WERE.
VIC AND I WEREN'T.
I WAS BEGINNING TO SUSPECT THAT, EVEN WHEN I STARTED NEEDING TO SHAVE EVERY DAY, I WOULD STILL BE WAY BEHIND.
HELLO?

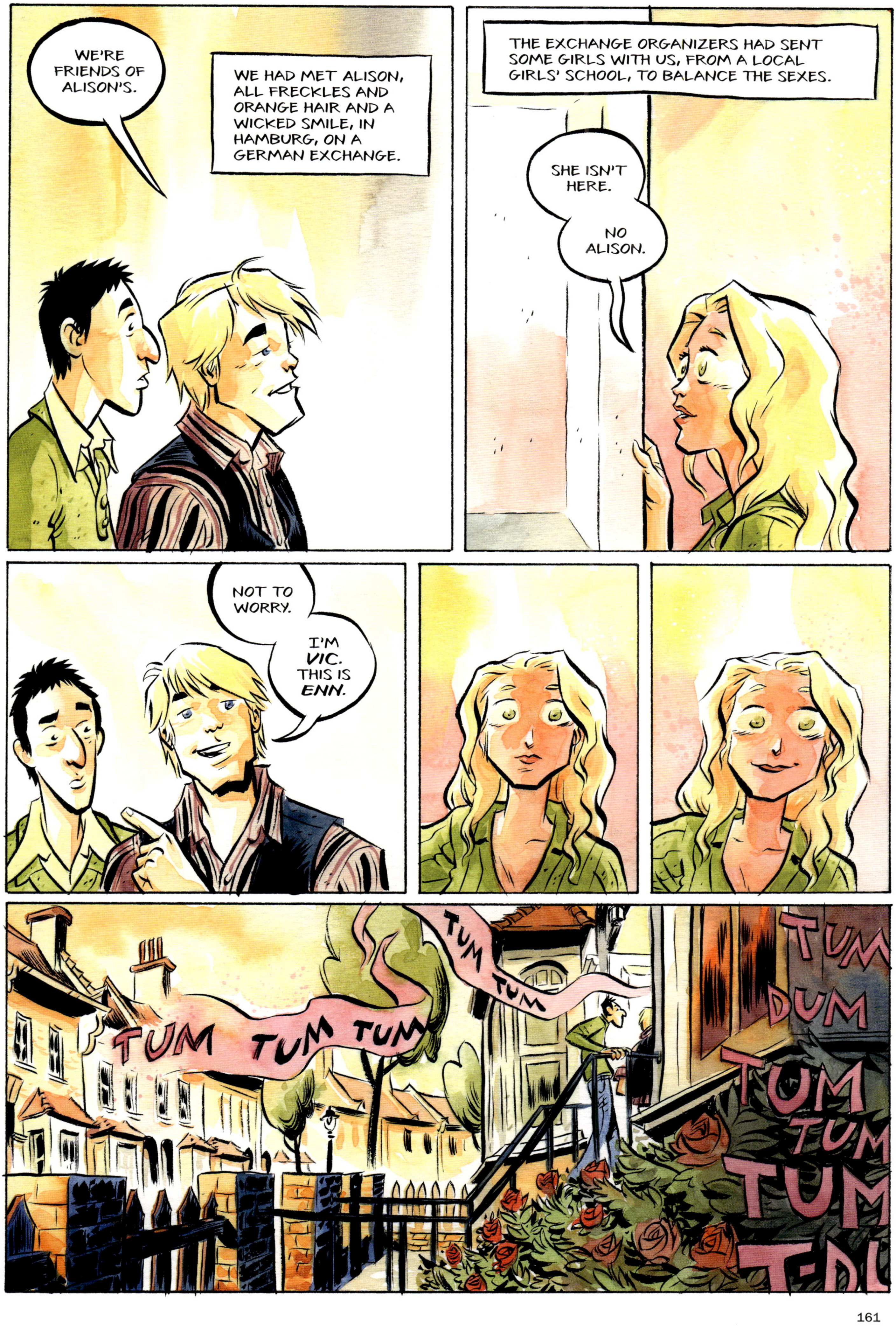
WE'RE FRIENDS OF ALISON'S.
WE HAD MET ALISON, ALL FRECKLES AND ORANGE HAIR AND A WICKED SMILE, IN HAMBURG, ON A GERMAN EXCHANGE.
THE EXCHANGE ORGANIZERS HAD SENT SOME GIRLS WITH US, FROM A LOCAL GIRLS' SCHOOL, TO BALANCE THE SEXES.
SHE ISN'T HERE.
NO ALISON.
NOT TO WORRY.
I'M *VIC.* THIS IS *ENN.*
TUM TUM TUM
TUM TUM
TUM DUM
TUM TUM TUM

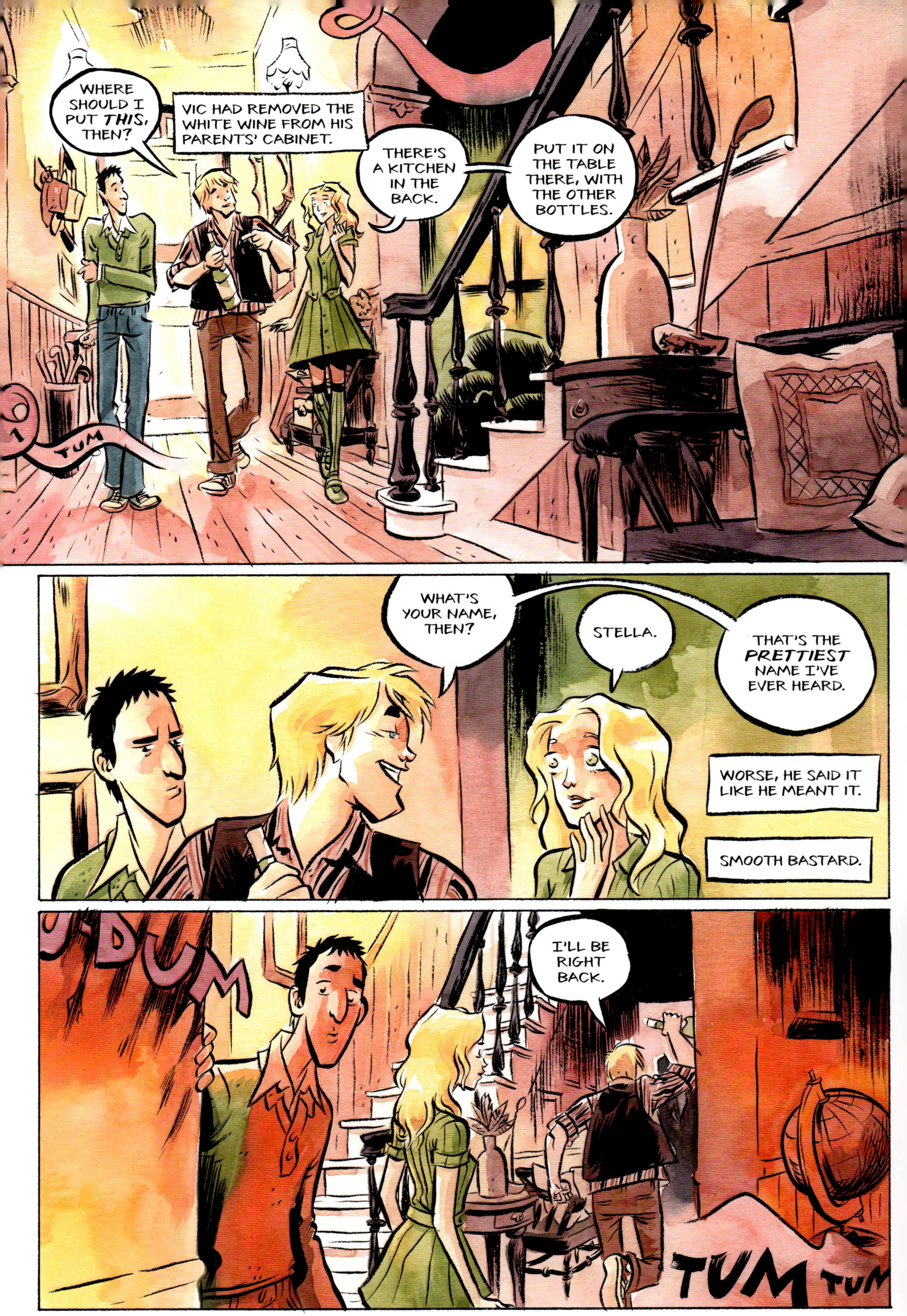
WHERE SHOULD I PUT THIS, THEN?
VIC HAD REMOVED THE WHITE WINE FROM HIS PARENTS' CABINET.
THERE'S A KITCHEN IN THE BACK.
PUT IT ON THE TABLE THERE, WITH THE OTHER BOTTLES.
TUM
WHAT'S YOUR NAME, THEN?
STELLA.
THAT'S THE PRETTIEST NAME I'VE EVER HEARD.
WORSE, HE SAID IT LIKE HE MEANT IT.
SMOOTH BASTARD.
I'LL BE RIGHT BACK.
TUM TUM

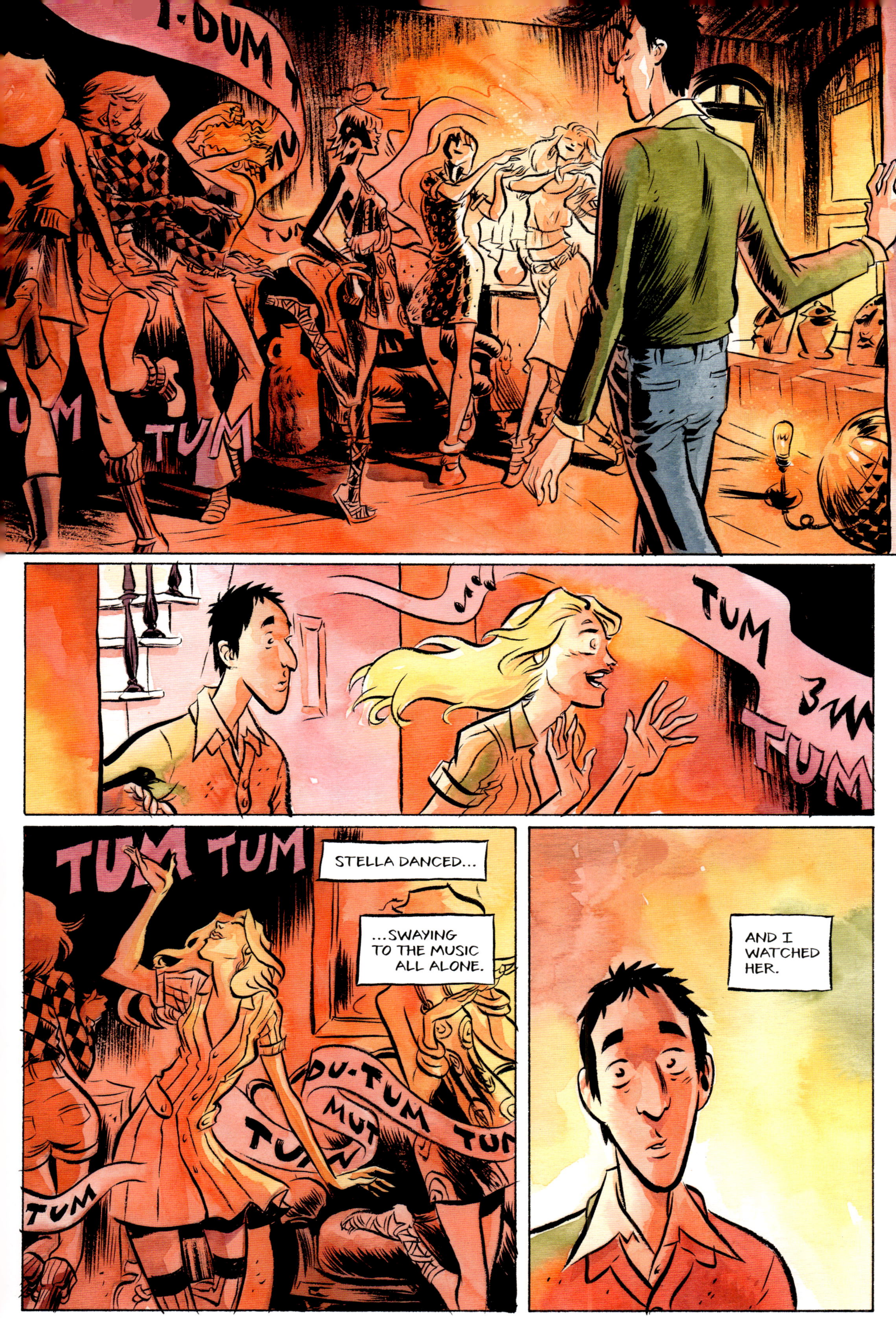
TUM
TUM
TUM
TUM TUM
STELLA DANCED...
...SWAYING TO THE MUSIC ALL ALONE.
DU-TUM
MUT
TUM
AND I WATCHED HER.

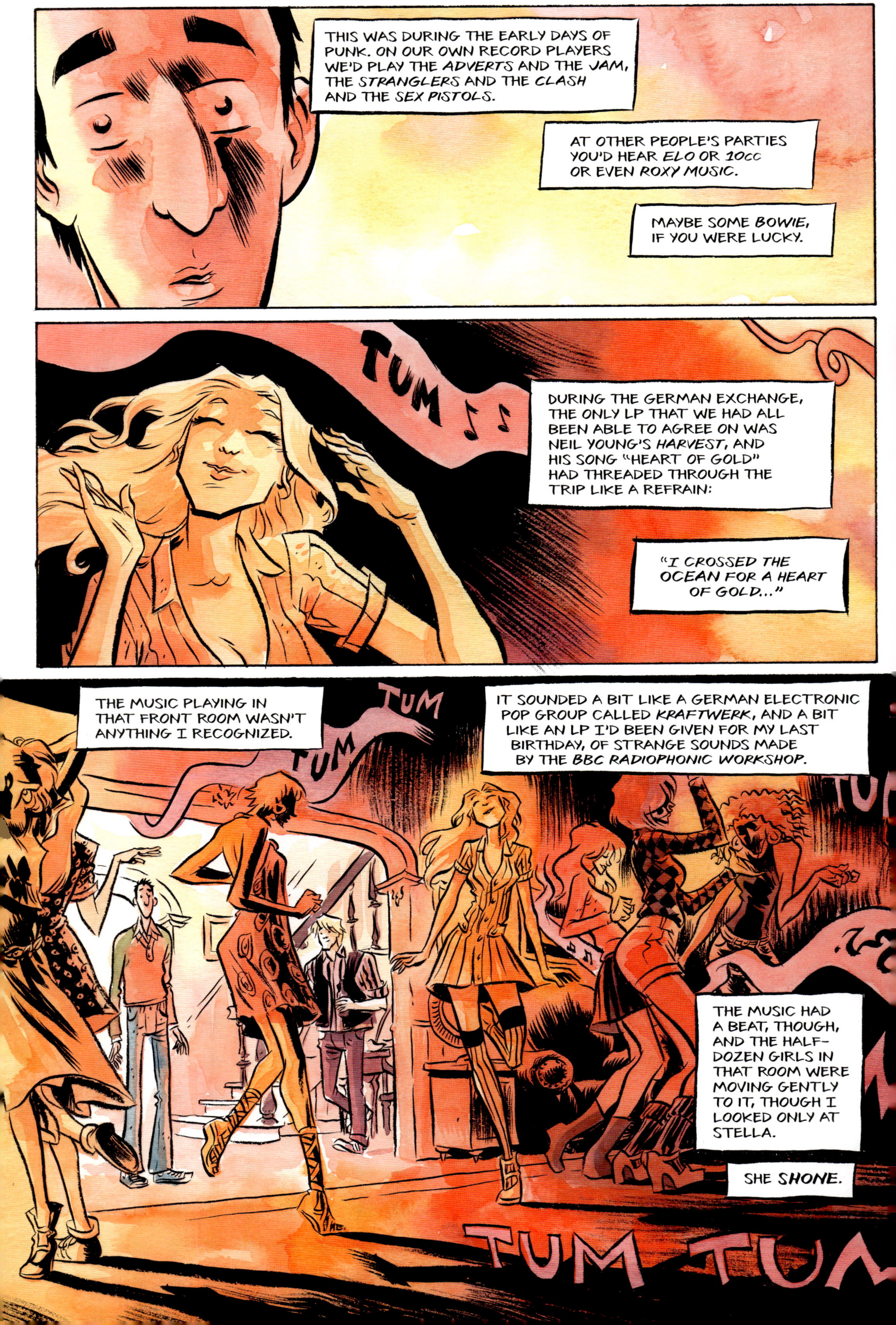
THIS WAS DURING THE EARLY DAYS OF PUNK. ON OUR OWN RECORD PLAYERS WE'D PLAY THE *ADVERTS* AND THE *JAM*, THE *STRANGLERS* AND THE *CLASH* AND THE *SEX PISTOLS*.
AT OTHER PEOPLE'S PARTIES YOU'D HEAR *ELO* OR *10cc* OR EVEN *ROXY MUSIC*.
MAYBE SOME *BOWIE*, IF YOU WERE LUCKY.
TUM
DURING THE GERMAN EXCHANGE, THE ONLY LP THAT WE HAD ALL BEEN ABLE TO AGREE ON WAS NEIL YOUNG'S *HARVEST*, AND HIS SONG "HEART OF GOLD" HAD THREADED THROUGH THE TRIP LIKE A REFRAIN:
"I CROSSED THE OCEAN FOR A HEART OF GOLD..."
THE MUSIC PLAYING IN THAT FRONT ROOM WASN'T ANYTHING I RECOGNIZED.
TUM TUM
IT SOUNDED A BIT LIKE A GERMAN ELECTRONIC POP GROUP CALLED *KRAFTWERK*, AND A BIT LIKE AN LP I'D BEEN GIVEN FOR MY LAST BIRTHDAY, OF STRANGE SOUNDS MADE BY THE *BBC RADIOPHONIC WORKSHOP*.
THE MUSIC HAD A BEAT, THOUGH, AND THE HALF-DOZEN GIRLS IN THAT ROOM WERE MOVING GENTLY TO IT, THOUGH I LOOKED ONLY AT STELLA.
SHE ***SHONE***.
TUM

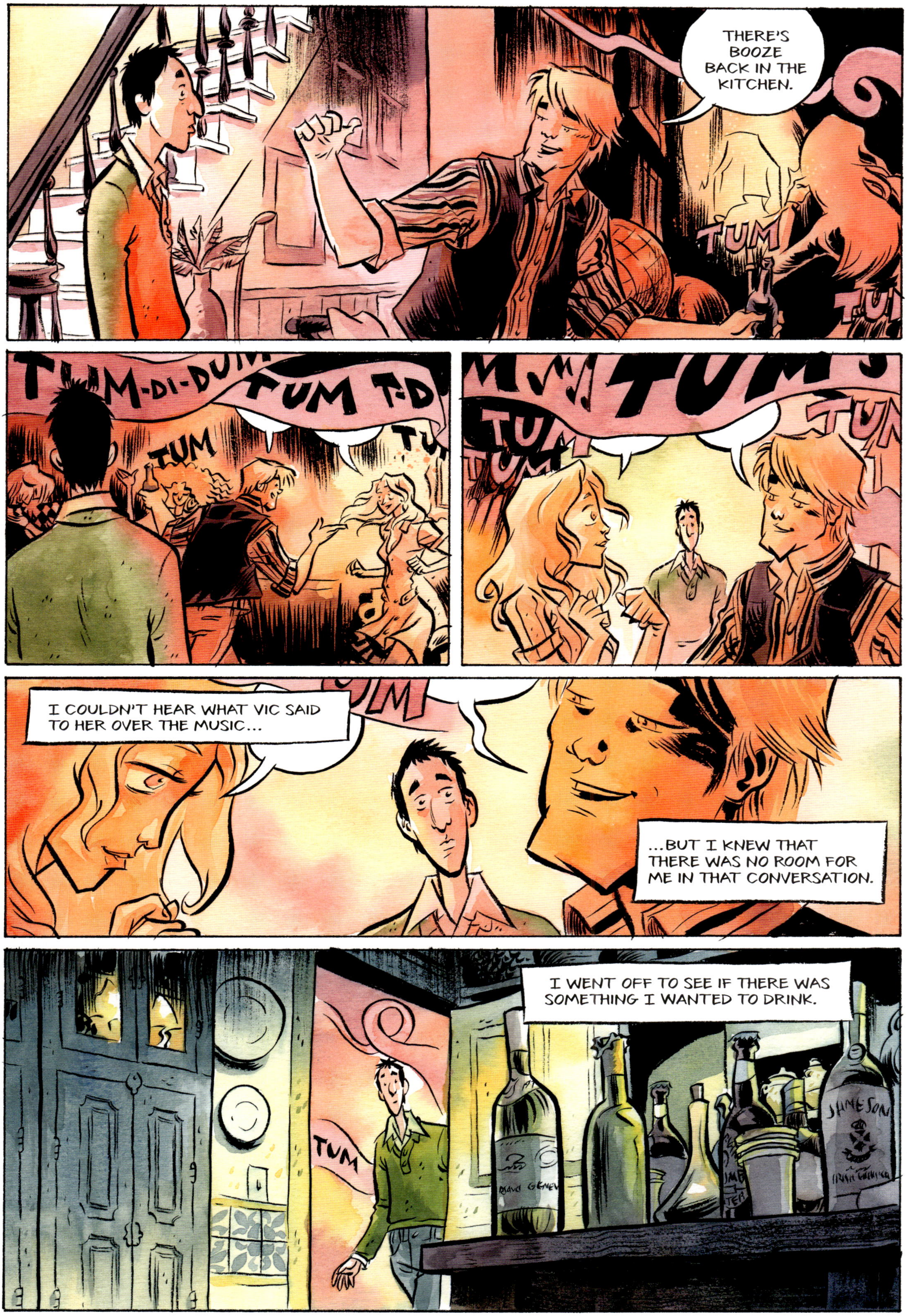
THERE'S BOOZE BACK IN THE KITCHEN.
TUM
TUM-DI-DUM TUM T-D
TUM
TUM
TUM
I COULDN'T HEAR WHAT VIC SAID TO HER OVER THE MUSIC...
...BUT I KNEW THAT THERE WAS NO ROOM FOR ME IN THAT CONVERSATION.
I WENT OFF TO SEE IF THERE WAS SOMETHING I WANTED TO DRINK.
TUM

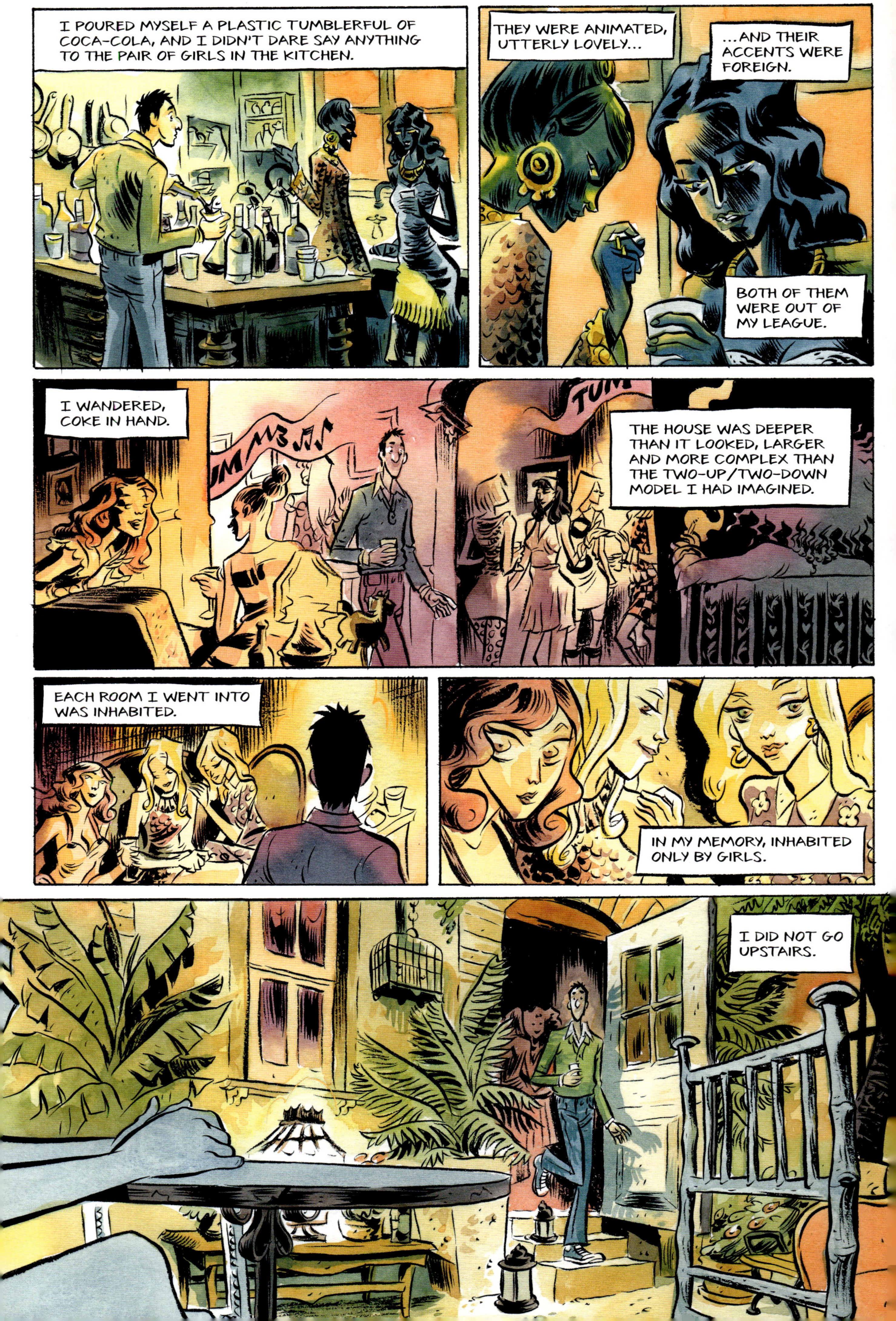
I POURED MYSELF A PLASTIC TUMBLERFUL OF COCA-COLA, AND I DIDN'T DARE SAY ANYTHING TO THE PAIR OF GIRLS IN THE KITCHEN.
THEY WERE ANIMATED, UTTERLY LOVELY...
...AND THEIR ACCENTS WERE FOREIGN.
BOTH OF THEM WERE OUT OF MY LEAGUE.
I WANDERED, COKE IN HAND.
THE HOUSE WAS DEEPER THAN IT LOOKED, LARGER AND MORE COMPLEX THAN THE TWO-UP/TWO-DOWN MODEL I HAD IMAGINED.
EACH ROOM I WENT INTO WAS INHABITED.
IN MY MEMORY, INHABITED ONLY BY GIRLS.
I DID NOT GO UPSTAIRS.

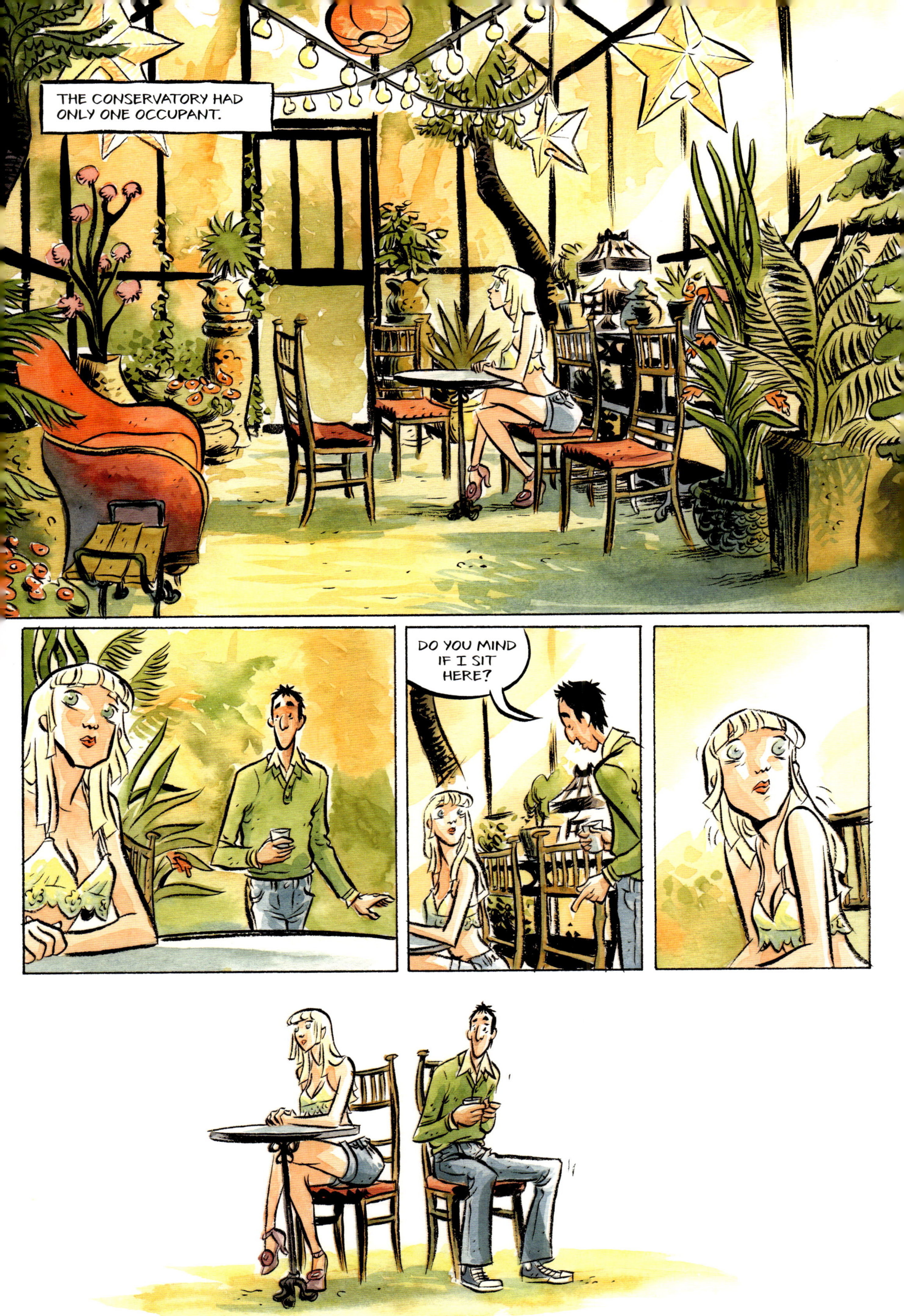
THE CONSERVATORY HAD ONLY ONE OCCUPANT.
DO YOU MIND IF I SIT HERE?

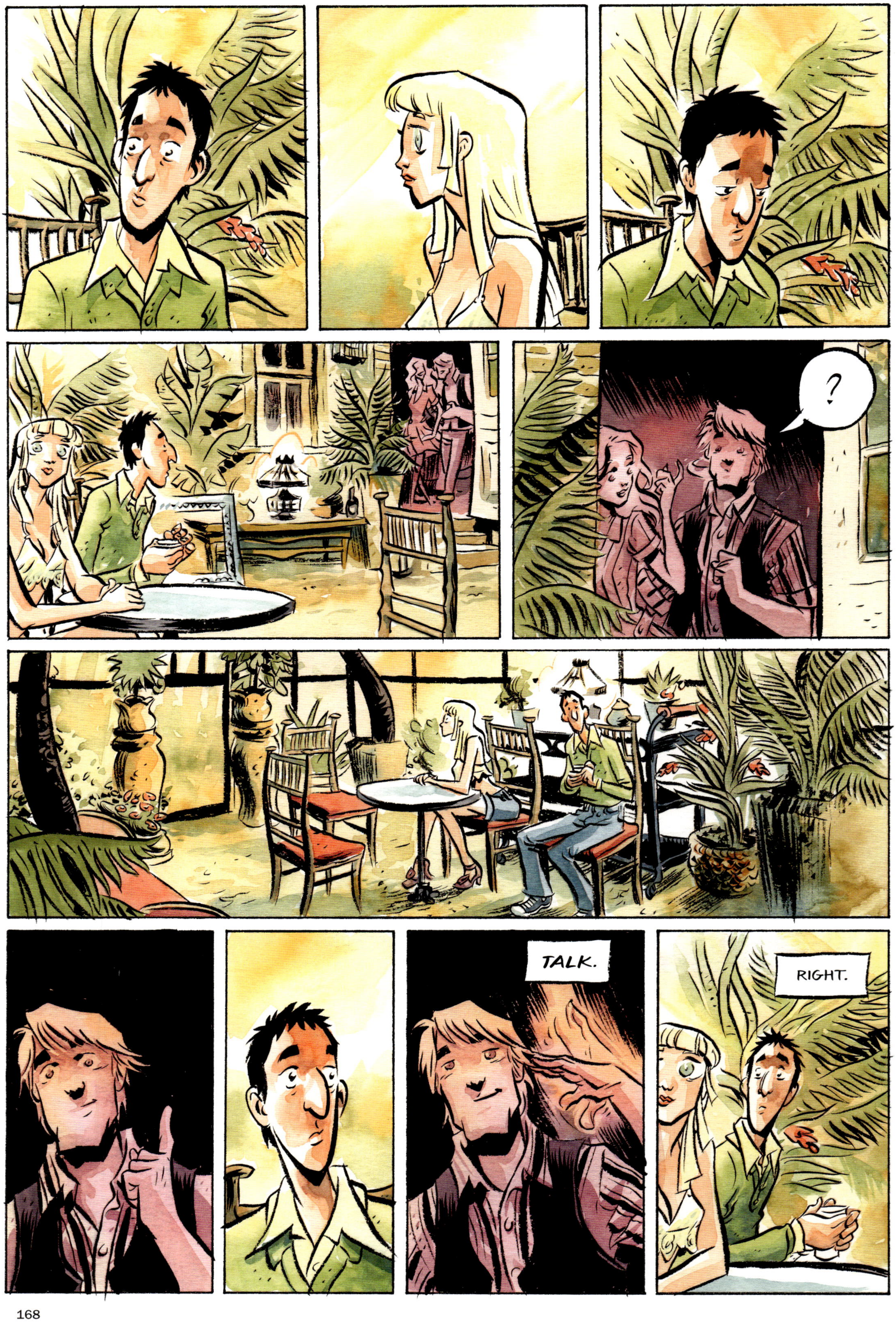
?
TALK.
RIGHT.

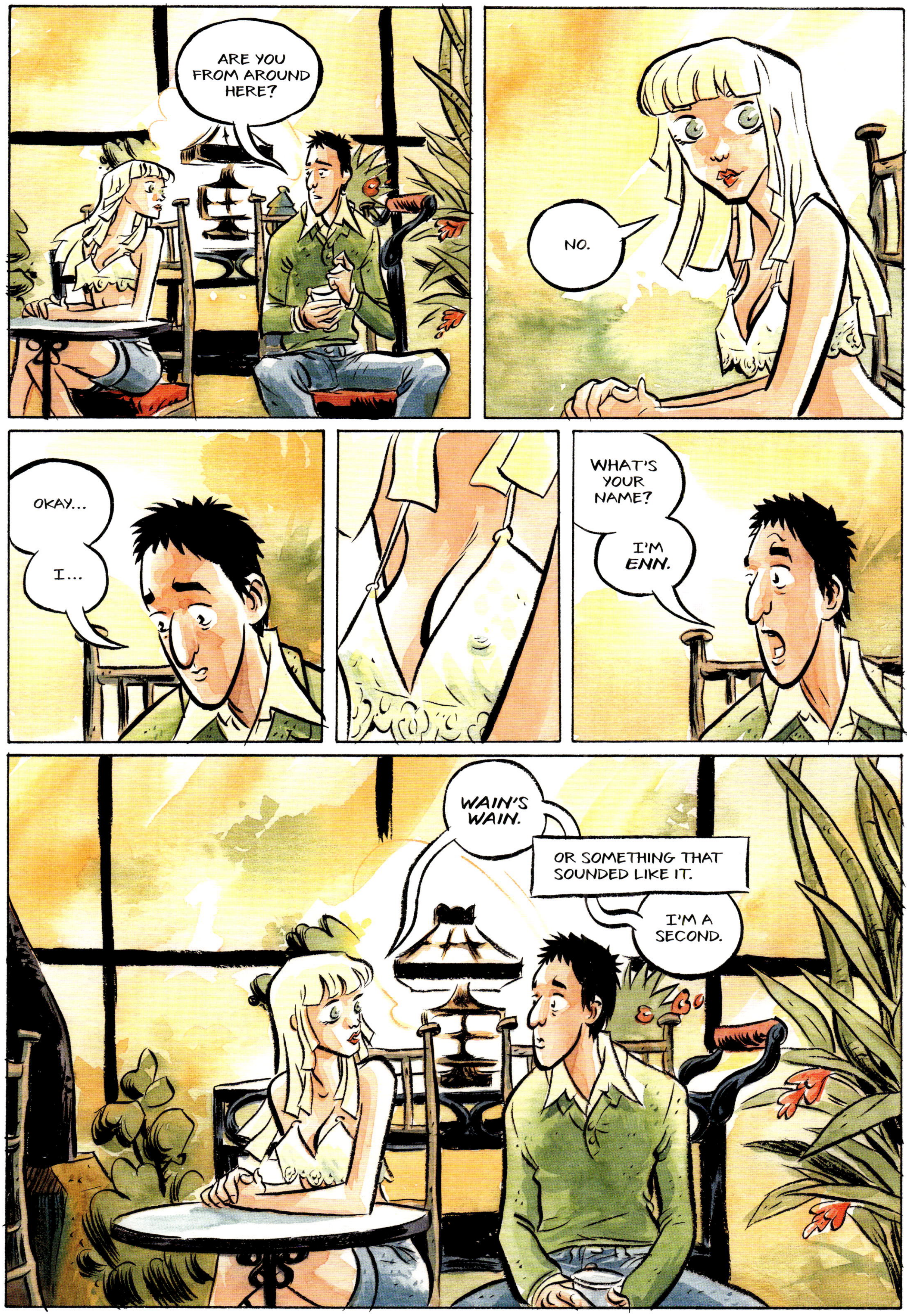
ARE YOU FROM AROUND HERE?
NO.
OKAY...
I...
WHAT'S YOUR NAME?
I'M ENN.
WAIN'S WAIN.
OR SOMETHING THAT SOUNDED LIKE IT.
I'M A SECOND.

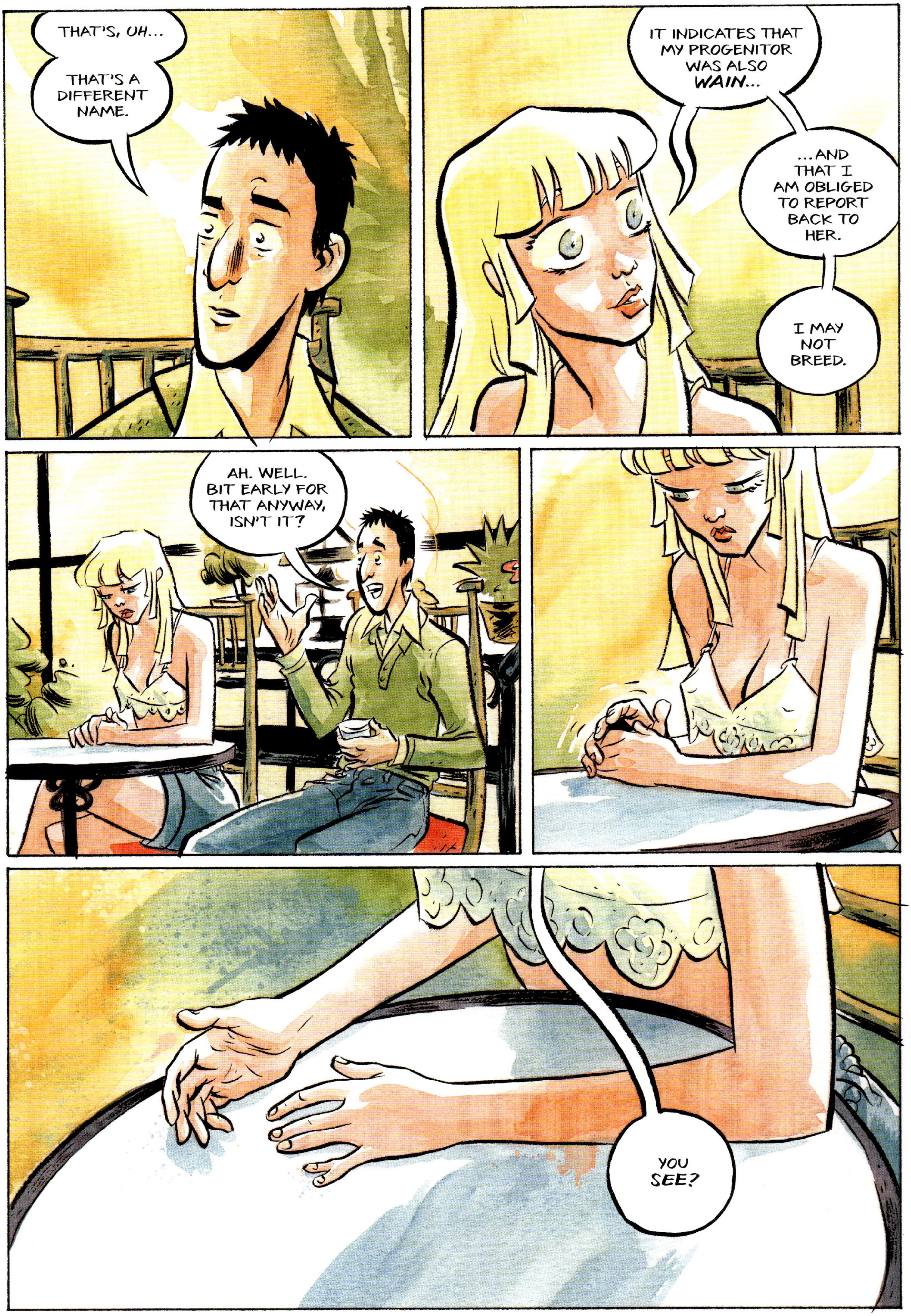
THAT'S, UH...
THAT'S A DIFFERENT NAME.
IT INDICATES THAT MY PROGENITOR WAS ALSO WAIN...
...AND THAT I AM OBLIGED TO REPORT BACK TO HER.
I MAY NOT BREED.
AH. WELL. BIT EARLY FOR THAT ANYWAY, ISN'T IT?
YOU SEE?

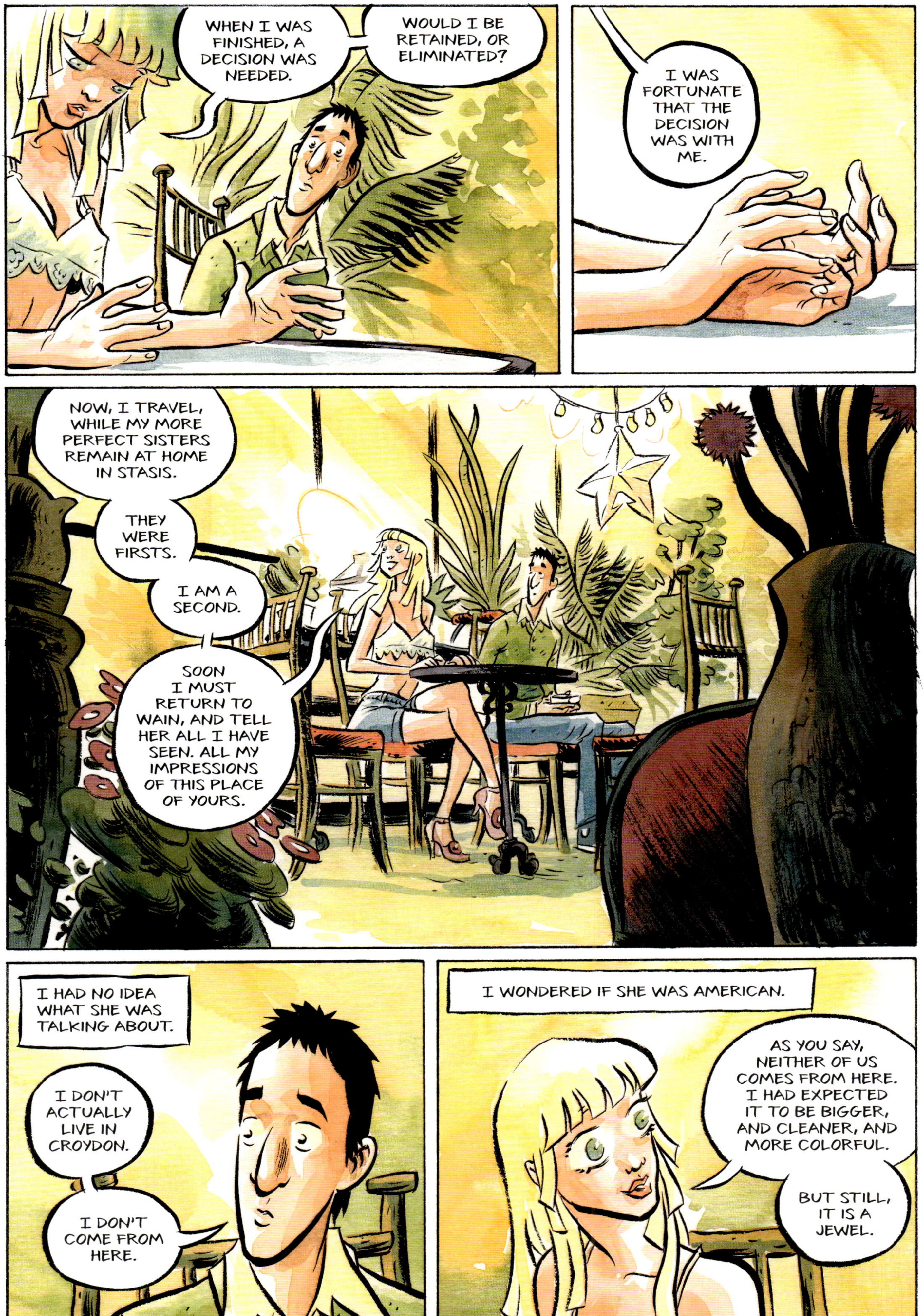
WHEN I WAS FINISHED, A DECISION WAS NEEDED.
WOULD I BE RETAINED, OR ELIMINATED?
I WAS FORTUNATE THAT THE DECISION WAS WITH ME.
NOW, I TRAVEL, WHILE MY MORE PERFECT SISTERS REMAIN AT HOME IN STASIS.
THEY WERE FIRSTS.
I AM A SECOND.
SOON I MUST RETURN TO WAIN, AND TELL HER ALL I HAVE SEEN. ALL MY IMPRESSIONS OF THIS PLACE OF YOURS.
I HAD NO IDEA WHAT SHE WAS TALKING ABOUT.
I DON'T ACTUALLY LIVE IN CROYDON.
I DON'T COME FROM HERE.
I WONDERED IF SHE WAS AMERICAN.
AS YOU SAY, NEITHER OF US COMES FROM HERE. I HAD EXPECTED IT TO BE BIGGER, AND CLEANER, AND MORE COLORFUL.
BUT STILL, IT IS A JEWEL.

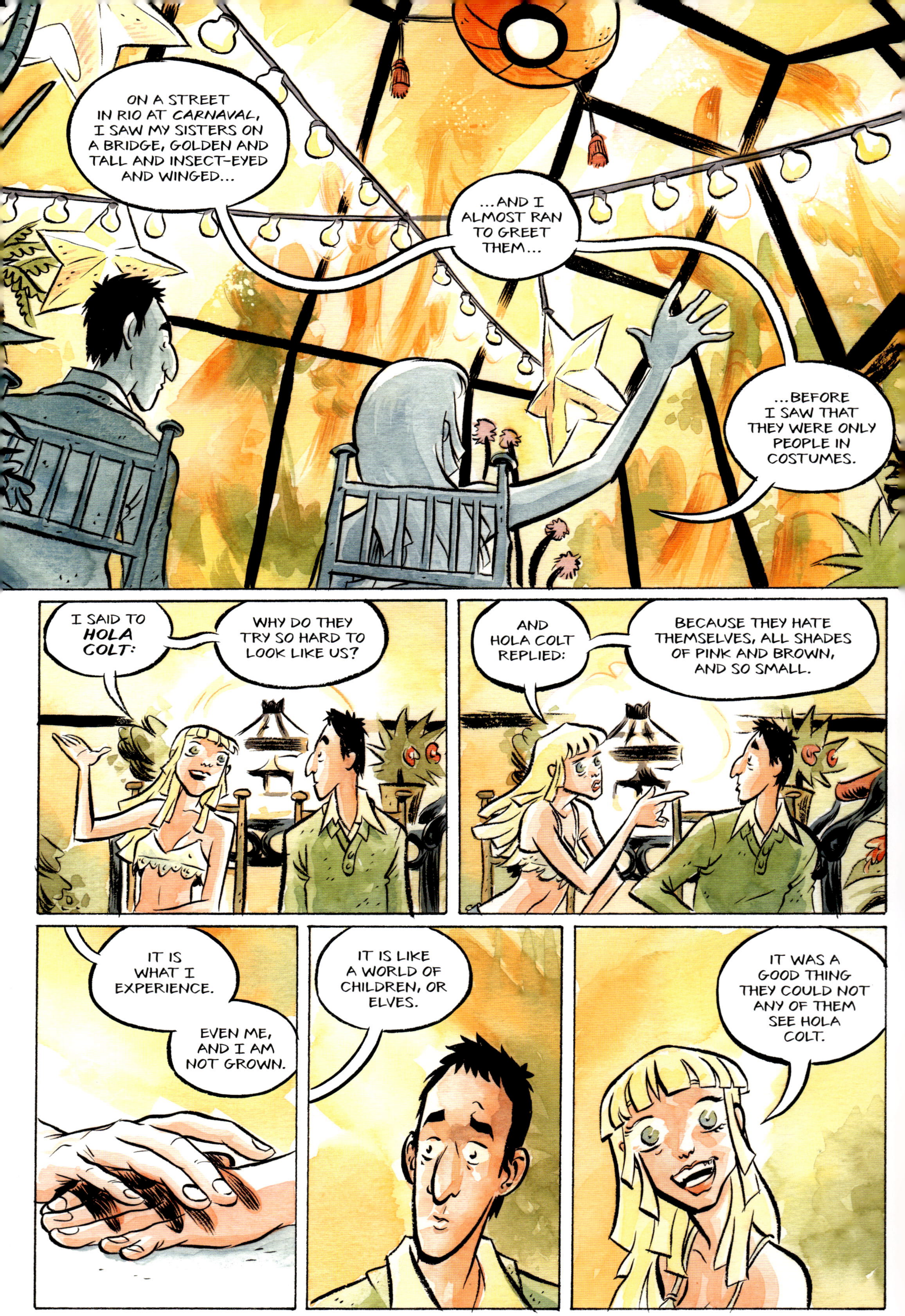
ON A STREET IN RIO AT CARNAVAL, I SAW MY SISTERS ON A BRIDGE, GOLDEN AND TALL AND INSECT-EYED AND WINGED...
...AND I ALMOST RAN TO GREET THEM...
...BEFORE I SAW THAT THEY WERE ONLY PEOPLE IN COSTUMES.
I SAID TO HOLA COLT:
WHY DO THEY TRY SO HARD TO LOOK LIKE US?
AND HOLA COLT REPLIED:
BECAUSE THEY HATE THEMSELVES, ALL SHADES OF PINK AND BROWN, AND SO SMALL.
IT IS WHAT I EXPERIENCE.
EVEN ME, AND I AM NOT GROWN.
IT IS LIKE A WORLD OF CHILDREN, OR ELVES.
IT WAS A GOOD THING THEY COULD NOT ANY OF THEM SEE HOLA COLT.

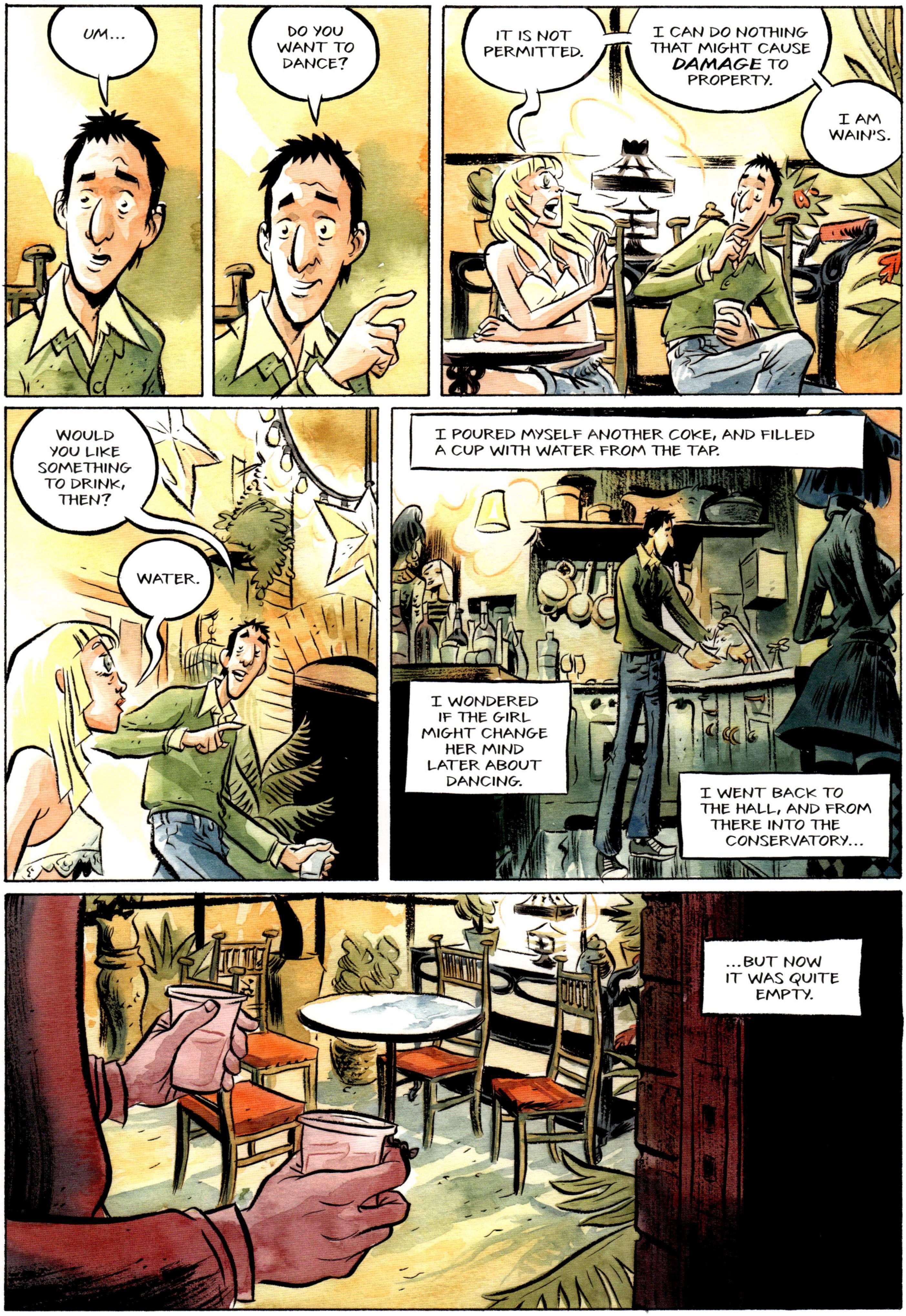
UM...
DO YOU WANT TO DANCE?
IT IS NOT PERMITTED.
I CAN DO NOTHING THAT MIGHT CAUSE DAMAGE TO PROPERTY.
I AM WAIN'S.
WOULD YOU LIKE SOMETHING TO DRINK, THEN?
WATER.
I POURED MYSELF ANOTHER COKE, AND FILLED A CUP WITH WATER FROM THE TAP.
I WONDERED IF THE GIRL MIGHT CHANGE HER MIND LATER ABOUT DANCING.
I WENT BACK TO THE HALL, AND FROM THERE INTO THE CONSERVATORY...
...BUT NOW IT WAS QUITE EMPTY.

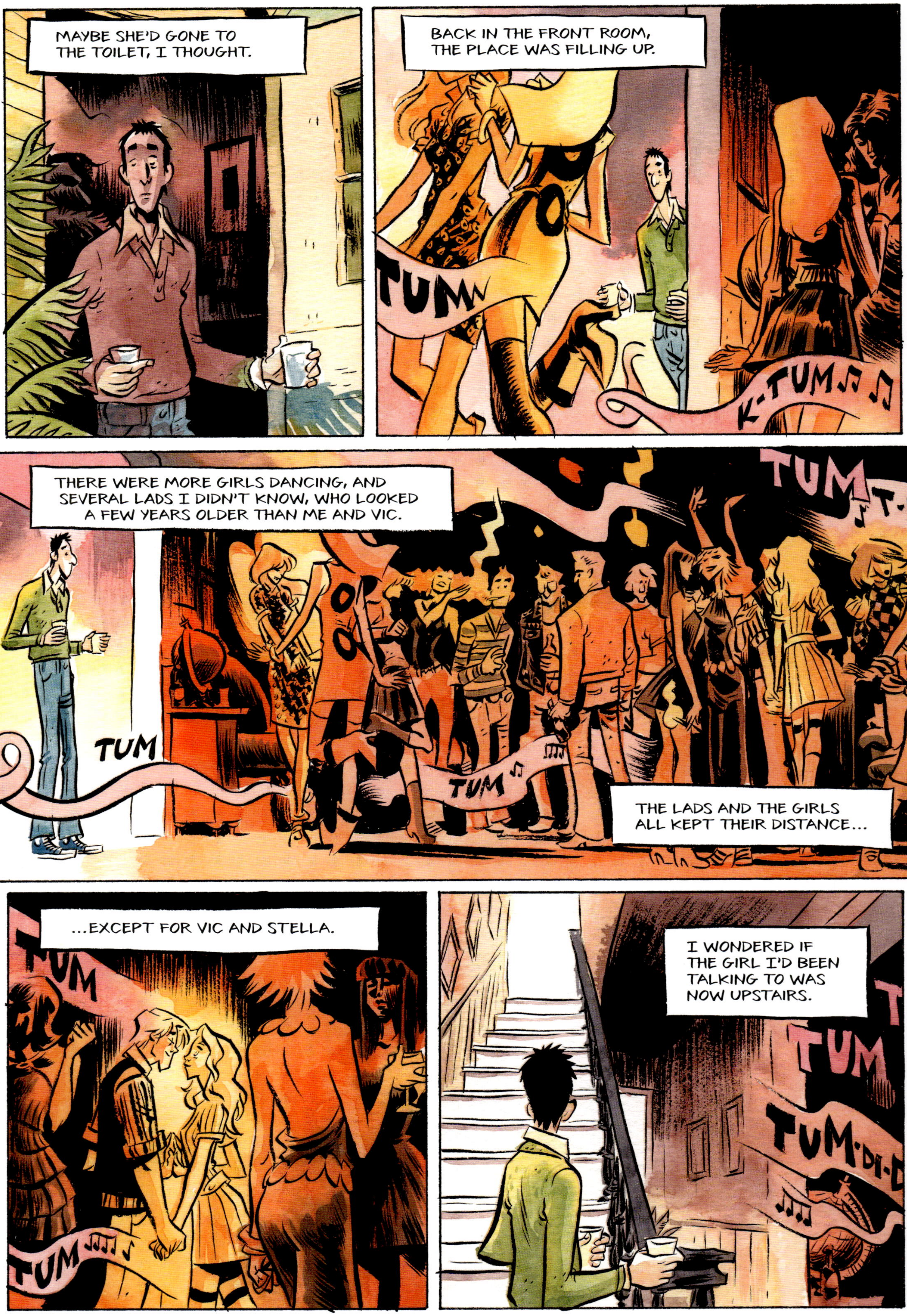
MAYBE SHE'D GONE TO THE TOILET, I THOUGHT.
BACK IN THE FRONT ROOM, THE PLACE WAS FILLING UP.
TUM
K-TUM
THERE WERE MORE GIRLS DANCING, AND SEVERAL LADS I DIDN'T KNOW, WHO LOOKED A FEW YEARS OLDER THAN ME AND VIC.
TUM
TUM
TUM
THE LADS AND THE GIRLS ALL KEPT THEIR DISTANCE...
...EXCEPT FOR VIC AND STELLA.
TUM
TUM
I WONDERED IF THE GIRL I'D BEEN TALKING TO WAS NOW UPSTAIRS.
TUM

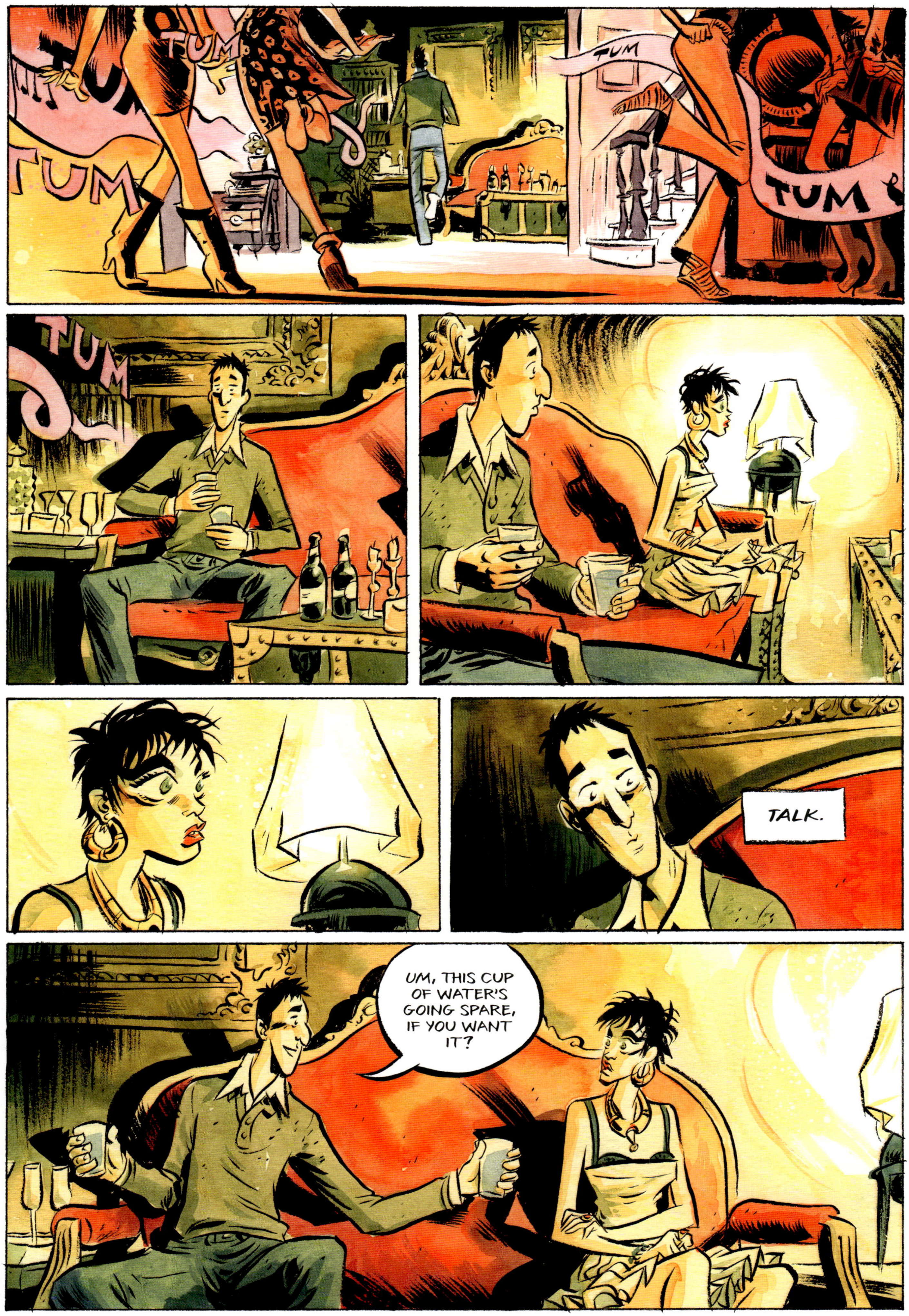
TUM
TUM
TUM
TUM
TUM
TALK.
UM, THIS CUP OF WATER'S GOING SPARE, IF YOU WANT IT?

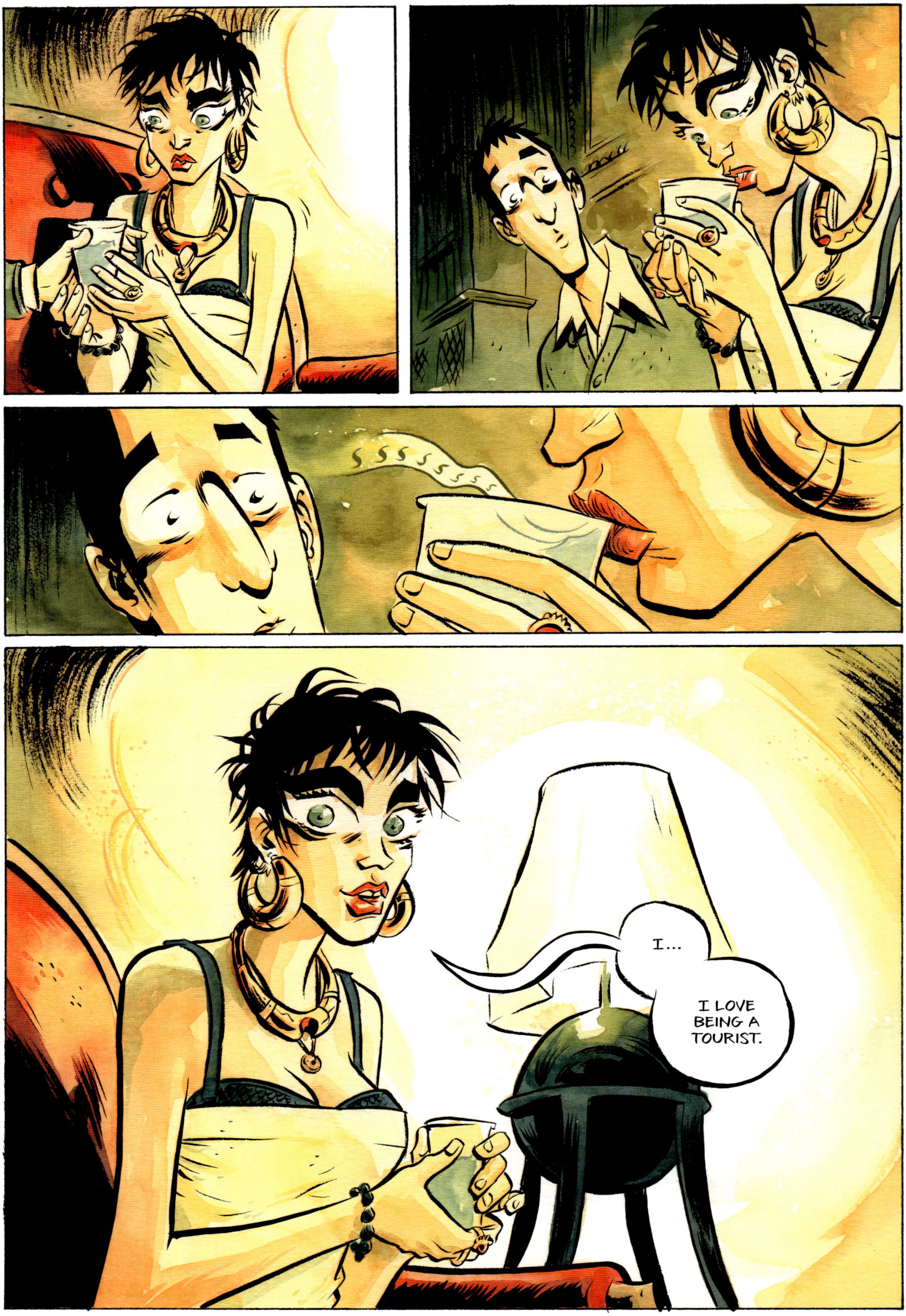
SSSSSSSS
I...
I LOVE BEING A TOURIST.

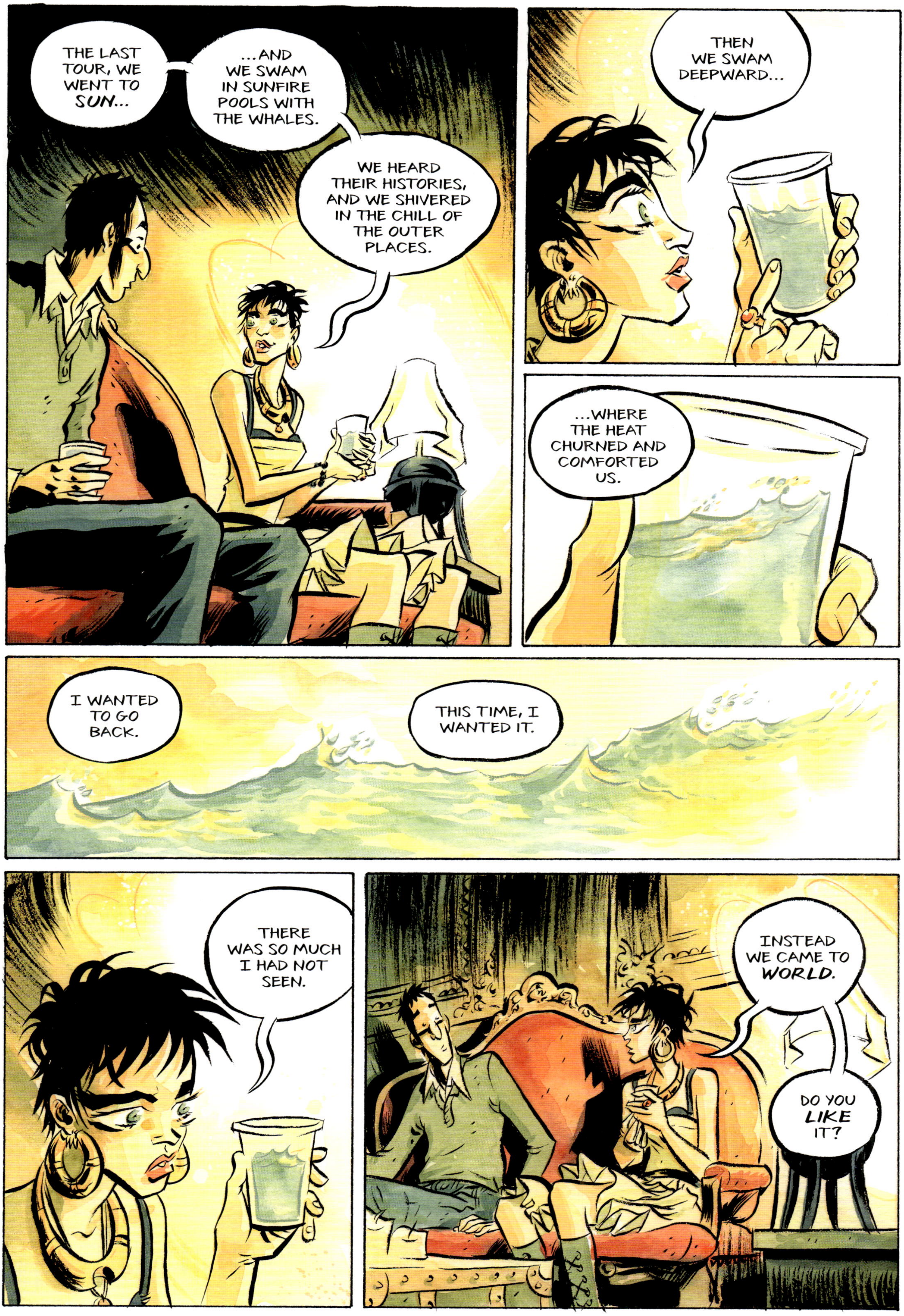
THE LAST TOUR, WE WENT TO SUN...
...AND WE SWAM IN SUNFIRE POOLS WITH THE WHALES.
WE HEARD THEIR HISTORIES, AND WE SHIVERED IN THE CHILL OF THE OUTER PLACES.
THEN WE SWAM DEEPWARD...
...WHERE THE HEAT CHURNED AND COMFORTED US.
I WANTED TO GO BACK.
THIS TIME, I WANTED IT.
THERE WAS SO MUCH I HAD NOT SEEN.
INSTEAD WE CAME TO WORLD.
DO YOU LIKE IT?

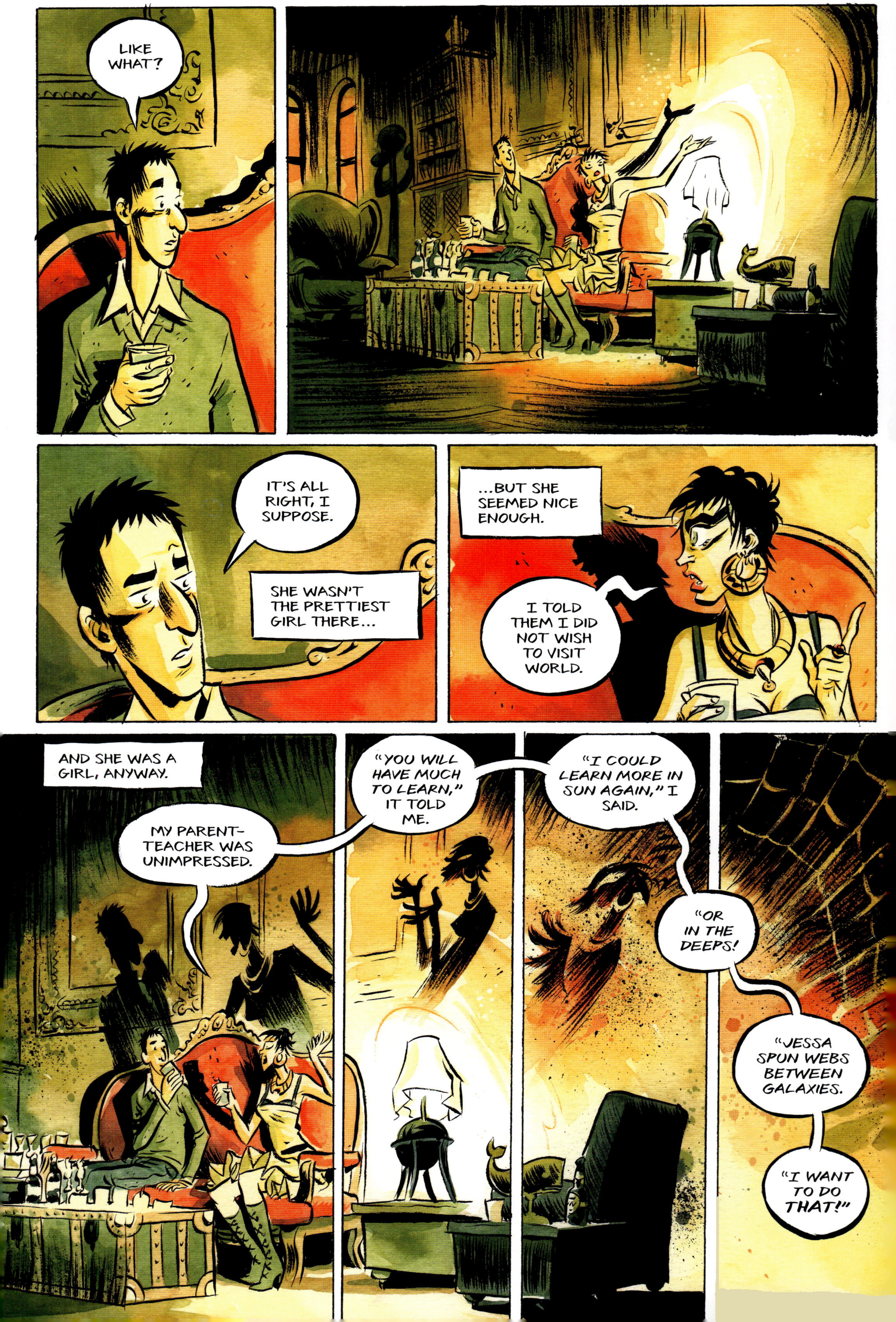
LIKE WHAT?
IT'S ALL RIGHT, I SUPPOSE.
SHE WASN'T THE PRETTIEST GIRL THERE...
...BUT SHE SEEMED NICE ENOUGH.
I TOLD THEM I DID NOT WISH TO VISIT WORLD.
AND SHE WAS A GIRL, ANYWAY.
MY PARENT-TEACHER WAS UNIMPRESSED.
"YOU WILL HAVE MUCH TO LEARN," IT TOLD ME.
"I COULD LEARN MORE IN SUN AGAIN," I SAID.
"OR IN THE DEEPS!
"JESSA SPUN WEBS BETWEEN GALAXIES.
"I WANT TO DO THAT!"

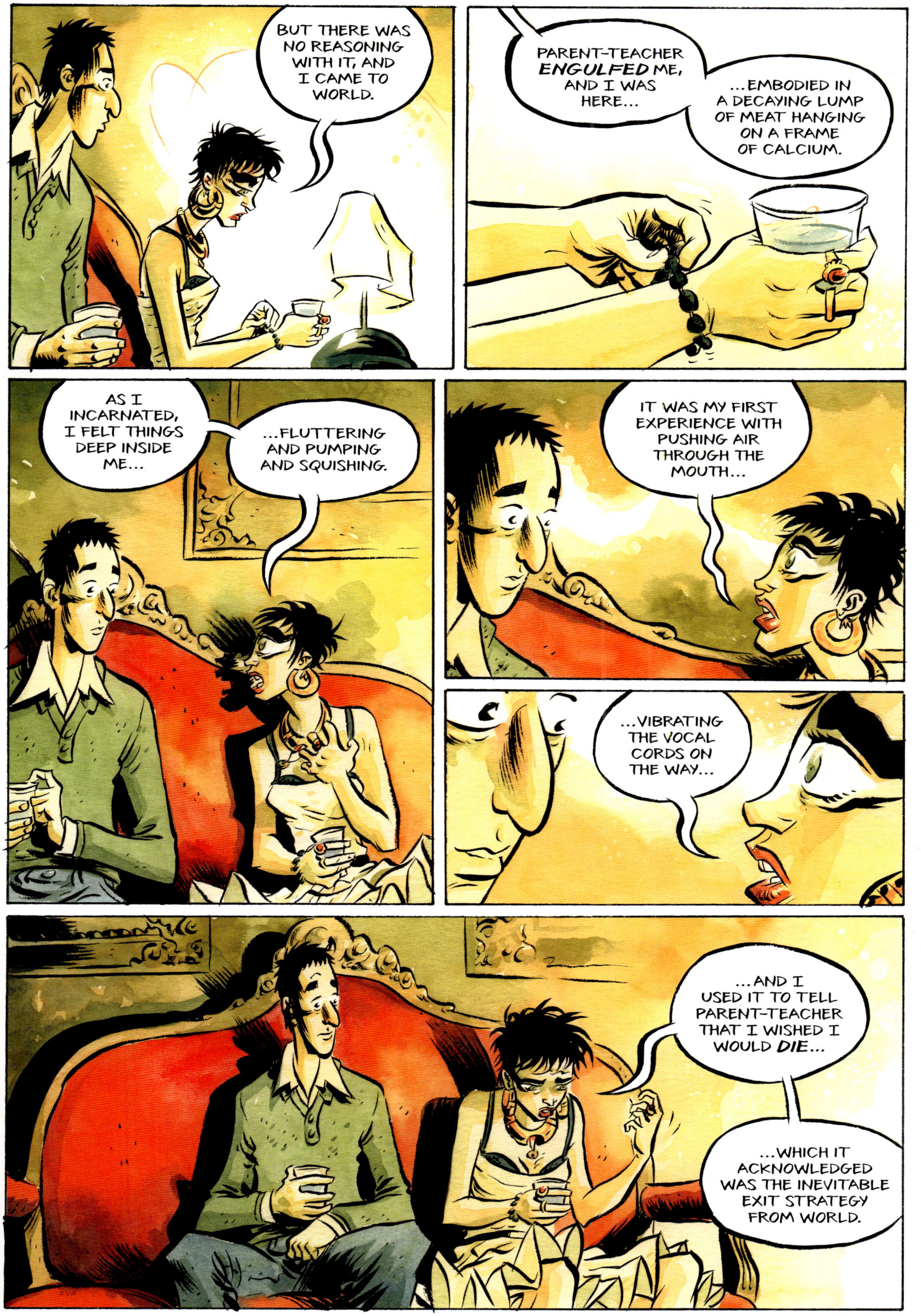
BUT THERE WAS NO REASONING WITH IT, AND I CAME TO WORLD.
PARENT-TEACHER ENGULFED ME, AND I WAS HERE...
...EMBODIED IN A DECAYING LUMP OF MEAT HANGING ON A FRAME OF CALCIUM.
AS I INCARNATED, I FELT THINGS DEEP INSIDE ME...
...FLUTTERING AND PUMPING AND SQUISHING.
IT WAS MY FIRST EXPERIENCE WITH PUSHING AIR THROUGH THE MOUTH...
...VIBRATING THE VOCAL CORDS ON THE WAY...
...AND I USED IT TO TELL PARENT-TEACHER THAT I WISHED I WOULD DIE...
...WHICH IT ACKNOWLEDGED WAS THE INEVITABLE EXIT STRATEGY FROM WORLD.

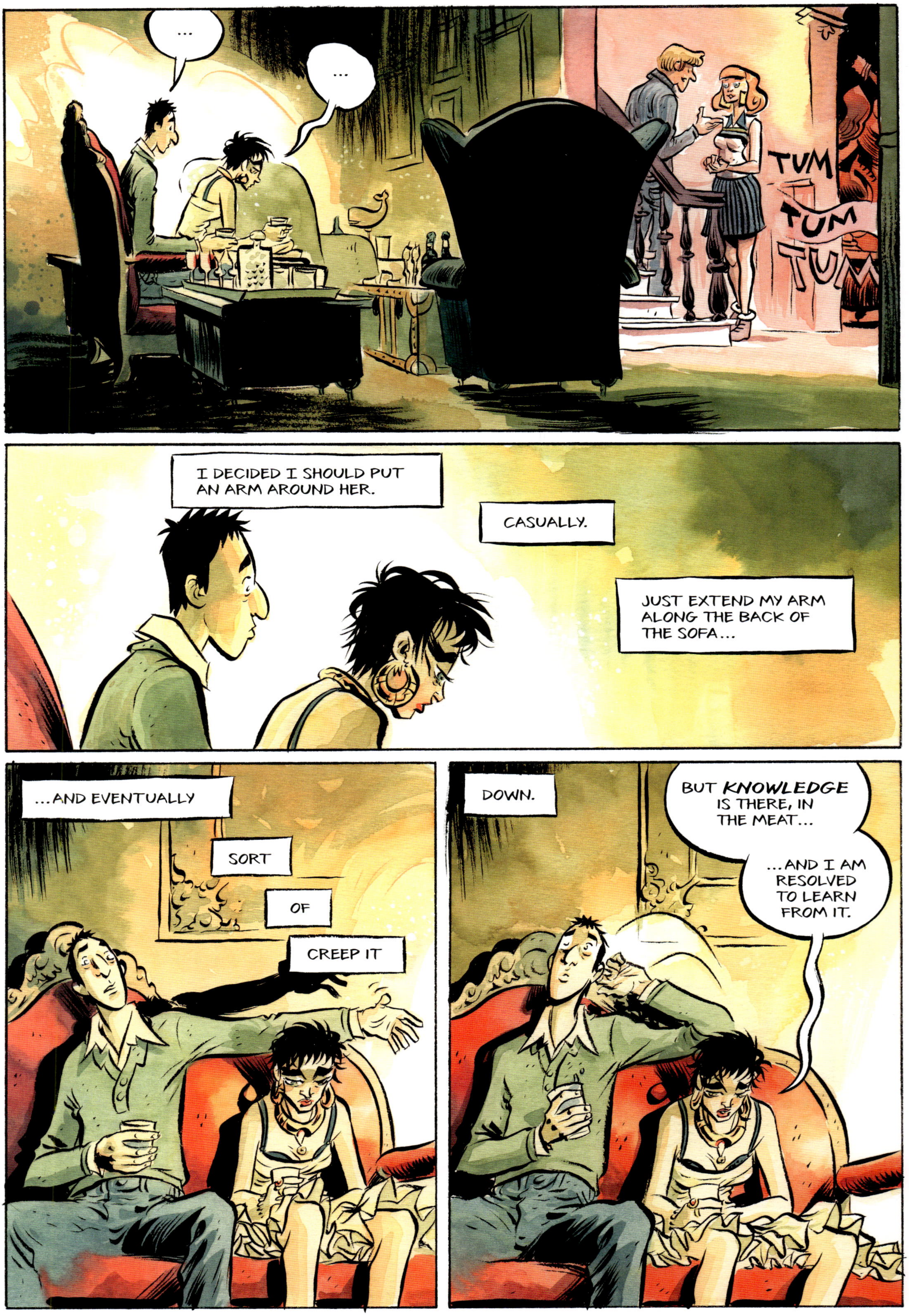
...
...
TUM
TUM
TUM
I DECIDED I SHOULD PUT AN ARM AROUND HER.
CASUALLY.
JUST EXTEND MY ARM ALONG THE BACK OF THE SOFA...
...AND EVENTUALLY
SORT
OF
CREEP IT
DOWN.
BUT KNOWLEDGE IS THERE, IN THE MEAT...
...AND I AM RESOLVED TO LEARN FROM IT.

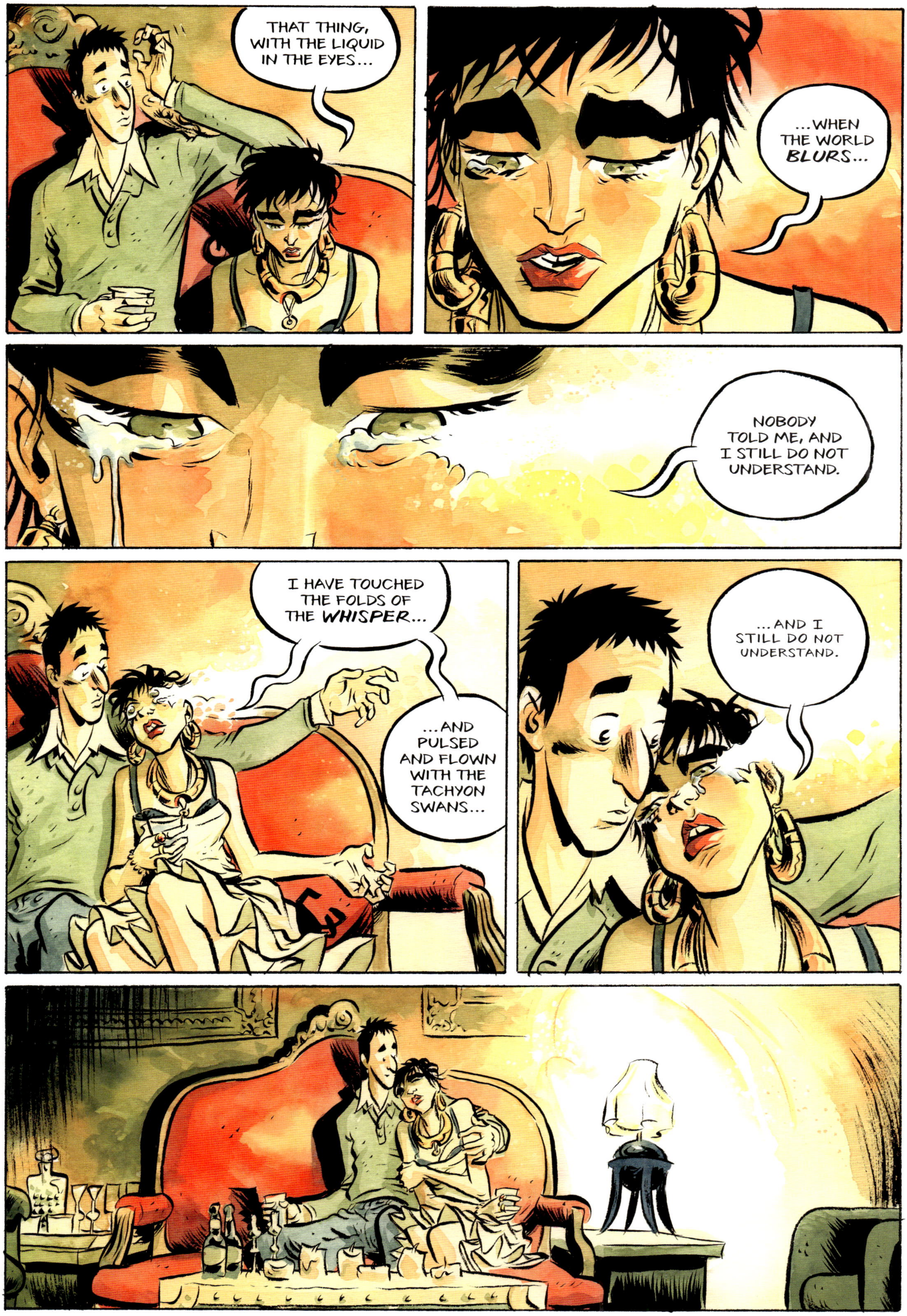

THAT THING, WITH THE LIQUID IN THE EYES...
...WHEN THE WORLD BLURS...
NOBODY TOLD ME, AND I STILL DO NOT UNDERSTAND.
I HAVE TOUCHED THE FOLDS OF THE WHISPER...
...AND PULSED AND FLOWN WITH THE TACHYON SWANS...
...AND I STILL DO NOT UNDERSTAND.

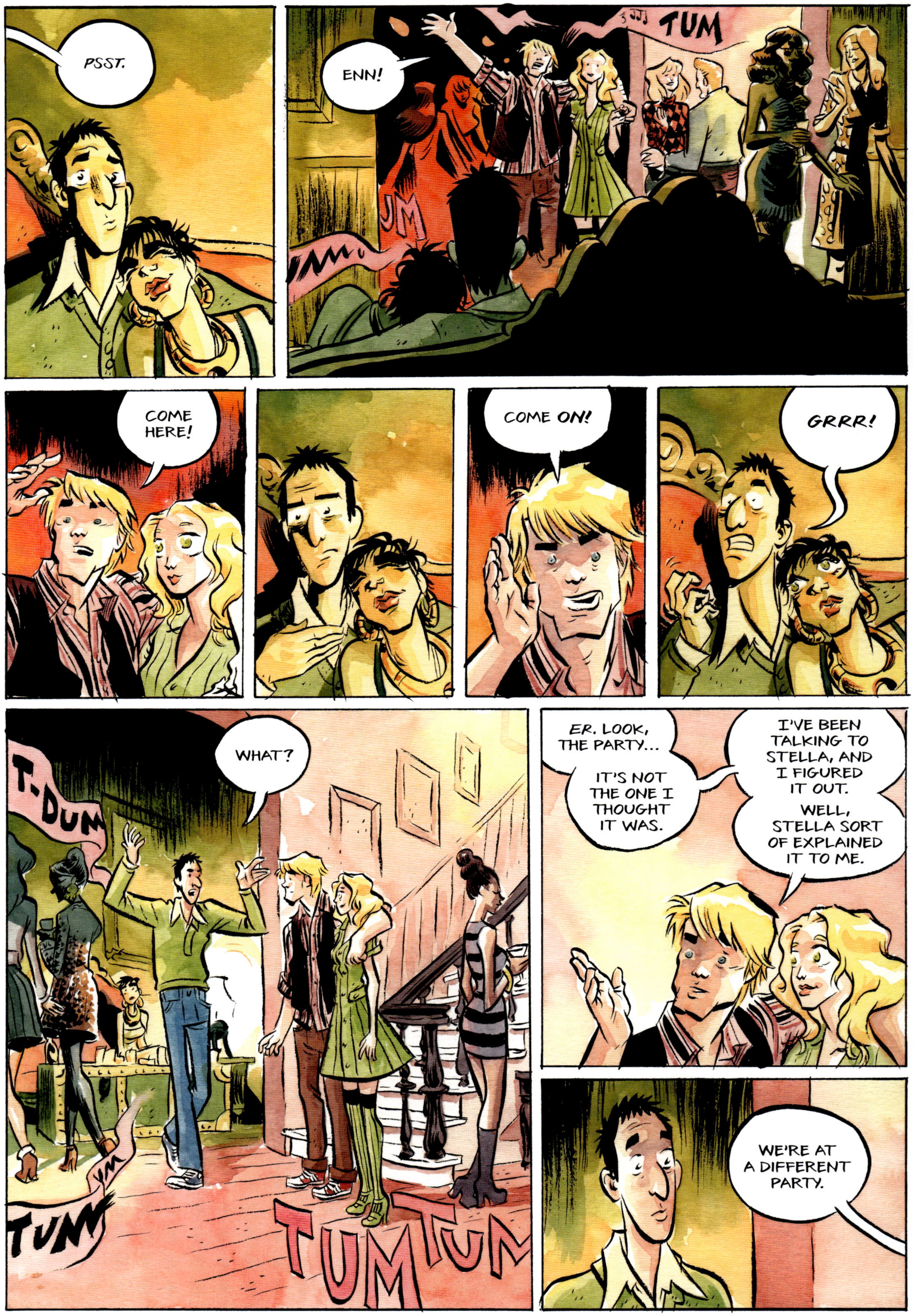
PSST.
ENN!
TUM
UM
TUM
COME HERE!
COME ON!
GRRR!
WHAT?
T-DUM
TUM
UM
TUMTUM
ER. LOOK, THE PARTY...
IT'S NOT THE ONE I THOUGHT IT WAS.
I'VE BEEN TALKING TO STELLA, AND I FIGURED IT OUT.
WELL, STELLA SORT OF EXPLAINED IT TO ME.
WE'RE AT A DIFFERENT PARTY.

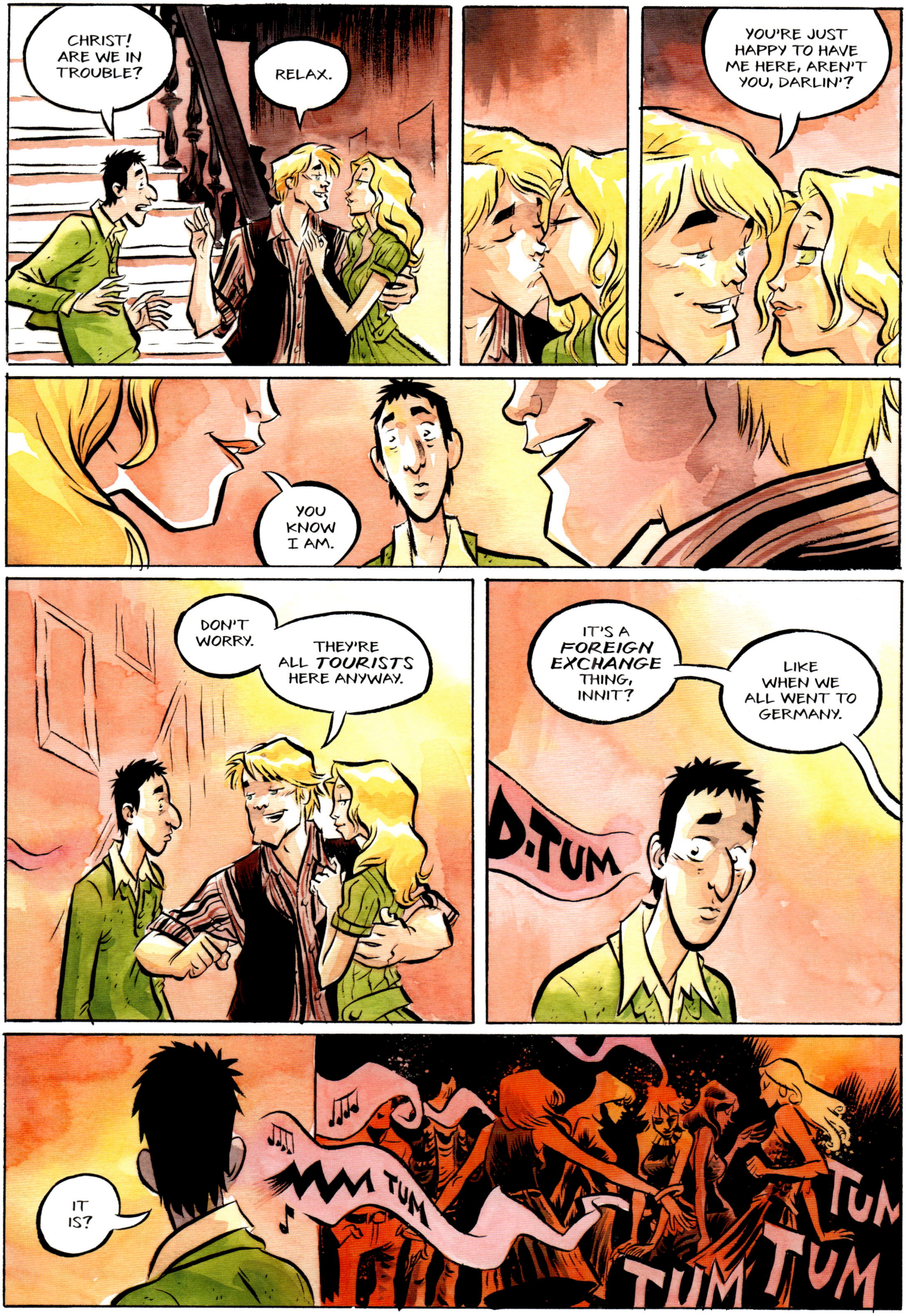
CHRIST! ARE WE IN TROUBLE?
RELAX.
YOU'RE JUST HAPPY TO HAVE ME HERE, AREN'T YOU, DARLIN'?
YOU KNOW I AM.
DON'T WORRY.
THEY'RE ALL *TOURISTS* HERE ANYWAY.
IT'S A *FOREIGN EXCHANGE* THING, INNIT?
LIKE WHEN WE ALL WENT TO GERMANY.
D-TUM
IT IS?
TUM
TUM
TUM TUM TUM

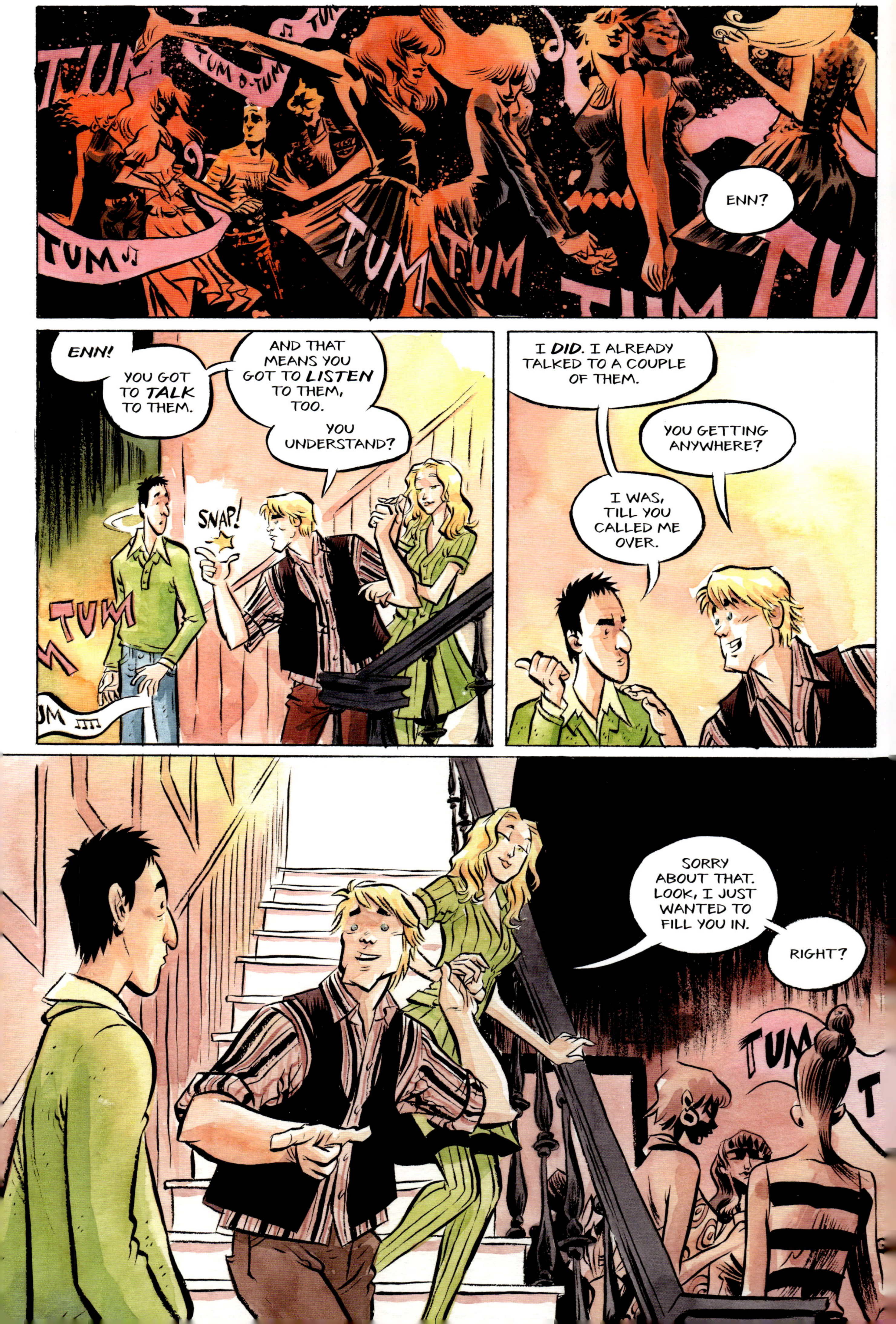
TUM
TUM-TUM
TUM-TUM
TUM
ENN?
TUM TUM
TUM TUM
ENN!
YOU GOT TO *TALK* TO THEM.
AND THAT MEANS YOU GOT TO *LISTEN* TO THEM, TOO.
YOU UNDERSTAND?
SNAP!
TUM
I *DID*. I ALREADY TALKED TO A COUPLE OF THEM.
YOU GETTING ANYWHERE?
I WAS, TILL YOU CALLED ME OVER.
SORRY ABOUT THAT. LOOK, I JUST WANTED TO FILL YOU IN.
RIGHT?
TUM

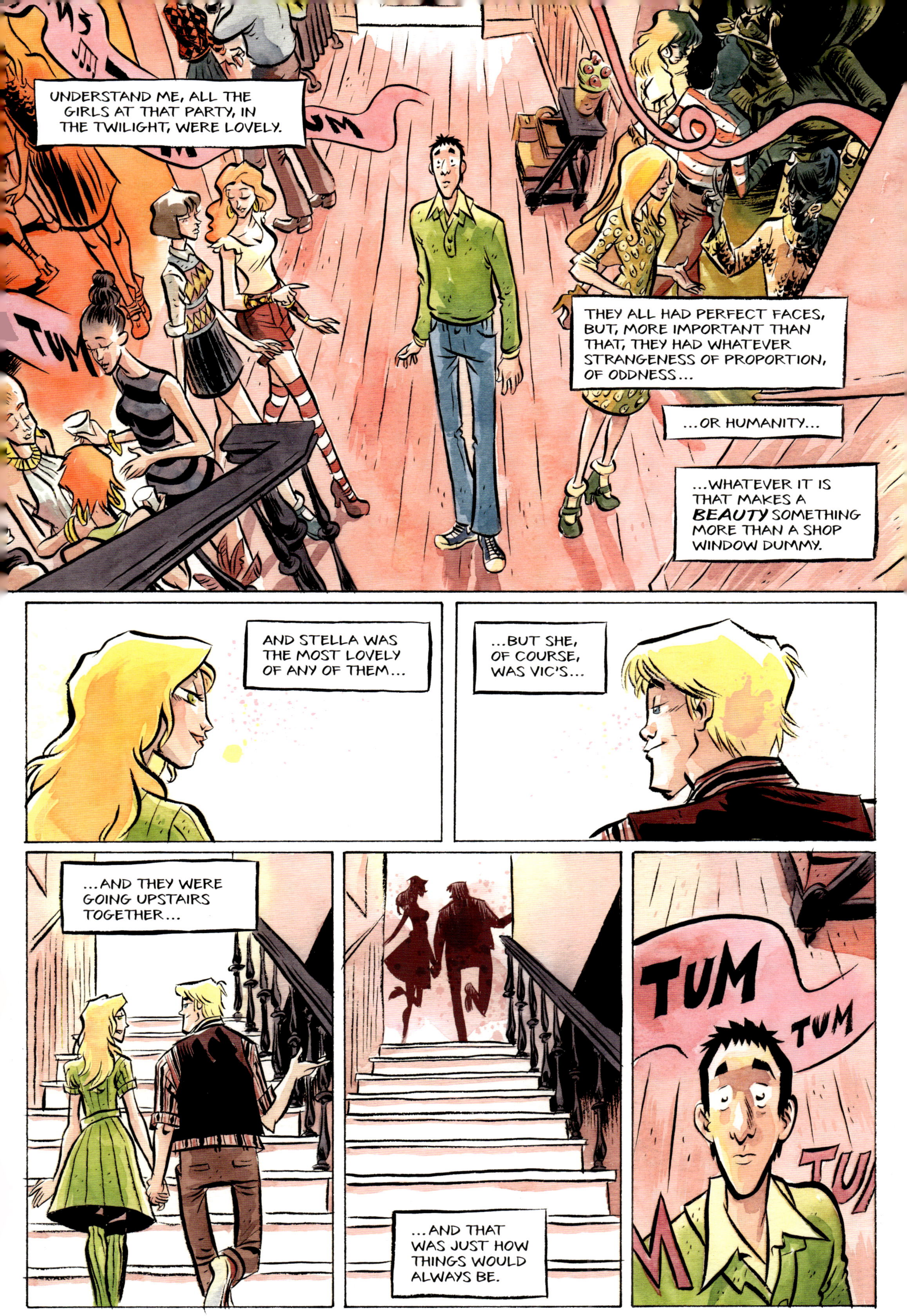
UNDERSTAND ME, ALL THE GIRLS AT THAT PARTY, IN THE TWILIGHT, WERE LOVELY.
TUM
TUM
THEY ALL HAD PERFECT FACES, BUT, MORE IMPORTANT THAN THAT, THEY HAD WHATEVER STRANGENESS OF PROPORTION, OF ODDNESS...
...OR HUMANITY...
...WHATEVER IT IS THAT MAKES A BEAUTY SOMETHING MORE THAN A SHOP WINDOW DUMMY.
AND STELLA WAS THE MOST LOVELY OF ANY OF THEM...
...BUT SHE, OF COURSE, WAS VIC'S...
...AND THEY WERE GOING UPSTAIRS TOGETHER...
...AND THAT WAS JUST HOW THINGS WOULD ALWAYS BE.
TUM
TUM

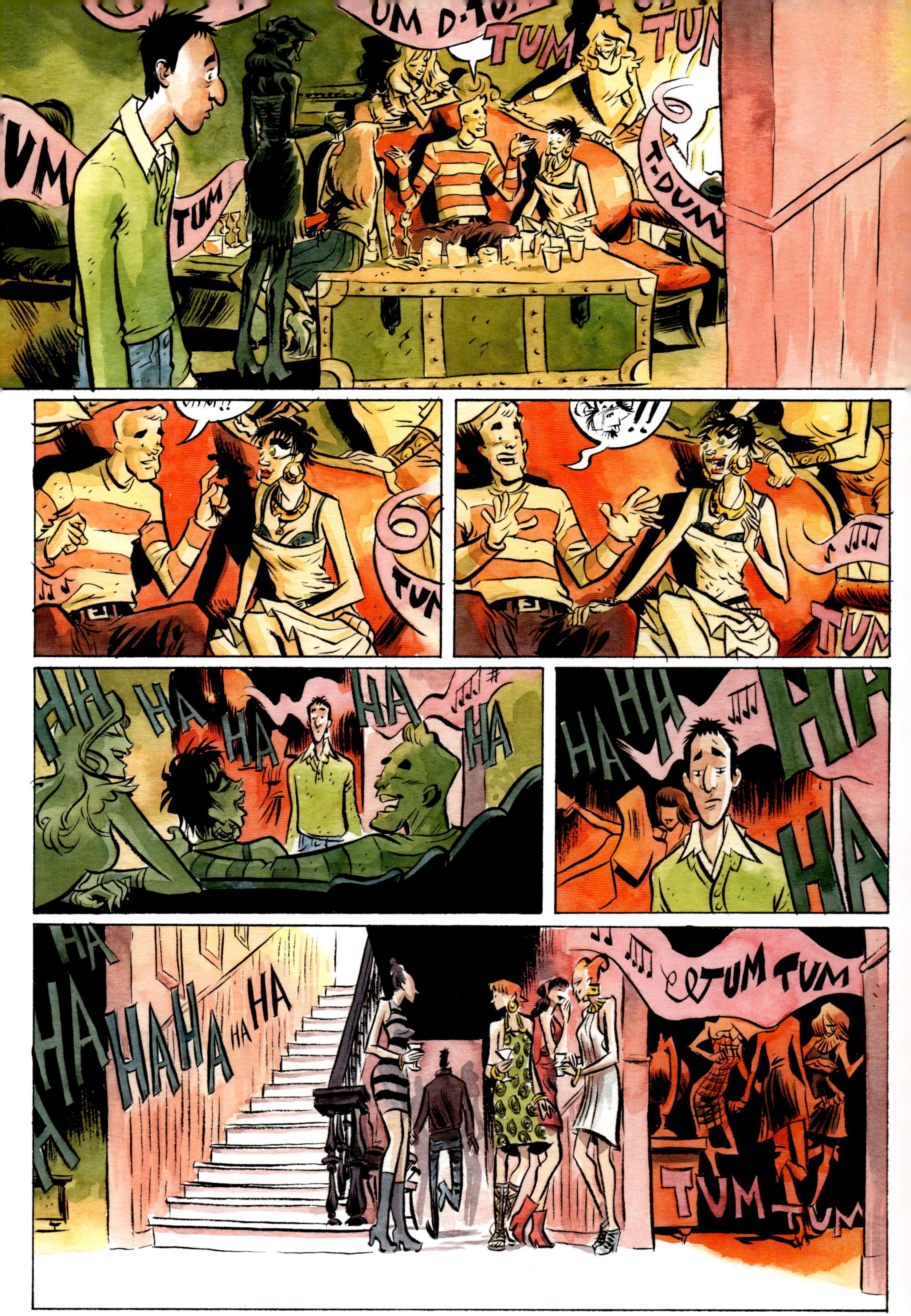

UM D-TUM
TUM
TUN
UM
TUM
T-DUN
TUM
TUM
HA HA HA HA HA HA
HA HA HA HA HA
HA HA HA HA HA HA
TUM TUM
TUM TUM

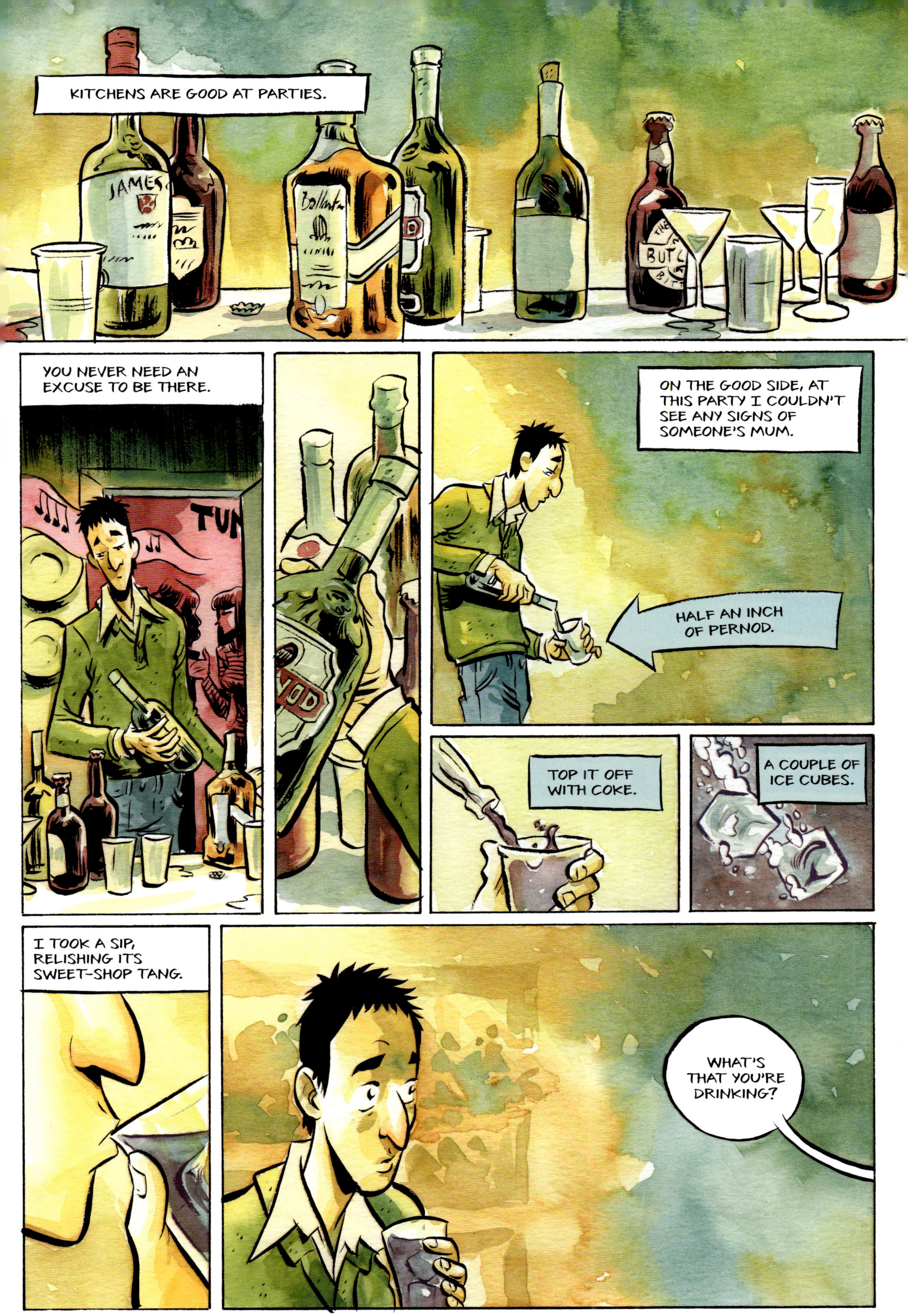
KITCHENS ARE GOOD AT PARTIES.
YOU NEVER NEED AN EXCUSE TO BE THERE.
ON THE GOOD SIDE, AT THIS PARTY I COULDN'T SEE ANY SIGNS OF SOMEONE'S MUM.
HALF AN INCH OF PERNOD.
TOP IT OFF WITH COKE.
A COUPLE OF ICE CUBES.
I TOOK A SIP, RELISHING ITS SWEET-SHOP TANG.
WHAT'S THAT YOU'RE DRINKING?

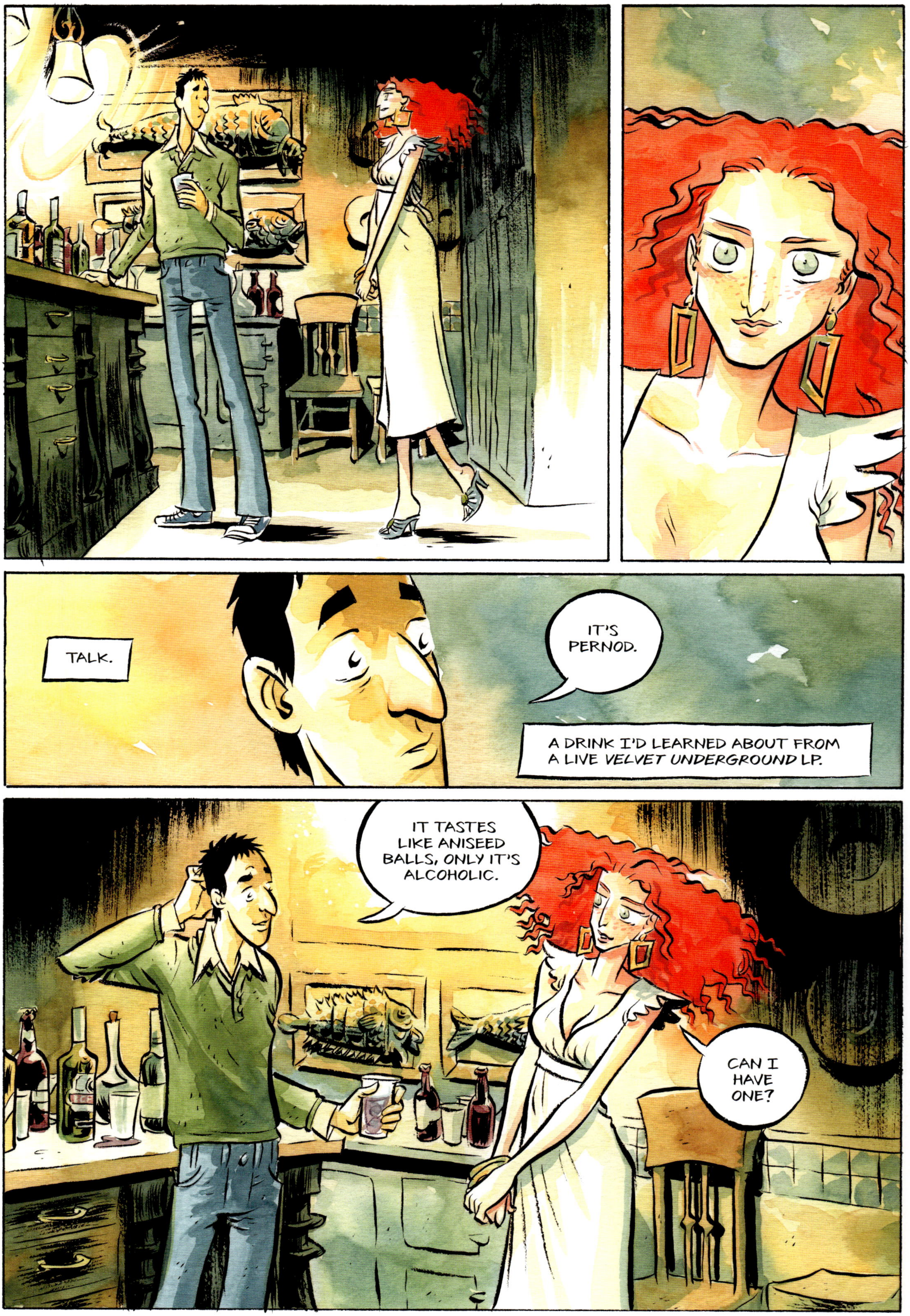
TALK.
IT'S PERNOD.
A DRINK I'D LEARNED ABOUT FROM A LIVE *VELVET UNDERGROUND* LP.
IT TASTES LIKE ANISEED BALLS, ONLY IT'S ALCOHOLIC.
CAN I HAVE ONE?

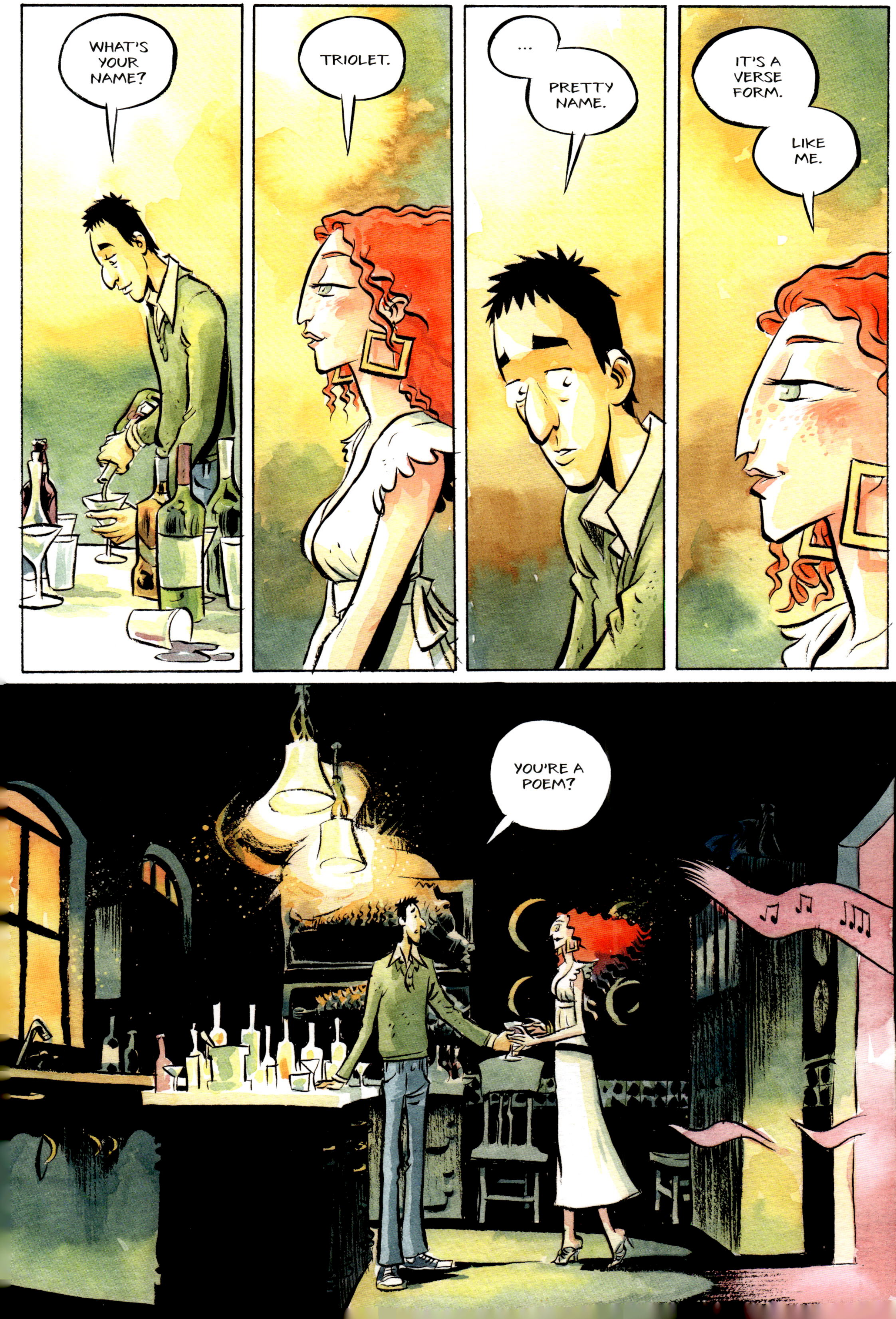
WHAT'S YOUR NAME?
TRIOLET.
...
PRETTY NAME.
IT'S A VERSE FORM.
LIKE ME.
YOU'RE A POEM?

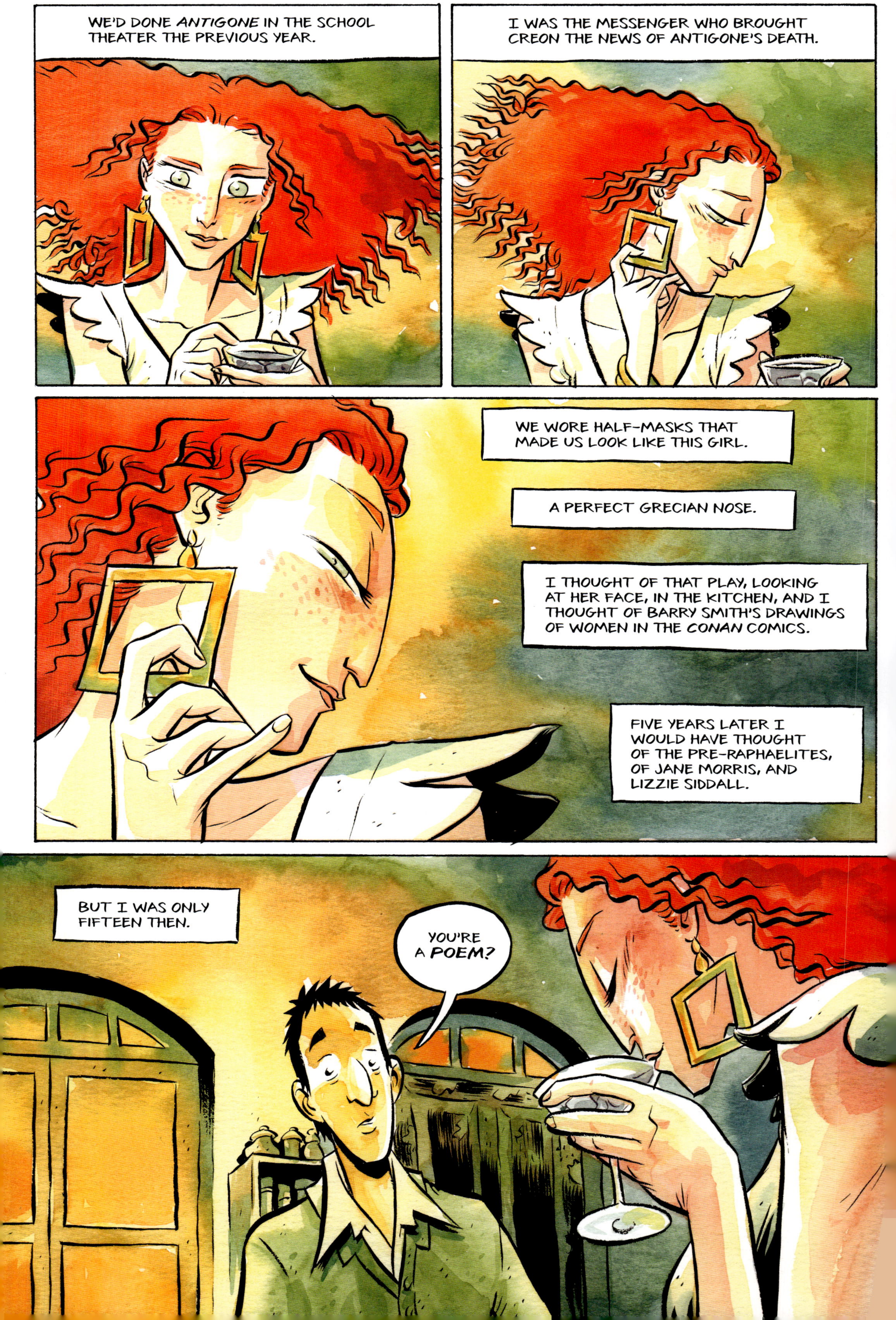
WE'D DONE *ANTIGONE* IN THE SCHOOL THEATER THE PREVIOUS YEAR.
I WAS THE MESSENGER WHO BROUGHT CREON THE NEWS OF ANTIGONE'S DEATH.
WE WORE HALF-MASKS THAT MADE US LOOK LIKE THIS GIRL.
A PERFECT GRECIAN NOSE.
I THOUGHT OF THAT PLAY, LOOKING AT HER FACE, IN THE KITCHEN, AND I THOUGHT OF BARRY SMITH'S DRAWINGS OF WOMEN IN THE *CONAN* COMICS.
FIVE YEARS LATER I WOULD HAVE THOUGHT OF THE PRE-RAPHAELITES, OF JANE MORRIS, AND LIZZIE SIDDALL.
BUT I WAS ONLY FIFTEEN THEN.
YOU'RE A ***POEM?***

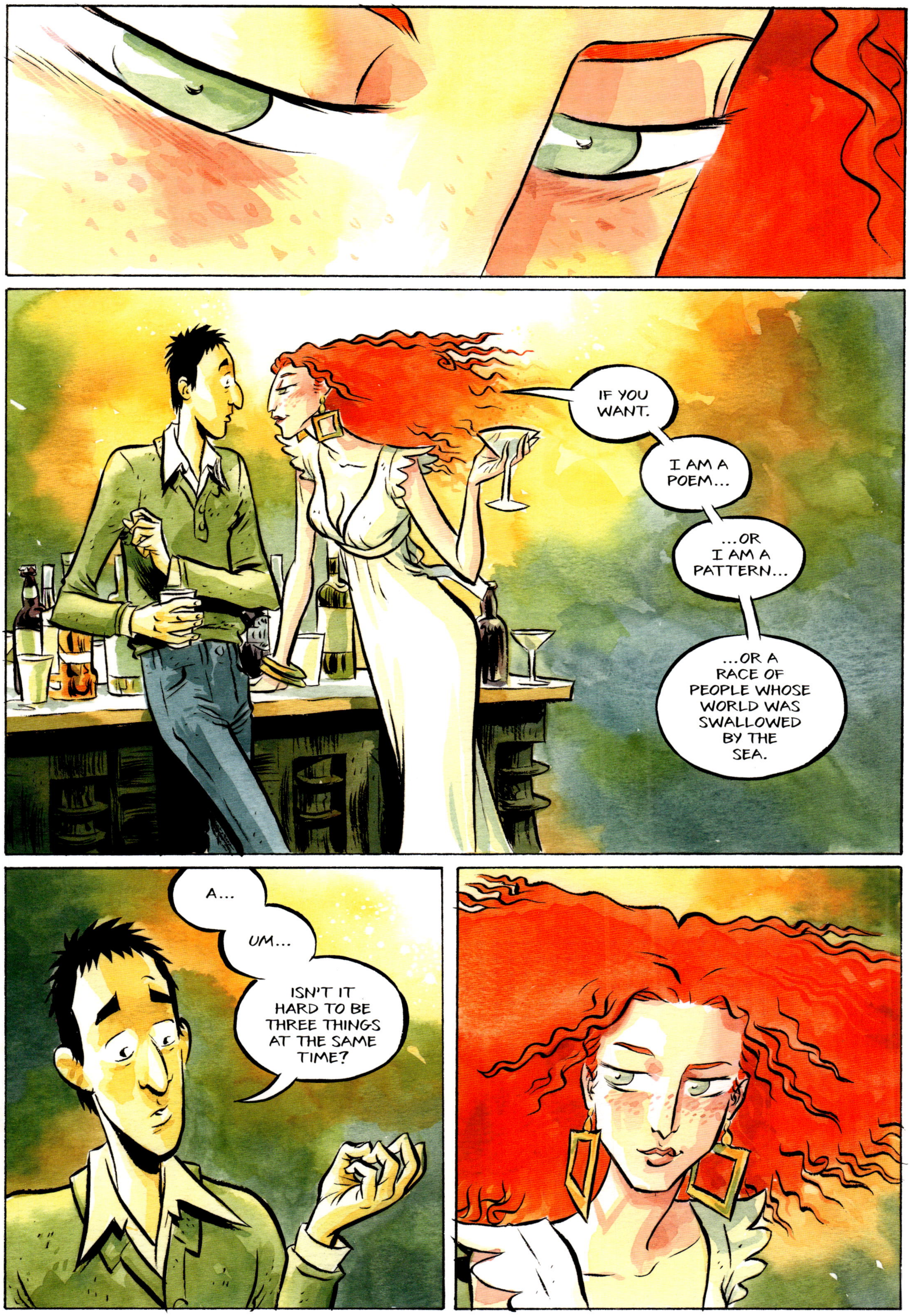
IF YOU WANT.
I AM A POEM...
...OR I AM A PATTERN...
...OR A RACE OF PEOPLE WHOSE WORLD WAS SWALLOWED BY THE SEA.
A...
UM...
ISN'T IT HARD TO BE THREE THINGS AT THE SAME TIME?

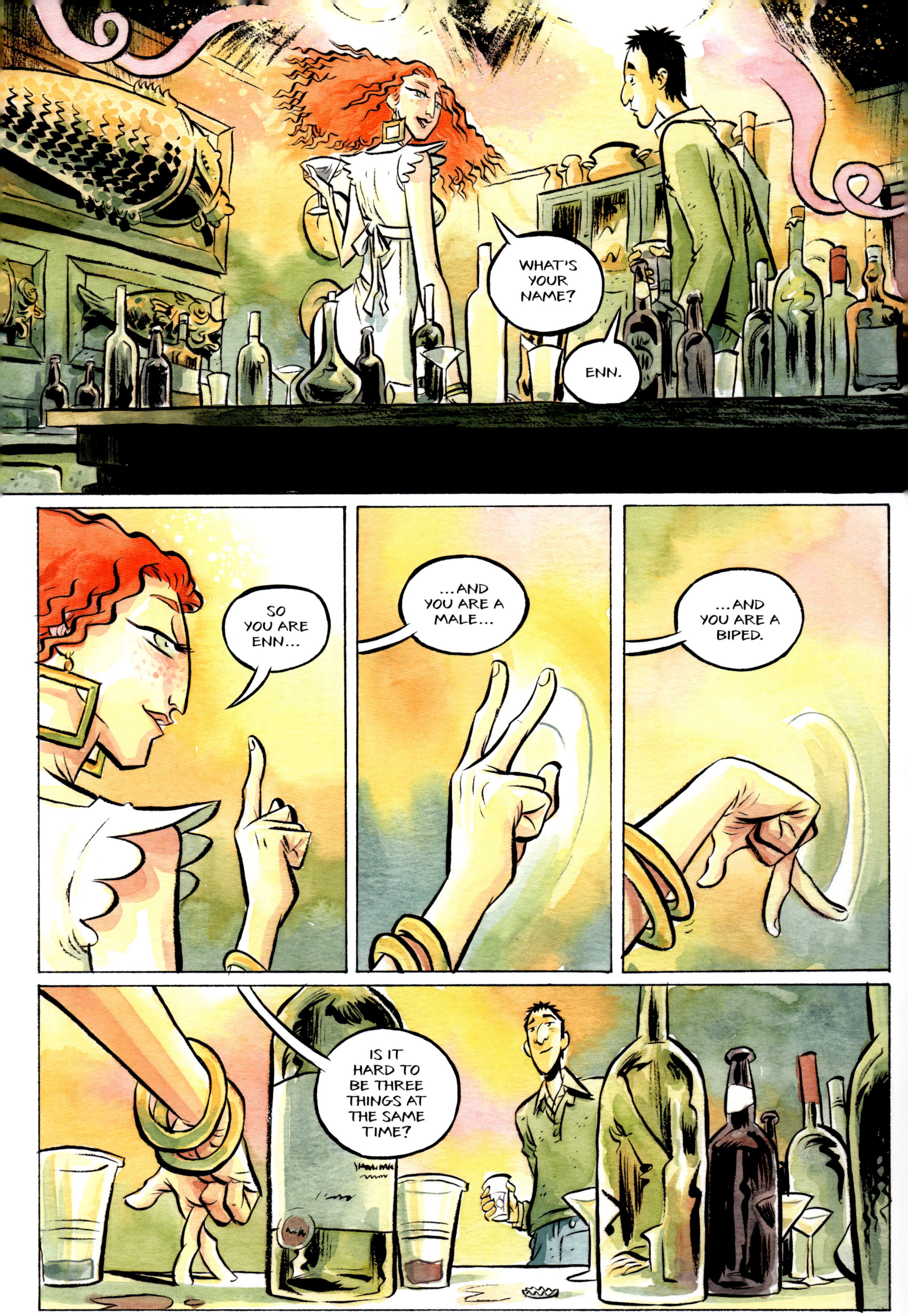
WHAT'S YOUR NAME?
ENN.
SO YOU ARE ENN...
...AND YOU ARE A MALE...
...AND YOU ARE A BIPED.
IS IT HARD TO BE THREE THINGS AT THE SAME TIME?

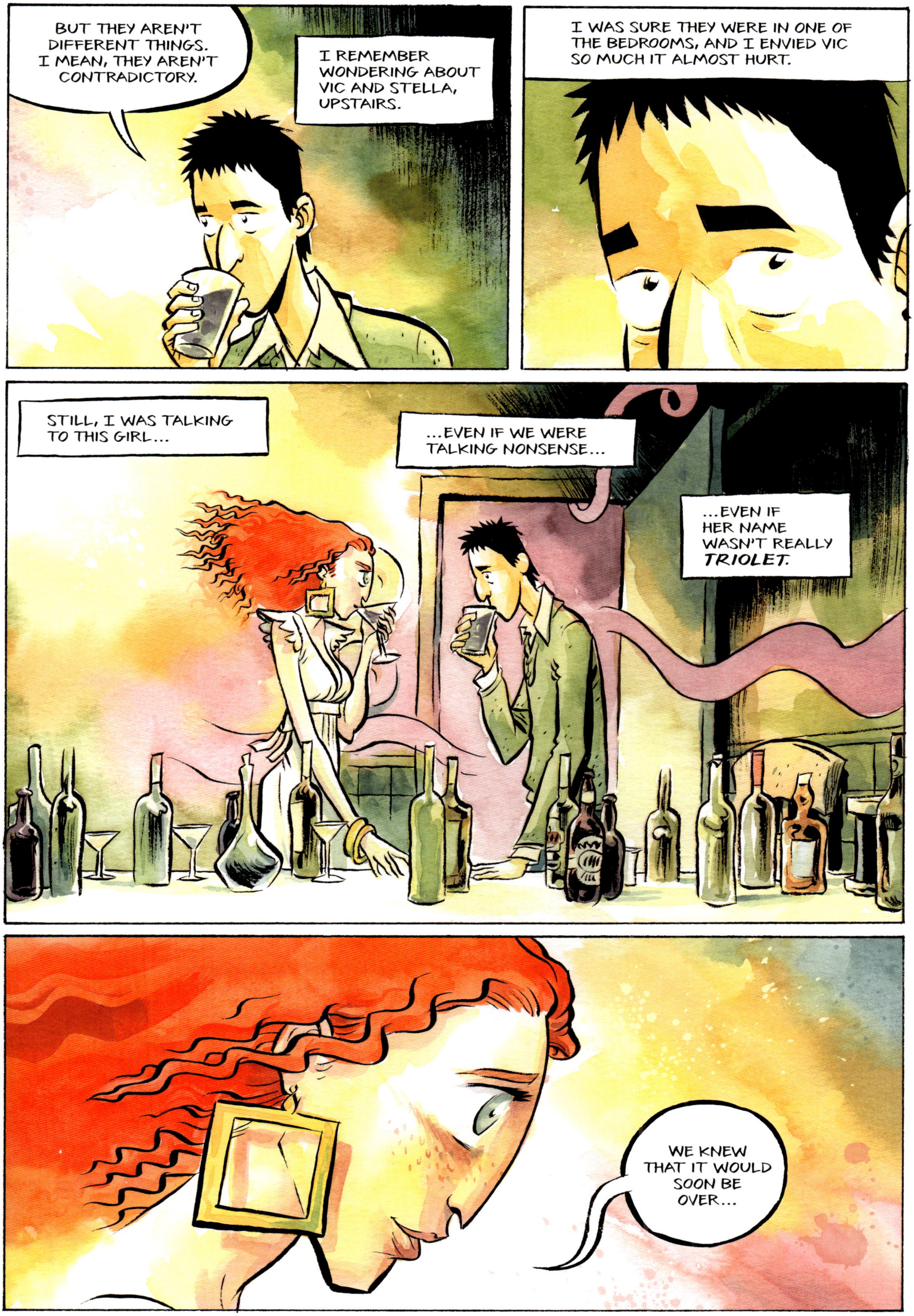
BUT THEY AREN'T DIFFERENT THINGS. I MEAN, THEY AREN'T CONTRADICTORY.
I REMEMBER WONDERING ABOUT VIC AND STELLA, UPSTAIRS.
I WAS SURE THEY WERE IN ONE OF THE BEDROOMS, AND I ENVIED VIC SO MUCH IT ALMOST HURT.
STILL, I WAS TALKING TO THIS GIRL...
...EVEN IF WE WERE TALKING NONSENSE...
...EVEN IF HER NAME WASN'T REALLY *TRIOLET.*
WE KNEW THAT IT WOULD SOON BE OVER...

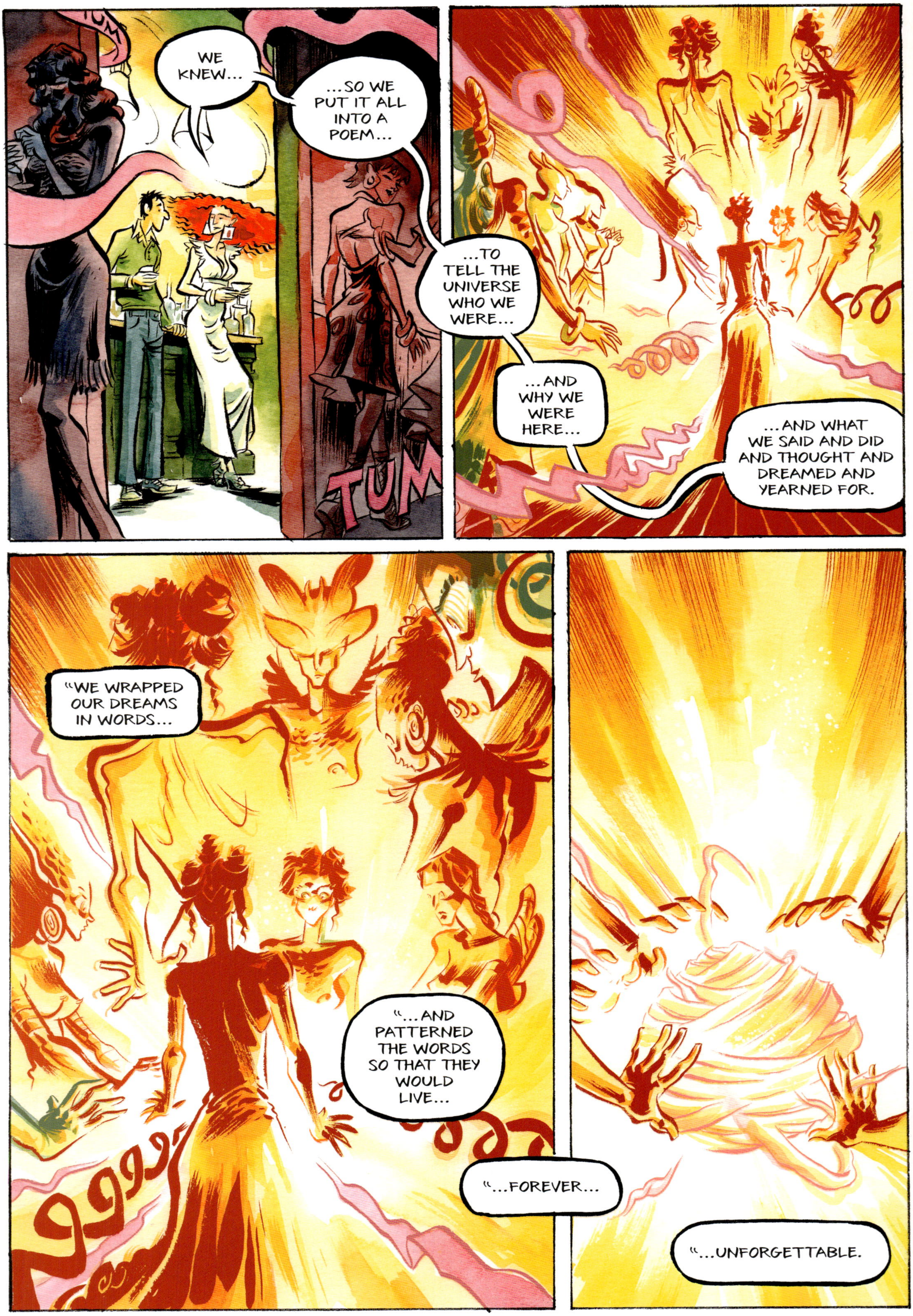
TUM
WE KNEW...
...SO WE PUT IT ALL INTO A POEM...
...TO TELL THE UNIVERSE WHO WE WERE...
...AND WHY WE WERE HERE...
...AND WHAT WE SAID AND DID AND THOUGHT AND DREAMED AND YEARNED FOR.
TUM
"WE WRAPPED OUR DREAMS IN WORDS...
"...AND PATTERNED THE WORDS SO THAT THEY WOULD LIVE...
"...FOREVER...
"...UNFORGETTABLE.

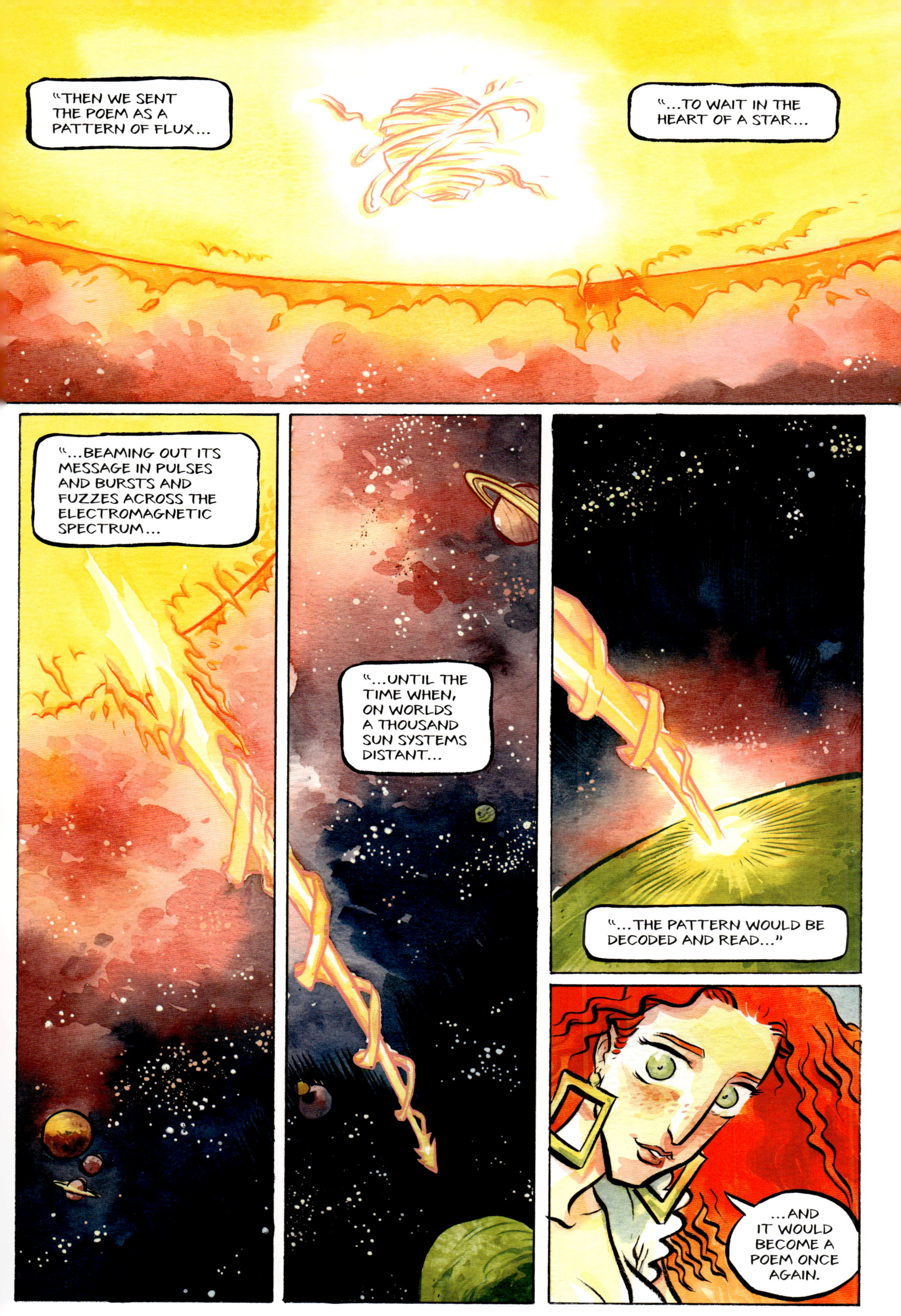
"THEN WE SENT THE POEM AS A PATTERN OF FLUX...
"...TO WAIT IN THE HEART OF A STAR...
"...BEAMING OUT ITS MESSAGE IN PULSES AND BURSTS AND FUZZES ACROSS THE ELECTROMAGNETIC SPECTRUM...
"...UNTIL THE TIME WHEN, ON WORLDS A THOUSAND SUN SYSTEMS DISTANT...
"...THE PATTERN WOULD BE DECODED AND READ..."
...AND IT WOULD BECOME A POEM ONCE AGAIN.

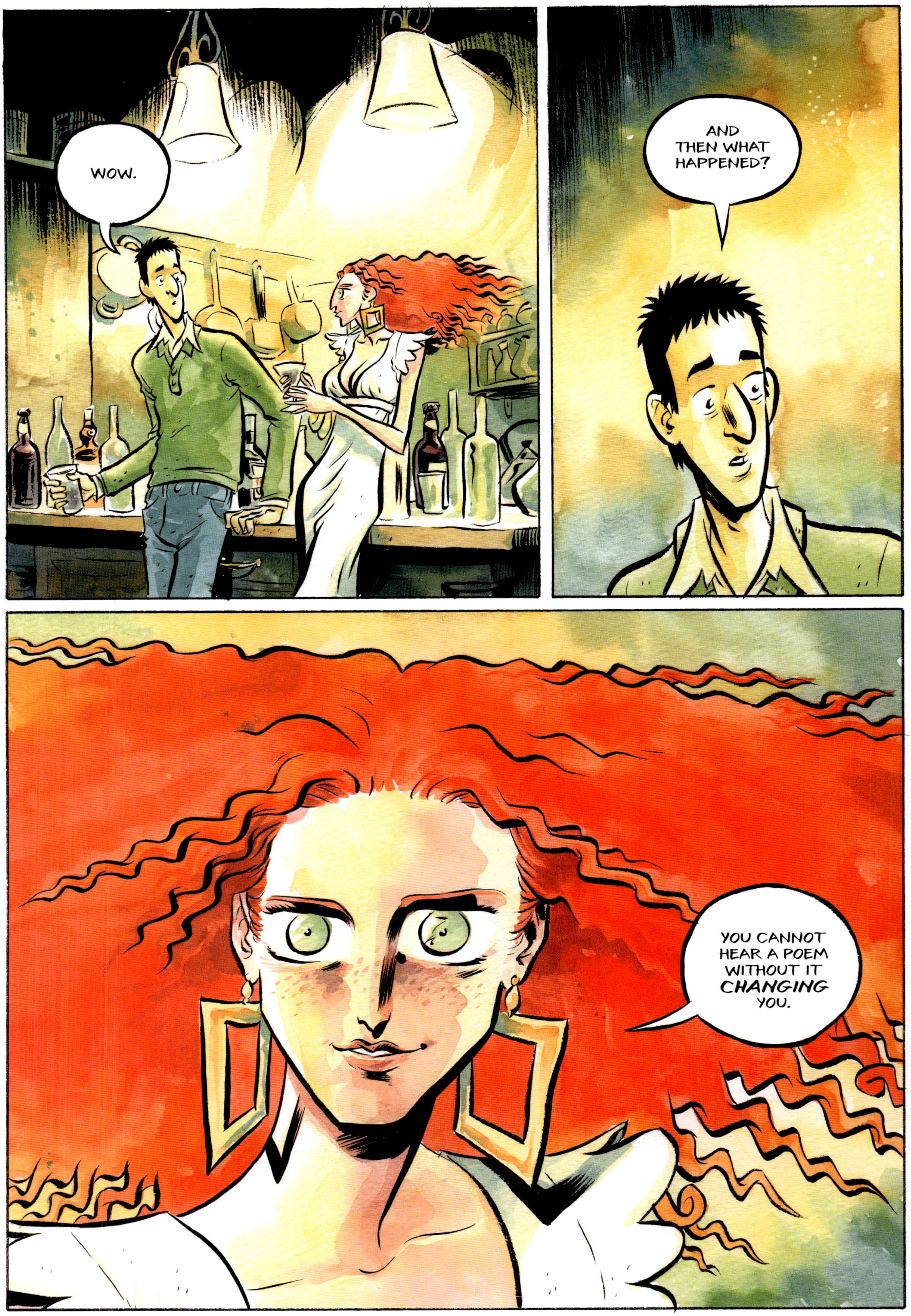
WOW.
AND THEN WHAT HAPPENED?
YOU CANNOT HEAR A POEM WITHOUT IT *CHANGING* YOU.

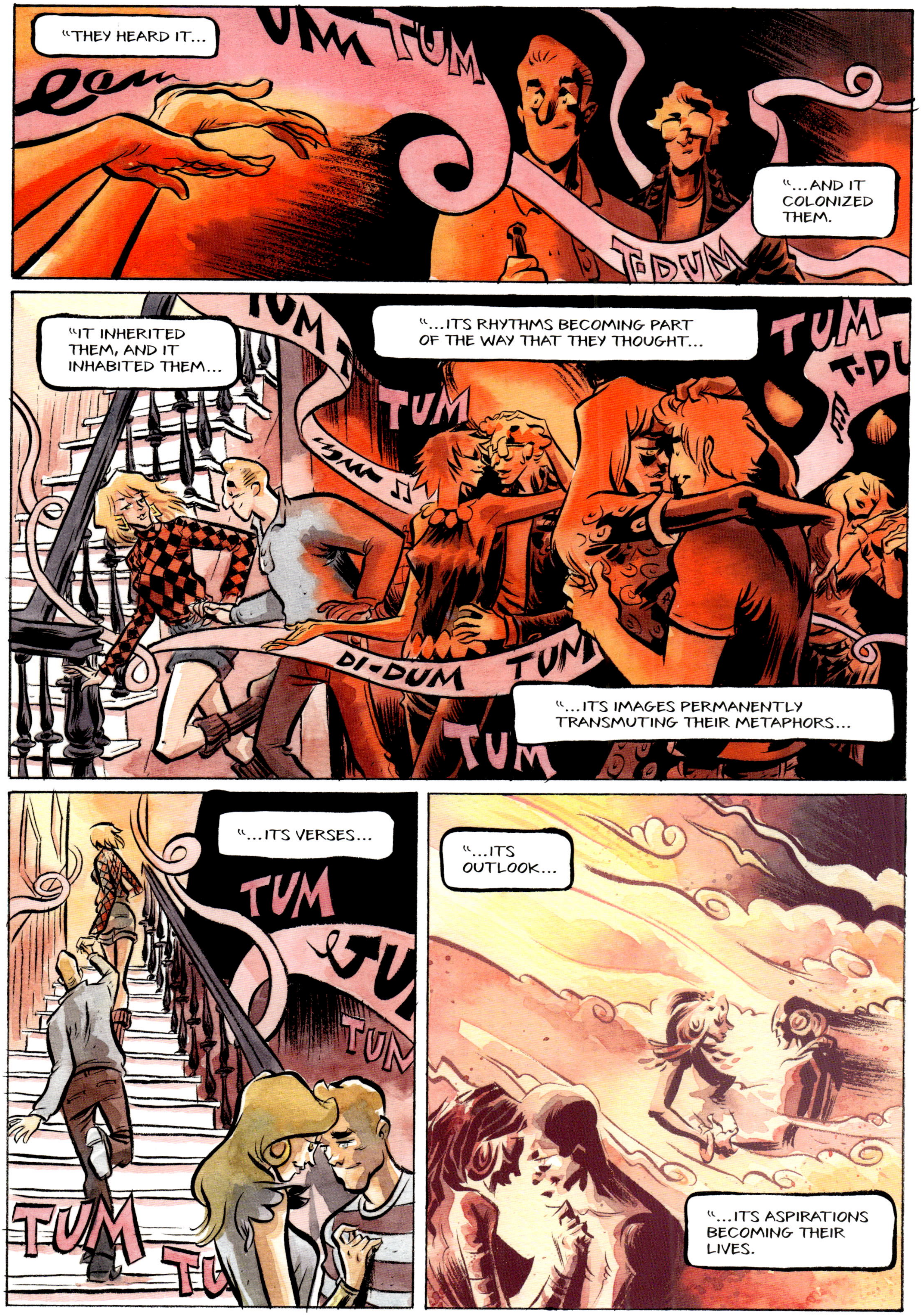
"THEY HEARD IT...
TUM
"...AND IT COLONIZED THEM.
T-DUM
"IT INHERITED THEM, AND IT INHABITED THEM...
"...ITS RHYTHMS BECOMING PART OF THE WAY THAT THEY THOUGHT...
TUM
TUM
DI-DUM
"...ITS IMAGES PERMANENTLY TRANSMUTING THEIR METAPHORS...
TUM
"...ITS VERSES...
TUM
TUM
"...ITS OUTLOOK...
"...ITS ASPIRATIONS BECOMING THEIR LIVES.

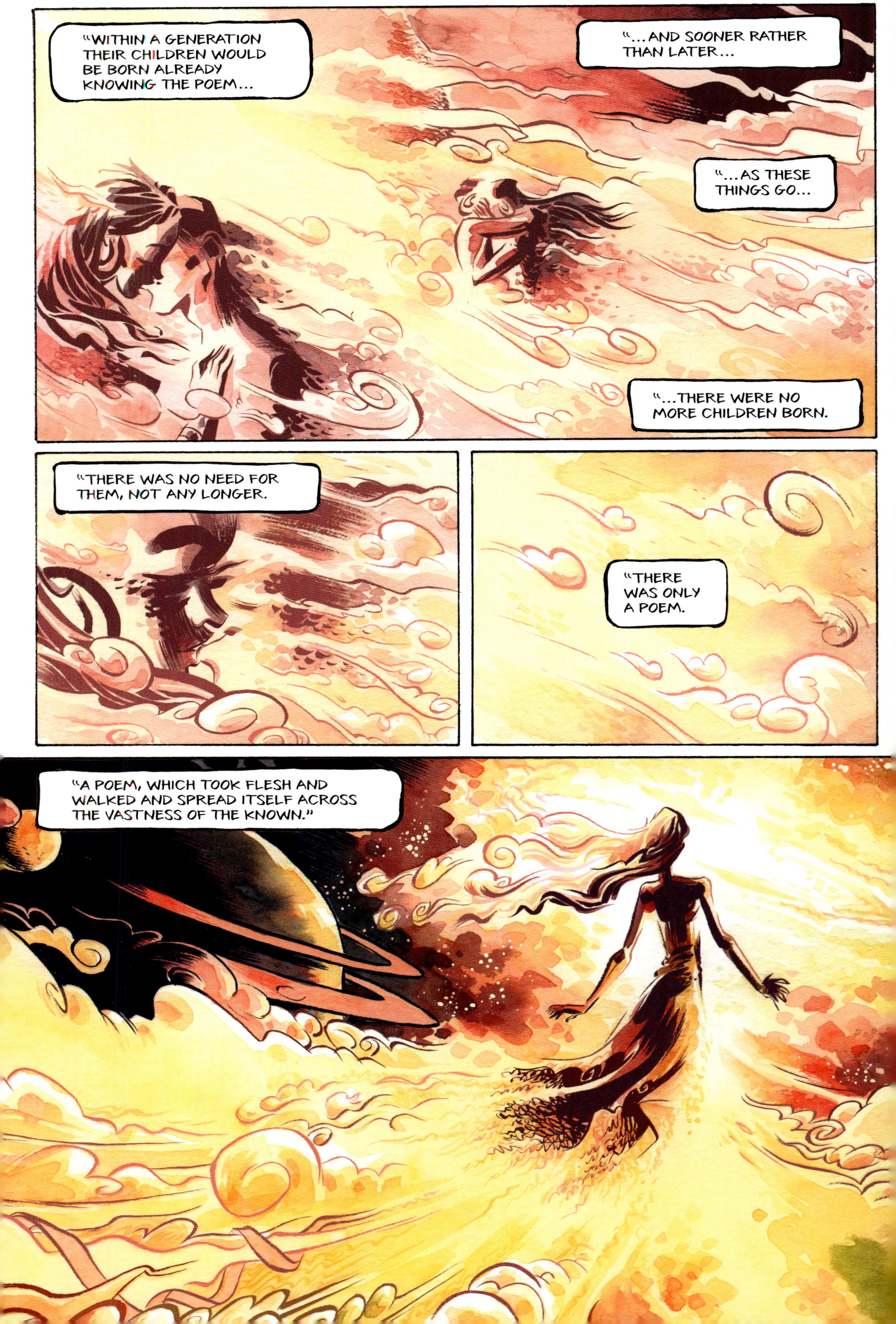
"WITHIN A GENERATION THEIR CHILDREN WOULD BE BORN ALREADY KNOWING THE POEM...
"...AND SOONER RATHER THAN LATER...
"...AS THESE THINGS GO...
"...THERE WERE NO MORE CHILDREN BORN.
"THERE WAS NO NEED FOR THEM, NOT ANY LONGER.
"THERE WAS ONLY A POEM.
"A POEM, WHICH TOOK FLESH AND WALKED AND SPREAD ITSELF ACROSS THE VASTNESS OF THE KNOWN."

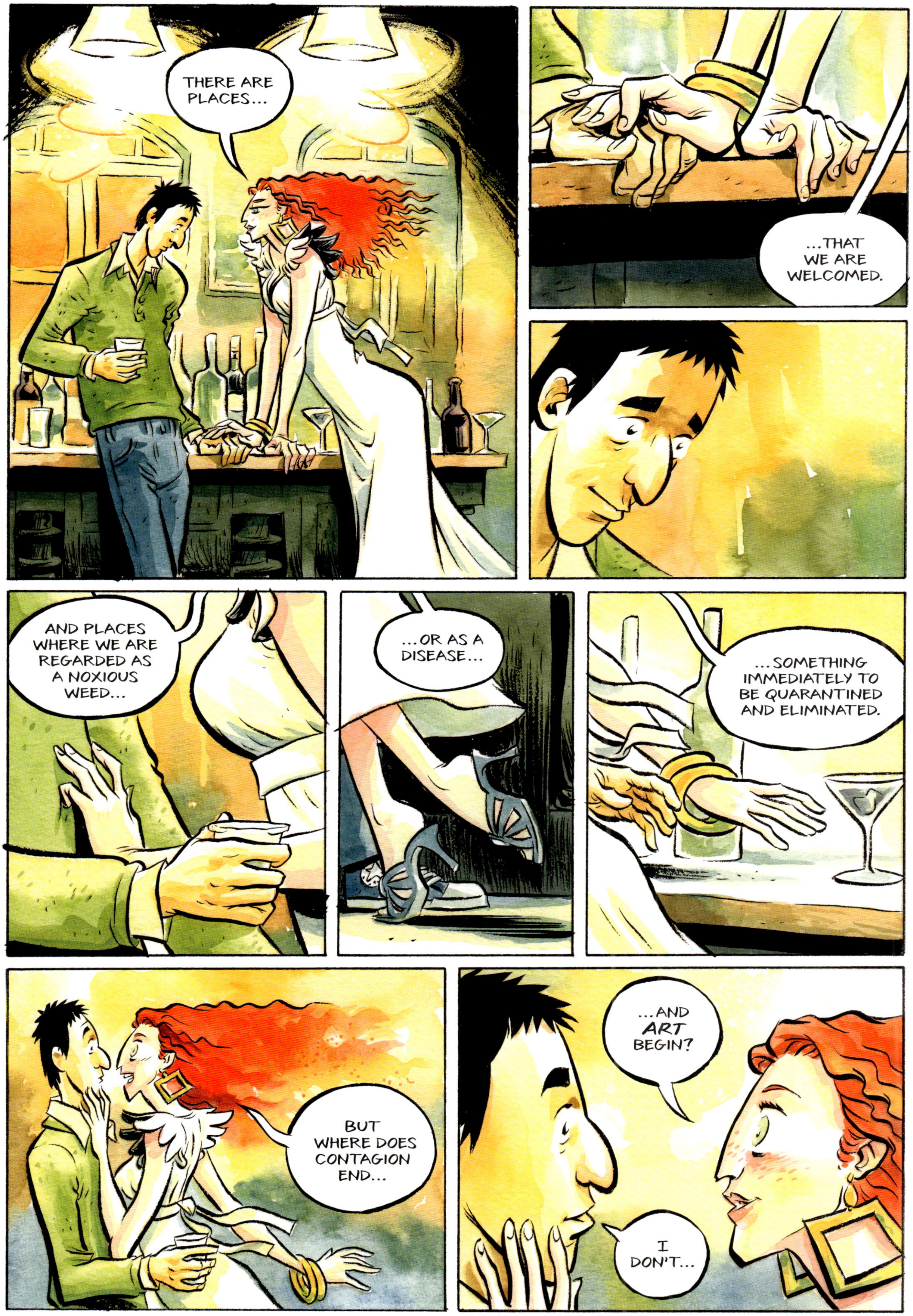
THERE ARE PLACES...
...THAT WE ARE WELCOMED.
AND PLACES WHERE WE ARE REGARDED AS A NOXIOUS WEED...
...OR AS A DISEASE...
...SOMETHING IMMEDIATELY TO BE QUARANTINED AND ELIMINATED.
BUT WHERE DOES CONTAGION END...
...AND ART BEGIN?
I DON'T...

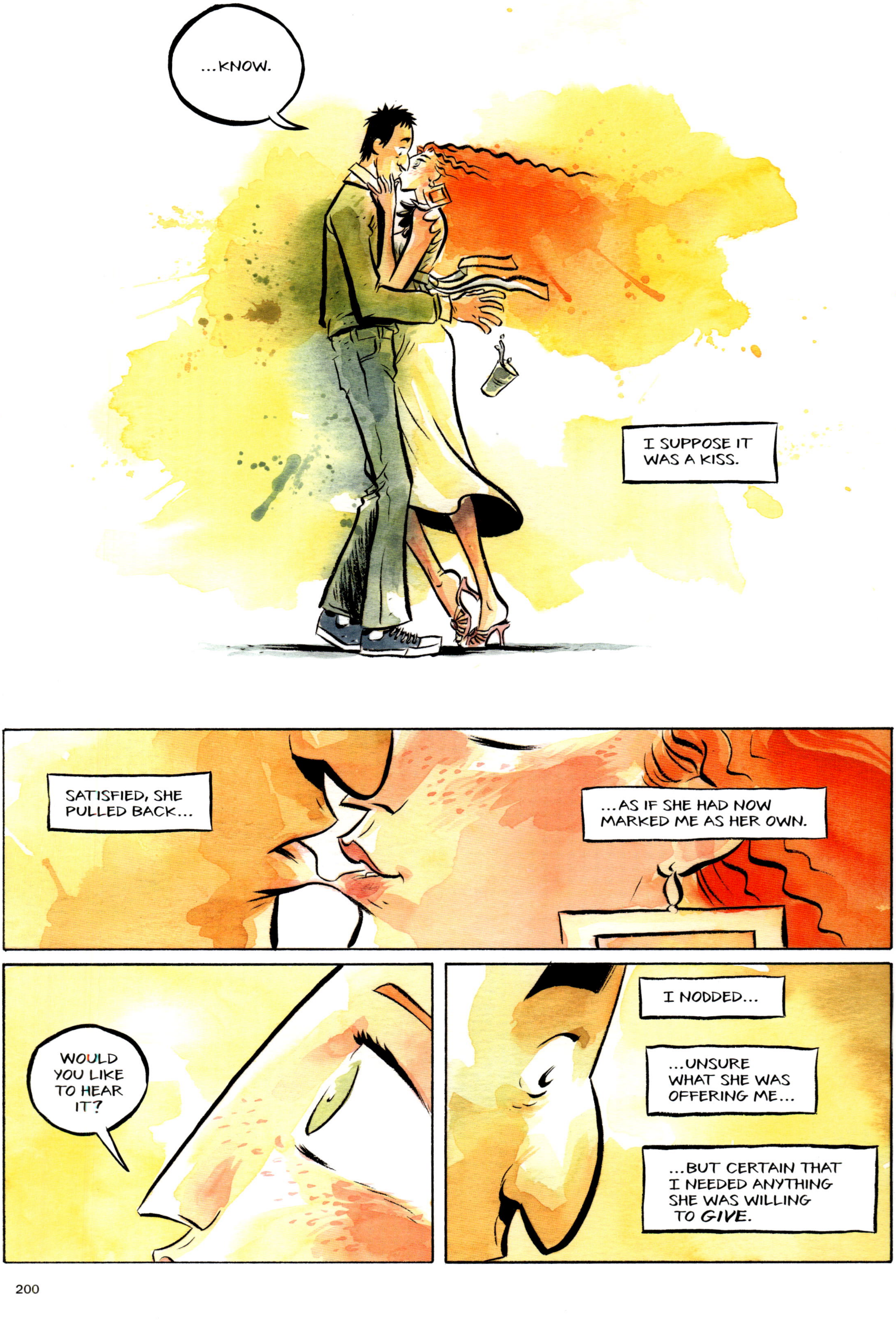
...KNOW.
I SUPPOSE IT WAS A KISS.
SATISFIED, SHE PULLED BACK...
...AS IF SHE HAD NOW MARKED ME AS HER OWN.
WOULD YOU LIKE TO HEAR IT?
I NODDED...
...UNSURE WHAT SHE WAS OFFERING ME...
...BUT CERTAIN THAT I NEEDED ANYTHING SHE WAS WILLING TO GIVE.

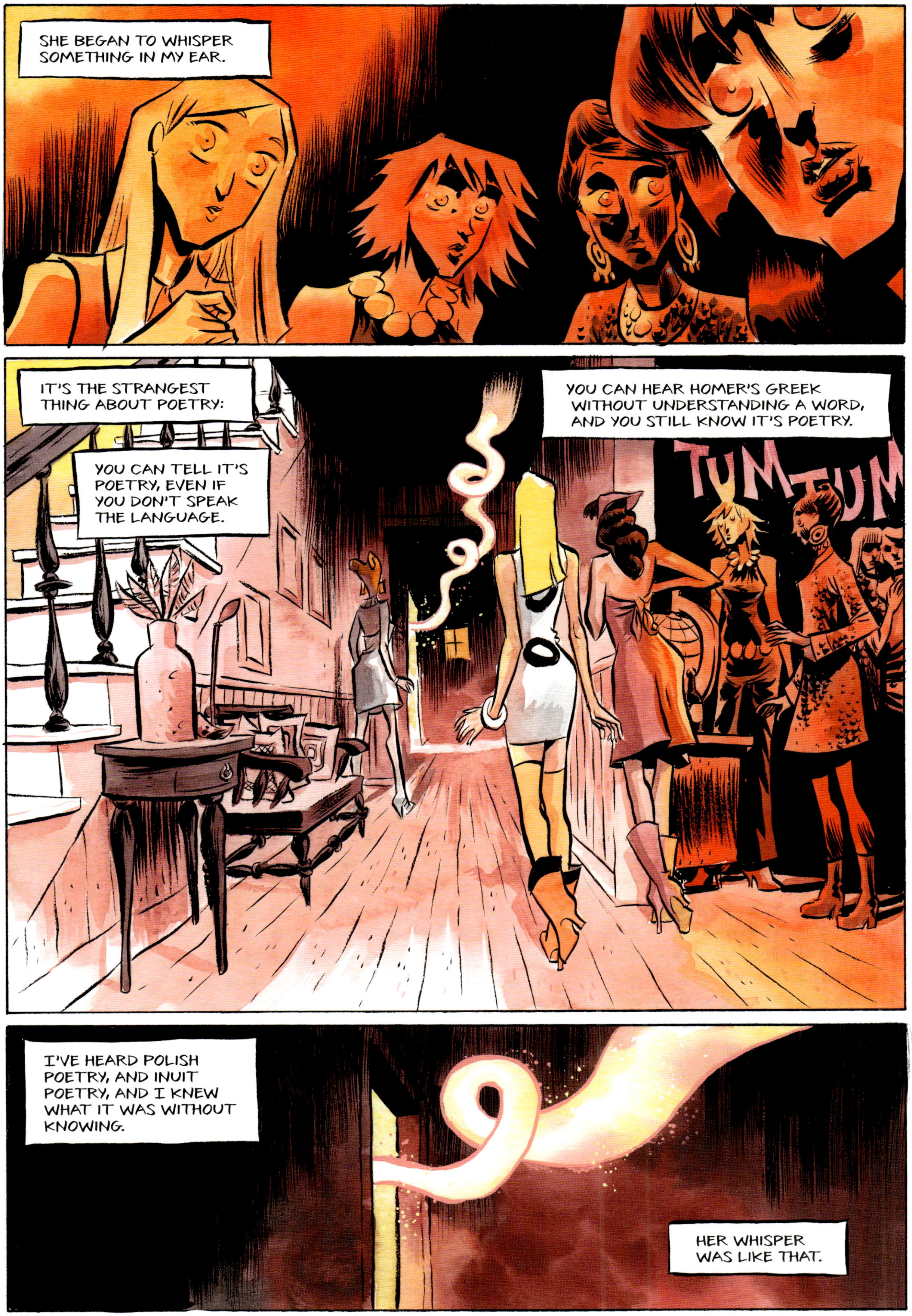
SHE BEGAN TO WHISPER SOMETHING IN MY EAR.
IT'S THE STRANGEST THING ABOUT POETRY:
YOU CAN TELL IT'S POETRY, EVEN IF YOU DON'T SPEAK THE LANGUAGE.
YOU CAN HEAR HOMER'S GREEK WITHOUT UNDERSTANDING A WORD, AND YOU STILL KNOW IT'S POETRY.
TUM TUM
I'VE HEARD POLISH POETRY, AND INUIT POETRY, AND I KNEW WHAT IT WAS WITHOUT KNOWING.
HER WHISPER WAS LIKE THAT.

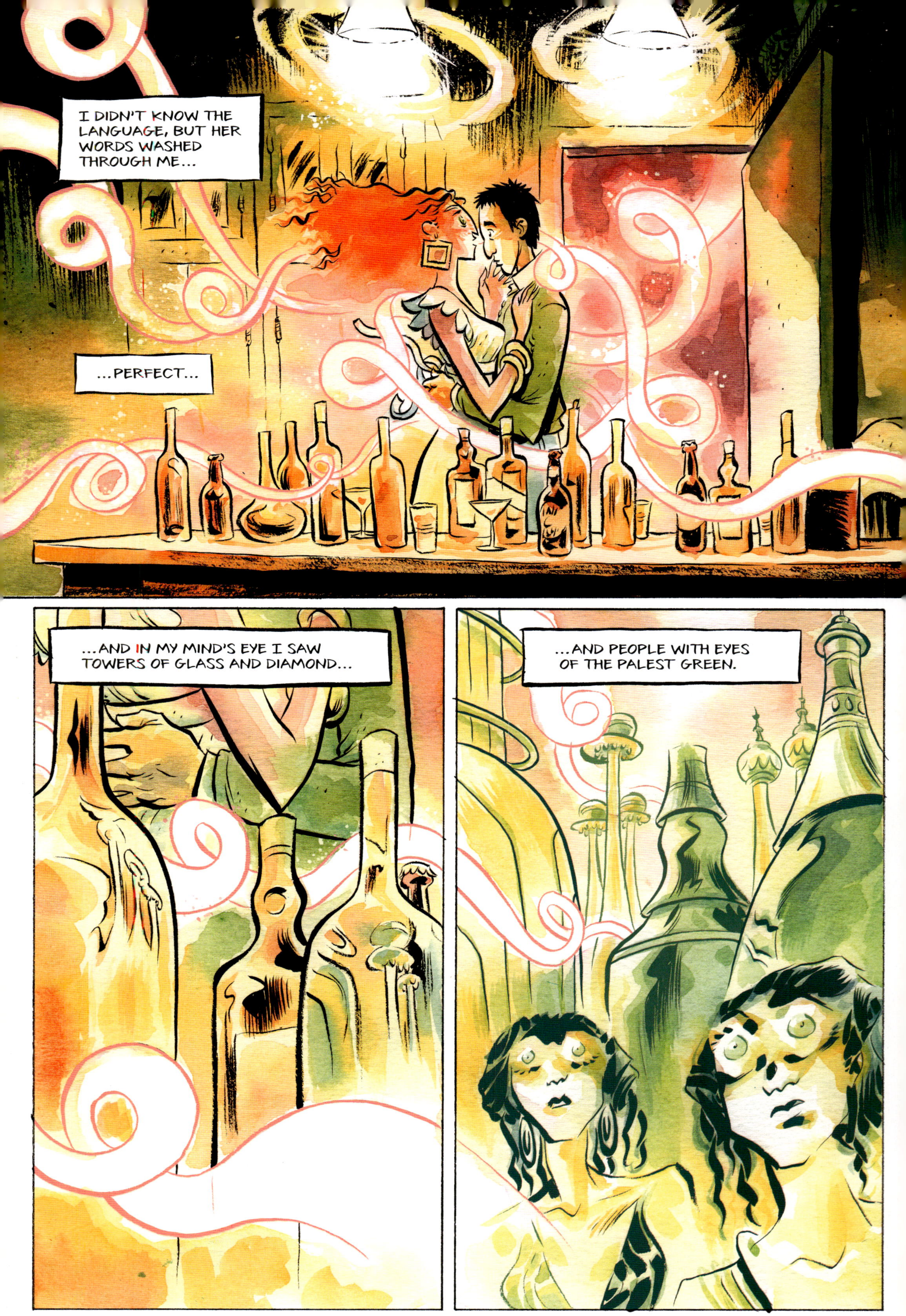
I DIDN'T KNOW THE LANGUAGE, BUT HER WORDS WASHED THROUGH ME...
...PERFECT...
...AND IN MY MIND'S EYE I SAW TOWERS OF GLASS AND DIAMOND...
...AND PEOPLE WITH EYES OF THE PALEST GREEN.

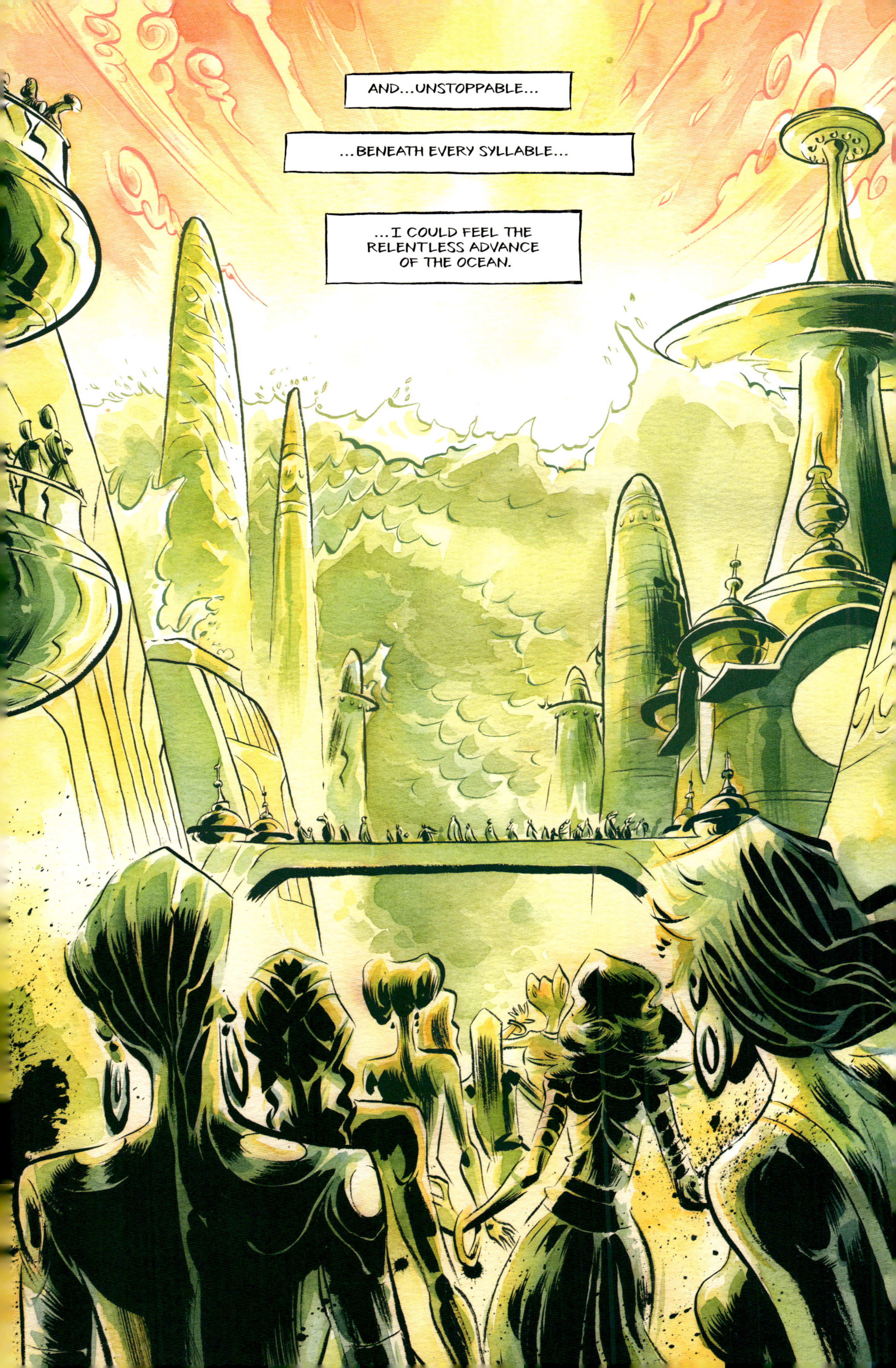
AND...UNSTOPPABLE...
...BENEATH EVERY SYLLABLE...
...I COULD FEEL THE RELENTLESS ADVANCE OF THE OCEAN.

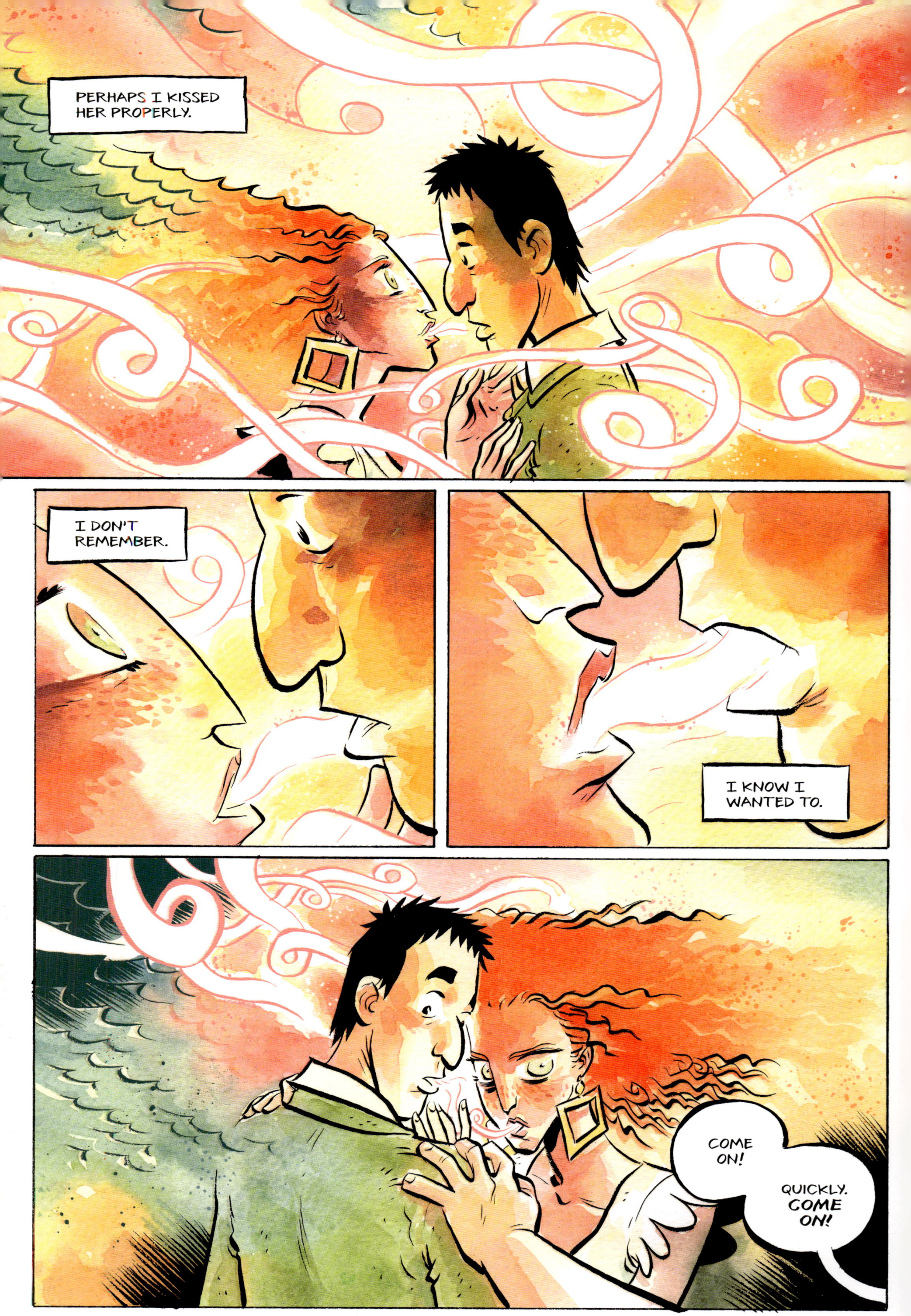
PERHAPS I KISSED HER PROPERLY.
I DON'T REMEMBER.
I KNOW I WANTED TO.
COME ON!
QUICKLY. COME ON!

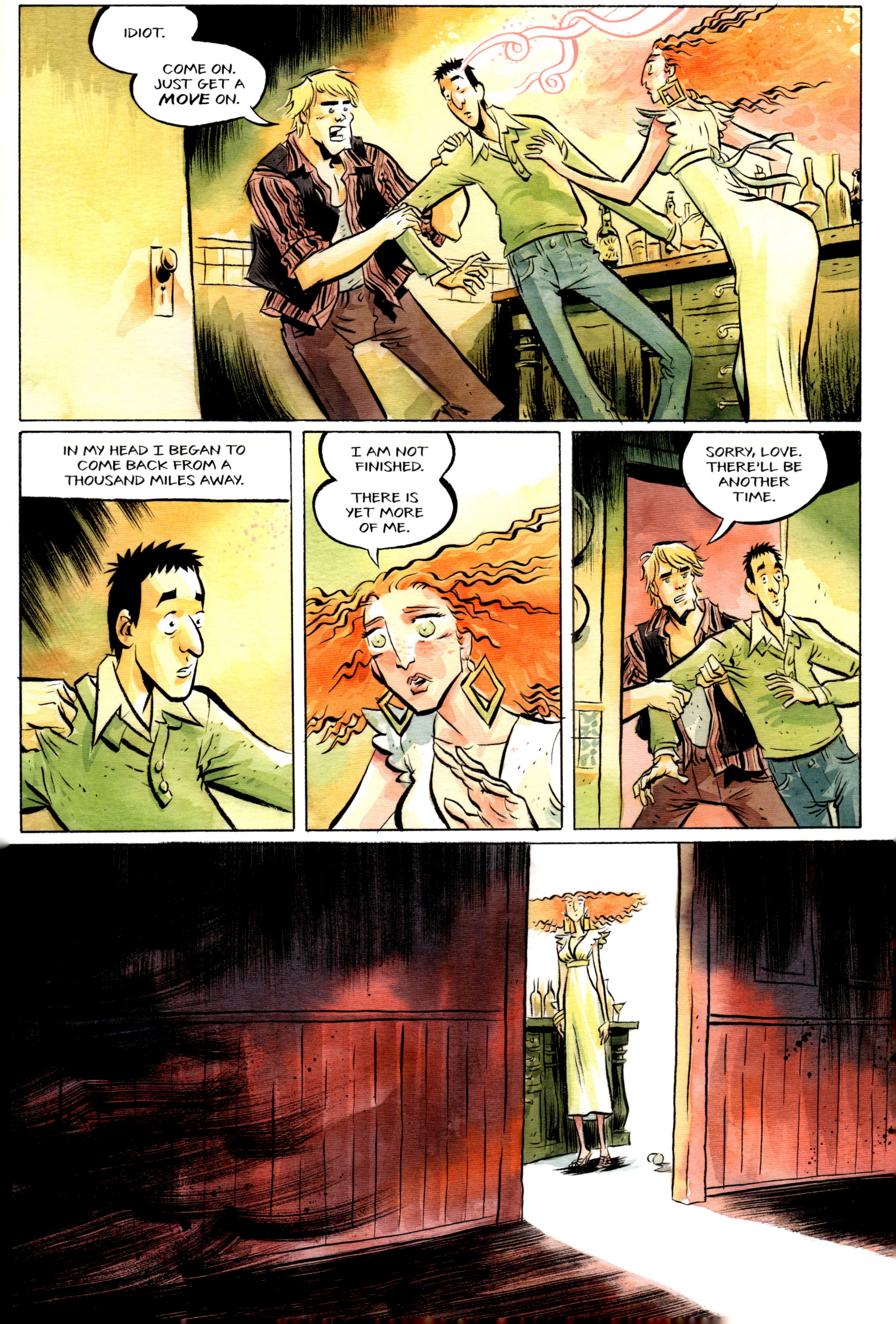
IDIOT.
COME ON. JUST GET A MOVE ON.
IN MY HEAD I BEGAN TO COME BACK FROM A THOUSAND MILES AWAY.
I AM NOT FINISHED.
THERE IS YET MORE OF ME.
SORRY, LOVE. THERE'LL BE ANOTHER TIME.

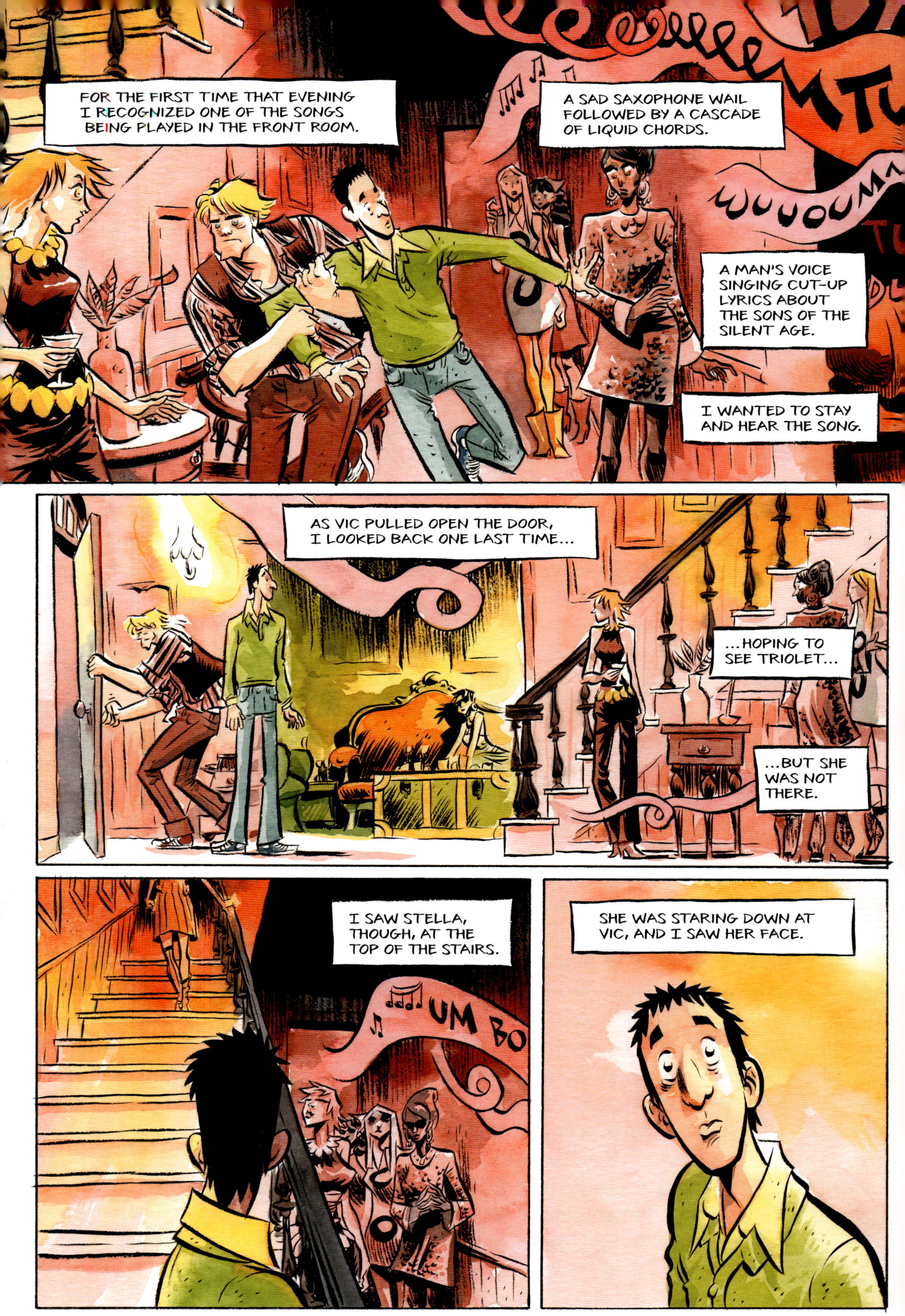
FOR THE FIRST TIME THAT EVENING I RECOGNIZED ONE OF THE SONGS BEING PLAYED IN THE FRONT ROOM.
A SAD SAXOPHONE WAIL FOLLOWED BY A CASCADE OF LIQUID CHORDS.
A MAN'S VOICE SINGING CUT-UP LYRICS ABOUT THE SONS OF THE SILENT AGE.
I WANTED TO STAY AND HEAR THE SONG.
AS VIC PULLED OPEN THE DOOR, I LOOKED BACK ONE LAST TIME...
...HOPING TO SEE TRIOLET...
...BUT SHE WAS NOT THERE.
I SAW STELLA, THOUGH, AT THE TOP OF THE STAIRS.
UM BO
SHE WAS STARING DOWN AT VIC, AND I SAW HER FACE.

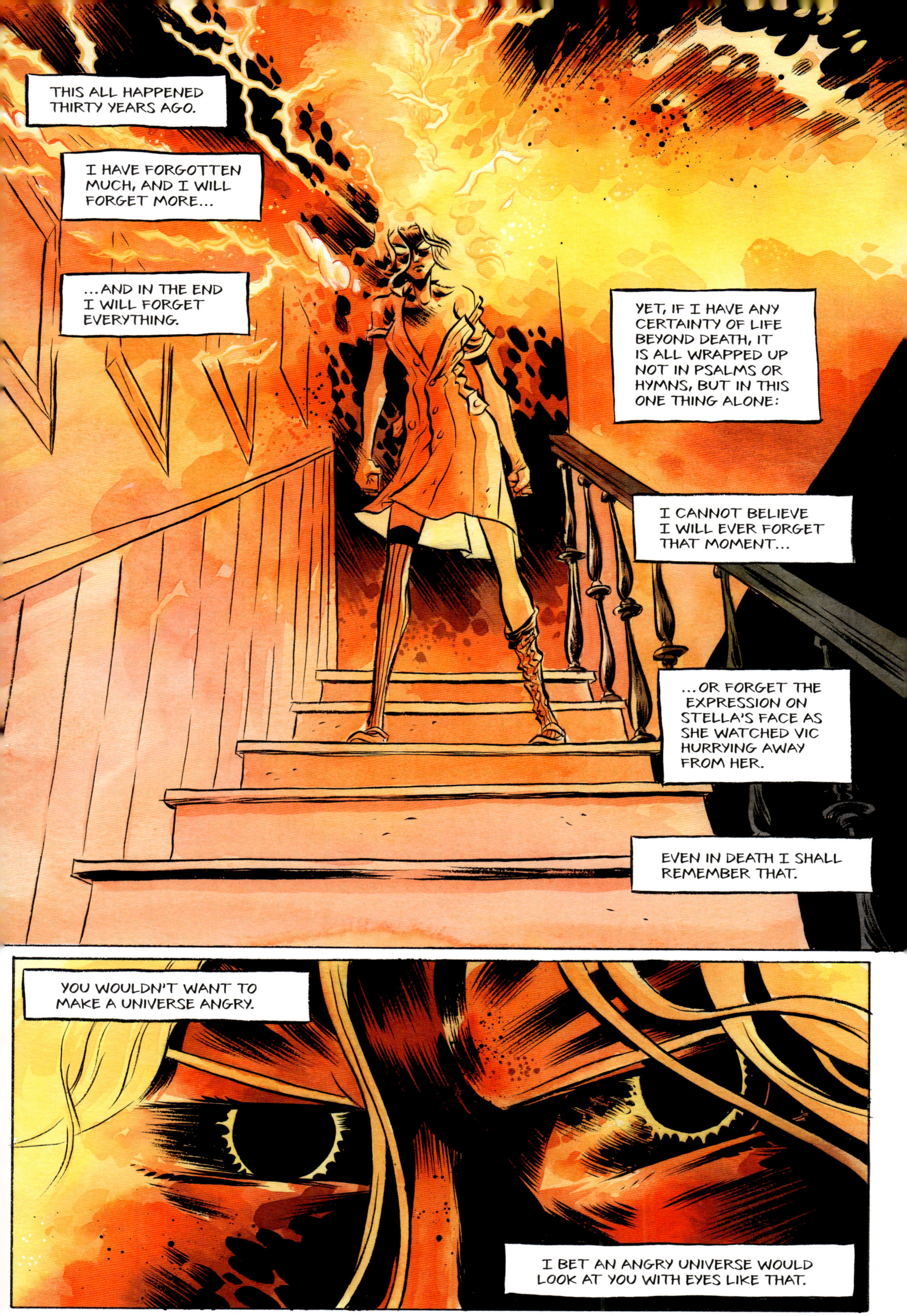
THIS ALL HAPPENED THIRTY YEARS AGO.
I HAVE FORGOTTEN MUCH, AND I WILL FORGET MORE...
...AND IN THE END I WILL FORGET EVERYTHING.
YET, IF I HAVE ANY CERTAINTY OF LIFE BEYOND DEATH, IT IS ALL WRAPPED UP NOT IN PSALMS OR HYMNS, BUT IN THIS ONE THING ALONE:
I CANNOT BELIEVE I WILL EVER FORGET THAT MOMENT...
...OR FORGET THE EXPRESSION ON STELLA'S FACE AS SHE WATCHED VIC HURRYING AWAY FROM HER.
EVEN IN DEATH I SHALL REMEMBER THAT.
YOU WOULDN'T WANT TO MAKE A UNIVERSE ANGRY.
I BET AN ANGRY UNIVERSE WOULD LOOK AT YOU WITH EYES LIKE THAT.

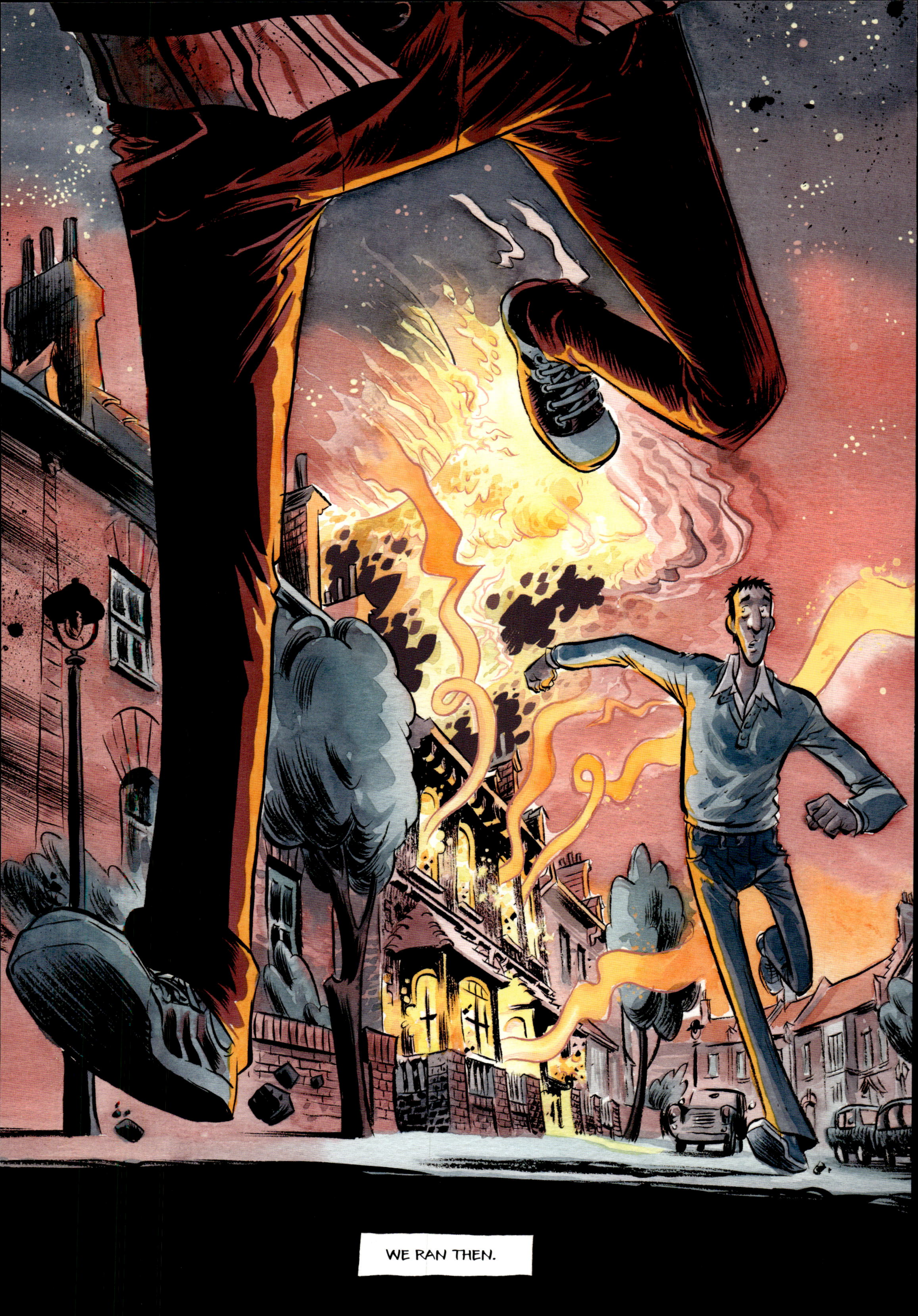
WE RAN THEN.

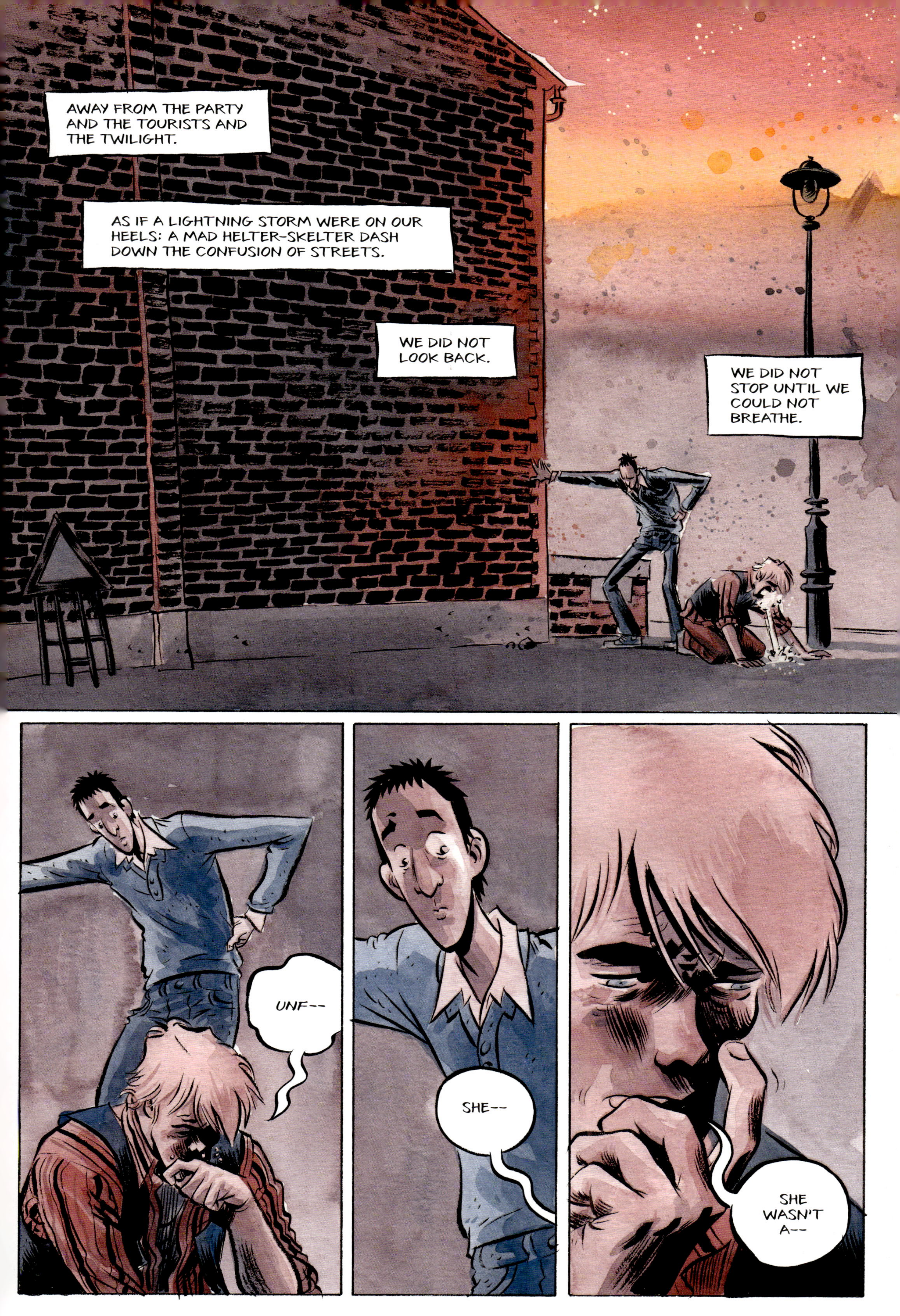
AWAY FROM THE PARTY AND THE TOURISTS AND THE TWILIGHT.
AS IF A LIGHTNING STORM WERE ON OUR HEELS: A MAD HELTER-SKELTER DASH DOWN THE CONFUSION OF STREETS.
WE DID NOT LOOK BACK.
WE DID NOT STOP UNTIL WE COULD NOT BREATHE.
UNF--
SHE--
SHE WASN'T A--

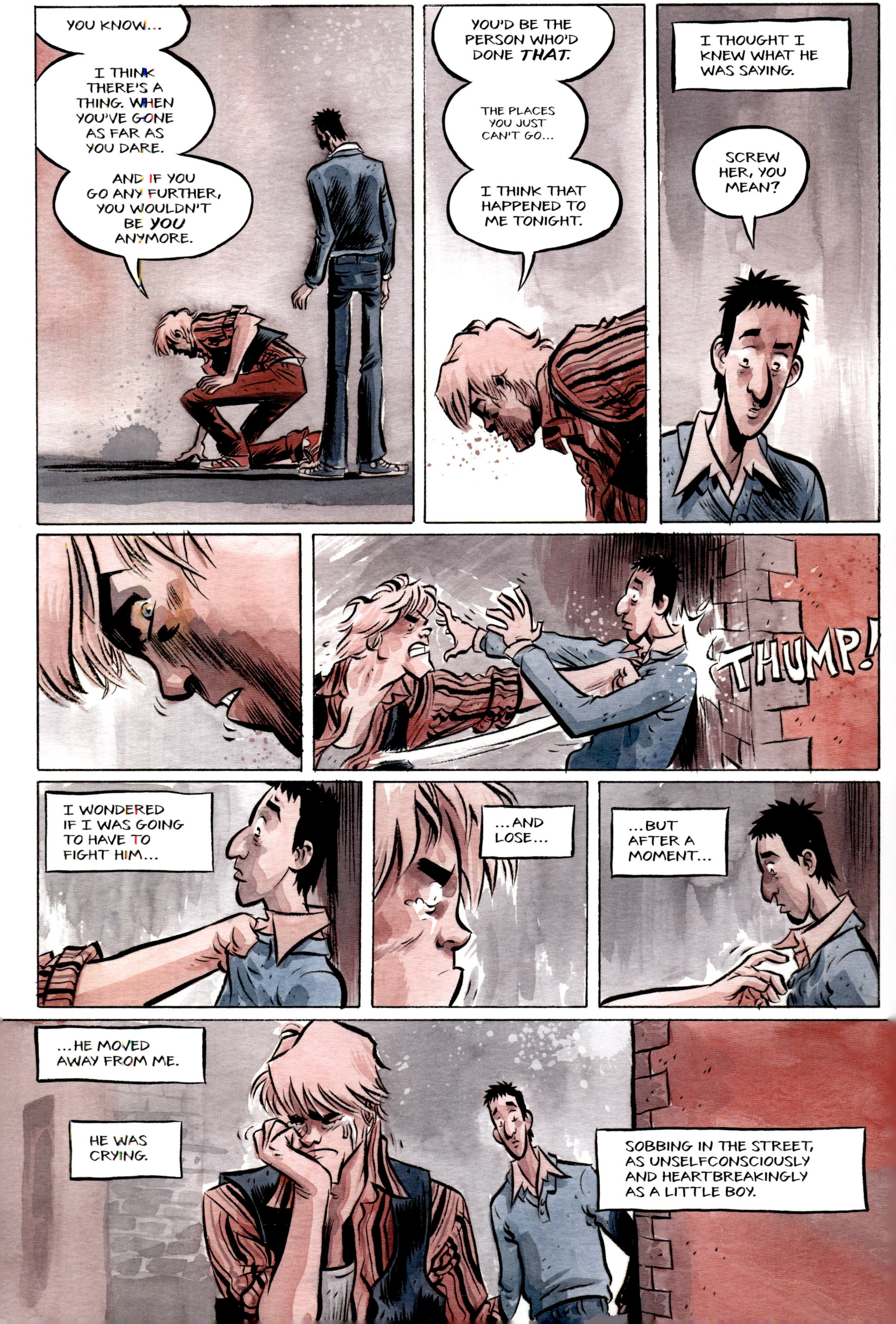
YOU KNOW...
I THINK THERE'S A THING. WHEN YOU'VE GONE AS FAR AS YOU DARE.
AND IF YOU GO ANY FURTHER, YOU WOULDN'T BE *YOU* ANYMORE.
YOU'D BE THE PERSON WHO'D DONE *THAT.*
THE PLACES YOU JUST CAN'T GO...
I THINK THAT HAPPENED TO ME TONIGHT.
I THOUGHT I KNEW WHAT HE WAS SAYING.
SCREW HER, YOU MEAN?
THUMP!
I WONDERED IF I WAS GOING TO HAVE TO FIGHT HIM...
...AND LOSE...
...BUT AFTER A MOMENT...
...HE MOVED AWAY FROM ME.
HE WAS CRYING.
SOBBING IN THE STREET, AS UNSELFCONSCIOUSLY AND HEARTBREAKINGLY AS A LITTLE BOY.

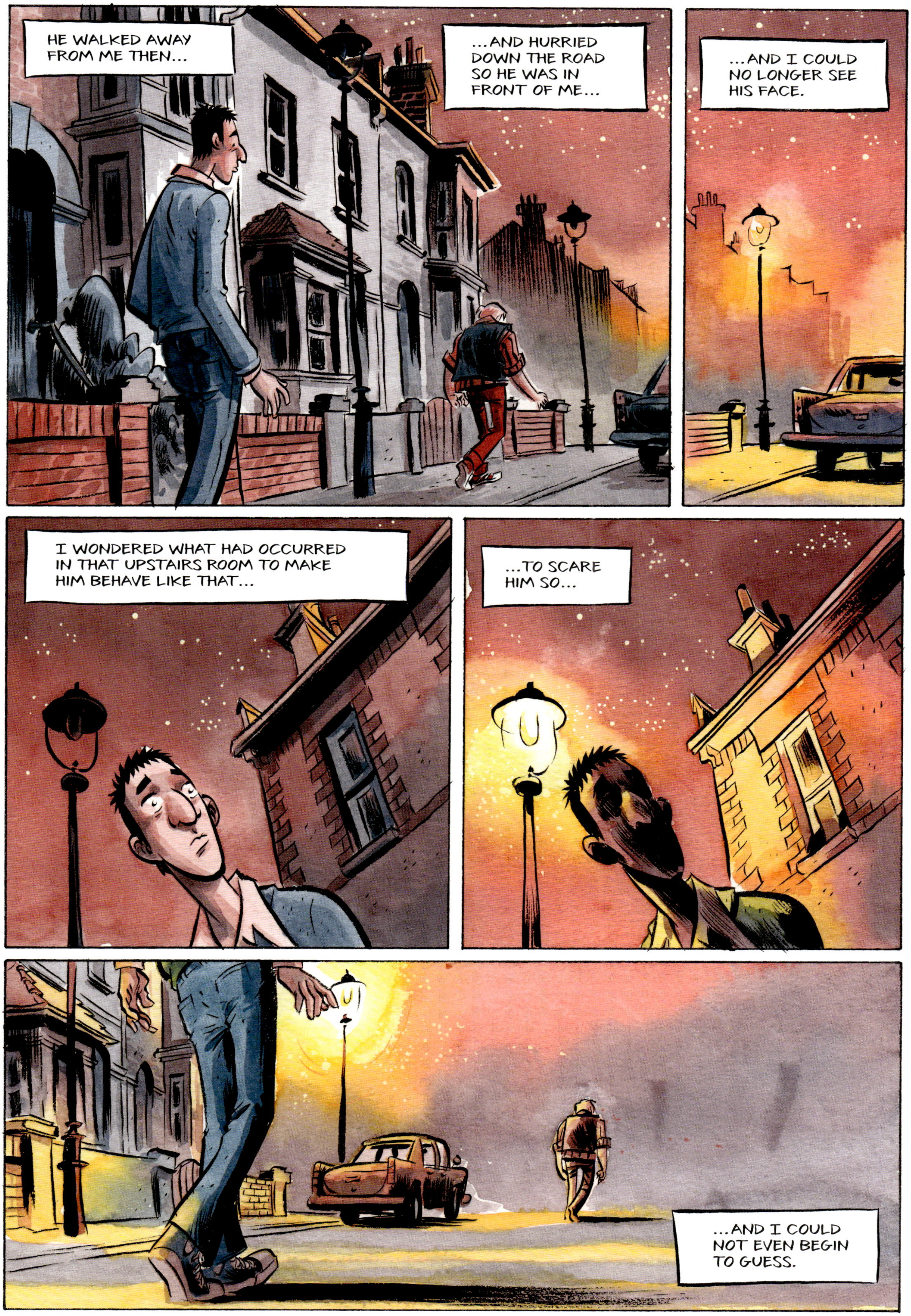
HE WALKED AWAY FROM ME THEN...
...AND HURRIED DOWN THE ROAD SO HE WAS IN FRONT OF ME...
...AND I COULD NO LONGER SEE HIS FACE.
I WONDERED WHAT HAD OCCURRED IN THAT UPSTAIRS ROOM TO MAKE HIM BEHAVE LIKE THAT...
...TO SCARE HIM SO...
...AND I COULD NOT EVEN BEGIN TO GUESS.

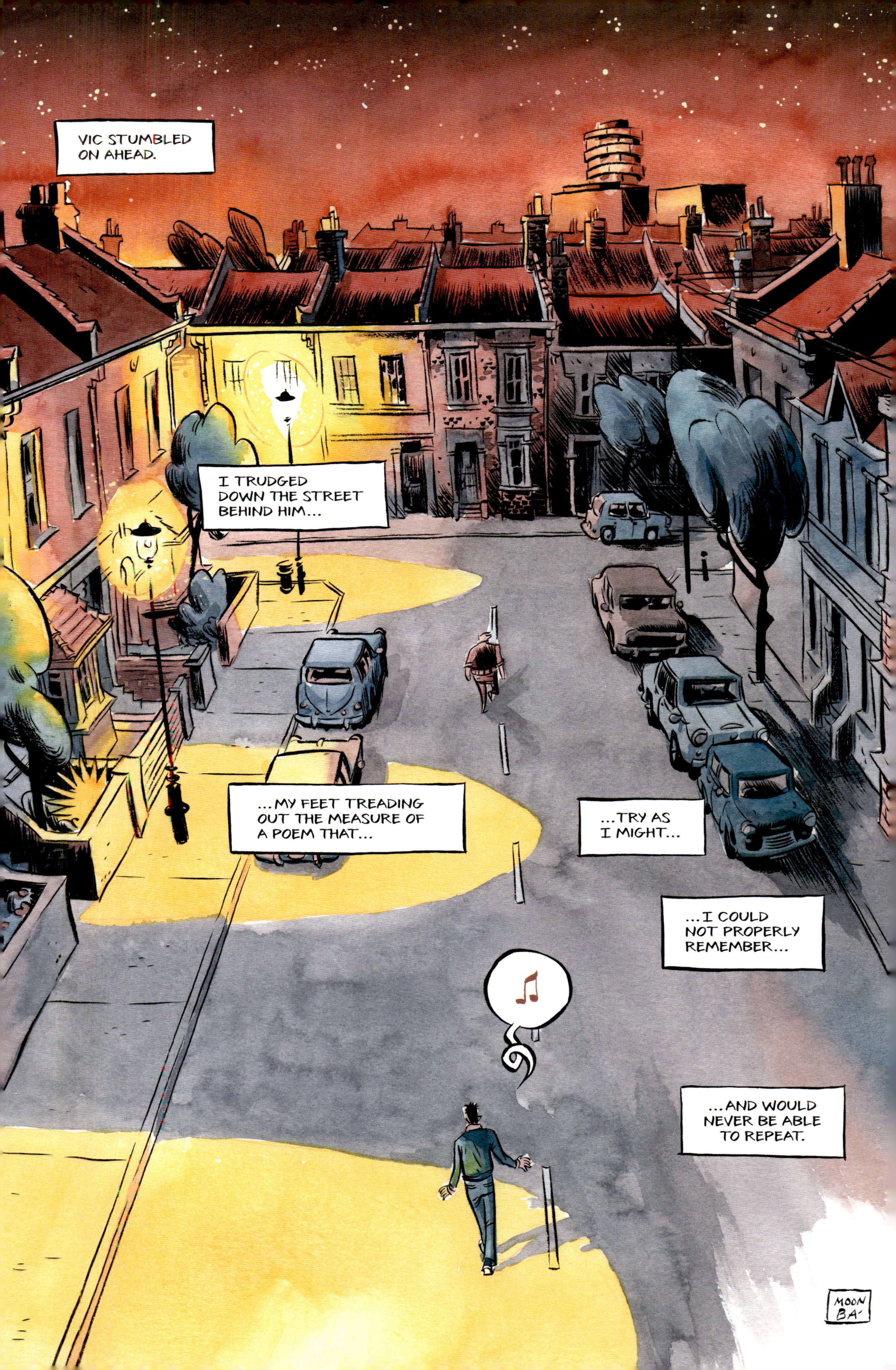
VIC STUMBLED ON AHEAD.
I TRUDGED DOWN THE STREET BEHIND HIM...
...MY FEET TREADING OUT THE MEASURE OF A POEM THAT...
...TRY AS I MIGHT...
...I COULD NOT PROPERLY REMEMBER...
...AND WOULD NEVER BE ABLE TO REPEAT.
MOON BÁ

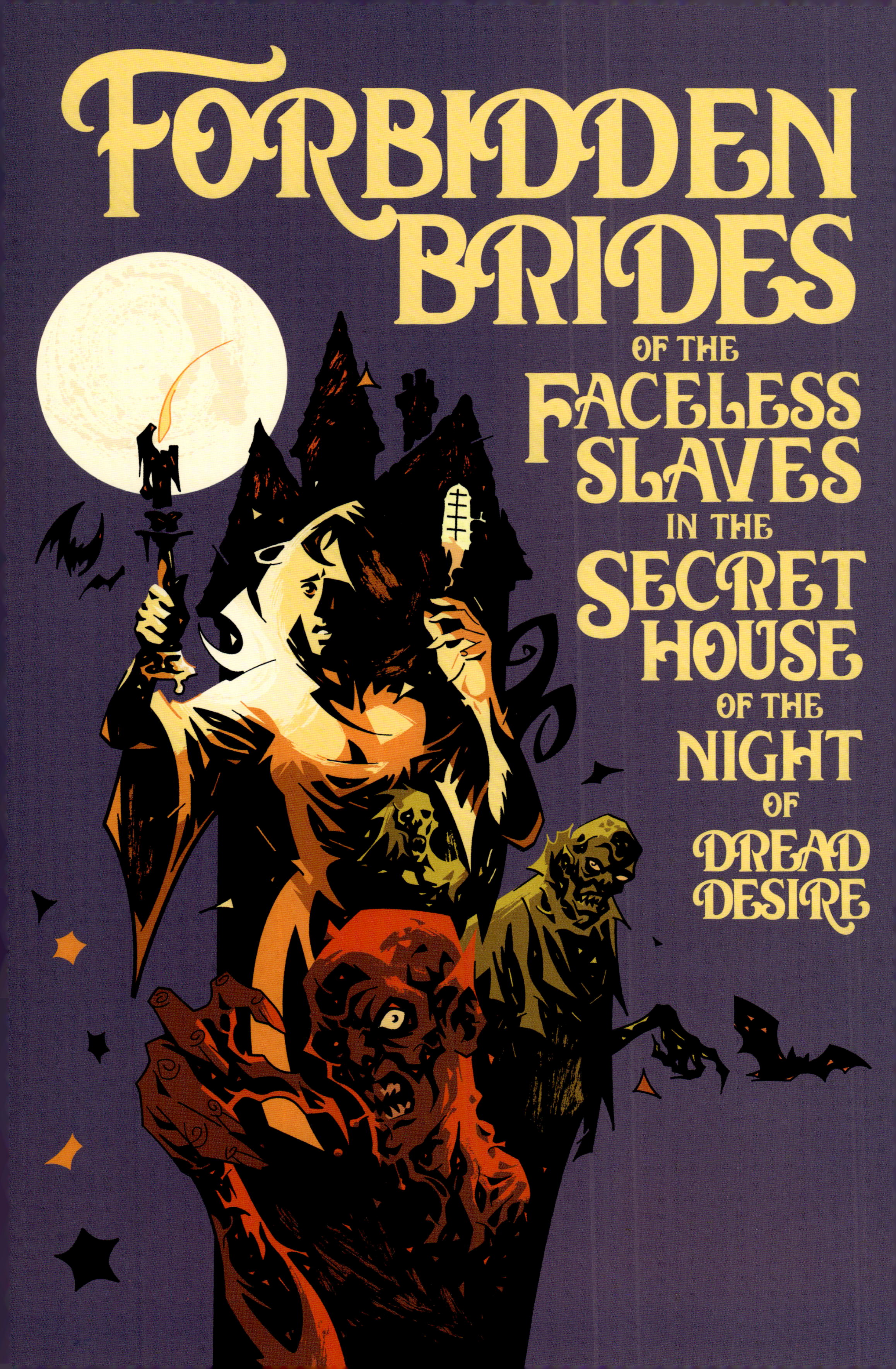
FORBIDDEN BRIDES
OF THE
FACELESS SLAVES
IN THE
SECRET HOUSE
OF THE
NIGHT
OF
DREAD DESIRE

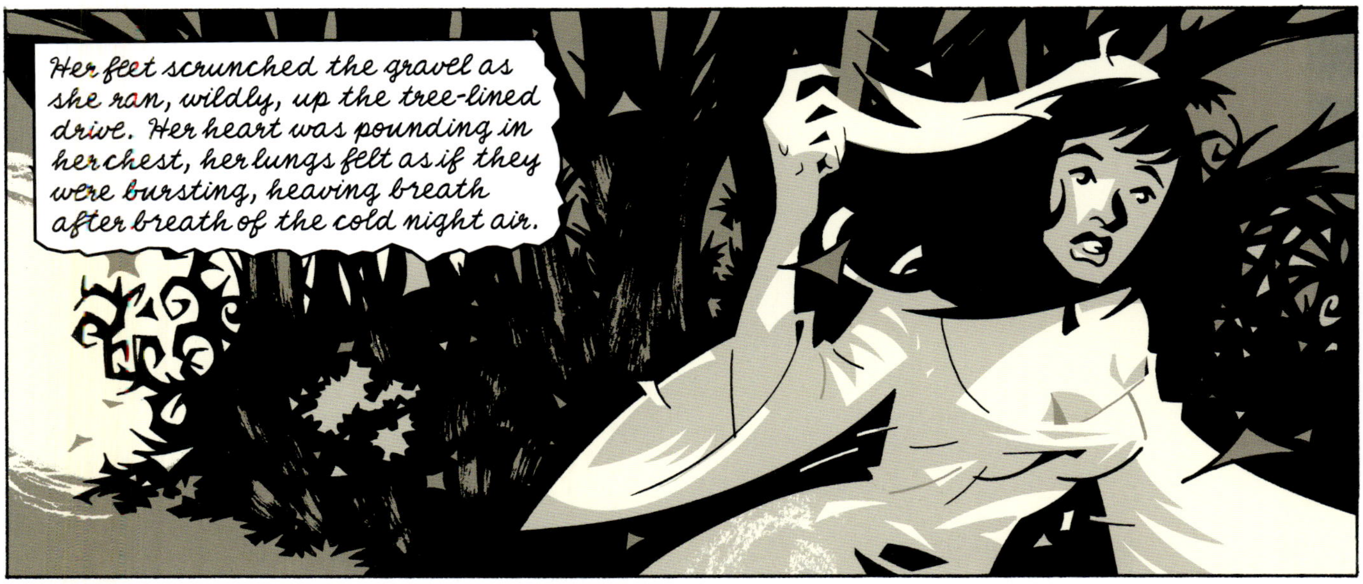
Her feet scrunched the gravel as she ran, wildly, up the tree-lined drive. Her heart was pounding in her chest, her lungs felt as if they were bursting, heaving breath after breath of the cold night air.
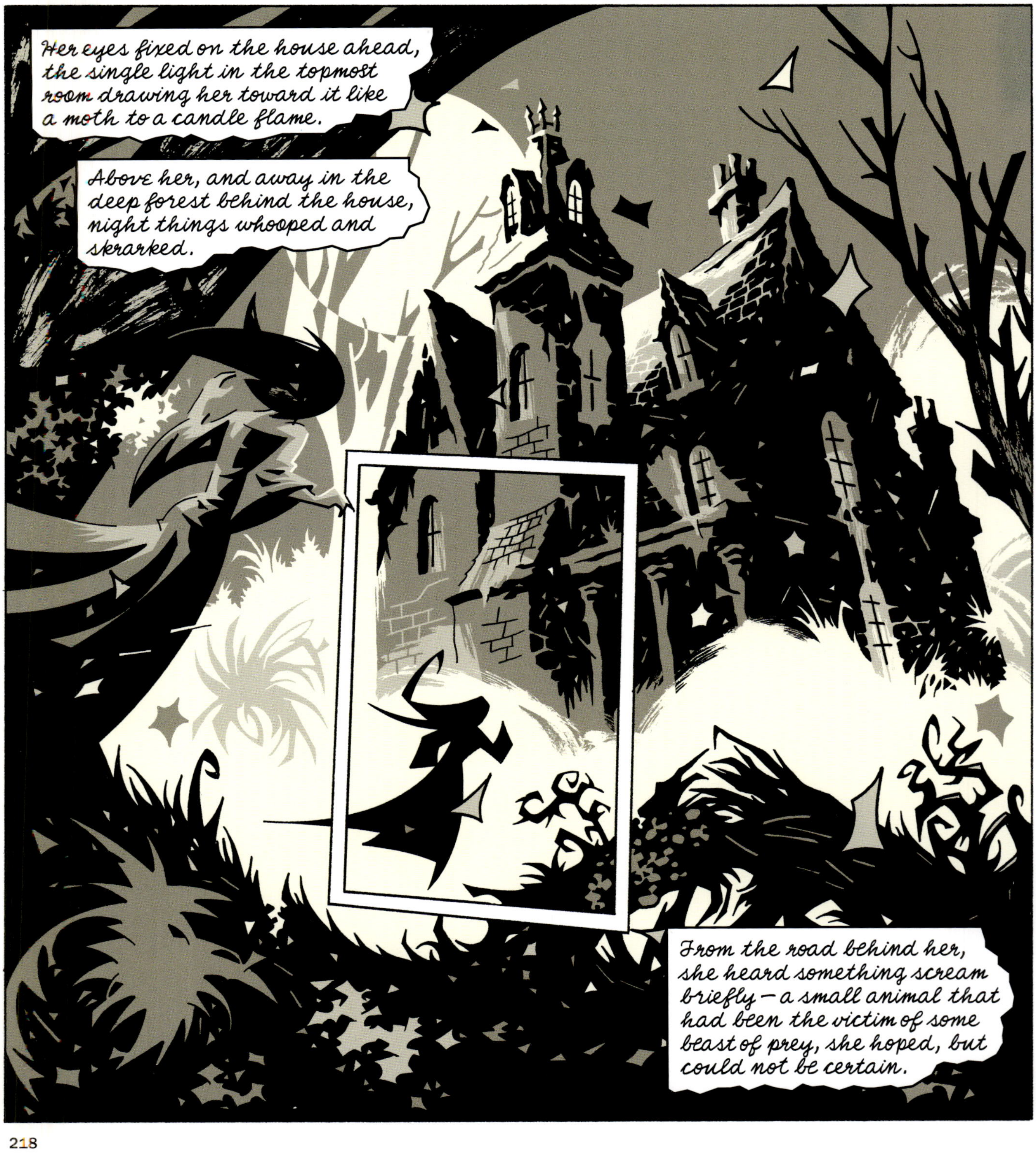
Her eyes fixed on the house ahead, the single light in the topmost room drawing her toward it like a moth to a candle flame.
Above her, and away in the deep forest behind the house, night things whooped and skrarked.
From the road behind her, she heard something scream briefly—a small animal that had been the victim of some beast of prey, she hoped, but could not be certain.

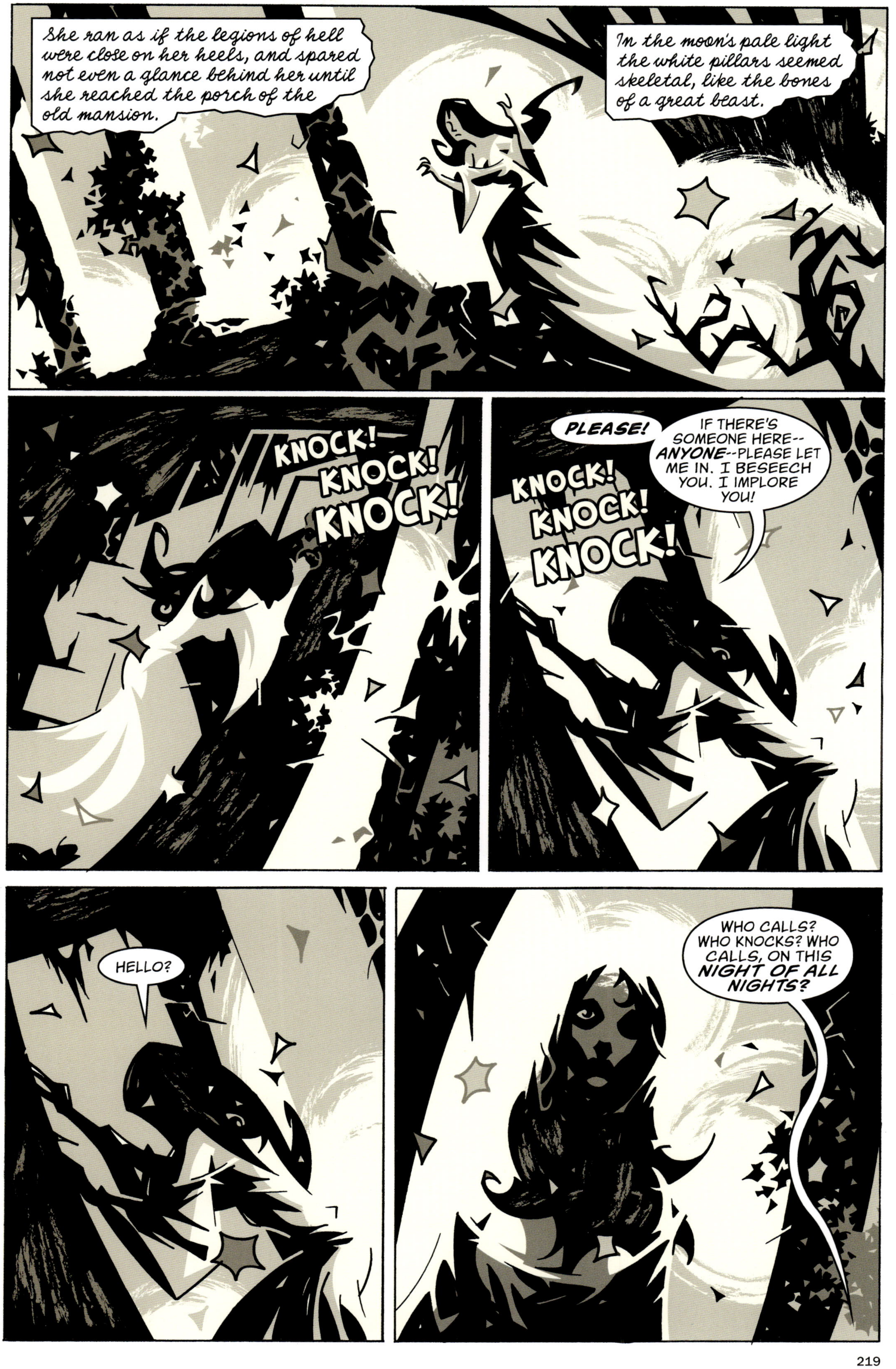
She ran as if the legions of hell were close on her heels, and spared not even a glance behind her until she reached the porch of the old mansion.
In the moon's pale light the white pillars seemed skeletal, like the bones of a great beast.
KNOCK! KNOCK! KNOCK!
PLEASE!
IF THERE'S SOMEONE HERE--ANYONE--PLEASE LET ME IN. I BESEECH YOU. I IMPLORE YOU!
KNOCK! KNOCK! KNOCK!
HELLO?
WHO CALLS? WHO KNOCKS? WHO CALLS, ON THIS NIGHT OF ALL NIGHTS?

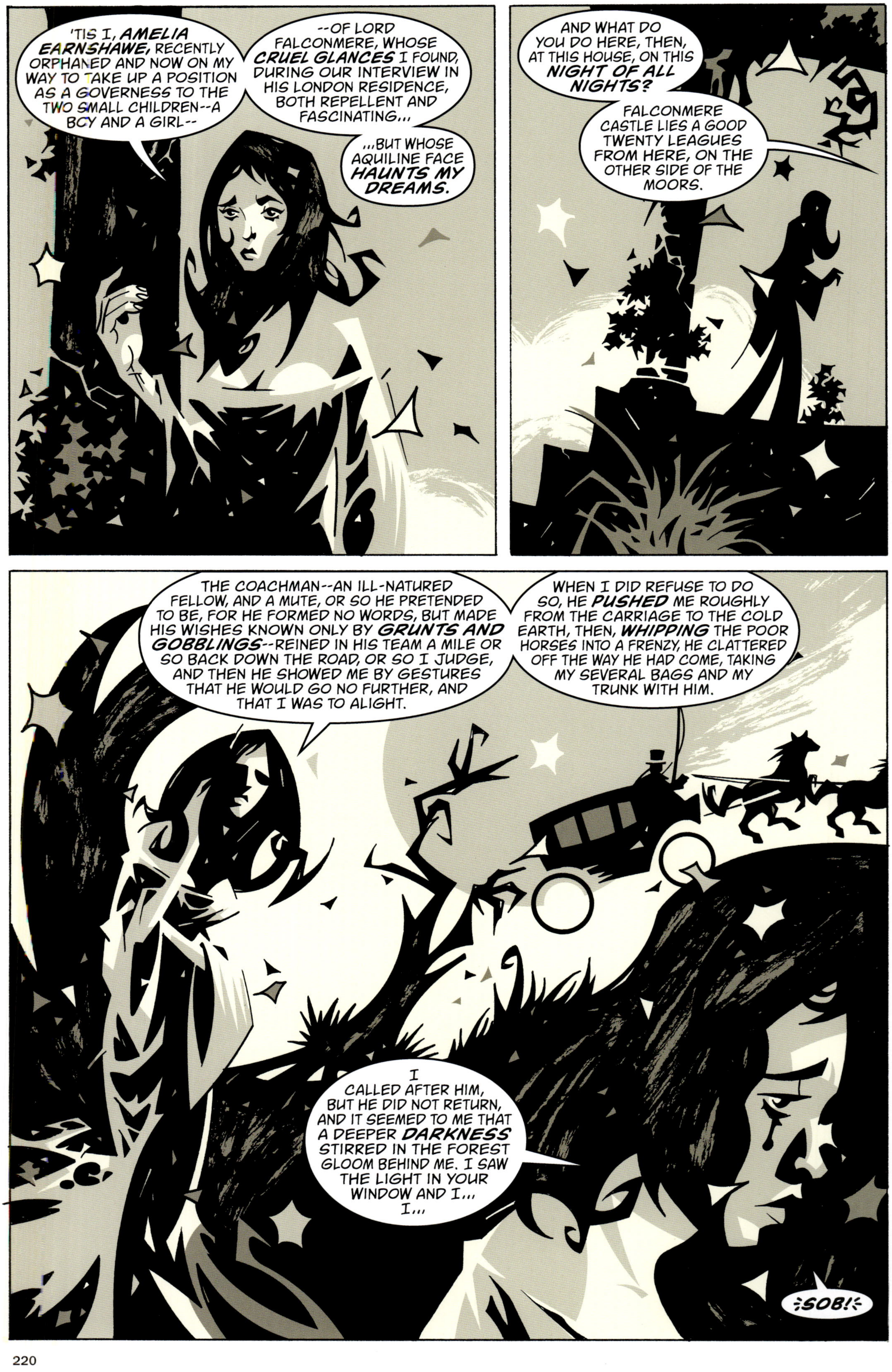
'TIS I, AMELIA EARNSHAWE, RECENTLY ORPHANED AND NOW ON MY WAY TO TAKE UP A POSITION AS A GOVERNESS TO THE TWO SMALL CHILDREN--A BOY AND A GIRL--
--OF LORD FALCONMERE, WHOSE CRUEL GLANCES I FOUND, DURING OUR INTERVIEW IN HIS LONDON RESIDENCE, BOTH REPELLENT AND FASCINATING...
...BUT WHOSE AQUILINE FACE HAUNTS MY DREAMS.
AND WHAT DO YOU DO HERE, THEN, AT THIS HOUSE, ON THIS NIGHT OF ALL NIGHTS?
FALCONMERE CASTLE LIES A GOOD TWENTY LEAGUES FROM HERE, ON THE OTHER SIDE OF THE MOORS.
THE COACHMAN--AN ILL-NATURED FELLOW, AND A MUTE, OR SO HE PRETENDED TO BE, FOR HE FORMED NO WORDS, BUT MADE HIS WISHES KNOWN ONLY BY GRUNTS AND GOBBLINGS--REINED IN HIS TEAM A MILE OR SO BACK DOWN THE ROAD, OR SO I JUDGE, AND THEN HE SHOWED ME BY GESTURES THAT HE WOULD GO NO FURTHER, AND THAT I WAS TO ALIGHT.
WHEN I DID REFUSE TO DO SO, HE PUSHED ME ROUGHLY FROM THE CARRIAGE TO THE COLD EARTH, THEN, WHIPPING THE POOR HORSES INTO A FRENZY, HE CLATTERED OFF THE WAY HE HAD COME, TAKING MY SEVERAL BAGS AND MY TRUNK WITH HIM.
I CALLED AFTER HIM, BUT HE DID NOT RETURN, AND IT SEEMED TO ME THAT A DEEPER DARKNESS STIRRED IN THE FOREST GLOOM BEHIND ME. I SAW THE LIGHT IN YOUR WINDOW AND I... I...
SOB!

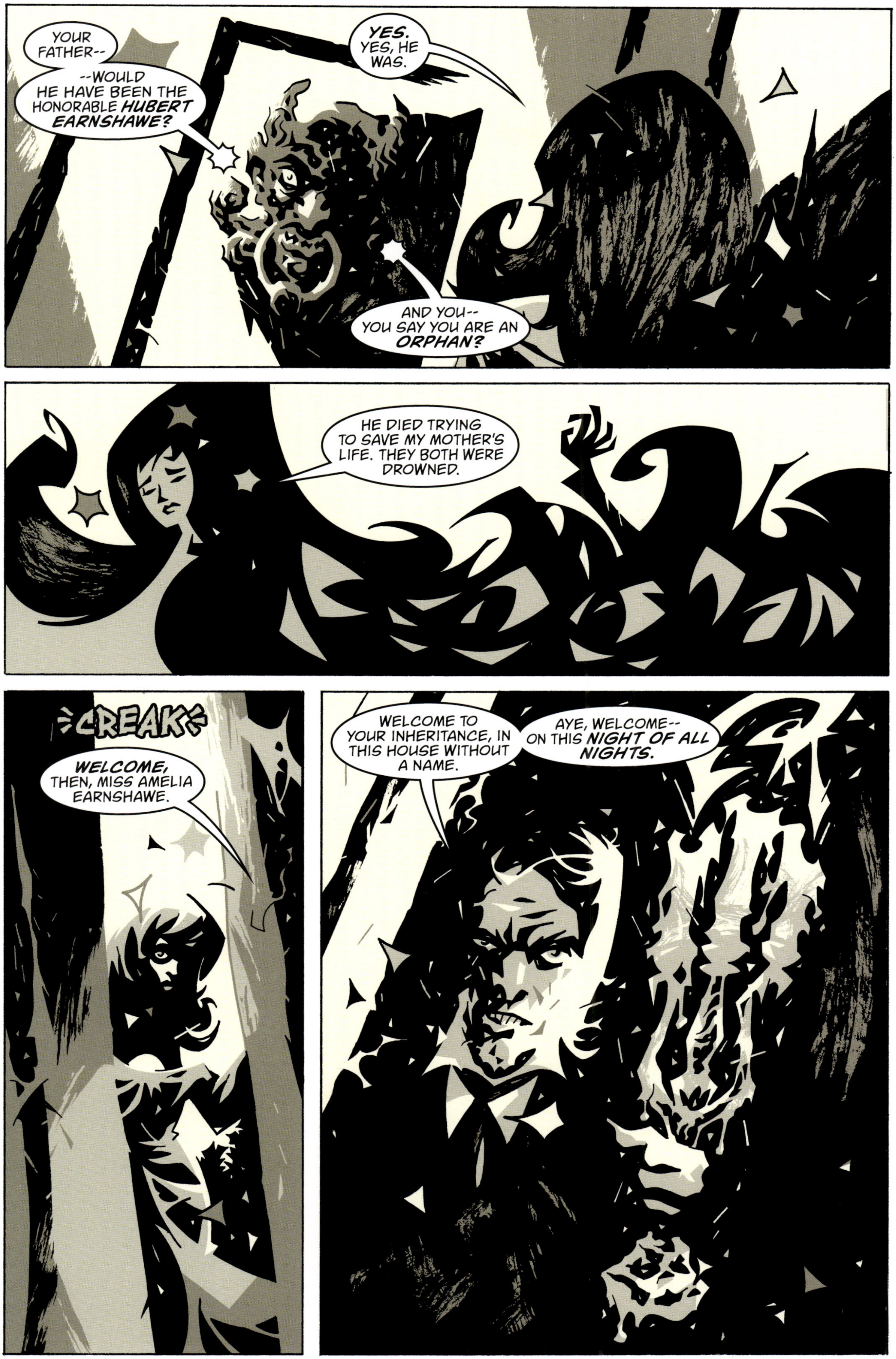
YOUR FATHER--
--WOULD HE HAVE BEEN THE HONORABLE *HUBERT EARNSHAWE?*
YES. YES, HE WAS.
AND YOU-- YOU SAY YOU ARE AN *ORPHAN?*
HE DIED TRYING TO SAVE MY MOTHER'S LIFE. THEY BOTH WERE DROWNED.
CREAK
WELCOME, THEN, MISS AMELIA EARNSHAWE.
WELCOME TO YOUR INHERITANCE, IN THIS HOUSE WITHOUT A NAME.
AYE, WELCOME-- ON THIS *NIGHT OF ALL NIGHTS.*

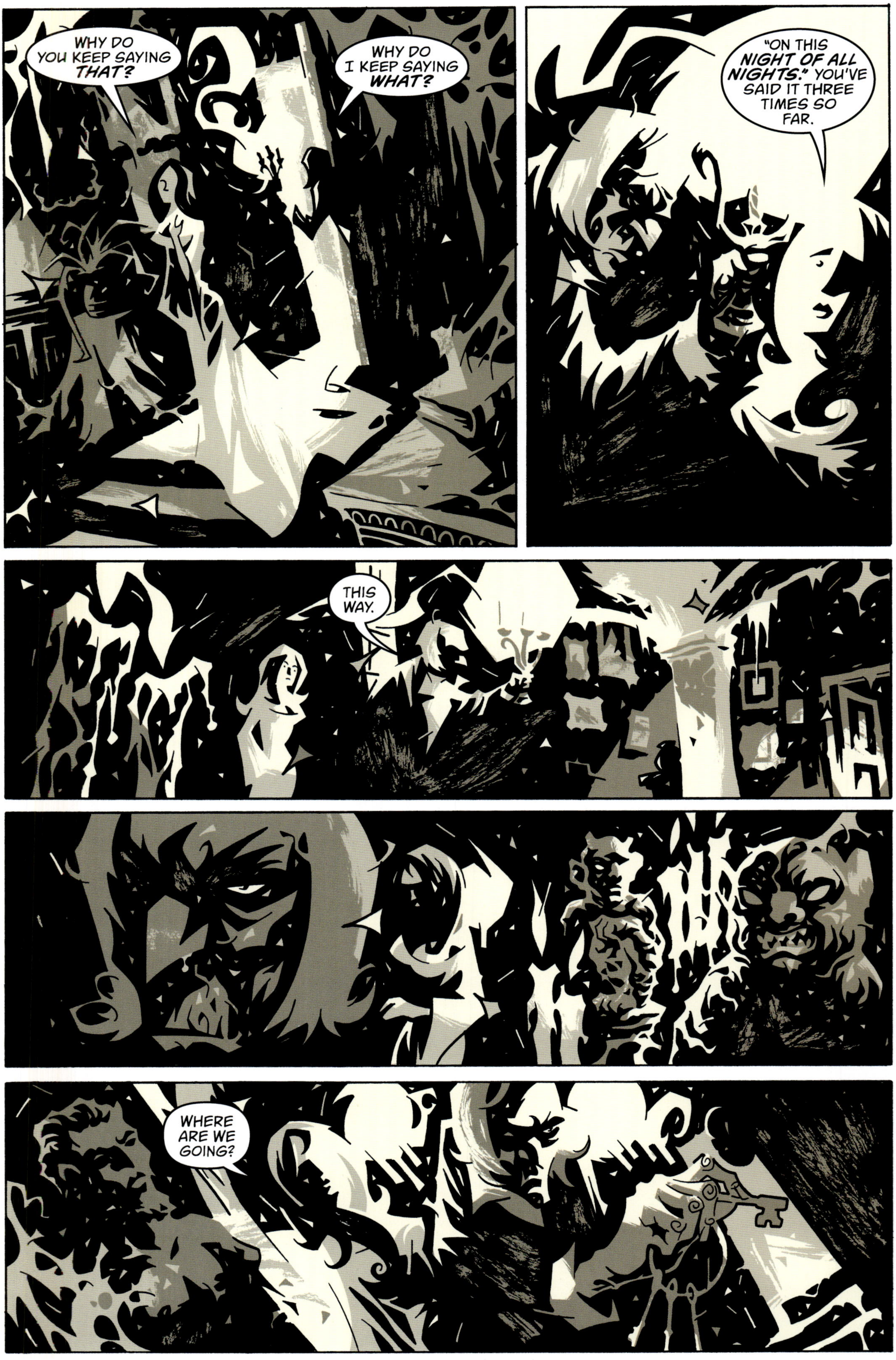
WHY DO YOU KEEP SAYING *THAT?*
WHY DO I KEEP SAYING *WHAT?*
"ON THIS *NIGHT OF ALL NIGHTS.*" YOU'VE SAID IT THREE TIMES SO FAR.
THIS WAY.
WHERE ARE WE GOING?

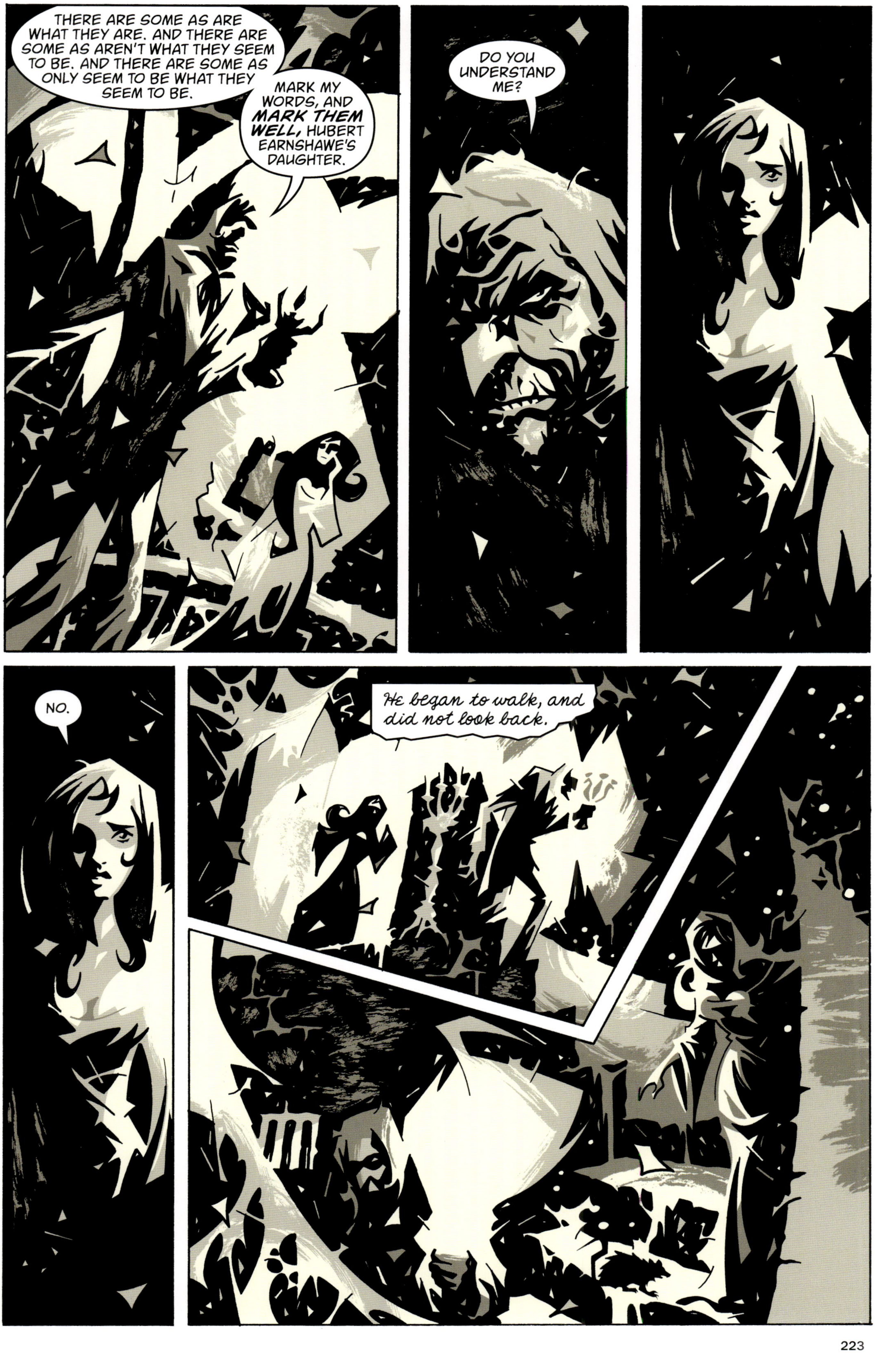

THERE ARE SOME AS ARE WHAT THEY ARE. AND THERE ARE SOME AS AREN'T WHAT THEY SEEM TO BE. AND THERE ARE SOME AS ONLY SEEM TO BE WHAT THEY SEEM TO BE.
MARK MY WORDS, AND MARK THEM WELL, HUBERT EARNSHAWE'S DAUGHTER.
DO YOU UNDERSTAND ME?
NO.
He began to walk, and did not look back.

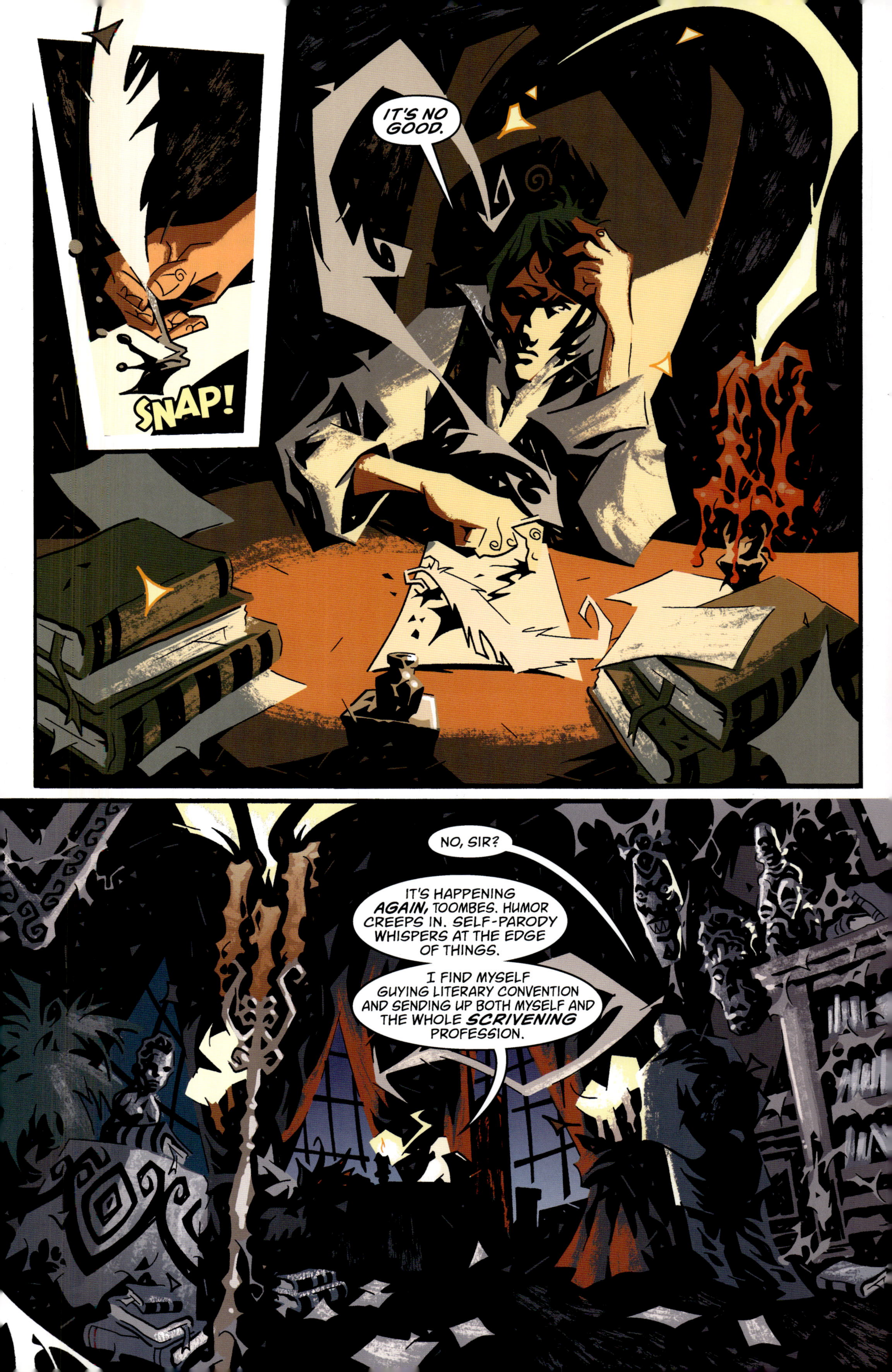
SNAP!
IT'S NO GOOD.
NO, SIR?
IT'S HAPPENING AGAIN, TOOMBES. HUMOR CREEPS IN. SELF-PARODY WHISPERS AT THE EDGE OF THINGS.
I FIND MYSELF GUYING LITERARY CONVENTION AND SENDING UP BOTH MYSELF AND THE WHOLE SCRIVENING PROFESSION.

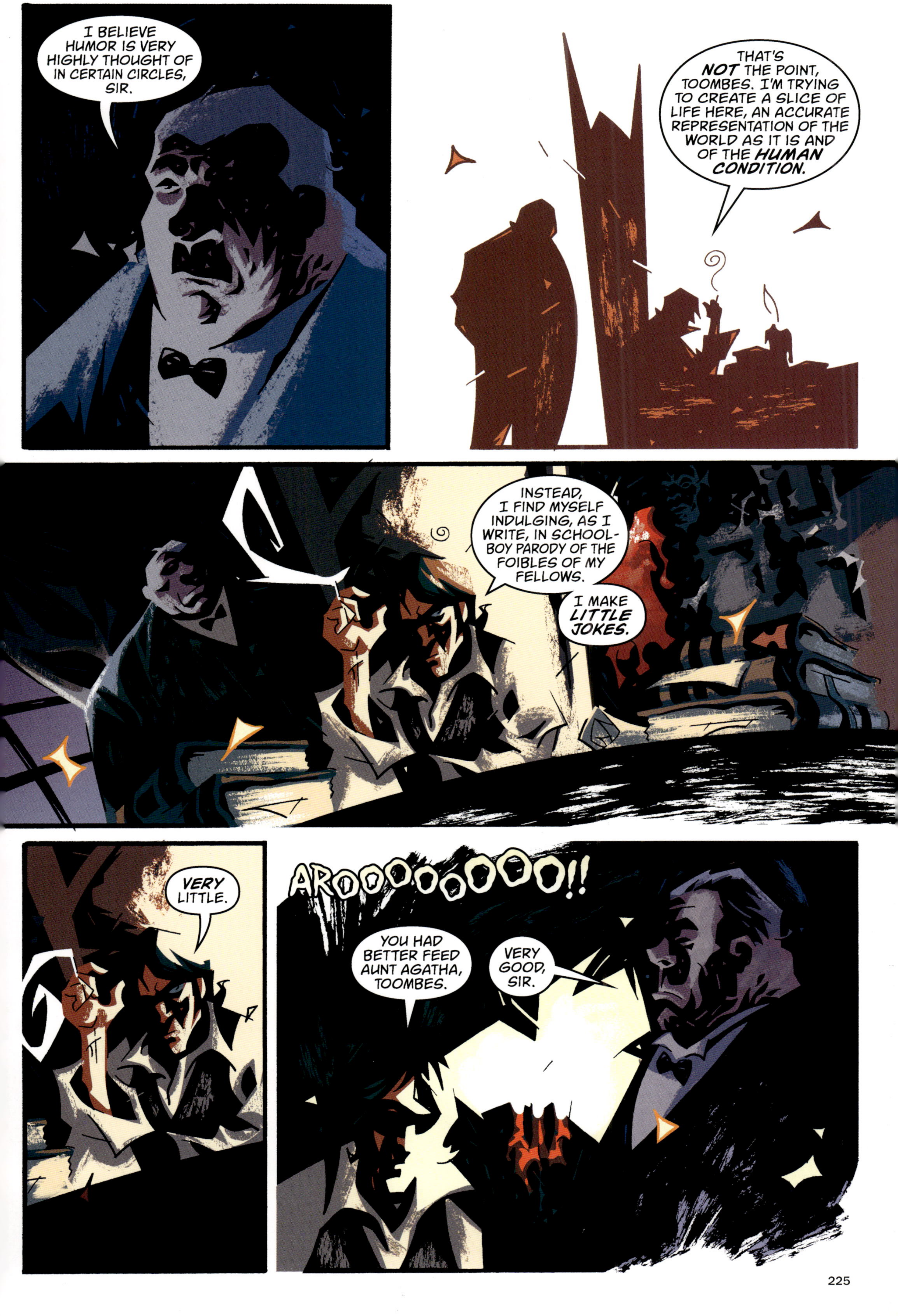
I BELIEVE HUMOR IS VERY HIGHLY THOUGHT OF IN CERTAIN CIRCLES, SIR.
THAT'S **NOT** THE POINT, TOOMBES. I'M TRYING TO CREATE A SLICE OF LIFE HERE, AN ACCURATE REPRESENTATION OF THE WORLD AS IT IS AND OF THE ***HUMAN CONDITION.***
INSTEAD, I FIND MYSELF INDULGING, AS I WRITE, IN SCHOOL-BOY PARODY OF THE FOIBLES OF MY FELLOWS.
I MAKE ***LITTLE JOKES.***
VERY LITTLE.
AROOOOOOOOO!!
YOU HAD BETTER FEED AUNT AGATHA, TOOMBES.
VERY GOOD, SIR.

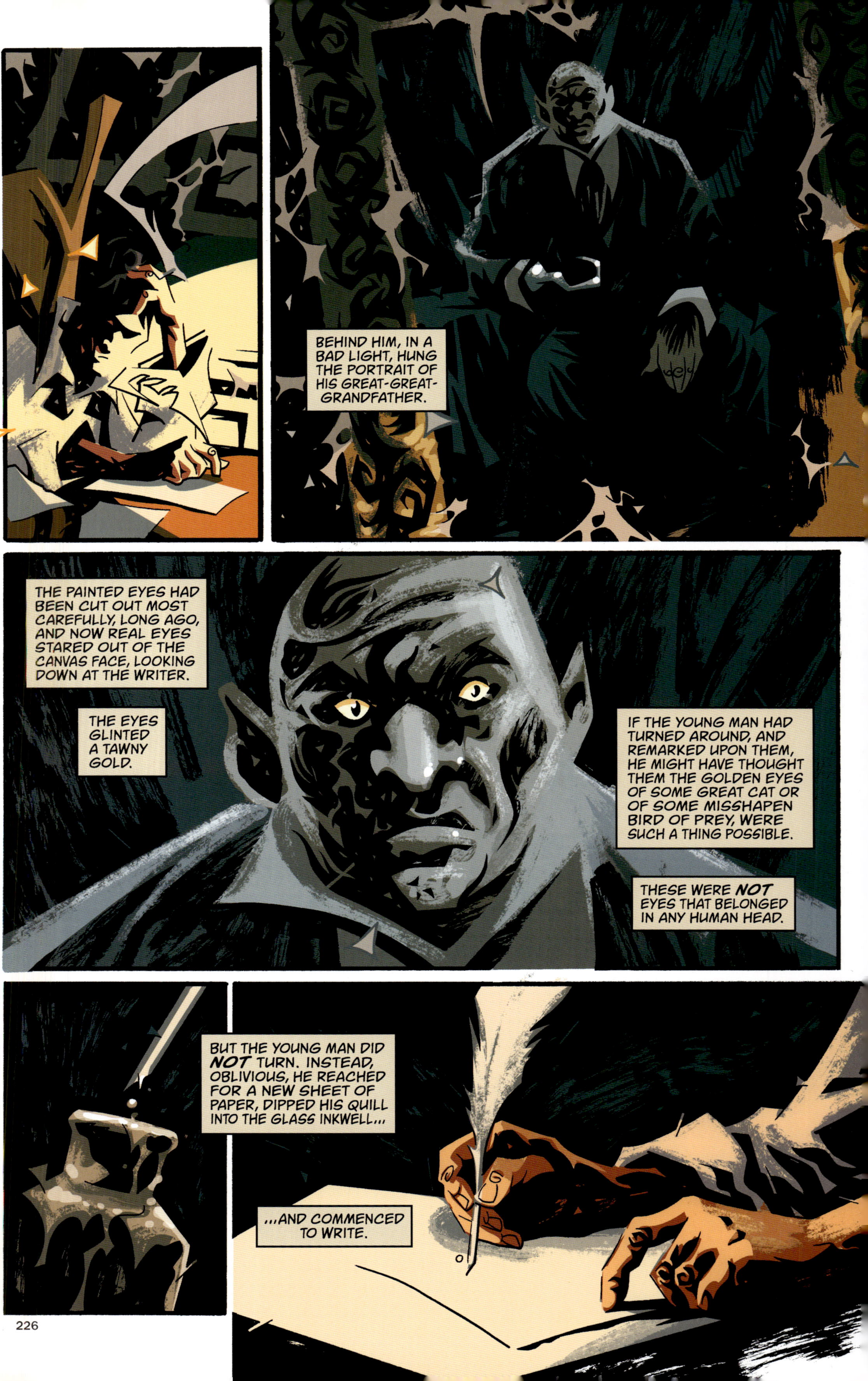
BEHIND HIM, IN A BAD LIGHT, HUNG THE PORTRAIT OF HIS GREAT-GREAT-GRANDFATHER.
THE PAINTED EYES HAD BEEN CUT OUT MOST CAREFULLY, LONG AGO, AND NOW REAL EYES STARED OUT OF THE CANVAS FACE, LOOKING DOWN AT THE WRITER.
THE EYES GLINTED A TAWNY GOLD.
IF THE YOUNG MAN HAD TURNED AROUND, AND REMARKED UPON THEM, HE MIGHT HAVE THOUGHT THEM THE GOLDEN EYES OF SOME GREAT CAT OR OF SOME MISSHAPEN BIRD OF PREY, WERE SUCH A THING POSSIBLE.
THESE WERE NOT EYES THAT BELONGED IN ANY HUMAN HEAD.
BUT THE YOUNG MAN DID NOT TURN. INSTEAD, OBLIVIOUS, HE REACHED FOR A NEW SHEET OF PAPER, DIPPED HIS QUILL INTO THE GLASS INKWELL...
...AND COMMENCED TO WRITE.

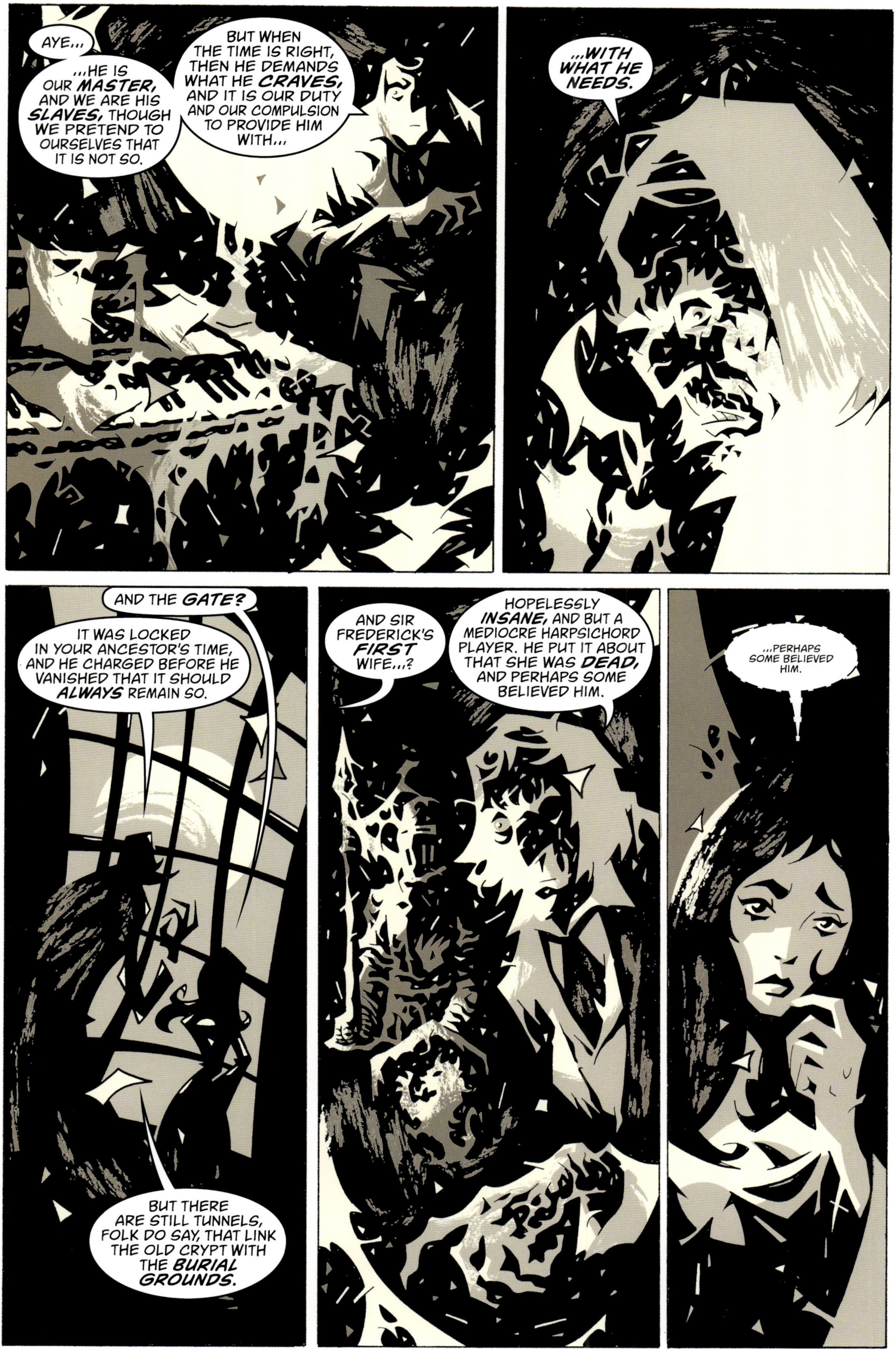
AYE...
...HE IS OUR MASTER, AND WE ARE HIS SLAVES, THOUGH WE PRETEND TO OURSELVES THAT IT IS NOT SO.
BUT WHEN THE TIME IS RIGHT, THEN HE DEMANDS WHAT HE CRAVES, AND IT IS OUR DUTY AND OUR COMPULSION TO PROVIDE HIM WITH...
...WITH WHAT HE NEEDS.
AND THE GATE?
IT WAS LOCKED IN YOUR ANCESTOR'S TIME, AND HE CHARGED BEFORE HE VANISHED THAT IT SHOULD ALWAYS REMAIN SO.
BUT THERE ARE STILL TUNNELS, FOLK DO SAY, THAT LINK THE OLD CRYPT WITH THE BURIAL GROUNDS.
AND SIR FREDERICK'S FIRST WIFE...?
HOPELESSLY INSANE, AND BUT A MEDIOCRE HARPSICHORD PLAYER. HE PUT IT ABOUT THAT SHE WAS DEAD, AND PERHAPS SOME BELIEVED HIM.
...PERHAPS SOME BELIEVED HIM.

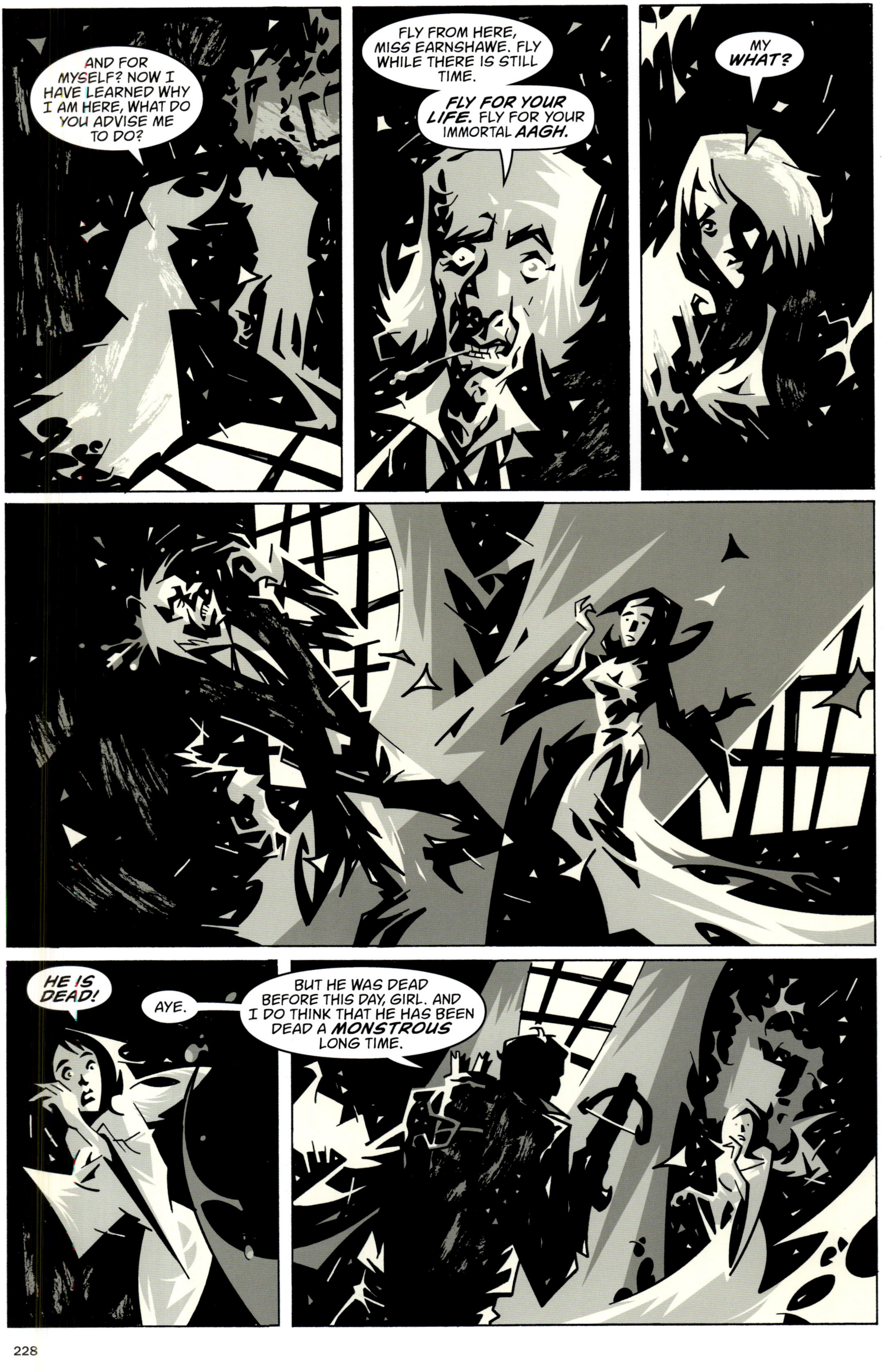
AND FOR MYSELF? NOW I HAVE LEARNED WHY I AM HERE, WHAT DO YOU ADVISE ME TO DO?
FLY FROM HERE, MISS EARNSHAWE. FLY WHILE THERE IS STILL TIME.
FLY FOR YOUR LIFE. FLY FOR YOUR IMMORTAL AAGH.
MY WHAT?
HE IS DEAD!
AYE.
BUT HE WAS DEAD BEFORE THIS DAY, GIRL. AND I DO THINK THAT HE HAS BEEN DEAD A MONSTROUS LONG TIME.

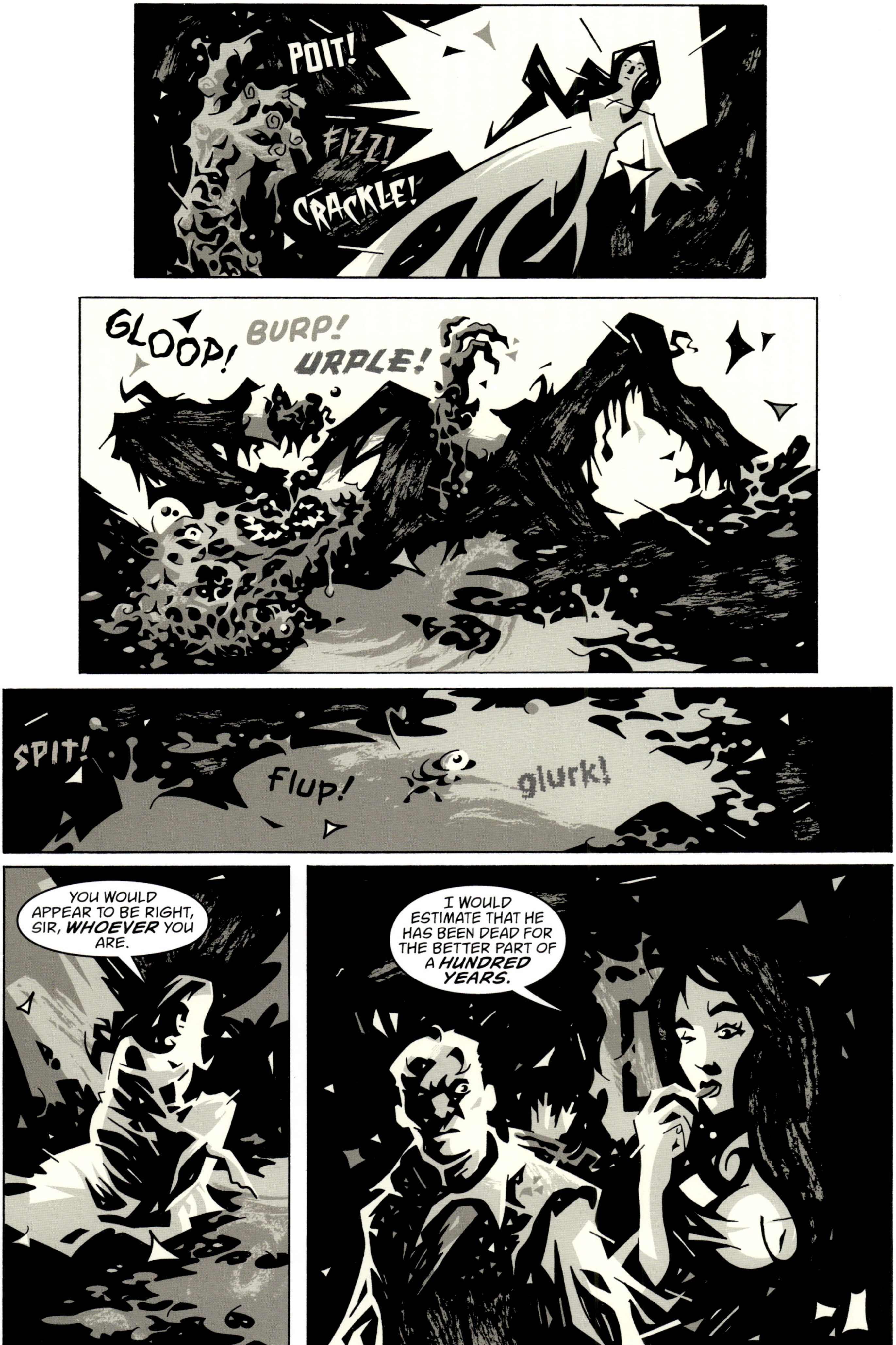
POIT!
FIZZ!
CRACKLE!
GLOOP!
BURP!
URPLE!
SPIT!
FLUP!
GLURK!
YOU WOULD APPEAR TO BE RIGHT, SIR, *WHOEVER* YOU ARE.
I WOULD ESTIMATE THAT HE HAS BEEN DEAD FOR THE BETTER PART OF A *HUNDRED YEARS.*

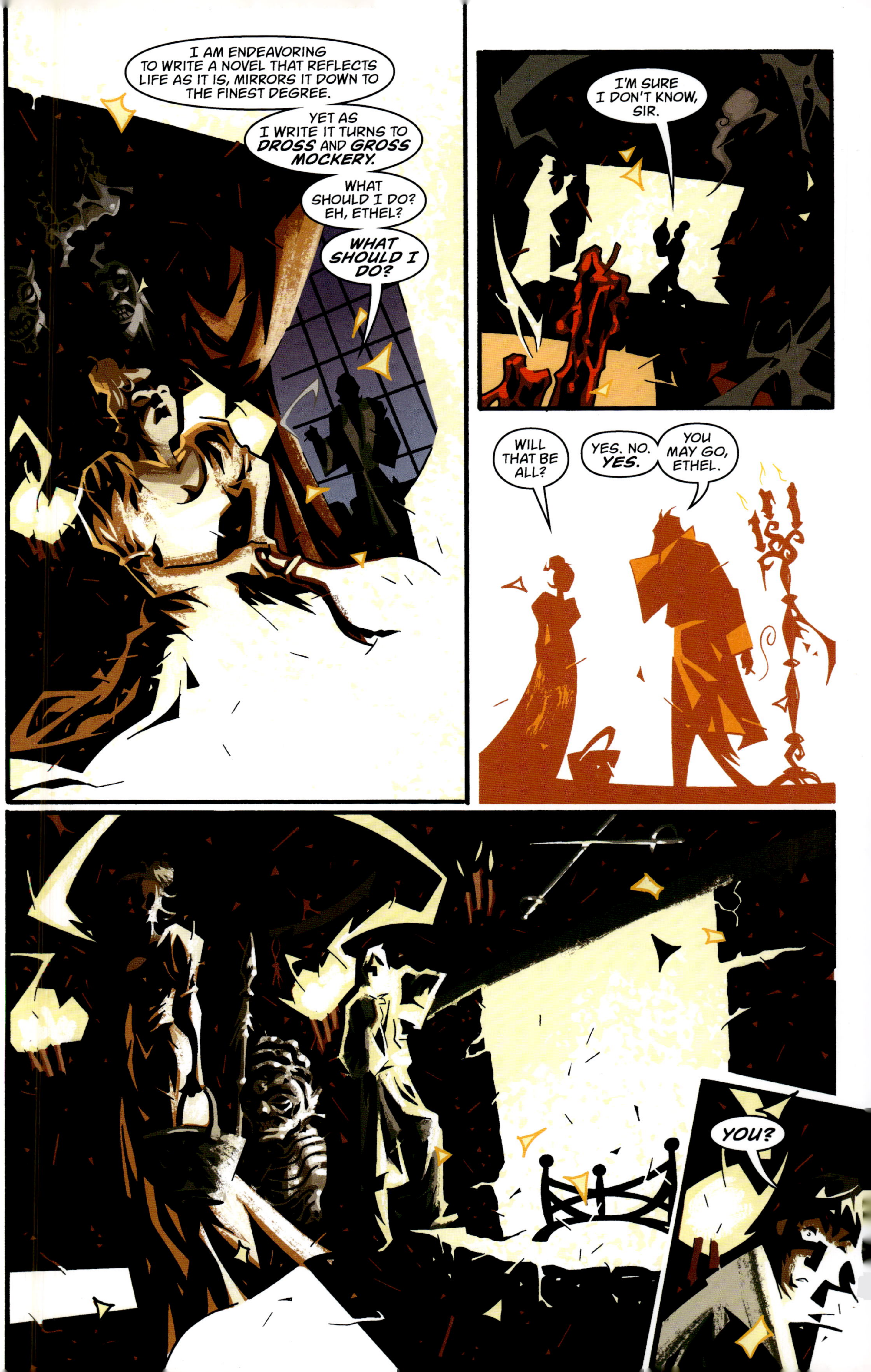
I AM ENDEAVORING TO WRITE A NOVEL THAT REFLECTS LIFE AS IT IS, MIRRORS IT DOWN TO THE FINEST DEGREE.
YET AS I WRITE IT TURNS TO *DROSS* AND *GROSS MOCKERY.*
WHAT SHOULD I DO? EH, ETHEL?
WHAT SHOULD I DO?
I'M SURE I DON'T KNOW, SIR.
WILL THAT BE ALL?
YES. NO. *YES.*
YOU MAY GO, ETHEL.
YOU?

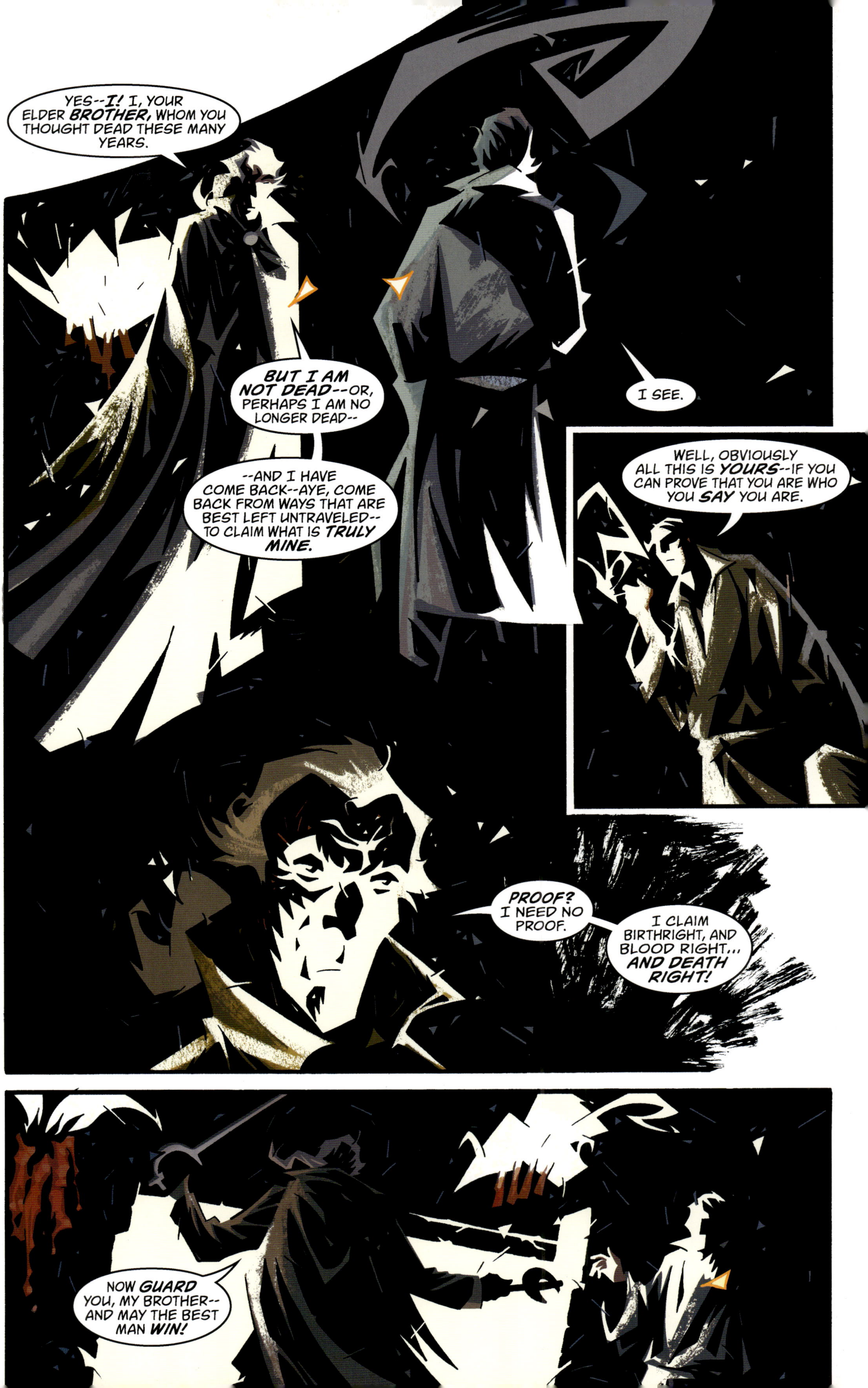
YES--I! I, YOUR ELDER BROTHER, WHOM YOU THOUGHT DEAD THESE MANY YEARS.
BUT I AM NOT DEAD--OR, PERHAPS I AM NO LONGER DEAD--
--AND I HAVE COME BACK--AYE, COME BACK FROM WAYS THAT ARE BEST LEFT UNTRAVELED--TO CLAIM WHAT IS TRULY MINE.
I SEE.
WELL, OBVIOUSLY ALL THIS IS YOURS--IF YOU CAN PROVE THAT YOU ARE WHO YOU SAY YOU ARE.
PROOF? I NEED NO PROOF.
I CLAIM BIRTHRIGHT, AND BLOOD RIGHT... AND DEATH RIGHT!
NOW GUARD YOU, MY BROTHER--AND MAY THE BEST MAN WIN!

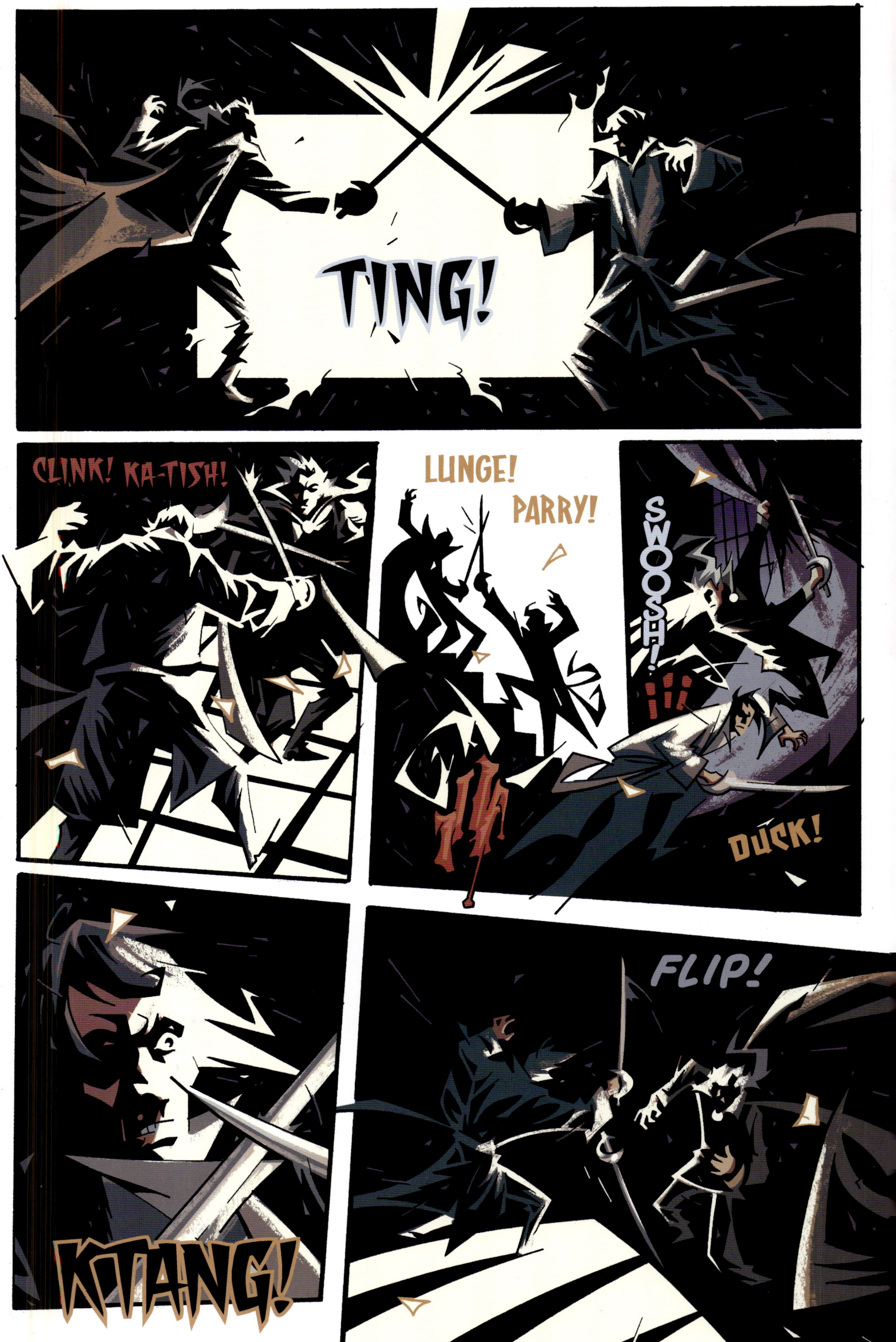
TING!
CLINK! KA-TISH!
LUNGE!
PARRY!
SWOOSH!
DUCK!
KTANG!
FLIP!

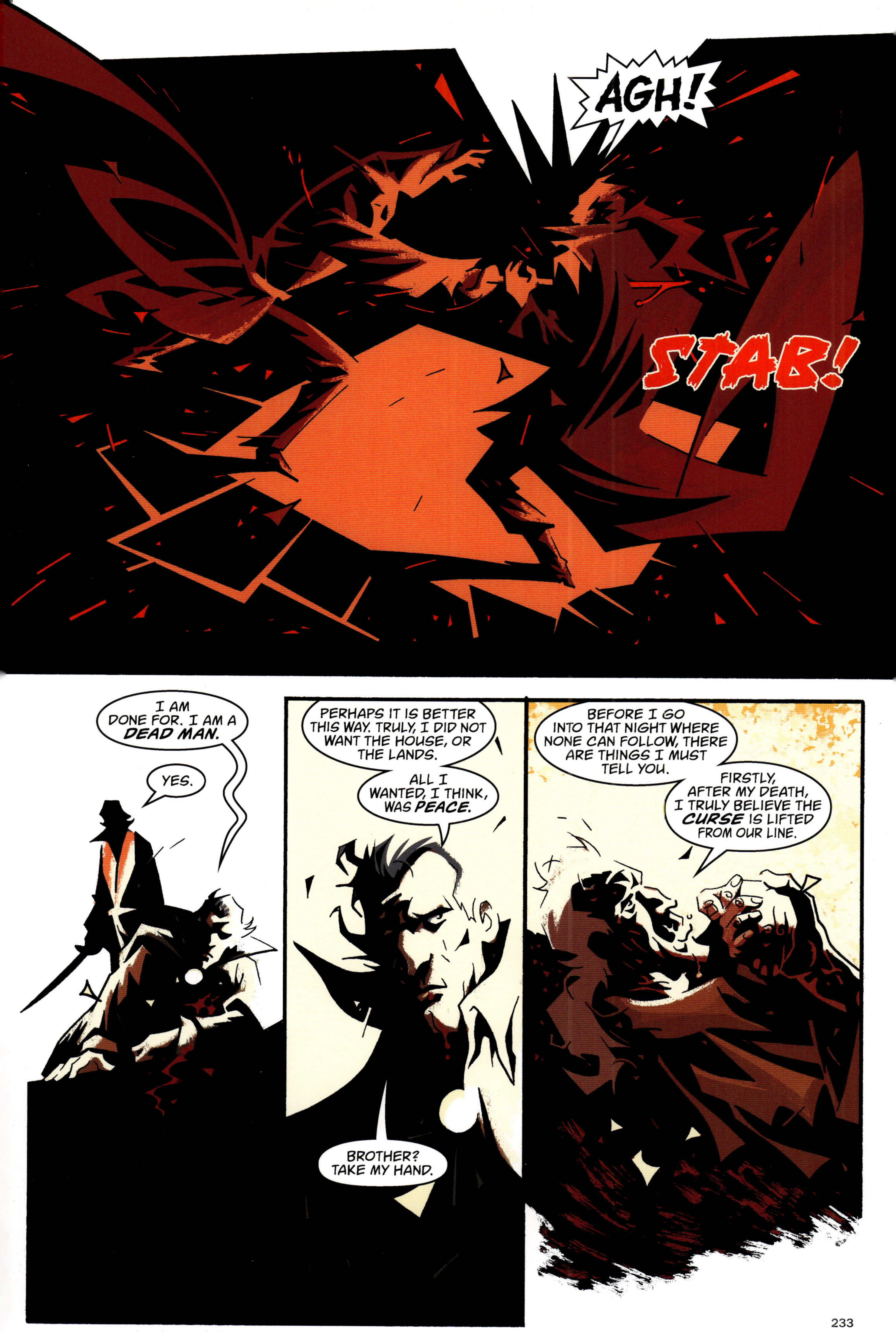
AGH!
STAB!
I AM DONE FOR. I AM A DEAD MAN.
YES.
PERHAPS IT IS BETTER THIS WAY. TRULY, I DID NOT WANT THE HOUSE, OR THE LANDS.
ALL I WANTED, I THINK, WAS PEACE.
BROTHER? TAKE MY HAND.
BEFORE I GO INTO THAT NIGHT WHERE NONE CAN FOLLOW, THERE ARE THINGS I MUST TELL YOU.
FIRSTLY, AFTER MY DEATH, I TRULY BELIEVE THE CURSE IS LIFTED FROM OUR LINE.

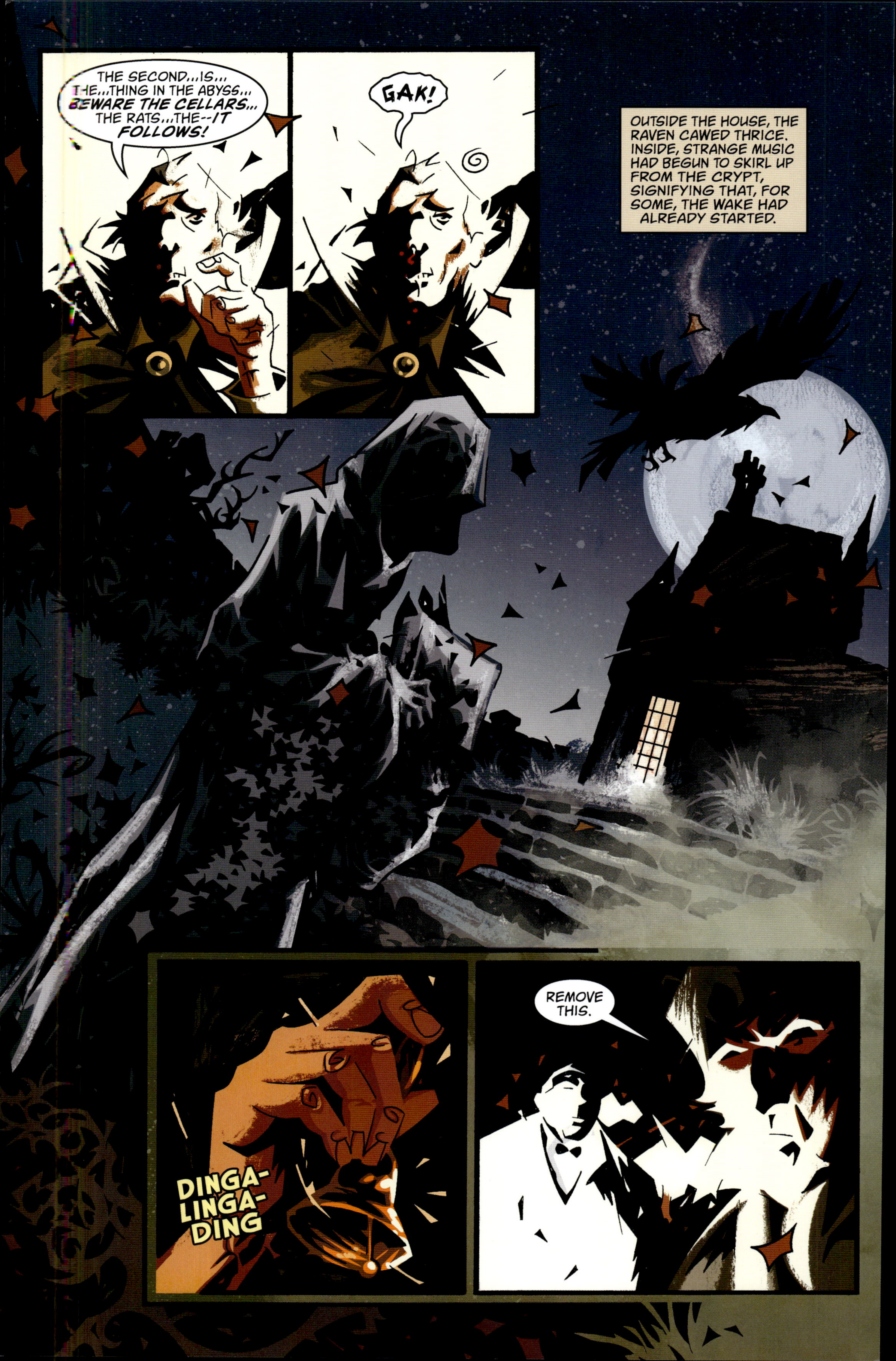
THE SECOND...IS... THE...THING IN THE ABYSS... BEWARE THE CELLARS... THE RATS...THE--IT FOLLOWS!
GAK!
OUTSIDE THE HOUSE, THE RAVEN CAWED THRICE. INSIDE, STRANGE MUSIC HAD BEGUN TO SKIRL UP FROM THE CRYPT, SIGNIFYING THAT, FOR SOME, THE WAKE HAD ALREADY STARTED.
DINGA-LINGA-DING
REMOVE THIS.

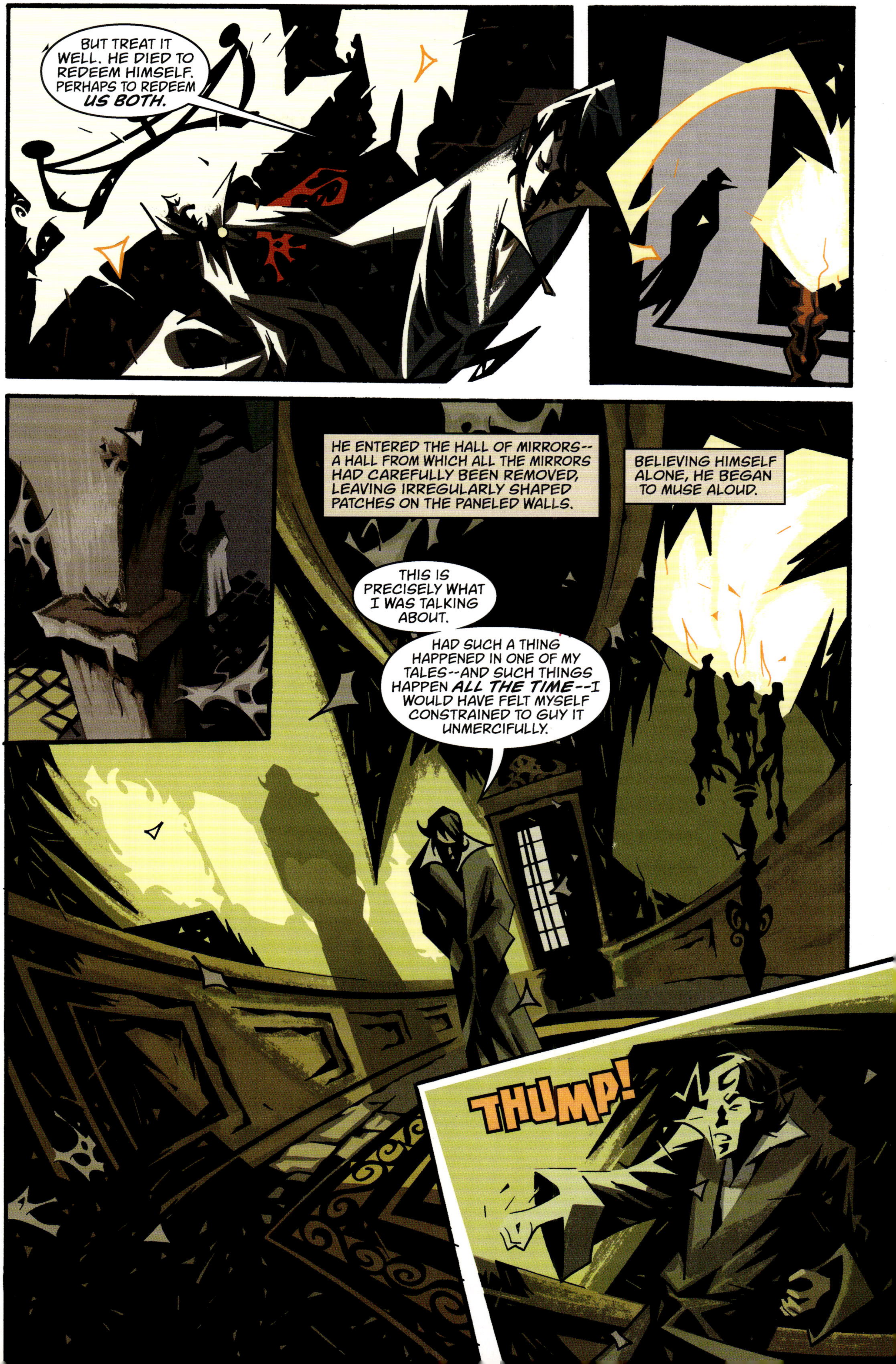
BUT TREAT IT WELL. HE DIED TO REDEEM HIMSELF. PERHAPS TO REDEEM *US BOTH.*
HE ENTERED THE HALL OF MIRRORS-- A HALL FROM WHICH ALL THE MIRRORS HAD CAREFULLY BEEN REMOVED, LEAVING IRREGULARLY SHAPED PATCHES ON THE PANELED WALLS.
BELIEVING HIMSELF ALONE, HE BEGAN TO MUSE ALOUD.
THIS IS PRECISELY WHAT I WAS TALKING ABOUT.
HAD SUCH A THING HAPPENED IN ONE OF MY TALES--AND SUCH THINGS HAPPEN *ALL THE TIME*--I WOULD HAVE FELT MYSELF CONSTRAINED TO GUY IT UNMERCIFULLY.
THUMP!

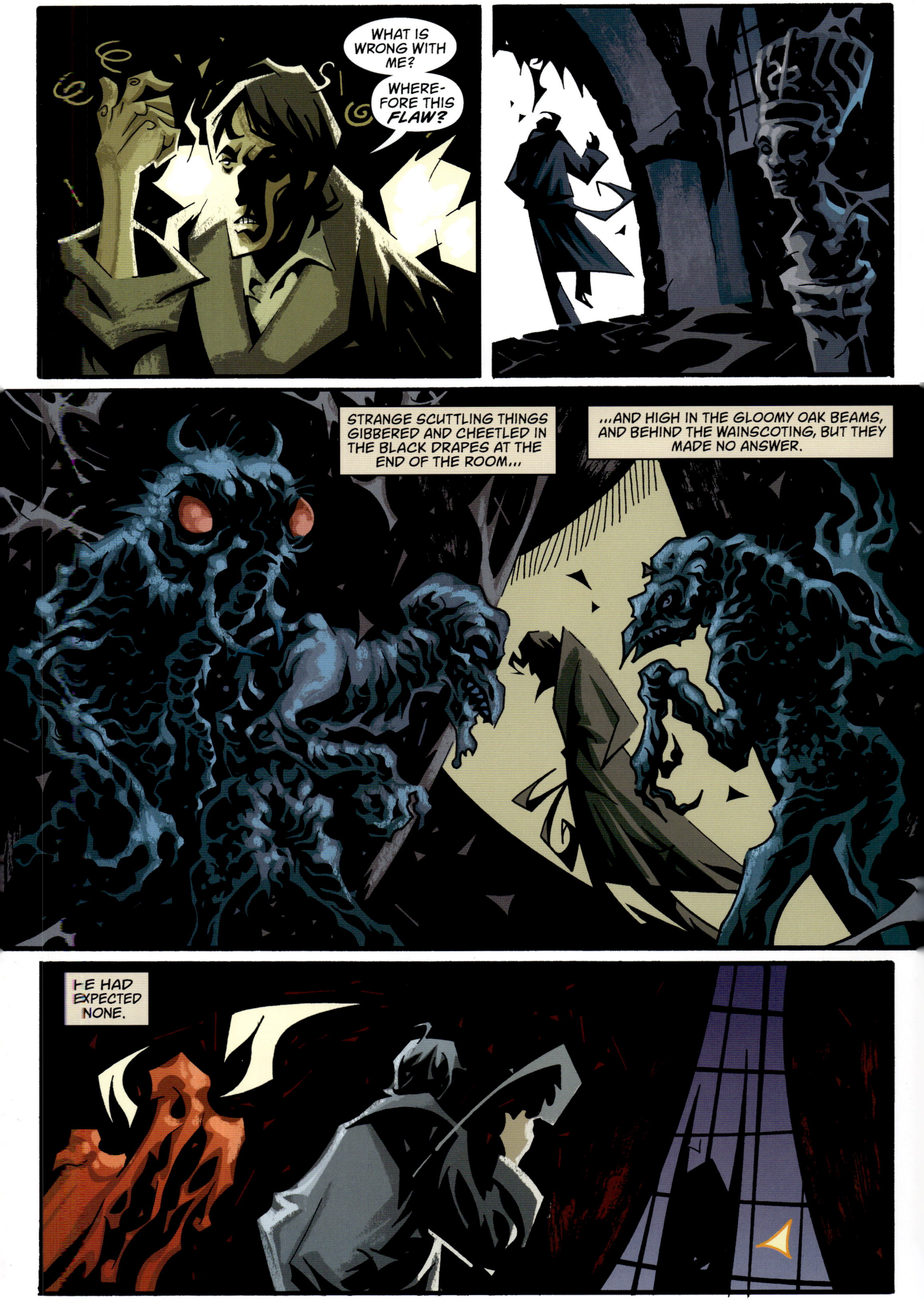
WHAT IS WRONG WITH ME?
WHERE-FORE THIS *FLAW?*
STRANGE SCUTTLING THINGS GIBBERED AND CHEETLED IN THE BLACK DRAPES AT THE END OF THE ROOM...
...AND HIGH IN THE GLOOMY OAK BEAMS, AND BEHIND THE WAINSCOTING, BUT THEY MADE NO ANSWER.
HE HAD EXPECTED NONE.

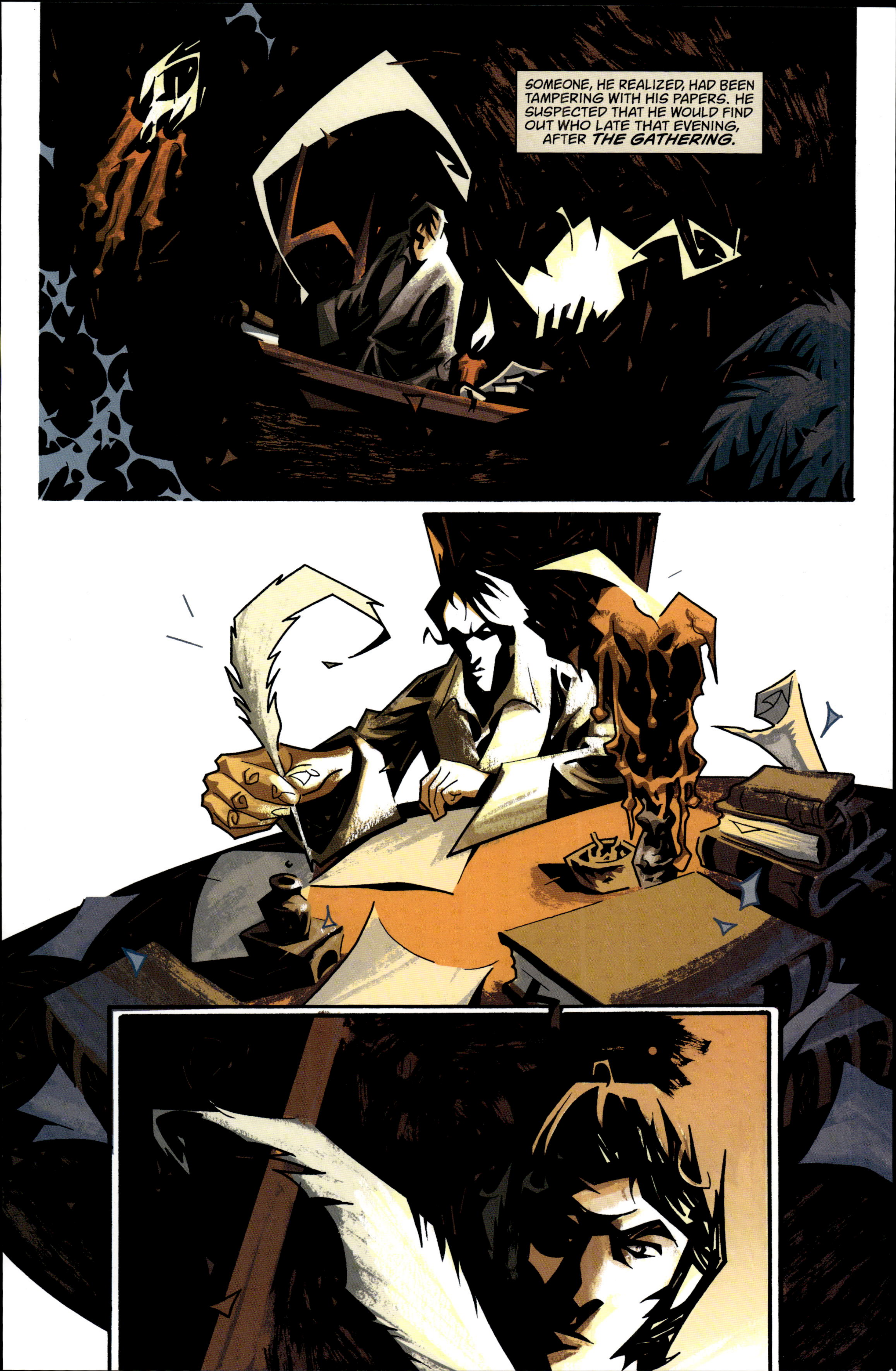
SOMEONE, HE REALIZED, HAD BEEN TAMPERING WITH HIS PAPERS. HE SUSPECTED THAT HE WOULD FIND OUT WHO LATE THAT EVENING, AFTER THE GATHERING.

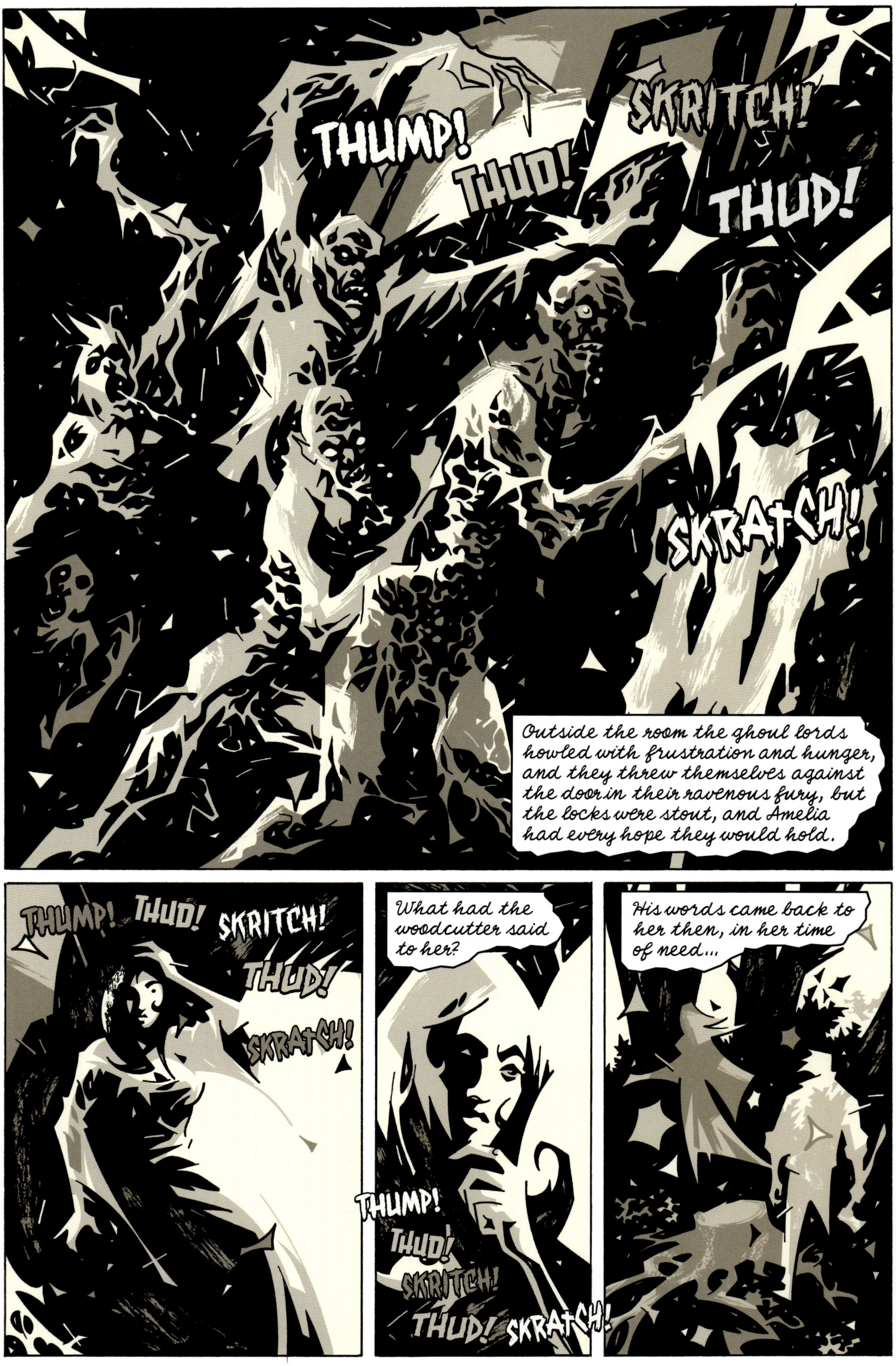
THUMP!
THUD!
SKRITCH!
THUD!
SKRATCH!
Outside the room the ghoul lords howled with frustration and hunger, and they threw themselves against the door in their ravenous fury, but the locks were stout, and Amelia had every hope they would hold.
THUMP! THUD! SKRITCH!
THUD!
SKRATCH!
What had the woodcutter said to her?
THUMP!
THUD!
SKRITCH!
THUD! SKRATCH!
His words came back to her then, in her time of need...

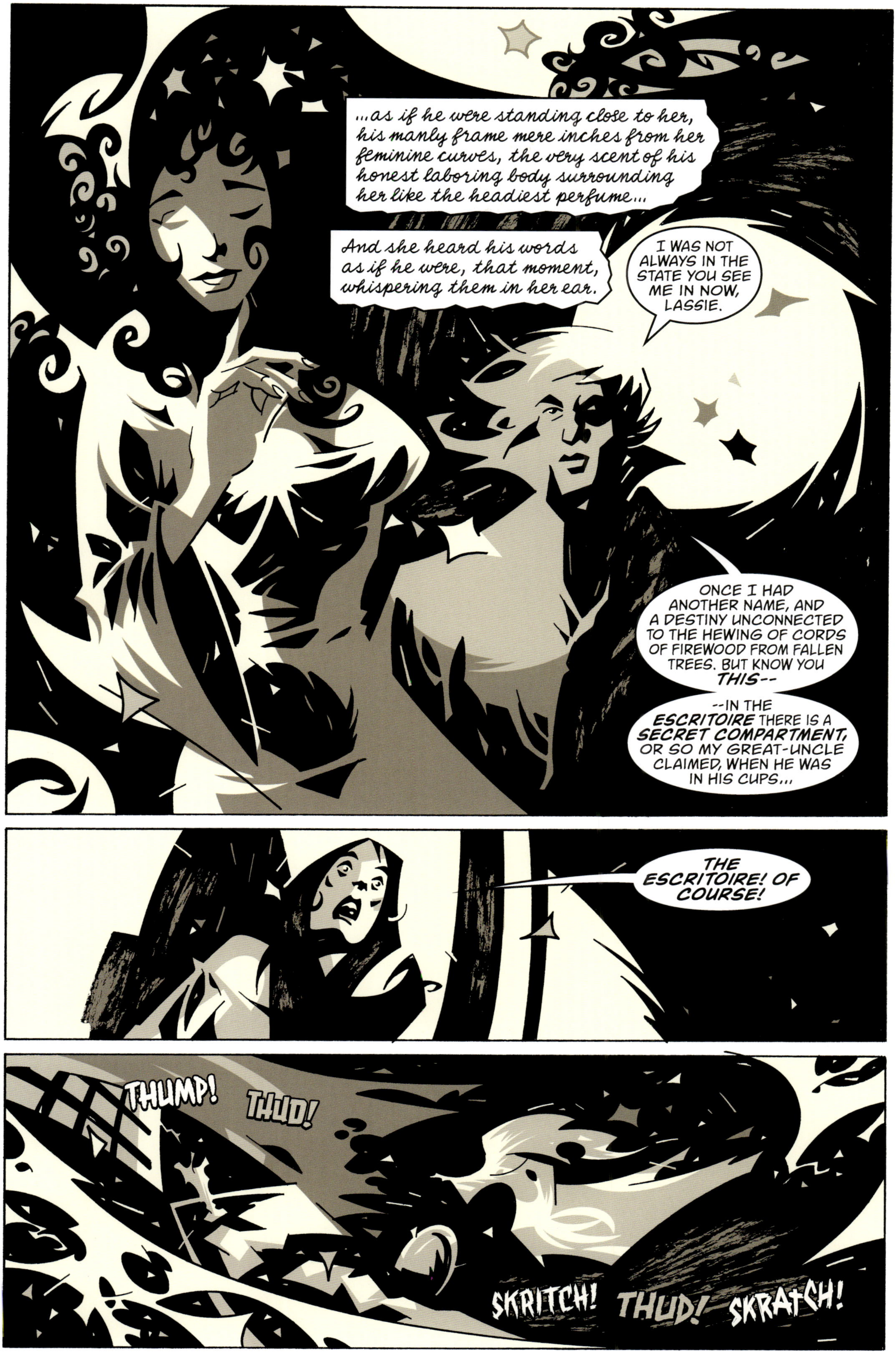
...as if he were standing close to her, his manly frame mere inches from her feminine curves, the very scent of his honest laboring body surrounding her like the headiest perfume...
And she heard his words as if he were, that moment, whispering them in her ear.
I WAS NOT ALWAYS IN THE STATE YOU SEE ME IN NOW, LASSIE.
ONCE I HAD ANOTHER NAME, AND A DESTINY UNCONNECTED TO THE HEWING OF CORDS OF FIREWOOD FROM FALLEN TREES. BUT KNOW YOU THIS--
--IN THE ESCRITOIRE THERE IS A SECRET COMPARTMENT, OR SO MY GREAT-UNCLE CLAIMED, WHEN HE WAS IN HIS CUPS...
THE ESCRITOIRE! OF COURSE!
THUMP! THUD!
SKRITCH! THUD! SKRATCH!

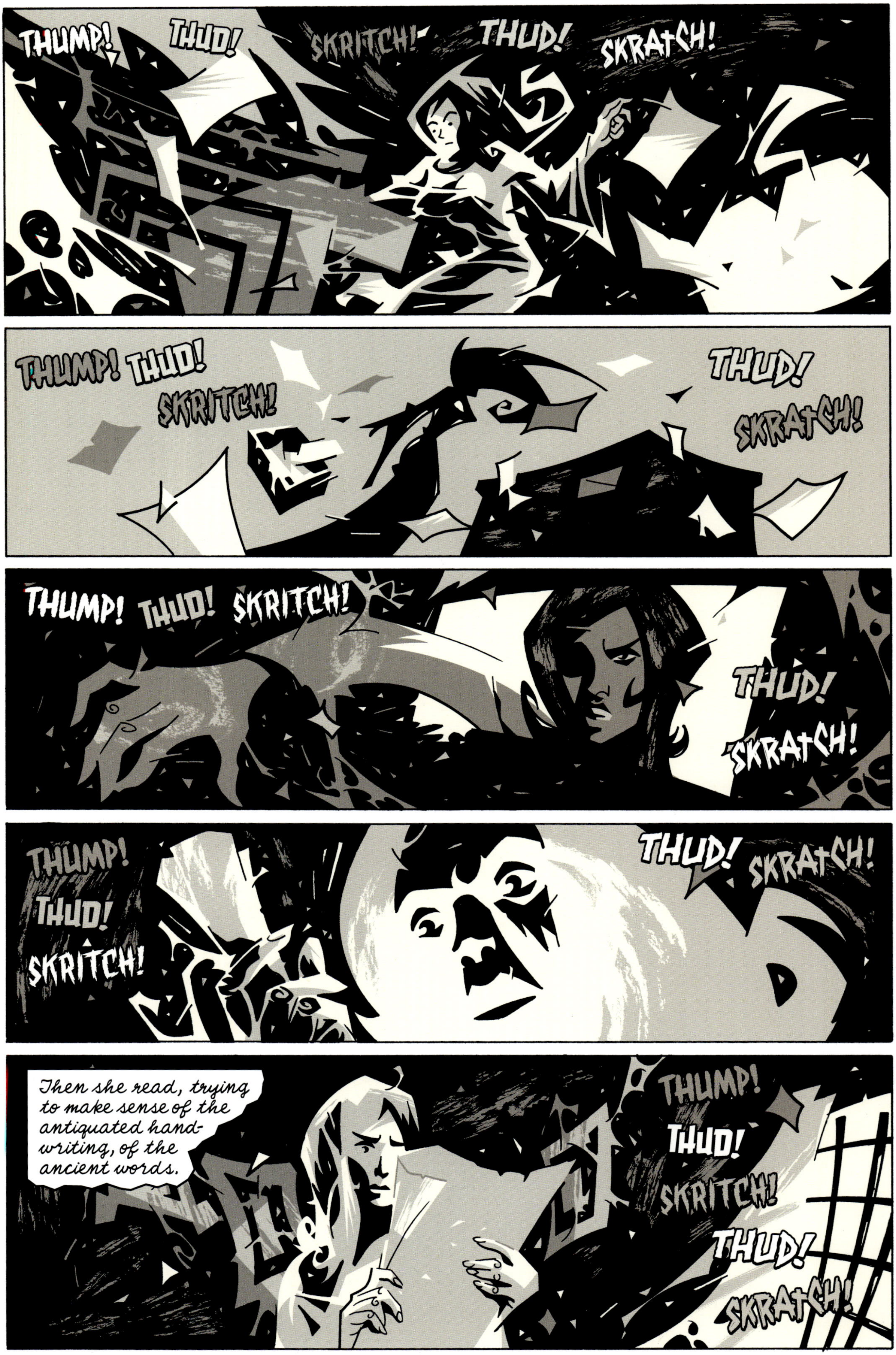
THUMP!
THUD!
SKRITCH!
THUD!
SKRATCH!
THUMP!
THUD!
SKRITCH!
THUD!
SKRATCH!
THUMP!
THUD!
SKRITCH!
THUD!
SKRATCH!
THUMP!
THUD!
SKRITCH!
THUD!
SKRATCH!
Then she read, trying to make sense of the antiquated handwriting, of the ancient words.
THUMP!
THUD!
SKRITCH!
THUD!
SKRATCH!

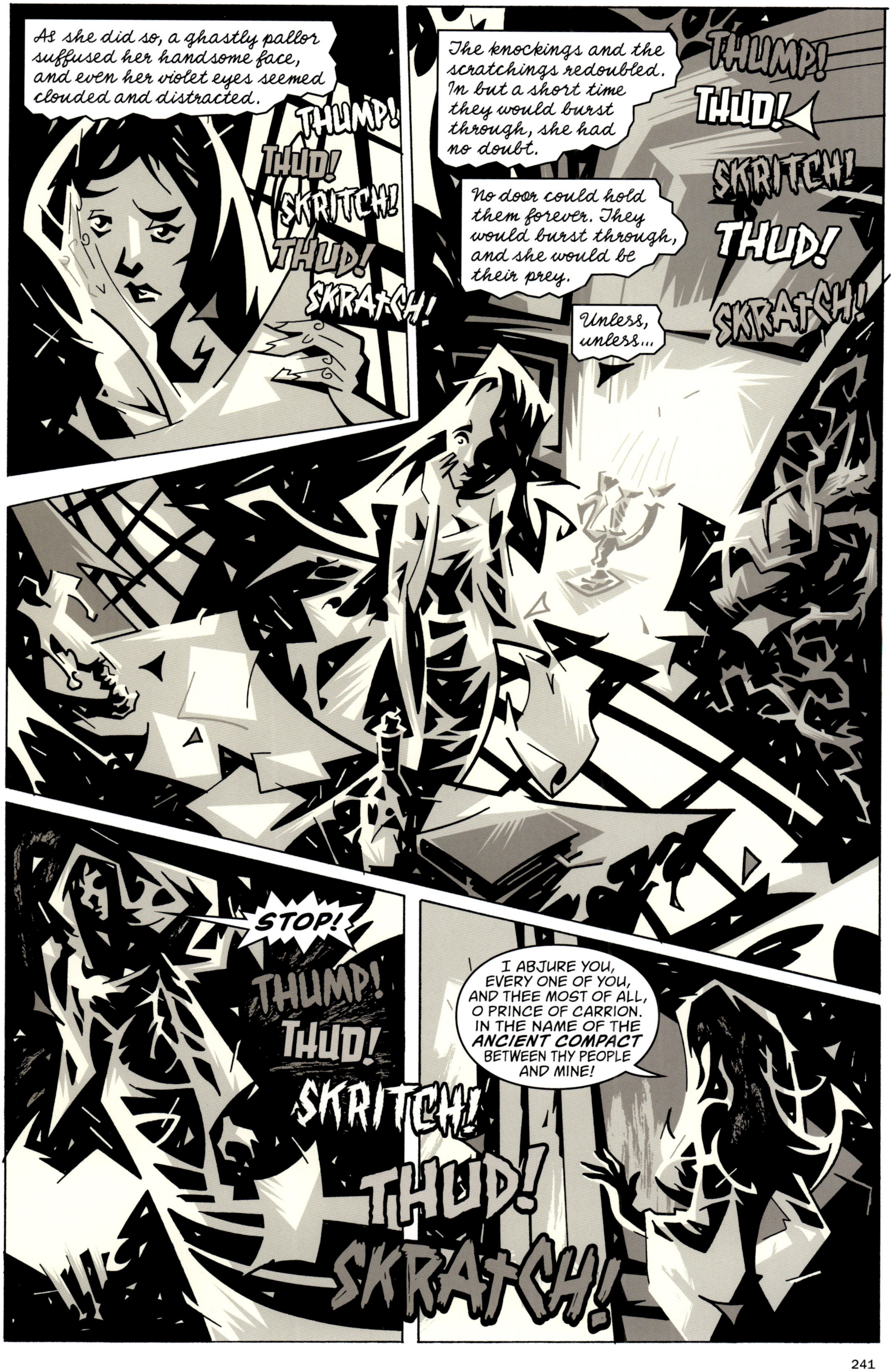
As she did so, a ghastly pallor suffused her handsome face, and even her violet eyes seemed clouded and distracted.
THUMP!
THUD!
SKRITCH!
THUD!
SKRATCH!
The knockings and the scratchings redoubled. In but a short time they would burst through, she had no doubt.
THUMP!
THUD!
SKRITCH!
THUD!
SKRATCH!
No door could hold them forever. They would burst through, and she would be their prey.
Unless, unless...
STOP!
THUMP!
THUD!
SKRITCH!
THUD!
SKRATCH!
I ABJURE YOU, EVERY ONE OF YOU, AND THEE MOST OF ALL, O PRINCE OF CARRION. IN THE NAME OF THE ANCIENT COMPACT BETWEEN THY PEOPLE AND MINE!

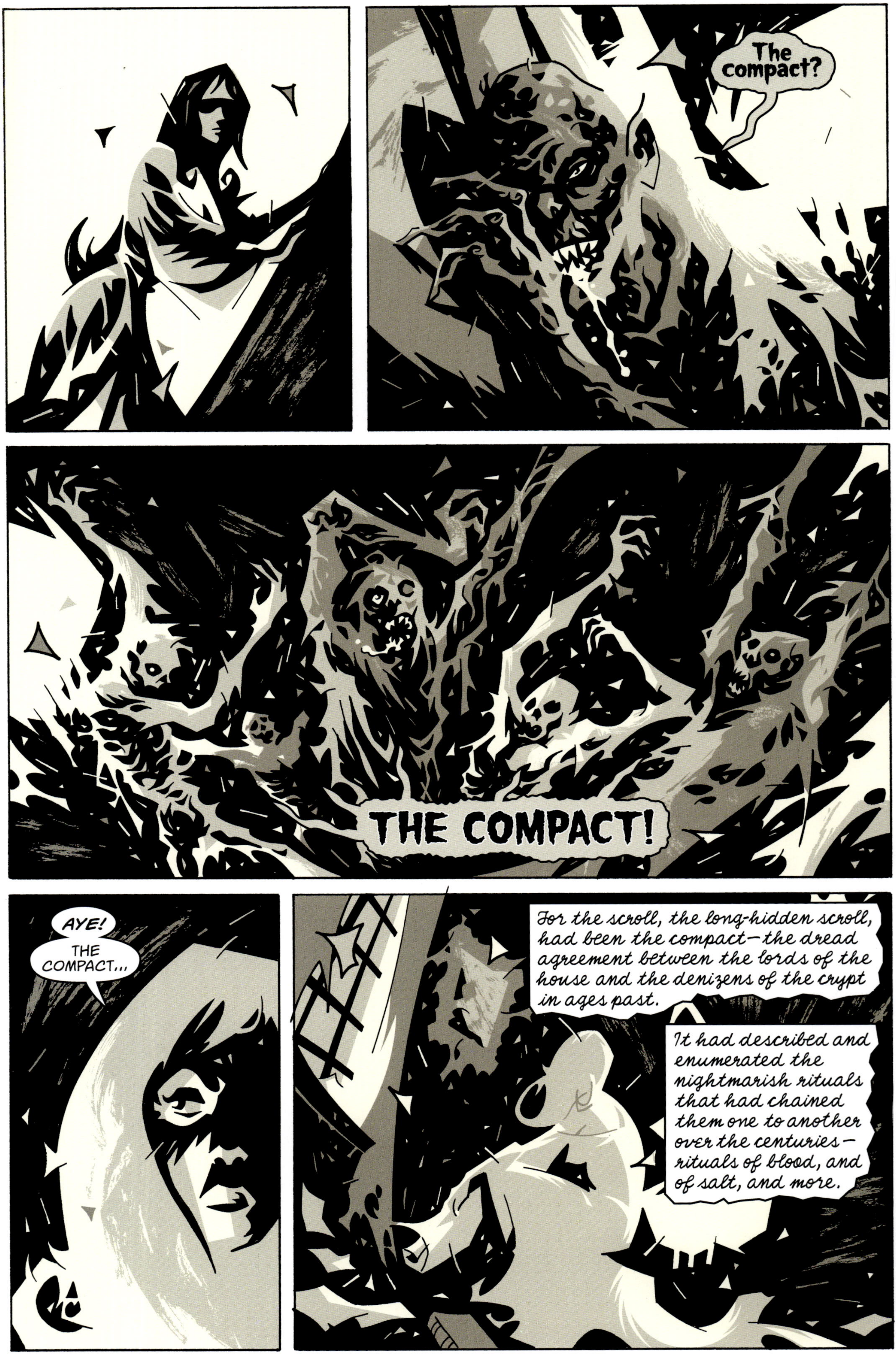
The compact?
THE COMPACT!
AYE! THE COMPACT...
For the scroll, the long-hidden scroll, had been the compact—the dread agreement between the lords of the house and the denizens of the crypt in ages past.
It had described and enumerated the nightmarish rituals that had chained them one to another over the centuries—rituals of blood, and of salt, and more.

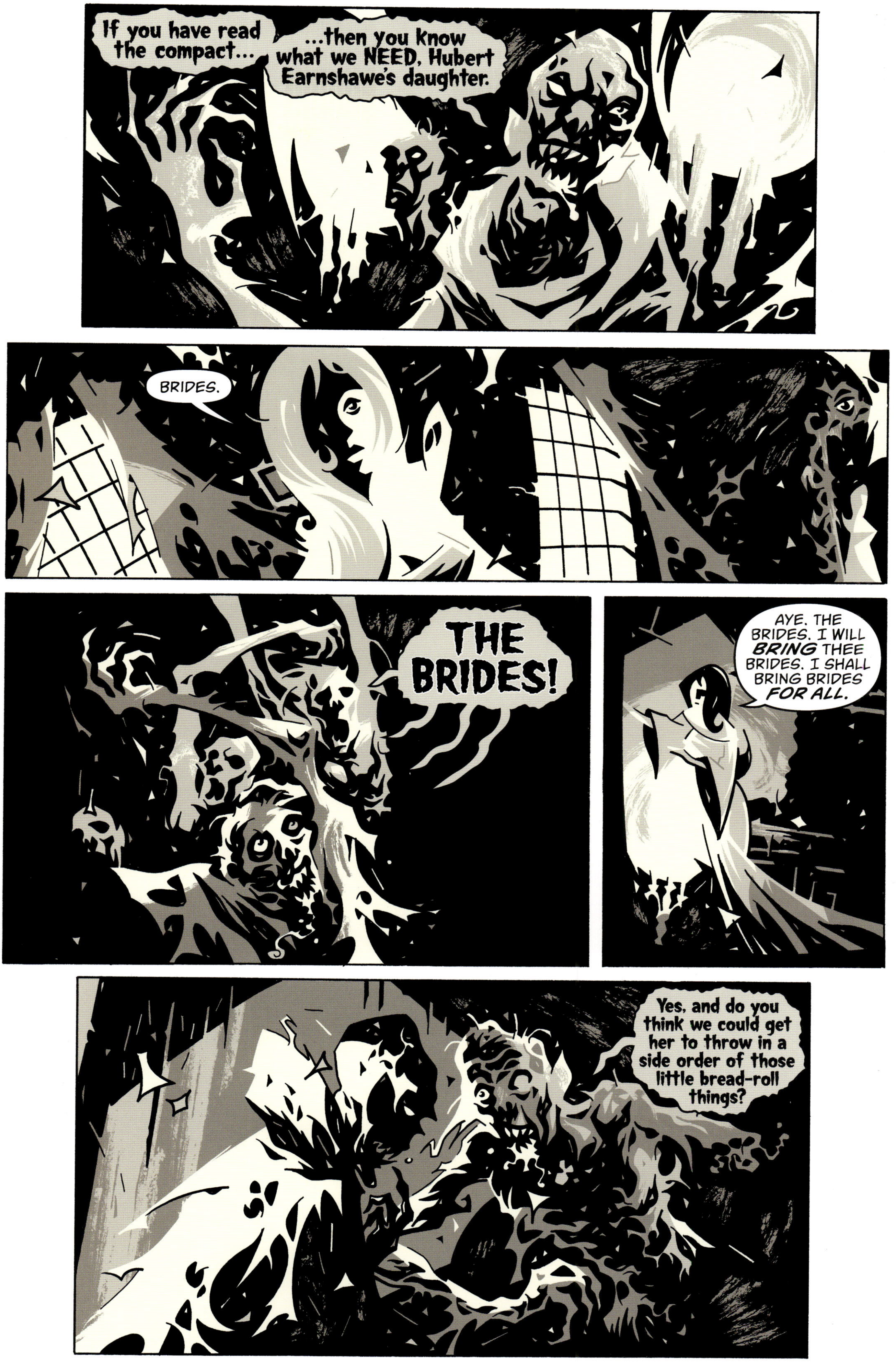
If you have read the compact...
...then you know what we NEED, Hubert Earnshawe's daughter.
BRIDES.
THE BRIDES!
AYE. THE BRIDES. I WILL BRING THEE BRIDES. I SHALL BRING BRIDES FOR ALL.
Yes, and do you think we could get her to throw in a side order of those little bread-roll things?

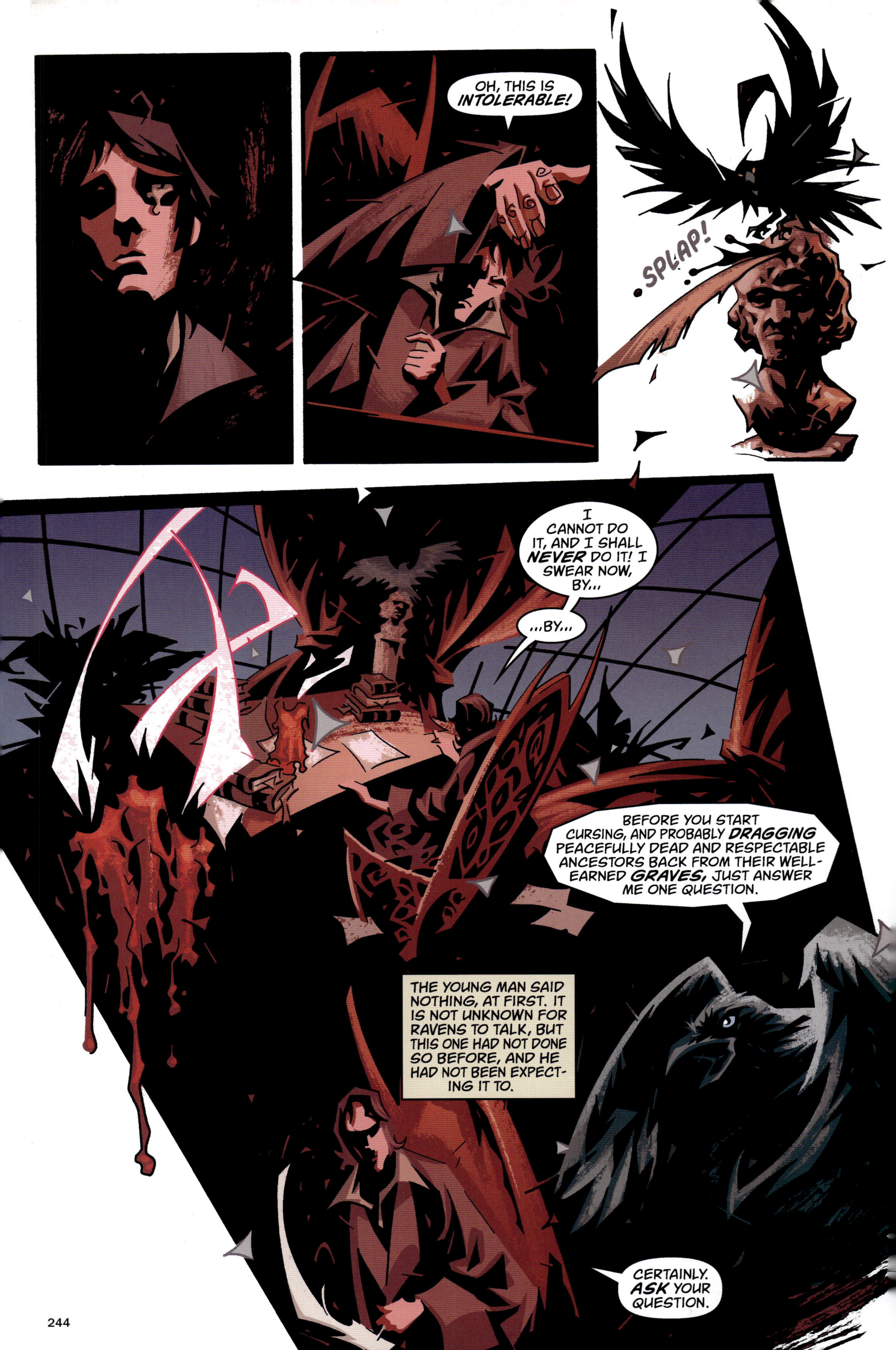
OH, THIS IS *INTOLERABLE!*
SPLAP!
I CANNOT DO IT, AND I SHALL **NEVER** DO IT! I SWEAR NOW, BY...
...BY...
BEFORE YOU START CURSING, AND PROBABLY **DRAGGING** PEACEFULLY DEAD AND RESPECTABLE ANCESTORS BACK FROM THEIR WELL-EARNED **GRAVES,** JUST ANSWER ME ONE QUESTION.
THE YOUNG MAN SAID NOTHING, AT FIRST. IT IS NOT UNKNOWN FOR RAVENS TO TALK, BUT THIS ONE HAD NOT DONE SO BEFORE, AND HE HAD NOT BEEN EXPECTING IT TO.
CERTAINLY. **ASK** YOUR QUESTION.

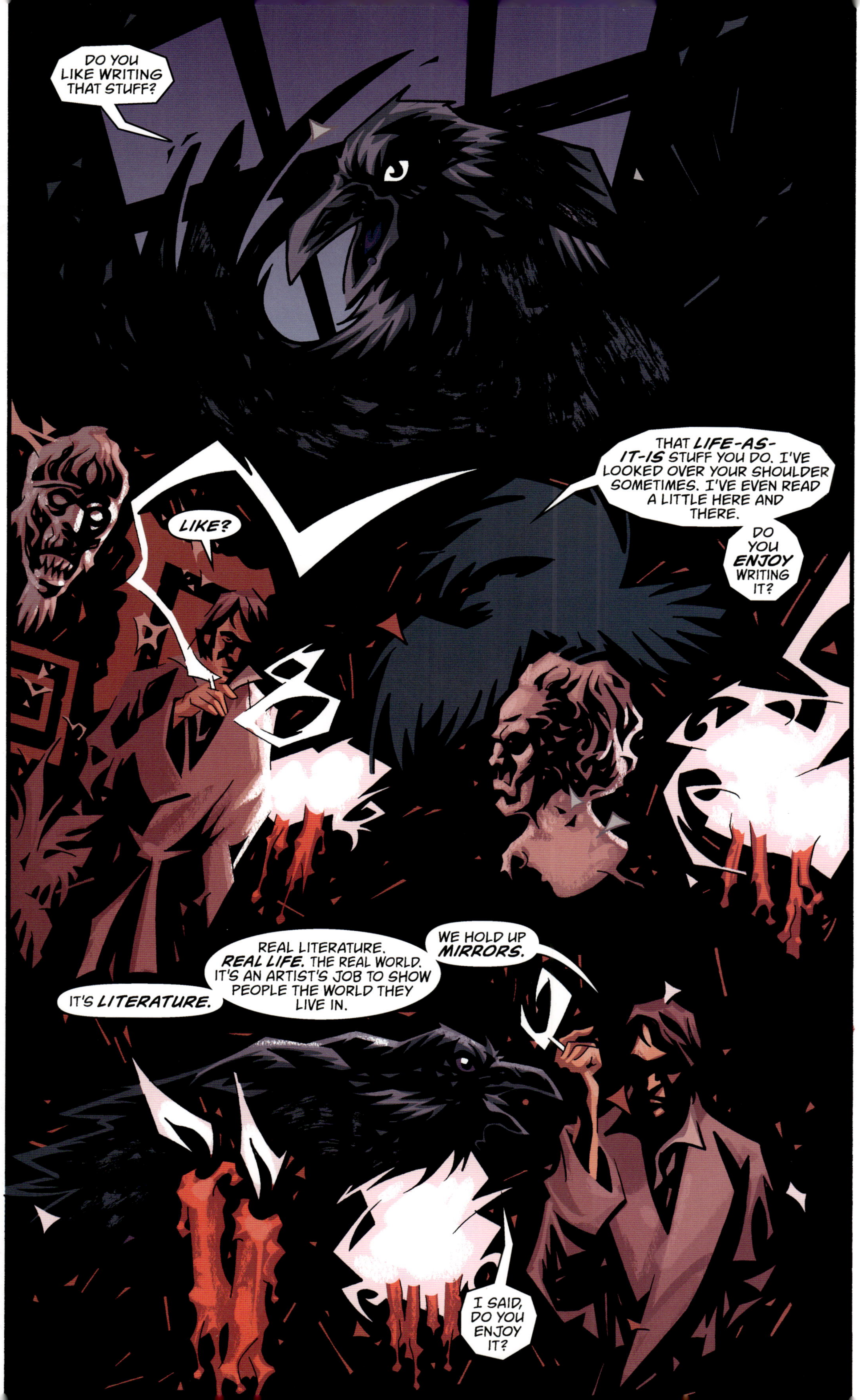
DO YOU LIKE WRITING THAT STUFF?
LIKE?
THAT LIFE-AS-IT-IS STUFF YOU DO. I'VE LOOKED OVER YOUR SHOULDER SOMETIMES. I'VE EVEN READ A LITTLE HERE AND THERE.
DO YOU ENJOY WRITING IT?
IT'S LITERATURE.
REAL LITERATURE. REAL LIFE. THE REAL WORLD. IT'S AN ARTIST'S JOB TO SHOW PEOPLE THE WORLD THEY LIVE IN.
WE HOLD UP MIRRORS.
I SAID, DO YOU ENJOY IT?

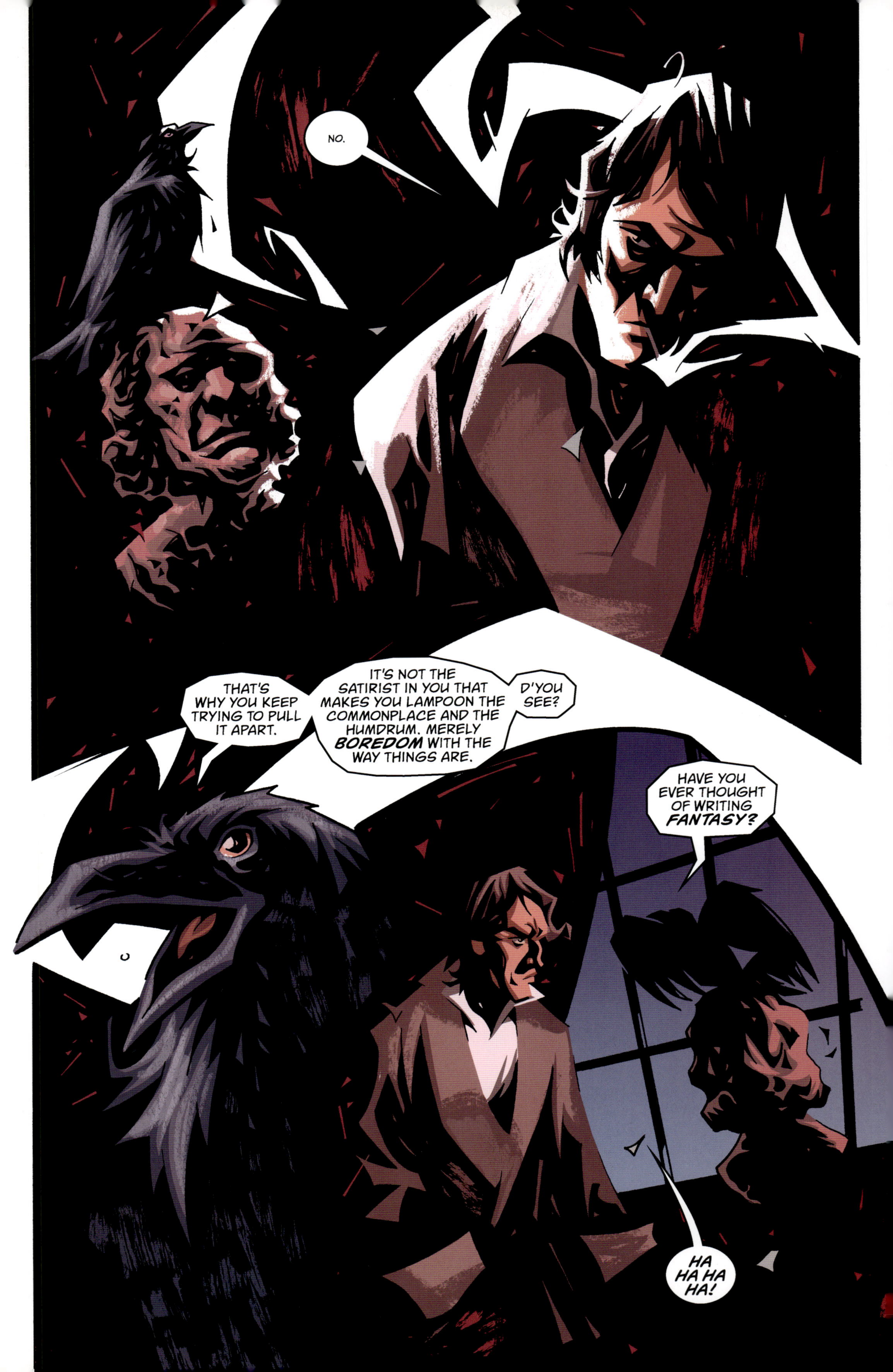
NO.
THAT'S WHY YOU KEEP TRYING TO PULL IT APART.
IT'S NOT THE SATIRIST IN YOU THAT MAKES YOU LAMPOON THE COMMONPLACE AND THE HUMDRUM. MERELY *BOREDOM* WITH THE WAY THINGS ARE.
D'YOU SEE?
HAVE YOU EVER THOUGHT OF WRITING *FANTASY?*
HA HA HA HA!

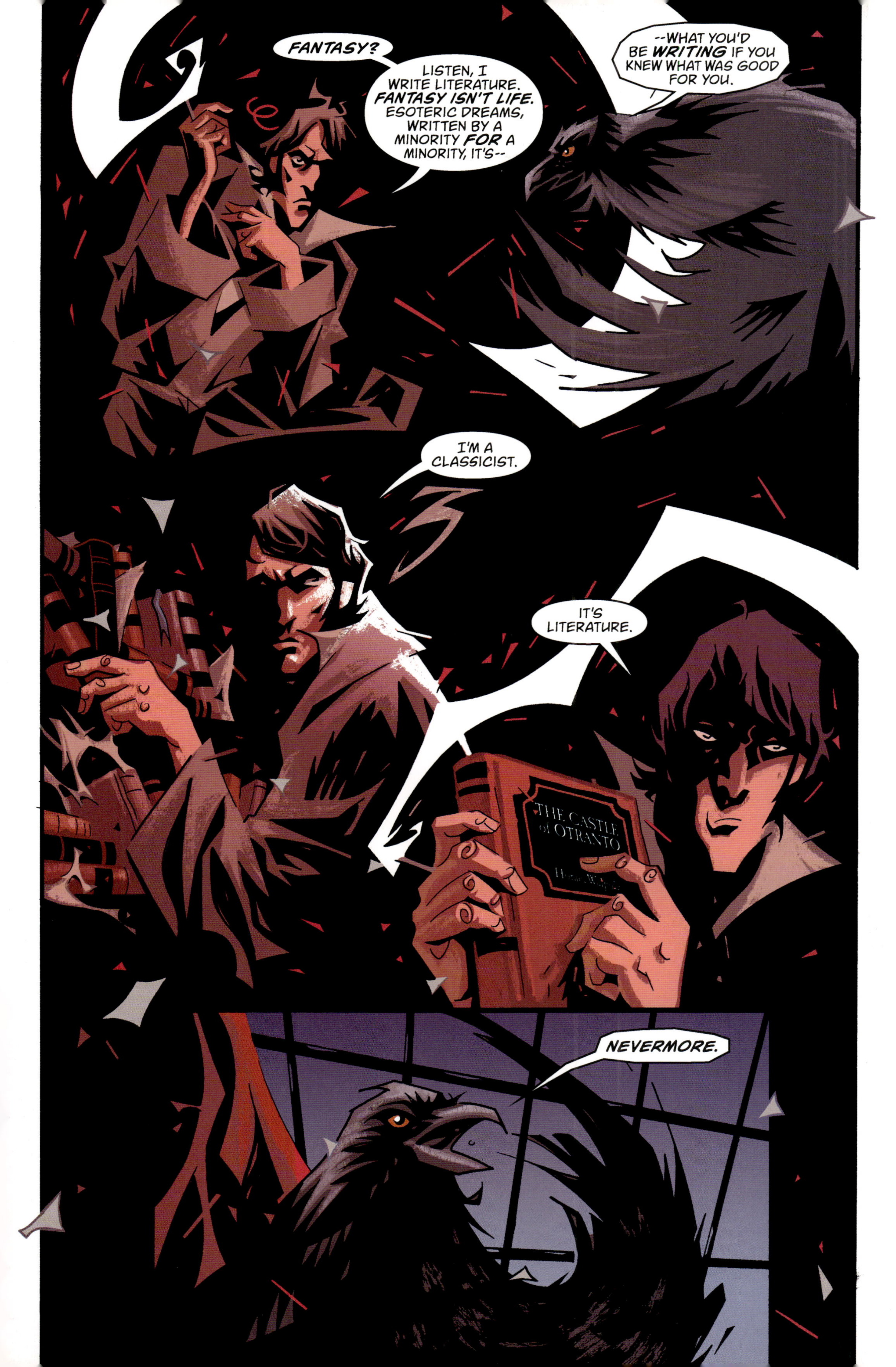
FANTASY?
LISTEN, I WRITE LITERATURE. FANTASY ISN'T LIFE. ESOTERIC DREAMS, WRITTEN BY A MINORITY FOR A MINORITY, IT'S--
--WHAT YOU'D BE WRITING IF YOU KNEW WHAT WAS GOOD FOR YOU.
I'M A CLASSICIST.
IT'S LITERATURE.
THE CASTLE of OTRANTO
NEVERMORE.

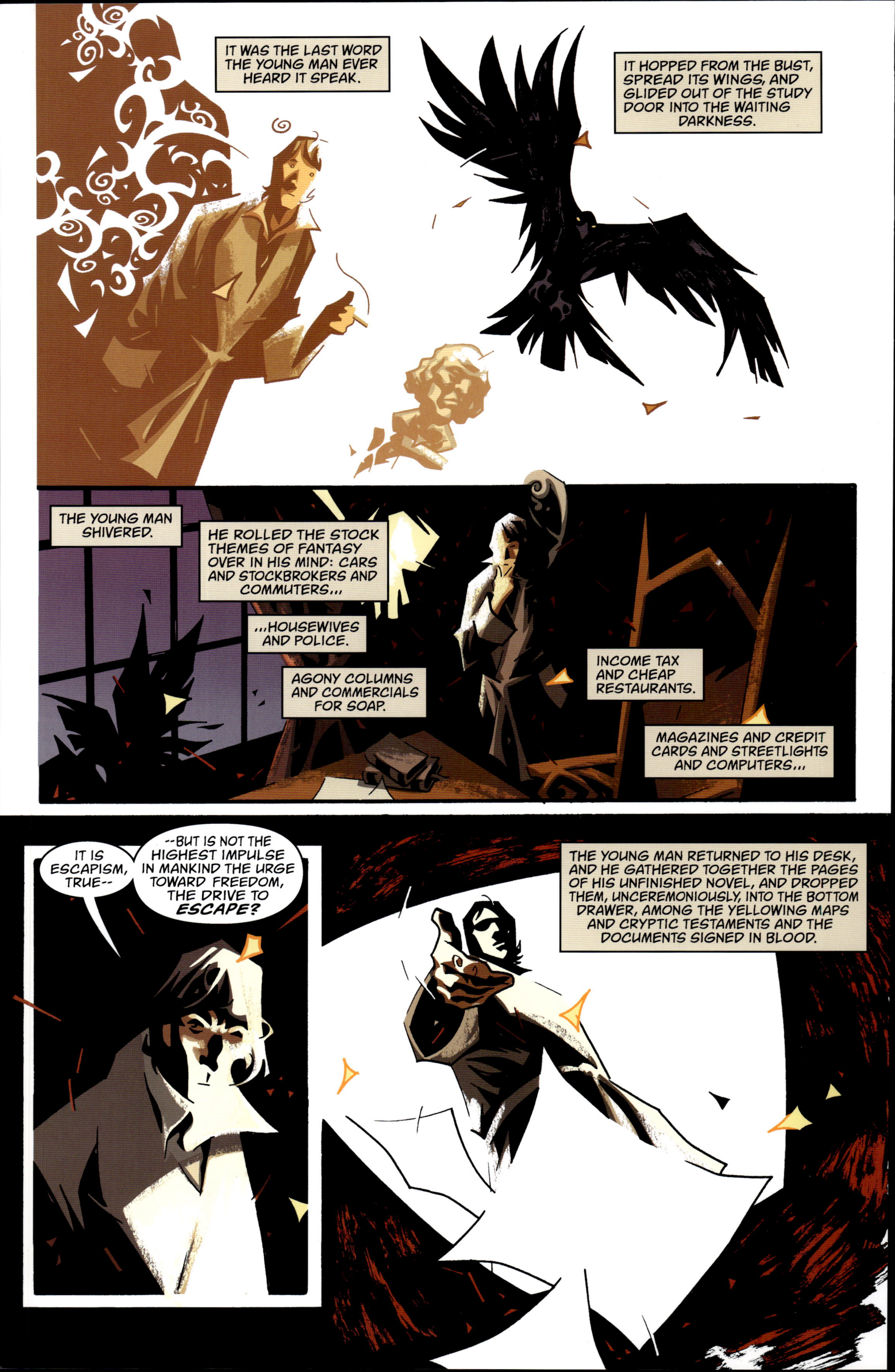
IT WAS THE LAST WORD THE YOUNG MAN EVER HEARD IT SPEAK.
IT HOPPED FROM THE BUST, SPREAD ITS WINGS, AND GLIDED OUT OF THE STUDY DOOR INTO THE WAITING DARKNESS.
THE YOUNG MAN SHIVERED.
HE ROLLED THE STOCK THEMES OF FANTASY OVER IN HIS MIND: CARS AND STOCKBROKERS AND COMMUTERS...
...HOUSEWIVES AND POLICE.
AGONY COLUMNS AND COMMERCIALS FOR SOAP.
INCOME TAX AND CHEAP RESTAURANTS.
MAGAZINES AND CREDIT CARDS AND STREETLIGHTS AND COMPUTERS...
IT IS ESCAPISM, TRUE--
--BUT IS NOT THE HIGHEST IMPULSE IN MANKIND THE URGE TOWARD FREEDOM, THE DRIVE TO ESCAPE?
THE YOUNG MAN RETURNED TO HIS DESK, AND HE GATHERED TOGETHER THE PAGES OF HIS UNFINISHED NOVEL, AND DROPPED THEM, UNCEREMONIOUSLY, INTO THE BOTTOM DRAWER, AMONG THE YELLOWING MAPS AND CRYPTIC TESTAMENTS AND THE DOCUMENTS SIGNED IN BLOOD.

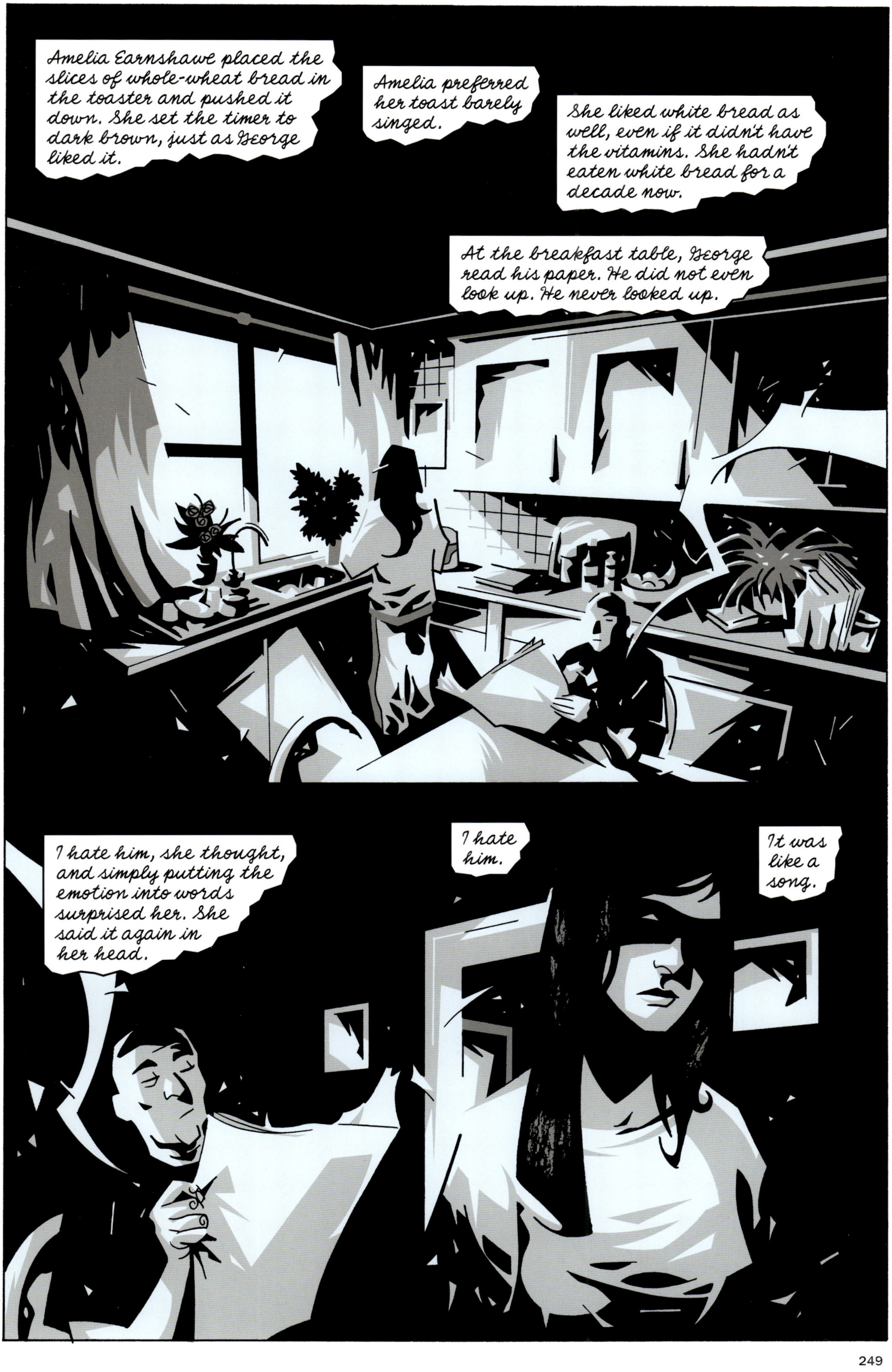
Amelia Earnshawe placed the slices of whole-wheat bread in the toaster and pushed it down. She set the timer to dark brown, just as George liked it.
Amelia preferred her toast barely singed.
She liked white bread as well, even if it didn't have the vitamins. She hadn't eaten white bread for a decade now.
At the breakfast table, George read his paper. He did not even look up. He never looked up.
I hate him, she thought, and simply putting the emotion into words surprised her. She said it again in her head.
I hate him.
It was like a song.

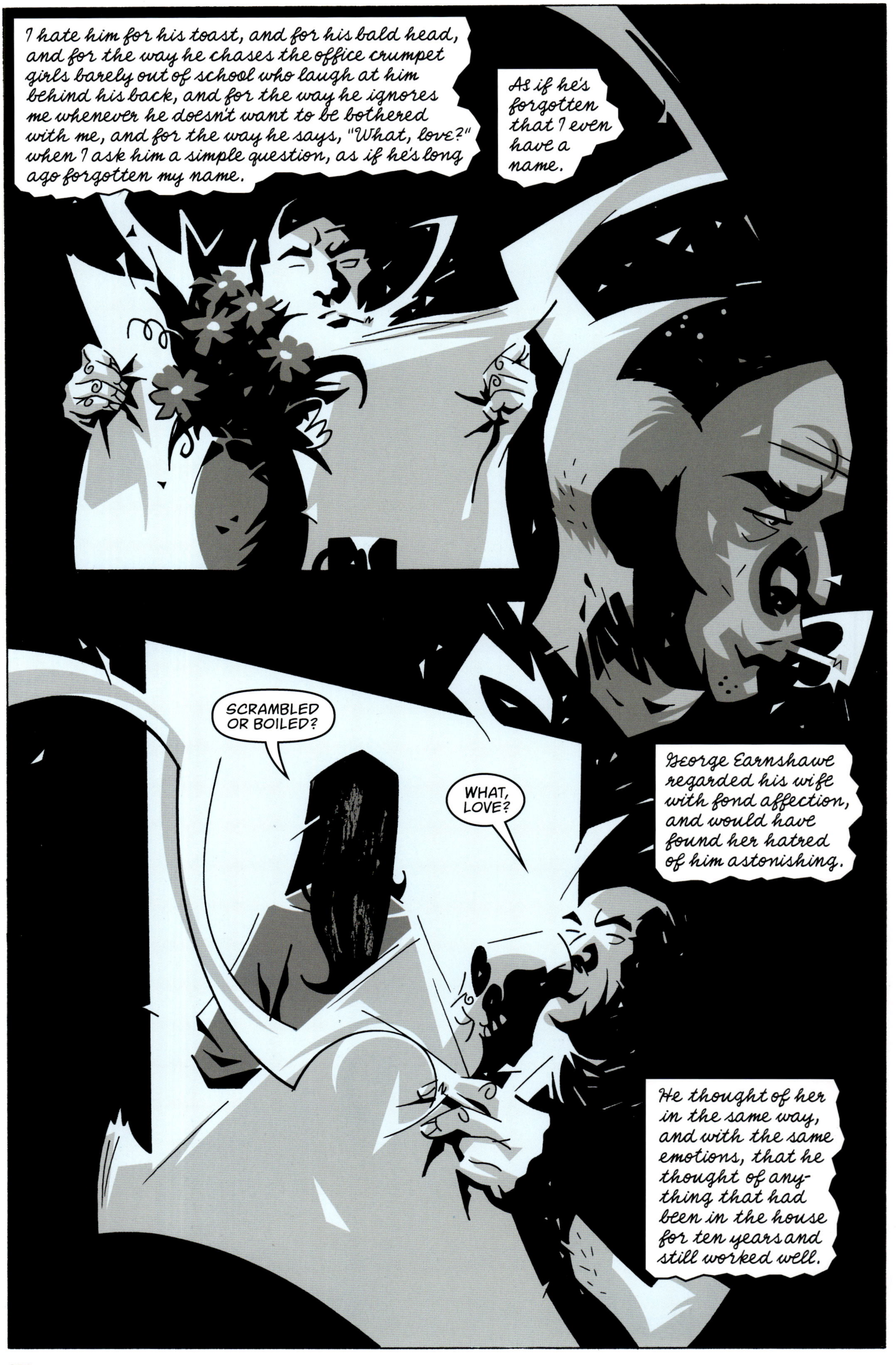
I hate him for his toast, and for his bald head, and for the way he chases the office crumpet girls barely out of school who laugh at him behind his back, and for the way he ignores me whenever he doesn't want to be bothered with me, and for the way he says, "What, love?" when I ask him a simple question, as if he's long ago forgotten my name.
As if he's forgotten that I even have a name.
SCRAMBLED OR BOILED?
WHAT, LOVE?
George Earnshawe regarded his wife with fond affection, and would have found her hatred of him astonishing.
He thought of her in the same way, and with the same emotions, that he thought of anything that had been in the house for ten years and still worked well.

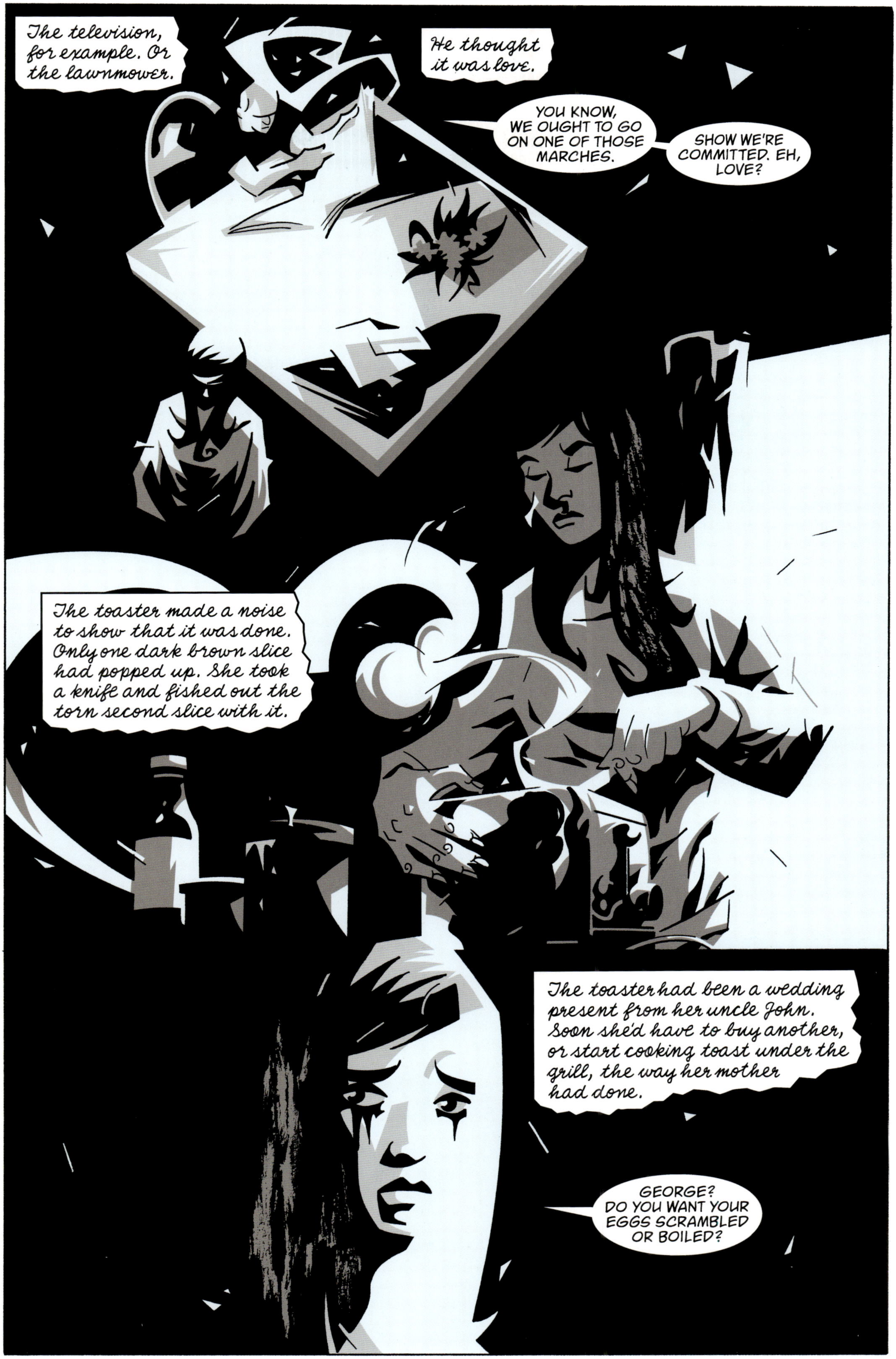
The television, for example. Or the lawnmower.
He thought it was love.
YOU KNOW, WE OUGHT TO GO ON ONE OF THOSE MARCHES.
SHOW WE'RE COMMITTED. EH, LOVE?
The toaster made a noise to show that it was done. Only one dark brown slice had popped up. She took a knife and fished out the torn second slice with it.
The toaster had been a wedding present from her uncle John. Soon she'd have to buy another, or start cooking toast under the grill, the way her mother had done.
GEORGE? DO YOU WANT YOUR EGGS SCRAMBLED OR BOILED?

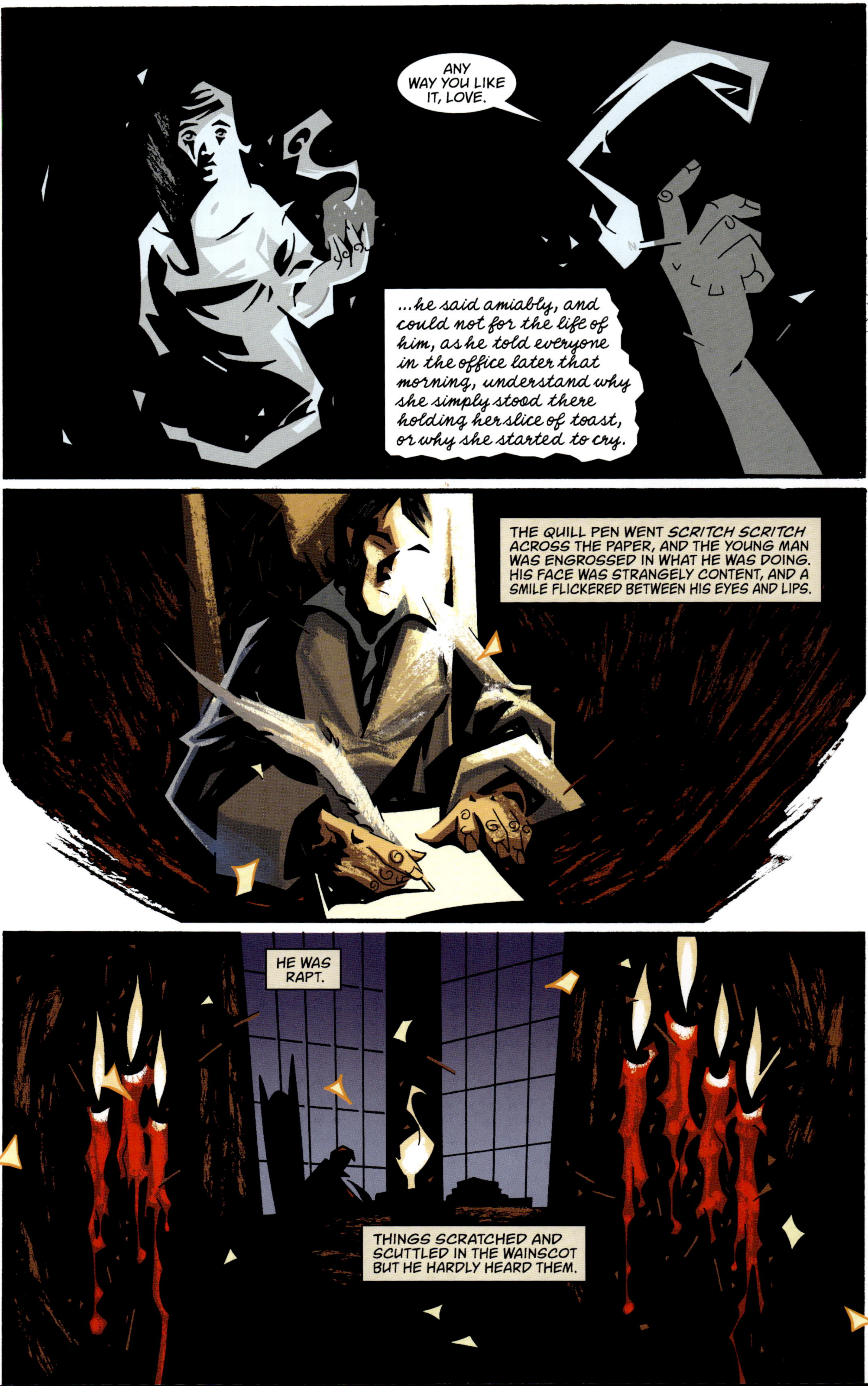
ANY WAY YOU LIKE IT, LOVE.
...he said amiably, and could not for the life of him, as he told everyone in the office later that morning, understand why she simply stood there holding her slice of toast, or why she started to cry.
THE QUILL PEN WENT SCRITCH SCRITCH ACROSS THE PAPER, AND THE YOUNG MAN WAS ENGROSSED IN WHAT HE WAS DOING. HIS FACE WAS STRANGELY CONTENT, AND A SMILE FLICKERED BETWEEN HIS EYES AND LIPS.
HE WAS RAPT.
THINGS SCRATCHED AND SCUTTLED IN THE WAINSCOT BUT HE HARDLY HEARD THEM.

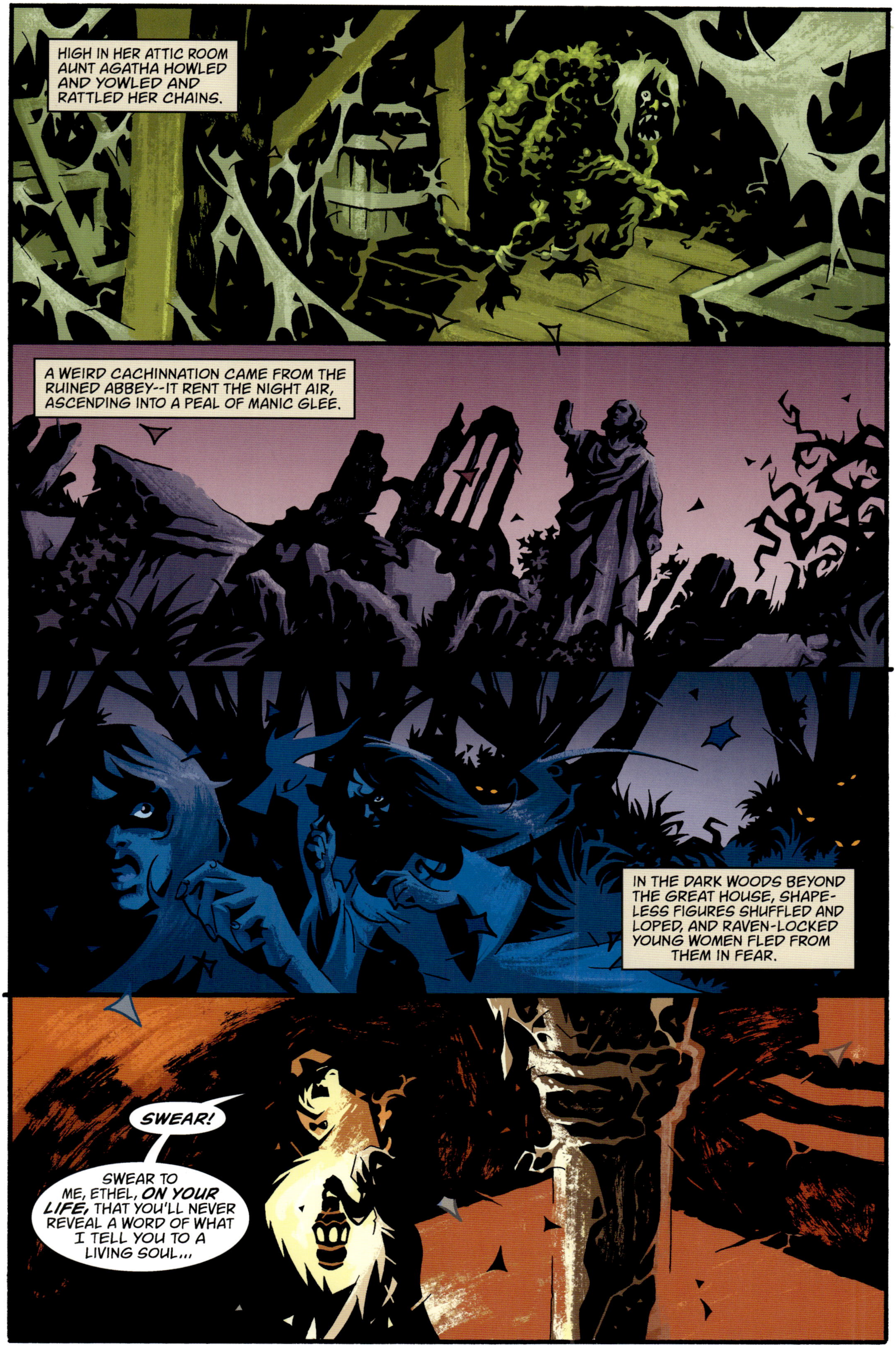
HIGH IN HER ATTIC ROOM AUNT AGATHA HOWLED AND YOWLED AND RATTLED HER CHAINS.
A WEIRD CACHINNATION CAME FROM THE RUINED ABBEY--IT RENT THE NIGHT AIR, ASCENDING INTO A PEAL OF MANIC GLEE.
IN THE DARK WOODS BEYOND THE GREAT HOUSE, SHAPE-LESS FIGURES SHUFFLED AND LOPED, AND RAVEN-LOCKED YOUNG WOMEN FLED FROM THEM IN FEAR.
SWEAR!
SWEAR TO ME, ETHEL, ON YOUR LIFE, THAT YOU'LL NEVER REVEAL A WORD OF WHAT I TELL YOU TO A LIVING SOUL...

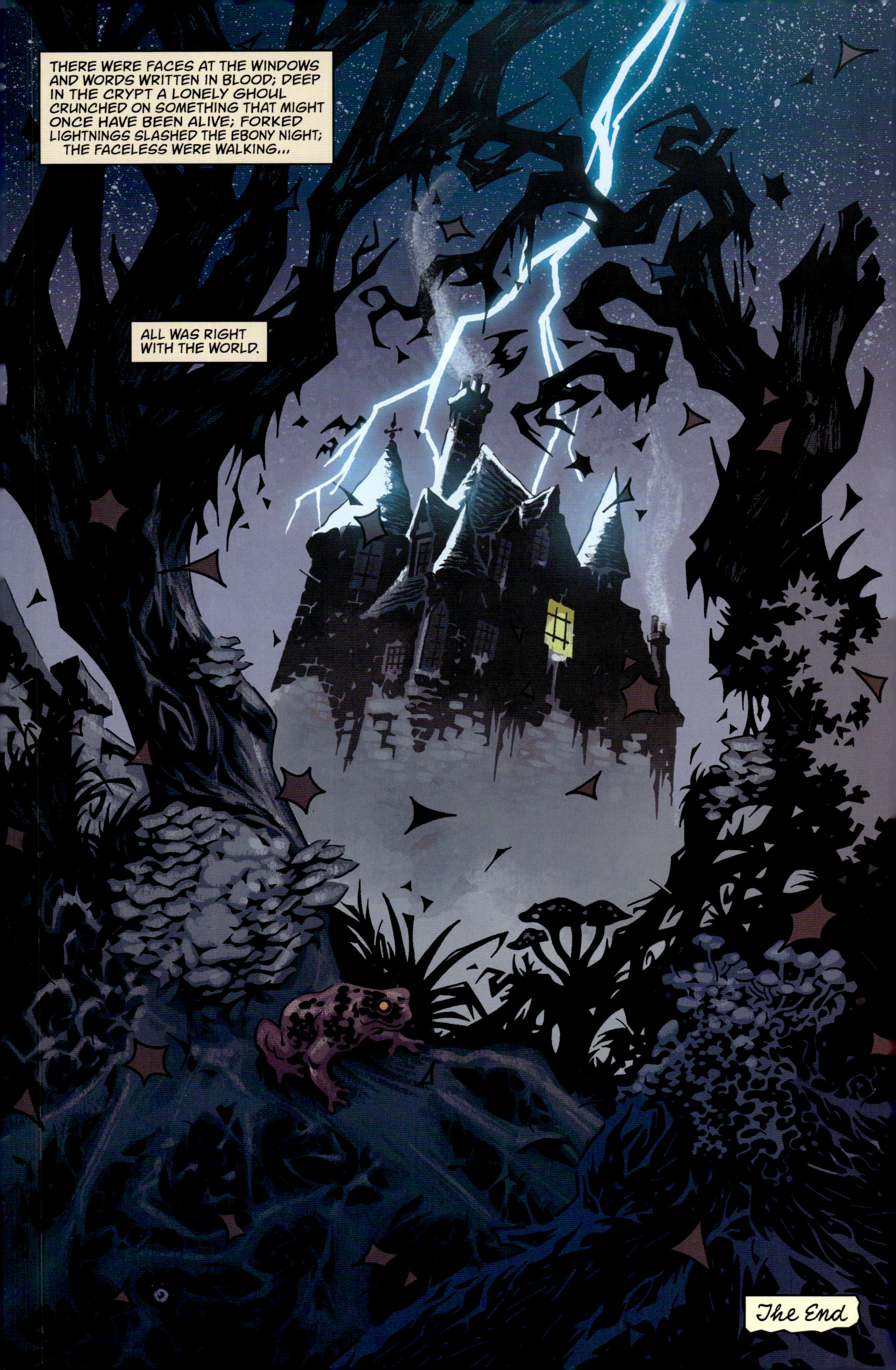
THERE WERE FACES AT THE WINDOWS AND WORDS WRITTEN IN BLOOD; DEEP IN THE CRYPT A LONELY GHOUL CRUNCHED ON SOMETHING THAT MIGHT ONCE HAVE BEEN ALIVE; FORKED LIGHTNINGS SLASHED THE EBONY NIGHT; THE FACELESS WERE WALKING...
ALL WAS RIGHT WITH THE WORLD.
The End

BONUS CONTENT

A STUDY IN EMERALD
PAGE 256

MURDER MYSTERIES
PAGE 267

FORBIDDEN BRIDES
OF THE FACELESS SLAVES IN THE SECRET HOUSE
OF THE NIGHT OF DREAD DESIRE
PAGE 306

A STUDY IN EMERALD SKETCHBOOK

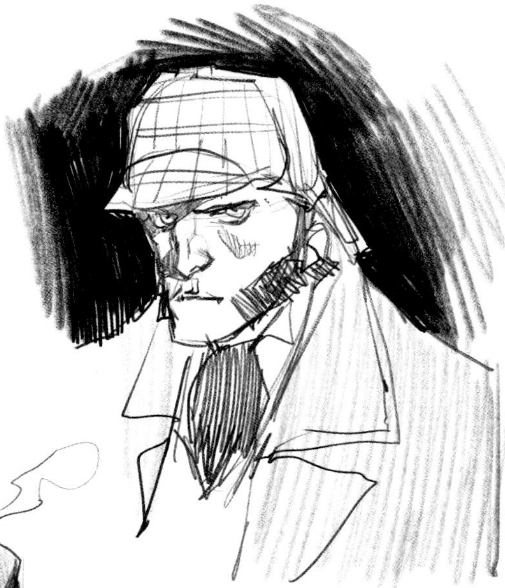

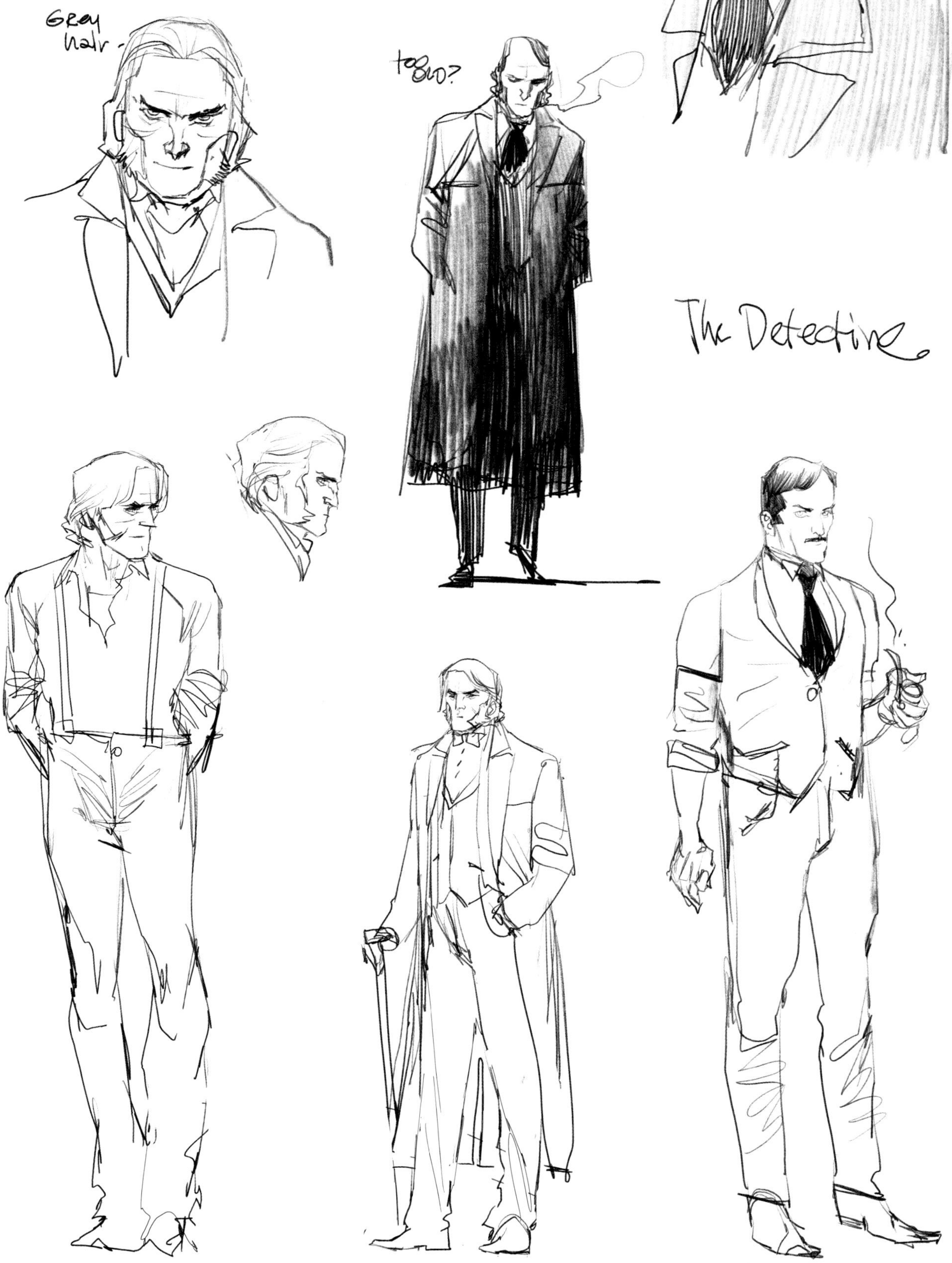
Grey hair -
too old?
The Detective

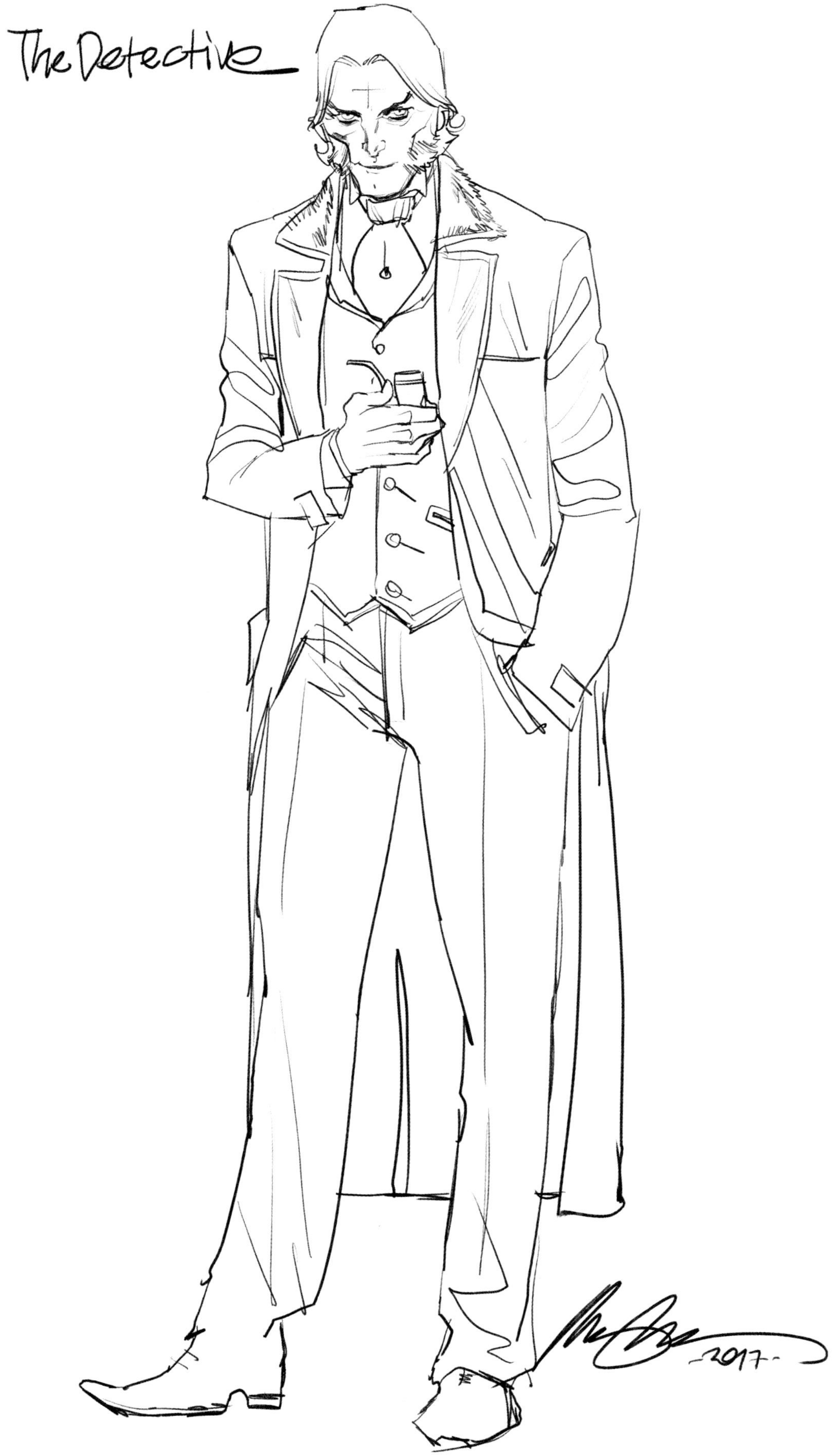
The Detective
2017

Early designs by Rafael Albuquerque for our mysterious protagonist—the Detective.

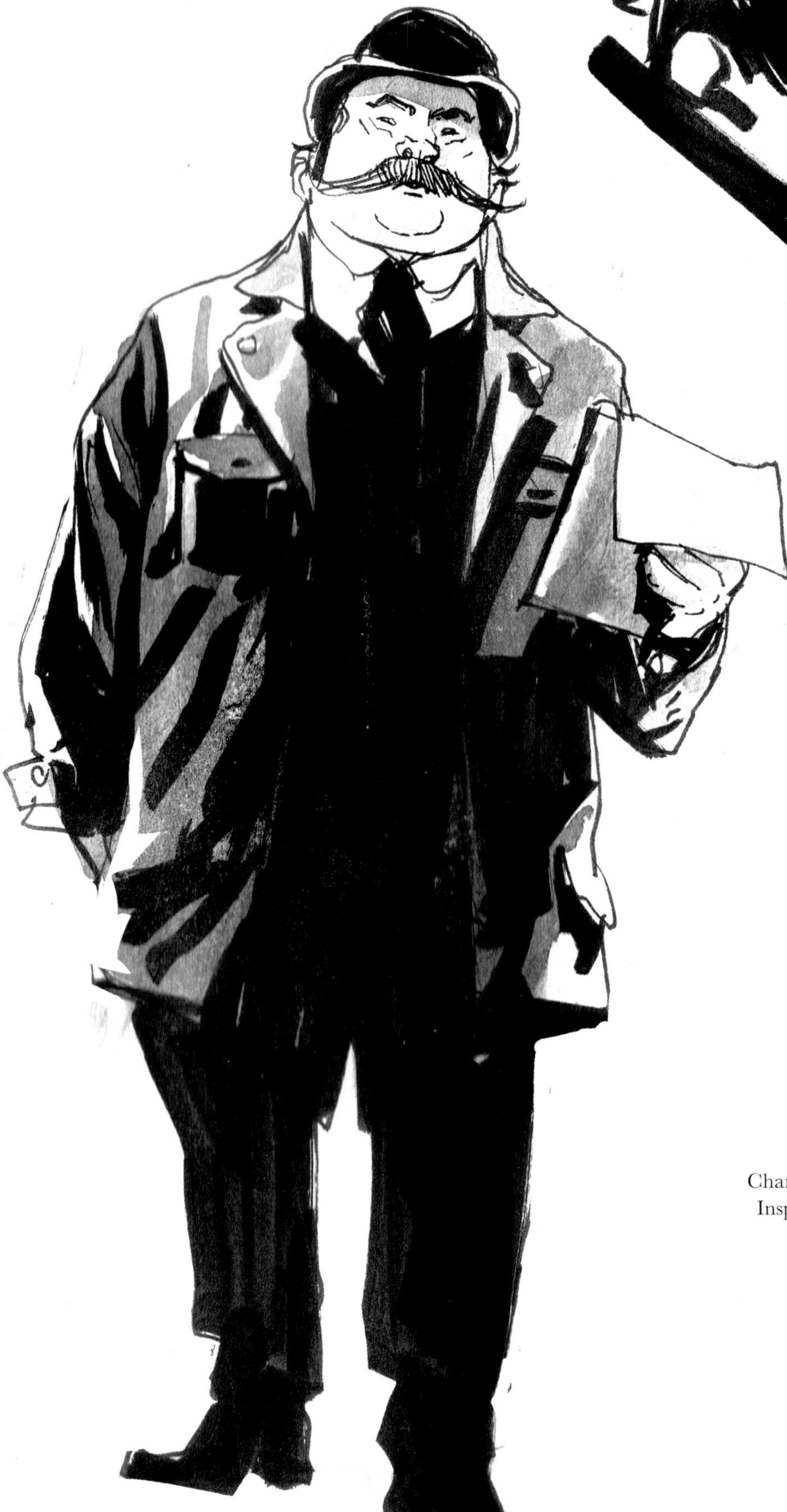

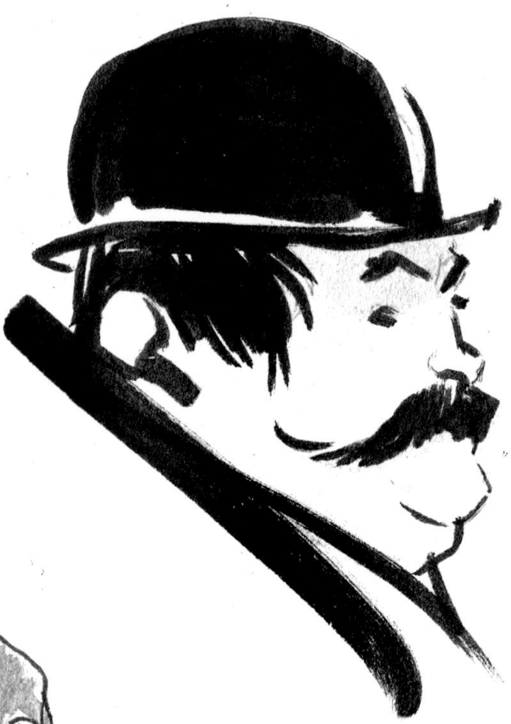

Character designs for
Inspector Lestrade.

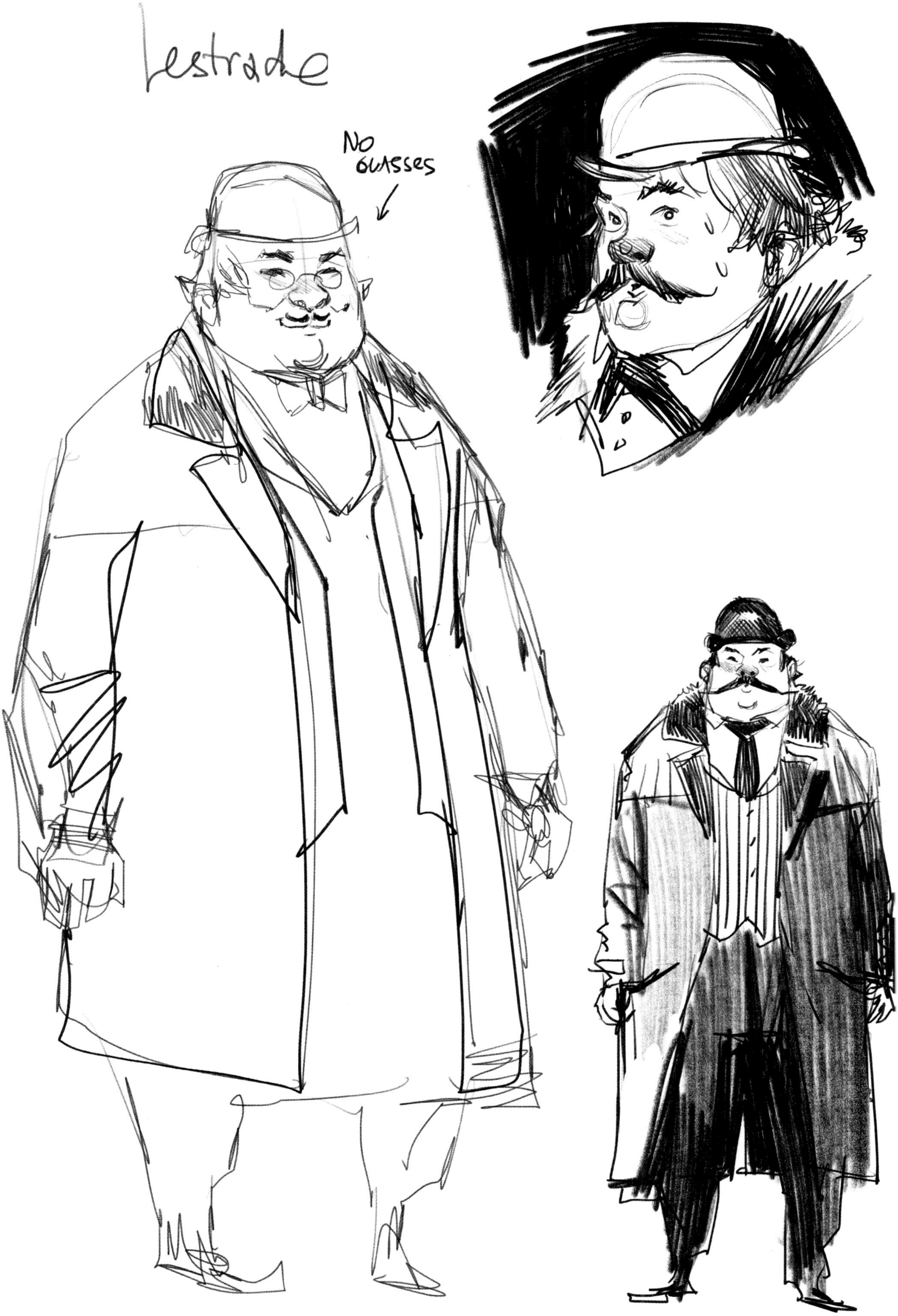
Lestrade
NO GLASSES

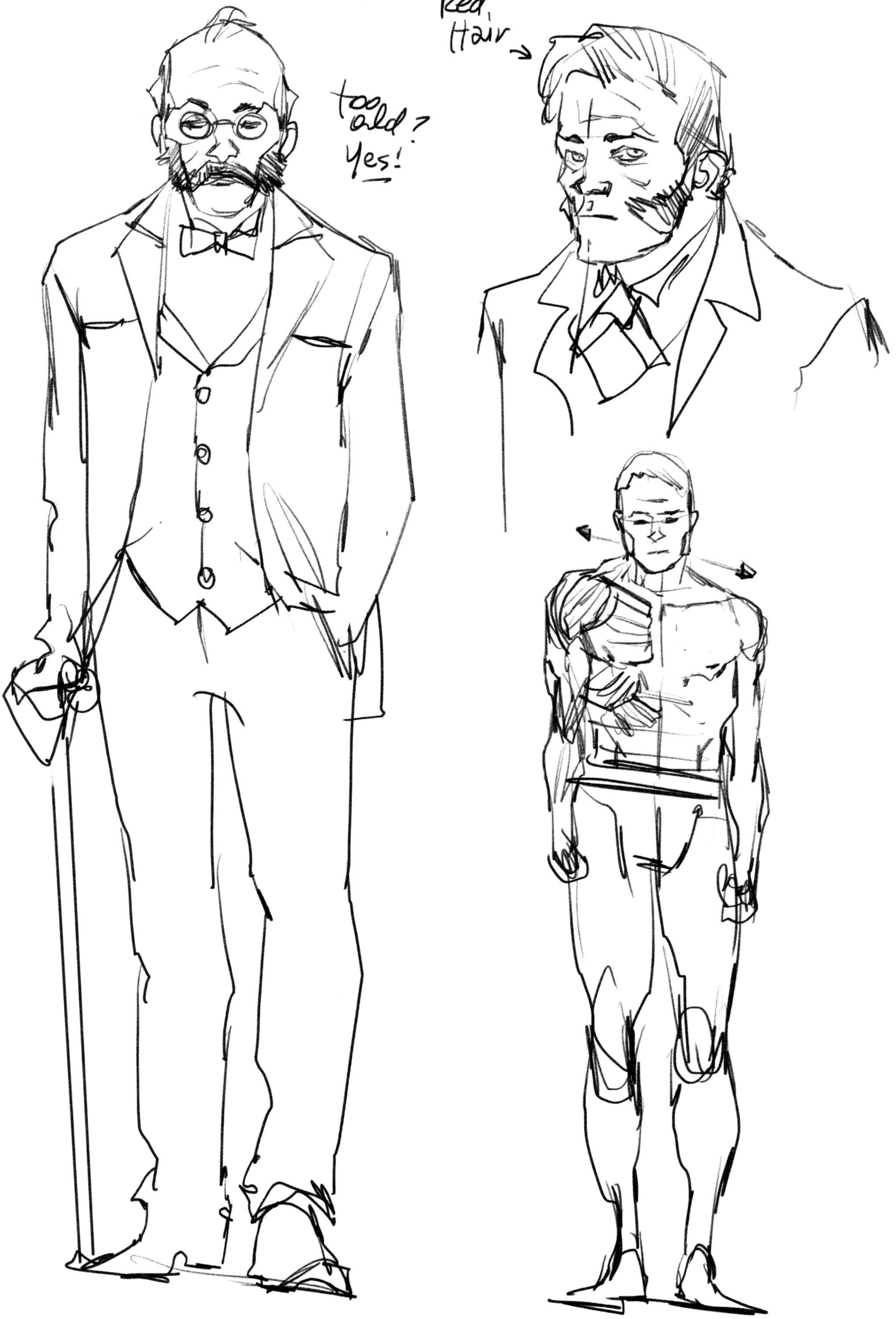
too old? Yes!
Red Hair

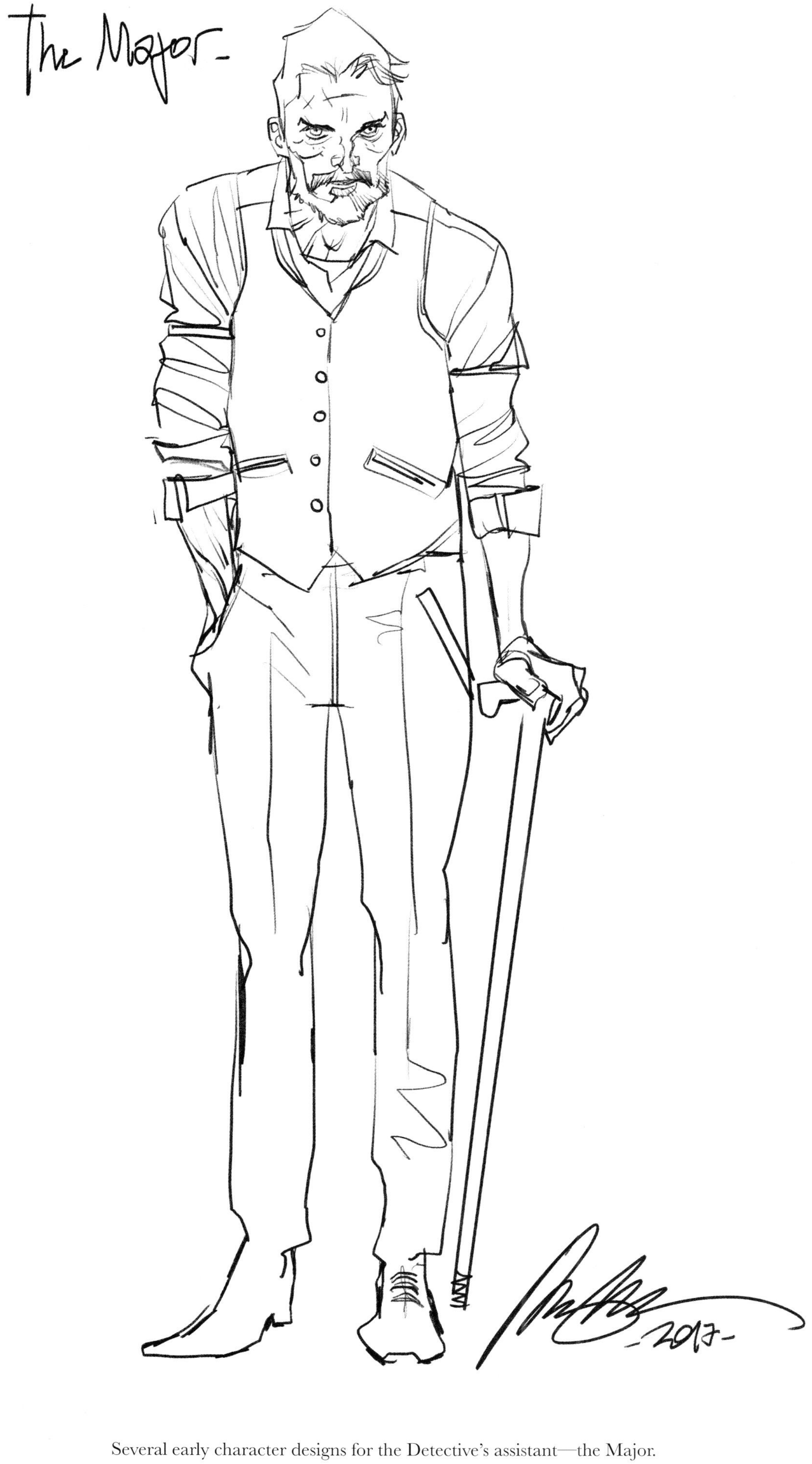
The Major-
-2017-

Several early character designs for the Detective's assistant—the Major.

The Major.

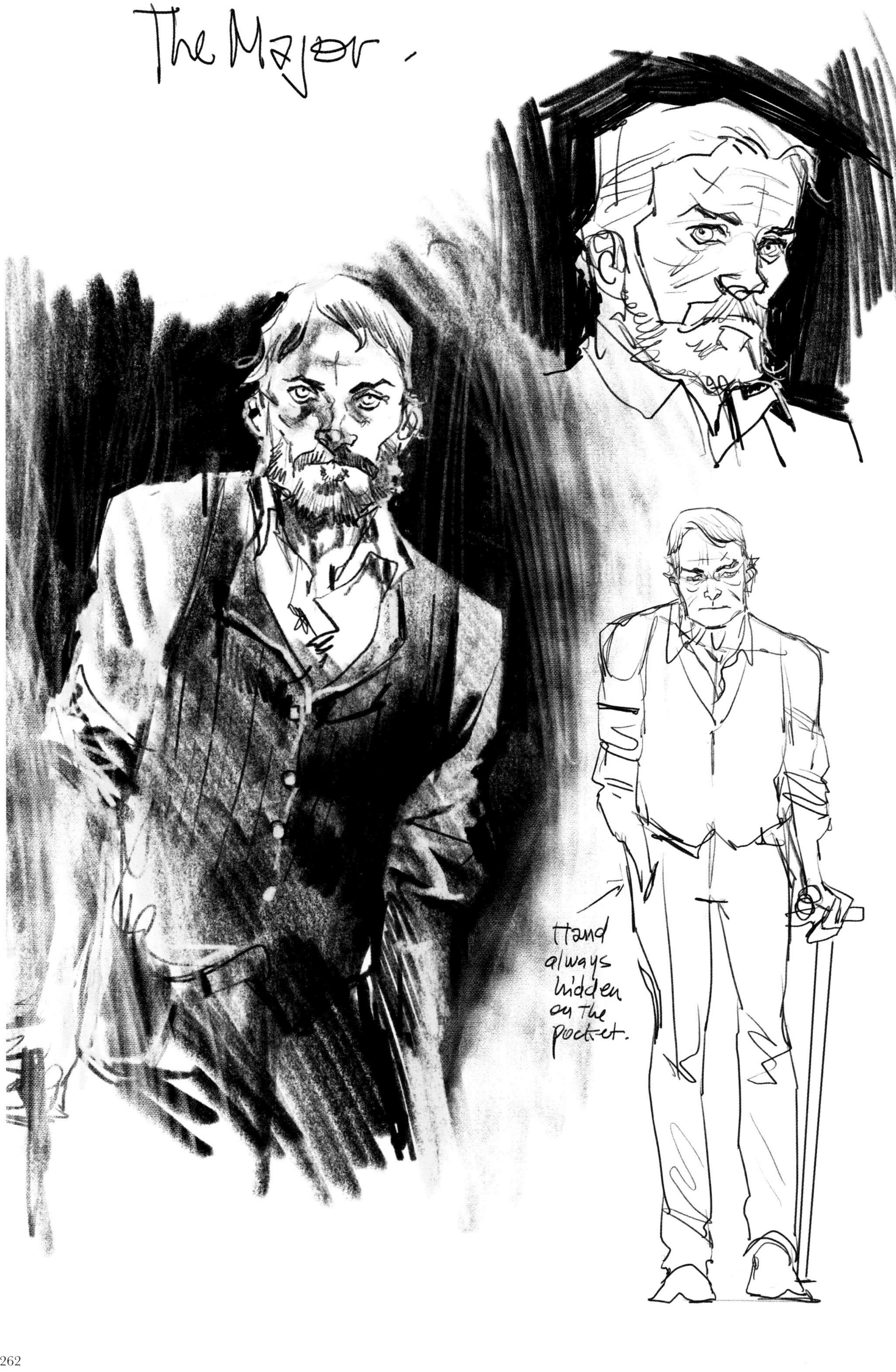
Hand always hidden on the pocket.

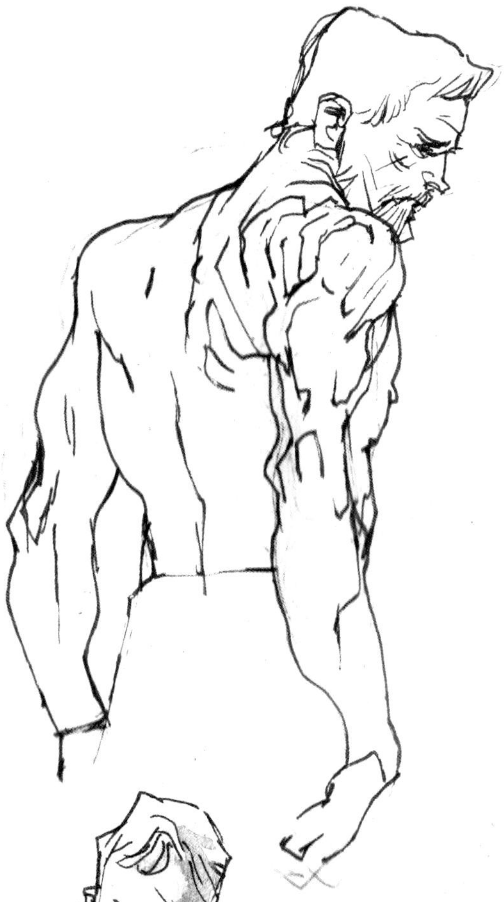

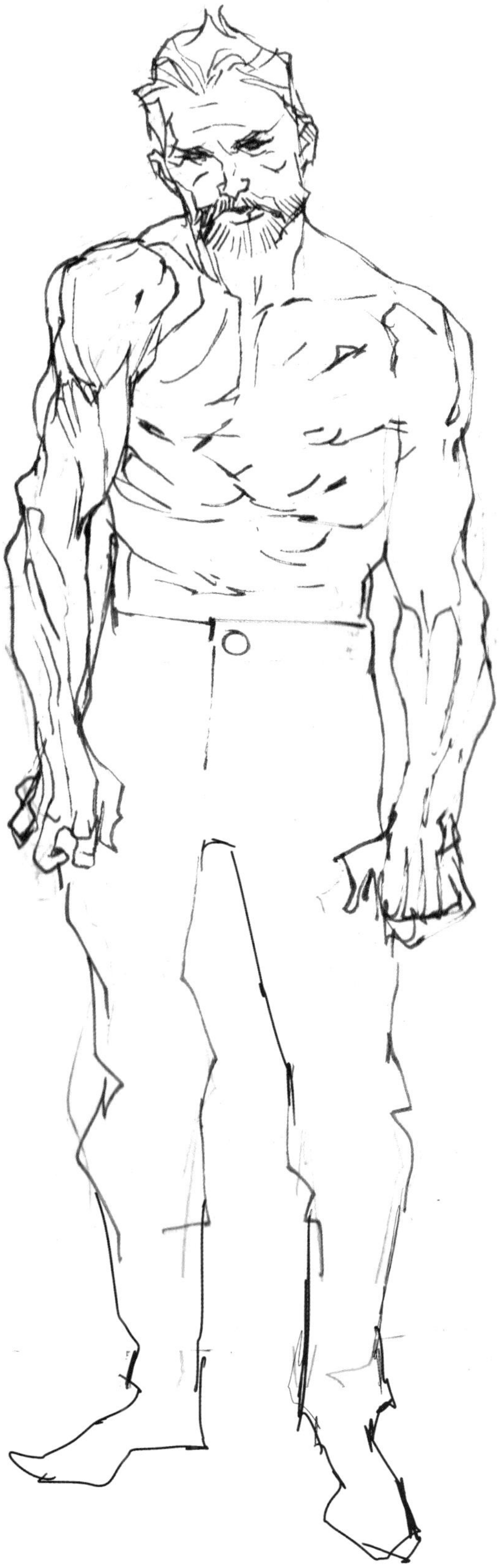

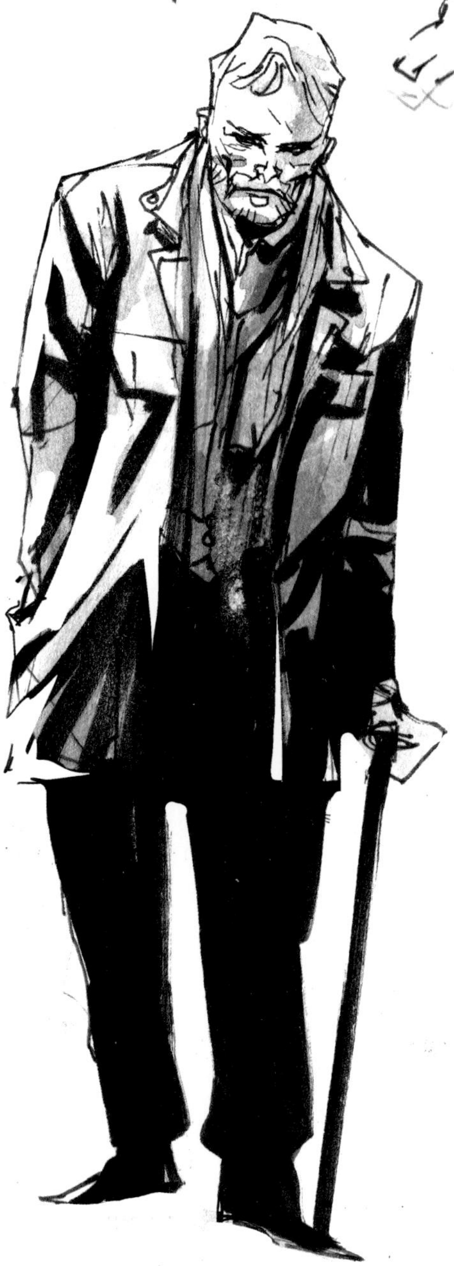

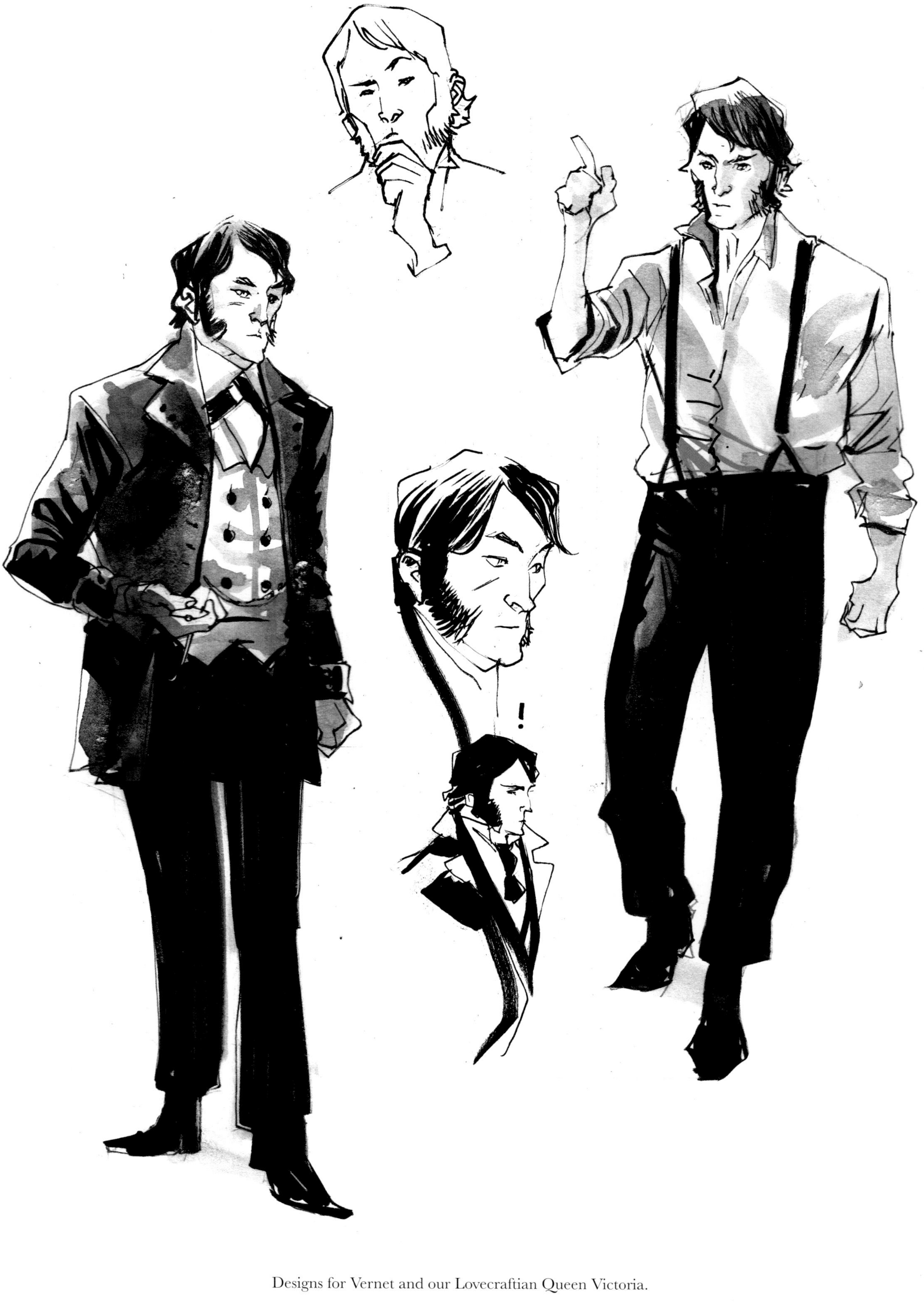

Designs for Vernet and our Lovecraftian Queen Victoria.

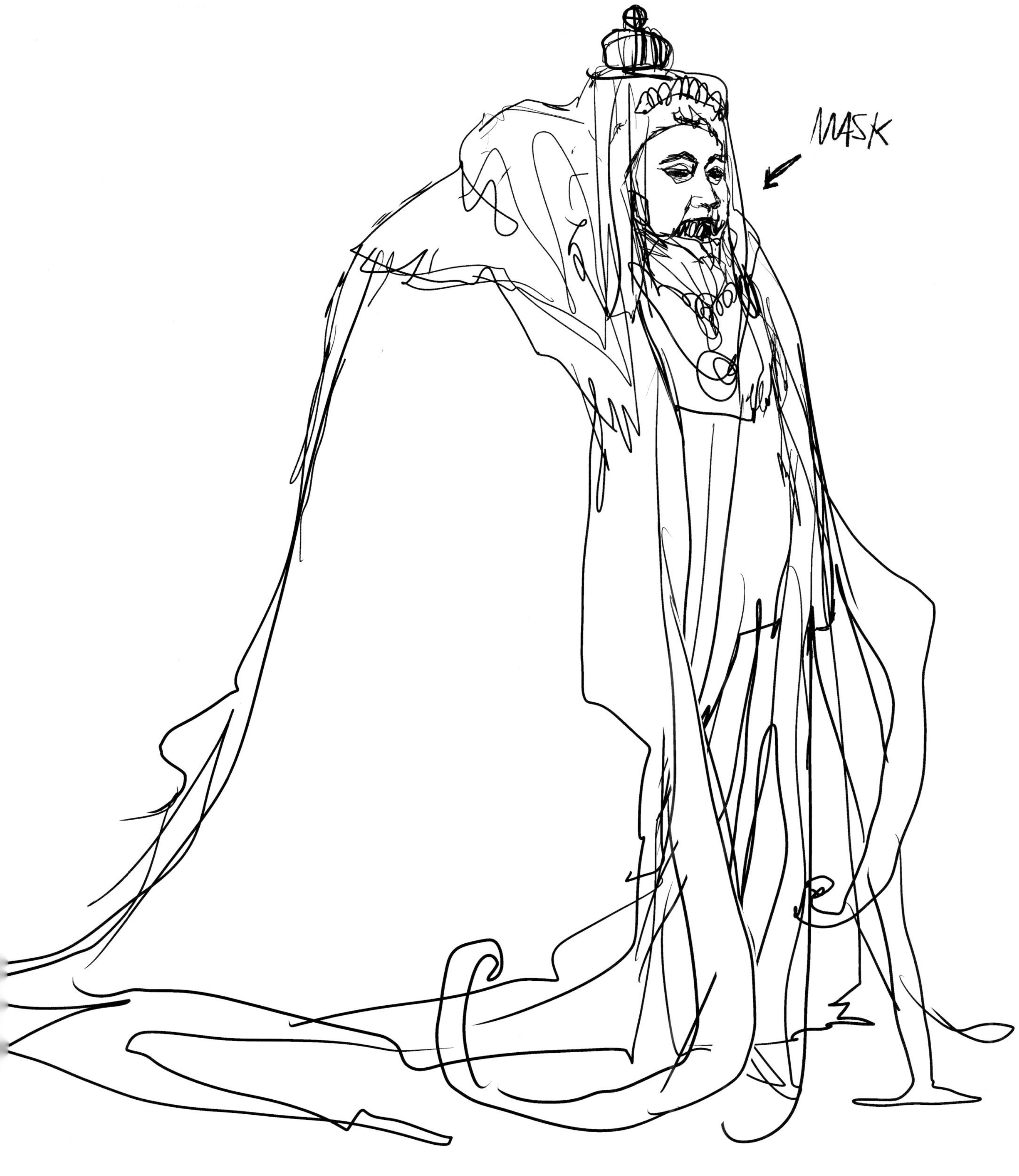
MASK

MYSTERIES DEMYSTIFIED
BY DURWIN S. TALON

A comics professional working since 1972, Philip Craig Russell has garnered deserved praise. He has received the highest industry honors, including the Eisner, the Harvey, and the Inkpot Award for Career Achievement. His graphic novels have been critically acclaimed in journals from the *School Library Journal* to *Publishers Weekly*. However, Russell's true success can be measured by his peers' acclaim.

P. Craig Russell is the comic artist's artist. He is meticulous with his images and his words, which makes his success as a comic book artist evident. There are no careless moments in his storytelling. Every element is placed deliberately and precisely to make the most of the story. Though he graduated from the University of Cincinnati with a degree in painting, his signature style is the fine, lyrical line that flowed from his early days with Marvel's *Dr. Strange* to DC's *Sandman*. However, it is his passion for literature and music that has made him renowned, leading to a number of award-winning adaptations including: the *Fairy Tales of Oscar Wilde*, Rudyard Kipling's *Jungle Book Stories*, Wolfgang Amadeus Mozart's *The Magic Flute*, and Richard Wagner's *The Ring of the Nibelung*.

He has also had an award-winning relationship with Neil Gaiman, with his short story "Death" receiving the 2004 Eisner Award. But Gaiman's *Murder Mysteries* serves as a proud example of Russell's work as a collaborator. While this story first appeared as a radio play and a short story, Russell not only adapted the work into the comic book form, but through his process, he used his indelible style to make it a successful story in the sequential art form.

SERVING THE STORY

MURDER MYSTERIES

"He stared at the floor. Then he stared up, proudly, aggressively. And he smiled.

"'I was.'

"'Do you want to tell me about it?'

"'No.' A shrug. 'But I suppose I must. Very well, then.

"'We worked together. And when we began to work on *Love*...we became lovers. It was his idea.

The creation of *Murder Mysteries* was a two-part process: the script was edited from two sources before the art could be created. Dialogue, captions, and thoughts drive the sequential narrative. However, when adapting a work of prose, the decisions can be much more difficult to make. Russell's process is one part inspiration and one part thoughtfulness.

PCR: My process reminds me of the old Archie Goodwin cartoon, where he had a drawing of himself just sitting there, face and shoulders, and said, "Someone asks me how I get my ideas." He's just sitting there with his head in one hand for three panels, and the last one he says, "Sometimes I use both hands."

[When adapting], I consider the source: am I adapting a prose story, or am I working from a script written for comics? [With written prose], part of it is just soaking up that writer's words and just trying to get all the marrow out of the bone. And I find that frequently there's a lot more in there than they've seen. It's not changing their ideas or their themes, it's just maybe polishing those words and finding pictures that underscore the words and amplify the words in a way that's not in their story, but is inherent in their story.

Sometimes with a script, the writer might have several word balloons in one panel, as two people are in a conversation. I will read this, and sometimes one single line out of several sentences in this one balloon will just pop out. It's so beautifully written and so telling that you look at it and say, "This line deserves its own room." So that's why I tend to almost double the amount of panels when I'm working with an original script for comics. I always have a lot more panels in than they have written—if it has forty panels, I'll do seventy-five.

When reading [the story] over and over and over, certain ideas pop out very quickly and quite easily, and other scenes take a lot more time to chisel away at. I think with pictures. I'll mull over a scene then I will roughly block out the whole story. Then I start work on those rough chunks one page at a time, picking out the most obvious "money shot" of that page, then work a number of different versions until the page comes out right. Once I have the sequence of events in that page, I'll roughly place those down in panels.

But then you have to make aesthetic decisions: is there a rhythm to these panels? If you turned the page upside down, would this arrangement of rectangles be pleasing? Sometimes it just looks like a layered sandwich, one tier after another, and nothing seems to stand out on the page. You want a continuous flow—not all panels are created equal—so I really try to get a storytelling rhythm going. And a visual rhythm. These panels should always be in the service of the story. *Always*.

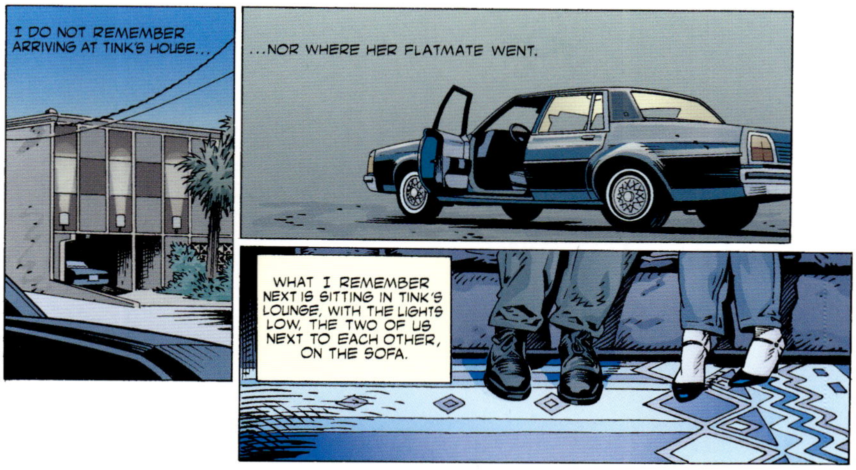
I DO NOT REMEMBER ARRIVING AT TINK'S HOUSE...
...NOR WHERE HER FLATMATE WENT.
WHAT I REMEMBER NEXT IS SITTING IN TINK'S LOUNGE, WITH THE LIGHTS LOW, THE TWO OF US NEXT TO EACH OTHER, ON THE SOFA.

Gaiman's *Murder Mysteries* was first written as a short prose story with the themes of deception and vengeance describing the first betrayal, the first heartbreak, and the first crime in God's own city of angels. The story encompasses two worlds: the streets of Los Angeles and heaven itself. The narrators are a young Brit stranded on his way back to England and the angel Raguel, the agent of the Lord's vengeance. With two narrators and two worlds, adapting this story proved to be tricky. Russell had both the *Murder Mysteries* short story and the radio play to rely on for inspiration and detail. Choosing moments or thoughts between the two sources, he highlighted words or moments, then began to assemble his roughs and visual notations. This would eventually be streamlined into the pages of the adaptation.

PCR: Well, by the time I was ready to actually do my adaptation I had both the [short story and the radio play] in hand. I mean, I had read this story about ten years ago, when I did the single illustration for it in the book of short stories. But once we geared up to do the graphic novel, Neil had written the radio play script. I found it interesting the things that Neil would expand on because he needed to or some things that he would drop for the radio play.

Murder Mysteries is an oblique story. It does not reveal itself quickly, which is part of its charm—that it's really well written. So the edge that I was walking on was that I wanted visually to make it not quite so oblique. There were certain things that I did want to make a little clearer.

"I do not remember arriving at Tink's house ...

... Nor where her flatmate went."

Like any good writer, visual storytellers must be able to define time and place. If an artist can establish an environment, characters can move from setting to setting as the story unfolds. With proper emphasis on background detail, the reader will never be lost. Story page 12 of *Murder Mysteries* establishes all of the locations used in Los Angeles.

PCR: I wanted to foreshadow a little bit, on the *nor where her flatmate went*, to show that empty car with the overhead light still on. [I wanted the reader] to get an idea—there's something about an empty car with the door standing open that's not right.

I also wanted to establish a shot of Tink's house. In the end [of *Murder Mysteries*], when he's on the plane and he's reading the newspaper, the photo [of the apartment] in the newspaper triggers some memory—and we know. Even though he's still oblivious ... the panel sets up an echo in his head somehow. It seemed important to me that we've actually seen [Tink's apartment] before.

```
/SFX/ THE SOUNDS OF LOS ANGELES CROSSFADE WITH

/SFX/THE SOUND OF RAGUEL'S AWAKENING, UNDER...

/MUS/THE WORD WAS GOD -- SILVER CITY THEME --

                    RAGUEL NARRATION
        The Word gave me a body, gave me eyes.
        And I opened my eyes, and I saw the light
        of the Silver City. I was in a room -- a
        silver room -- and there wasn't anything
        in it except me. In front of me was a
        window, that went from floor to ceiling,
        open to the sky, and through the window I
        could see the spires of the City, and at
        the edge of the City, the Dark. I don't
        know how long I waited there.
                         (MORE)
                                                 (CONTINUED)
```

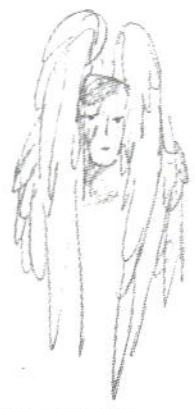

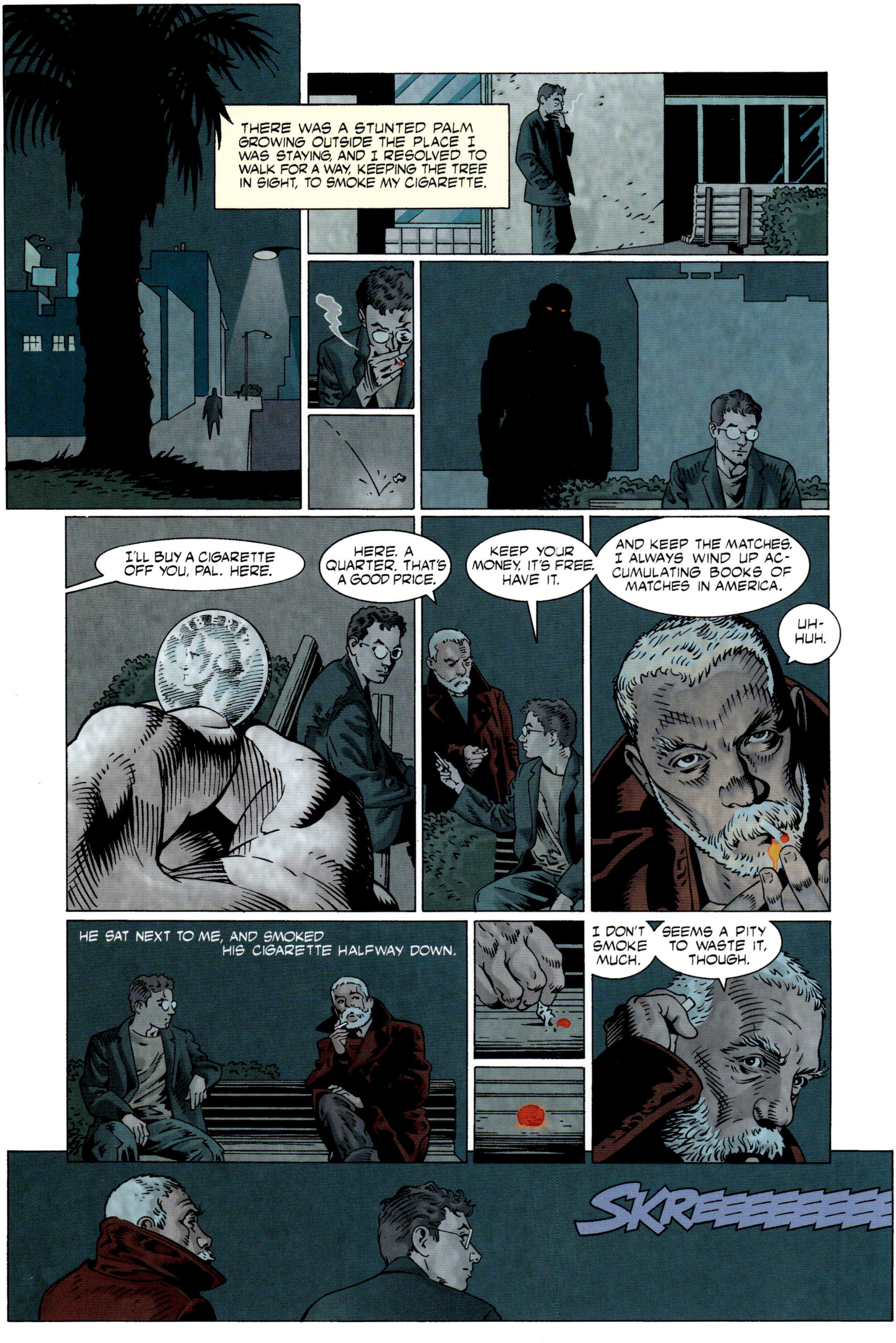
THERE WAS A STUNTED PALM GROWING OUTSIDE THE PLACE I WAS STAYING, AND I RESOLVED TO WALK FOR A WAY, KEEPING THE TREE IN SIGHT, TO SMOKE MY CIGARETTE.
I'LL BUY A CIGARETTE OFF YOU, PAL. HERE.
HERE. A QUARTER. THAT'S A GOOD PRICE.
KEEP YOUR MONEY. IT'S FREE. HAVE IT.
AND KEEP THE MATCHES. I ALWAYS WIND UP ACCUMULATING BOOKS OF MATCHES IN AMERICA.
UH-HUH.
HE SAT NEXT TO ME, AND SMOKED HIS CIGARETTE HALFWAY DOWN.
I DON'T SMOKE MUCH.
SEEMS A PITY TO WASTE IT, THOUGH.
SKREEEEEEEE

SERVING THE STORY

"Here. A quarter. That's a good price."

An open dialogue with Neil Gaiman proved invaluable in creating a unified vision. This marriage between words and pictures proved crucial to creating themes that would be carried consistently throughout the duration of the story. In story page 17 of Murder Mysteries, a simple solution independent of the source materials was developed because of this dialogue.

PCR: If you look on the first story page at the bottom, [a sign reads] "Be an Angel Give Generously." That's one of the things that Neil pointed out to me early on. He said, "Don't forget it's Christmas. It may be LA and it's hot, but it's Christmas." And it's kind of dreary. So you see that sweating Santa Claus at the bottom, you're already repeating those notes that we started the story out with, the little purple musical notes. And you have that fallen angel. Now we hear that music again and that reference to the angel, only now it's all gritty. When he gets into the apartment, there are the angels that the little girl is drawing. And then I put that shabby little Christmas tree with that little tin angel on top, which reminded me of the angel we had when I was a kid. So you go from these beautiful angels to the shabby little tin angel, then we see the real angel dead on the ground. But clear towards the end, after all this stuff has happened and he's back on the street, where he says, "I walked back to the place I was staying, to the house by the stunted palm tree. I thought about angels and about Tink … and I wondered whether love and death went hand in hand." At the last minute I interpolated that middle panel to give you another clue as to what might have happened in that apartment. We see that tree knocked over with the lights, and that little tin angel on the ground, which, again, relates to the first murder in heaven, the real angel. So that happened at the very last minute, and I was sort of hopping up and down. "Ooh! Ooh! The little angel!"

Another point was that Liberty coin, when he's handing him that coin and says, "I'll buy a cigarette off you, pal." I was simply drawing a quarter, and it had Liberty on it. So later on, I just had an upshot of all those wires and cables that you see over the street, and a street sign. And I called Neil. I said, "What should we put on the street sign? It should relate somehow to the story." And neither of us came up with something. And then, the next day I thought: "Well, of course. Liberty." Because he's talking about his freedom, sort of, a number of times in there. So it just tied in with that quarter. He offers him freedom, and that's what he gets.

Russell is an avid reader. He respects the power of words in both the narrative and sequential art forms. He plans the space for the words in the layout stage to dictate the rhythm of the narrative. By doing this, there is a clear path the reader follows through the page. To Russell, the art serves to support the words.

PCR: I plan [balloon] lettering by hand, and the rhythm of those word balloons as part of the design.

Sometimes something as simple as a word balloon in the corner of the panel, but [deleting] the panel line around the edges of it, having the balloon *open*, lets a little air into the page. That's one less area that you're blocking off, and it gives a little relief to the eye. Mike Mignola and Kevin Nowlan do that a lot.

I also leave a lot of empty space behind the word balloons and I carefully design the word balloons into the story. I think that's one of the reasons some artists say that you're expecting a lot from the reader —because they're not designing the word balloons. They're doing these drawings and just sort of indicating where the balloons go later. But you really have to do more than that.

It's only when I was starting to work on *The Ring* that I really started thinking about [dialogue in panels]—and that was the year I did about six hundred pages of layouts. I've tended to break it up so that every person has their own panel when they're speaking and talking and answering. And I was even sort of contemptuous of pages where there'd be ten people in the panel and they all have a word balloon. But I realized that you can use that as a tool to speed time up. So there were these ensemble scenes in *The Ring* where there are six or seven people [in a panel], and they're all talking—and I would use it when you wanted the action. I mean, everyone was talking at the same time—it was a very quick sort of thing. So I've tried to be more aware of when to use [multiple dialogue balloons in a single panel] to give an impression of time, faster or slower.

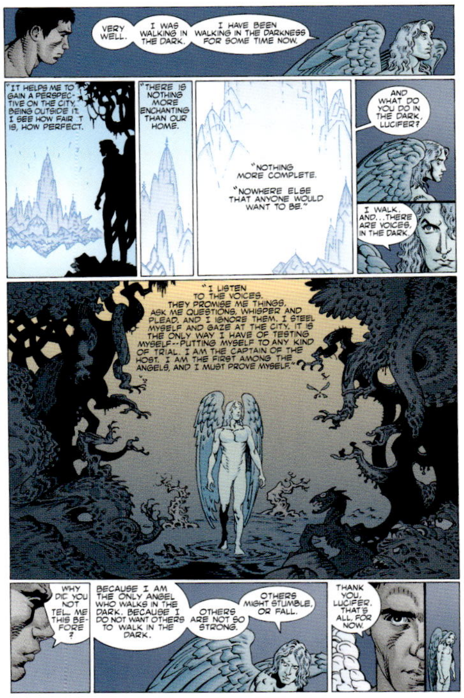
VERY WELL.
I WAS WALKING IN THE DARK.
I HAVE BEEN WALKING IN THE DARKNESS FOR SOME TIME NOW.
"IT HELPS ME TO GAIN A PERSPECTIVE ON THE CITY, BEING OUTSIDE IT. I SEE HOW FAIR IT IS, HOW PERFECT.
"THERE IS NOTHING MORE ENCHANTING THAN OUR HOME.
"NOTHING MORE COMPLETE.
"NOWHERE ELSE THAT ANYONE WOULD WANT TO BE."
AND WHAT DO YOU DO IN THE DARK, LUCIFER?
I WALK. AND...THERE ARE VOICES, IN THE DARK.
"I LISTEN TO THE VOICES. THEY PROMISE ME THINGS, ASK ME QUESTIONS, WHISPER AND PLEAD. AND I IGNORE THEM. I STEEL MYSELF AND GAZE AT THE CITY. IT IS THE ONLY WAY I HAVE OF TESTING MYSELF--PUTTING MYSELF TO ANY KIND OF TRIAL. I AM THE CAPTAIN OF THE HOST. I AM THE FIRST AMONG THE ANGELS, AND I MUST PROVE MYSELF."
WHY DID YOU NOT TELL ME THIS BEFORE?
BECAUSE I AM THE ONLY ANGEL WHO WALKS IN THE DARK. BECAUSE I DO NOT WANT OTHERS TO WALK IN THE DARK.
OTHERS ARE NOT SO STRONG.
OTHERS MIGHT STUMBLE, OR FALL.
THANK YOU, LUCIFER. THAT'S ALL, FOR NOW.

"I walk. And …

there are voices, in the dark."

Last, the process of comics can be instinctual. Even when words have been written, spoken, and processed, all the best plans can be deviated from when faced with a better idea. The job of a storyteller is to always allow for the possibility of inspiration.

PCR: You also have to be willing to back up and look for another solution if something is not working. In my first take on [story] page 45, in what was panel 5, [the dialogue] was originally combined with what is now panel 6: "I walk. And … there are voices, in the dark." When I lettered that out and started drawing it, I realized it was just too crowded with the way I was drawing the panel, so I thought, "Well, that first line could be removed and given its own separate panel." So I separated that little panel before. Sometimes when you're forced to come up with a solution, you come up with something better. And I think coming in on the close-up of him, when he says, "I walk. And … there are voices in the dark," ends up being stronger than if I had actually had enough room in the first place to do that. So sometimes you're glad you have these gumption blocks.

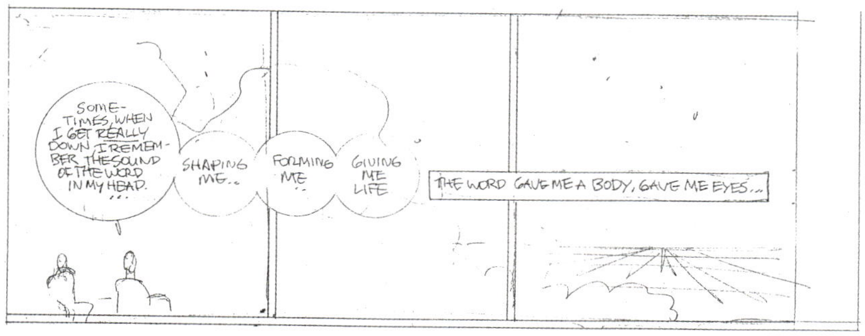
SOME-TIMES, WHEN I GET REALLY DOWN I REMEMBER THE SOUND OF THE WORD IN MY HEAD...
SHAPING ME..
FORMING ME
GIVING ME LIFE
THE WORD GAVE ME A BODY, GAVE ME EYES...

"Sometimes when I get* really *down,

I remember the sound of the word in my head...

shaping me ... forming me ... giving me life."

Planning the delivery of the words is crucial in maintaining the integrity of the story and this is even evident in the roughs stage. However, the way the words are delivered can also be designed. This technique is most evident when the fallen Raguel converses with the young Brit.

PCR: When he says, "Sometimes when I get really down, I remember the sound of the Word in my head ... shaping me ... forming me ... giving me life," I give several word balloons to a single sentence to break it up. The shaping, forming, and giving seemed to be three separate actions, so each one gets its due. But it also is there to lead your eye across those panels. And while he's talking about shaping and forming, you have all these clouds behind him, an amorphous shape. Then the panel, "The Word gave me a body, gave me eyes," and we have the stars, where he's talking about the eyes, the stars, and LA, and all the lights. And then it fades into black and into the light as he says, "I opened my eyes." It's just a way of preparing you, of leading you into the story, into the universe and the stars and the heavens, and using the word balloons to help move you through it.

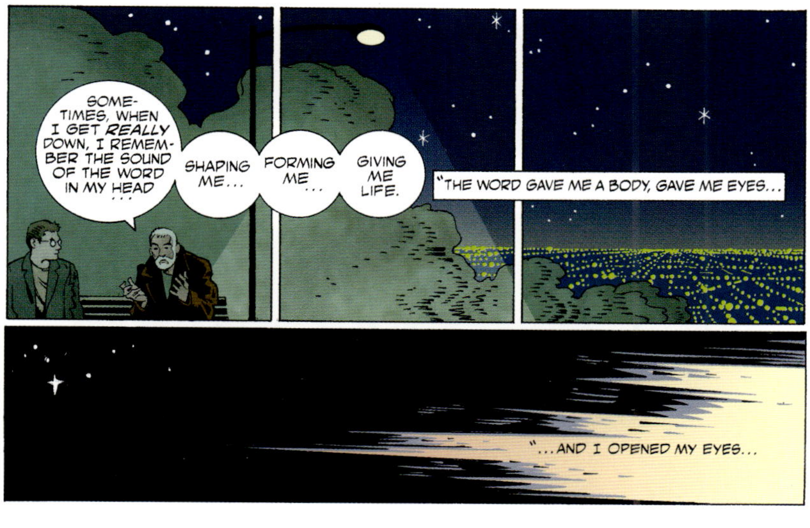
SOME-TIMES, WHEN I GET REALLY DOWN, I REMEMBER THE SOUND OF THE WORD IN MY HEAD ...
SHAPING ME...
FORMING ME ...
GIVING ME LIFE.
"THE WORD GAVE ME A BODY, GAVE ME EYES...
"...AND I OPENED MY EYES...

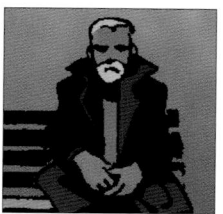

"Sure. Sure. Tell me a story."

Starting with the short story *Murder Mysteries* photocopied onto 11 x 17 inch paper, Russell begins the roughs process by blocking out paragraphs that will translate into comics pages. These roughs crowd the margins and are drawn no larger than two inches tall. However, this thumbnail stage is crucial for the roughs, and then the penciling and inking stages that follow.

I SAT BACK
IN ENGLAND
HE COUGHED
FIRST THING
SHAPING

I SAT BACK ON THE BENCH, AND THE NIGHT WAS WARM. IN ENGLAND, A FREEZING NEW DAY WOULD ALREADY HAVE BEGUN: ANOTHER HANDFUL OF OLD PEOPLE, AND THOSE WITHOUT HOMES, WOULD HAVE DIED, IN THE NIGHT, FROM THE COLD.
SURE.
SURE.
TELL ME A STORY
HE COUGHED, GRINNED WHITE TEETH—A FLASH IN THE DARKNESS...
—AND HE BEGAN
FIRST THING I REMEMBER WAS THE WORD.
AND THE WORD WAS GOD.
SOMETIMES, WHEN I GET REALLY DOWN, I REMEMBER THE SOUND OF THE WORD IN MY HEAD...
SHAPING ME...
FORMING ME
GIVING ME LIFE
THE WORD GAVE ME A BODY, GAVE ME EYES...
...AND I OPENED MY EYES...

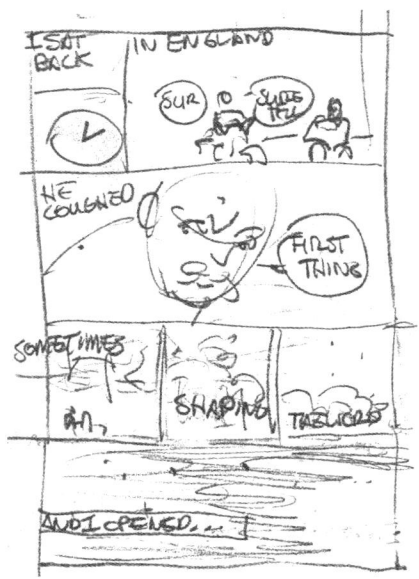

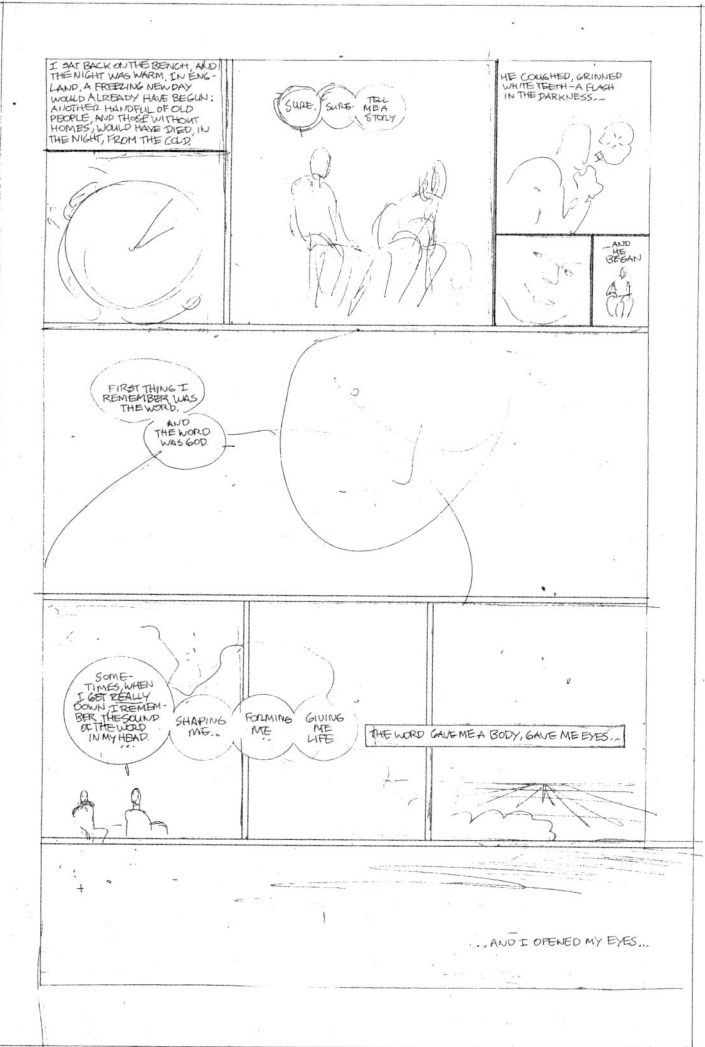

ANGELS AND VISITATIONS

the Darkness begins, and it was there, under a vast silver spire, that we descended to the street, and I saw the dead angel.

"The body lay, crumpled and broken, on the silver sidewalk. Its wings were crushed underneath it and a few loose feathers had already blown into the silver gutter.

"The body was almost dark. Now and again a light would flash inside it, an occasional flicker of cold fire in the chest, or in the eyes, or in the sexless groin, as the last of the glow of life left it for ever.

"Blood pooled in rubies on its chest and stained its white wing-feathers crimson. It was very beautiful, even in death.

"It would have broken your heart.

"Lucifer spoke to me, then. 'You must find who was responsible for this, and how; and take the Vengeance of the Name on whomever caused this thing to happen.'

"He really didn't have to say anything. I knew that already. The hunt, and the retribution, it was what I was created for, in the Beginning; it was what I *was*.

I LIFTED
YOU DID THIS

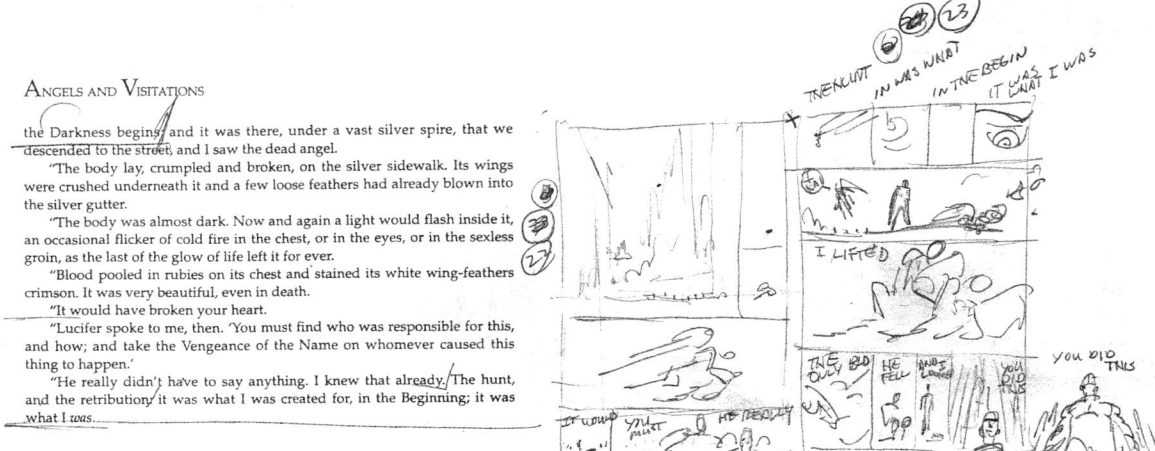

"It was what I was created for, in the beginning."

At the heart of most comics is the use of a grid. It is designed to help organize panels into an arrangement on the page. Using horizontal tiers, storytellers can separate events, time, or place. Relying on vertical columns, storytellers can then play with emphasis. Simply put, the larger a panel, the larger the moment. The rest of the panels on the page must somehow relate to and support this moment.

PCR: There are a lot of tricks in your bag to make a multipaneled page work. I've seen people who had three panels on a page and it's like a jungle of thorns, you can't even get into it. And you can do twelve or fourteen panels on a page and have [the storytelling] made very clear.

One of the things you can do is vary the panel size. Pick the panel on the page that might be larger than the rest, and then all of the other panels relate to it in some way. If you can't create a focal panel and are just doing panel after panel, then everything is competing for attention. If you're doing a lot of small panels in a row, you certainly shouldn't be putting a new background and a change of scene in every single one. If I do three or four panels in a row, it might be the same person talking with just a change of expression on the face.

Being able to change panel sizes creates a [storytelling] rhythm, and as a storyteller, I can make the panel size reflect the emotions of the characters. There are purists who believe that every panel should be the same size … nine-panel, six-panel, or whatever they're doing. And obviously, you can do great work that way—I mean, you could do a great painting using one color. But it seems to me, ultimately, boring. It seems to be throwing out one of the most effective tools we have that's the most unique to this form. It's like tension and release, and forte and piano, in music.

The original roughs for story page 25 opened with Raguel realizing his powers as an instrument of retribution. Since these panels work as a unit of action, this tier of action was repositioned to end story page 24 with a dramatic note.

PCR: There are three panels at the top [of the roughs] just coming in closer on the angel. Or you might think of it as four, three coming in closer and then the [close-up of the eye]. So those four panels work as a unit.

I think sometimes when you're doing these scenes, each page is autonomous and they all work within the story as a whole, but within the page you seem to have separate scenes, and certain things need to work as a unit. You're looking at it as not just as individual panels, but as groupings of panels. And you think of four panels in a row of the same person, it works as a single unit. So, when he says, "The hunt … and the retribution … it was what I was created for, in the beginning … it was what I was." That in itself is its own little drama, its own little unit there.

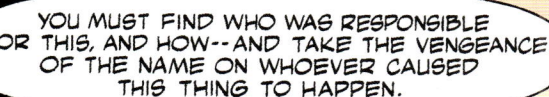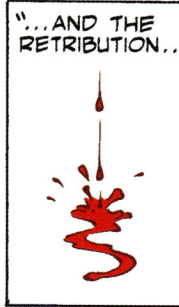

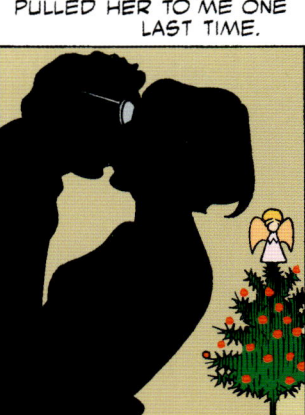

PANELS AND GRIDS

"A blank here, in my mind."

The use of a grid is crucial to clear storytelling. However, breaking the rules can also be effective. On page 15 of the story, Russell expands the height of a gutter to divide time and space while developing the story in a unique way.

PCR: That whole point seemed to be that there's this enormous piece missing. So why not try to visually show that instead of just relying on words? So you should try to get the reader to have the feeling, visually, that something is missing out of the story. Don't just tell them; come up with a way to show it. I deliberately put that square of copy down from the center, not just centering it, but so that the heavier part of the blank is above there. I didn't want it dead center because it would dominate that space. So I moved that down from the exact middle point and started it, and then the "perhaps" has its own little separate thing, and then widening out. In that last panel when he says, "I do know, however," I wanted to accentuate that horizontal feeling and balance it with what was above it there.

So that helps to make the last panel and the blank sort of a unit that works. But it's hard, sometimes, to stop and just let that space be a space.

All successful comics have vision, but the best comics also have a cadence, timing. The way the viewer reads the panels, the speed at which the words are read, and the way images are absorbed can be controlled by the storyteller. Russell modulates panel sizes much as a musician relies on phrasing to accentuate notes. Panel arrangements that are not merely formulaic can be symphonic to the eyes.

PCR: I've learned a lot from classical music, especially the romantic era. The way ideas and themes are developed and grow and mutate into other themes. There is this constant movement—even when there's something surprising—every idea unfolds into the next. A theme has an entrance and an exit almost like the character in a play.

Getting one picture to relate to the next is very fluid, which is almost, at least in the modern art world, a very conservative, almost nineteenth-century way of approaching arts. Twentieth-century developments were much more into a sharp, quick juxtaposition of one idea against the other without much transition. And I'm very linear and transitional. I think the good thing about that is that the viewer usually knows where they are in my story. And I've read other artists whose artwork I really like, but after three pages my eyes glaze over [because] I can't make the connection between the image and the writing.

CARASEL WAS A REMARKABLE DESIGNER. IF HE HAD ONE FAILING, IT WAS THAT HE THREW HIMSELF TOO DEEPLY INTO HIS WORK.
SARAQUAEL?
YOU'RE SHIVERING...
...SARAQUAEL...
AM I?

"Am I?"

On story page 47 of *Murder Mysteries*, Russell separates Saraquael in the last and smallest panel. However, the emotion resonating in this panel gives it more impact than any other panel on the page. The moment's power is a tribute to Russell's editing and then synthesizing his source material with his own vision to create this scene. This moment exists in the radio play but not in the short story.

PCR: I wanted to isolate Saraquael. Those two panels could have been a single panel, with the three angels in it, and "You're shivering … Saraquael … Am I?" [as two word balloons]. But, by creating a narrower panel, that gives us a chance for him to pull his arms up around him and isolate him from the others. He's not with them anymore.

Also, I'm [directing the eye] from that large close-up of Raguel. So you start with Raguel's face and the eyes looking to our right, towards Saraquael. And then up to, "You're shivering," and then you go down. You can just draw an arc from Raguel's eyes, through those word balloons, to the "Am I?" [word balloon] and down the little tail on the end.

YOU WALK ON THE EDGE OF THE CITY ?
YES.
THAT'S ALL I WANT TO KNOW...
...FOR NOW.
WHO ELSE HAVE YOU TALKED TO ?

"You walk on the edge of the city?"

Inspired by the music world, Russell has a storytelling style that can be described as lyrical. He possesses graceful line work and his panel arrangements have a melodic quality. Some moments are sustained while others are subdivided. On story page 36, the concept of timing is explored.

PCR: I spent a lot of time on these last four panels—arranging that lettering and the movement of time. So after the "You walk on the edge of the city?" panel, there is a silent panel.

I could have done that without the gutter between them, but putting the gutter in there forces you to see that next panel as a beat of time in which he is not answering. If we don't have the gutter and then in the next panel he says, "Yes," you don't really get an impression that he is hesitating. So just by putting that (silent panel) in there, it slows down the time, because he's pausing. And then (another example of graphic beats) in the next panel, when he says, "For now," and, "Who else have you talked to?" He answers immediately.

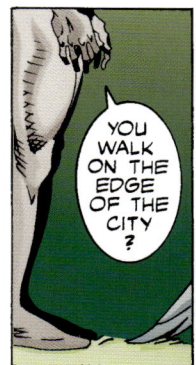

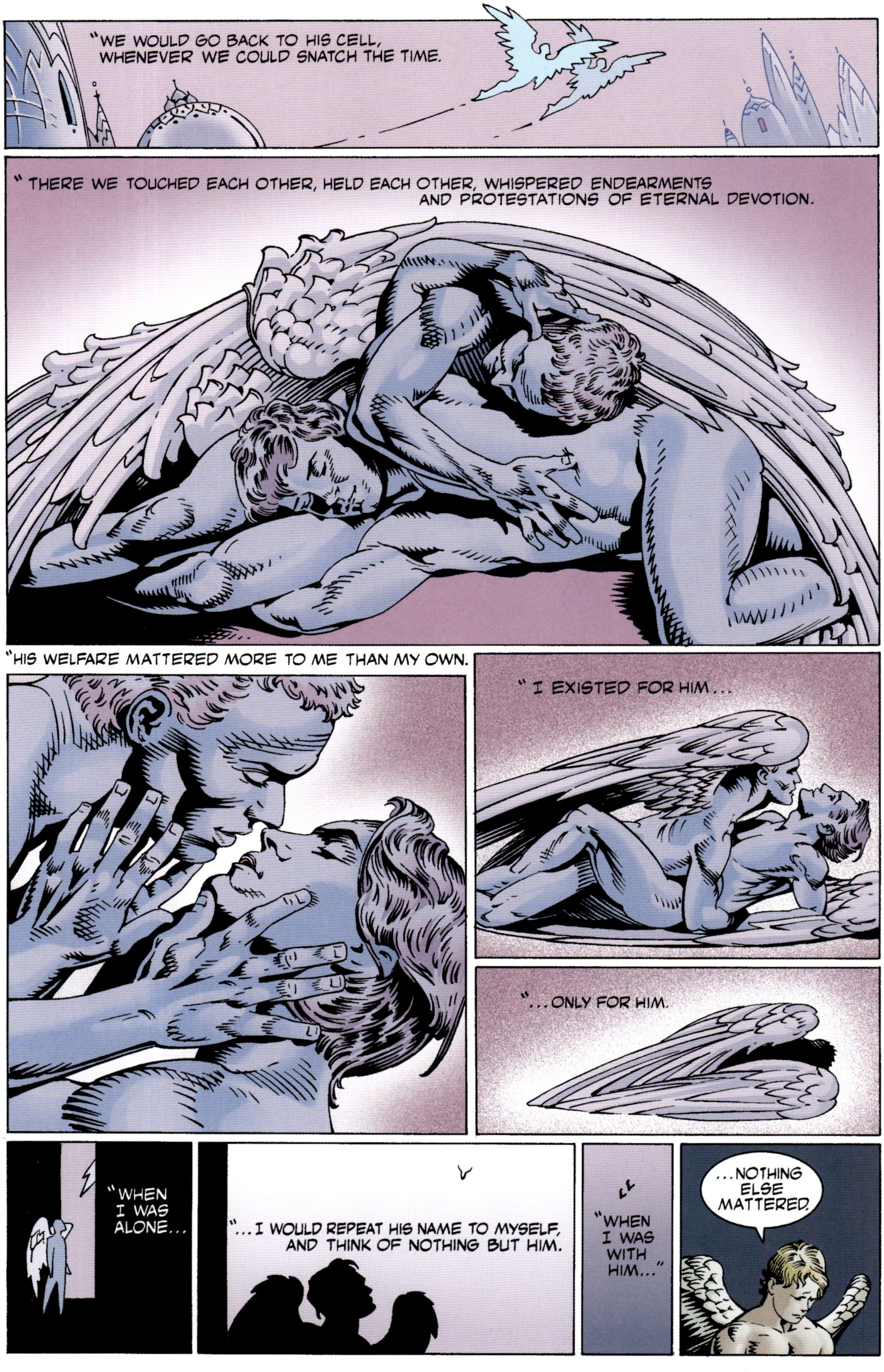
"WE WOULD GO BACK TO HIS CELL, WHENEVER WE COULD SNATCH THE TIME.
"THERE WE TOUCHED EACH OTHER, HELD EACH OTHER, WHISPERED ENDEARMENTS AND PROTESTATIONS OF ETERNAL DEVOTION.
"HIS WELFARE MATTERED MORE TO ME THAN MY OWN.
"I EXISTED FOR HIM...
"...ONLY FOR HIM.
"WHEN I WAS ALONE...
"...I WOULD REPEAT HIS NAME TO MYSELF, AND THINK OF NOTHING BUT HIM.
"WHEN I WAS WITH HIM..."
...NOTHING ELSE MATTERED.

PACING AND PHRASING

"When I was alone ...

I would repeat his name to myself,

and think of nothing but him.

When I was with him ...

nothing else mattered."

There is a balance a storyteller must strike when adapting someone else's work—between respect and results. Russell is a comic book artist who understands how to use panels to get the most from a story. On story page 49, breaking up dialogue over several panels instead of forcing the moment to be contained into one panel underscores Russell's talent as a visual storyteller.

PCR: Sometimes lines in a script all work as one short paragraph. As a storyteller, you might be tempted to just have a talking head [deliver all of the lines], which seem so important. I think those are frequently the moments where the writer is at his best, and yet they're the moments that resist visualization the most— I found that in *The Ring of the Nibelung* all the time. There were all sorts of things that were purely musical but that really needed to find some kind of visual structure for. I felt like the lines needed to split up, that they need to be dramatized on their own, almost like its own little four-panel story.

However, the images working up to this scene were almost completely visual. And here, Russell had to use his imagination to tell this story visually, as there were no real descriptions to use in the source material.

PCR: Since angels don't have a sexuality, I couldn't be too explicit on the love-making scene. So I left it to the imagination, as these wings almost sort of make a heart. And what they're doing in there, we'll never know.

P. Craig Russell has an understanding of color through his extensive painting background. He has worked with some of the finest colorists in comics and chooses to have an active hand in the coloring stage—if only to facilitate the story. Color is an important storytelling tool, one that is often overlooked. Russell views color as one of the most important tools in his bag of tricks.

PCR: The colorist and I go over the story page by page, sometimes panel by panel. My initial input is more conceptual; I'll talk about times of day if it's in the story. I'll ask for special effects sometimes, a certain glow. Sometimes I'll ask for noise or texture on a panel. Artists are sometimes discouraged from talking to anybody else on the project except the editor. There are editors who see this as sort of a power issue—they'll talk to the colorist, thank you very much. That's just ridiculous. You want the creative team to be talking to each other. You want people to be working on the same piece.

IT WAS DECEMBER, AND THE CALIFORNIA WEATHER WAS WARM AND PLEASANT.
ENGLAND, HOWEVER, WAS IN THE GRIP OF FOGS AND SNOWSTORMS, AND NO PLANES WERE LANDING THERE.
EACH DAY I'D PHONE THE AIRPORT, AND EACH DAY I'D BE TOLD TO WAIT ANOTHER DAY.
BE AN ANGEL GIVE GENEROUSLY
THIS HAD GONE ON FOR ALMOST A WEEK.

"It was December, and the California weather was warm and pleasant."

The first duty of color is to help establish a scene. In *Murder Mysteries*, color helps to establish physical details and environment. With a narrative that jumps from narrator to narrator and from heaven to earth, it becomes a priority to assign colors. Story page 7 exemplifies this concept. Palettes can be created to not only keep scenes consistent, but to standardize these choices for consistent use at a later time.

PCR: We used color to [define] the time of day and the flashback scenes. LA should be more muted, more realistic, less color, and grayed out to contrast with the scenes in heaven. We want that real clear contrast between the two phases of the story, partly because they should be, and also for clarity, so that the reader recognizes when they're in a different place.

We've done this for so many years that [Lovern and I] have kind of a repertoire of palettes. Now I can just say, "Do the blue night motif that we used from some of the *Jungle Book*, and then in *The Ring*." It's just a certain way of coloring at night, a certain set of blues, and flesh in the shadow. It's really lovely, and he knows exactly what I mean. And every project we seem to come up with maybe one or two more [palettes] that are new.

We had a series of greens in that *Lucifer* #50 that I said, "Ah! That goes in the bag. We'll be using that again." So it helps. You do want to be coming up with fresh stuff because you never know what the situation is going to be in the story. There's always going to be something that demands something we haven't done before.

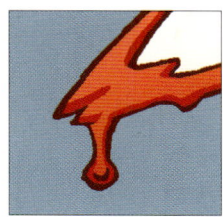

"It was what I was created for,

in the beginning."

A storyteller can shape decisions in the coloring stage. Moments of anger and other powerful emotions can be illustrated in black and white, but color can heighten these moments. On story page 24, these emotions are clarified by perceptive color choices.

PCR: This is the kind of thing, if you gave [the page] to the colorist just as a black-and-white piece of paper and didn't tell him anything, reading [the dialogue], a competent colorist would probably pick up on it anyhow. I think they would figure out that the blank panel, panel 10, was to be all red. But, sort of like a parent telling their child to be careful, I go over even the obvious stuff, just to be sure.

"THE HUNT...
"...AND THE RETRIBUTION...
"...IT WAS WHAT I WAS CREATED FOR, IN THE BEGINNING...
"...IT WAS WHAT I WAS."

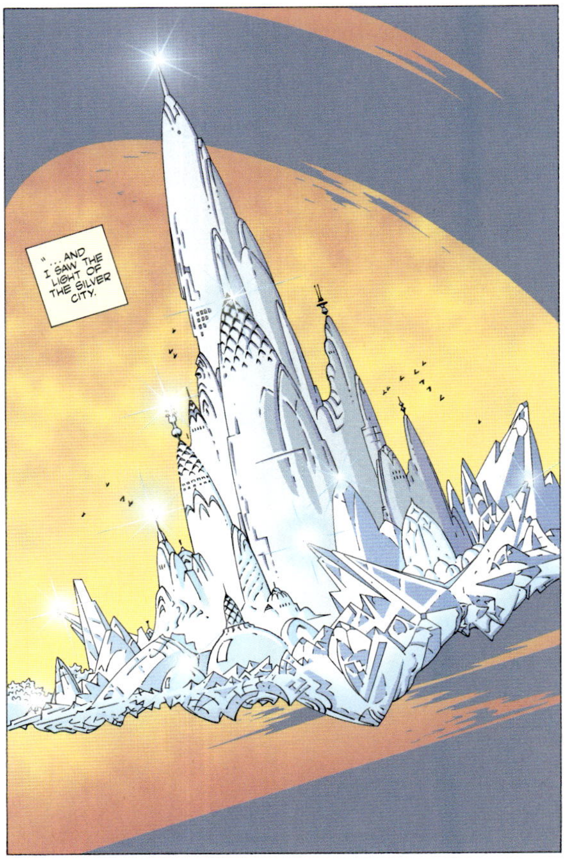
"...AND I SAW THE LIGHT OF THE SILVER CITY."

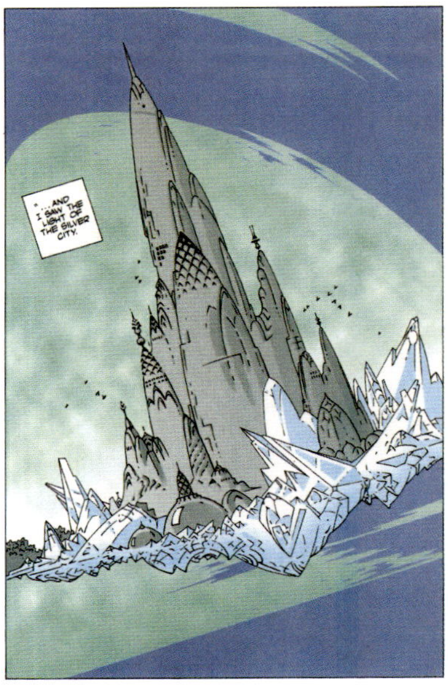
"...AND I SAW THE LIGHT OF THE SILVER CITY."

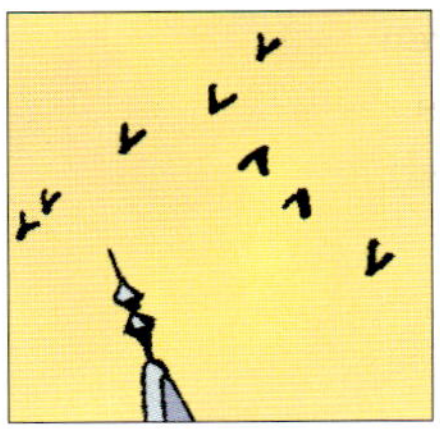

"And I saw the light of the silver city."

Sometimes, when creating comics, the storyteller must become the art director. If a vision is clear in the artist's mind, then they must direct to preserve the clarity. Story page 20 was actually colored twice to achieve the right feeling. It was a difficult decision, but one that paid off for the story.

PCR: That first one was his first take on it, and I thought, "That's not working." So sometimes I'll ask for a complete redo of something. I'll say, "He's opening his eyes, yes, it's not drab, but we need more depth. It should feel like early morning, and warmer. At the same time that it's kind of coolly silver, there should be something warmer." And the second time Lovern nailed it.

CREATING FLOW

Directing the reader from panel to panel, then page to page, is the first duty of a sequential artist. Grids and gutters certainly help organize eye movement, but the way characters move on a page can also help direct action and narration. Excessive detail can confuse the reader, and though Russell can render breathtaking backgrounds in every panel, he often relies on negative space to expedite flow.

PCR: You can also direct the eye in certain ways so that you're not lost. Eye movement is directed in a line—hopefully a pleasing yet a confident line—that leads you through the page. [As a storyteller] you're demanding a lot more from yourself. If you're demanding a lot from the reader, you haven't solved the problem.

Hal Foster and Jeff Jones [are] absolute geniuses at negative space. I was also inspired by the Japanese woodblock artists of the seventeenth, eighteenth century. There was [*ukiyo-e* prints] with three geishas walking down the road in all of these patterned kimonos. You would look to the shape of the negative space in relation to the edges of [the subject]. The nothingness, the rhythm of the shapes ... There was never a moment when your eye wasn't activated, and yet at the same time soothed. It was energetic, and yet it was never confusing. And you could follow these kimonos, almost like the coastline of a continent, and you had the feeling that there was nothing left to chance. It was always carefully planned, these spaces, and yet there was never the feeling of it being labored.

"And then it fell into place. I saw the whole picture ..."

During the climax of *Murder Mysteries*, the reader finally understands the consequences of the original murder. Story pages 53–56 underscore how all of these storytelling devices—pacing, word balloons, panels, and color—come together to carry the reader towards the end. It's the turning point of the story, and Russell lets the words drive the narrative.

PCR: Towards the end, we see Zephkiel, who, of course, is God. And he is just another character in the story until Raguel realizes and says, "I returned to myself once more." And you see Phanuel on his knees, and Lucifer just sort of observing, and then that strange light in the eyes of Zephkiel on the bottom. After that, after Lucifer leaves, you never see God again, because once you know who he is, you can't look in the face. So he disappears. Once we realize who it is, he disappears from the story. And we see him as a silhouette, and then all of his word balloons after that are all off panel. And at one point, when he says, "I looked into his old, old eyes," and I wonder if he should even have done that, but I guess, since he's an angel, they can. But he covers his eyes, sort of shields them, when he says, "It was my function."

 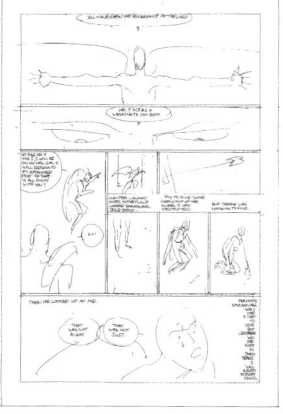 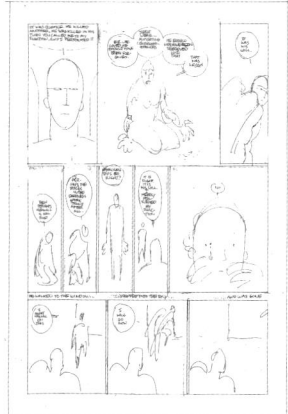 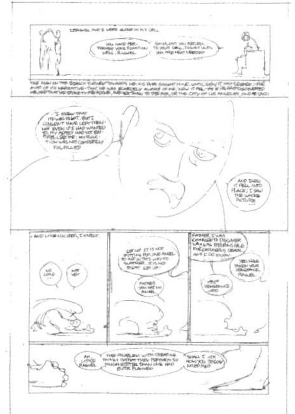

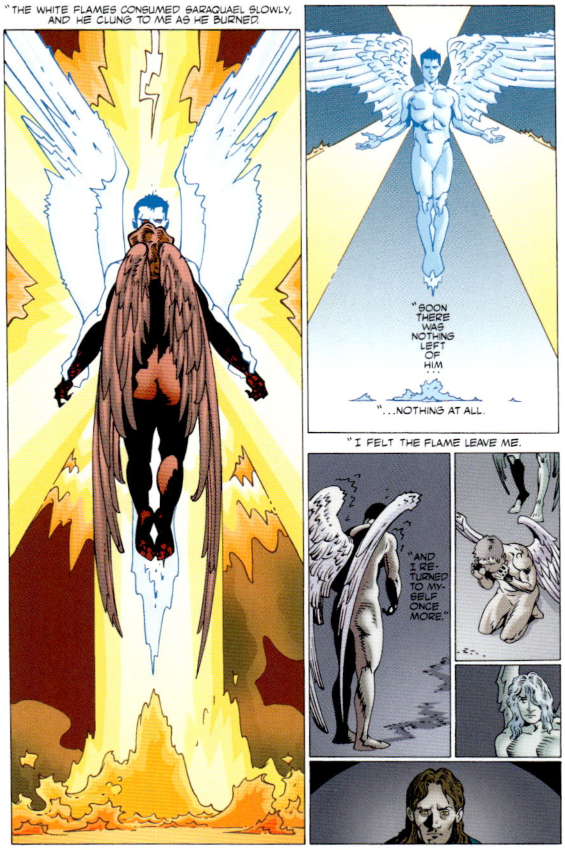
"THE WHITE FLAMES CONSUMED SARAQUAEL SLOWLY, AND HE CLUNG TO ME AS HE BURNED.
"SOON THERE WAS NOTHING LEFT OF HIM . . .
". . .NOTHING AT ALL.
"I FELT THE FLAME LEAVE ME.
"AND I RETURNED TO MYSELF ONCE MORE."

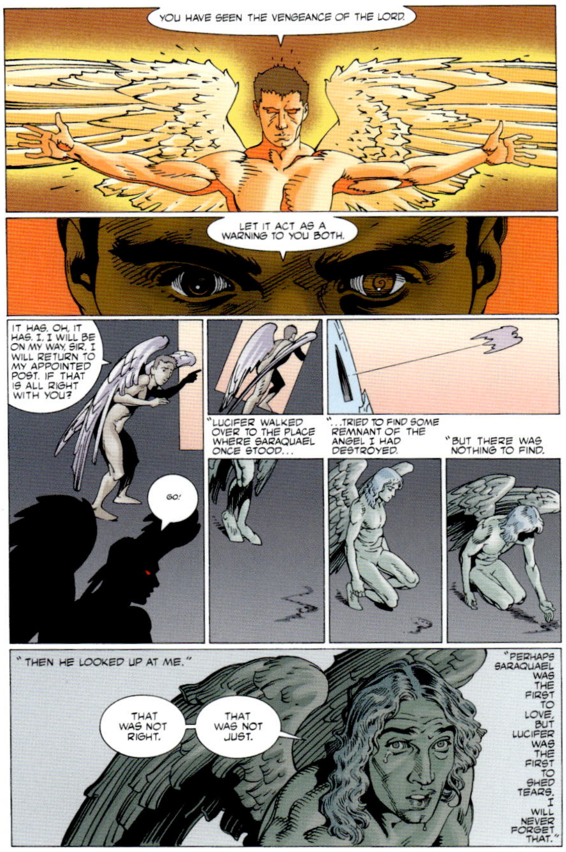
YOU HAVE SEEN THE VENGEANCE OF THE LORD.
LET IT ACT AS A WARNING TO YOU BOTH.
IT HAS. OH, IT HAS. I, I WILL BE ON MY WAY, SIR. I WILL RETURN TO MY APPOINTED POST. IF THAT IS ALL RIGHT WITH YOU?
GO!
"LUCIFER WALKED OVER TO THE PLACE WHERE SARAQUAEL ONCE STOOD...
"...TRIED TO FIND SOME REMNANT OF THE ANGEL I HAD DESTROYED.
"BUT THERE WAS NOTHING TO FIND.
"THEN HE LOOKED UP AT ME."
THAT WAS NOT RIGHT.
THAT WAS NOT JUST.
"PERHAPS SARAQUAEL WAS THE FIRST TO LOVE, BUT LUCIFER WAS THE FIRST TO SHED TEARS. I WILL NEVER FORGET THAT."

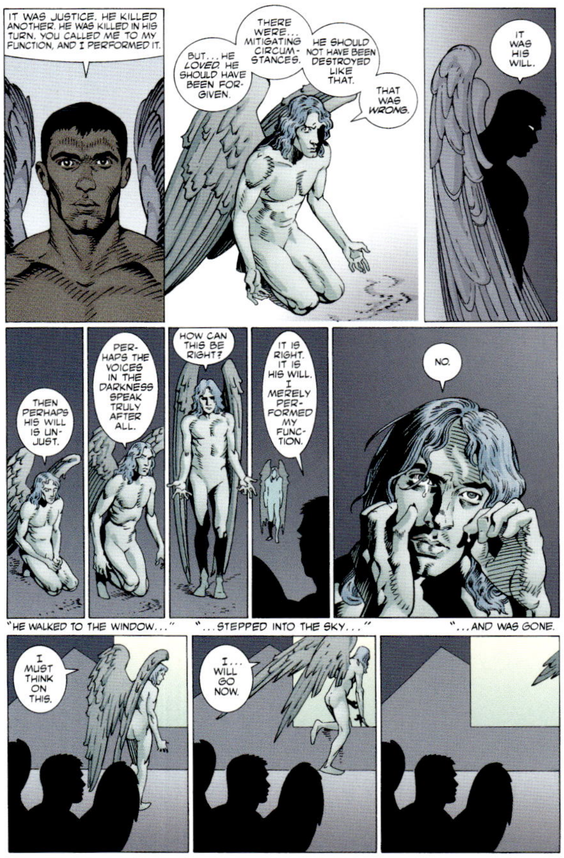
IT WAS JUSTICE. HE KILLED ANOTHER. HE WAS KILLED IN HIS TURN. YOU CALLED ME TO MY FUNCTION, AND I PERFORMED IT.
BUT... HE LOVED. HE SHOULD HAVE BEEN FORGIVEN.
THERE WERE... MITIGATING CIRCUMSTANCES.
HE SHOULD NOT HAVE BEEN DESTROYED LIKE THAT.
THAT WAS WRONG.
IT WAS HIS WILL.
THEN PERHAPS HIS WILL IS UNJUST.
PERHAPS THE VOICES IN THE DARKNESS SPEAK TRULY AFTER ALL.
HOW CAN THIS BE RIGHT?
IT IS RIGHT. IT IS HIS WILL. I MERELY PERFORMED MY FUNCTION.
NO.
"HE WALKED TO THE WINDOW..."
I MUST THINK ON THIS.
"...STEPPED INTO THE SKY..."
I... WILL GO NOW.
"...AND WAS GONE.

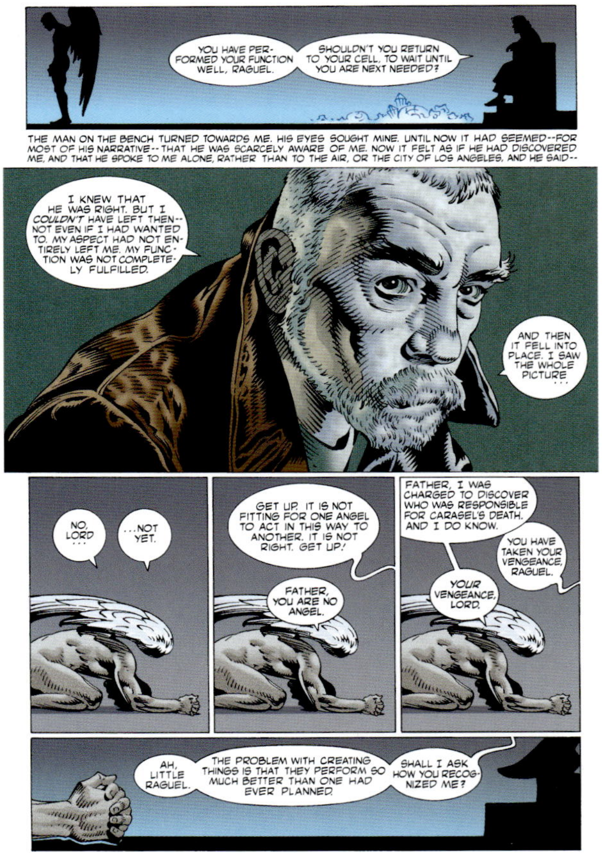
YOU HAVE PERFORMED YOUR FUNCTION WELL, RAGUEL.
SHOULDN'T YOU RETURN TO YOUR CELL, TO WAIT UNTIL YOU ARE NEXT NEEDED?
THE MAN ON THE BENCH TURNED TOWARDS ME. HIS EYES SOUGHT MINE. UNTIL NOW IT HAD SEEMED--FOR MOST OF HIS NARRATIVE--THAT HE WAS SCARCELY AWARE OF ME. NOW IT FELT AS IF HE HAD DISCOVERED ME, AND THAT HE SPOKE TO ME ALONE, RATHER THAN TO THE AIR, OR THE CITY OF LOS ANGELES, AND HE SAID--
I KNEW THAT HE WAS RIGHT. BUT I COULDN'T HAVE LEFT THEN--NOT EVEN IF I HAD WANTED TO. MY ASPECT HAD NOT ENTIRELY LEFT ME. MY FUNCTION WAS NOT COMPLETELY FULFILLED.
AND THEN IT FELL INTO PLACE. I SAW THE WHOLE PICTURE . . .
NO, LORD
. . .NOT YET.
GET UP. IT IS NOT FITTING FOR ONE ANGEL TO ACT IN THIS WAY TO ANOTHER. IT IS NOT RIGHT. GET UP!
FATHER, YOU ARE NO ANGEL.
FATHER, I WAS CHARGED TO DISCOVER WHO WAS RESPONSIBLE FOR CARASEL'S DEATH. AND I DO KNOW.
YOUR VENGEANCE, LORD.
YOU HAVE TAKEN YOUR VENGEANCE, RAGUEL.
AH, LITTLE RAGUEL.
THE PROBLEM WITH CREATING THINGS IS THAT THEY PERFORM SO MUCH BETTER THAN ONE HAD EVER PLANNED.
SHALL I ASK HOW YOU RECOGNIZED ME?

"…And I knew that

I would soon be home."

In the original radio play, the narrator possessed a more agitated voice, confined in his cell, his life over. But after consulting with the writer, Russell was encouraged to take creative liberties to make the most appropriate ending to the *Murder Mysteries* graphic novel.

I FEEL AS IF I'VE RECEIVED A GIFT, UNASKED, FROM ANOTHER PERSON--A HOUSE, A WIFE, CHILDREN, A VOCATION.

PCR: (Story page 65) is almost a perversely happy ending. In the beginning of the story, when he's talking from the present time, we see him in his little cell behind those windows, looking out into the yard. It's like he's in the same place that Raguel was, in his little cell. There's all these people in little boxes. Using the motif of the feathers, he seems to be calm and knows that he's going to be home. But there's still something, just by [the panels] getting smaller and smaller and this blackness around him, just growing. And the previous page, he's on the airplane and that tiny little dot against the void and this memory is gone, and that piece of his past is gone. So here he is in the black, and getting smaller in this little silver room, that's when we bring in this rain of feathers that recalls the murder at the beginning of the story, so it's still all around him, somehow. I try to come up with some visual motifs that work on their own in the course of the story, that help to just make it visually knitted together. So when he says in that first line, "This is all true," you see already those feathers fading out in the sky behind him. So you have those in the very beginning of the story, and then at the end it's just like it starts snowing again. I think I may have talked to Neil about the ending, and it was sort of a contradiction. We went for the calmer ending.

MURDER MYSTERIES SKETCHBOOK

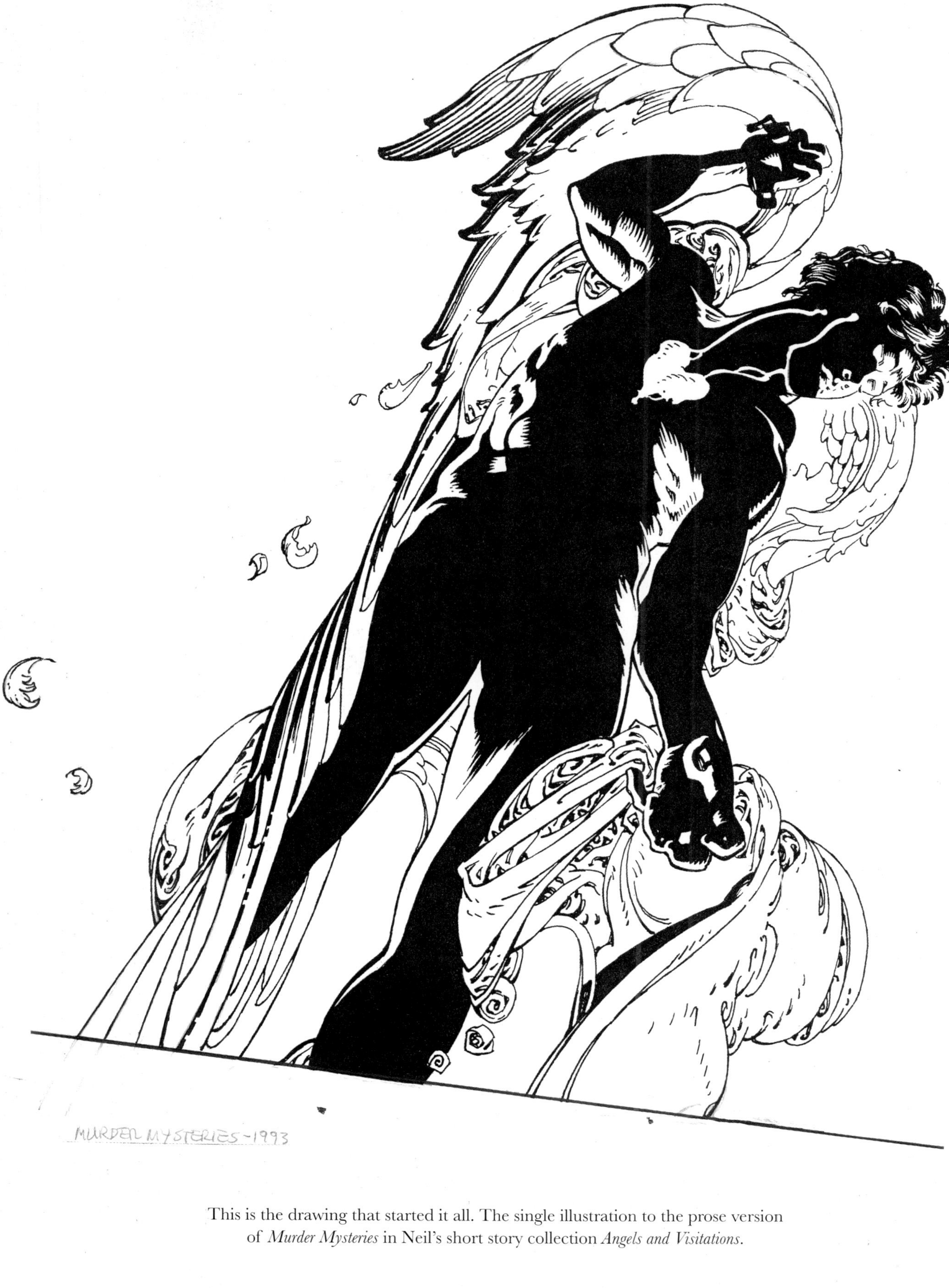
MURDER MYSTERIES -1993

This is the drawing that started it all. The single illustration to the prose version of *Murder Mysteries* in Neil's short story collection *Angels and Visitations*.

THIS IS MAD
YOU DON'T
FOR
NO
GOD
HMMH

THIS IS ALL TRUE
TEN YEARS AGO
ENGLAND
THIS HAD GONE ON
I WAS LOOKING AS IF I'VE
NOTHING
IF IT'S TRUE
THIS HAD

MURDER MYSTERIES
THIS IS ALL
BE AN ANGEL - GIVE GENEROUSLY
MURDER MYSTERIES
MURDER MYSTERIES

Murder Mysteries

The Fourth Angel says:

Of this order I am made one,
From Mankind to guard this place
That through their Guilt they have foregone,
For they have forfeited His Grace;
Therefore all this must they shun
Or else my Sword they shall embrace
And myself will be their Foe
To flame them in the Face.

Chester Mystery Cycle:
The Creation, and Adam and Eve, 1461.

This is true.

Ten years ago, give or take a year, I found myself on an enforced stopover in Los Angeles, a long way from home. It was December, and the California weather was warm and pleasant/England, however, was in the grip of fogs and snowstorms, and no planes were landing there. Each day I'd phone the airport, and each day I'd be told to wait another day.

This had gone on for almost a week.

I was barely out of my teens. Looking around today at the parts of my life left over from those days, I feel uncomfortable, as if I've received a gift, unasked, from another person: a house, a wife, children, a vocation. Nothing to do with me, I could say, innocently. If it's true that every seven years each cell in your body dies and is replaced, then I have truly inherited my life

139

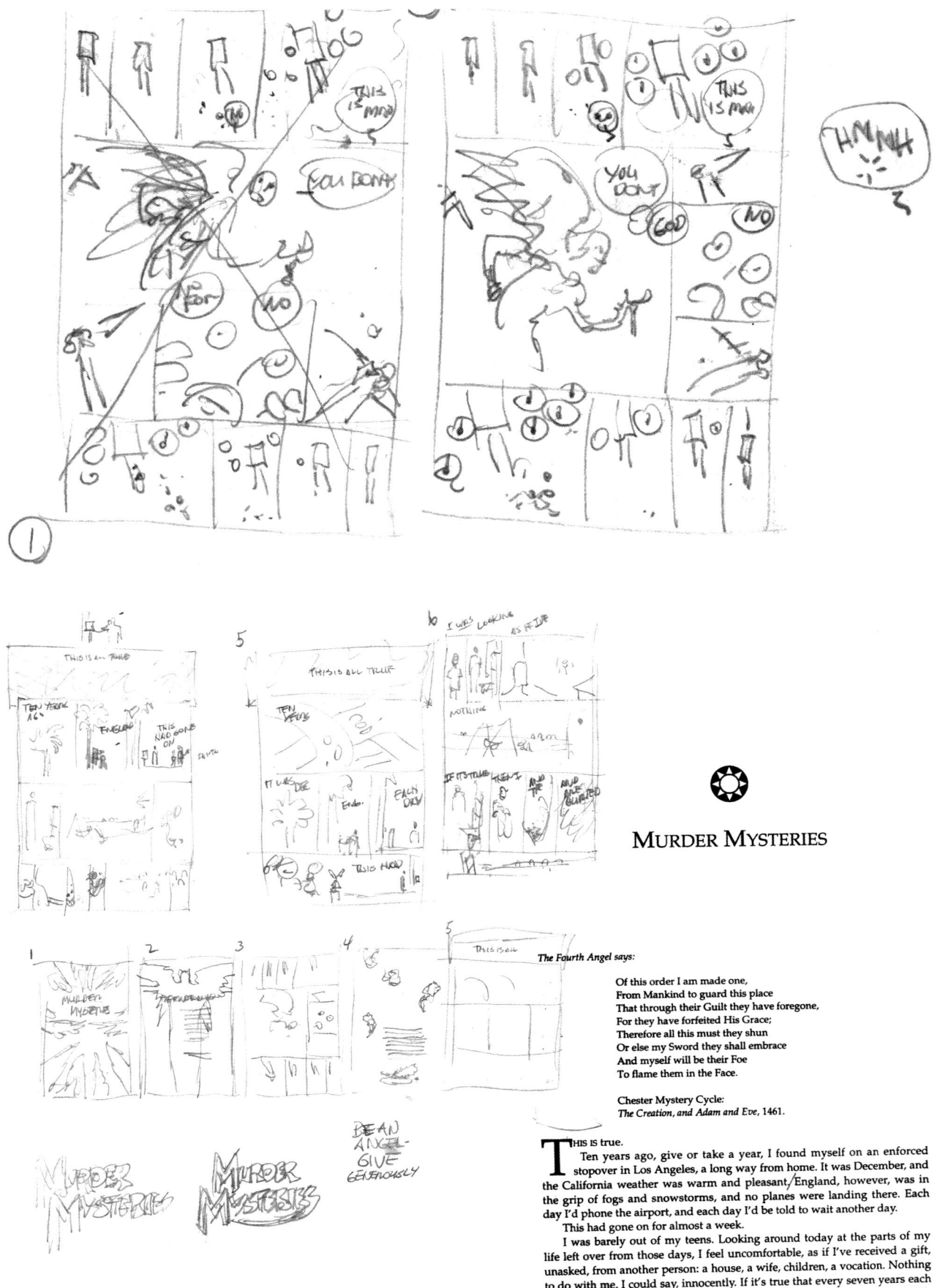

First page of Neil's radio play version of *Murder Mysteries*. The slash marks between sentences show my first thoughts on breaking down sentences and paragraphs into word balloons and panels.

Angels and Visitations

"Susan's upstairs, asleep," said Tink. "She's all I live for. Would you like to see her?"

"I don't mind."

We went upstairs. Tink led me into a darkened bedroom. There were child-scrawl pictures all over the walls — wax-crayoned drawings of winged fairies and little palaces — and a small, fair-haired girl was asleep in the bed.

"She's very beautiful," said Tink, and kissed me. Her lips were still slightly sticky. "She takes after her father."

We went downstairs. We had nothing else to say, nothing else to do. Tink turned on the main light. For the first time I noticed tiny crows' feet at the corners of her eyes, incongruous on her perfect, Barbie-doll face.

"I love you," she said.

"Thank you."

"Would you like a ride back?"

"If you don't mind leaving Susan alone...?"

She shrugged, and I pulled her to me for the last time.

At night, Los Angeles is all lights. And shadows.

A blank, here, in my mind. I simply don't remember what happened next. She must have driven me back to the place where I was staying — how else would I have gotten there? I do not even remember kissing her goodbye. Perhaps I simply waited on the sidewalk and watched her drive away.

Perhaps.

I do know, however, that once I reached the place I was staying I just stood there, unable to go inside, to wash and then to sleep, unwilling to do anything else.

I was not hungry. I did not want alcohol. I did not want to read, or talk. I was scared of walking too far, in case I became lost, bedeviled by the repeating motifs of Los Angeles, spun around and sucked in so I could never find my way home again. Central Los Angeles sometimes seems to me to be nothing more than a pattern, like a set of repeating blocks: a gas station, a few homes, a mini-mall (donuts, photo developers, laundromats, fast-foods), and repeat until hypnotised; and the tiny changes in the mini-malls and the houses only se

I thought

pulled out a pa

I lit one, in

Murder Mysteries

There was a stunted palm tree growing outside the place I was staying, and I resolved to walk for a way, keeping the tree in sight, to smoke my cigarette, perhaps even to think; but I felt too drained to think. I felt very sexless, and very alone.

A block or so down the road there was a bench, and when I reached it I sat down. I threw the stub of the cigarette onto the pavement, hard, and watched it shower orange sparks.

Someone said, "I'll buy a cigarette off you, pal. Here."

A hand, in front of my face, holding a quarter. I looked up.

He did not look old, although I would not have been prepared to say how old he was. Late thirties, perhaps. Mid-forties. He wore a long, shabby coat, colorless under the yellow street lamps, and his eyes were dark.

"Here. A quarter. That's a good price."

I shook my head, pulled out the packet of Marlboros, offered him one. "Keep your money. It's free. Have it."

He took the cigarette. I passed him a book of matches (it advertised a telephone sex line; I remember that), and he lit the cigarette. He offered me the matches back, and I shook my head. "Keep them. I always wind up accumulating books of matches in America."

"Uh-huh." He sat next to me, and smoked his cigarette. When he had smoked it halfway down, he tapped the lighted end off on the concrete, stubbed out the glow, and placed the butt of the cigarette behind his ear.

"I don't smoke much," he said. "Seems a pity to waste it, though."

A car careened down the road, veering from one side to the other. There were four young men in the car: the two in the front were both pulling at the wheel, and laughing. The windows were wound down, and I could hear their laughter, and the two in the back seat (*"Gaary, you asshole! What the fuck are you onnn mannnn?"*) and the pulsing beat of a rock song. Not a song I recognised. The car looped around a corner, out of sight.

Soon the sounds were gone, too.

"I owe you," said the man on the bench.

"Sorry?"

"I owe you something. For the cigarette. And the matches. You wouldn't take the money. I owe you."

I shrugged, embarrassed. "Really, it's just a cigarette. I figure, if I give people cigarettes, then if ever I'm out, maybe people will give me cigarettes."

143

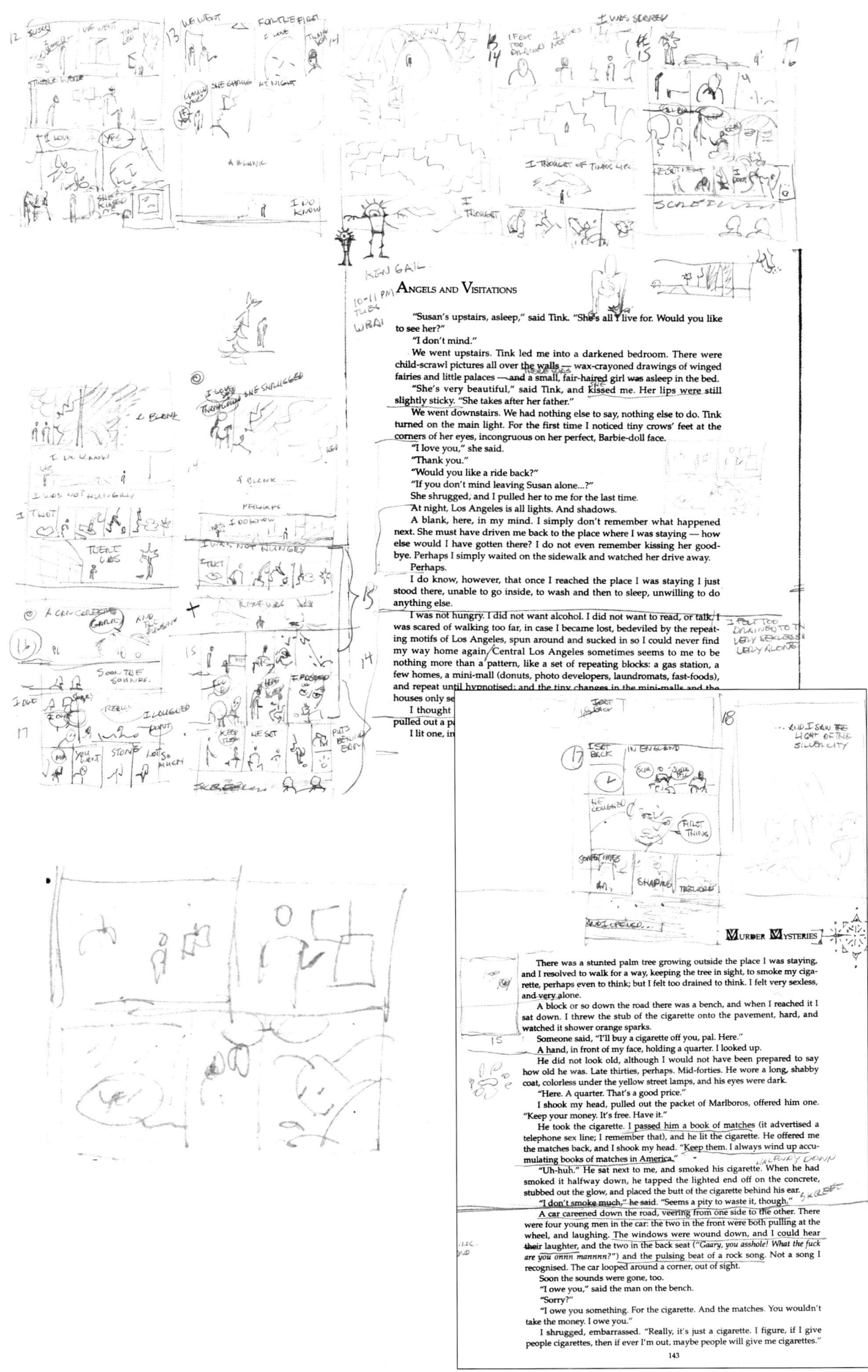

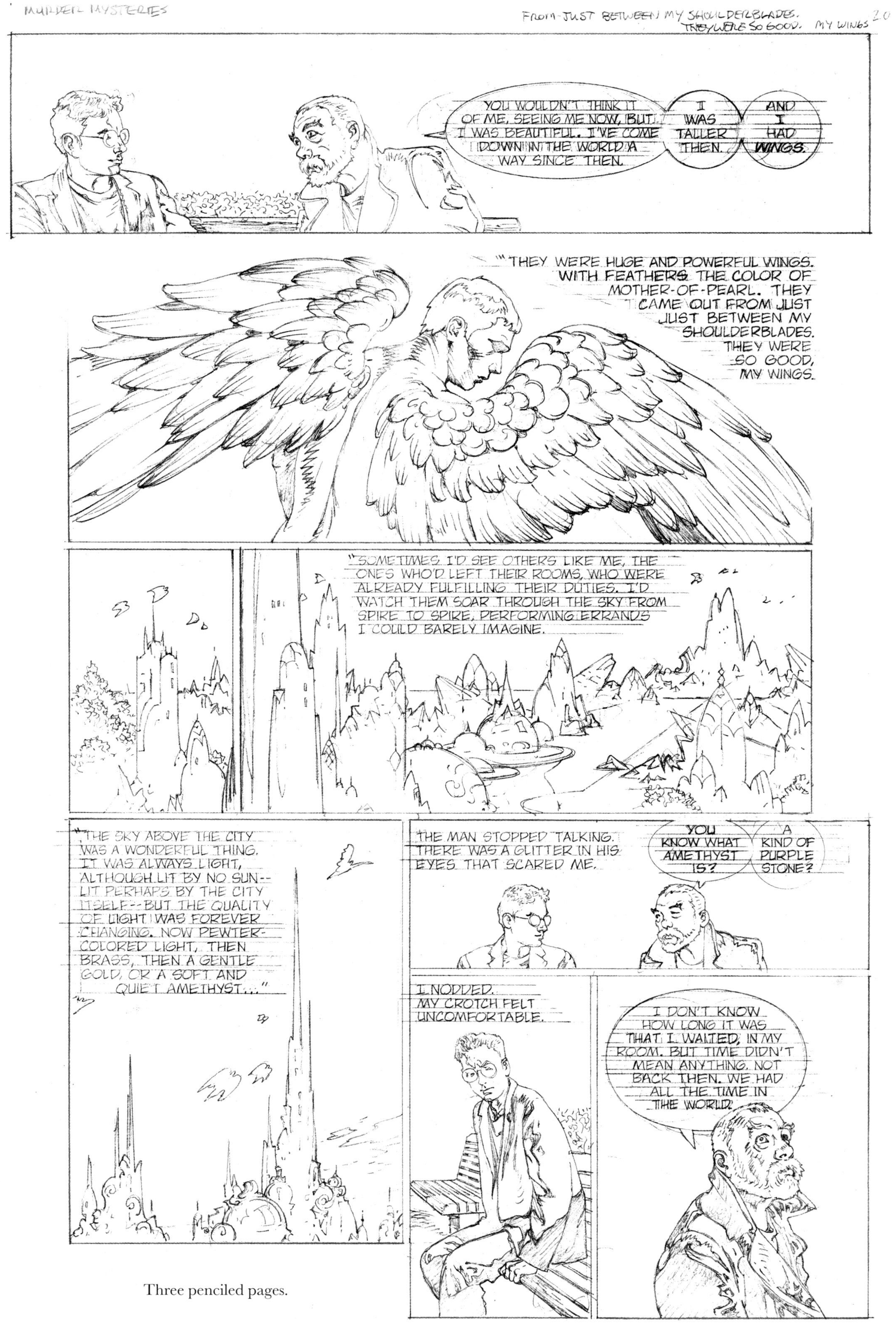
MURDER MYSTERIES
FROM-JUST BETWEEN MY SHOULDERBLADES. THEY WERE SO GOOD. MY WINGS
20
YOU WOULDN'T THINK IT OF ME, SEEING ME NOW, BUT I WAS BEAUTIFUL. I'VE COME DOWN IN THE WORLD A WAY SINCE THEN.
I WAS TALLER THEN.
AND I HAD WINGS.
"THEY WERE HUGE AND POWERFUL WINGS. WITH FEATHERS THE COLOR OF MOTHER-OF-PEARL. THEY CAME OUT FROM JUST JUST BETWEEN MY SHOULDERBLADES. THEY WERE SO GOOD, MY WINGS.
"SOMETIMES I'D SEE OTHERS LIKE ME, THE ONES WHO'D LEFT THEIR ROOMS, WHO WERE ALREADY FULFILLING THEIR DUTIES. I'D WATCH THEM SOAR THROUGH THE SKY FROM SPIRE TO SPIRE, PERFORMING ERRANDS I COULD BARELY IMAGINE.
"THE SKY ABOVE THE CITY WAS A WONDERFUL THING. IT WAS ALWAYS LIGHT, ALTHOUGH LIT BY NO SUN-- LIT PERHAPS BY THE CITY ITSELF--BUT THE QUALITY OF LIGHT WAS FOREVER CHANGING. NOW PEWTER-COLORED LIGHT, THEN BRASS, THEN A GENTLE GOLD, OR A SOFT AND QUIET AMETHYST..."
THE MAN STOPPED TALKING. THERE WAS A GLITTER IN HIS EYES THAT SCARED ME.
YOU KNOW WHAT AMETHYST IS?
A KIND OF PURPLE STONE?
I NODDED. MY CROTCH FELT UNCOMFORTABLE.
I DON'T KNOW HOW LONG IT WAS THAT I WAITED, IN MY ROOM. BUT TIME DIDN'T MEAN ANYTHING. NOT BACK THEN. WE HAD ALL THE TIME IN THE WORLD.

Three penciled pages.

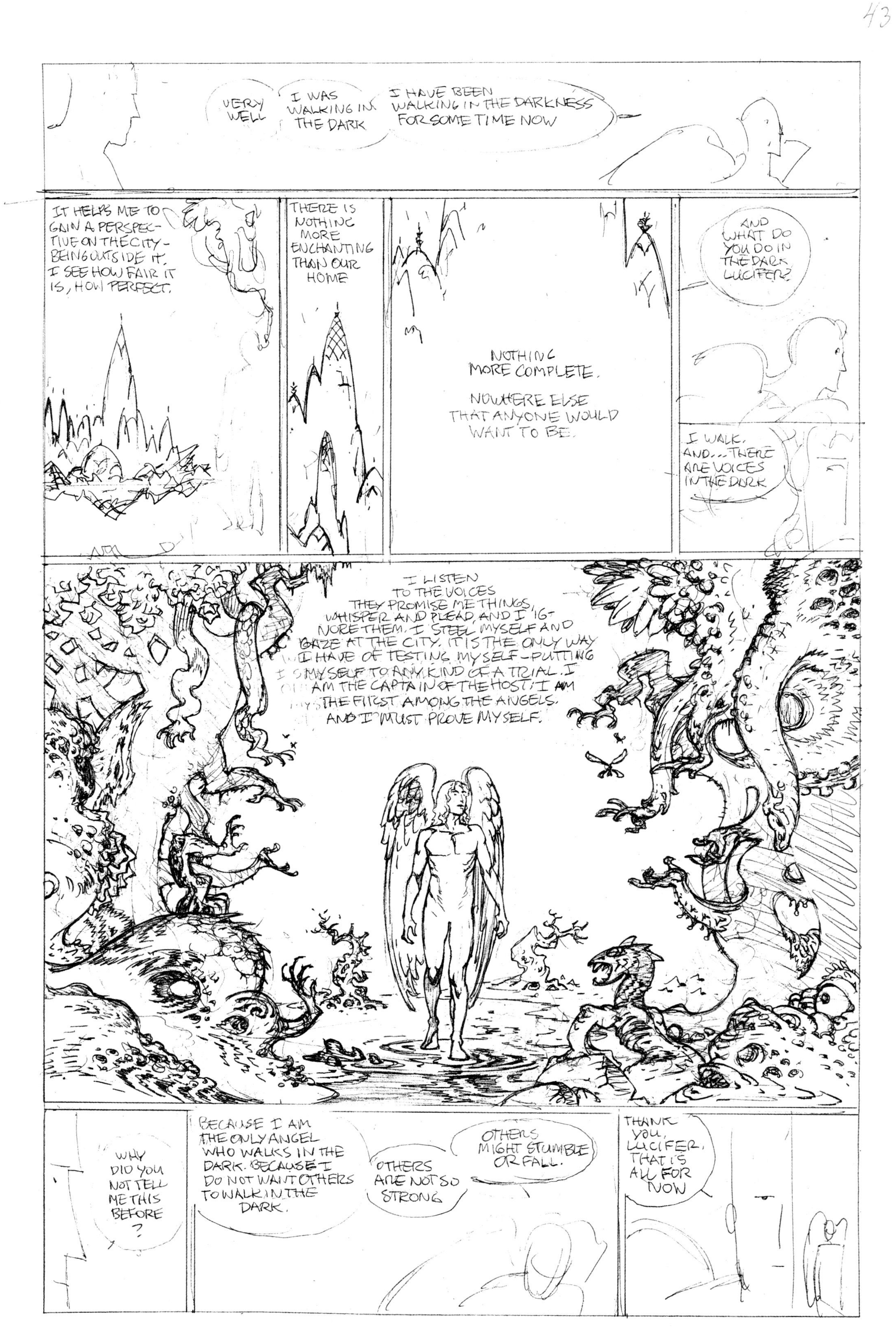
43
VERY WELL
I WAS WALKING IN THE DARK
I HAVE BEEN WALKING IN THE DARKNESS FOR SOME TIME NOW
IT HELPS ME TO GAIN A PERSPECTIVE ON THE CITY - BEING OUTSIDE IT. I SEE HOW FAIR IT IS, HOW PERFECT.
THERE IS NOTHING MORE ENCHANTING THAN OUR HOME
NOTHING MORE COMPLETE.
NOWHERE ELSE THAT ANYONE WOULD WANT TO BE.
AND WHAT DO YOU DO IN THE DARK LUCIFER?
I WALK. AND... THERE ARE VOICES IN THE DARK
I LISTEN TO THE VOICES THEY PROMISE ME THINGS, WHISPER AND PLEAD, AND I IGNORE THEM. I STEEL MYSELF AND GAZE AT THE CITY. IT IS THE ONLY WAY I HAVE OF TESTING MYSELF - PUTTING MYSELF TO ANY KIND OF A TRIAL. I AM THE CAPTAIN OF THE HOST; I AM THE FIRST AMONG THE ANGELS. AND I MUST PROVE MYSELF.
WHY DID YOU NOT TELL ME THIS BEFORE ?
BECAUSE I AM THE ONLY ANGEL WHO WALKS IN THE DARK. BECAUSE I DO NOT WANT OTHERS TO WALK IN THE DARK.
OTHERS ARE NOT SO STRONG
OTHERS MIGHT STUMBLE OR FALL.
THANK YOU, LUCIFER. THAT IS ALL FOR NOW

Pencil page, inked page, and a color note page. Lovern and I discuss coloring over the phone and online.
I rarely, if ever, produce hard copy color notes. This was one of those rare times.

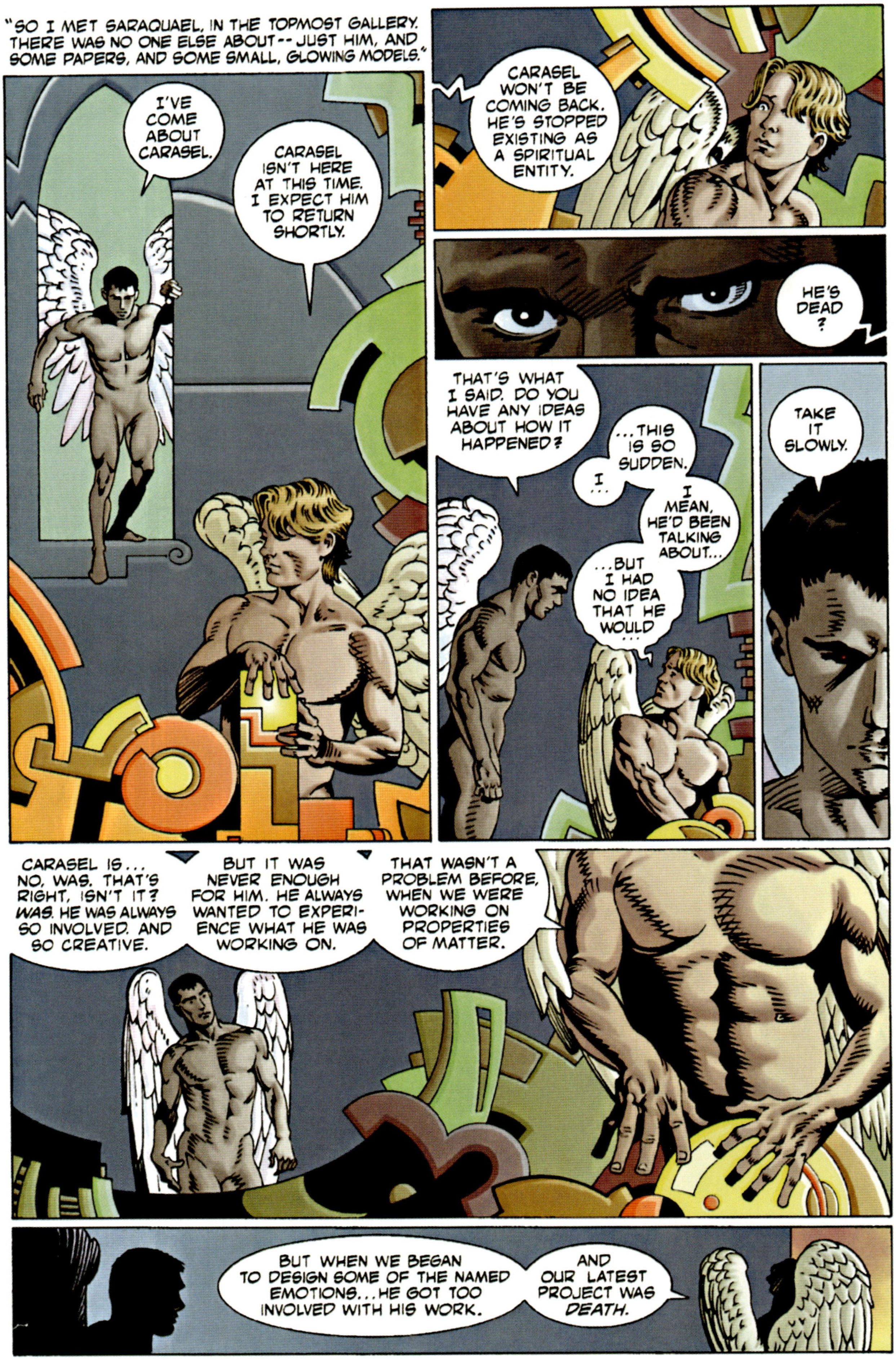
"SO I MET SARAQUAEL, IN THE TOPMOST GALLERY. THERE WAS NO ONE ELSE ABOUT-- JUST HIM, AND SOME PAPERS, AND SOME SMALL, GLOWING MODELS."
I'VE COME ABOUT CARASEL.
CARASEL ISN'T HERE AT THIS TIME. I EXPECT HIM TO RETURN SHORTLY.
CARASEL WON'T BE COMING BACK. HE'S STOPPED EXISTING AS A SPIRITUAL ENTITY.
HE'S DEAD ?
THAT'S WHAT I SAID. DO YOU HAVE ANY IDEAS ABOUT HOW IT HAPPENED?
I ...
...THIS IS SO SUDDEN.
I MEAN, HE'D BEEN TALKING ABOUT...
...BUT I HAD NO IDEA THAT HE WOULD ...
TAKE IT SLOWLY.
CARASEL IS... NO, WAS. THAT'S RIGHT, ISN'T IT? WAS. HE WAS ALWAYS SO INVOLVED. AND SO CREATIVE.
BUT IT WAS NEVER ENOUGH FOR HIM. HE ALWAYS WANTED TO EXPERIENCE WHAT HE WAS WORKING ON.
THAT WASN'T A PROBLEM BEFORE, WHEN WE WERE WORKING ON PROPERTIES OF MATTER.
BUT WHEN WE BEGAN TO DESIGN SOME OF THE NAMED EMOTIONS...HE GOT TOO INVOLVED WITH HIS WORK.
AND OUR LATEST PROJECT WAS DEATH.

First draft coloring and second draft coloring. Note that we added warmth to panels four to seven in the second draft.

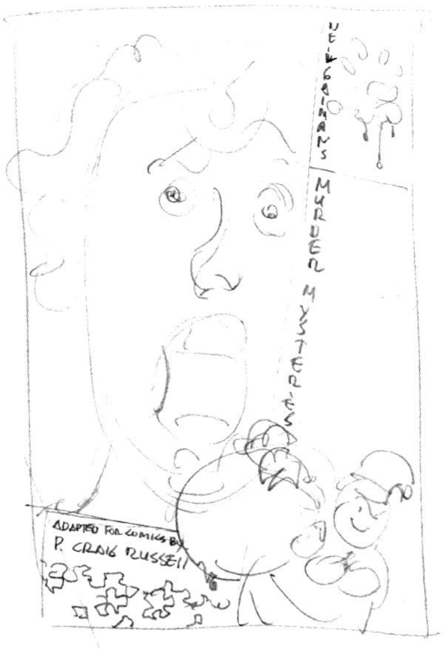
NEIL GAIMAN'S
MURDER MYSTERIES
ADAPTED FOR COMICS BY
P. CRAIG RUSSELL

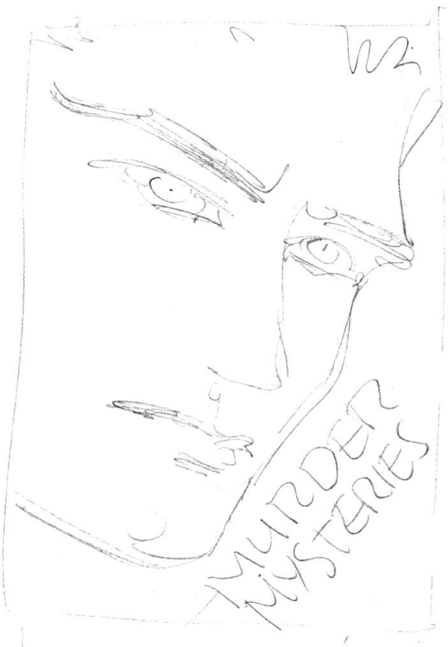
MURDER MYSTERIES

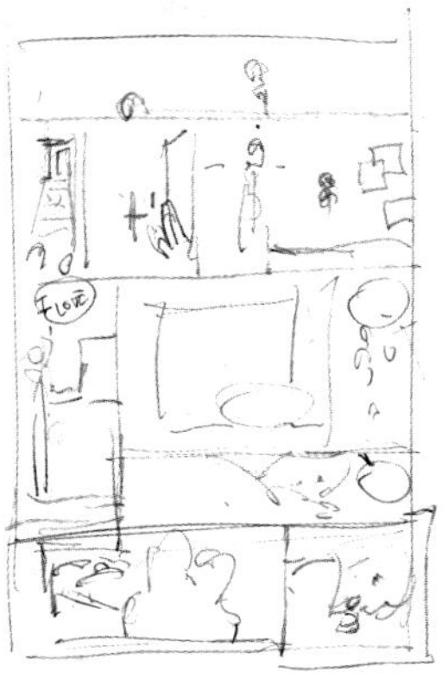

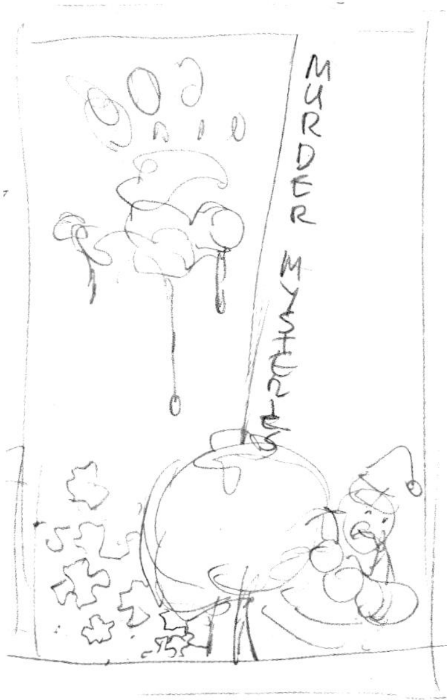
MURDER MYSTERIES

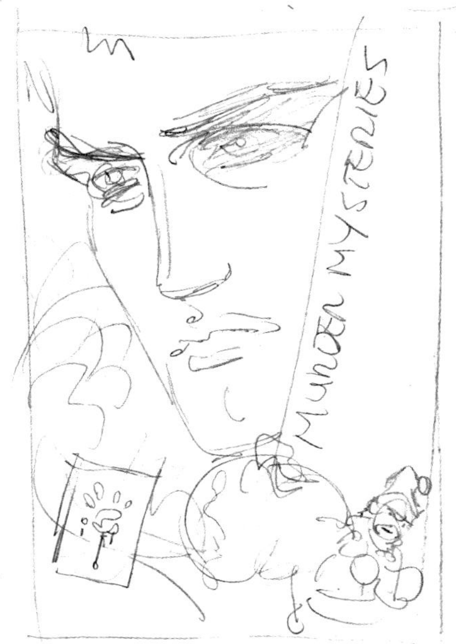
MURDER MYSTERIES

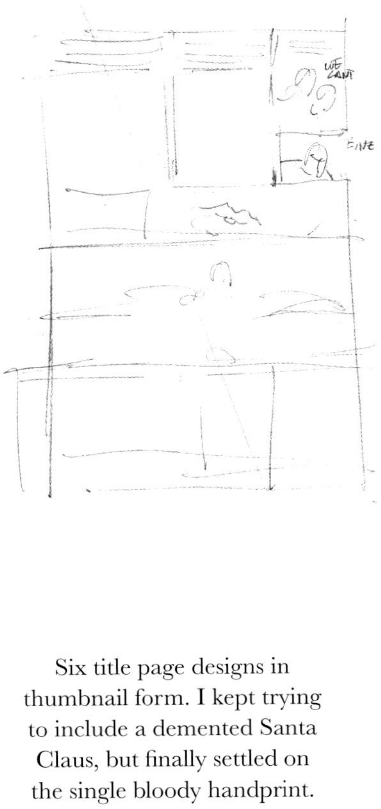

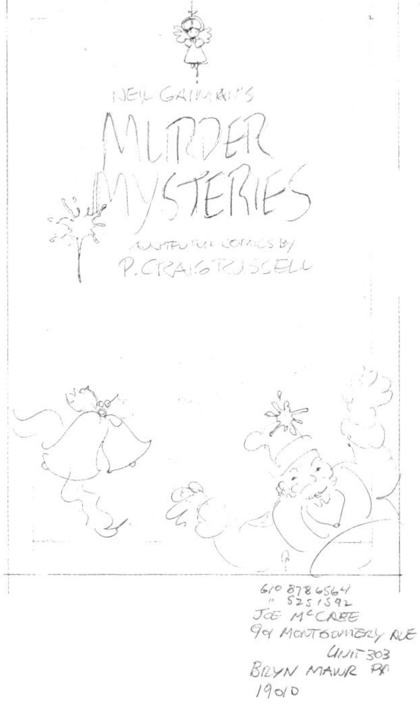
NEIL GAIMAN'S
MURDER MYSTERIES
P. CRAIG RUSSELL
BRYN MAWR PA

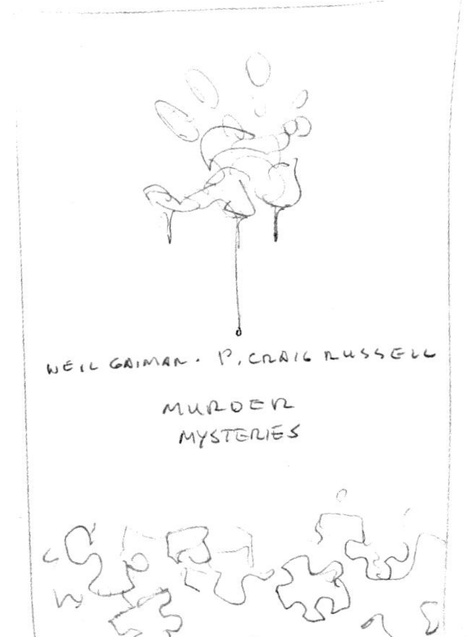
NEIL GAIMAN · P. CRAIG RUSSELL
MURDER
MYSTERIES

Six title page designs in thumbnail form. I kept trying to include a demented Santa Claus, but finally settled on the single bloody handprint.

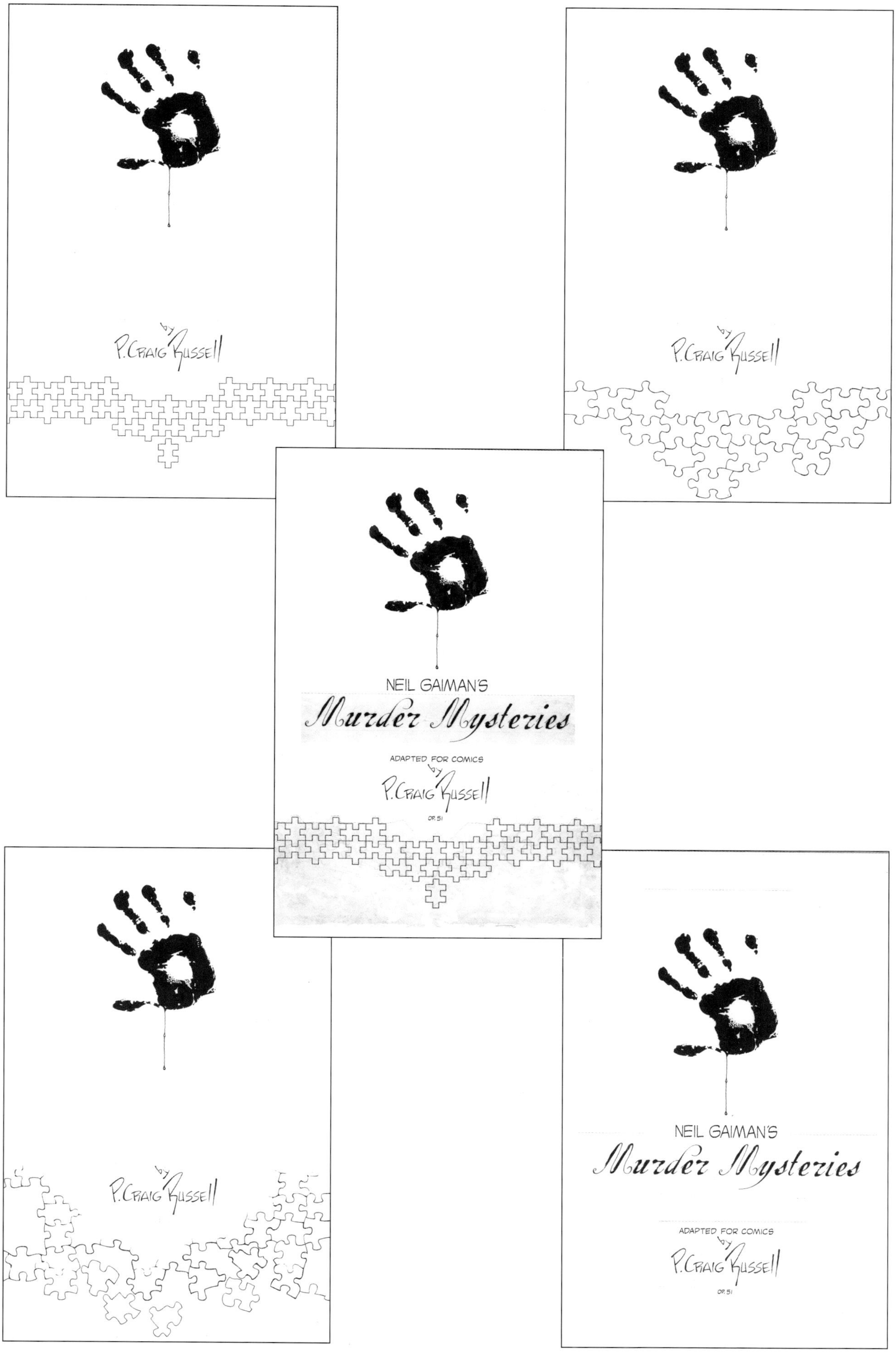
by P. Craig Russell
by P. Craig Russell
NEIL GAIMAN'S
Murder Mysteries
ADAPTED FOR COMICS by P. Craig Russell
OP. 51
by P. Craig Russell
NEIL GAIMAN'S
Murder Mysteries
ADAPTED FOR COMICS by P. Craig Russell
OP. 51

Five full-size title pages.

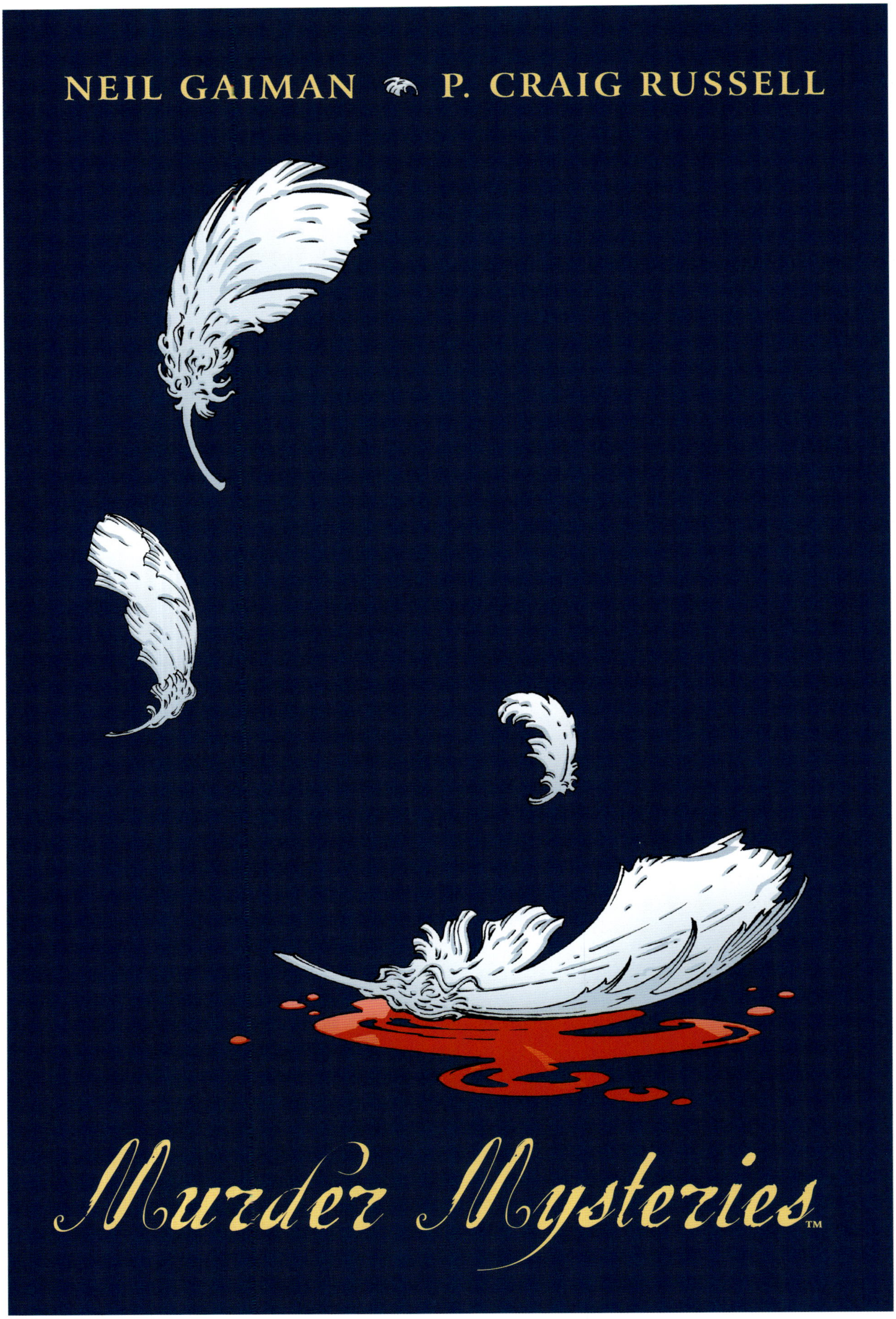
NEIL GAIMAN
P. CRAIG RUSSELL
Murder Mysteries™

Original cover for the first edition of *Murder Mysteries*.

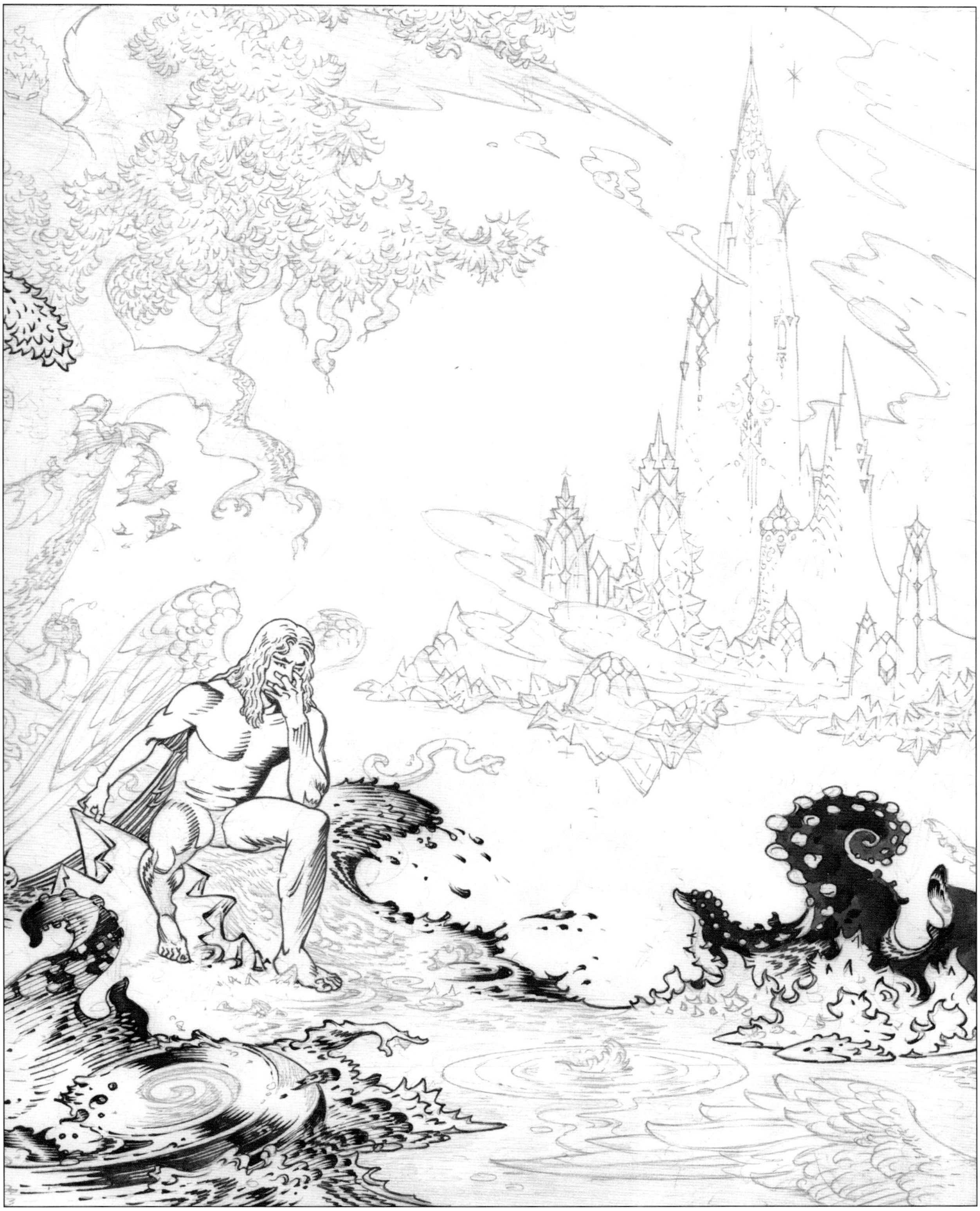

The cover process for this collection.

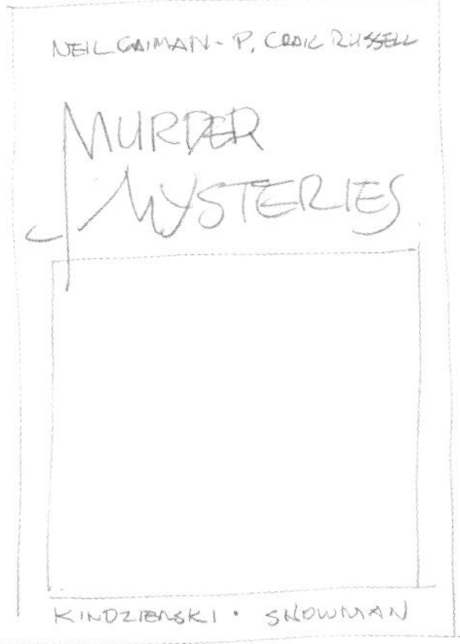
NEIL GAIMAN - P. CRAIG RUSSELL
MURDER MYSTERIES
KINDZIERSKI • SNOWMAN

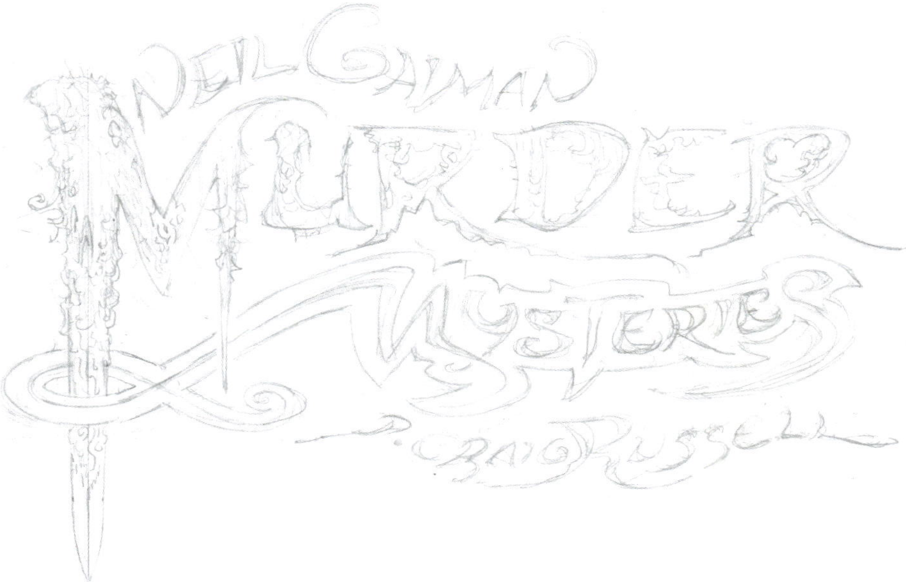
NEIL GAIMAN
MURDER
MYSTERIES
P. CRAIG RUSSELL

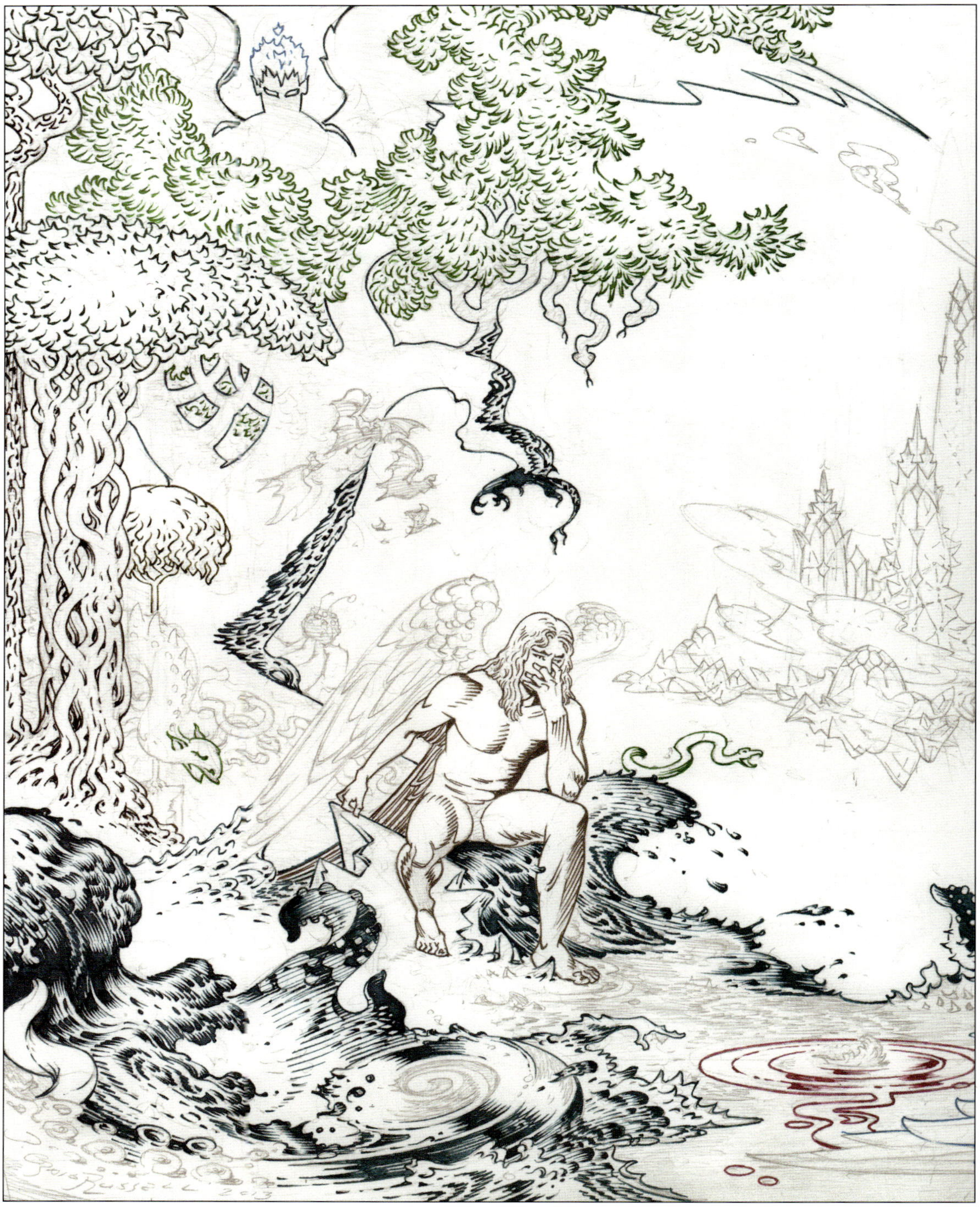

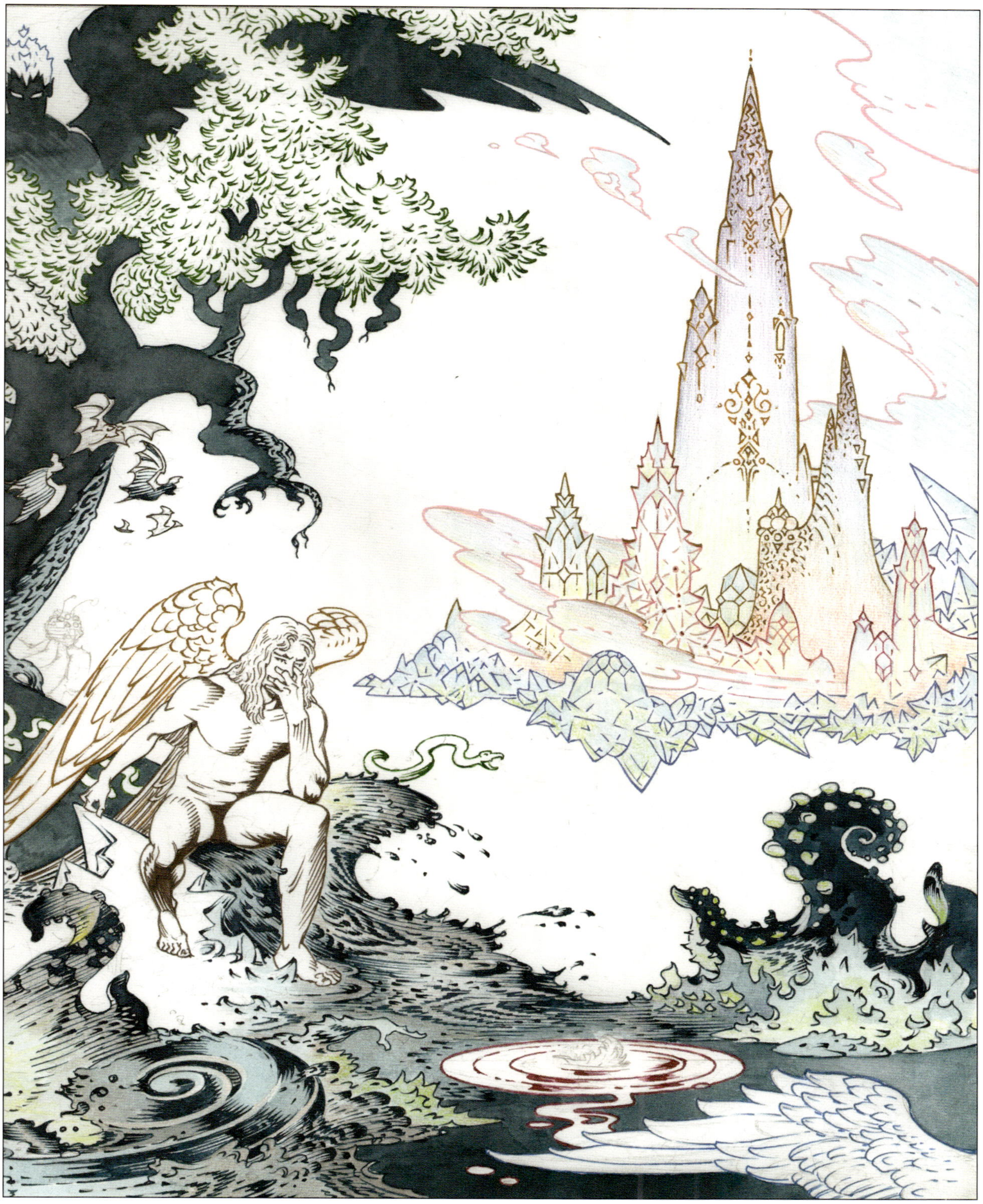

FORBIDDEN BRIDES

SKETCHBOOK

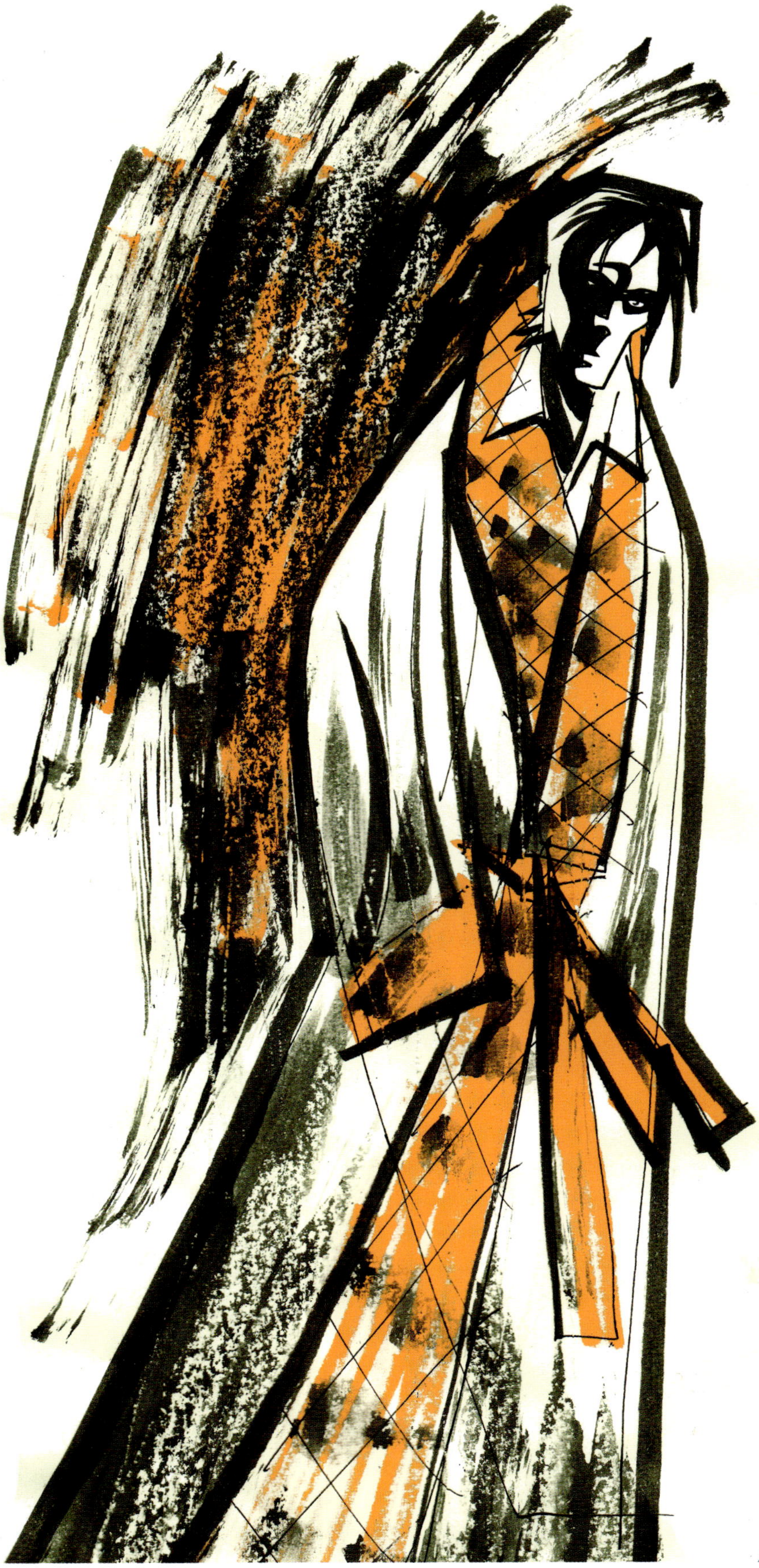

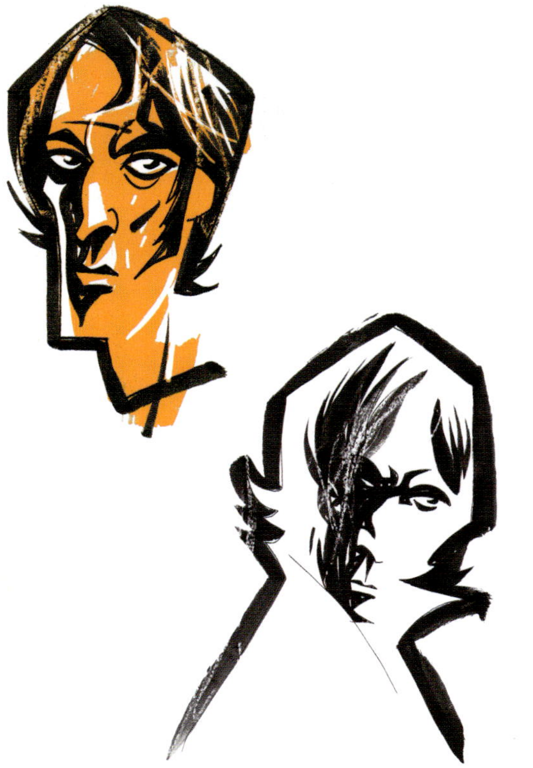

THE AUTHOR

Neil wasn't that specific in describing the author. For me, that's a definite plus. I love this part of the process, though occasionally I can't make up my mind, like this time. So my wife chose for me.

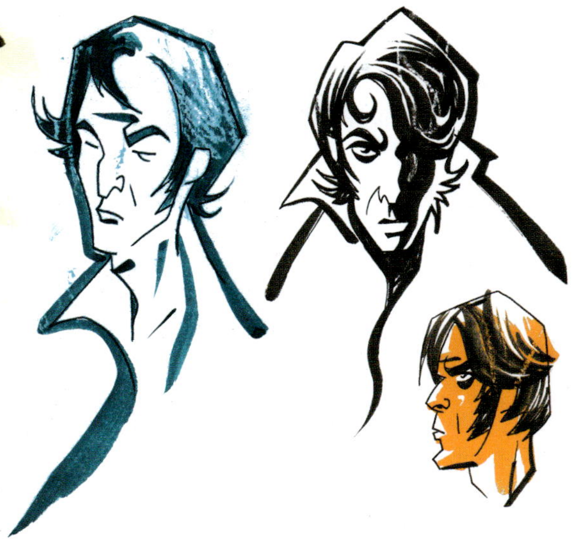

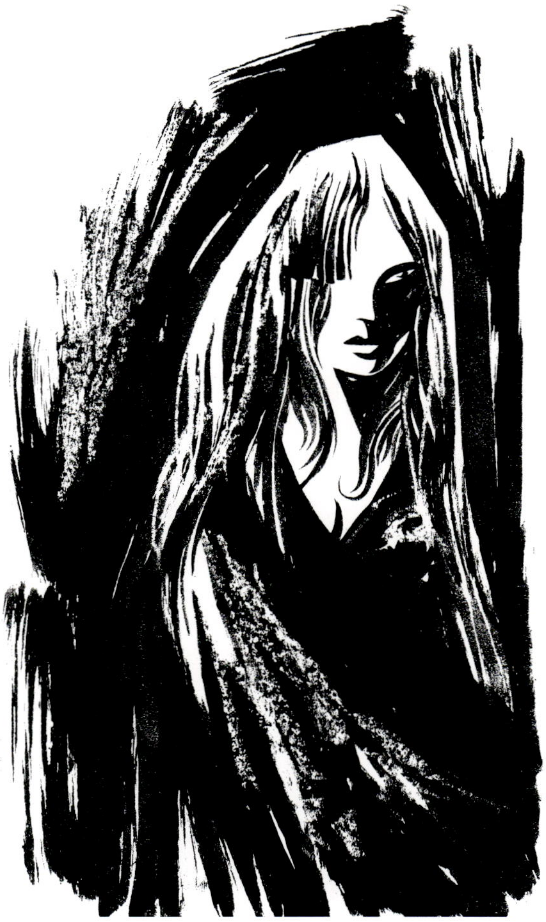

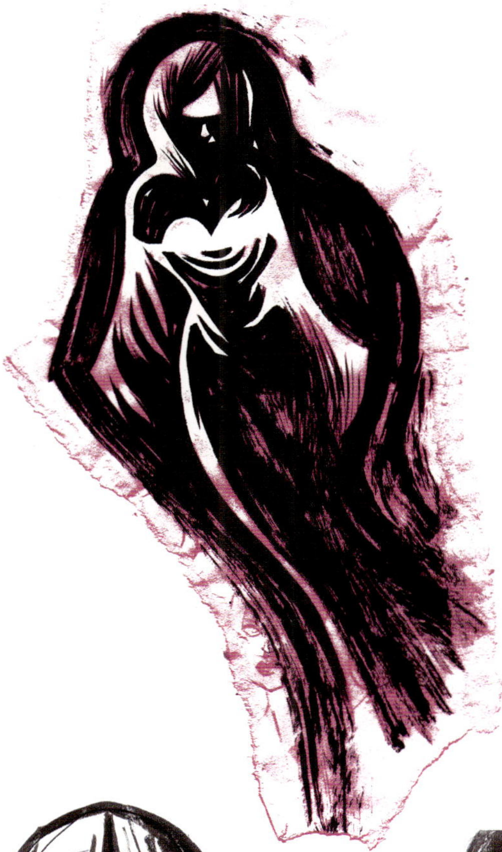

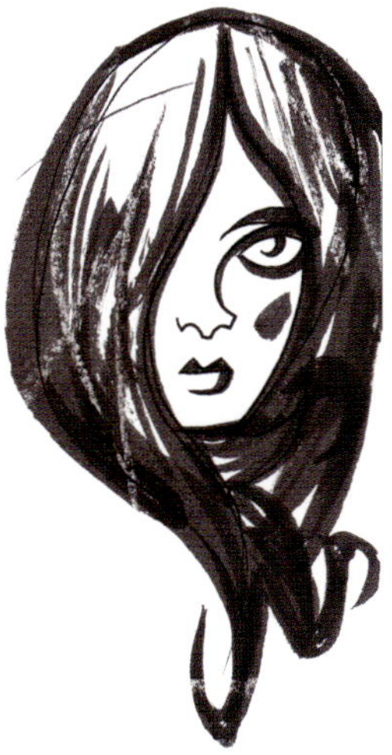

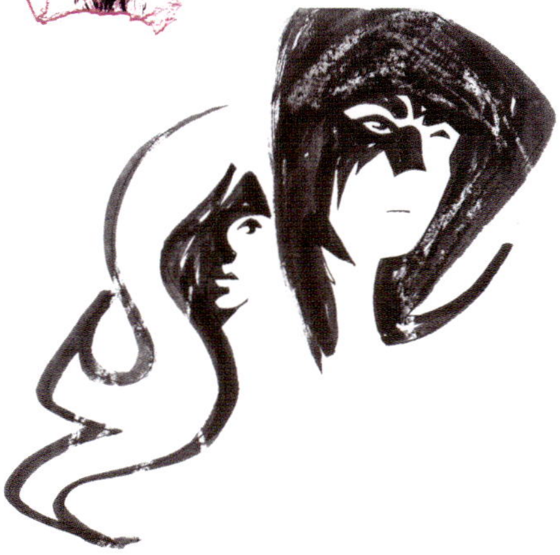

AMELIA

Amelia is pretty much your archetypal wary woman on a gothic romance paperback book cover. And I was also picturing various B- and C-list starlets from Hammer vampire movies.

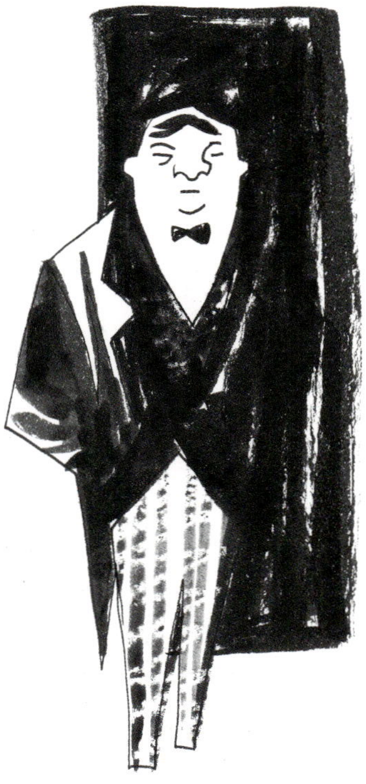

THE BUTLER

Originally based on English actor Geoffrey Palmer. All condescending brows and bloodhound jowls. Ended up looking like Richard Nixon. Never a good thing. Dropped that idea.

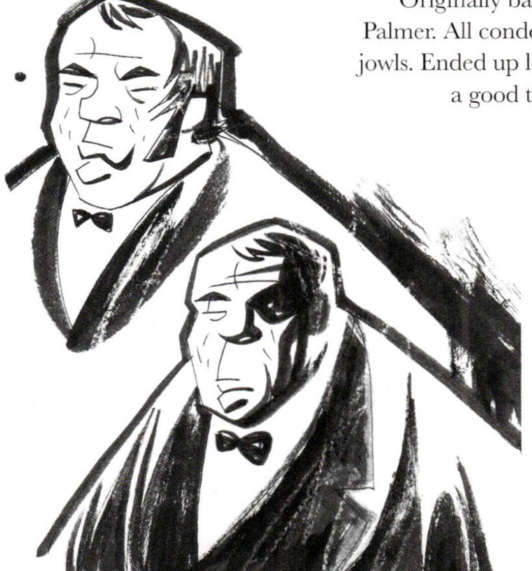

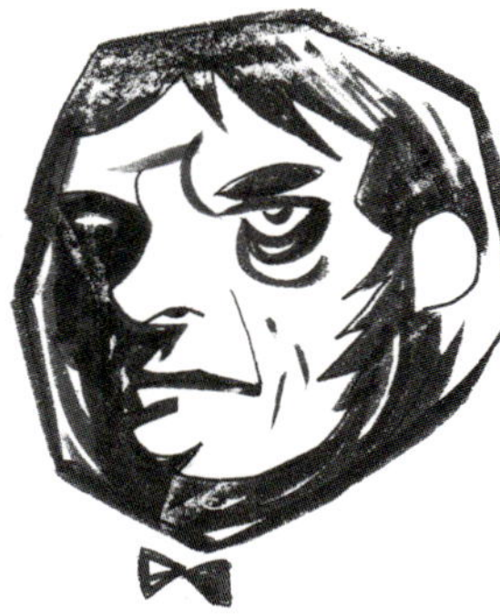

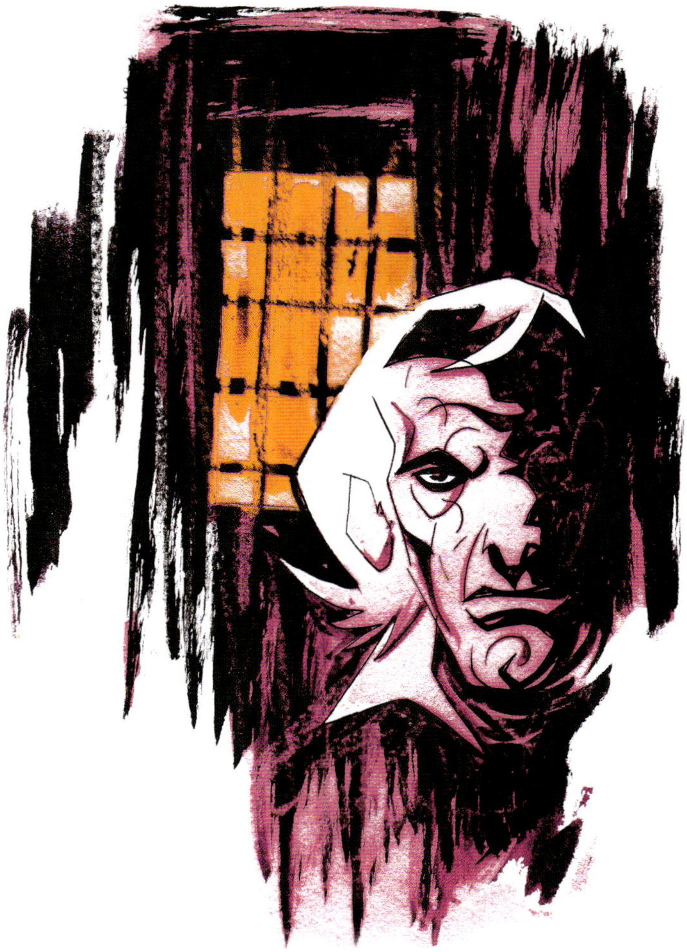

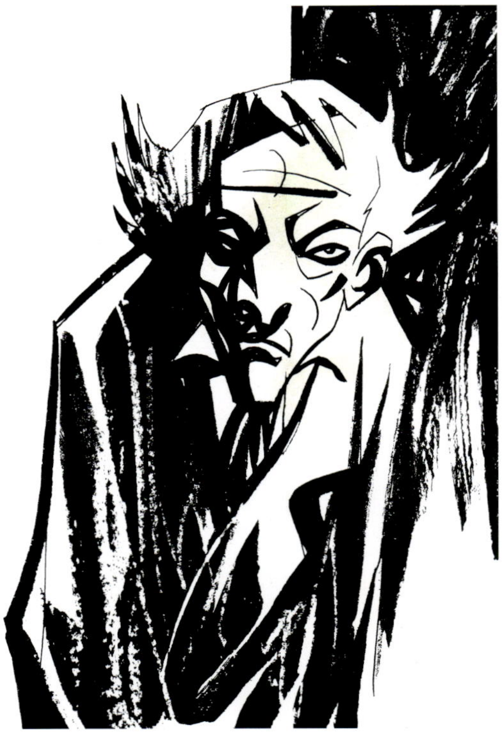

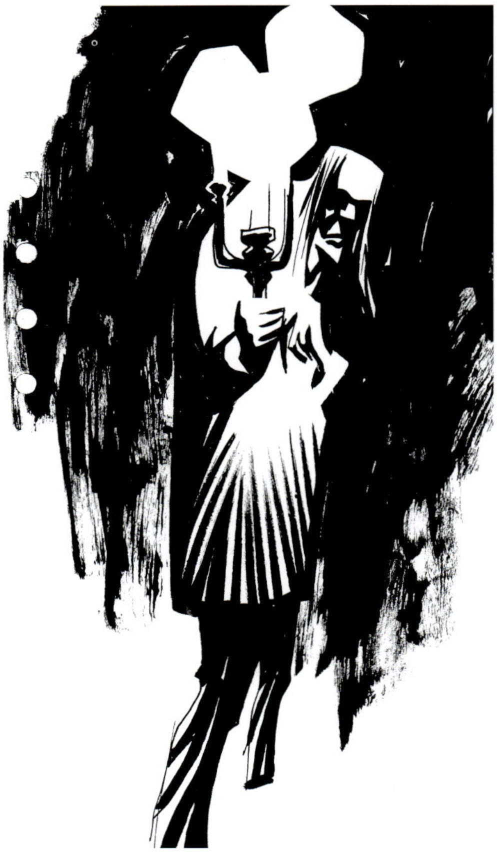

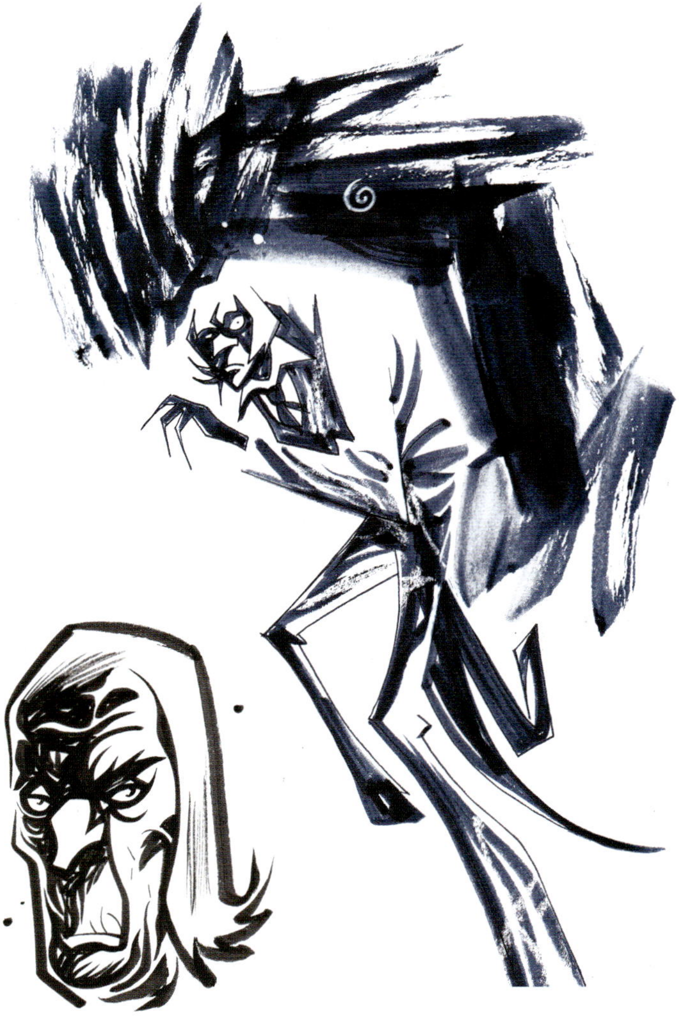

THE CARETAKER

Much easier. Bony and bent—that gaunt and sinister face answering many a door at midnight. Squint, and it's almost Uncle Creepy.

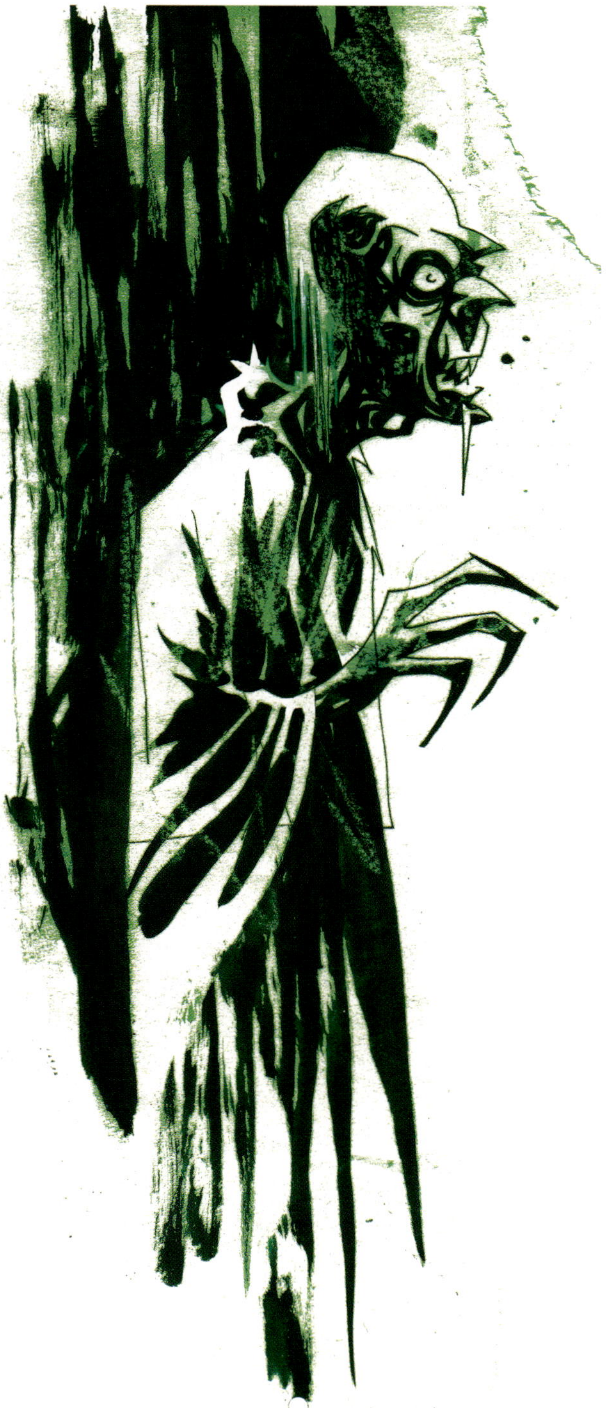

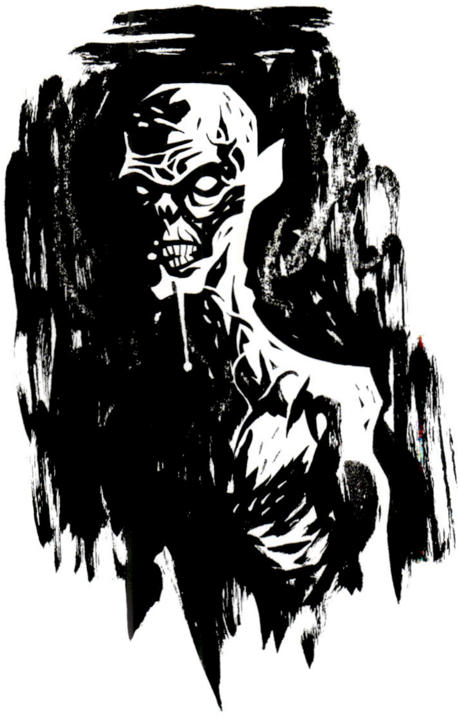

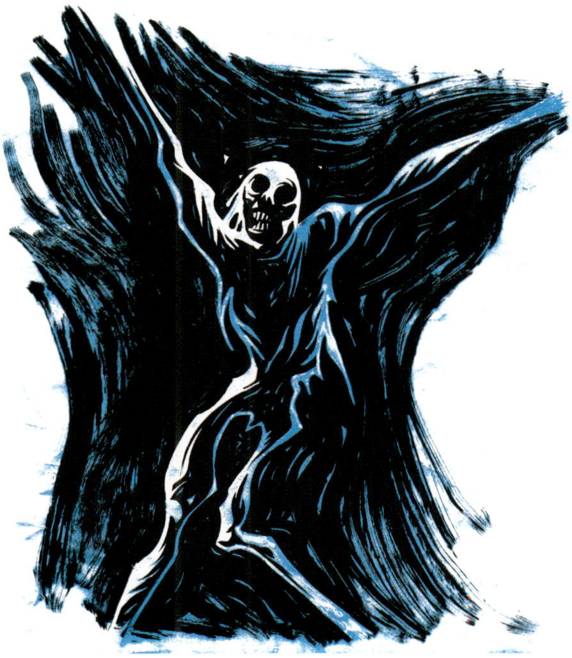

THE GHOULS

I could've filled this book with ghoul sketches. Indulged myself way too much. I even gave them names and pondered their origins and day-to-day lifestyle. Why were some dressed in monk robes? Where were the girl ghouls?

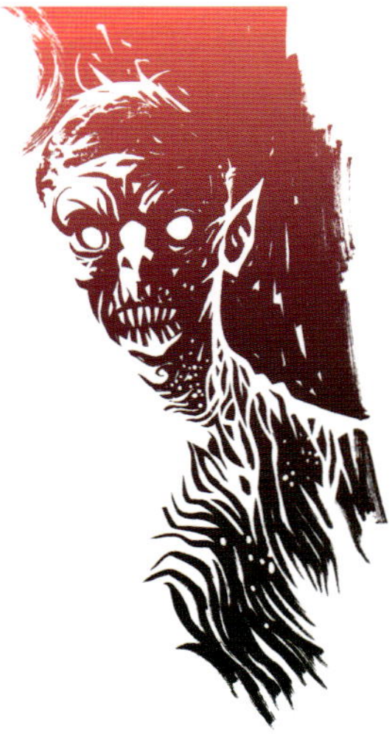

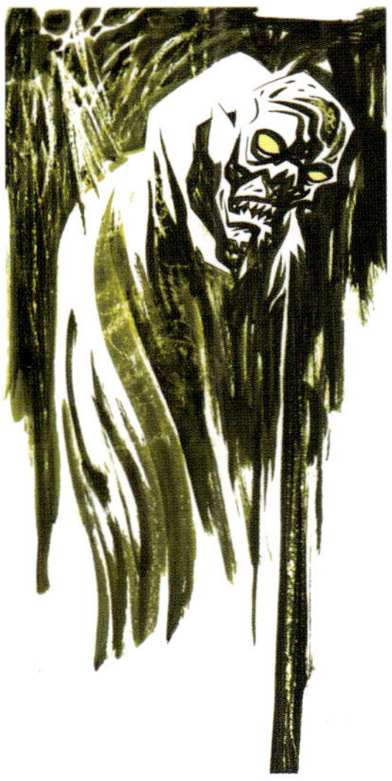

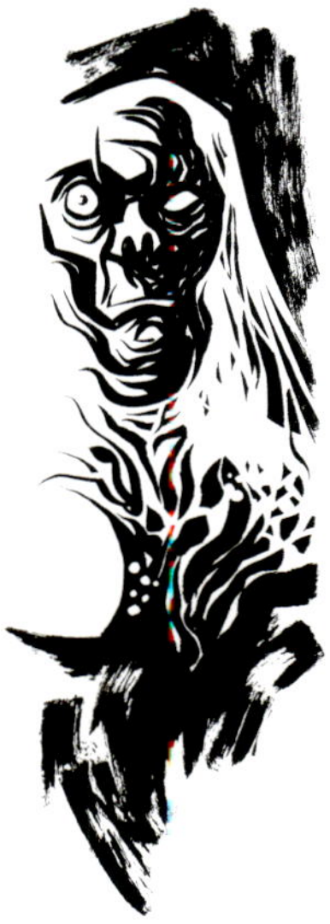

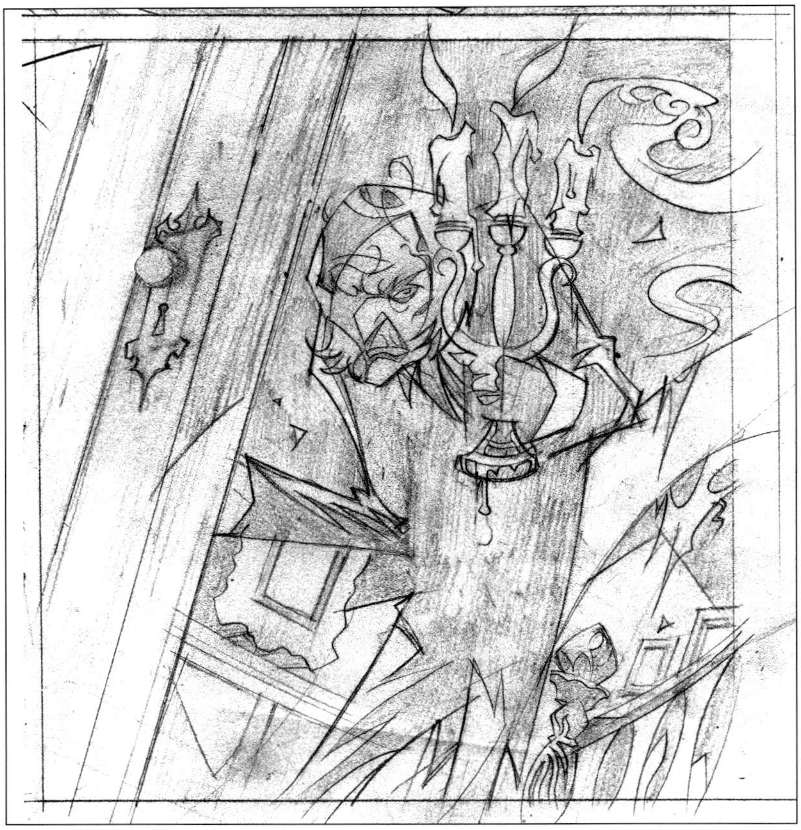

UNUSED PANEL

It was a good panel, but I don't think it had enough impact. Not for the reveal. Kick myself I forgot to use the pose further on.

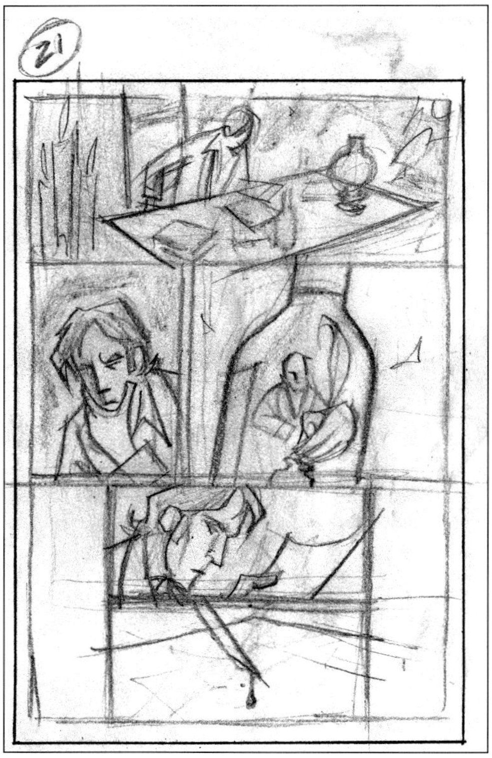

21

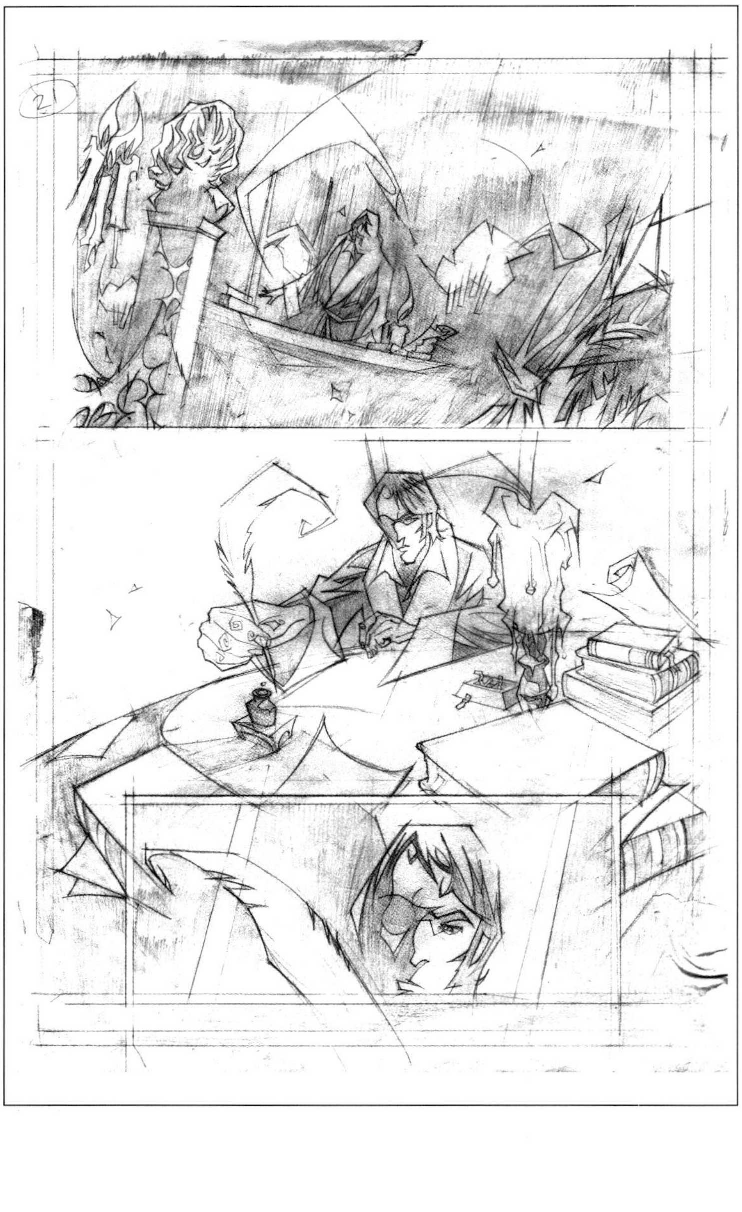

21

LAYOUTS VS. FINISHED PENCILS

Usually I follow my thumbnails closely, but the page needed less fuss and more drama. I also decided he wouldn't drink wine on the job (perhaps preferring an opium pipe). See, me overthinking it again.

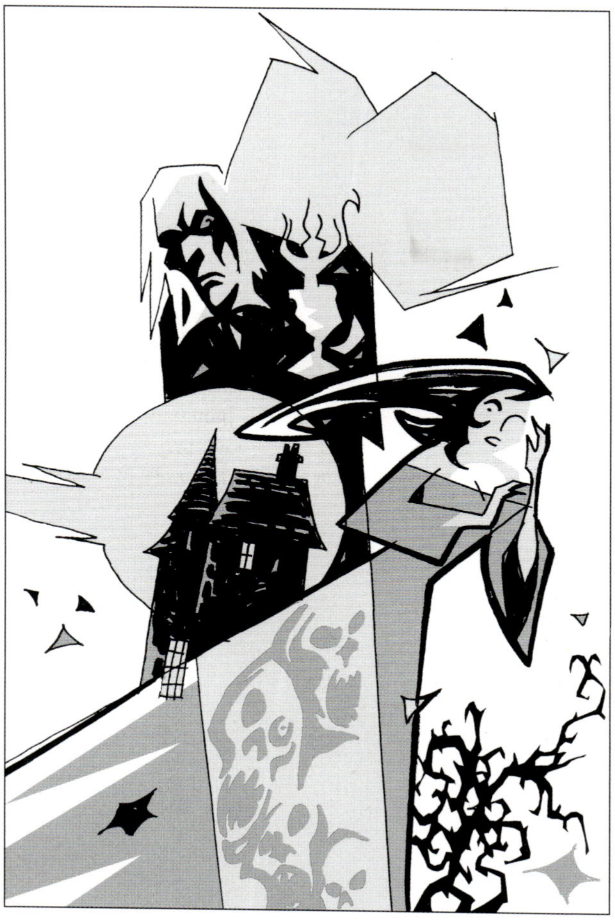

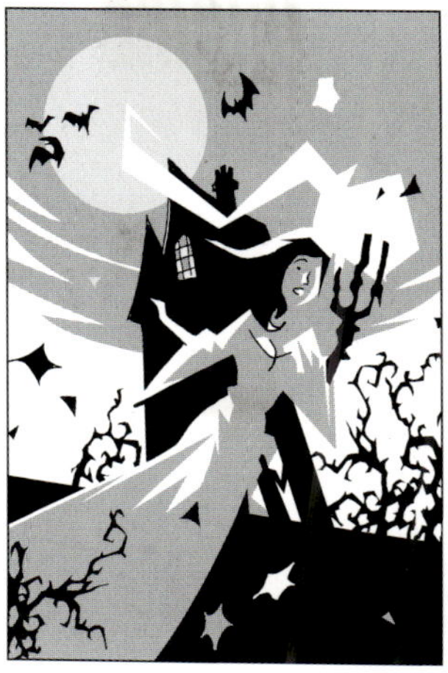

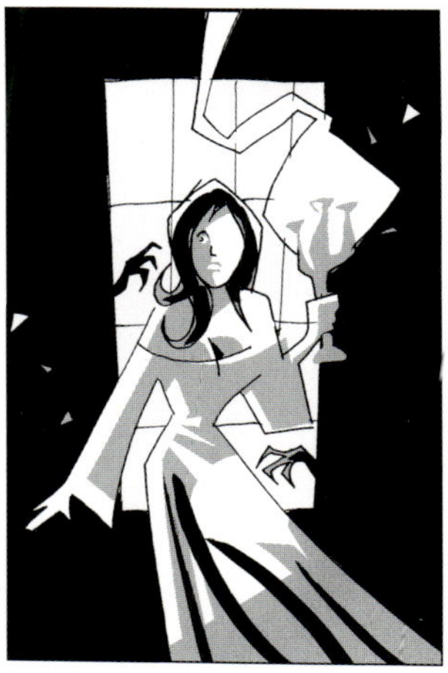

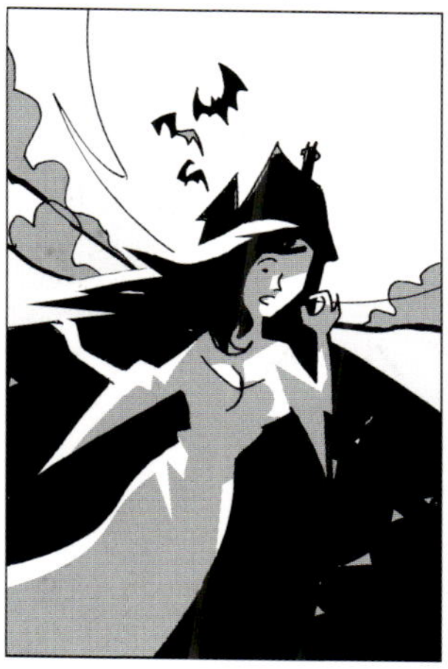

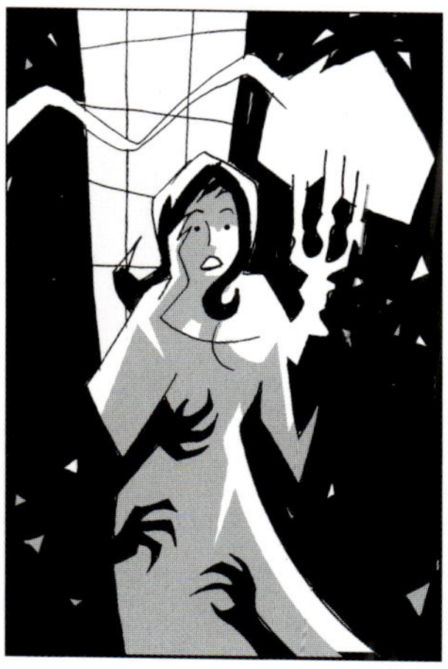

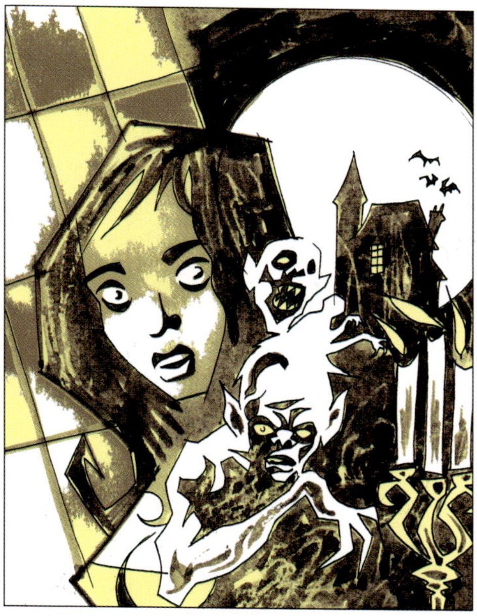

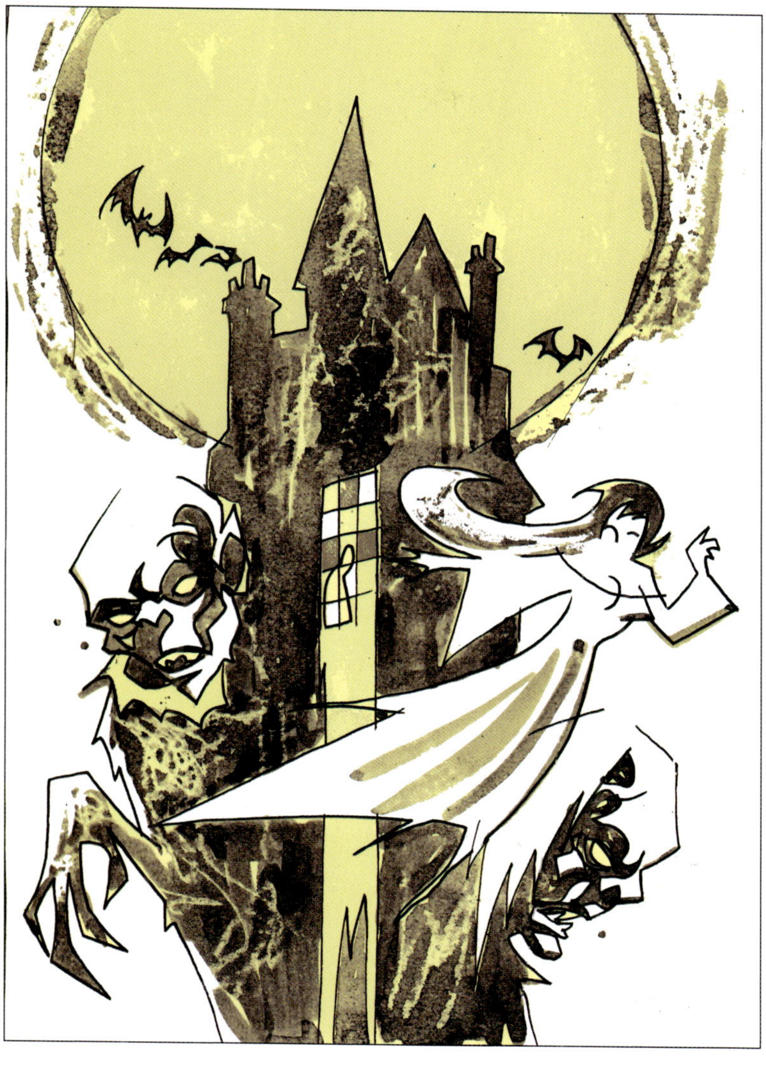

COVER

The cover was the toughest I've done. I wanted the composition to be as simple as possible, but choosing what to put in and leave out proved a major headache. So many, many variables. Wife helped again.

MORE TITLES FROM THE NEIL GAIMAN LIBRARY

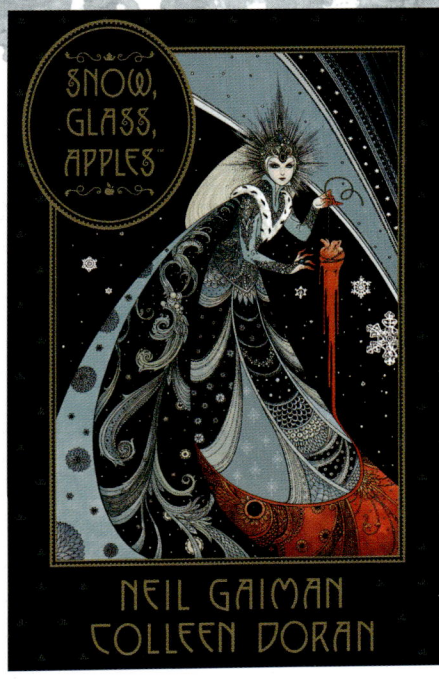  

NEIL GAIMAN LIBRARY VOLUME 1
Neil Gaiman and various artists
$49.99 | ISBN 978-1-50671-593-3

LIKELY STORIES
Neil Gaiman and Mark Buckingham
$17.99 | ISBN 978-1-50670-530-9

AMERICAN GODS: SHADOWS
Neil Gaiman, P. Craig Russell,
Scott Hampton, and others
$29.99 | ISBN 978-1-50670-386-2

AMERICAN GODS: MY AINSEL
Neil Gaiman, P. Craig Russell,
Scott Hampton, and others
$29.99 | ISBN 978-1-50670-730-3

AMERICAN GODS: THE MOMENT OF THE STORM
Neil Gaiman, P. Craig Russell, Scott Hampton, and others
$29.99 | ISBN 978-1-50670-731-0

ONLY THE END OF THE WORLD AGAIN
Neil Gaiman, P. Craig Russell, and Troy Nixey
$19.99 | ISBN 978-1-50670-612-2

MURDER MYSTERIES
2nd Edition
Neil Gaiman, P. Craig Russell, and Lovern Kinderski
$19.99 | ISBN 978-1-61655-330-2

THE FACTS IN THE CASE OF THE DEPARTURE OF MISS FINCH
2nd Edition
Neil Gaiman and Michael Zulli
$13.99 | 978-1-61655-949-6

NEIL GAIMAN'S HOW TO TALK TO GIRLS AT PARTIES
Neil Gaiman, Fábio Moon, and Gabriel Bá
$17.99 | ISBN 978-1-61655-955-7

NEIL GAIMAN'S TROLL BRIDGE
Neil Gaiman and Colleen Doran
$14.99 | ISBN 978-1-50670-008-3

FORBIDDEN BRIDES OF THE FACELESS SLAVES IN THE SECRET HOUSE OF THE NIGHT OF DREAD DESIRE
Neil Gaiman and Shane Oakley
$17.99 | ISBN 978-1-50670-140-0

CREATURES OF THE NIGHT
2nd Edition
Neil Gaiman and Michael Zulli
$12.99 | ISBN 978-1-50670-025-0

SIGNAL TO NOISE
Neil Gaiman and Dave McKean
$24.99 | ISBN 978-1-59307-752-5

HARLEQUIN VALENTINE
2nd Edition
Neil Gaiman and John Bolton
$12.99 | ISBN 978-1-50670-087-8

NEIL GAIMAN'S A STUDY IN EMERALD
Neil Gaiman and Rafael Albuquerque
$17.99 | ISBN 978-1-50670-393-0

THE PROBLEM OF SUSAN AND OTHER STORIES
Neil Gaiman, P. Craig Russell, Paul Chadwick, and others
$17.99 | ISBN 978-1-50670-511-8

SNOW, GLASS, APPLES
Neil Gaiman and Colleen Doran
$17.99 | ISBN 978-1-50670-979-6

AVAILABLE AT YOUR LOCAL COMICS SHOP OR BOOKSTORE.
To find a comics shop in your area, visit comicshoplocator.com. For more information, visit DarkHorse.com

Likely Stories © Neil Gaiman. Text and illustrations of Only the End of the World Again™ © Neil Gaiman, P. Craig Russell, and Troy Nixey. Text of Murder Mysteries™ © Neil Gaiman. Adaptation and illustrations of Murder Mysteries™ © P. Craig Russell. Signal to Noise © Neil Gaiman & Dave McKean. Cover art © Dave McKean. Text of Harlequin Valentine™ © Neil Gaiman. Illustrations of Harlequin Valentine™ © John Bolton. The Facts in the Case of the Departure of Miss Finch™ text © Neil Gaiman, art © Michael Zulli. Miss Finch is a trademark of Neil Gaiman. How to Talk to Girls at Parties™ © Neil Gaiman. Artwork © Fábio Moon and Gabriel Bá. Neil Gaiman's Troll Bridge™ © Neil Gaiman, artwork © Colleen Doran. Forbidden Brides of the Faceless Slaves in the Nameless House of the Night of Dread Desire™ text © Neil Gaiman, art © Shane Ivan Oakley. The Price™ © Neil Gaiman. Daughter of Owls™ © Neil Gaiman. Artwork © Michael Zulli. Creatures of the Night is a trademark of Neil Gaiman. American Gods™ © Neil Gaiman. A Study In Emerald™ © Neil Gaiman. The Problem of Susan and Other Stories™ © Neil Gaiman. Snow, Glass, Apples™ © Neil Gaiman. Artwork © Colleen Doran. Dark Horse Books® and the Dark Horse logo are registered trademarks of Dark Horse Comics LLC. All rights reserved. (BL 6043)